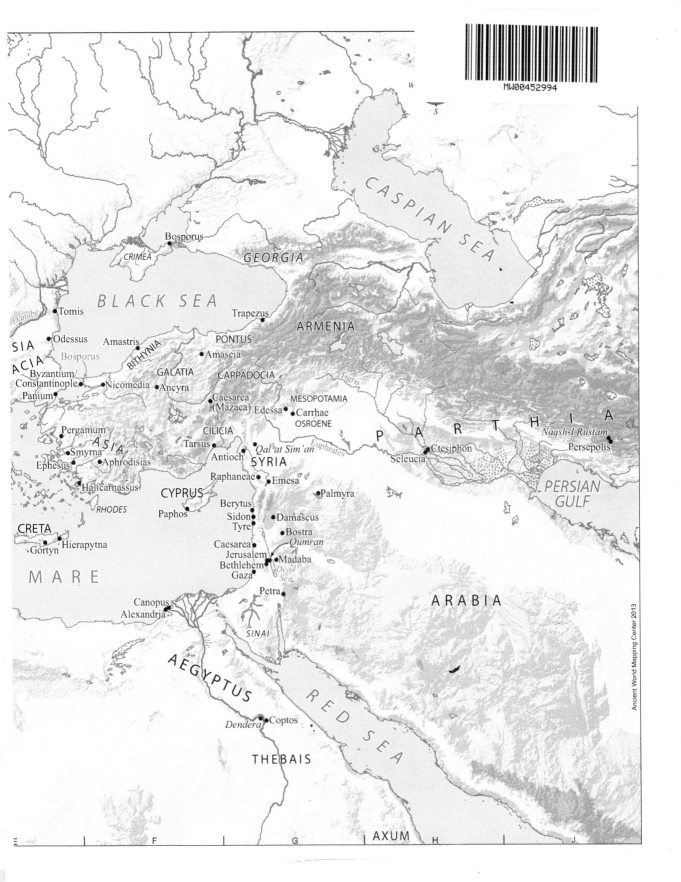

MW00452994

W

S

CASPIAN SEA

CRIMEA

Bosporus

GEORGIA

BLACK SEA

Danube Tomis

Trapezus

ARMENIA

SIA

ACIA Odessus

Amastris BITHYNIA

PONTUS

Bosporus

Byzantium/
Constantinople Nicomedia

GALATIA

Amaseia

Ancyra

CAPPADOCIA

Panium

Caesarea
(Mazaca) Edessa

MESOPOTAMIA

Carrhae

Tigris

OSROENE

P   A   R   T   H   I   A

Naqsh-I Rustam

Pergamum

ASIA

Smyrna

CILICIA

Tarsus

Antioch

Qalʾat Simʾan

SYRIA

Euphrates

Seleucia

Ctesiphon

Persepolis

Ephesus

Aphrodisias

Raphaneae

Emesa

Palmyra

PERSIAN
GULF

Halicarnassus

CYPRUS

RHODES

Paphos

Berytus

Sidon

Tyre

Damascus

Bostra

CRETA

Caesarea

Qumran

Gortyn Hierapytna

Jerusalem

Madaba

Bethlehem

Gaza

*Dead
Sea*

ARABIA

MARE

Petra

Canopus

Alexandria

SINAI

Nile

AEGYPTUS

R E D

S E A

Dendera Coptos

THEBAIS

Ancient World Mapping Center 2013

E   F   G   AXUM   H   J

A New Latin Primer

Mary C. English

Georgia L. Irby

New York :: Oxford

OXFORD UNIVERSITY PRESS

Oxford University Press is a department of the University of Oxford.
It furthers the University's objective of excellence in research,
scholarship, and education by publishing worldwide.

Oxford   New York
Auckland   Cape Town   Dar es Salaam   Hong Kong   Karachi
Kuala Lumpur   Madrid   Melbourne   Mexico City   Nairobi
New Delhi   Shanghai   Taipei   Toronto

With offices in
Argentina   Austria   Brazil   Chile   Czech Republic   France   Greece
Guatemala   Hungary   Italy   Japan   Poland   Portugal   Singapore
South Korea   Switzerland   Thailand   Turkey   Ukraine   Vietnam

For titles covered by Section 112 of the US Higher Education
Opportunity Act, please visit www.oup.com/us/he for the
latest information about pricing and alternate formats.

Published by Oxford University Press
198 Madison Avenue, New York, New York 10016
http://www.oup.com

Library of Congress Cataloging-in-Publication Data
English, Mary C., author.
   A new Latin primer / by Mary C. English and Georgia L. Irby.
      pages cm
   ISBN 978-0-19-998201-1 (pbk.)
   1. Latin language--Readers. 2. Latin language--Grammar. I. Irby, Georgia
Lynette, 1965- author. II. Title.
   PA2095.E544 2015
   478.6'421--dc23
                                                      2015010440

Printing number: 9 8 7 6 5 4 3 2

Printed in the United States of America
on acid-free paper

Contents

3. THIRD DECLENSION NOUNS AND ADJECTIVES
THE LEGENDS OF EARLY ROME   27

4. VOCATIVE CASE, IMPERATIVES, AND PERSONAL PRONOUNS
ROMAN POETS AND THE BUSINESS OF POETRY   42

27. PERFECT AND PLUPERFECT SUBJUNCTIVES AND CUM CLAUSES
VIRTUS, DIGNITAS, et PIETAS

28. PURPOSE CLAUSES
MAGIC AND THE OCCULT

Preface

A NEW LATIN PRIMER offers beginning students a solid overview of Latin grammar, syntax, and vocabulary. For the most part, it features a traditional, grammar-based approach to the language and emphasizes vocabulary from standard classical authors. Grammatical explanations are spare and to the point, and they are illustrated by unadapted Latin examples so that students learn from Roman authors how to employ the syntax under discussion. Each of the thirty-six lessons contains twelve short practice sentences (eight from Latin to English; four from English to Latin) as well as fifteen passages of unadapted Latin from a wide variety of important classical and medieval authors (Catullus, Vergil, Horace, Ovid, Martial, Caesar, Cicero, Livy, Sallust, Tacitus, Augustus, Seneca the Younger, Pliny the Younger, Pliny the Elder, Augustine, Bede, *inter alios*). These passages are formatted with unfamiliar vocabulary and explanatory notes provided immediately below the readings so that students can transition easily from this textbook to more advanced Latin courses. All of the selections in a single lesson are tailored to one or two specific aspects of Roman culture or history. Thus they remind the students that the study of Latin provides firsthand access to the texts that shape our understanding of the Roman world. The cultural sections are as crucial to our textbook as the grammatical explanations, and instructors should budget time to review these essays in class. We feel strongly that an introductory sequence in Latin should offer students a window into Roman literature and culture; grammar and translation exercises should be viewed as a means to that end and not as the primary objective of the class.

We intend for the *Primer* to be used as flexibly as possible: as an introductory course over two or three semesters, as a self-study volume, or as an intensive review. Some instructors may wish to assign all of the passages in a given lesson, while others may prefer to assign a selection of them, reserving the Extra Passages for quizzes and exams. Some lessons may take one class period (e.g., *NLP* 1), others several (e.g., *NLP* 2 and 3). In our experience, most lessons should take two days: one for grammar and drills, another for translating passages. The companion Workbook to *A New Latin Primer* features a variety of drills, additional practice sentences, directed English-to-Latin translation practice, and word games to reinforce grammar, vocabulary, and culture. We invite students and teachers to use these exercises in full or to select from them as it seems best.

In formatting the *Primer*, we have used the *Oxford Classical Texts* (OCTs) for the Latin text. To aid students in pronunciation and the identification of forms, we have included macrons for all of the passages in the text and glossaries. We have followed the governing principle of the *Oxford Latin Dictionary* and marked all vowels that are long by nature. For the inscriptions, we have retained the texts as they have come down to us, but we have expanded all abbreviations, indicated by parentheses (e.g., *NLP* 1.12 and 1.13), and we have provided notes for scribal errors in grammar and syntax (e.g., *NLP* 1.7). The major collections of inscriptions used in the *Primer* include *CIL* (*Corpus Inscriptionum Latinarum*), *ILS* (*Inscriptiones Latinae Selectae*), and *RIB* (*Roman Inscriptions of Britain*).

Like the *Little Latin Reader*, the *New Latin Primer* is the product of our combined vision, and all aspects of this book result from our joint and equal contributions. Furthermore, many individuals helped make *A New Latin Primer* possible. We would like to thank Charles Cavaliere, our editor at Oxford University Press, and his assistant Christi Sheehan, who both provided many wonderful suggestions for this book. We would also like to thank the following people who reviewed (and, in some cases, class-tested) the manuscript in various stages of development and provided invaluable feedback: Gareth Williams, Columbia University; Mary Pendergraft, Wake Forest University; Donald E. Connor, Trinity School; Blaise Nagy, College of the Holy Cross; T. Davina McClain, Northwestern State University; John Henkel, Georgetown College; Linda W. Gillison, University of Montana–Missoula; John Klopacz, Stanford University; Madeleine M. Henry, Purdue University; John Carlevale, Berea College; Emily E. Batinski, Louisiana State University; Elizabeth Anne Manwell, Kalamazoo College; Zoe Kontes, Kenyon College; Prudence Jones, Montclair State University; Keely Lake, Wayland Academy; and Katherine Panagakos, Stockton University.

We also owe a debt to our Latin students over the years who inspired us to undertake this project and who field-tested the book at various stages in its development (a special thanks to Georgia Irby's Beginning and Intermediate Latin students at William and Mary, fall 2013–spring 2015, especially Grace Albrecht, Callie Angle, Sara Barlow, Dereck Basinger, Megan Bland, Laura Cooley, Rochelle Evans, Aaron Finkle, William Gaskins, Susannah Haury, Justin Jones, Joe Maniaci, Erin Miao, Paige Newsome, Sam Nussbaum, Alex Olson, Francesca Orfila, Jasmane Ormond, Joseph Palame, Kristen Roper, Jason Scott-Sheets, and Ben Zhang, who all provided us with crucial feedback and caught countless infelicities). We extend additional gratitude to Tejas Arelare, Thomas Barto, Maura Brennan, Greg Callaghan, John Donahue, Brett Evans, Jason Fulbrook, Pam Hawkes, Joyce Holmes, C.J. Kamp, Emily (Rossow) Kamp, John Oakley, Duane Roller, Molly Swetnam-Burland, Russ Walker, and the crew of the Godspeed at Jamestown, Virginia for their support and encouragement over the years, and to Georgia's graduate school mentors, James C. Anderson and Christoph F. Konrad, whose influence is (hopefully) evident in many of the cultural essays. Special debts of gratitude go to Barbette Spaeth for her thoughtful observations arising from beta-testing the book with her Beginning Latin class at William and Mary, 2014–2015, and to Jessamyn Rising, for her rigorous proofing and salutary recommendations. Most of all, we would like to thank our families: Carol L. Irby, Georgia Irby's aunt, so much like her brother, John L. Robinson, her nautical mentor and best friend, and her mother Patricia A. Irby, who so eagerly and supportively endured myriad updates; and Aditya and Theodore Arjuna Adarkar, loving husband and son of Mary English, and Howard and Mary English, her parents, who supported this project day after day and cheered it on to completion.

About the Authors

MARY C. ENGLISH (BA, College of the Holy Cross; MA and PhD, Boston University) is Associate Professor of Classics and General Humanities at Montclair State University, where she has taught Latin and Greek at all levels as well as courses in mythology, ancient drama, and theater history. Most recently, with Dr. Georgia L. Irby, she authored *A Little Latin Reader* (Oxford University Press, 2011). She also has written numerous articles and book chapters on the staging of ancient comedy and the reception of Greek drama by contemporary American playwrights.

GEORGIA L. IRBY (BA and MA, University of Georgia; PhD, University of Colorado, Boulder) is Associate Professor of Classical Studies and Fellow of the College of the Liberal Arts at the College of William and Mary, where she teaches Latin and Greek at all levels, as well as courses on the history of science, Greek and Roman civilization, mythology, epic, tragedy, and historiography in translation. Most recently, with Dr. Mary C. English, she authored *A Little Latin Reader* (Oxford University Press, 2011). She has also written many articles and book chapters on Greek and Roman cartography, medicine, religion, mythology, and pedagogy. She is currently editing *The Blackwell Companion to Ancient Science, Medicine and Technology* (forthcoming). In her "spare time" she crews on the *Godspeed*, a seventeenth-century replica square-rigged ship out of Jamestown, Virginia.

Introduction

A BRIEF HISTORY OF THE LATIN LANGUAGE

Latin is a member of the Indo-European family of languages, sharing grammatical structure and root vocabulary with other languages spoken in Europe, parts of central Asia, and the Indian subcontinent, such as Greek, German, Russian, Anglo-Saxon, and even Sanskrit. Not all European languages are Indo-European; Basque, for example, predates the spread of Indo-European languages westward into Spain and developed in isolation from them. Likewise, Hungarian and Finnish are related to each other, but they also developed in isolation from Indo-European languages.

Indo-European languages share many common features of grammar, syntax, and base vocabulary, and the most common words are easily recognized from one language to the next. Let us consider just one example, the word for "mother":

- **English**: mother
- **Sanskrit**: mātar
- **Greek**: mētēr
- **Latin**: māter
- **Anglo-Saxon**: mōdor
- **Old Irish**: máthir
- **Lithuanian**: mote
- **Russian**: mat

In all of these languages, the word for "mother" is similar in spelling and pronunciation. All of these words for "mother" derive from the root word *méh₂tēr* in Proto-Indo-European, the earliest reconstructable incarnation of this language family. Consequently, we call Indo-European languages "cognate" because they are related to each other linguistically and derived from the same parent language, Proto-Indo-European. The words themselves (like our variant Indo-European words for "mother") are also called "cognate".

As Rome grew and extended into the larger Mediterranean world, Roman officials and soldiers brought with them not only their system of government, institutions, and wares, but they also introduced their language, Latin, to the western Mediterranean. Just like Greek in the east, Latin became the language of administration and commerce in the west. To deal with Rome, one had to learn Latin. Both the Greeks and the Romans were proud of their languages and often notoriously refused to learn other languages. Educated Greeks condescended to learn Latin as a matter of survival, but Cato the Elder refused to use Greek, a language which he knew well but considered unworthy of Roman dignity.

As Latin spread, it began to mingle with local languages, influencing and reshaping them. Today the modern Romance languages ("from Rome," "according to Roman practice") are spoken in lands that were strongholds of the Roman Empire: Spanish in Spain (Hispania), French in France (Gallia), Italian in Italy (Italia), Romanian in Romania (Dacia), and Portuguese in Portugal (Lusitania). These languages, cognate with one another, are derivatives of Latin. Rome never gained a secure foothold in Germany; Britain, although thoroughly Romanized, was abandoned by the Romans in the fifth century CE, before local Celtic languages had been stamped out and forgotten. Latin's influence on the English language is indirect, through Medieval French, introduced when Duke William II from Normandy in northern coastal France defeated the Anglo-Saxon King Harold II ("Card Face") on October 14, 1066 at Hastings in southern England. These political ties were eventually severed in 1204, and, although English was still spoken in the homes of the peasants and managed to reassert itself as the language of politics and business, English had been irrevocably changed by an influx of redundant and "courtly" words (e.g., the hoof stock bleating in the courtyard might be a lamb or a sheep, but on the plate it was known by the French-derived "mutton").

THE NATURE OF THE LATIN LANGUAGE

Two terms, grammar and syntax, are important for our discussions about Latin. Grammar involves the forms of words (e.g., singular versus plural). Compare *a student learns Latin* (singular subject with singular verb) and *students learn Latin* (plural subject with plural verb). Syntax involves how words fit together into coherent sentences (subjects, direct objects, etc.).

English is a word-ordered language wherein meaning is conveyed by the word's position within the sentence. Subjects are usually first, and verbs next, followed by direct objects. From our example above (*students learn Latin*), *students* is the subject, explaining who does the learning, *learn* is the verb, explaining what action occurs in our sentence, and *Latin* is the direct object, explaining what is being learned. Reversing the word order renders a sentence that is illogical: *Latin learns students*.

In Latin, endings ("inflection"), rather than word order, convey meaning. As a result, words can appear in any order at all. English carries a vestige of inflection in its system of pronouns. Consider the following sentences in English:

> Marcus and Flavia are siblings.
> **He** sees Flavia.
> Flavia protects **him**.
> Flavia returns **his** toy.

He, *him*, and *his* all replace Marcus in their respective sentences. Notice how the spelling changes slightly, depending on whether Marcus performs the action (*he*), is affected by the action (*him*), or possesses an object (*his*). In these cases, the word order could be altered slightly without affecting the meaning, though the new sentences may sound stilted. For example: *He Flavia sees* (Marcus is still doing the seeing, and Flavia is still being seen); *Him Flavia protects* (Flavia is still doing the protecting, and Marcus is still being protected); *His toy Flavia returns* (the toy still belongs to Marcus). Consider the following Latin example: ***tenet error amantem*** ("uncertainty holds a lover"). The first word *tenet* is the verb, explaining the action of the sentence, the subject *error*, which performs the action of "holding," appears in the middle, and the direct object *amantem*, the person being held by uncertainty, is at the end. No matter in what order the words appear, the meaning and translation remain the same. Because of this, Latin (along with many other Indo-European languages) is characterized as "inflected." Despite this fact, Latin sentences often follow the standard word order of subject, direct object, verb, and this basic word order can provide essential clues to help the reader disentangle phrases and clauses in longer, more complex sentences.

BASIC PARTS OF SPEECH

Recognizing words by their parts of speech is one of many skills necessary for reading and translating challenging Latin passages. There are eight parts of speech, and only four of them are "inflected" (i.e., change their spelling/endings according to their meaning within a sentence).

> **Verb**: describes an action or state of being: *Hīc **habitat** fēlīcitās.* ("Luck **lives** here"). The verb *habitat* explains what Luck does.
>
> **Noun:** person, place, thing, idea: *Hīc habitat **fēlīcitās**.* ("**Luck** lives here"). The noun *fēlīcitās* explains who is doing the living.
>
> **Pronoun**: replaces a noun: *Amō **tē, Facilis*** ("I love **you,** Facilis"). The pronoun *tē* replaces *Facilis.*
>
> **Adjective**: modifies a noun or pronoun: *Magus **malus** est.* ("The magician is **bad**"). The adjective *malus* describes the magician.
>
> **Adverb**: modifies a verb, adverb, or adjective: *Hīc habitat fēlīcitās.* ("Luck lives **here**"). The adverb *hīc* explains where Luck lives.
>
> **Preposition**: denotes a spatial or temporal relationship to a noun: *Fēlix **cum** Fortūnātā.* ("Felix **with** Fortunata"). The preposition *cum* explains the spatial relationship between Felix and Fortunata.
>
> **Conjunction**: joins two words or clauses: *Clōdius hīc **et** ubici amābiliter* ("Clodius amiably here **and** everywhere").
>
> **Interjection**: expression of emotion, surprise or pleasure: *vae!* ("woe!")

In the required vocabulary lists for each lesson, vocabulary words are arranged by part of speech (nouns, pronouns, adjectives, verbs, adverbs, prepositions, conjunctions, interjections), and within each part of speech, words are further organized by declension or conjugation group as appropriate.

THE LATIN ALPHABET AND PRONUNCIATION

The Roman alphabet evolved over time, as some letters were added and others dropped out (the emperor Claudius, in fact, tried unsuccessfully to introduce three new letters to the alphabet, though some inscriptions from his reign still show his letters). Some letters were almost interchangeable (*g* and *c*). And the letters *y* and *z* came into the Latin alphabet from Greek in the late 1st century BCE. The alphabet known to our Romans lacked the letters *j* and *w*.

Many sources do describe the sounds of the Latin language, so we can be reasonably certain about pronunciation.

Vowels: Some vowels are short, and others are long. In *A New Latin Primer*, long vowels will be marked by macrons. The difference in the pronunciation between long and short vowels is one of quantity, not quality, and long vowels will take twice as long to pronounce.

a: like "car"	**ā**: like "bought"
e: like "get"	**ē**: like "clay"
i: like "tin"	**ī**: like "green"
o: like "hot"	**ō**: like "drove"
u: like "foot"	**ū**: like "food"

N.B. Although the Romans occasionally indicated long vowels with a stroke (*Róma*), by doubling the vowel (*Rooma*), or by writing it larger than the other letters (*rOmanus*), this practice was not consistent, and the Romans did not use macrons. We include them here as an aid to both pronunciation and identification (compare: *venit* ["he/she/it comes"] and *vēnit* ["he/she/it has come"]; or *liber* ["book"] and *līber* ["free"]). Our approach has been conservative, and we mark only those vowels that are long by nature, in accord with the governing principle of the *Oxford Latin Dictionary*.

Diphthongs: Some combinations of two vowels work together to produce a single sound.

ae: like "mile"
au: like "spouse"
 ei: like "tame"
eu: like "mew"
oe: like "toil"
 ui: like "Louis" (rare: found only in the following forms: *huius, cuius, huic, cui*)

Consonants: For the most part, the consonants are much the same in Latin and English. Note the following qualifications:

> **c** and **g** are always hard in Classical Latin: like "coat" and "gone"
>
> **q** is always followed by a consonantal *u*: like "quick" and "quiz"
>
> **r** is always rolled (as in Spanish) and was called the *littera canīna* (the dog-letter) because it sounded like a growling dog
>
> **s** is always unvoiced (as in "send") and never is pronounced with "z" variant (as in "tease")
>
> **ch**, **ph**, and **th** are from aspirated Greek consonantal characters, and the "h" is pronounced as a puff of air: like "**ch**orus", "to**p h**at", and "pet **h**amster"
>
> **v** is pronounced like English *w*
>
> **i** as a consonant will be followed by another vowel and pronounced like an English "y": *Iulius, Troia*. Some texts transliterate this *i* as the letter *j*, which did not exist in the Latin alphabet of classical times (*Julius, Troja*)

Syllables: A Latin word has as many syllables as it has vowels and diphthongs. To divide Latin words into syllables, consider the following:

> Two contiguous vowels or a vowel next to a diphthong divide into two syllables: *tu-us, tu-ae*.
>
> A single consonant between two vowels/diphthongs is pronounced with the second vowel: *do-cē-re, ni-hil, Trō-ia, Iu-li-us*.
>
> If two or more consonants separate vowels/diphthongs, generally the consonants divide between the two syllables: *mit-tō, pu-el-la*.
>
> A "stop" (**b, c, d, g, p, t**) + a "liquid" (**l, r**) count as a single consonant and will go with the second vowel/diphthong: *a-grī, ves-tra, ex-clu-dō, tem-plum*.
>
> In compound words, the composite parts remain intact: *ab-esse, ex-eō, ex-i-stō*.
>
> **ch**, **gu**, **ph**, **th**, and **qu** always count as a single consonant: *ar-**chi**-tec-tus, at-**que**, lin-**gu**a, re-lin-**qu**us*.
>
> **x**, however, counts as a double consonant and is split between the two syllables: *du-xit = duc-sit, vexō = vec-sō*.

Accentuation: As in English, Latin words are pronounced by giving one syllable a little extra emphasis. Consider the following:

In words of two syllables, the accent falls on the first syllable: *ni-hil, tu-us.*

In words of three or more syllables, the accent falls on the penult (second to last syllable) **if** the penult is long (e.g., has a macron, is a diphthong, or is followed by two consonants): *po-ē-ta, po-ē-tā-rum, do-cē-re, Mī-nō-tau-rus, pu-el-la.*

In words of three or more syllables, the accent falls on the antepenult (third to last syllable) **if** the penult is short: *ca-pi-mus, fē-lī-ci-tās, pa-tri-bus, vo-lu-cris.*

Present Tense

1. In Latin, the endings of verbs reveal their subjects. In fact, there is often no need to express the subject of a sentence with a pronoun as we do in English. Consider the following examples:

habitō = I live (-**ō** indicates the subject is "I")
docēs = You (singular) teach (-**s** indicates the subject is "you")
audit = He/She/It hears (-**t** indicates the subject is "he/she/it")
amāmus = We love (-**mus** indicates the subject is "we")
capitis = You (plural) take (-**tis** indicates the subject is "you")
mittunt = They send (-**nt** indicates the subject is "they")

In other words, verb endings convey **PERSON** (1st = I/we; 2nd = you; 3rd = he/she/it/they) and **NUMBER** (singular and plural). Study this simple table:

Person	Singular	Plural
1st	-**ō**/-**m**	-**mus**
2nd	-**s**	-**tis**
3rd	-**t**	-**nt**

2. Each Latin verb falls into one of four categories known as **CONJUGATIONS**. The **INFINITIVE** ("to love," "to hear," etc.) signifies to which conjugation a Latin verb belongs. There are four possible infinitive endings for regular verbs: -**āre**, -**ēre**, -**ere**, -**īre**. Here are the infinitives for our paradigm verbs:

First Conjugation: **amāre** = to love
Second Conjugation: **docēre** = to teach

Third Conjugation: **mittere** = to send
Fourth Conjugation: **audīre** = to hear

3. The **PRESENT TENSE** describes current as well as ongoing actions and can be translated in several ways depending upon the context. For example, *docent* can mean "they teach," "they are teaching," "they do teach," and "they continue to teach." In Latin, the present stem is formed by dropping the ending (**-āre, -ēre, -ere, -īre**) from the verb's infinitive.

Infinitive	Base
amāre	**am-**
docēre	**doc-**
mittere	**mitt-**
capere	**cap-**
audīre	**aud-**

The vowel between this stem and the personal endings (learned above) changes depending upon the verb's conjugation. It is helpful to memorize one verb in the present tense from each conjugation to serve as a model for other verbs.

FIRST CONJUGATION

Person	Singular	Plural
1st	am**ō**: I love	am**āmus**: we love
2nd	am**ās**: you love	am**ātis**: you (plural) love
3rd	am**at**: he/she/it loves	am**ant**: they love

SECOND CONJUGATION

Person	Singular	Plural
1st	doce**ō**: I teach	doc**ēmus**: we teach
2nd	doc**ēs**: you teach	doc**ētis**: you (plural) teach
3rd	doc**et**: he/she/it teaches	doc**ent**: they teach

THIRD CONJUGATION

Person	Singular	Plural
1st	mittō: I send	mittimus: we send
2nd	mittis: you send	mittitis: you (plural) send
3rd	mittit: he/she/it sends	mittunt: they send

FOURTH CONJUGATION

Person	Singular	Plural
1st	audiō: I hear	audīmus: we hear
2nd	audīs: you hear	audītis: you (plural) hear
3rd	audit: he/she/it hears	audiunt: they hear

N.B. Vowels before *-nt* and *-t* are short. Thus, for first, second, and fourth conjugation verbs, the macron will drop off the final vowel in the 3rd person singular and plural forms.

4. There is a subset of the third conjugation called "-io verbs." In the present tense, these verbs conjugate largely like third conjugation verbs, but they follow the model for fourth conjugation verbs in the 1st person singular and 3rd person plural.

THIRD CONJUGATION (-IO)

Person	Singular	Plural
1st	capiō: I take	capimus: we take
2nd	capis: you take	capitis: you (plural) take
3rd	capit: he/she/it takes	capiunt: they take

5. The verb "to be" is irregular in both Latin and English. Although the stem in the present tense alternates between *su-* and *e(s)-*, the verb uses the same basic endings as regular verbs.

Person	Singular	Plural
1st	sum: I am	sumus: we are
2nd	es: you are	estis: you (plural) are
3rd	est: he/she/it is	sunt: they are

6. Most verbs have four principal parts in their dictionary entries:

amō	I love	1st person singular, present tense
amāre	to love	present active infinitive
amāvī	I have loved, I loved	1st person singular, perfect tense (action is completed)
amātus	having been loved	perfect passive participle (a verbal adjective)

Some verbs (e.g., **fugiō, fugere, fūgī**: flee) have only three principal parts. Many of these verbs are intransitive (i.e., they do not take a direct object in Latin). Other variations from the standard pattern of four principal parts will be explained in subsequent Lessons.

7. Three of the four conjugations follow regular patterns for their principal parts, with a few exceptions.

> First Conjugation: **-ō, -āre, -āvī, -ātus**
> Second Conjugation: **-eō, -ēre, -uī, -(i)tus**
> Fourth Conjugation: **-iō, -īre, -īvī, -ītus**

The stems of third conjugation verbs often change significantly for the third and fourth principal parts. Consider the following examples:

> Third Conjugation: **mittō, -ere, mīsī, missus**: send
> Third Conjugation (-io): **capiō, -ere, cēpī, captus**: take, capture

8. Even though the third and fourth principal parts will not be explained in detail until *NLP* Lessons 13 and 18, it is best to commit all four forms of the required verbs to memory now.

I. Required Vocabulary

NOUNS
  nihil: nothing

VERBS
  amō, -āre, -āvī, -ātus: like, love

dō, dare, dedī, datus: give (N.B. The "a" in the infinitive ending is short and serves as the linguistic evidence that, earlier in the history of the Latin language, the verbs of what we now call the first conjugation were subdivided into -are and -āre verbs.)

habitō, -āre, -āvī, -ātus: live, dwell

doceō, -ēre, docuī, doctus: teach, instruct
videō, -ēre, vīdī, vīsus: see, look at, watch

capiō, -ere, cēpī, captus: take, seize, capture
fugiō, -ere, fūgī: flee, escape, run away
mittō, -ere, mīsī, missus: send, let go

audiō, -īre, -īvī, -ītus: hear
sciō, -īre, -īvī, -ītus: know

sum, esse, fuī, futūrus: be

CONJUNCTIONS AND ADVERBS
et: and (**et … et**: both … and)
hīc: here
nōn: not

II. Translate the following sentences from Latin to English or English to Latin.

1. Nōn audītis.
2. Hīc habitāmus.
3. Nihil capis.
4. Hīc docent.
5. Sciō.
6. Nihil mittunt.
7. Hīc es.
8. Nihil dō.
9. We see.
10. I both love and run away.
11. She knows nothing.
12. You (plural) do not live here.

Latin Inscriptions

From the beginnings of written language, people have scribbled messages onto walls, or etched inscriptions on stone, metal, bricks, glass, pottery, mosaic tesserae, and wooden tablets. The study of inscriptions is called "epigraphy" from the Greek *epigraphein* ("to write on"), and about 200,000 inscriptions in Latin have been collected. Representing the voices of a variety of people, from humble provincials at the furthest reaches of the Roman Empire (Britain, Turkey, North Africa) to the emperors themselves, inscriptions chronicle idle musings, personal vendettas, sporting rivalries, election campaigns, and poignant epitaphs for deceased loved ones. A particularly rich collection of inscriptions from Pompeii survived under its protective layer of ash after the eruption of Vesuvius in 79 CE until its rediscovery in 1748.

Inscriptions in the Latin-speaking world covered a gamut of styles. Official inscriptions were sometimes deeply incised with regular block letters painted red, or they were erected on public buildings in bronze letters. Individuals could hire professional stonecutters to inscribe tombstones, but the results were not always regular. Personal votives and simple objects dedicated by ordinary people were frequently inscribed more crudely, painted, scratched, or incised with rough and barely legible cursive characters. Professionals, on the other hand, employed a mostly regularized system of abbreviations, probably to cut costs. We have fully expanded these abbreviations in *NLP*. For example, one stonecutter wrote *Venus es, Ve,* which we have expanded to *Venus es, Ve(nus).* Many of the personal inscriptions, especially along the outskirts of the Empire, also reflect local pronunciation and interesting grammatical anomalies and errors.

Although the Roman epigraphic record spans a millennium, most inscriptions date to the first three centuries CE. About 180,000 inscriptions have been collected in twenty volumes of the *Corpus Inscriptionum Latinarum (CIL),* the first of which was published in 1893. Other valuable collections of inscriptions include *Inscriptiones Latinae Selectae (ILS),* three large volumes published from 1892 to 1916, and *Roman Inscriptions of Britain (RIB),* an ongoing project whose first volume appeared in 1965. Inscriptions have been discovered in the context of formal archaeological digs, during city infrastructure improvement, and even in backyards. New inscriptions continue to come to light every year.

SUGGESTIONS FOR FURTHER READING:

Franklin, James L. *Pompeis difficile est: Studies in the Political Life of Imperial Pompeii.*
University of Michigan, 2001.
Hartnett, Matthew. *By Roman Hands: Inscriptions and Graffiti for Students of Latin.*
Focus, 2008.
Keppie, Lawrence. *Understanding Roman Inscriptions.* Johns Hopkins, 1991.
LaFleur, Richard A. *Scribblers, Sculptors, and Scribes.* HarperCollins, 2010.
Wallace, Rex E. *An Introduction to Wall Inscriptions from Pompeii to Herculaneum.*
Bolchazy-Carducci, 2005.

PASSAGES

1.1. *CIL* IV 1454: Pompeii. Etched in a bakery above the oven.

Hīc habitat fēlīcitās.

Notes: **fēlīcitās, -ātis**, f: happiness, good fortune, success.

1.2. *CIL* IV 2331: Pompeii. On a pillar in a peristyle garden, carefully painted above a labyrinth.

Labyrinthus. Hīc habitat Mīnōtaurus.

Notes: **Labyrinthus, -ī**, m: the labyrinth, constructed by Daedalus for King Minos of Crete to contain the monstrous child of his wife Pasiphaë; **Mīnōtaurus, -ī**, m: the half-human, half-bull son of Pasiphaë, who slept with the Cretan Bull and conceived this monster.

1.3. *CIL* IV 1222: Pompeii. On a door. The perils of love.

Amāmus. Invidēmus.

Notes: **invideō, -ēre, -vīdī, -vīsus**: envy, be jealous.

1.4. *CIL* IV 10234: Pompeii. Part of a longer inscription on a wall.

Amō tē, Facilis.

Notes: **tē**: you; **Facilis, -is**, m/f: a name meaning "easy."

1.5. *CIL* **IV 2409a:** Pompeii. On an atrium wall. An ignoramus.

Stronius Stronnius nīl scit.

Notes: **Stronius Stronnius, Stroniī Stronniī**, m: a Roman man's name; **nīl** = *nihil*.

1.6. *CIL* **IV 2351:** Pompeii. On an atrium wall. A coward on the run!

Polucarpus fugit.

Notes: **Polucarpus, -ī**, m: a Greek man's name meaning "rich in fruit" (our Polucarpus may have been a gladiator).

1.7. *CIL* **IV 5358:** Pompeii. A successful date.

Secundus cum Prīmigeniā conveniunt.

Notes: **Secundus, -ī**, m: a Roman man's name meaning "second" or "favorable"; **cum Prīmigeniā**: "with Primigenia" (*Prīmigenia, -iae, f*: a Roman woman's name, "first-born"); **conveniō, -īre, -vēnī, -ventus**: come together, meet (here the verb should be *convenit* to agree with the singular subject *Secundus*, but the author has construed *cum Prīmigeniā* as part of the subject and rendered the verb as plural).

1.8. *CIL* **IV 3031a:** Pompeii. On a column in the Vicoletto of Mercury. Lessons learned.

Dare et accipere (et) prohibēre.

Notes: **accipiō, -ere, accēpī, acceptus**: take, receive; **prohibeō, -ēre, -uī**: hold back, restrain, hinder.

1.9. *CIL* **IV 1816:** Pompeii. On a basilica. What happened to your hair?!

Epaphra, glaber es.

Notes: **Epaphra, -ae**, m: a man's name from a Greek word meaning "frothy"; **glaber, glabra, glabrum**: bald.

1.10. *CIL* **IV 1625:** Pompeii. On a tavern wall. A redundant compliment.

Venus es, Ve(nus).

Notes: **Venus, Veneris**, f: loveliness (in general), the goddess of beauty and sexual attraction.

1.11. *CIL* IV 10093c: Pompeii. Scribbled onto a wall. A timeworn insult.

Brū(t)us canis est.

Notes: **Brūtus, -ī**, m: a Roman cognomen ("third name") to distinguish individual families within a *gens* ("clan"). Two famous Romans belonged to this family: Lucius Iunius Brutus, who liberated Rome from despotic Etruscan kings in 509 BCE, and Didius Iunius Brutus, among the senators who assassinated Julius Caesar in 44 BCE; **canis, -is**, m/f: dog.

1.12. *CIL* IV 10597: Herculaneum. Scribbled onto the wall of a bath. Compliment or curse?

Cosmus cas(tus) (est).

Notes: **Cosmus, -ī**, m: a man's name from a Greek word meaning "world, order, universe"; **castus, -a, -um**: clean, pure, chaste.

1.13. *CIL* IV 1435: Pompeii. On a column in the Vicoletto of Mercury. A lucky tenant.

(Fēli)x (es)t Ianuārius Fūficius, quī hīc habitat.

Notes: **fēlix, fēlīcis**: lucky; **Ianuārius Fūficius, Ianuāriī Fūficiī**, m: a Roman man's name; **quī**: who.

1.14. *CIL* VI 29609: Rome. Columbarium tablet found near the Via Latina (cremated remains were stored in columbaria). Part of a longer inscription in which a young girl named Utilis ("a practical girl") hopes for immortality from the grave. The lines are adapted from a Greek epigram.

Cinis sum. Cinis terra est. Terra dea est. Ergō ego mortuua nōn sum.

Notes: **cinis, cineris**, m: ash; **terra, -ae**, f: earth, ground, soil; **dea, -ae**, f: goddess; **ergō**: therefore; **ego**: I; **mortuua** = *mortua* from *mortuus, -a, -um*: dead.

1.15. *CIL* IV 9226: Pompeii. Scribbled on a wall next to a caricature of a laurel-bedecked man.

Rūfus est (imperātor).

Notes: **Rūfus, -ī**, m: a Roman man's name meaning "red, ruddy"; **imperātor, -ōris**, m: general, monarch of the Roman Empire.

First and Second Declension Nouns and Adjectives

PART 1: NOUNS

1. As you noticed in *NLP* 1, there are no articles ("the," "a," or "an") in Latin. You must supply the article according to the context.

2. The ending of a Latin noun conveys its grammatical role in the sentence. This feature, combined with the fact that a verb's subject is often indicated only by the ending of the verb, renders word order in Latin almost irrelevant (although Latin sentences often follow this order: subject, direct object, verb). This apparent lack of word order can prove challenging because English relies so heavily on word order to convey meaning.

3. Latin has six basic categories, or cases, for the grammatical functions of nouns. The basic functions of each case are described below. Future lessons will explain in greater detail the more nuanced uses of these cases.

The **NOMINATIVE CASE** signifies either the subject of a clause, a predicate adjective, or a subject complement.

> *CIL* IV 2331 (*NLP* 1.2): **Hīc habitat <u>Mīnōtaurus</u>**. The <u>Minotaur</u> lives here.
> *Mīnōtaurus* is the subject of the sentence and in the nominative case.

> Pliny the Elder, *Naturalis Historia* 24.151: **Cicūta quoque <u>venēnum</u> est**. Hemlock is also a <u>poison</u>.
> *venēnum* is a subject complement and in the nominative case.

The **GENITIVE CASE** signifies the relationship between two nouns and often indicates possession. Nouns in the genitive case are frequently translated into English as the object of the preposition "of." N.B. The "of" is implied in the case ending and is not explicitly expressed in Latin.

> Caesar, *de Bello Civili* 3.94.5: **Castrōrum praesidia confirmō**. I strengthen the camp's defenses.
>> *Castrōrum* is a possessive noun and in the genitive case.

> *CIL* IV 4289: **Puel(l)ārum decus Celadus**. Celadus (is) the glory of the girls.
>> *Puel(l)ārum* is the object of the English preposition "of" and in the genitive case.

The **DATIVE CASE** signifies an indirect object and is used for other expressions involving "to/for" and, for the most part, a person. N.B. The "to/for" is implied in the case ending and is not explicitly expressed in Latin.

> Cicero, *ad Familiares* 14.1.6: **Tulliolae et Cicerōnī salūtem dīc**. Say hello to little Tullia and Cicero, Jr.
>> *Tulliolae* and *Cicerōnī* are the indirect objects of *dīc* and in the dative case.

> *CIL* VI 30786: **Neptūnō Aug(ustō) et Nymphīs sacrum**. (An offering) sacred to Augustan Neptune and the Nymphs.
>> *Neptūnō Aug(ustō)* and *Nymphīs* indicate "to" whom the offering is sacred and in the dative case.

The **ACCUSATIVE CASE** signifies either a direct object, which receives the action of the verb, or the object of certain prepositions (e.g., "to," "near," "across") that are explicitly expressed by a separate Latin word.

> *CIL* IV 10697: **Fortūnātus amat Amplianda(m)**. Fortunatus loves Amplianda.
>> *Ampliandam* is the direct object of *amat* and in the accusative case.

> Caesar, *de Bello Gallico* 1.10.4: **Hī sunt extrā prōvinciam trans Rhodanum prīmī**. These are the first people beyond the province across the Rhone.
>> *prōvinciam* is the object of the Latin preposition *extrā*, and *Rhodanum* is the object of the Latin preposition *trans*; both nouns are in the accusative case.

The **ABLATIVE CASE** signifies an object of one of the following prepositions: "with," "from," "by," and "in." Sometimes the preposition is explicitly expressed by a separate Latin word; other times it is implied in the case ending.

> *CIL* IV 5358 (*NLP* 1.7): **Secundus cum <u>Prīmigeniā</u> conveniunt**. Secundus meets with <u>Primigenia</u>.
>
> > *Prīmigeniā* is the object of the Latin preposition *cum* and in the ablative case.

> Tacitus, *Agricola* 12.3: **Caelum <u>crēbrīs imbribus</u> ac <u>nebulīs</u> foedum**. The sky (is) foul <u>with frequent rain and clouds</u>.
>
> > *crēbrīs imbribus* and *nebulīs* are the objects of an implied "with" and in the ablative case.

The **VOCATIVE CASE** signifies direct address.

> *CIL* IV 1816 (*NLP* 1.9): **<u>Epaphra</u>, glaber es**. <u>Epaphra</u>, you are bald.
>
> > *Epaphra* is in the vocative case.

> Cicero, *ad Familiares* 14.3.5: **Valē, <u>mea Terentia</u>**. Goodbye, <u>my Terentia</u>.
>
> > *mea Terentia* is in the vocative case.

4. Every Latin noun falls into one of five sets, or declensions, and each declension has its own case endings. The genitive singular ending indicates the declension group of a Latin noun (the genitive singular is different in each declension group: **-ae, -ī, -is, -ūs, -ēī**). All Latin nouns also have gender (masculine, feminine, neuter). Grammatical gender is an arbitrary function of the language and rarely has a connection to natural gender (e.g., the inanimate object "door" [*iānua, -ae*] happens to be feminine and "animal" [*animal, animālis*] happens to be neuter).

5. The dictionary entry for Latin nouns consists of the nominative singular, the genitive singular (often abbreviated), and the gender. Consider the following examples:

puella, -ae, f: girl (**-ae** indicates first declension)
annus, -ī, m: year (**-ī** indicates second declension)
māter, mātris, f: mother (**-is** indicates third declension)
lacus, -ūs, m: lake (**-ūs** indicates fourth declension)
rēs, -eī, f: thing, matter, situation (**-ēī** indicates fifth declension)

It is essential to know to what declension a noun belongs so that you can employ the proper set of case endings. The genitive singular form also gives the base to which other case endings are attached. The base is found by dropping the genitive singular ending.

Declension	Genitive Form	Genitive Ending	Base
1st	**puellae**	-ae	**puell-**
2nd	**annī**	-ī	**ann-**
3rd	**mātris**	-is	**mātr-**
4th	**lacūs**	-ūs	**lac-**
5th	**reī**	-ēī	**r-**

You will learn the case endings for the first and second declensions in this lesson. The other declensions will be covered in *NLP* 3 and 10.

6. Nouns of the first declension end in **-a** in the nominative singular and feature -a- in most of the case endings. These nouns are usually feminine, but a small number of them, often referring to occupations typically held by men in Rome, are masculine (e.g., **poēta**: poet; **agricola**: farmer; **nauta**: sailor; **convīva**: guest; and **pīrāta**: pirate). Most women's names

FIRST DECLENSION NOUNS

Case	puella, -ae, f: girl	poēta, -ae, m: poet
Singular		
Nominative	puell**a**	poēt**a**
Genitive	puell**ae**	poēt**ae**
Dative	puell**ae**	poēt**ae**
Accusative	puell**am**	poēt**am**
Ablative	puell**ā**	poēt**ā**
Vocative	puell**a**	poēt**a**
Plural		
Nominative	puell**ae**	poēt**ae**
Genitive	puell**ārum**	poēt**ārum**
Dative	puell**īs**	poēt**īs**
Accusative	puell**ās**	poēt**ās**
Ablative	puell**īs**	poēt**īs**
Vocative	puell**ae**	poēt**ae**

belong to the first declension and are, predictably, feminine (e.g., Livia, Lucretia, Julia, and Terentia). Some men's names also belong to the first declension (e.g., Seneca, Sulla, Agrippa, and Epaphra, our friend from *NLP* 1.9), but are masculine like *agricola* and *poēta*.

7. In the first declension, the endings for the genitive singular, dative singular, nominative plural, and vocative plural are identical (-**ae**). Likewise, the endings for the dative and ablative plurals (-**īs**) are identical, as are the nominative and vocative singulars (-**a**). In instances where the ending can signify two or more cases, context will help you to determine which case is being employed. The verb will often provide valuable clues.

8. Nouns of the second declension typically end in -**us** or -**um** in the nominative singular. Most of these nouns are either masculine (-**us**) or neuter (-**um**). A small number are feminine, including trees, gems, and some place names: **laurus**: laurel tree; **pīnus**: pine, fir tree; **amethystus**: amethyst; and **Aegyptus**: Egypt. A few very common second declension masculine nouns end in -**r** (not -**us**) in the nominative singular (**puer**: boy; **vir**: man; and **ager**: field [N.B. *ager* features a stem change to *agr-*]). A few

SECOND DECLENSION NOUNS

Case	annus, -ī, m: year	laurus, -ī, f: laurel tree	vir, virī, m: man	ager, agrī, m: field	vīnum, -ī, n: wine
Singular					
Nominative	ann**us**	laur**us**	vir	ager	vīn**um**
Genitive	annī	laurī	virī	agrī	vīnī
Dative	annō	laurō	virō	agrō	vinō
Accusative	ann**um**	laur**um**	vir**um**	agr**um**	vīn**um**
Ablative	annō	laurō	virō	agrō	vinō
Vocative	ann**e**	laur**e**	vir	ager	vīn**um**
Plural					
Nominative	annī	laurī	virī	agrī	vīna
Genitive	ann**ōrum**	laur**ōrum**	vir**ōrum**	agr**ōrum**	vīn**ōrum**
Dative	ann**īs**	laur**īs**	vir**īs**	agr**īs**	vīn**īs**
Accusative	ann**ōs**	laur**ōs**	vir**ōs**	agr**ōs**	vīna
Ablative	ann**īs**	laur**īs**	vir**īs**	agr**īs**	vīn**īs**
Vocative	annī	laurī	virī	agrī	vīna

neuter nouns end in **-us** (not **-um**) in the nominative and accusative singulars (**pelagus**: sea; **vulgus**: crowd).

9. Note that the endings of typical second declension neuter nouns differ from the masculine ones in only a few cases: **-um** (not -us/-e) in the nominative and vocative singular, **-a** (not -ī) in the nominative and vocative plural, and **-a** (not -ōs) in the accusative plural. In addition, the endings for the masculine genitive singular and the masculine nominative plural (-ī) are identical, as well as neuter nominative plural and neuter accusative plural (-**a**), the dative and ablative singular (-**ō**), and the dative and ablative plural (-**īs**). N.B. For the few neuter nouns that take **-us** in the nominative singular, the accusative and vocative singular endings are also **-us** (the neuter accusative is always identical to its corresponding nominative).

10. This table summarizes the case endings for first and second declension nouns:

Case	1st Declension f/m		2nd Declension m/f		2nd Declension n	
	Singular	Plural	Singular	Plural	Singular	Plural
Nominative	-a	-ae	-us/-r	-ī	-um	-a
Genitive	-ae	-ārum	-ī	-ōrum	-ī	-ōrum
Dative	-ae	-īs	-ō	-īs	-ō	-īs
Accusative	-am	-ās	-um	-ōs	-um	-a
Ablative	-ā	-īs	-ō	-īs	-ō	-īs
Vocative	-a	-ae	-e/-r	-ī	-um	-a

PART 2: ADJECTIVES

11. A Latin adjective must agree with the noun it modifies in case, number, and gender. First and second declension Latin adjectives take their feminine endings from the first declension and their masculine and neuter endings from the second declension. First and second declension adjectives follow two patterns:

- adjectives in *-us, -a, -um*
- adjectives with their masculine singular in *-er* (these adjectives frequently undergo a stem change)

FIRST AND SECOND DECLENSION ADJECTIVES
(-us, -a, -um)

Case	Masculine	Feminine	Neuter
Singular			
Nominative	bon**us**	bon**a**	bon**um**
Genitive	bon**ī**	bon**ae**	bon**ī**
Dative	bon**ō**	bon**ae**	bon**ō**
Accusative	bon**um**	bon**am**	bon**um**
Ablative	bon**ō**	bon**ā**	bon**ō**
Vocative	bon**e**	bon**a**	bon**um**
Plural			
Nominative	bon**ī**	bon**ae**	bon**a**
Genitive	bon**ōrum**	bon**ārum**	bon**ōrum**
Dative	bon**īs**	bon**īs**	bon**īs**
Accusative	bon**ōs**	bon**ās**	bon**a**
Ablative	bon**īs**	bon**īs**	bon**īs**
Vocative	bon**ī**	bon**ae**	bon**a**

FIRST AND SECOND DECLENSION ADJECTIVES
WITH A STEM CHANGE

Case	Masculine	Feminine	Neuter
Singular			
Nominative	noster	nostr**a**	nostr**um**
Genitive	nostr**ī**	nostr**ae**	nostr**ī**
Dative	nostr**ō**	nostr**ae**	nostr**ō**
Accusative	nostr**um**	nostr**am**	nostr**um**
Ablative	nostr**ō**	nostr**ā**	nostr**ō**
Vocative	noster	nostr**a**	nostr**um**
Plural			
Nominative	nostr**ī**	nostr**ae**	nostr**a**
Genitive	nostr**ōrum**	nostr**ārum**	nostr**ōrum**
Dative	nostr**īs**	nostr**īs**	nostr**īs**
Accusative	nostr**ōs**	nostr**ās**	nostr**a**
Ablative	nostr**īs**	nostr**īs**	nostr**īs**
Vocative	nostr**ī**	nostr**ae**	nostr**a**

12. The dictionary entry for first and second declension adjectives consists of the nominative singular masculine, feminine, and neuter (often abbreviated **-us, -a, -um**). Consider the following examples:

> **bonus, -a, -um**: good
> *bonus* is masculine, nominative, singular
> *bona* is feminine, nominative, singular
> *bonum* is neuter, nominative, singular

> **noster, nostra, nostrum**: our
> *noster* is masculine, nominative, singular
> *nostra* is feminine, nominative, singular
> *nostrum* is neuter, nominative, singular
> (Note the stem change to *nostr-*.)

13. Adjectives sometimes have the same endings as the nouns they modify. When they do, it is easy to determine which words in a Latin sentence modify one another. Consider the following examples:

> *CIL* IV 9199: **Mag<u>us</u> mal<u>us</u> est**. The magician is evil.

> Catullus 1.1 (*NLP* 4.1): **Cui dōnō lepid<u>um</u> nov<u>um</u> libell<u>um</u>?** To whom do I give the charming new little book?

Adjectives often have different endings from the nouns they modify because the adjective belongs to one declension and the noun to another. Nevertheless, they always agree with the nouns they modify in case, number, and gender. Consider the following examples:

> Vergil, *Georgics* 2.18: **Parnāsi<u>a</u> laur<u>us</u>**. A Parnassian laurel tree.
> Both *laurus* and *Parnāsia* have the same case, number, and gender: nominative, singular, and feminine; however, *laur<u>us</u>* is a feminine noun in the second declension whereas *Parnāsi<u>a</u>* is an adjective with first declension endings.

Cicero, *pro Roscio Amerino* 146: **Quis pīrāta tam barbarus** . . . What pirate (was) so savage . . .

> Both *pīrāta* and *barbarus* have the same case, number, and gender: nominative, singular, and masculine; however, *pīrāta* is a masculine noun in the first declension whereas *barbarus* is an adjective with second declension endings.

14. In Latin, adjectives can also function as nouns. When adjectives act in this capacity, they are called **SUBSTANTIVES**. Consider the following examples:

> Livy, *ab Urbe Condita* 22.57.6: **Gallus et Galla, Graecus et Graeca in forō bovāriō sub terram vīvī dēmissī sunt**. A <u>Gallic man</u> and a <u>Gallic woman</u>, and a <u>Greek man</u> and a <u>Greek woman</u> were buried (literally: "thrust down under the earth") alive in the cattle market.
>
> > *Gallus* alone stands for *Gallus vir; Galla* alone stands for *Galla fēmina; Graecus* alone stands for *Graecus vir; Graeca* alone stands for *Graeca fēmina.*

> Caesar, *de Bello Gallico* 7.42.3: **Bona cīvium Rōmānōrum dīripiunt**. They snatch the <u>property</u> of Roman citizens.
>
> > *Bona* alone stands for "good things," "goods," and, by extension, "possessions" or "property."

> Vergil, *Aeneid* 4.569–70: **Varium et mūtābile semper fēmina**. A woman is always an inconstant and changeable thing.
>
> > *Varium* and *mūtābile* do not modify *fēmina* because they are neuter, not feminine. Here, these two words act as substantives: an accurate translation is only achieved by adding the English word "thing" to their basic meanings.

15. In Latin (and English), a noun or adjective can serve as an **APPOSITIVE**, renaming or further describing a noun. Appositives are often triggered by verbs of naming or calling. Consider the following examples:

CIL VI 3097 (*NLP* 6.13): **Deō Mercuriō.** To the god Mercury.

Both *deō* and *Mercuriō* are in the dative case. The noun *Mercuriō* stands in apposition to *deō* and pinpoints the identity of the god.

Pliny the Elder, *Naturalis Historiae* 4.75: **Angustiās "Hellespontum" vocant.** They call the narrows the "Hellespont."

Both *angustiās* and *Hellespontum* are in the accusative case. The singular noun *Hellespontum* describes the plural noun *angustiās* by giving its proper name.

I. Required Vocabulary

NOUNS

> **fēmina, -ae**, f: woman
> **patria, -iae**, f: fatherland, country
> **poēta, -ae**, m: poet
> **puella, -ae**, f: girl
> **unda, -ae**, f: water, stream, wave
> **vīta, -ae**, f: life
>
> **ager, agrī**, m: field
> **animus, -ī**, m: soul, mind
> **annus, -ī**, m: year
> **vīnum, -ī**, n: wine
> **vir, virī**, m: man, husband

ADJECTIVES

> **bonus, -a, -um**: good; **bona, -ōrum**, n (plural): goods, possessions (substantive)
> **certus, -a, -um**: certain, resolved, decided
> **longus, -a, -um**: long, vast, spacious
> **magnus, -a, -um**: great
> **malus, -a, -um**: bad, evil
> **meus, mea, meum**: mine
> **miser, misera, miserum**: wretched, unhappy, miserable
> **noster, nostra, nostrum**: our
> **tuus, tua, tuum**: your (singular)
> **vester, vestra, vestrum**: your (plural)

VERBS

teneō, -ēre, tenuī, tentus: hold, maintain, detain

faciō, -ere, fēcī, factus: make, do
relinquō, -ere, relīquī, relictus: leave behind, desert, abandon

PREPOSITIONS

in (+ ablative): in, on
in (+ accusative): into, onto, against

CONJUNCTIONS

nec: and . . . not
-que: and (this type of conjunction, called an "enclitic," attaches to the
end of a word and joins that word to the previous word, phrase, or
sentence)
-que . . . -que: both . . . and
sed: but
tamen: nevertheless, nonetheless, however, but

II. Translate the following sentences from Latin to English or English to Latin.

1. Patria mea est magna.
2. Poētae bonī fēminās virōsque docent.
3. Nihil certum videō.
4. In animīs nostrīs magna tenēmus.
5. Brūte, bonus nōn es.
6. Vīnum animum bonum nōn facit.
7. Hīc habitāmus et agrōs vidēmus.
8. Vītam miseram fugitis.
9. I take my possessions.
10. The bad poet gives the men wine.
11. We leave behind the long year.
12. Miserable minds know evil things.

Publius Ovidius Naso (43 BCE–17 CE)

Sex, scandal, solitude—these three words summarize the turbulent life of Publius Ovidius Naso ("The Nose"), Rome's most prolific and sensational poet. Despite his father's protests, Ovid rejected the traditional career path of law and Roman political life and devoted himself to poetry under the patronage of Marcus Valerius Messalla Corvinus (64 BCE–8 CE), a wealthy army general and politician, who, although friendly enough with the emperor, supported a circle of Roman poets outside Augustus's direct control. Almost all of Ovid's publications revealed his countercultural tendencies. Most scandalous was his *Ars Amatoria* (2 CE), a didactic poem in three books that gave detailed advice to men and women on the art of seduction and other amatory, and often extramarital, pursuits. This publication, in particular, is thought to have angered Augustus, who wanted to promote a program of moral improvement, which, among other things, criminalized adultery. Even when Ovid tried to redeem himself by turning to epic verse in his *Metamorphoses*, he did not produce a stately masterpiece evoking the heroic tradition of Vergil's *Aeneid*, but he rather unfolded a complicated chronicle of Greco-Roman mythological tales that most likely failed, once again, to impress the emperor. (In the stories of Jupiter's adulterous affairs and whimsical abuses of power, for example, Ovid made allusions to Augustus's totalitarian, and perhaps abusive, authority over the Roman people.) Almost immediately after the publication of the *Metamorphoses* in 8 CE, Augustus exiled Ovid to Tomis, a remote area on the Black Sea. No one knows exactly why Ovid was banished, although the more outlandish theories involve some sort of dalliance between Ovid and Augustus's granddaughter Julia, who was exiled that same year. Whatever the reason, the witty and urbane Ovid despised life in Tomis and launched an extensive campaign for his recall. Despite his efforts, Ovid was never allowed to return to his beloved Rome, and he died in exile around 17 CE. His poems from exile reveal a creative spirit crushed by a political regime and an artist amazed that cosmopolitan Rome could punish him so severely for free expression.

Ovid's rebellious poetic voice and his cruel exile have inspired countless generations of artists. Echoes of his work appear in the verses of Dante, Petrarch, Chaucer, Shakespeare, Milton, and Cervantes. Ovid's influence on the visual arts is no less profound, as the paintings and sculptures of Botticelli, Poussin, Rembrandt,

Rubens, Picasso, and Dalí testify. Most remarkable, however, is that Ovid remains a vibrant muse for artists today. In his novel *An Imaginary Life* (Vintage, 1996), David Malouf explores what adjustments Ovid, the wry and sophisticated urban mythmaker, had to make living among a remote people who actually believed in myths. In *After Ovid: New Metamorphoses* (Farrar, Straus, and Giroux, 1996), Michael Hofmann and James Lasdun collect the work of more than forty contemporary poets who take Ovid's *Metamorphoses* as a springboard for their creations. Philip Terry compiled a similar collection of short stories entitled *Ovid Metamorphosed* (Vintage, 2001) that features such fiction powerhouses as Joyce Carol Oates and Margaret Atwood. Award-winning playwright Mary Zimmerman transformed the most popular tales of Ovid's epic poem into her own *Metamorphoses* (Northwestern University Press, 2002), a play that mesmerized Broadway audiences for 400 performances. All these works reinforce the vibrancy and immediacy of Ovid's poetry and the captivating "celebrity" persona he crafted for himself in those verses.

SUGGESTIONS FOR FURTHER READING:

Boyd, Barbara. *Ovid's Literary Loves: Influence and Innovation in the* Amores. University of Michigan Press, 1997.

Hardie, Philip R., ed. *Cambridge Companion to Ovid*. Cambridge, 2006.

Knox, Peter E., ed. *Oxford Readings in Ovid*. Oxford, 2007.

Martindale, Charles, ed. *Ovid Renewed: Ovidian Influences on Literature and Art from the Middle Ages to the Twentieth Century*. Cambridge, 1990.

McGowan, Matthew M. *Ovid in Exile: Power and Poetic Redress in the* Tristia *and* Epistulae ex Ponto. Brill, 2009.

Newlands, Carole E. *Playing with Time: Ovid's* Fasti. Cornell, 1995.

Volk, Katharina. *Ovid*. Wiley-Blackwell, 2010.

PASSAGES

2.1. Ovid, *Tristia* **4.10.3.** In this poem from exile, Ovid recounts his entire life story. Meter: elegiac couplets (dactylic hexameter line).

Sulmo mihī patria est, gelidīs ūberrimus undīs.

Notes: **Sulmō, -ōnis**, m: Ovid's birthplace, a town east of the Apennine Mountains, about 90 miles from Rome; **mihī**: to me (dative singular), here, "my"; **gelidus, -a, -um**: icy, frosty; **ūberrimus, -a, -um**: extremely abundant, very copious.

2.2. Ovid, *Ars Amatoria* 1.631. Here, Ovid gives advice to men pursuing potential lovers. Meter: elegiac couplets (dactylic hexameter line).

Nec timidē prōmitte: trahunt prōmissa puellās.

Notes: **timidē**: timidly; **prōmitte**: "promise!" (imperative singular from *prōmittō, -ere, -mīsī, -missus*); **trahō, -ere, traxī, tractus**: drag, draw (here, "get"); **prōmissum, -ī**, n: promise.

2.3. Ovid, *Ars Amatoria* 1.237. Here, Ovid recommends dinner parties as good places to meet women. Meter: elegiac couplets (dactylic hexameter line).

Vīna parant animōs faciuntque calōribus aptōs.

Notes: **parō, -āre, -āvī, -ātus**: prepare; **calor, -ōris**, m: heat, passion, love (*calōribus*: dative plural); **aptus, -a, -um** (+ dative): fitting (for), suitable (to), amenable (to) (in apposition with an implied "them").

2.4. Ovid, *Heroides* 1.3. In his *Heroides*, Ovid fabricates poignant love letters from mythological heroines to their lovers. Penelope writes to Odysseus, lamenting that she has not had even a letter from him since the fall of Troy. Meter: elegiac couplets (dactylic hexameter line).

Trōia iacet certē, Danaīs invīsa puellīs.

Notes: **Trōia, -ae**, f: the famous town of Asia Minor where the Greeks fought for the return of the beautiful Helen; **iaceō, -ēre, iacuī, iactus**: lie, lie dead; **certē**: certainly, at least; **Danaus, -a, -um**: Greek; **invīsus, -a, -um**: hateful (to), detested (by).

2.5. Ovid, *Metamorphoses* 10.264. Even when Ovid turned to epic and its loftier themes, he could not resist the sensational aspects of Greco-Roman mythology. The sculptor Pygmalion, disgusted by the women in his city, crafts a beautiful statue of the ideal woman with whom he falls in love. Here, he decorates his statue with appropriate courtship gifts. The modern playwright George Bernard

Shaw re-creates this story in his *Pygmalion*, which became the inspiration for Lerner and Loewe's beloved musical *My Fair Lady*. Meter: dactylic hexameter.

Dat digitīs gemmās, dat longa monīlia collō.

Notes: **digitus, -ī**, m: finger; **gemma, -ae**, f: jewel, precious stone; **monīle, -is**, n: necklace (*monīlia*: accusative plural); **collum, -ī**, n: neck.

2.6. Ovid, *Metamorphoses* 3.464. Narcissus finds a love as perfect as himself, only to discover that he has become infatuated with his own reflection. Here, Ovid relates Narcissus's immediate reaction to this revelation. Meter: dactylic hexameter.

"Flammās moveōque ferōque."

Notes: **flamma, -ae**, f: flame (of desire); **moveō, -ēre, mōvī, mōtus**: move, "inspire"; **ferō, ferre, tulī, lātus**: carry, endure, "feel."

2.7. Ovid, *Metamorphoses* 4.143–44. When Pyramus arrives to meet his lover Thisbe, he sees her bloody scarf (she had fled from a lion that was feasting on a kill). Believing her dead, he commits suicide. Moments later, Thisbe appears and, here, tries to rouse the dead Pyramus. Shakespeare dramatizes this tale in *A Midsummer Night's Dream* and updates it in *Romeo and Juliet*. Meter: dactylic hexameter.

"Pȳrame, respondē! Tua tē, cārissime, Thisbē
nōminat."

Notes: **Pȳramus, -ī**, m: a Greek man's name; **respondē**: "answer!" (imperative singular from *respondeō, -ēre, respondī, responsus*); **tē**: you (accusative singular); **cārissimus, -a, -um**: dearest, most beloved; **Thisbē, Thisbēs**, f: a Greek woman's name; **nōminō, -āre, -āvī, -ātus**: call.

2.8. Ovid, *Metamorphoses* 2.167–68. Phaethon has asked to drive the chariot of the sun as proof that Phoebus, the sun god, really is his father. Phoebus warns his son that the vehicle is too difficult for anyone else to drive, but Phaethon persists, and his father relents. The divine horses, easily detecting Phaethon's inexperience, scorch the earth. Meter: dactylic hexameter.

Ruunt trītumque relinquunt
quadriiugī spatium.

Notes: **ruō, -ere, ruī, rutus**: rush out, hasten; **trītus, -a, -um**: frequented, trodden; **quadriiugī, -ōrum**, m (plural): a team (*iugum, -ī,* n) of four (*quadr-*) horses; **spatium, -iī**, n: racetrack, course.

2.9. Ovid, *Metamorphoses,* **10.23.** On her wedding day, the lovely Eurydice was fatally bitten by a snake. Her husband, the talented musician Orpheus, is so stricken with grief that he travels to the underworld to retrieve her. Here, he pleads with Pluto and Proserpina to release Eurydice from death. Meter: dactylic hexameter.

"Causa viae est coniunx."

Notes: **causa, -ae**, f: cause, reason; **via, -ae**, f: path, road, street, "journey"; **coniunx, coniugis**, m/f: spouse.

2.10. Ovid, *Fasti* **1.164.** In the *Fasti,* Ovid explicates the festivals of the Roman religious year. Here, he describes how the new year begins at the winter solstice when days grow longer and the sun seems to be born anew. Meter: elegiac couplets (pentameter line).

Principium capiunt Phoebus et annus idem.

Notes: **principium, -iī**, n: beginning; **Phoebus, -ī**, m: Apollo, the Sun god; **idem**: "the same" (accusative singular neuter).

2.11. Ovid, *Heroides* **7.7.** In this letter, Dido confronts her lover Aeneas. Meter: elegiac couplets (dactylic hexameter line).

Certus es īre tamen miseramque relinquere Dīdōn?

Notes: **īre**: to go; **Dīdō, -ūs**, f: queen of Carthage (*Dīdōn*: Greek accusative).

2.12. Ovid, *Epistulae ex Ponto* **1.4.19.** Ovid writes this poignant, autobiographical collection of letters from exile at Tomis on the Black Sea, a bleak place on the edge of the Empire where the courtly and urbane Ovid was miserable. Meter: elegiac couplets (dactylic hexameter line).

Mē quoque dēbilitat seriēs inmensa malōrum.

Notes: **mē**: me (accusative singular); **quoque**: also; **dēbilitō, -āre, -āvi, -ātus**: disable, weaken; **seriēs, -ēī**, f: series, succession (*seriēs*: nominative singular); **inmensa** = *immensa* from *immensus, -a, -um*: immense, unending, immeasurable.

EXTRA PASSAGES: DAILY LIFE

Below are three inscriptions that address the same themes from everyday life that we see in Ovid: love and hate as well as life's simple pleasures.

2.13. *CIL* IV 3131: Pompeii. Etched onto a column.

Figulus amat Idaia(m).

Notes: **Figulus, -ī**, m: a man's name meaning "potter" or "bricklayer"; **Idaia, Idaiae**, f: a woman's name.

2.14. *CIL* IV 4429: Pompeii. Between two doorways.

M(arcī) Iūnī insula sum.

Notes: **Marcus Iūnius, Marcī Iūniī**, m: a man's name; **insula, -ae**, f: apartment building.

2.15. *CIL* VI 15258: Rome. Part of an epitaph to the 52-year-old Tiberius Claudius Secundus erected by his loving wife, Merope Caesaris.

Balnea, vīna, Venus corrumpunt corpora nostra, set vītam faciunt b(alnea), v(īna), V(enus).

Notes: **balneum, -ī**, n: bathing place; **Venus, Veneris**, f: loveliness (in general), the goddess of beauty and sexual attraction; **corrumpō, -ere, -rūpī, -ruptus**: destroy, annihilate; **corpus, corporis**, n: body (*corpora*: accusative plural); **set** = *sed*.

Third Declension
Nouns and Adjectives

ı

PART 1: THIRD DECLENSION NOUNS

1. Nouns of the third declension have no regular case ending for the nominative singular. These nouns can be masculine, feminine, or neuter. It is easiest just to memorize the gender as you learn new third declension nouns, but you may notice some patterns, especially for feminine nouns in the third declension, which include abstractions (**virtūs**) and nouns that end in

THIRD DECLENSION NOUNS

Case	māter, mātris, f: mother	rex, rēgis, m: king	corpus, corporis, n: body
Singular			
Nominative	māter	rex	corpus
Genitive	māt**ris**	rē**gis**	corpor**is**
Dative	mātr**ī**	rēg**ī**	corpor**ī**
Accusative	māt**rem**	rē**gem**	corpus
Ablative	māt**re**	rē**ge**	corpor**e**
Vocative	māter	rex	corpus
Plural			
Nominative	māt**rēs**	rē**gēs**	corpor**a**
Genitive	māt**rum**	rē**gum**	corpor**um**
Dative	māt**ribus**	rēg**ibus**	corpor**ibus**
Accusative	māt**rēs**	rē**gēs**	corpor**a**
Ablative	māt**ribus**	rēg**ibus**	corpor**ibus**
Vocative	māt**rēs**	rē**gēs**	corpor**a**

-**ās** (e.g., **aetās**, **cīvitās**). N.B. Many third declension nouns undergo a stem change, so it is particularly important to take note of the genitive singular, which gives the base to which the remaining endings are attached.

N.B. In future lessons, the dictionary entries of many third declension nouns will be abbreviated. For example:

amor, -ōris, m: love (the genitive singular is **amōris**)
castitās, -ātis, f: chastity (the genitive singular is **castitātis**)
factiō, -iōnis, f: band (the genitive singular is **factiōnis**)
hostis, -is, m/f: enemy (the genitive singular is **hostis**)

PART 2: I-STEM NOUNS

2. There is a subset of third declension nouns known as i-stems. For the most part, i-stem nouns have the same case endings as regular third declension nouns, except that the genitive plural will be -**ium** (not -**um**) for

THIRD DECLENSION I-STEM NOUNS

Case	urbs, urbis (-ium), f: city	ignis, ignis (-ium), m: fire	mare, maris (-ium), n: sea
Singular			
Nominative	urbs	ignis	mare
Genitive	urb**is**	ign**is**	mar**is**
Dative	urb**ī**	ign**ī**	mar**ī**
Accusative	urb**em**	ign**em**	mare
Ablative	urb**e**	ign**ī** (igne)	mar**ī**
Vocative	urbs	ignis	mare
Plural			
Nominative	urb**ēs**	ign**ēs**	mar**ia**
Genitive	urb**ium**	ign**ium**	mar**ium**
Dative	urb**ibus**	ign**ibus**	mar**ibus**
Accusative	urb**ēs** (urb**īs**)	ign**īs** (ign**ēs**)	mar**ia**
Ablative	urb**ibus**	ign**ibus**	mar**ibus**
Vocative	urb**ēs**	ign**ēs**	mar**ia**

all genders; the accusative plural will be either -ēs or -īs for masculine
and feminine i-stem nouns; the ablative singular will usually be -ī (not -e)
and the nominative, vocative, and accusative plurals will be -ia (not -a)
for neuter i-stem nouns.

3. *NLP* and some, but not all, dictionaries will signify that a noun is i-stem
   by including the genitive plural: **nūbēs, -is (-ium)**, f: cloud.

4. Certain types of third declension nouns are almost always i-stem:

   Parasyllabic masculine and feminine nouns (i.e., nouns with the same
   number of syllables in the nominative and genitive singular):

   > **ignis, -is (-ium)**, m: fire
   > **fīnis, -is (-ium)**, m: end, boundary
   > **cīvis, -is (-ium)**, m/f: citizen
   > **hostis, -is (-ium)**, m: enemy

   Masculine and feminine nouns that end in **-s** or **-x** in the nominative
   singular:

   > **urbs, urbis (-ium)**, f: city
   > **nox, noctis (-ium)**, f: night
   > **pars, partis (-ium)**, f: part, portion
   > **cohors, cohortis (-ium)**, m: cohort

   Masculine and feminine nouns that end in **-ns**:

   > **cliens, clientis (-ium)**, m: client
   > **gens, gentis (-ium)**, f: family, clan
   > **mens, mentis (-ium)**, f: mind

   Neuter nouns that end in **-e**, **-al**, or **-ar**:

   > **mare, maris (-ium)**, n: sea
   > **animal, animālis (-ium)**, n: animal
   > **exemplar, -āris (-ium)**, n: pattern

5. Do not worry too much about the i-stem nouns. Even the Romans had trouble with them! Many nouns lost some of their i-stem endings for regular third declension endings. It is far more important to recognize the i-stems forms in context.

6. The following table gives all the possible case endings for third declension nouns, regular and i-stem:

Case	3rd Declension m/f		3rd Declension n	
	Singular	Plural	Singular	Plural
Nominative	(varies)	-ēs	(varies)	-a/-ia
Genitive	-is	-um/-ium	-is	-um/-ium
Dative	-ī	-ibus	-ī	-ibus
Accusative	-em	-ēs/-īs	(varies)	-a/-ia
Ablative	-e	-ibus	-e/ī	-ibus
Vocative	(varies)	-ēs	(varies)	-a/-ia

PART 3: THIRD DECLENSION ADJECTIVES

7. There are three basic patterns for the nominative singular forms of third declension adjectives:

> **ācer, acris, acre**: sharp, fierce (three terminations / endings):
> *ācer* is masculine, nominative, singular
> *acris* is feminine, nominative, singular
> *acre* is neuter, nominative, singular
>
> **brevis, brevis, breve**: small, short (two terminations):
> *brevis* is masculine or feminine, nominative, singular
> *breve* is neuter, nominative, singular
>
> **potens**: strong, powerful (one termination):
> *potens* can be either masculine, feminine, or neuter, nominative, singular

Third declension adjectives with two terminations in the nominative singular are often abbreviated in the dictionary as **brevis, -e**. Third declension adjectives with only one termination in the nominative singular are listed in the dictionary with their genitive singular in parentheses: **potens (-entis)**.

8. Third declension adjectives have almost the same case endings as third declension i-stem nouns, except that masculine and feminine adjectives always have -ī (not -e) in the ablative singular. Study the following table:

THIRD DECLENSION ADJECTIVES

Case	Masculine	Feminine	Neuter
Singular			
Nominative	brevis	brevis	breve
Genitive	brevis	brevis	brevis
Dative	brevī	brevī	brevī
Accusative	brevem	brevem	breve
Ablative	brevī	brevī	brevī
Vocative	brevis	brevis	breve
Plural			
Nominative	brevēs	brevēs	brevia
Genitive	brevium	brevium	brevium
Dative	brevibus	brevibus	brevibus
Accusative	brevēs/brevīs	brevēs/brevīs	brevia
Ablative	brevibus	brevibus	brevibus
Vocative	brevēs	brevēs	brevia

9. As you have already learned in *NLP* 2, adjectives have to match their nouns in case, number, and gender, but not necessarily in declension. Consider the following examples:

CIL VII 249 [*ILS* 3162; *RIB* 584]: **Pāciferō Martī Ēlegaurba posuit ex vōtō.** Elegaurba has placed (this altar) to <u>Mars the Peace-bringer</u> according to her vow.
    Both *Pāciferō* and *Martī* have the same case, number, and gender: dative, singular, and masculine; however, *Martī* is a noun in the third declension whereas *Pāciferō* is an adjective with second declension endings.

Pliny the Elder, *Naturalis Historia* 8.146: **(Canēs) sōlī nōmina sua, sōlī <u>vōcem domesticam</u> agnoscunt.** Only (dogs) know their own names, only (dogs know) a <u>familiar voice</u>.
    Both *vōcem* and *domesticam* have the same case, number, and gender: accusative, singular, and feminine; however, *vōcem* is a noun in the third

declension whereas *domesticam* is an adjective with first declension endings.

Martial 5.24.2: <u>**Hermēs** *omnibus* **ērudītus** *armīs*</u>. <u>Hermes</u> (is) <u>skilled</u> in <u>all weapons</u>.

Both *Hermēs* and *ērudītus* have the same case, number, and gender: nominative, singular, and masculine; however, *Hermēs* is a noun in the third declension whereas *ērudītus* is an adjective with second declension endings.

Both *omnibus* and *armīs* have the same case, number, and gender: ablative, plural, and neuter; however, *armīs* is a noun in the second declension whereas *omnibus* is an adjective with third declension endings.

I. Required Vocabulary

NOUNS

arma, -ōrum, n (plural): arms, weapons
bellum, -ī, n: war (**bellum gerere**: to wage war)
imperium, -iī, n: command, dominion, power
populus, -ī, m: people
regnum, -ī, n: kingdom, realm, sovereignty

caput, capitis, n: head
corpus, corporis, n: body
frāter, frātris, m: brother
ignis, ignis (-ium), m: fire
mare, maris (-ium), n: sea
māter, mātris, f: mother
nōmen, nōminis, n: name
pater, patris, m: father, senator
rex, rēgis, m: king
scelus, sceleris, n: crime
soror, sorōris, f: sister
urbs, urbis (-ium), f: city
uxor, uxōris, f: wife

ADJECTIVES

Rōmānus, -a, -um: Roman

brevis, -e: short

omnis, -e: whole, entire, every (singular), all (plural)

VERBS

rogō, -āre, -āvī, -ātus: ask, ask for, endorse

vocō, -āre, -āvī, -ātus: call, summon

habeō, -ēre, habuī, habitus: have, consider, wear

absolvō, -ere, -solvī, -solūtus: release (from), set free (from); complete, finish

agō, -ere, ēgī, actus: do, drive, accomplish, guide, spend, act

gerō, -ere, gessī, gestus: carry on, manage, wear, endure, suffer

PREPOSITIONS

ā/ab (+ ablative): from, away from, by (*ā* precedes words that begin with consonants; *ab* precedes words that begin with vowels)

ad (+ accusative): to, toward, for (the purpose of)

cum (+ ablative): with

per (+ accusative): through

ADVERBS

deinde or **dein**: then, next

II. Translate the following sentences from Latin to English or English to Latin.

1. Mātrēs patrēsque in urbe hīc nōn habitant.
2. Scelera frātris magna sunt.
3. Nihil uxōrī tuae dās.
4. Corpus meum armīs absolvō.
5. Vīta brevis est et urbem fugimus.
6. Rēgem miserum vidētis.
7. Nōmen bonum meum in bellō relinquō.
8. Fēmina omnia agit.
9. Romulus and Remus wage war.
10. The body is big, the mind good.
11. You (plural) summon the Roman people.
12. I endorse my brother as king.

The Legends of Early Rome

Sensitive about how young their civilization was in comparison with that of the Greeks, the Romans traced their origins back to a hero who fought for Troy against the Greeks: Aeneas, son of the goddess Venus. After the Trojan War (c. 1200 BCE), with a small group of Trojan survivors, Aeneas wandered through the Mediterranean in search of a new homeland and had many adventures on his way to Italy. After spending a year in Carthage with the lovely queen Dido, Aeneas abandoned her to seek his own destiny, thereby incurring the legendary enmity between Carthage and Rome. Upon reaching Italy, Aeneas waged a new war against the local nobleman Turnus, who was betrothed to Lavinia, daughter of King Latinus and the key to empire in central Italy. Aeneas prevailed in this struggle and named his new city Lavinium after his young bride. Vergil gives the fullest account of this myth in the *Aeneid*, but Aeneas' adventures are also recounted by Livy as well as by Ovid.

After several centuries, Rome herself was founded by Aeneas' descendant Romulus (April 21, 753 BCE), who, along with his twin Remus, was born to the Vestal Virgin Rhea Silvia and the god Mars. The twins were abandoned at birth and raised by a shepherd. The brothers argued while building their city, and Romulus prevailed. To people his new city, Romulus accepted exiles, wanderers, and political outcasts. Neighboring tribes were reticent to deal with a city of criminals, much less to intermarry with them, so Romulus was compelled to employ unconventional methods to find wives for his citizens. He invited the neighboring tribe of the Sabines to a festival of games and kidnapped the Sabine women while they were watching the performances. When the Sabines finally returned to Rome to fight for their daughters, the women had already begun families with their Roman husbands, and, according to Livy, they stopped the fighting and called for a truce.

With Romulus began the regal period of Roman history (753–509 BCE), and, as the first of the seven kings of Rome, he established the Roman senate and political structure. According to legend, other kings established the religious fabric (Numa Pompilius), infrastructure (Ancus Marcus), and legal system (Servius Tullius). This regal period thrived for over two hundred years. However, the last king, L. Tarquinius Superbus, was a tyrannical Etruscan who, according to Livy, kept the city at war and the people in near servitude. In 509 BCE, public disaffection finally resulted in war when the king's son, Sextus Tarquinius, raped Lucretia, the beautiful wife of the Roman general Collatinus. Declaring herself to be pure in her soul, though not in her body, Lucretia bade her husband to seek revenge, and she committed suicide so future Roman women would not be able to use her example to hide their own crimes (i.e., by crying "rape" to cover up adultery). Collatinus and his friend Brutus (the ancestor of Julius Caesar's young friend) led the Roman army against the Etruscan royalty, toppled the king, and founded the Roman Republic.

The legends of the fledging Republic reflect the same Roman ideals of patriotism, freedom, and chastity that flourished in later periods. Perhaps the most compelling example involves a variant of the Lucretia story. In 451 BCE, Rome suspended its traditional republican government and fell under the control of the *Decemvirī*, a group of ten appointed magistrates. The leader of this group, Appius Claudius, desired Verginia, whose father was a well-regarded plebian. Verginia's reputation was impeccable, and she was betrothed to another important plebian, Lucius Icilius. Appius recruited his client Marcus Claudius to declare that Verginia was born a slave in Appius Claudius's household and stolen by Verginius as a child. The case appeared before Appius himself, who granted custody to Marcus Claudius. Verginius killed his daughter to protect her honor and freedom rather than hand her over to the evil judge. In reaction to Verginia's tragic fate, the Roman people rose against the powerful aristocrats to establish a revised Republic, allowing for greater equality between the classes.

SUGGESTIONS FOR FURTHER READING:

Cameron, Alan. *Greek Mythography in the Roman World*. Oxford, 2005.
Carandini, Andrea. *Rome: Day One*. Translated by Stephen Sartarelli. Princeton, 2011.
Gardner, Jane F. *Roman Myths*. British Museum and University of Texas, 1993.
Wiseman, T.P. *Remus: A Roman Myth*. Cambridge, 1995.

PASSAGES

3.1. Livy, *ab Urbe Condita* 1.1.11. After defeating Turnus, Aeneas settles in Italy and marries Lavinia, the daughter of the local Latin king.

Oppidum condunt; Aenēās ab nōmine uxōris "Lāvīnium" appellat.

Notes: **oppidum, -ī,** n: town; **condō, -ere, condidī, conditus:** build, found, establish (construe "Trojans" as the subject of *condunt*); **Aenēās, -ae,** m: Aeneas; **Lāvīnium, -ī,** n: Aeneas' home in Italy; **appellō, -āre, -āvī, -ātus:** call (construe *oppidum* as the direct object).

3.2. Livy, *ab Urbe Condita* 1.3.10–11. Livy records the succession of rulers between Aeneas (c. 1200 BCE) and Numitor (c. 775 BCE), whose jealous and evil brother Amulius usurps power and kills his nephew. (He also sentences his niece Rhea Silvia to a lifetime of chastity as a Vestal Virgin.)

Pulsō frātre, Amūlius regnat. Addit scelerī scelus: stirpem frātris virīlem interēmit.

Notes: **pulsō . . . frātre:** "his brother having been driven off" (ablative absolute); **regnō, -āre, -āvī, -ātus:** reign, rule; **addō, -ere, addidī, additus:** add; **stirps, stirpis (-ium),** m/f: offspring, descendant; **virīlis, -e:** male, masculine; **interēmit:** "he (Amulius) killed" (*interēmit:* perfect tense of *interimō, -ere, -ēmī, -emptus:* kill, abolish).

3.3. Ovid, *Fasti* 2.369–70. Ovid relates the following story to explain why men celebrate the Lupercalia in the nude. Robbers attacked Romulus and Remus while they were sacrificing a goat to Faunus, a goat-horned god of the greenwood, similar to the Greek Pan. While the goat was cooking on the spit, the brothers exercised in the nude until a shepherd alerted them of the assault. Meter: elegiac couplets.

Pastor ab excelsō "Per dēvia rūra iuvencōs,
        Rōmule, praedōnēs, et Reme," dixit "agunt."

Notes: **pastor, -ōris,** m: shepherd; **excelsum, -ī,** n: height, high ground; **dēvius, -a, -um:** remote; **rūs, rūris,** n: country, countryside; **iuvencus, -ī,** m: young bull, steer; **praedō, -ōnis,** m: robber; **dixit:** "he (the shepherd) said" (*dixit:* perfect tense of *dīcō, -ere, dixī, dictus:* say, speak).

3.4. Ovid, *Fasti* 4.817–18. Feuding over which one would rule the city (as twins, neither could claim to be firstborn), Romulus and Remus decided to search for omens in the skies (described here). Livy reports that a further struggle ensued regarding the omen's interpretation: Remus claimed victory because he saw his birds first; Romulus also asserted victory because he saw more birds. Meter: elegiac couplets.

> Sex Remus, hic volucrēs bis sex videt ordine; pactō
> > stātur, et arbitrium Rōmulus urbis habet.

Notes: **sex** (indeclinable): six; **hic**: this man (here, Romulus); **volucer, volucris**, m: bird; **bis**: twice; **ordō, ordinis**, m: line, row; **pactō stātur**: "they stand by the pact" (literally: "a stand is made by the pact"); **arbitrium, -iī**, n: power, control.

3.5. Ovid, *Ars Amatoria* 1.115–16. Since his new city lacks marriageable women, Romulus decides to invite women from the nearby Sabine community to a day of games at Rome. As the festivities begin, Romulus's men surprise the women and take them captive. Meter: elegiac couplets.

> Prōtinus exiliunt, animum clāmōre fatentēs,
> > virginibus cupidās iniciuntque manūs.

Notes: **prōtinus**: immediately; **exiliō, -īre, -uī**: jump out; **clāmor, -ōris**, m: shout; **fatens (-entis)**: confessing, admitting, acknowledging (N.B. adjectives with verbal properties often take a direct object; construe *animum* as the direct object of *fatentēs*); **virgō, virginis**, f: girl, maiden, virgin; **cupidus, -a, -um**: desirous, eager, zealous; **iniciō, -ere, -iēcī, -iectus**: put (something in accusative case) on (someone in dative case); **manus, -ūs**, f: hand (*manūs*: accusative plural).

3.6. Livy, *ab Urbe Condita* 1.13.4. Romulus and the Romans finally negotiate peace with the Sabines.

> Nec pācem modo sed cīvitātem ūnam ex duābus faciunt. Regnum
> consociant: imperium omne conferunt Rōmam.

Notes: **nec . . . modo**: not only; **pax, pācis**, f: peace; **cīvitās, -ātis**, f: city-state; **ūnus, -a, -um**: one; **ē/ex** (+ ablative): out of, from; **duo, duae, duo**: two (*duābus*: ablative plural); **consociō, -āre, -āvī, -ātus**: share; **conferō, -ferre, -tulī, -lātus**: bring together; **Rōmam**: "to Rome."

3.7. Livy, *ab Urbe Condita* 1.58.7. The virtuous Lucretia tells her husband Collatinus that she has been raped by the lustful Sextus Tarquinius, son of Lucius Tarquinius Superbus ("Tarquin the Proud"), the seventh and last king of Rome.

"Vestīgia virī aliēnī, Collātīne, in lectō sunt tuō; cēterum corpus est tantum violātum, animus insons."

Notes: **vestīgium, -iī**, n: footprint, footstep, track, trace; **aliēnus, -a, -um**: another, foreign, strange; **Collātīnus, -ī**, m: husband of Lucretia; **lectus, -ī**, m: bed; **cēterum**: but, however; **tantum**: only; **violātus, -a, -um**: violated; **insons (-ontis)**: innocent.

3.8. Livy, *ab Urbe Condita* 1.58.10. Lucretia decides to commit suicide rather than live with the shame of the crime committed against her.

"Ego mē etsī peccātō absolvō, suppliciō nōn līberō."

Notes: **ego**: I (nominative singular); **mē**: "myself" (accusative singular); **etsī**: even if (N.B. *etsī* does not appear as the first word of its clause as it does in the English translation); **peccātum, -ī**, n: sin; **supplicium, -iī**, n: punishment; **līberō, -āre, -āvī, -ātus**: free (from), release (from).

3.9. Livy, *ab Urbe Condita* 2.2.4. Collatinus's friend Brutus incites the crowds to expel the corrupt king and his family, and Brutus and Collatinus are declared the first Consuls of the Roman Republic. In the early days of the Republic, however, people grow worried that Collatinus, a Tarquin by birth and distant relative of the hated king, might harbor sympathies for the ousted regal family. Brutus summons an assembly and asks Collatinus to step aside for Rome's peace of mind.

Sollicitamque suspīciōne plēbem Brūtus ad contiōnem vocat.

Notes: **sollicitus, -a, -um**: worried, anxious (N.B. adjectives with verbal properties can be expanded by adverbs, prepositional phrases, or nouns in the ablative case); **suspīciō, -iōnis**, f: suspicion, mistrust; **plebs, plēbis**, f: rabble, common people; **Brūtus, -ī**, m: friend of Lucretia's husband Collatinus; **contiō, -iōnis**, f: public meeting, assembly.

3.10. Livy, *ab Urbe Condita* **2.2.7.** Brutus acknowledges Collatinus's service to the Republic, but, nevertheless, requests that he abandon his consulship. Collatinus, urged especially by his father-in-law, Spurius Lucretius, reluctantly agrees, and Publius Valerius is elected Consul in his place.

"Absolve beneficium tuum, aufer hinc rēgium nōmen."

Notes: **absolve:** "complete!" (imperative singular of *absolvō*); **beneficium, -iī,** n: kindness, service, help; **aufer:** "remove!" (imperative singular of *auferō, -ferre, abstulī, ablātus:* remove, take away); **hinc:** from here; **rēgius, -a, -um:** royal, kingly.

3.11. Livy, *ab Urbe Condita* **3.48.5.** Livy alludes to the rape of Lucretia when he recounts the fate of Verginia, whose father Lucius Verginius killed her rather than hand her over to the salacious decemvir Appius Claudius. (Chaucer recasts this story in "The Physician's Tale" of his *Canterbury Tales*.)

Pectus deinde puellae transfīgit, respectansque ad tribūnal "Tē," inquit, "Appī, tuumque caput sanguine hōc consecrō."

Notes: **pectus, pectoris,** n: chest; **transfīgō, -ere, -fīxī, -fictus:** pierce; **respectans (-antis):** looking back; **tribūnal, -ālis (-ium),** n: platform, judgment seat; **tē:** you (accusative singular); **inquit:** "he (Verginius) said"; **Appius, -iī,** m: Appius Claudius, the corrupt leader of the *Decemviri* (a college of ten men commissioned to codify the Roman constitution and legal code in 451–450 bce, whose work resulted in the *Twelve Tables*. During these years, the *Decemviri* had sole governance of the state, alternating every ten days in their authority. The regular magistracies were reinstated in 449 BCE when the *Decemviri* resigned); **Appī:** vocative singular; **sanguis, sanguinis,** m: blood, descendant, bloodshed, murder; **hōc:** this (ablative singular); **consecrō, -āre, -āvī, -ātus:** curse, consecrate, doom to destruction.

3.12. Livy, *ab Urbe Condita* **3.48.7.** Verginia's body is displayed to the Roman people, who in turn drive out the *Decemviri* and restore the Republican system of government.

Icilius Numitōriusque exsangue corpus sublātum ostentant populō; scelus Appī, puellae infēlīcem formam, necessitātem patris dēplōrant.

Notes: **Icilius, -iī,** m: Verginia's fiancé; **Numitōrius, -iī,** m: Verginia's grandfather; **exsanguis, -e:** bloodless, pale; **sublātus, -a, -um:** displayed, lifted up; **ostentō, -āre, -āvī, -ātus:** show, display; **infēlix (infēlīcis):** unhappy, unlucky; **forma, -ae,** f: beauty, shape, figure; **necessitās, -ātis,** f: necessity, compulsion; **dēplōrō, -āre, -āvī, -ātus:** despair over, mourn.

EXTRA PASSAGES: OCCUPATIONS

These inscriptions from Pompeii highlight common jobs held by average people during the Roman Empire. The terms for these professions often belong to the third declension.

3.13. *CIL* **IV 710:** Pompeii. A campaign poster.

C(aium) Cuspium Pansam aed(īlem) aurificēs ūniversī rog(ant).

Notes: **Caius Cuspius Pansa, Caiī Cuspiī Pansae,** m: a Roman man's name (the cognomen [see *NLP* 1.11] *Pansa* means "splay-footed," where the feet are flat and turned out); **aedīlis, -is,** m: aedile, a Roman politician in charge of streets, traffic, markets, and public games; **aurifex, -ficis,** m: goldsmith; **ūniversus, -a, -um:** all, the whole group.

3.14. *CIL* **IV 9131:** Pompeii. A parody of Vergil's *Aeneid* 1.1 (*Arma virumque canō:* "I sing of arms and a man") inscribed on the house of the fuller Marcus Fabius Ululitremulus.

Fullōnēs ululamque canō nōn arma virumq(ue).

Notes: **fullō, -ōnis,** m: fuller, clothes-cleaner, launderer; **ulula, -ae,** f: owl, sacred to Minerva and a symbol of the fullers' trade; **canō, -ere, cecinī, cantus:** sing (of).

3.15. *CIL* **IV 8623:** Pompeii. The "Sator" square, a series of five palindromes that read the same both horizontally and vertically. (The macrons, however, are not consistent, and hence are not marked here.) Scholars have rearranged the words to make a complete and sensible Latin sentence: *Arepo sator rōtās opera tenet.* This square has also been interpreted as having a hidden Christian message: the letters can be rearranged in a cross to spell *Pater Noster AO* ("Our Father, the alpha and omega") twice.

R O T A S
O P E R A
T E N E T
A R E P O
S A T O R

Notes: **rōta, -ae**, f: wheel; **opus, operis**, n: work, task, labor; **Arepo, -ōnis**, m: a Roman man's name; **sator, -ōris**, m: sower, planter.

Vocative Case, Imperatives, and Personal Pronouns

PART 1: VOCATIVE CASE

1. The **VOCATIVE CASE** is the case of direct address. As you learned in *NLP* 2 and 3, vocative endings are identical to the nominative endings, with the exception of second declension nouns and adjectives that end in **-us** and -ius. For these two groups, the vocative singular endings are -**e** and -**ī** respectively. In addition, the adjective **meus, mea, meum** ("my, mine") has an irregular vocative masculine singular form, **mī**; and the second declension noun **deus** ("god") has an irregular vocative plural, **dī**. Consider the following examples:

CIL VI 10150: **Marciāne, vincās!** Marcianus, may you win!
    Marciāne is the vocative singular of the second declension noun *Marciānus*.

CIL IV 4764: **Perārī, fūr es.** Perarius, you are a thief.
    Perārī is the vocative singular of the second declension noun *Perarius*.

Cicero, *de Officiis* 3.121: **Valē igitur, mī Cicerō.** Farewell, therefore, my Cicero.
    Mī Cicerō is the vocative singular of *meus Cicerō*.

Ovid, *Amores* 2.19.18: **Oscula, dī magnī, quālia quotque dabat!** Great gods, what kind and how many (were) the kisses she was giving!
    Dī magnī is the vocative plural of *deus magnus*.

Review carefully the charts in *NLP* 2 and 3 for the vocative case endings of first, second, and third declension nouns and adjectives.

PART 2: IMPERATIVES

2. Direct address often appears in the same sentence as a simple command, i.e., a verb in the **IMPERATIVE MOOD**. Consider the following examples:

Ovid, *Metamorphoses* 4.143 (*NLP* 2.7): **Pȳrame, respondē!** <u>Pyramus</u>, <u>respond</u>!
  Pȳrame is the vocative of *Pȳramus*; *respondē* is the singular imperative of *respondeō*.

Cicero, *pro Milōne* 77.1: **Atque audīte, cīvēs!** And <u>listen</u>, <u>citizens</u>!
  Cīvēs is the plural vocative of *cīvis*; *audīte* is the plural imperative of *audiō*.

3. The singular imperative is formed from the present tense base plus the appropriate connecting vowel. The plural imperative is formed by adding -**te** to the singular imperative (note, however, that for third conjugation verbs, both regular and -io, the final -**e** of the singular imperative changes to -**i** before adding -**te**). For the most part, imperatives are 2nd person. Study this table:

Verb	Singular Imperative	Plural Imperative	Translation
amō, -āre	**amā**	**amāte**	love!
doceō, -ēre	**docē**	**docēte**	teach!
mittō, -ere	**mitte**	**mittite**	send!
capiō, -ere	**cape**	**capite**	take!
audiō, -īre	**audī**	**audīte**	listen!

4. Some very common verbs have irregular imperatives, especially in the singular.

Verb	Singular Imperative	Plural Imperative	Translation
dīcō, -ere	**dīc**	**dīcite**	speak!
dūcō, -ere	**dūc**	**dūcite**	lead!
faciō, -ere	**fac**	**facite**	make! do!
ferō, ferre	**fer**	**ferte**	carry!
sum, esse	**es**	**este**	be!

N.B. All verbs have **MOOD**, a term used to describe the verb's "state of being" or the manner whereby its action occurs. Verbs describing statements of fact, like those you learned in NLP 1, are in the **INDICATIVE MOOD**.

5. Latin does not usually negate an imperative by adding **nōn** before the verb. You will learn how to express negative commands in *NLP* 11 and 27.

6. It is easy to confuse direct address with other exclamations. Latin often employs the accusative case for short emotional outbursts that function much like interjections (**ACCUSATIVE OF EXCLAMATION**). In the first two examples below, note that the endings clearly indicate that the expression is accusative, not vocative. In the second two examples, the accusative neuter endings could easily be mistaken for vocative neuter endings, but the context indicates an emotional exclamation, not direct address.

Ovid, *Amores* 1.1.25: **Mē miserum!** O wretched me!

Cicero, *pro Caelio* 71.1: **Ō stultitiam!** O folly!

Cicero, *in Catilinam* 1.2: **Ō tempora, ō mōrēs!** O the times, O the customs!

Tacitus, *Annales* 11.34.1: **Ō facinus! Ō scelus!** O the crime! O the wickedness!

PART 3: PERSONAL PRONOUNS (FIRST AND SECOND PERSON)

7. **PERSONAL PRONOUNS** refer to particular people from the perspective of the speaker or narrator (i.e., "I," "we," "you," "he," "she," "it," "they," etc.). In this lesson, you will learn only the first and second person pronouns. Consider the following examples:

Ovid, *Metamorphoses* 1.482: **Dēbēs <u>mihi</u>, nāta, nepōtēs.** Daughter, you owe grandchildren <u>to me</u>.

Ovid, *Metamorphoses* 2.597: **<u>Nōs</u> vānum spernimus ōmen.** <u>We</u> scorn a false omen.

Martial 1.5 (*NLP* 11.1): **Dō <u>tibi</u> naumachiam, <u>tū</u> dās epigrammata <u>nōbīs</u>.** I give <u>to you</u> a naval battle, <u>you</u> give epigrams <u>to me</u> (literally "to us"; the plural here is used out of respect for the speaker, the emperor Domitian).

Cicero, *ad Familiares* 14.14.2: **<u>Vōs</u>, meae cārissimae animae, quam saepissimē ad <u>mē</u> scrībite.** <u>You</u>, my dearest souls (Tullia and Terentia), write to <u>me</u> as often as possible.

N.B. As we learned in *NLP* 1, Latin often omits nominative personal pronouns, especially first and second person subjects, which are conveyed through the endings on verbs. If they are used, as in the second example above, they often give extra emphasis to the subject.

8. Personal pronouns have their own declensions that must be memorized. **FIRST PERSON PRONOUNS** refer to the speaker ("I," "we"). **SECOND PERSON PRONOUNS** refer to the addressee ("you"). For each set of pronouns, singular and plural, the forms for all genders are the same.

FIRST PERSON PRONOUNS

Case	Singular	Plural
Nominative	**ego**	**nōs**
Genitive	**meī**	**nostrum (nostrī)**
Dative	**mihi (mihī, mī)**	**nōbīs**
Accusative	**mē**	**nōs**
Ablative	**mē**	**nōbīs**

SECOND PERSON PRONOUNS

Case	Singular	Plural
Nominative	**tū**	**vōs**
Genitive	**tuī**	**vestrum (vestrī)**
Dative	**tibi (tibī)**	**vōbīs**
Accusative	**tē**	**vōs**
Ablative	**tē**	**vōbīs**

Because the first and second person pronouns decline so similarly in Latin, it is easy to confuse them. Pay close attention to the first letter of the pronoun: the letters "m"/"n" designate the first person (I/me/we); the letters "t"/"v" designate the second person (you).

N.B. It is important to distinguish these personal pronouns from the following related adjectives:

meus, mea, meum: my
noster, nostra, nostrum: our
tuus, tua, tuum: your
vester, vestra, vestrum: your

9. Personal pronouns in the ablative case are usually attached directly to the preposition *cum* (*mēcum, tēcum, nōbiscum, vōbiscum*). Consider the following examples:

Ovid, *Metamorphoses* 10.570: **Pedibus contendite <u>mēcum</u>.** Compete <u>with me</u> on feet (i.e., in a race).

Cicero, *ad Atticum* 16.6.2: **Cūr ego tēcum nōn sum?** Why am I not <u>with you</u>?

Cicero, *pro Archia* 16: **Pernoctant <u>nōbiscum</u>.** They are passing the night <u>with us</u>.

Caesar, *de Bello Gallico* 7.50.4: **Mē ūnā <u>vōbiscum</u> servāre nōn possum.** I am not able to save myself along <u>with you</u>.

I. Required Vocabulary

NOUNS

lingua, -ae, f: tongue, language
Mūsa, -ae, f: a Muse, a goddess of artistic inspiration
Rōma, -ae, f: city of Rome

deus, -ī, m: god (N.B. This noun often has irregular forms: *dī* for nominative and vocative plurals, *deum* for genitive plural, and *dīs* for dative and ablative plurals.)
libellus, -ī, m: little book
modus, -ī, m: way, method, manner, measure, rhythm
praesidium, -iī, n: defense, protection, guard
puer, puerī, m: boy
verbum, -ī, n: word

amor, -ōris, m: love
carmen, carminis, n: song, poem
decus, decoris, n: honor, glory
opus, operis, n: work, task, labor
virgō, virginis, f: maiden, virgin

ADJECTIVES

doctus, -a, -um: learned, clever
novus, -a, -um: new

sacer, sacra, sacrum: holy, consecrated, accursed

sanctus, -a, -um: holy, sacred, blameless

tener, tenera, tenerum: delicate, tender, soft

dulcis, -e: sweet, pleasant

gravis, -e: heavy, serious, painful

VERBS

cantō, -āre, -āvī, -ātus: sing, play

moveō, -ēre, mōvī, mōtus: move

dīcō, -ere, dixī, dictus: say, speak (of), mention, call, appoint

premō, -ere, pressī, pressus: press, oppress, control, pursue

CONJUNCTIONS AND ADVERBS

atque: and also

aut: or (**aut . . . aut**: either . . . or)

diū: for a long time

modo: just now

nunc: now

II. Translate the following sentences from Latin to English or English to Latin.

1. Ō Mūsa, tū praesidium et dulce decus meum es.
2. Ō dī magnī, audīte carmina nostra!
3. Libellum novum doctumque rēgī da!
4. Ō poētae, puellās atque puerōs docēte!
5. Rōmule et Reme, nōs bellum longum atque grave vōbiscum nōn gerimus.
6. Nunc omnia fac!
7. Ō sorōrēs frātrēsque, miseram urbem fugite!
8. Ō breve et bonum carmen!
9. Leave behind (plural) your work and possessions!
10. Say (singular) nothing to your father!
11. O mother, be good!
12. Sing (plural) sweet words!

Roman Poets and the Business of Poetry

One medieval manuscript preserves the poems of Catullus (84–54 BCE) and links us to the verses that launched one of the most exciting and innovative periods in Latin poetic composition. Catullus and his contemporaries, known as the Neoterics, took their inspiration from the giants of Greek lyric poetry—Sappho, Alcaeus, Alcman, Archilochus—and they composed Latin poems in Greek meters, a difficult task because the Latin language does not easily fit into these Greek lyric forms. Catullus, whose poems reveal the versatility of lyric verse, is most famous for a series of poems about his tumultuous love affair with Lesbia, a married *femme fatale* whom many believe to be Clodia, the sister of the politically ambitious Publius Clodius Pulcher and wife of Quintus Caecilius Metellus Celer. Catullus, however, did not restrict himself to amatory verse: he wrote poems about poetry, springtime, his military service in Bithynia, his brother's death, Cicero, and Caesar; he penned marriage hymns, traditional songs of worship, and even a small epic. Unlike his poetic successors, Catullus was not bound to a literary patron, nor did he seem concerned about the publication and distribution of his work. His poems are thus characterized by an independent spirit, written as much for his own enjoyment as for posterity.

With the innovations of the Neoterics, poetic activity in Rome began to flourish. In 37 BCE, Vergil published his *Eclogues*, ten pastoral poems inspired by Theocritus, which juxtapose the idyllic landscape of shepherds with the social and political upheaval of the waning Republic. However, after Augustus assumed power, literary patronage became a significant issue for poets in Rome. Maecenas, Augustus's cultural director, recruited Vergil to serve as one of the official poets of the Empire. In this capacity, Vergil wrote his *Georgics*, a didactic poem in the tradition of Hesiod's *Works and Days*, and he embarked upon his *magnum opus*, the *Aeneid*, a glorious epic poem in the tradition of Homer's *Iliad* and *Odyssey*, linking Augustus's Julian clan to Aeneas' son Iulus (an alternate name for Ascanius), the grandson of Venus. Despite the power and poignancy of the *Aeneid*, many scholars view the work as an artistic departure from Vergil's more politically provocative *Eclogues*. The same type of shift can be seen in the poems of Horace, whom Maecenas also brought into his circle of poets. The acerbic wit of Horace's early works—*Sermones* (35 BCE) and *Epodes* (31 BCE)—seems to be missing from the highly polished lyric verse of his four books of *Carmina* (23 and 15 BCE), containing poems praising Augustus and traditional Roman values. However, Maecenas did not recruit all the great poets of the Augustan Age. Another prominent Roman to emerge from the tumultuous 30s BCE, Marcus Valerius Messalla Corvinus, became the patron of Tibullus, Lygdamus, Sulpicia, and the controversial Ovid (see *NLP* 2), and this literary circle represented a countercultural poetic voice that worked in subtle (and sometimes not so subtle) opposition to Augustus's cultural agenda.

For many generations, Vergil, Horace, and Ovid were considered the gold standard of Latin poetry, but recent work on poets of the later imperial periods has revealed some overlooked treasures. Martial (c. 38–104 CE) published fourteen books of epigrams and other short poems that rivaled, or even surpassed, Catullus's most provocative verses. Martial also recognized the value of courting political favor: early in his career (80 CE), he wrote *Liber Spectaculorum*, a book of poems commemorating the opening of the Colosseum under Vespasian; later, he flattered the emperor Domitian in order to safeguard his livelihood (although his opinions of the emperor cooled once that reign ended). Likewise, Martial's contemporary, Statius, composed a prize-winning poem on Domitian's German and Dacian campaigns. Such overt flattery probably contributed to Statius's prolific and versatile career: he wrote two epics, the *Thebaid* and the *Achilleid*; and the *Silvae*, a large collection of occasional poems. Although Martial and Statius have been criticized as flatterers, perhaps their concern was warranted. The satiric poet Juvenal, known for his caustic commentary on imperial life, is thought to have been exiled by Domitian (or possibly Trajan) for insulting a famous actor in the emperor's court.

SUGGESTIONS FOR FURTHER READING:

Griffin, Jasper. *Latin Poets and Roman Life*. University of North Carolina, 1986.
Miller, John F. *Apollo, Augustus, and the Poets*. Cambridge, 2009.
Wilkinson, L. P. *Golden Latin Artistry*. Cambridge, 1963.
Williams, Gordon. *Tradition and Originality in Roman Poetry*. Oxford, 1968.

PASSAGES

4.1. Catullus 1.1–3. Catullus dedicates his poems to Cornelius Nepos, who wrote a three-volume history of Rome as well as a series of biographies. Meter: hendecasyllabics.

Cui dōnō lepidum novum libellum
āridā modo pūmice expolītum?
Cornēlī, tibi.

Notes: **cui**: "to whom?" (dative singular); **dōnō, -āre, -āvī, -ātus**: give as a present, bestow; **lepidus, -a, -um**: charming, pleasant; **āridus, -a, -um**: dry; **pūmex, -icis**, m/f: pumice stone; **expolītus, -a, -um**: smooth, polished; **Cornēlius, -iī**, m: a Roman man's name.

4.2. Catullus 14.12. For a Saturnalia gift Catullus has received a vile book of poems from his friend and fellow poet Calvus! Meter: hendecasyllabics.

Dī magnī, horribilem et sacrum libellum!

Notes: **horribilis, -e**: dreadful, vile.

4.3. Catullus 12.10–11. Catullus demands that Marrucinus Asinius return his napkin. If his treasured keepsake is not returned immediately, Catullus threatens drastic action. Meter: hendecasyllabics.

Quārē aut hendecasyllabōs trecentōs
exspectā, aut mihi linteum remitte.

Notes: **quārē**: wherefore, therefore; **hendecasyllabī, -ōrum**, m (plural): a poetic rhythm with eleven syllables per line; **trecentī, -ae, -a** (plural): three hundred; **exspectō, -āre, -āvī, -ātus**: wait for, await, fear the arrival of; **linteum, -ī**, n: linen napkin; **remittō, -ere, -mīsī, -missus**: return.

4.4. Catullus 42.10–13. One of Catullus's "lady" friends (a *moecha*) refuses to return a tablet full of hendecasyllabic verses. Catullus commands the verses themselves to act on his behalf. Meter: hendecasyllabics.

Circumsistite eam, et reflāgitāte,
"Moecha pūtida, redde cōdicillōs,
redde, pūtida moecha, cōdicillōs!"

Notes: **circumsistō, -ere, -stetī**: surround; **eam**: her (accusative singular, referring to the *moecha*); **reflāgitō, -āre, -āvī, -ātus**: demand back again; **moecha, -ae**, f: adulteress; **pūtidus, -a, -um**: rotten, stinking; **reddō, -ere, reddidī, redditus**: give back, return, restore, exchange; **cōdicillī, -ōrum**, m (plural): little writing tablets.

4.5. Horace, *Carmina* **1.1.1–2.** Horace dedicates this book of verse to his patron Maecenas. Meter: First Asclepiadean.

> Maecēnās atavīs ēdite rēgibus,
> ō et praesidium et dulce decus meum.

Notes: **Maecēnās, -ātis**, m: Rome's most famous patron of poets; **atavus, -ī**, m: ancestor (in apposition with *rēgibus*); **ēditus, -a, -um**: uplifted, born.

4.6. Martial 1.2.7–8. Martial gives directions to the shop that sells his poems. Meter: elegiac couplets.

> Lībertum doctī Lūcensis quaere Secundum
> > līmina post Pācis Palladiumque forum.

Notes: **lībertus, -ī**, m: freedman; **Lūcensis, -is**, m: a Roman man's name; **quaerō, -ere, quaesīvī, quaesītus**: look for, seek (carefully note the form); **Secundus, -ī**, m: a Roman man's name; **līmen, līminis**, n: entrance; **post** (+ accusative): behind; **pax, pācis**, f: peace, referring here to the Temple of Peace (*Templum Pācis*), begun by Vespasian in 71 CE after his conquest of Judea. The temple and its attached library showcased Vespasian's treasures from Judea, including perhaps the Menorah from the Jewish Temple in Jerusalem. Pliny the Elder (*Naturalis Historia* 36.102) described this temple as one of the three most beautiful monuments in Rome; **Palladius, -a, -um**: Palladian, "of Pallas," an epithet of the Greek goddess Athena, equivalent to the Roman Minerva; **forum, -ī**, n: open square, marketplace, forum (the Palladian Forum was the precinct that surrounded Vespasian's Temple of Peace).

4.7. Ovid, *Amores* **3.1.35–36.** Ovid imagines an argument between Tragedy and Elegy. Here, light-hearted Elegy speaks to somber Tragedy. Meter: elegiac couplets.

> "Quid gravibus verbīs, animōsa Tragoedia," dixit,
> > "mē premis? An numquam nōn gravis esse potes?"

Notes: **Quid**: why?; **animōsus, -a, -um**: full of hot air, blustering; **Tragoedia, -iae**, f: Tragedy; **dixit**: "she (Elegy) said" (perfect tense of *dīcō*); **an**: or; **numquam**: never; **potes**: "are you able to?"

4.8. Ovid, *Amores* **1.1.13.** Cupid, whose powers are extensive, has compelled Ovid to craft amatory, not epic, verse. Meter: elegiac couplets (dactylic hexameter line).

Sunt tibi magna, puer, nimiumque potentia regna.

Notes: **sunt tibi**: "you have" (dative of possession); **nimium**: too much, excessively; **potens (potentis)**: powerful, strong.

4.9. Ovid, *Amores* **1.9.1–2.** Ovid argues that the lover, and by extension erotic poetry, has martial (or even epic!) qualities. Meter: elegiac couplets.

Mīlitat omnis amans, et habet sua castra Cupīdō;
    Attice, crēde mihī, mīlitat omnis amans.

Notes: **mīlitō, -āre, -āvī, -ātus**: serve as a soldier; **amans, amantis (-ium)**, m/f: lover; **suus, sua, suum**: his own; **castra, -ōrum**, n (plural): military camp; **Cupīdō, Cupīdinis**, m: son of Venus, a god of love; **Atticus, -ī**, m: a Roman man's name; **crēdō, -ere, -didi, -ditus** (+ dative): believe, trust.

4.10. Ovid, *Amores* **1.1.27–28.** Ovid declares that he fully intended to be an epic poet, but Cupid stole a metrical foot from him and changed his epic meter into elegiac couplets. Here, Ovid describes the precise rhythmical form of the couplet. Meter: elegiac couplets.

Sex mihi surgat opus numerīs, in quinque resīdat:
    ferrea cum vestrīs bella valēte modīs!

Notes: **sex** (indeclinable): six (here, construe with *numerīs*); **surgat**: "let (the work) rise" (from *surgō, -ere, surrexī, surrectus*); **numerus, -ī**, m: measure, number; **quinque** (indeclinable): five (here, construe with *numerīs*); **resīdat**: "let it fall" (from *resīdō, -ere, -sēdī*); **ferreus, -a, -um**: iron, stern, cruel; **valeō, -ēre, -uī**: be strong, goodbye, farewell.

4.11. Ovid, *Tristia* **3.14.1–2.** From the grim shores of the Black Sea, Ovid beseeches a friend in Rome (perhaps Caius Julius Hyginus at the Palatine library) to circulate his books: exile is Ovid's punishment; but his books should be spared! Meter: elegiac couplets.

Cultor et antistes doctōrum sancte virōrum,
    quid facis, ingeniō semper amīce meō?

Notes: **cultor, -ōris**, m: cultivator, friend, supporter; **antistes, antistitis**, m/f: priest, priestess, master; **quid**: what? (accusative singular, direct object of *facis*); **ingenium, -iī**, n: character, wit, genius; **semper**: always, every time; **amīcus, -a, -um** (+ dative): friendly (to).

4.12. Ovid, *Amores* **2.1.3–4.** Ovid wants only an audience that will appreciate his erotic poetry. Meter: elegiac couplets.

> Hoc quoque iussit Amor—procul hinc, procul este, sevērae!
> Nōn estis tenerīs apta theātra modīs.

Notes: **hoc**: this (accusative singular); **quoque**: also; **iussit**: "(Love) ordered" (perfect tense of *iubeō, -ēre, iussī, iussus*); **procul**: at a distance; **hinc**: from here; **sevērus, -a, -um**: strict, rigid, stern, "prudish" (here, understand *fēminae*); **aptus, -a, -um** (+ dative): appropriate (for), suited (to); **theātrum, -ī**, n: theater, "audience."

EXTRA PASSAGES: HYMNS OF WORSHIP

In the following passages, we see glimpses of the ancient gods not so much as characters in myth, as in Ovid's *Metamorphoses* and *Heroides*, but as the inspiration for traditional hymns of worship and other more playful lyric compositions.

4.13. Horace, *Carmina* **4.1.1–2.** Horace begs Venus to pity him and instead turn her attention to another victim, Paullus Fabius Maximus, a younger man better able to endure the hardships of love. Meter: Second Asclepiadean.

> Intermissa, Venus, diū
> rursus bella movēs? Parce, precor, precor.

Notes: **intermissus, -a, -um**: interrupted, suspended; **rursus**: again; **parcō, -ere, pepercī** (+ dative): spare, be merciful (to) (understand *mihi*, "me" as the dative object of *parce*); **precor**: "I pray," "I beg (of you)" (*precor* is a deponent verb: see *NLP* 21).

4.14. Horace, *Carmina* 1.21.1–4. Horace pays homage to Latona and her Olympian children, Diana and Apollo. Meter: Fourth Asclepiadean.

Diānam, tenerae, dīcite, virginēs;
intonsum, puerī, dīcite Cynthium
Lātōnamque suprēmō
      dīlectam penitus Iovī.

Notes: **Diāna, -ae,** f: goddess of the hunt; **intonsus, -a, -um:** unshorn, long-haired; **Cynthius, -a, -um:** Cynthian, referring to Mount Cynthus on Delos where Apollo and Diana were born; **Lātōna, -ae,** f: mother of Apollo and Diana; **suprēmus, -a, -um:** highest, uppermost; **dīlectus, -a, -um** (+ dative): beloved (to), dear (to); **penitus:** deeply; **Iuppiter, Iovis,** m: the supreme god of the Romans.

4.15. Catullus 34.17–20. Catullus extols Diana's influence over the harvest cycle. Meter: glyconic stanzas.

Tū cursū, dea, menstruō
mētiens iter annuum,
rustica agricolae bonīs
tecta frūgibus explēs.

Notes: **cursus, -ūs,** m: course (*cursū*: ablative singular); **dea, -ae,** f: goddess; **menstruus, -a, -um:** monthly; **mētiens (-entis):** measuring out; **iter, itineris,** n: journey; **annuus, -a, -um:** yearly; **rusticus, -a, -um:** rural, simple; **agricola, -ae,** m: farmer; **tectum, -ī,** n: shelter, dwelling, abode; **frux, frūgis,** f: fruit, crop; **expleō, -ēre, -ēvī, -plētus:** fill up (with), fill, complete.

Genitive Case

1. Nouns in the genitive case depend on other nouns. They are often translated into English as the object of the preposition "of." (N.B. The "of" is implied in the case ending and is not explicitly expressed in Latin.) In this Lesson, you will learn some of the more common uses of the genitive case. There is no need to identify the precise function of every genitive you encounter in the readings. Focus instead on learning the types of words and patterns that trigger genitive constructions so that you can read complex Latin passages with greater ease. In addition, review the tables in *NLP* 2 and 3 for the genitive case endings of first, second, and third declension nouns and adjectives.

2. Nouns in the genitive case frequently express **POSSESSION** and identify the person or thing to which another noun belongs. Likewise, a possessive genitive can identify the source or origin of a particular noun.

   Livy, *ab Urbe Condita* 1.58.7 (*NLP* 3.7): **Vestīgia <u>virī aliēnī</u>, Collātīne, in lectō sunt tuō.** The traces <u>of another man</u>, Collatinus, are in your bed.
   > The genitive *virī aliēnī* tells us to whom the traces (*vestīgia*) belong.

   Vergil, *Aeneid* 11.604: **Virginis ala <u>Camillae</u>.** The virgin <u>Camilla's</u> cavalry wing.
   > The genitive *virginis Camillae* tells us who is in charge of the cavalry wing (*ala*).

   Inscriptions du port d'Ostie (1952), A 25: **Q(uintus) Appius <u>Q(uintī)</u> f(īlius) Sāturnīnus.** Quintus Appius Saturninus, son <u>of Quintus</u>.
   > The genitive *Quintī* identifies the father, or "source," of Quintus Appius Saturninus.

3. Nouns in the genitive case can depend on other nouns that express some kind of action or state of being (e.g., **amor, amōris**, m: love; **causa, -ae**,

f: cause; **pugna, -ae**, f: fight). A **SUBJECTIVE GENITIVE** *performs* the implied action of the noun upon which it depends. Conversely, an **OBJECTIVE GENITIVE** *receives* the implied action of the noun upon which it depends.

Petronius, *Satyricon* 67: **Dum altera <u>dīligentiam</u> <u>mātris familiae</u> iactat, altera dēliciās et <u>indīligentiam</u> <u>virī</u>.** While one woman discusses the <u>industry</u> of the *mater familiās*, the other (discusses) the mistresses and <u>inattention of (her) husband</u>.

> The subjective genitives *mātris familiae* and *virī* tell us who was attentive and who was not; the nouns on which they depend (*dīligentiam* and *indīligentiam*) suggest the **action** of "being attentive" (or "inattentive").

Ovid, *Heroides* 7.195: **Praebuit Aenēās et <u>causam</u> <u>mortis</u> et ensem.** Aeneas offered both the <u>reason</u> for her (Dido's) <u>death</u> and the sword.

> The objective genitive *mortis* helps identify what Aeneas caused; the noun on which *mortis* depends (*causam*) suggests the **action** of "causing."

4. Nouns in the genitive case can identify a part of a group or collection. This genitive construction (**PARTITIVE GENITIVE** or **GENITIVE OF THE WHOLE**) depends on words of quantity that can be generic (e.g., **pars, partis**, f: part; **numerus, -ī**, m: number), ambiguous (e.g., **quis**, **quid**: anyone/thing; **aliquis, aliquid**: someone/thing; **nihil**: none; **satis**: enough), or that can refer to a specific number (**duo, duae, duo**: two).

Caesar, *de Bello Gallico* 5.12.1: **<u>Britanniae</u> <u>pars</u> interior ...** The interior <u>part</u> of <u>Britain</u> ...

> The genitive *Britanniae* identifies the part of which province Caesar is discussing.

CIL V 8974: **<u>Nīl</u> <u>malī</u> est, ubi nīl est.** There is <u>no</u> <u>evil</u> (literally: nothing [of] evil) where there is nothing.

> The noun *nihil*, abbreviated *nīl*, triggers the partitive genitive *malī*: there is no part of all the evil that exists.

Cicero, *ad Atticum* 3.20.2: **Rogātiō Sestī neque <u>dignitātis</u> <u>satis</u> habet nec <u>cautiōnis</u>.** Sestius's bill has neither <u>enough</u> (of) <u>merit</u> nor (of) foresight.

> The indefinite quantity *satis* triggers the partitive genitives *dignitātis* and *cautiōnis*: there is not enough "merit and caution" in Sestius's bill.

5. Nouns in the genitive case can express the **VALUE** or **WORTH** of another noun. These genitives can be rather general (**magnī, parvī, tantī, nihilī,** etc.) or very precise (e.g., **assis** from *as, assis*, m: a Roman coin, "penny") and often follow verbs indicating worth or estimation (e.g., **putō, habeō,** etc.).

Apuleius, *Apologia* 23.1: **Sī haec exempla <u>nihilī</u> putās** ... If you consider these examples <u>worth nothing</u> ...
> The genitive *nihilī* gives a general estimation of how little the examples are worth.

Catullus 5.3: **Omnēs <u>ūnīus</u> aestimēmus <u>assis</u>**! Let us value all (the rumors) <u>as worth a single "penny."</u>
> The genitive *ūnīus assis* ("worth a single penny") gives a very specific estimation of the rumors that Catullus considers worthless.

6. Nouns in the genitive case can describe the **MATERIAL** or **QUALITY** of another noun when modified by an adjective.

Caesar, *de Bello Gallico* 3.5.2: **Vir et <u>consilī magnī</u> et <u>virtūtis</u>** ... A man both <u>of great judgment and virtue</u> ...
> The genitive phrase *consilī magnī et virtūtis* describes Gaius Volusenus, a distinguished military tribune in Caesar's army.

Cicero, *in Verrem* 2.3.103: **Cognoscētis Entellinōrum, hominum <u>summī labōris</u> <u>summaeque industriae</u>, dolōrem et iniūriās.** You will know the anguish and insults of the Entelli, a people <u>of the greatest toil</u> and <u>the greatest diligence</u>.
> The genitives *summī labōris* and *summae industriae* describe the work ethic of the Entelli.

7. Nouns in the genitive case can describe the crime of which someone is charged (**GENITIVE OF CHARGE**). These genitives follow verbs of accusing, condemning, charging, or acquitting (e.g., **condemnō, damnō,** etc.).

Cicero, *in Catilinam* 1.4: **Mē ipse <u>inertiae nēquitiaeque</u> condemnō.** I myself condemn myself <u>of idleness and worthlessness.</u>
> The genitives *inertiae nēquitiaeque* tell us for what crimes Cicero blames himself.

Livy, *ab Urbe Condita* 10.31.9: **Aliquot mātrōnās ad populum <u>stuprī</u> damnātās pecūniā multāvit.** He (Quintus Fabius Gurges) punished some women, charged with <u>adultery</u> before the people, with a fine.

The genitive *stuprī* tells us the crime for which the women were charged.

8. Certain adjectives and verbs introduce nouns in the genitive case (**GENITIVE WITH SPECIAL ADJECTIVES AND VERBS**). Such words will be indicated by "(+ genitive)" in our glossaries and notes. Some common adjectives that govern the genitive include the following:

avidus, -a, -um: greedy (for)
capax (capācis): capable (of)
conscius, -a, -um: conscious (of)
memor (memoris): mindful (of)
nescius, -a, -um: ignorant (of)
oblītus, -a, -um: forgetful (of)
perītus, -a, -um: skilled (in)
plēnus, -a, -um: full (of)
potens (potentis): powerful (over)

Some common verbs that govern the genitive include the following:

egeō: I lack, am in need (of)
indigeō: I lack, need
misereor: I pity
oblīviscor: I forget
meminī: I remember

Cicero, *pro Archia* 5: **Erat Itālia tunc <u>plēna</u> <u>Graecārum artium ac disciplīnārum</u>.** Italy at that time was <u>full</u> of Greek arts and disciplines.

The adjective *plēna* governs the genitives *Graecārum artium* and *disciplīnārum*.

Ovid, *Heroides* 7.191: **Soror Anna, <u>meae</u> male <u>conscia</u> <u>culpae</u>.** Sister Anna, unfortunately <u>conscious</u> <u>of my (Dido's) crime</u>.

The adjective *conscia* governs the genitive *meae culpae*.

Suetonius, *Vita Augusti* 99: **Livia, <u>nostrī coniugiī</u> <u>memor</u> vīve, ac valē!** Livia, live <u>mindful</u> <u>of our marriage</u>, and farewell!

The adjective *memor* governs the genitive *nostrī coniugiī*.

Cicero, *ad Familiares* 9.3.2: **. . . ut medicīnae egeāmus. . . .** that <u>we are in need</u> <u>of medicine</u>.

The verb *egeāmus* governs the genitive *medicīnae*.

N.B. Although such adjectives and verbs are **usually** followed by a noun in the genitive case, sometimes these same adjectives and verbs are not completed by genitive nouns.

Aulus Gellius, *Atticae Noctes* 4.16: **Sed hoc planē <u>indigeō</u> <u>discere</u>**. But I clearly <u>need</u> <u>to learn</u> this.

The verb *indigeō* is completed by the complementary infinitive *discere* instead of a noun in the genitive case.

Horace, *Carmina* 3.1.16: **Omne <u>capax</u> movet urna nōmen**. The <u>capacious</u> urn moves every name.

The adjective *capax* simply modifies the noun *urna* and is not completed by a word in the genitive case.

I. Required Vocabulary

NOUNS

fīlia, -iae, f: daughter

consilium, -iī, n: plan, counsel, good judgment, advice

castitās, -ātis, f: chastity, virtue

coniunx, coniugis, m/f: spouse, husband, wife

dolor, -ōris, m: pain, grief

dux, ducis, m/f: leader, general

frons, frontis (-ium), m: brow, forehead

iuvenis, -is, m: youth, young man

multitūdō, multitūdinis, f: multitude, number, crowd

pars, partis (-ium), f: part

ADJECTIVES

multus, -a, -um: great, many

tantus, -a, -um: so great, so much

VERBS

condemnō, -āre, -āvī, -ātus: condemn, blame, disprove

putō, -āre, -āvī, -ātus: think, suppose, consider

colō, -ere, coluī, cultus: inhabit, cultivate, worship
scrībō, -ere, scripsī, scriptus: write

veniō, -īre, vēnī, ventus: come

PREPOSITIONS

causā (+ genitive): for the sake of (the ablative singular of the noun *causa* often serves as a "postposition," i.e., a preposition that follows, instead of precedes, its object)

ē/ex (+ ablative): out of, from, on account of, by reason of (*ē* precedes words that begin with consonants; *ex* precedes words that begin with vowels)

grātiā (+ genitive): for the sake of (the ablative singular of the noun *grātia* can also serve as a postposition)

prō (+ ablative): for, on behalf of, in place of, in front of

CONJUNCTIONS AND ADVERBS

ac: and in addition, and also, and
bene: well
iam: now, already (**nōn iam**: no longer)
nam, namque: for, indeed, really
tantum: only

II. Translate the following sentences from Latin to English or English to Latin.

1. Amōris coniugisque causā patriam relinquō.
2. Iūlia, soror magnae castitātis ac animī certī, nōn iam hīc habitat.
3. Fīliae patris bonī libellōs brevēs scrībunt.
4. Multōrum opera nōn colimus.
5. Nihil dolōris in iuvenibus nostrīs vidētis.
6. Iam fēminārum omnis multitūdō ad Rōmulī urbem venit.
7. Consilium magnī putāmus.
8. Frātrēs mātrem sceleris condemnant.
9. For the sake of your wife you (singular) are cultivating love.
10. I am a good leader and a woman of great glory.
11. They do not consider virtue worth so much.
12. The mother of the king condemns the evil daughter of the crime.

Roman Marriage and Motherhood

Defined by their relationships with men and almost always under the legal authority of a male relative, Roman women were viewed as daughters, wives, and mothers. Alone of Roman women, the Vestal Virgins enjoyed a unique exemption from the expectations of marriage and motherhood. Roman women were also under tremendous pressure to bear children, both for the sake of the state (providing citizens to magnify the glory of Rome) and for the sake of their families (providing male heirs to preserve the family name, traditions, and estate). Especially among the elite, Roman marriages were arranged, often for the purpose of brokering political or financial deals. Augustus, for example, who had no sons of his own, arranged three marriages for his daughter Julia in the hopes of acquiring a male heir. On the wedding night, the groom gave his bride gifts of fire and water, symbolizing his protection, and the bride brought with her a spindle and distaff, the tools for spinning thread for weaving, the primary occupation of the legally wed Roman wife. Should the marriage dissolve in divorce, as common then as now, most women returned to their birth families, with their dowries but without their children. The father's claim was always considered greater.

Despite the constraints of male authority, women in Rome, especially those married to prominent politicians, often wielded remarkable influence over their husbands and, by extension, over public affairs and not-so-private intrigues. Many of these same women also lobbied ruthlessly for the education and advancement of their children. Cornelia, the daughter of the famous general Scipio Africanus (who defeated Rome's Carthaginian foe Hannibal) and mother of twelve, including Gaius and Tiberius Gracchus, personally oversaw her children's education after her husband's death. She even refused a proposal of marriage from Ptolemy VII, ruler of Egypt. The feisty and ambitious Fulvia, the most politically active woman in the late Republic, remained faithful to her third husband, Marc Antony (to his death), even after their divorce, his remarriage, and his long-term affair with and "marriage" to Cleopatra. Augustus's sister Octavia was a loving and selfless mother who agreed to raise Cleopatra's children with Marc Antony (her second husband). Octavia bitterly mourned the untimely demise of her own son Marcellus, who had been chosen to inherit the Empire from his uncle. Augustus's queenly wife Livia, on the other hand, proved an indifferent mother, strongly preferring her firstborn son Tiberius to Drusus, her second, and she rancorously despised her own grandson Germanicus. Despite these character flaws, Augustus shamelessly showcased Livia as a model for Roman women: she did everything from dictating fashion trends and hairstyles to underwriting public works. Agrippina the Elder, granddaughter of Augustus, not only accompanied her husband Germanicus to his posts in Germany and Gaul, but, after Germanicus's suspicious death in Syria, she also positioned herself in Tiberius's circle so that her sons would be seen as prime candidates for the principate. Tiberius grew cautious of her ambition and even tried to poison her at a dinner party. When that failed, he had her arrested and tortured in prison until she died in her cell. Nonetheless, her son Caligula followed Tiberius as emperor. On the one hand, Caligula's second cousin Messalina, who had married Claudius, Caligula's uncle and successor, was a popular public figure in her husband's court and a watchful mother to her son Britannicus—she took drastic measures to eliminate all potential threats to Britannicus's succession; she is also reported to have engaged in extremely scandalous behavior, including sex competitions and orgies.

For the most part, the stories of these Roman women come to us from male authors, and we possess very few firsthand accounts that document the lives of Roman women from their own perspectives. However, some women did find their own public voices. Hortensia, the daughter of Cicero's rival Hortensius, was a capable orator in her own right. Sulpicia, the niece of the important literary patron Messalla Corvinus, composed sophisticated elegies in elegant Latin. And, as numerous inscriptions testify, many women, furthermore, erected epitaphs for their loved ones, sponsored games, and underwrote the restoration of public buildings.

SUGGESTIONS FOR FURTHER READING:

Cohen, Ada and Jeremy B. Rutter, eds. *Constructions of Chidhood in Ancient Greece and Italy.* Hesperia Supplement 41. American School of Classical Studies at Athens, 2007.

Dixon, Suzanne. *The Roman Mother.* Routledge, 1990.

Fantham, Elaine, Helene Foley, Natalie Boymen Kampen, Sarah B. Pomeroy, and H.A. Shapiro. *Women in the Classical World.* Oxford, 1995.

Lefkowitz, Mary and Maureen B. Fant, eds. *Women's Life in Greece and Rome: A Source Book in Translation,* 3rd ed. Johns Hopkins, 2005.

Petersen, Lauren Hackworth and Patricia Salzman-Mitchell, eds. *Mothering and Motherhood in Ancient Greece and Rome.* University of Texas, 2012.

Raia, Ann, Cecelia Luschnig, and Judith Lynn Sebesta. *The Worlds of Roman Women*. Focus Publishing, 2005. (There is an excellent online companion for this book with images and additional texts: *http://www2.cnr.edu/home/araia/companion.html*.)

Treggiari, Susan. *Roman Marriage: Iusti Coniuges from the Time of Cicero to the Time of Ulpian*. Oxford, 1991.

PASSAGES

5.1. Cicero, *ad Familiares* 14.19.1. On 27 November 48 BCE, writing from Brundisium to his wife Terentia, Cicero expresses concern about the failing health of their daughter Tullia.

In maximīs meīs dolōribus excruciat mē valētūdō Tulliae nostrae.

Notes: **maximus, -a, -um**: greatest, very great; **excruciō, -āre, -āvī, -ātus**: torture, torment exceedingly; **valētūdō, valētūdinis**, f: health.

5.2. Tacitus, *Agricola* 4.1. Tacitus provides a flattering portrait of Iulia Procilla, the mother of Agricola, Tacitus's father-in-law and longtime governor of Britain.

Māter Iūlia Procilla fuit rārae castitātis.

Notes: **fuit**: "(his mother) was" (perfect tense of *sum*); **rārus, -a, -um**: uncommon, rare, unusual.

5.3. Tacitus, *Annales* 1.69.1. Germanicus's wife, Agrippina the Elder, aids her husband on the German front.

Sed fēmina ingens animī mūnia ducis per eōs diēs induit.

Notes: **ingens (-entis)**: huge, enormous, remarkable; **mūnia, -iōrum**, n (plural): duties, functions; **per eōs diēs**: "in those days"; **induō, -ere, -duī, -dūtus**: clothe, surround, engage in.

5.4. Statius, *Silvae* 1.2.113–14. In an *epithalamium*, or wedding hymn, for the marriage of Violentilla and Statius's patron Lucius Arruntius Stella, Venus describes Violentilla's beauty and her striking Flavian hairstyle. Meter: dactylic hexameter.

> "Celsae procul aspice frontis honōrēs
> suggestumque comae."

Notes: **celsus, -a, -um**: high, lofty, proud; **procul**: at a distance; **aspiciō, -ere, -spexī, -spectus**: see, behold, observe; **honor, -ōris**, m: honor, glory, distinction; **suggestum, -ī**, n: platform, pile, heap; **coma, -ae**, f: hair.

5.5. Seneca, *de Consolatione ad Helviam* 19.5. In a letter to his mother, Seneca praises an unnamed aunt, whom he characterizes affectionately as a second mother. On a return trip from Egypt, this woman and her husband suffered a shipwreck, and Seneca's aunt risked her own safety to drag her husband's body ashore for burial.

> Ō quam multārum ēgregia opera in obscūrō iacent!

Notes: **quam**: "how!"; **multārum**: substantive; **ēgregius, -a, -um**: exceptional, distinguished; **obscūrum, -ī**, n: darkness, obscurity; **iaceō, -ēre, iacuī, iactus**: lie, rest, lie dead.

5.6. Pliny the Younger, *Epistulae* 4.19.2. In a letter to his wife's aunt, Pliny describes the devotion of his third wife Calpurnia.

> Amat mē, quod castitātis indicium est. Accēdit hīs studium litterārum, quod ex meī cāritāte concēpit. Meōs libellōs habet, lectitat, ēdiscit etiam.

Notes: **quod**: which (nominative singular; the antecedent is the clause *amat mē*); **indicium, -iī**, n: evidence, sign, token; **accēdō, -ere, -cessī, -cessus**: be added; **hīs**: to these things (dative plural); **studium, -iī**, n: eagerness, zeal (*studium* is subject of *accēdit*); **litterae, -ārum**, f (plural): literature; **quod**: which (accusative singular); **cāritās, -ātis**, f: affection; **concēpit**: "(she) undertook" (perfect tense of *concipiō, -ere, -cēpī, -ceptus*); **lectitō, -āre, -āvī, -ātus**: read and reread; **ēdiscō, -ere, -didicī**: learn by heart.

5.7. Petronius, *Satyricon* **37.7.** Encolpius asks a fellow banqueter about Fortunata, the wife of the affluent freedman Trimalchio, who hosts the outlandish dinner party described by Petronius. Fortunata does not mince words and is quite open about showing favor or disfavor.

Est sicca, sōbria, bonōrum consiliōrum: tantum aurī vidēs. Est tamen malae linguae, pīca pulvīnāris. Quem amat, amat; quem nōn amat, nōn amat.

Notes: **siccus, -a, -um**: dry, firm, solid; **sōbrius, -a, -um**: sober, reasonable; **aurum, -ī**, n: gold; **pīca, -ae**, f: magpie (a clever, chatty, and acquisitive bird of the crow family); **pulvīnar, -āris**, n: couch; **quem**: whom (accusative singular masculine).

5.8. Juvenal, *Saturae* **6.85–86.** Eppia, the wealthy wife of a Roman senator, runs away with a gladiator. Meter: dactylic hexameter.

Inmemor illa domūs et coniugis atque sorōris
nīl patriae indulsit.

Notes: **inmemor (-oris)**: forgetful, unmindful; **illa**: that woman, she (Eppia); **domus, -ūs**, f: house, home (*domūs*: genitive singular); **nīl** = *nihil*; **indulsit**: "(she) has conceded (to)" (perfect tense of *indulgeō, -ēre, -dulsī*).

5.9. Suetonius, *Vita Domitiani* **4.1.** Roman women did not only pursue gladiators, they were gladiators! Domitian sponsored all sorts of spectacles in the arena, including bouts between female fighters.

Nam vēnātiōnēs gladiātōrēsque et noctibus ad lychnūchōs, nec virōrum modo pugnās sed et fēminārum.

Notes: This phrase depends on an understood *commīsit*: "he (Domitian) sponsored"; **vēnātiō, -iōnis**, f: staged hunt; **gladiātor, -ōris**, m: gladiator; **et** = *etiam*: even; **noctibus**: "at night"; **ad lychnūchōs**: "by lamp stands"; **nec modo . . . sed et**: not only . . . but also; **pugna, -ae**, f: fist-fight, battle.

5.10. *CIL* VI 10072: Rome. Rufina honors her mother.

D(īs) M(ānibus) Ponpeiae Trofhime vestiāria Rufīna fīlia matrī b(ene) m(eritō) f(ēcit). Uxor Narcisiōnis, conditor gregis ryssātae.

Notes: **dī mānēs, deōrum mānium**, m (plural): the spirits of the dead; **Ponpeia Trofhima, Ponpeiae Trofhim(a)e**, f: a Roman woman's name (*Trofhima* is a Greek name meaning "nurturing"); **vestiāria, -iae**, f: a dealer in clothes; **Rufīna, -ae**, f: a Roman woman's name ("ruddy," "red"); **meritō**: deservedly, rightly; **fēcit**: "(Rufina) made (this)" (perfect tense of *faciō*); **Narcisiō, -iōnis**, m: a Roman man's name, recalling the narcissus flower and the self-loving mythological character of the same name; **conditor, -ōris**, m: founder, "sponsor"; **grex, gregis**, m: herd, flock, troop; **ryssātae** = **russātae** from *russātus, -a, -um*: dressed in red, referring to the Red Faction of the Circus at Rome (see *NLP* 14).

5.11. Cicero, *pro Cluentio* 15. In 66 BCE, Cicero defends Cluentius against a (ludicrous, to Cicero's mind) charge of poisoning his stepfather, Oppianicus, lodged by his own mother, Sassia! Cicero calls Sassia's character into question and here vividly describes how Sassia seduced her daughter's husband.

Nōn līmen cubiculī! Nōn cubīle fīliae! Nōn parietēs dēnique ipsōs, superiōrum testēs nuptiārum!

Notes: **līmen, līminis**, n: threshold; **cubiculum, -ī**, n: bedchamber; **cubīle, -is**, n: bed, marriage bed; **pariēs, parietis**, m: wall; **dēnique**: finally; **ipsōs**: "the very" (accusative plural with *parietēs*); **superior, -ōris**: higher, earlier, former; **testis, -is**, m: witness; **nuptiae, -iārum**, f (plural): marriage, wedding.

5.12. Lucan, *Pharsalia* 2.341–43. Octavian's stepsister Marcia had married Marcus Porcius Cato, who then decided to divorce her so that his friend Quintus Hortensius Hortalus could marry her instead. Seeking the legal and social protections of legitimate marriage after Hortalus's death, Marcia here begs her first husband, Cato, to take her back. Although he did restore her to his household, it is unclear if they actually remarried. Meter: dactylic hexameter.

"Dā foedera priscī
illībāta torī, dā tantum nōmen ināne
cōnūbiī."

Notes: **foedus, foederis**, n: treaty, alliance; **priscus, -a, -um**: ancient, former; **illībātus, -a, -um**: unimpaired, intact, undefiled; **torus, -ī**, m: bed, marriage couch; **inānis, -e**: empty; **cōnūbium, -iī**, n: marriage, legal Roman marriage rites.

EXTRA PASSAGES: WOMEN OF MYTH AND LEGEND

No less compelling than historical women (or their fictional representations) were the heroines of Roman myth and legend, some of whom you met in *NLP* 3. Below we see again that Roman writers such as Vergil and Livy traced the values of Roman womanhood to the legendary heroines of early Rome.

5.13. Vergil, *Aeneid* **11.583–84.** Even though many Italian mothers want the *bellatrix* (warrioress) Camilla as a daughter-in-law, she prefers an independent life. Meter: dactylic hexameter.

> Aeternum tēlōrum et virginitātis amōrem intemerāta colit.

Notes: **aeternus, -a, -um**: everlasting, eternal; **tēlum, -ī**, n: weapon, missile, javelin, spear; **virginitās, -ātis**, f: virginity; **intemerātus, -a, -um**: inviolate, undefiled.

5.14. Livy, *ab Urbe Condita* **1.4.2.** To preserve her honor, Rhea Silvia, the mother of Romulus and Remus, claims that she was raped by a god.

> Martem incertae stirpis patrem nuncupat.

Notes: **Mars, Martis**, m: god of war and one of the divine founders of the Roman race; **incertus, -a, -um**: doubtful, uncertain; **stirps, stirpis (-ium)**, f: family, race, lineage; **nuncupō, -āre, -āvī, -ātus**: name, pronounce openly.

5.15. Livy, *ab Urbe Condita* **1.9.9.** The Sabines accept an invitation to attend games at Rome (see *NLP* 3.5).

> Iam Sabīnōrum omnis multitūdō cum līberīs ac coniugibus venit.

Notes: **līberī, -ōrum**, m (plural): children.

Dative Case

1. For the most part, nouns in the dative case express the relationship between a verb and a noun indirectly affected by that verb. As you learn the more common uses of the dative case, focus again not on memorizing grammatical terminology but on learning the types of words and patterns that trigger dative constructions so that you can recognize these nouns in context. In addition, review the tables in *NLP* 2 and 3 for the dative case endings of first, second, and third declension nouns and adjectives.

2. Nouns in the dative case often indicate an **INDIRECT OBJECT**, the person or thing that is indirectly affected by the action of the verb. Indirect objects often follow verbs that mean "to give" (e.g., *dō, dōnō, dēdicō*) or "to speak" (e.g., *dīcō, narrō*).

   Ovid, *Metamorphoses* 10.264 (*NLP* 2.5): **Dat digitīs gemmās, dat longa monīlia collō**. (Pygmalion) gives gems to (his statue's) fingers, he gives long necklaces to (her) neck.
   > *Digitīs* and *collō* are in the dative case and tell us which body parts Pygmalion adorned with jewelry.

   Caesar, *de Bello Gallico* 7.11.9: **Praedam mīlitibus dōnat**. He gives plunder to the soldiers.
   > *Mīlitibus* is in the dative case and tells us to whom Caesar gives plunder.

3. Nouns in the dative case can indicate the person from whose point of view or to whose benefit or disadvantage something occurs. This use of the dative case is often called **DATIVE OF REFERENCE**.

Catullus 86.1: **Quintia formōsa est <u>multīs</u>**. Quintia is pretty <u>to many</u>.

Multīs is in the dative case and tells us from whose perspective Quintia is attractive.

CIL VI 10125: **<u>Cithāroedae coniugī optimae</u> C. Cornēlius Nerītus fēcit et <u>sibi</u>**. C. Cornelius Neritus made (this epitaph) <u>for his excellent wife</u>, a cithara player, and <u>for himself</u>.

Cithāroedae coniugī optimae and sibi are in the dative case and tell us for whose benefit Neritus erected an epitaph.

Catullus 101.5: **Quandoquidem fortūna <u>mihi</u> tēte abstulit ipsum** . . . Since fortune has stolen you yourself away <u>from me</u> . . .

Mihi is in the dative case and tells to whose disadvantage fortune has worked.

4. Nouns in the dative case can express **PURPOSE** or function.

Ovid, Ars Amatoria 1.49: **Māteriam <u>longō</u> quī quaeris <u>amōrī</u>** . . . You who seek the material <u>for a long love-affair</u> . . .

Longō amōrī is in the dative case and expresses for what reason the reader seeks material.

Livy, ab Urbe Condita 5.54.4: **Dī hominēsque hunc <u>urbī condendae</u> locum ēlēgērunt**. The gods and men chose this place <u>for establishing a city</u>.

Urbī condendae is the dative case and expresses for what purpose the place was chosen.

5. Both a dative of reference and dative of purpose can appear together in the same clause. The resulting construction is known as the **DOUBLE DATIVE**.

Catullus 12.15–16: **Mīsērunt <u>mihi</u> <u>mūnerī</u> Fabullus / et Verānius**. Fabullus and Veranus sent (that napkin) <u>as a gift</u> <u>for me</u>.

Mihi is a dative of reference; mūnerī is a dative of purpose.

Horace, *Carmina* 2.4.1: **Nē sit ancillae tibi amor pudōrī**. May the love of a slave girl not be <u>a source of shame</u> <u>to you</u>.

Tibi is a dative of reference; *pudōrī* is a dative of purpose.

6. Although Latin relies on the genitive case to indicate possession, nouns in the dative case can also convey **POSSESSION**, especially with forms of *sum, esse*.

Ovid, *Amores* 1.1.13 (*NLP* 4.8): **Sunt tibi magna, puer, nimiumque potentia regna**. <u>Your</u> kingdoms, boy, are great and excessively powerful. (Or, You, boy, have great and excessively powerful kingdoms.)

Tibi is in the dative case and tells us to whom the kingdoms belong.

Ovid, *Tristia* 4.10.3 (*NLP* 2.1): **Sulmo mihī patria est**. Sulmo is <u>my</u> homeland.

Mihi is in the dative case and tells us for whom Sulmo is home.

7. Nouns in the dative case follow certain common adjectives (**DATIVE WITH SPECIAL ADJECTIVES**):

amīcus, -a, -um: friendly (to), devoted (to)
aptus, -a, -um: appropriate (for), suited (to)
cārus, -a, -um: dear (to)
fidēlis, -e: faithful (to)
grātus, -a, -um: pleasing (to), agreeable (to)
invīsus, -a, -um: hateful (to)
nōtus, -a, -um: familiar (to), well known (to)
pār (paris): equal (to)
similis, -e: similar (to)

These adjectives will be marked "(+ dative)" in our glossaries and notes.

Ovid, *Heroides* 1.3 (*NLP* 2.4): **Trōia iacet certē, Danaīs invīsa puellīs**. Troy certainly lies dead, hateful <u>to Greek girls</u>.

The adjective *invīsa* governs the dative *Danaīs puellīs*.

Ovid, *Amores* 2.4 (*NLP* 4.12): **Nōn estis <u>tenerīs</u> apta theātra <u>modīs</u>.** You (prudish women) are not audiences fit <u>for tender verses</u>.

The adjective *apta* governs the dative *tenerīs modīs*.

Pliny, *Naturalis Historia* 9.24: **Delphīnus nōn <u>hominī</u> tantum amīcum animal, vērum et mūsicae <u>artī</u>.** The dolphin (is) an animal devoted not only <u>to man</u>, but also <u>to the art</u> of music.

The adjective *amīcum* governs the datives *hominī* and *artī*.

N.B. Although such adjectives are **often** followed by a noun in the dative case, sometimes these same adjectives (are) not completed by dative nouns.

Ovid, *Metamorphoses* 2.649: **Tū quoque, <u>cāre</u> pater, nunc inmortālis.** You also, <u>dear</u> father, (are) now immortal.

Cāre simply modifies *pater* and is not completed by a noun in the dative case.

Cicero, *ad Atticum* 4.1.5: **<u>Similis</u> et frequentia et plausus mē usque ad Capitōlium celēbrāvit.** Both a <u>similar</u> crowd and (<u>similar</u>) applause accompanied me all the way to the Capitolium.

Similis simply modifies *frequentia* and *plausus* and is not completed by a noun in the dative case.

8. Several special verbs take an object not in the accusative case but in the dative case (**DATIVE WITH SPECIAL VERBS**). Some of the more common verbs include:

crēdō: I believe
imperō: I command, control
noceō: I harm
parcō: I spare
pāreō: I obey
placeō: I please
resistō: I oppose, I withstand

serviō: I am slave (to), I serve

studeō: I am eager (for), I care (for)

These verbs will be marked "(+ dative)" in our glossaries and notes.

Ovid, *Amores* 1.9.2 (*NLP* 4.9): **Attice, crēde <u>mihī</u>, mīlitat omnis amans.** Atticus, believe <u>me</u>, every lover serves as a soldier.

The verb *crēde* governs the dative *mihī*.

Horace, *Carmina* 3.9.16: **Sī parcent <u>puerō</u> fāta <u>superstitī</u> . . .** If the fates will spare <u>the surviving boy</u> . . .

The verb *parcent* (future tense of *parcō*) governs the dative *puerō superstitī*.

N.B. Although such verbs are **often** followed by a noun in the dative case, sometimes these same verbs are not completed by dative nouns.

Cicero, *ad Atticum* 13.20.3: **Scīre igitur <u>studeō</u>.** Therefore I <u>am eager</u> to know. *Studeō* is completed by the complementary infinitive *scīre* rather than a noun in the dative case.

Caesar, *de Bello Gallico* 5.1.8: **Caesar obsidēs <u>imperat</u>.** Caesar <u>demands</u> hostages.

Imperat is completed by the direct object *obsidēs* rather than a noun in the dative case.

9. Many **COMPOUND VERBS** that begin with prefixes such as **ad-**, **ante-**, **con-**, **in-**, **inter-**, **ob-**, **post-**, **prae-**, **pro-**, **sub-**, or **super-** take a dative indirect object to complete them. Sometimes, as in the second example below, these verbs govern an accusative direct object and a dative indirect object.

Augustus, *Res Gestae* 34.3: **Auctōritāte <u>omnibus</u> praestitī.** I exceeded <u>everyone</u> in authority.

The compound verb *praestitī* (perfect tense of *praestō*) takes a dative indirect object (*omnibus*) to complete its action.

Ovid, *Ars Amatoria* 1.116 (*NLP* 3.5): <u>**Virginibus**</u> **cupidās iniciuntque manūs**. They (the Roman men) put their greedy hands <u>on the virgins</u>.

The compound verb *iniciunt* takes both an accusative direct object (*cupidās manūs*) and a dative indirect object (*virginibus*).

I. Required Vocabulary

NOUNS

fortūna, -ae, f: fortune
terra, -ae, f: land

caelum, -ī, n: sky

color, -ōris, m: color, hue, complexion
Dīs, Dītis, m: Pluto, god of the underworld
genus, generis, n: origin, lineage, kind
mānēs, -ium, m (plural): spirits of the dead (often cited in inscriptions
    with *deus*: **D(īs) M(ānibus)**, "to the spirits of the dead")
mors, mortis (-ium), f: death
virtūs, virtūtis, f: valor, manliness, virtue
vox, vōcis, f: voice

ADJECTIVES

alius, alia, aliud: other, another (**aliī . . . aliī**: some . . . others)
amīcus, -a, -um: friendly (+ dative) (**amīcus, -ī**, m and **amīca, -ae**, f:
    friend)

levis, -e: light, unambitious, fickle
similis, -e (+ dative): like, similar

VERBS

commendō, -āre, -āvī, -ātus: commit, entrust
imperō, -āre, -āvī, -ātus (+ dative): command, control

crēdō, -ere, crēdidī, crēditus (+ dative): believe, trust
legō, -ere, lēgī, lectus: pick, choose, read
vīvō, -ere, vixī, victus: live, be alive

PREPOSITIONS

sine (+ ablative): without
suprā (+ accusative): above (as adverb: previously, above)

CONJUNCTIONS AND ADVERBS

enim: for, indeed
ergō: therefore
etiam: as yet, still, but also (N.B. *etiam* is sometimes abbreviated *et*)
neque: and not (**neque . . . neque**: neither . . . nor)
quod: because
quoque: also
sī: if
sīc: thus, in this manner

II. Translate the following sentences from Latin to English or English to Latin.

1. Māter bona libellum fīliae dulcī dat.
2. Mors misera tamen iuvenibus malō est.
3. Carmina enim operibus poētārum aliōrum similia legimus.
4. Ō ducēs, virīs fēminīsque Rōmānīs amīcī, bellum sīc gerite.
5. Ergō rex doctus nostrae urbī modo imperat.
6. Fortūnam coniugī tuō commendās.
7. Virtūs decorī ducibus est.
8. Consiliō patris bonī tantum crede.
9. Sister, give your brother weapons.
10. The good leader now commands a large and beautiful country.
11. The king wages war on behalf of the Roman people.
12. I entrust the protection of the city to wretched men.

Death, Mourning, and Roman Funeral Practices

The Romans mourned, but not too much. According to Paulus, who codified centuries of Roman law, one could mourn a parent or child over the age of six for a full year, children age six and under for six months only (*Opiniones* 1.21.13). Excessive mourning for young children was considered effeminate. Nonetheless, Roman writers composed eloquent epitaphs for parents, children, friends, and even slaves and political figures. These testimonials range from the simple and poignant to the extravagant, and they bear witness to the same vicissitudes of fortune that plague us today: children died from accidents and disease, women died in childbirth, men died in battle, and many died from the exigencies of poverty.

Strict laws governed Roman burial practices and the treatment of graves. For reasons of common sense and sanitation, burials were strictly prohibited within the city walls, and to this day one can see the cities of the dead, or "necropoleis," that have grown up along the roadsides outside of Rome. Funerals took a variety of forms, from the simple practices of the poor to the ostentatious state funerals of the wealthy and famous. For an initiation fee (which might include an amphora of good wine!) and modest monthly dues, many Romans joined funeral clubs to help defray the costs of their own funerals. Such clubs provided social activities with monthly meetings and dinner parties, and also guaranteed mourners at a member's funeral, even if the member died out of town. The Greek historian Polybius (who lived in Rome during the middle of the second century BCE) describes an elite funeral which included a period of lying in state, a procession to the burial plot, pallbearers, musicians, and mourners, who themselves were often professionals (6.53–54). Wealthy funerals often included gladiator games to honor the deceased (such scenes are common on children's sarcophagi). Many aristocratic families also maintained collections of wax masks of their ancestors. Usually showcased in the family house, these masks were publicly displayed when a prominent family member died. Upkeep of the gravesite was the responsibility of the heir, and to desecrate a grave was considered the ultimate sacrilege, punishable by a sentence to work in the mines (the harshest of all punishments for lower-class Roman citizens and slaves: see *NLP* 15). During the prescribed period of mourning, family members abstained from attending dinner parties, wearing white or purple, and donning elaborate jewelry. The Roman festival calendar also included two festivals to commemorate the dead: the *Parentalia* in February, when the deceased received their annual meal from their descendants (Ovid, *Fasti* 2.533–616), and the *Lemuria* in May, when Romans engaged in rituals to rid their homes of malevolent spirits (Ovid, *Fasti* 5.419–92), similar to our Halloween.

The Romans, like the Greeks, had many views of the afterworld. Those who followed the Stoic philosophy believed that a person's soul survived death intact. Their rival sect, the Epicureans, advanced a strictly materialistic worldview. At death, a person's atoms—body and soul—dissipated and returned to the universe to be recombined into new bodies and new souls. In *Aeneid* 6, Vergil offers a complex and vivid geography of the underworld with precincts for criminals, those who died before their time, and blessed heroes. Many Romans believed in the immortality of the soul and the possibility of life after death. Yet some denied this prospect, or at least they expressed healthy skepticism.

SUGGESTIONS FOR FURTHER READING:

Edwards, Catherine. *Death in Ancient Rome.* Yale, 2007.
Erasmo, Mario. *Reading Death in Ancient Rome.* Ohio State, 2008.
Erasmo, Mario. *Death: Antiquity and Its Legacy.* Oxford, 2012.
Hope, Valerie M. *Death in Ancient Rome: A Sourcebook.* Routledge, 2007.
Toynbee, J. M. C. *Death and Burial in the Roman World.* Johns Hopkins, 1971.

PASSAGES

6.1. Statius, *Silvae* 5.3.28. Statius tells us that his father taught Greek and Latin literature at Naples, attracted many students, and was equal to any literary challenge, in both prose and poetry. In 79 CE Statius's father died. Here he invokes his father, like a Muse, to inspire his eulogy. Meter: dactylic hexameter.

Dā vōcem magnō, pater, ingeniumque dolōrī.
Notes: **ingenium, -iī,** n: talent, ability.

6.2. Vergil, *Aeneid* 9.485–86. In Aeneas' war with Turnus, two young Trojan soldiers, Nisus and Euryalus, propose a nighttime mission into the enemy

Rutulian camp. Among their plunder was a beautiful golden helmet that Euryalus had snatched from the head of a slain enemy. As the sun rose, the gleam of the helmet attracted enemy attention. The Rutulians killed both men. Here, Euryalus's mother laments his untimely (and foolish) death. Meter: dactylic hexameter.

Heu, terrā ignōtā canibus data praeda Latīnīs
ālitibusque iacēs!

Notes: **heu**: alas; **ignōtus, -a, -um**: unknown, overlooked; **canis, -is**, m/f: dog; **datus, -a, -um**: given (to); **praeda, -ae**, f: plunder, prey (in apposition with the subject); **Latīnus, -a, -um**: Latin; **āles, ālitis**: winged (here used substantively, "birds"); **iaceō, -ēre, iacuī**: lie.

6.3. **Propertius,** *Elegiae* **3.18.11–12.** Augustus, who had no sons of his own, orchestrated a marriage between his daughter Julia to her cousin Marcellus, the son of Augustus's sister Octavia. Augustus raised Marcellus up through the ranks of government from an early age, and the young man seemed to show a great deal of promise for leadership. In 23 BCE, Marcellus died at age 19, sending (most of) the imperial family into mourning and inspiring literary commemoration. This passage comes from Propertius's elegy on Marcellus's death. Meter: elegiac couplets.

Quid genus aut virtūs aut optima prōfuit illī
        māter?

Notes: **quid**: how? to what extent?; **optimus, -a, -um**: best; **prōfuit**: "(family, etc.) was profitable (to)" (perfect tense of *prōsum, prōdesse, prōfuī* [+ dative]); **illī**: "to that man" (dative singular, referring to Marcellus).

6.4. **Horace,** *Carmina* **1.28.17–18.** Speaking his own epitaph, a sailor who has drowned at sea begs for a proper burial. Here he explains how some young men die. Meter: Alcmanic strophe.

Dant aliōs Furiae torvō spectācula Martī;
        exitiō est avidum mare nautīs.

Notes: **Furiae, -iārum**, f (plural): the Furies, avenging spirits; **aliōs**: note the gender (substantive); **torvus, -a, -um**: savage, gloomy, grim; **spectāculum, -ī**, n: sight, show, spectacle (*spectācula*: in apposition with *aliōs*); **Mars, Martis**, m: the Roman god of war; **exitium, -iī**, n: destruction, ruin, death; **avidus, -a, -um**: greedy, gluttonous; **nauta, -ae**, m: sailor.

6.5. Petronius, *Satyricon* **71.** In the *Satyricon*, Trimalchio, an absurdly wealthy ex-slave, hosts an ostentatious banquet. He is also obsessed with death, and here he stages his own funeral, making bequests to his slaves so that they will love him now as though he were already dead.

"Philargyrō etiam fundum legō et contubernālem suam, Cāriōnī quoque insulam et vīcēsimam et lectum strātum. Nam Fortūnātam meam hērēdem faciō, et commendō illam omnibus amīcīs meīs."

Notes: **Philargyrus, -ī**, m: a Greek man's name; **fundus, -ī**, m: ground, farm, estate; **legō**: "I bequeath"; **contubernālis, -is**, m/f: comrade, mate (often used for a long-term romantic partner); **suam**: "his own"; **Cāriō, -iōnis**, m: a Greek man's name; **insula, -ae**, f: apartment building; **vīcēsima, -ae**, f: a five percent "freedom tax" on the value of a manumitted slave; **lectus, -ī**, m: couch, bed; **strātus, -a, -um**: made smooth, covered; **Fortūnāta, -ae**, f: Trimalchio's wife (see *NLP* 5.7); **hērēs, hērēdis**, m/f: heir; **illam**: her (accusative singular feminine).

6.6. Pliny the Elder, *Naturalis Historia* **16.139.** Because he had accidentally killed his pet stag, Cyparissus, one of Apollo's young lovers, begged that he be allowed to mourn his pet forever. Apollo transformed the inconsolable boy into the cypress, the tree of mourning (Ovid, *Metamorphoses* 10.106-43). It was commonly accepted that the cypress tree symbolizes mourning, as Pliny the Elder attests in his "scientific" account of all the trees known to the Romans.

Dītī sacra et ideō fūnebrī signō ad domōs posita.

Notes: understand *cyparissus* (cypress tree/wreath) as the subject and *est* as the verb; **ideō**: for this reason, consequently, therefore; **fūnebris, -e**: funereal; **signum, -ī**, n: sign, standard, mark; **ad domōs**: "at homes"; **positus, -a, -um**: placed, positioned.

6.7. Vergil, *Aeneid* **6.298–300.** As Aeneas travels to the underworld, he encounters the aged ferryman Charon, whose boat transports the souls of the deceased over the river Styx. Meter: dactylic hexameter.

Flūmina servat
terribilī squālōre Charōn, cui plūrima mentō
cānitiēs inculta iacet.

Notes: **flūmen, flūminis**, n: stream, river; **servō, -āre, -āvī, -ātus**: watch over, protect; **terribilis, -e**: frightful, dreadful; **squālor, -ōris**, m: roughness, stiffness; **Charōn, Charontis**, m: the ferryman of the underworld; **cui**: "on whose" (dative singular, construe with *mentō*); **plūrimus, -a, -um**: most, very many, much (in singular); **mentum,**

-ī, n: chin; **cānitiēs, -iēī**, f: grayness, gray hair, old age (nominative singular); **incultus, -a, -um**: uncultivated, neglected; **iacet**: see *NLP* 6.2.

6.8. Vergil, *Aeneid* **2.793–95.** As the Trojans flee from the burning city of Troy, Aeneas' wife Creusa becomes separated from her family. When Aeneas discovers her absence, he returns to look for her. Creusa has already died, and her ghost entrusts Aeneas with the care of their young son, Ascanius. Here, Aeneas tries to embrace Creusa's specter, but his efforts are futile. Meter: dactylic hexameter.

Ter cōnātus ibī collō dare bracchia circum;
ter frustrā comprensa manūs effūgit imāgō,
pār levibus ventīs volucrīque simillima somnō.

Notes: **ter**: three times; **cōnātus** (*sum*): "I tried" (+ a complementary infinitive); **ibī**: there; **collum, -ī**, n: neck; **bracchium, -iī**, n: arm; **circumdō, -dare, -dedī, -datus**: place around, encircle (here the prefix of the compound verb has been separated from its base; this poetic device is called *tmesis*); **frustrā**: in vain; **comprensus, -a, -um**: grasped; **manus, -ūs**, f: hand (accusative plural); **effūgit**: "(the image) slipped from" (perfect tense of *effugiō, -ere, -fūgī*); **imāgō, imāginis**, f: image, form, figure; **pār (paris)** (+ dative): equal (to); **ventus, -ī**, m: wind; **volcer, -cris, -cre**: winged, swift; **simillimus, -a, -um** (+ dative): most like (to), very similar (to); **somnus, -ī**, m: sleep.

6.9. *CIL* **VIII 27279:** Dougga, Africa. Children honor their deceased father.

D(īs) M(ānibus) s(acrum). Sī vīvunt anim(a)e corp(ore) condītō, vīvet pater noster noster sed sine nōs.

Notes: **anima, -ae**, f: breath, spirit; **condītus, -a, -um**: buried, hidden; **vīvet**: "(our father) will live" (future tense of *vīvō*); the stonecutter has repeated the adjective *noster*, perhaps accidentally. It is also possible that the deceased may have had two children—the stonecutter providing one *noster* for each child; **nōs**: a slip for the ablative *nōbīs*.

6.10. *CIL* **I.2 1219:** Rome. This grave monument for a young girl speaks to the ephemeral nature of life on earth.

Prīmae Pompēiae ossua heic. Fortūna spondet multa multīs, praestat nēminī; vīve in diēs et hōrās, nam proprium est nihil. Salvius et Hērōs dant.

Notes: **prīmus, -a, -um**: firstborn; **Pompēia, -ae**, f: a Roman girl's name; **ossua** = **ossa** from *os, ossis*, n: bone; **heic** = *hīc*; **spondeō, -ēre, spopondī, sponsus**: promise; **praestō, -āre, -stitī, -stitus**: supply, furnish, fulfill (understand *nihil* as the direct object of *praestat*); **nēmo, nēminis**, m/f: no one; **in diēs et hōrās**: "for the days and hours"; **proprius, -a, -um**: one's own, "our own"; **Salvius, -iī**, m: a Roman man's name; **Hērōs**, probably a slightly garbled form of *Hērō, -ūs*, f: a Greek woman's name (we assume that Salvius and Heros are Pompeia's grieving parents); **dant**: understand "this funereal monument" as the direct object.

6.11. Cicero, *ad Familiares* 4.6.1. In February of 44 BCE, Cicero's beloved daughter Tullia died a month after giving birth to her second son. Cicero's friend and fellow orator Servius Sulpicius wrote an eloquent letter of condolence, but Cicero replied that his grief was still acute.

> Vix resistō dolōrī, quod ea mē sōlātia dēficiunt.

Notes: **vix**: scarcely, hardly; **resistō, -ere, -stitī** (+ dative): oppose, withstand; **ea**: those (construe with *sōlātia*); **sōlātium -iī**, n: consolation, comfort, solace, relief (here, the ones that comfort most people); **dēficiō, -ere, -fēcī, -fectus**: desert, abandon, fail.

6.12. Vergil, *Aeneid* 4.700–704. After being abandoned by Aeneas, Dido resolves to kill herself, an untimely death that brings grief to Juno, the patron goddess of Carthage. Sent by Juno to hasten Dido's difficult and painful death, Iris here performs the last rites, including the dedication of a lock of hair to the gods of the underworld, Pluto and Proserpina. Meter: dactylic hexameter.

> Ergō Īris croceīs per caelum roscida pennīs
> mille trahens variōs adversō sōle colōrēs
> dēvolat et suprā caput astitit. "Hunc ego Dītī
> sacrum iussa ferō tēque istō corpore solvō."
> Sīc ait et dextrā crīnem secat.

Notes: **Īris, Īridis**, f: Juno's messenger, the goddess of the rainbow; **croceus, -a, -um**: saffron-colored, golden; **roscidus, -a, -um**: dewy, moistened; **penna, -ae**, f: wing; **mille**: a thousand (indeclinable, construe with *colōrēs*); **trahens (-entis)**: drawing (accusative) from (ablative); **varius, -a, -um**: varied, manifold; **adversus, -a, -um**: facing, opposite; **sōl, sōlis**, m: sun; **dēvolō, -āre, -āvī, -ātus**: fly down; **astitit**: "(she) stood" (perfect tense from *adstō, -āre, adstitī*); **hunc**: "this (lock of hair)" (accusative singular masculine); **iussus, -a, -um**: bidden, ordered (by Juno); **ferō, ferre, tulī, lātus**: bear, carry; **istō**: "from that (body) of yours" (ablative singular neuter); **solvō, -ere, solvī, solūtus**: release, set free (someone in the accusative) from (something in the ablative); **ait**: "she spoke"; **dexter, dextra, dextrum**: right (hand); **crīnis, -is (-ium)**, m: lock of hair; **secō, -āre, -āvī, -ātus**: cut, cleave, slice.

EXTRA PASSAGES: INVOKING THE GODS

In addition to dedications for deceased loved ones, the Romans also honored the gods with messages on stone, either to secure their goodwill before a trip, wedding, or battle, to thank them for favors, or in response to visions and dreams.

6.13. *CIL* **VI 30978:** Rome. A traveler asks for help.

Caecilius viātor deō Mercuriō.

Notes: **Caecilius, -iī,** m: a Roman man's name (perhaps derived from *caecus, -a, -um*: blind); **viātor, -ōris,** m: traveler; **Mercurius, -iī,** m: the Roman god Mercury, who protected messengers, vendors, thieves, and other people who traveled.

6.14. *CIL* **VI 30991:** Rome. Covering one's bases.

Diīs, deabus, penātibus, familiāriabus et Iovī cēterīsve diibus.

Notes: **Diīs** = *dīs*; **dea, -ae,** f: goddess (*deabus*: irregular dative plural); **penātēs, -ium,** m (plural): the Latin gods who protected the household and the family; **familiāris, -e:** belonging to the slaves of a household, familiar (here *familiāribus* refers to the *dī familiārēs*: another set of gods who protected the household; the stonecutter has misspelled *familiāribus* by adding an extra "a" to the dative plural ending); **Iuppiter, Iovis,** m: Jupiter; **cēterus, -a, -um:** remaining, other, rest; **-ve:** or (enclitic like *-que*); **diibus** = *dīs* (another irregular dative plural).

6.15. *CIL* **VI 784 [*ILS* 3168]:** Rome. A Roman woman responds to a dream.

Venerī Pudīcae [C]laudia Maximill[a] ex vīsō dōnum posuit.

Notes: **Venus, Veneris,** f: the Roman goddess of beauty and sex; **pudīcus, -a, -um:** modest, chaste, virtuous; **Claudia Maximilla, Claudiae Maximillae,** f: a Roman woman's name (*Maximilla*: a diminutive of *maximus, -a, -um*: greatest; "sweet little greatest girl"); **vīsum, -ī,** n: appearance, vision; **dōnum, -ī,** n: gift, present; **posuit:** "(she) placed" (perfect tense from *pōnō*).

Accusative, Ablative, and Locative Cases

1. For the most part, nouns in the accusative and ablative cases govern a wide variety of expressions that come into English as prepositional phrases. In this Lesson, you will learn the more common uses of the accusative and ablative cases. Focus again not on memorizing grammatical terminology but on learning the types of words and patterns that trigger these constructions so that you can recognize them in context. In addition, review the tables in *NLP* 2 and 3 for the accusative and ablative case endings of first, second, and third declension nouns and adjectives.

PART 1: ACCUSATIVE CASE

2. As we have seen since *NLP* 2, a noun in the **ACCUSATIVE CASE** often signifies a **DIRECT OBJECT**, the person or thing that is directly affected by the action of the verb.

3. In Latin, a second noun in the accusative case can often be a **PREDICATE ACCUSATIVE** or **OBJECT COMPLEMENT**, which renames the direct object. Object complements typically follow verbs of naming, calling, and making, such as:

appellō: I name
faciō: I make
vocō: I call

Other verbs sometimes require two objects to complete the action:

cēlō: I hide
doceō: I teach
moneō: I warn
poscō: I demand
rogō: I ask, endorse

Petronius, *Satyricon* 71 (*NLP* 6.4): **Nam <u>Fortūnātam</u> <u>meam hērēdem</u> faciō** . . .
For I (Trimalchio) am making <u>Fortunata</u> <u>my heir</u>.
> Both *meam hērēdem* and *Fortūnātam* are in the accusative case:
> *Fortūnātam* is the direct object of *faciō* and *meam hērēdem* renames her
> by explaining what she becomes.

CIL IV 710 (*NLP* 3.13): **<u>C(aium) Cuspium Pansam</u> <u>aed(īlem)</u> aurificēs
ūniversī rog(ant).** All the goldworkers endorse <u>Caius Cuspius Pansa</u> as <u>aedile</u>.
> Both *C(aium) Cuspium Pansam* and *aed(īlem)* are in the accusative case:
> *C(aium) Cuspium Pansam* is the direct object of *rog(ant)* and *aed(īlem)*
> explains for what office he receives endorsement.

4. Since *NLP* 2, we have seen that nouns in the accusative case frequently
   follow certain **PREPOSITIONS**. The most common of these prepositions,
   in (into) and **ad** (to, toward), indicate motion toward a specific place.
   With the names of towns, small islands, peninsulas, **domum** (home,
   homeward), and **rūs** (to the country), the preposition **ad** is omitted.

Ovid, *Fasti* 2.388: **Geminōs <u>in loca sōla</u> ferunt**. They carry the twins
(Romulus and Remus) <u>into remote places</u>.
> *Loca sōla* is in the accusative case, following the preposition *in*, and tells
> us to what location the twins are carried.

Tacitus, *Germania* 7.2: **<u>Ad mātrēs</u>, <u>ad coniugēs</u> vulnera ferunt.** <u>To their
mothers</u>, <u>to their wives</u>, they bring their wounds.
> *Mātrēs* and *coniugēs* are in the accus ative case, following the preposition
> *ad*, and tell us to whom the Germans go when they are wounded in battle.

Livy, *ab Urbe Condita* 8.12.9: **Ipse quoque triumphī ante <u>victōriam</u> flāgitātor Rōmam rediit**. He himself (Aemilius), demander of a military triumph, also returned <u>to Rome</u> before the <u>victory</u>.

> *Rōmam* is in the accusative case (the preposition *ad* is omitted) and tells us to what city Aemilius returned. *Victōriam* is in the accusative case after the preposition *ante*.

5. Nouns in the accusative case can also express the **DURATION** or **EXTENT OF TIME** over which an event occurs.

Caesar, *de Bello Civili* 3.18.1: **Bibulus <u>multōs diēs</u> terrā prohibitus** . . . Bibulus, prohibited from the land <u>for many days</u> . . .

> *Multōs diēs* is in the accusative case and tells us for how long Bibulus was prevented from making landfall.

Vergil, *Aeneid* 8.481–82: **Hanc <u>multōs</u> flōrentem <u>annōs</u> rex deinde superbō / imperiō et saevīs tenuit Mezentius armīs**. The King Mezentius then held this (city), flourishing <u>for many years</u> with an arrogant command and savage weapons.

> *Multōs annōs* is in the accusative case and tells us for how long Mezentius reigned.

PART 2: ABLATIVE CASE

6. In general, the **ABLATIVE CASE** governs three types of constructions:

> **LOCATIVE** constructions that signify the place and time of particular events
>
> **INSTRUMENTAL** constructions that indicate how or by what means an event takes place
>
> **SEPARATION** constructions that indicate the source from which or out of which an event occurs

7. Nouns in the ablative case often indicate the **PLACE WHERE** an action occurs as well as the **PLACE AWAY FROM WHICH** an action occurs. This type of ablative construction typically follows such prepositions as the following:

ā/ab: from, away from
ē/ex: out of, from
in: in, on (N.B. *in* with the ablative indicates place where; *in* + accusative indicates motion toward)
sub: under

As we saw above, with the names of towns, small islands, peninsulas, and a handful of other expressions such as **domō** (from home), **rūre** (from the countryside), **lītore** (on the shore), and **terrā marīque** (on land and sea), the preposition is often omitted.

Caesar, *de Bello Civili* 1.5.5: **Profugiunt statim ex urbe tribūnī plēbis.** Immediately the tribunes of the plebs flee from the city.
   Urbe is in the ablative case, following the preposition *ex*, and tells us from where the tribunes escape.

Tacitus, *Germania* 20.1: **In omnī domō nūdī ac sordidī in hōs artūs, in haec corpora, quae mirāmur, excrescunt.** In every house, naked and dirty, they (German children) grow into these limbs (and) into these bodies, which we admire.
   Omnī domō is in the ablative case, following the preposition *in*, and tells us in what place the German children grow.

8. Nouns in the ablative case often indicate the **TIME WHEN** or **WITHIN WHICH** an event occurs.

Horace, *Carmina* 3.7.29: **Prīmā nocte domum claude . . .** At first night (at dusk) lock up (your) house . . .
   Prīmā nocte is in the ablative case and tells us when to lock up the house.

Catullus 13.1–2 (*NLP* 13.14): **Cēnābis bene, mī Fabulle, apud mē/<u>paucīs</u>, sī tibi dī favent, <u>diēbus</u>** ... You will dine well, my Fabullus, at my house <u>within a few days</u>, if the gods favor you ...

> *Paucīs diēbus* is in the ablative case and tells us within which time frame Fabullus will dine at Catullus's house.

9. Nouns in the ablative case can indicate the **MEANS** or physical **INSTRUMENT** by which an event occurs. For this construction, the prepositions "with" and "by" are not expressed in Latin.

Caesar, *de Bello Civili* 1.11.4: **Pisaurum, Fānum, Ancōnam <u>singulīs cohortibus</u> occupat.** He (Caesar) occupies Pisaurum, Fanum, and Ancona <u>with one cohort each</u>.

> *Singulīs cohortibus* is in the ablative case and tells us by what physical means Caesar occupies these towns of northeastern Italy.

Catullus 1.1–2 (*NLP* 4.1): **Cui dōnō lepidum novum libellum / <u>āridā</u> modo <u>pūmice</u> expolītum?** To whom do I give this new charming little book, just now polished <u>with a dry pumice stone</u>?

> *Āridā pūmice* is in the ablative case and tells us with what physical instrument Catullus polished his charming book of poetry.

10. Abstract nouns in the ablative case can also express the **MANNER** by which an action occurs. For this construction, the preposition "with" typically is not expressed in Latin; however, Latin authors sometimes (but not always) include the preposition **cum** when the ablative noun is modified by an adjective (in these cases *cum* often appears between the noun and adjective).

Tacitus, *Germania* 19.1: **Ergō <u>saeptā pudicitiā</u> agunt** ... Therefore, they live <u>with guarded chastity</u> ...

> *Saeptā pudicitiā* is in the ablative case and tells us in what way the Germans live.

Caesar, *de Bello Gallico* 5.18.5: **Sed <u>eā celeritāte</u> atque <u>eō impetū</u> mīlitēs iērunt** . . . But the soldiers advanced <u>with this speed</u> and <u>with this attack</u> . . .

> *Eā celeritāte* and *eō impetū* are in the ablative case and tell us in what ways Caesar's soldiers attacked.

Caesar, *de Bello Gallico* 5.44.14: **<u>Summā cum laude</u> sēsē intrā mūnītiōnēs recipiunt.** They retreat (literally: take themselves back) within their fortifications <u>with the highest praise</u>.

> *Summā cum laude* is in the ablative case and tells us in what way Caesar's soldiers return to camp. N.B. the preposition **cum** is expressed and appears between the noun and adjective.

11. Nouns in the ablative case can express the idea of **ACCOMPANIMENT**. In this construction, the preposition **cum** (with) is typically expressed in Latin.

Ovid, *Amores* 1.1.28 (*NLP* 4.10): **Ferrea <u>cum vestrīs</u> bella valēte <u>modīs</u>!** Goodbye, ironclad wars <u>with your (epic) meters</u>!

> *Vestrīs modīs* is in the ablative case, following the preposition *cum*, and tells us what meters accompany ironclad wars.

Livy, *ab Urbe Condita* 1.9.9 (*NLP* 5.15): **Iam Sabīnōrum omnis multitūdō <u>cum līberīs</u> ac <u>coniugibus</u> venit.** Now the entire throng of Sabines arrives <u>with (their) children and wives</u>.

> *Līberīs* and *coniungibus* are in the ablative case, following the preposition *cum*, and tell us what people accompany the Sabines to the games at Rome.

12. Nouns in the ablative case often indicate the **CAUSE** or reason why an event occurs.

Catullus 3.17–18: **<u>Tuā</u> nunc <u>operā</u> meae puellae/flendō turgidulī rubent ocellī.** Now <u>because of your work</u>, the swollen eyes of my girlfriend grow red from weeping.

> *Tuā operā* is in the ablative case and tells us why Lesbia weeps.

Tacitus, *Annales* 1.3.3: . . . **mors fātō propera vel novercae Liviae dolus abstulit.** . . . a death speedy <u>because of fate</u> or the deception of his stepmother Livia removed (Gaius).

> *Fātō* is in the ablative case and gives one reason for Gaius's early death.

13. Nouns in the ablative case are often used to describe additional attributes of other nouns (**ABLATIVE OF DESCRIPTION**). For this construction, the preposition "with" is not expressed in Latin.

    Tacitus, *Germania* 6.1: **Scūta tantum lectissimīs colōribus distinguunt.** They (the Germans) decorate their shields only <u>with the choicest colors</u>.
    > *Lectissimīs colōribus* is in the ablative case and describes the attributes of the German shields.

    Catullus 64.106: **cōnigeram <u>sūdantī cortice</u> pīnum** . . . a cone-bearing pine <u>with its sweating bark</u> . . .
    > *Sūdantī cortice* is in the ablative case and describes the attributes of the pine tree.

14. Nouns in the ablative case can indicate **SEPARATION**. These ablative expressions often appear without a Latin preposition and follow verbs of freeing, lacking, and depriving, such as **solvō:** I free; **careō:** I lack; and **egeō:** I lack, want (N.B. *egeō* can also be construed with the genitive case). Other times, they require the Latin preposition **ā/ab** (from, away from) or **ē/ex** (from, out of).

    Caesar, *de Bello Gallico* 6.38.1: **<u>Cibō</u> caruerat.** He had lacked <u>food</u>.
    > *Cibō* is in the ablative case and tells us what Caesar's lieutenant was without.

    Vergil, *Aeneid* 4.703 (*NLP* 6.12): **Tēque <u>istō corpore</u> solvō.** And I (Iris) free you (Dido) <u>from that body of yours</u>.
    > *Istō corpore* is in the ablative case and tells us from what Dido is freed.

15. Nouns in the ablative case can indicate the **SOURCE** or origin of a particular noun. The preposition may or may not be expressed in the Latin.

Horace, *Carmina* 1.1 (*NLP* 4.5): **Maecēnās <u>atavīs</u> ēdite <u>rēgibus</u>** . . . Maecenas, born <u>from royal ancestors</u> (literally: from ancestors as kings) . . .

Atavīs rēgibus is in the ablative case and tells us Maecenas' origins.

Pliny the Elder, *Naturalis Historia* 8.89: **Nec aliud animal ex <u>minōre orīgine</u> in māiōrem crescit magnitūdinem.** And no other animal (the crocodile) grows into a greater size <u>from a smaller beginning</u>.

Minōre orīgine is in the ablative case, following the preposition *ex*, and tells us the meager origin of the crocodile.

PART 3: LOCATIVE CASE

16. As we learned above, the ablative case often indicates the **PLACE WHERE** an action occurs. However, the **LOCATIVE CASE** indicates location for a small subset of "place" words: towns, cities, small islands, **domus, -ūs**, f: house; **humus, -ī**, f: ground; **rūs, rūris**, n: country, farm. Consider the following examples:

Ovid, *Amores* 3.1.12: **Palla iacēbat <u>humī</u>.** Her cloak was lying <u>on the ground</u>.

Humī is in the locative case and tells us where the cloak was lying.

Catullus 68.34: **Rōmae vīvimus.** We live at Rome.

Rōmae is in the locative case and tells us where Catullus lives.

17. The locative case ending for singular nouns of the first and second declension is identical to the genitive singular; the locative ending for third declension nouns (and plural nouns of the first and second declension) is identical to the corresponding ablative form. Consider the following examples:

Athēnīs: at Athens (locative of *Athēnae, -ārum*, f [plural])
Carthāgine: at Carthage (locative of *Carthāgō, Carthāginis*, f)
Ephesī: at Ephesus (locative of *Ephesus, -ī*, f)
Rōmae: at Rome (locative of *Rōma, -ae*, f)

domī: at home (locative of *domus, -ūs*, f)
humī: on the ground (locative of *humus, -ī*, f)
rūrī: in the country (locative of *rūs, rūris*, n)

I. Required Vocabulary

NOUNS

aqua, -ae, f: water (by extension "aqueduct")
memoria, -iae, f: recollection, memory

castra, -ōrum, n (plural): (military) camp
equus, -ī, m: horse
locus, -ī, m: place
numerus, -ī, m: number
officium, -iī, n: service, duty
oppidum, -ī, n: town
perīculum, -ī, n: danger
proelium, -iī, n: battle
signum, -ī, n: sign, standard, mark

animal, -ālis (-ium), n: a living being, an animal
eques, equitis, m: horseman, knight
homo, hominis, m: human being
hostis, -is (-ium), m/f: enemy
iter, itineris, n: journey, route
legiō, -iōnis, f: legion
mīles, mīlitis, m: soldier; (referring to a group) soldiery
rūs, rūris, n: country, countryside
sermō, -ōnis, m: conversation, discourse
sōl, sōlis, m: the sun
tempus, temporis, n: time (**brevī tempore**: soon); (plural) temples
(of head)

ADJECTIVES

hūmānus, -a, -um: human
tōtus, -a, -um: all, entire, complete

VERBS

accipiō, -ere, -cēpī, -ceptus: receive, accept

constituō, -ere, -stituī, -stitūtus: place, establish, decide

PREPOSITIONS

dē (+ ablative): down from, about, concerning

CONJUNCTIONS AND ADVERBS

ita: thus, so

nōn sōlum . . . sed etiam: not only . . . but also

quidem: certainly, at least, indeed

saepe: often

undique: from all sides, on all sides

vel: or, for instance

vel . . . vel: either . . . or

vērō: in fact, certainly, without doubt

II. Translate the following sentences from Latin to English or English to Latin.

1. Legiōnēs quidem prō castrīs rūrī constituimus.
2. Hostēs ad oppidum magnō cum perīculō movent.
3. Bellum memoriam vītae dulcis sacram facit.
4. In proeliīs magnum numerum equōrum undique vidētis.
5. Hominēs tantum bonōs officiō absolvō.
6. Ergō ad castra sine animālibus equitibusque venīs.
7. Ō mīlitēs, arma signaque capite et consiliō meō crēdite!
8. Oppidī causā tamen bellum in hostēs malōs gerimus.
9. We flee out of the city away from the enemies with the cavalrymen.
10. I free my mother and father from the command of the king.
11. On a long journey, a horse is often a source of great danger to the soldier.
12. Teach (singular) the people short and sweet songs.

The Roman Army

The Roman Empire was built on the back of a ruthlessly efficient army whose watchwords were discipline, obedience, and courage. Punishments for cowardice were fierce and swift, and cowardly units would be literally decimated (every tenth man, chosen at random, was executed). From an all-volunteer, land-holding citizen army of the early Republic to the professional behemoth created by Marius in the waning years of the second century BCE, the army was essential to Rome's identity. The two highest regular offices in Rome were in essence military posts whose duties included the security of the city (praetorship) and foreign diplomacy and warfare (consulship). The special prerogative of higher office, *imperium*, comprised the right to lead an army, among other things.

Evidence for the Roman army is particularly rich, from vignettes in Vergil and Lucan to descriptions of marches and battles recorded by Livy, Caesar, Sallust, Tacitus, and others, to a remarkably vibrant archaeological record. Wherever the army went, camps were built. Extant are weapons (javelins, short swords, shields, armor) and structures (headquarters, billets for the commanding officer, barracks, granaries, latrines, hospitals). Also surviving are standards (*signa*) around which troops would rally in battle, tack and armor for warhorses, fragments of artillery machines, hobnailed sandals, fragments of clothing, and cooking pots. In addition to the archaeological record, we have a visual account in the minutely carved helix on Trajan's column, commemorating that emperor's Dacian victories in 113 CE. This particular monument shows many aspects of life in the Roman army, from the glorious to the mundane: Trajan addressing his soldiers; a military parade; troops on the march with their equipment in "hobo" bundles carried over the left shoulders; men building bridges; troops in battle; Roman battle formations, including the "tortoise" wherein soldiers held their shields defensively—men on the front line held their shields to their front, the men on the sides held their shields out to the side, soldiers within the formation held their shields overhead, all together creating an "armored tank" of shields for the protection of the unit; Dacians besieging a Roman camp; medics tending to the wounded on the battlefield; Dacian prisoners of war, including women and children, being marched to Rome to be sold into slavery (as was common for the "weaker" members of a conquered people; enemy combatants were usually executed). Finally, there also survives the *de Re Militari* of Publius Flavius Vegetius Renatus, c. 400 CE. In four books, Vegetius describes recruitment and training; equipment and striking camp; the organization and administration of the legion and the duties of various officers; tactics and strategy for many situations, including how to resist war elephants and scythed chariots; fortifications; siege strategies for attack and defense; and the tenets of naval warfare. Vegetius eulogizes the army of the early Empire, especially with regard to training and discipline, and he bemoans the shortcomings of the army of his own day as a plea for reform.

The Roman army consisted of both citizen and allied branches. *Legiōnēs*, drawn strictly from citizen enlistments, enjoyed higher pay and a shorter term of service than the allied (non-citizen) *auxilia*. Auxiliary soldiers did, however, receive a grant of citizenship upon discharge. In battle, heavily armed *legiōnēs* served as infantry. Their armor was mass-produced throughout the empire (one factory has been discovered at Exmoor in Britain), and pay deductions were imposed to cover the government's expenses. *Auxilia*, consisting of non-Roman allies recruited in the provinces (from as early as the second century BCE), comprised about half of the total fighting force and served as both infantry and cavalry, under the command of Roman officers promoted from the legions.

Rome was hardly under constant warfare, and a standing army in Italy would have proved dangerous. From the 20s BCE, the army answered directly to the emperor, who stationed his troops far from the city, especially along the imperial frontiers (i.e., Britain, Germany, Dacia, Moesia, Noricum, and Syria). Provincial troops engaged in many peacetime activities: they served as administrators on the governor's staff and as customs officers; they constructed and maintained municipal infrastructure, such as baths, roads, and aqueducts (including the aqueduct at Caesarea Maritima in Israel); they served as land surveyors and engineers (Roman troops were responsible for building Hadrian's Wall, the Antonine Wall, and the German *Limes*/frontier wall); finally, they also served as a police force in particularly rebellious provinces like Judea.

SUGGESTIONS FOR FURTHER READING:

Campbell, Brian. *The Emperor and the Roman Army, 31 B.C.–A.D. 235*. Oxford, 1984.
Campbell, Brian. *The Roman Army: 31 B.C.–A.D. 337: A Sourcebook*. Routledge, 1994.
Campbell, Brian. *Warfare and Society in Imperial Rome, 31 B.C.–A. D. 280*. Routledge, 2002.

Erdkamp, Paul. *A Companion to the Roman Army.* Wiley-Blackwell, 2011.

Goldsworthy, Adrian Keith. *The Roman Army at War 100 BC–AD 200.* Oxford, 1998.

Keppie, Lawrence. *The Making of the Roman Army.* University of Oklahoma, 1984.

Warry, John Gibson. *Warfare in the Classical World: An Illustrated Encyclopedia of Weapons, Warriors and Warfare in the Ancient Civilisations of Greece and Rome.* University of Oklahoma, 1995.

Webster, Graham. *The Roman Imperial Army of the 1st and 2nd Centuries AD.* 3rd ed. University of Oklahoma, 1998.

PASSAGES

7.1. Vegetius, *de Re Militari* 1.2. Despite the fact that cowards and brave men are born in all places, on the evidence of ancient medical science Vegetius argues that some climates produce better soldiers than others.

Contrā septentriōnālēs populī, remōtī ā sōlis ardōribus, inconsultiōrēs quidem, sed tamen largō sanguine redundantēs, sunt ad bella promptissimī.

Notes: **contrā**: on the contrary; **septentriōnālis, -e**: northern; **remōtus, -a, -um**: withdrawn, distant; **ardor, -ōris**, m: flame, burning, heat; **inconsultior, -e**: rather rash, rather imprudent; **largus, -a, -um**: abundant, plentiful; **sanguis, sanguinis**, m: blood; **redundans (-antis)**: overflowing, streaming; **promptissimus, -a, -um**: most prepared.

7.2. Vegetius, *de Re Militari* 1.21. Military training was essential to the safety and morale of the troops. No less important was the regularized construction of camps, both permanent and on the march, which provided a sense of regularity, continuity, and "home."

Quippe, sī rectē constitūta sunt castra, ita intrā vallum sēcūrī mīlitēs diēs noctēsque peragunt.

Notes: **quippe**: indeed, surely; **rectē**: correctly, rightly; **constitūtus, -a, -um**: established, arranged; **intrā** (+ accusative): within; **vallum, -ī**, n: palisade, fortification, defense; **sēcūrus, -a, -um**: free from care, unconcerned; **diēs noctēsque**: "days and nights" (accusative plural); **peragō, -ere, -ēgī, -actus**: pass through, spend.

7.3. Vergil, *Aeneid* **9.174–75.** As Aeneas' army prepares for war in Italy, they provide a model of Roman discipline and self-control, in contrast with the Rutulian enemy, who often neglect their military duties, enjoying their wine or spending their evenings gambling. Here, we see the Trojan army readying itself for battle. Meter: dactylic hexameter.

> Omnīs per mūrōs legiō sortīta perīclum
> excubat exercetque vicēs.

Notes: **mūrus, -ī**, m: wall; **sortītus, -a, -um**: chosen by lot; **perīclum** = *perīculum*; **excubō, -āre, -āvī, -ātus**: keep watch (for); **exerceō, -ēre, -uī, -itus**: supervise, stand guard; **vicēs**: "in turns."

7.4. Caesar, *de Bello Gallico* **7.81.3.** Gallic reinforcements have arrived at Alesia, in Gallia Lugdunensis (central France) to give aid to Vercingetorix and his beseiged citizens. While these reinforcements drive the Roman troops from the siegeworks, Vercingetorix rallies the troops from within his hilltop city.

> Eōdem tempore, clāmōre exaudītō, dat tubā signum suīs
> Vercingetorix atque ex oppidō ēdūcit.

Notes: **eōdem**: "at the same (time)"; **clāmōre exaudītō**: "a shout heard" (ablative absolute); **tuba, -ae**, f: war trumpet; **suīs**: "to his own (troops)" (dative plural); **ēdūcō, -ere, -duxī, -ductus**: draw out, lead out.

7.5. Livy, *ab Urbe Condita* **9.13.2.** During the usual course of a battle, it is the *signifer* who relays battlefield orders. But in 320 BCE, during Rome's second Samnite War, Quintus Publilius Philo's soldiers are too eager to await orders.

> Vādunt igitur in proelium urgentēs signiferōs.

Notes: **vādō, -ere, vāsī**: hasten, rush (understand *mīlitēs* as the subject); **igitur**: therefore; **urgens (-entis)**: urging, pressing, plying; **signifer, -ī**, m: standard-bearer (construe as the direct object of *urgentēs*).

7.6. Vegetius, *de Re Militari* **3.24.** Pyrrhus of Lucania in southern Italy was the first to use war elephants against the Roman army, at Heraclea in 280 BCE. Vegetius provides a history of these intimidating and fascinating animals and the tactics used against them in battle.

Elafantī in proeliīs magnitūdine corporum, barrītūs horrōre, formae ipsīus novitāte hominēs equōsque conturbant.

Notes: **elafantī** = *elephantī* from *elephantus, -ī*, m/f: elephant; **magnitūdō, magnitūdinis,** f: size; **barrītus, -ūs,** m: war cry, trumpeting (*barrītūs*: genitive singular); **horror, -ōris,** m: roughness, dread, fright; **forma, -ae,** f: shape, beauty; **ipsīus**: "of their very (form)" (genitive singular); **novitās, -ātis,** f: newness, novelty; **conturbō, -āre, -āvī, -ātus**: disturb, throw into disorder.

7.7. Livy, *ab Urbe Condita* **23.43.6.** During the Second Punic War, the Carthaginian general Hannibal advanced on Rome from Spain through the Alps, with thirty-seven war elephants, most of whom perished on the journey. Here, in 215 BCE, Hannibal awaits his son's arrival at Nola, in southern Italy, with reinforcements, including elephants.

Eōdem Hannō ex Bruttiīs cum supplēmentō Carthāgine advectō atque elephantīs venit.

Notes: **eōdem**: there, to the same place; **Hannō, -ōnis,** m: Hannibal's son; **Bruttiī, -iōrum,** m (plural): (the territory of) the inhabitants of southern Italy; **supplēmentum, -ī,** n: body of recruits, reinforcements; **Carthāgō, Carthāginis,** f: Hannibal's capital city in northern Africa (now a suburb of modern Tunis in Tunisia); **advectus, -a, -um**: conveyed (from).

7.8. Caesar, *de Bello Gallico* **7.70.2.** In 52 BCE, Caesar employs German mercenaries against the Gauls trying to destroy Caesar's siegeworks at Alesia.

Labōrantibus nostrīs Caesar Germānōs summittit legiōnēsque prō castrīs constituit.

Notes: **labōrans (-antis)**: struggling; **nostrīs**: "to our men" (substantive); **Germānus, -ī,** m: German; **summittō, -ere, -mīsī, -missus**: send as help.

7.9. Caesar, *de Bello Civili* **3.94.5.** In the summer of 48 BCE, Pompey and Caesar met in battle at Pharsalus in central Greece. Caesar was short of both men and supplies, and Pompey had hoped to starve Caesar into surrender, but he reluctantly engaged in battle succumbing to the pressure of his senatorial officers. Pompey's defeat was overwhelming, and the battle was decisive. In this passage, Pompey's infantry has already lost ground. Pompey addresses his troops before retiring to his tent and eventually fleeing camp and abandoning his army.

"Ego reliquās portās circumeō et castrōrum praesidia confirmō."

Notes: **reliquus, -a, -um**: remaining, rest; **porta, -ae**, f: gate; **circumeō, -īre, -iī, -itus**: go around, surround; **confirmō, -āre, -āvī, -ātus**: strengthen.

7.10. Caesar, *de Bello Gallico* **7.88.3.** Caesar finally enjoys a definitive victory at Alesia, and Vercingetorix's troops desert.

Hostēs terga vertunt; fugientibus equitēs occurrunt. Fit magna caedēs.

Notes: **tergum, -ī**, n: back, rear; **vertō, -ere, vertī, versum**: turn; **fugiens (-ientis)**: fleeing, escaping (here used as a substantive); **occurrō, -ere, -currī, -cursus** (+ dative): meet with, encounter; **fiō, fierī, factus sum**: happen; **caedēs, -is (-ium)**, f: killing, slaughter.

7.11. Caesar, *de Bello Gallico* **7.90.2.** After the siege of Alesia, as he begins winter preparations, Caesar takes steps to ensure the peace.

Imperat magnum numerum obsidum. Legiōnēs in hīberna mittit. Captīvōrum circiter vīgintī mīlia Aeduīs Arvernīsque reddit.

Notes: **obses, obsidis**, m/f: hostage; **hīberna, -ōrum**, n (plural): winter quarters; **captīvus, -ī**, m: captive; **circiter**: about, approximately; **vīgintī mīlia**: twenty thousand; **Aeduī, -ōrum**, m (plural): a tribe of central Gaul who joined Vercingetorix against Caesar; **Arvernī, -ōrum**, m (plural): Vercingetorix's tribe in southern Gaul; **reddō, -ere, -didī, -ditus**: return.

7.12. Livy, *ab Urbe Condita* **7.32.17.** In 343 BCE, the Consul Marcus Valerius Corvus led the fight against the Samnites, who had opposed Roman expansion into central Italy. After a stunning victory at Mount Gaurus, Corvus amassed 40,000 Samnite shields and 170 battle standards into a battlefield trophy before returning to Rome, where he celebrated a triumph, a formal parade awarded by the Senate to a victorious general. Here, we read the climax of Corvus's pre-battle pep talk to his troops.

"Nunc, quod instat—dīs bene iuvantibus—novum atque integrum
dē Samnītibus triumphum mēcum petite."

Notes: **quod instat**: "as for that which is at hand"; **dīs . . . iuvantibus**: "if the gods are helping" (ablative absolute); **integer, integra, integrum**: complete, entire, fresh; **Samnītēs, -ium**, m (plural): the Samnite people who inhabited central Italy; **triumphus, -ī**, m: triumph, victory, victory parade; **petō, -ere, -īvī, -ītus**: seek, aim for.

EXTRA PASSAGES: ANIMALS

The Romans found it easier (and safer) to examine their own values and vices through the prism of animals. Some were valued for their "humanity" (like Pallas' warhorse and the studious and religious elephant). Others were reviled, like the aggressive crocodile and the crafty, almost Greek-like fox. You will learn more about animals in the ancient world in *NLP* 19.

7.13. Vergil, *Aeneid* **11.89–90.** At Pallas' funeral, the young warrior's mount, Aethon, is personified as mourning for his slain master. We are meant to think of Achilles' horses, who also mourned the death of Patroclus and were consoled by Zeus (*Iliad* 17.441–55). Meter: dactylic hexameter.

Post bellātor equus, positīs insignibus, Aethōn
it lacrimans guttīsque ūmectat grandibus ōra.

Notes: **post**: afterward; **bellātor, -ōris**: warlike, courageous; **positīs insignibus**: "his ceremonial finery set aside" (ablative absolute); **it**: "he (Aethon) goes"; **lacrimans (-antis)**: weeping; **gutta, -ae**, f: drop, tear; **ūmectō, -āre, -āvī, -ātus**: moisten; **grandis, -e**: great, large, abundant; **ōs, ōris**, n: mouth, face, countenance, expression.

7.14. Pliny the Elder, *Naturalis Historia* **8.1.** Pliny devotes thirty-five chapters to this remarkably sensitive, intelligent, and docile giant, describing elephants in the wild, the differences between Indian and African elephants, and the history of the human use of elephants. Here the elephant is personified as an idealized Roman and as a scholar.

Maximum est elephans proximumque hūmānīs sensibus, quippe intellectus illīs sermōnis patriī et imperiōrum obēdientia, officiōrum—quae didicēre memoriā—amōris et glōriae voluptās, immō vērō, quae etiam in homine rāra: probitās, prūdentia, aequitās, religiō quoque sīderum sōlisque ac lūnae venerātiō.

Notes: **maximus, -a, -um**: largest, greatest (construe with an understood *animal*); **elephans, -antis**, m: elephant; **proximus, -a, -um** (+ dative): closest (to); **sensus, -ūs**, m: sense, feeling (*sensibus*: dative plural); **quippe**: indeed, surely; **intellectus, -ūs**, m: comprehension, understanding (supply *est* as the verb); **illīs**: to/for them (dative plural); **patrius, -a, -um**: paternal, ancestral; **obēdientia, -iae**, f: obedience, compliance; **quae**: which (neuter accusative plural, referring back to *officiōrum*); **didicēre**: "they have learned" (perfect tense of *discō, -ere, didicī*); **glōria, -iae**, f: glory, fame; **voluptās, -ātis**, f: pleasure, enjoyment; **immō**: indeed; **quae**: "things which (are)"; **rārus, -a, -um**: rare, scant, infrequent; **probitās, -ātis**, f: honesty, uprightness; **prūdentia, -iae**, f: sagacity, discretion; **aequitās, -ātis**, f: equity, fairness; **religiō, -iōnis**, f: respect, awe, religious scruple; **sīdus, sīderis**, n: constellation; **lūna, -ae**, f: the moon; **venerātiō, -iōnis**, f: reverence, respect.

7.15. *Aberdeen Bestiary* **16r.** The author of the *Aberdeen Bestiary* drew his inspiration from a long tradition of Greek and Roman writers, including Pliny the Elder, who utilized animals for moral examples. The *Aberdeen Bestiary* is a Christian text, and most animals are seen in terms of good and evil, like our fox below.

Est enim volūbilis pedibus, et nunquam rectō itinere sed tortuōsīs anfractibus currit. Est et fraudulentum animal et ingeniōsum.

Notes: **volūbilis, -e**: revolving, changing, swirling (construe with *vulpēs* [from *vulpēs, -is* [*-ium*], f: fox]); **pēs, pedis**, m: foot; **nunquam**: never; **rectus, -a, -um**: straight, direct; **tortuōsus, -a, -um**: full of turns, intricate, involved; **anfractus, -ūs**, m: turning, bend, revolution (*anfractibus*: ablative plural); **currō, -ere, cucurrī, cursus**: run; **fraudulentus, -a, -um**: deceitful; **ingeniōsus, -a, -um**: clever, cunning.

Imperfect Tense

1. The imperfect tense describes past ongoing actions and can be translated in several ways depending upon the context. For example, *docēbant* can mean "they were teaching," "they taught," "they kept teaching," and "they used to teach." Consider the following examples:

Suetonius, *Vita Augusti* 81: **Neque frīgora neque aestūs facile tolerābat**. He (Augustus) easily <u>tolerated</u> neither cold spells nor heat waves.

Suetonius, *Vita Augusti* 91: **Somnia neque sua neque aliēna dē sē neglegēbat**. He (Augustus) <u>was neglecting</u> neither his own nor others' dreams about himself.

Suetonius, *Vita Neronis* 55: <u>**Erat illī**</u> **aeternitātis perpetuaeque fāmae cupīdō, sed inconsulta**. <u>There was</u> for him (Nero) a desire for immortality and everlasting renown, but (it was) ill-advised.

Martial 5.21.1–2: **Quintum prō Decimō, prō Crassō, Rēgule, Macrum/ante salūtābat rhētor Apollodotus**. Formerly, Regulus, the orator Apollodotus <u>used to greet</u> "Quintus" instead of "Decimus" and "Macer" instead of "Crassus." (That is to say, Apollodotus continuously got their names wrong!)

Tacitus, *Historiae* 2.91: **Ventitābat in senātum**. He (Vitellius) <u>kept coming</u> into the Senate.

2. In Latin, almost all verbs have the same endings for the imperfect tense. Simply add the personal endings that you learned in *NLP* 1 to the imperfect signifier **-ba-**.

Study the table below.

Person	Singular	Plural
1st	-bam	-bāmus
2nd	-bās	-bātis
3rd	-bat	-bant

3. To form the imperfect tense, add the imperfect tense endings (above) to the present stem, formed by dropping the ending (-**āre**, -**ēre**, -**ere**, -**īre**) from the verb's infinitive. The vowel between the present stem and the imperfect tense endings changes depending upon the verb's conjugation. It is helpful to memorize one verb in the imperfect tense from each conjugation to serve as a model for other verbs.

IMPERFECT TENSE OF FIRST CONJUGATION

Person	Singular	Plural
1st	amā**bam**: I was loving	amā**bāmus**: we were loving
2nd	amā**bās**: you were loving	amā**bātis**: you (plural) were loving
3rd	amā**bat**: he/she/it was loving	amā**bant**: they were loving

IMPERFECT TENSE OF SECOND CONJUGATION

Person	Singular	Plural
1st	docē**bam**: I was teaching	docē**bāmus**: we were teaching
2nd	docē**bās**: you were teaching	docē**bātis**: you (plural) were teaching
3rd	docē**bat**: he/she/it was teaching	docē**bant**: they were teaching

IMPERFECT TENSE OF THIRD CONJUGATION

Person	Singular	Plural
1st	mittē**bam**: I was sending	mittē**bāmus**: we were sending
2nd	mittē**bās**: you were sending	mittē**bātis**: you (plural) were sending
3rd	mittē**bat**: he/she/it was sending	mittē**bant**: they were sending

IMPERFECT TENSE OF THIRD CONJUGATION (-IO)

Person	Singular	Plural
1st	capiē**bam**: I was taking	capiē**bāmus**: we were taking
2nd	capiē**bās**: you were taking	capiē**bātis**: you (plural) were taking
3rd	capiē**bat**: he/she/it was taking	capiē**bant**: they were taking

IMPERFECT TENSE OF FOURTH CONJUGATION

Person	Singular	Plural
1st	audiēbam: I was hearing	audiēbāmus: we were hearing
2nd	audiēbās: you were hearing	audiēbātis: you (plural) were hearing
3rd	audiēbat: he/she/it was hearing	audiēbant: they were hearing

4. The irregular verb "to be" is one of the few Latin verbs that does not have **-ba-** as part of its imperfect endings.

IMPERFECT TENSE OF *ESSE*

Person	Singular	Plural
1st	eram: I was	erāmus: we were
2nd	erās: you were	erātis: you (plural) were
3rd	erat: he/she/it was	erant: they were

I. Required Vocabulary

NOUNS

āra, -ae, f: altar

forma, -ae, f: shape, beauty

nātūra, -ae, f: nature, character, temperament

porta, -ae, f: gate, strait

via, viae, f: path, road, street

līberī, -ōrum, m (plural): children

studium, -iī, n: pursuit, enthusiasm, zeal

templum, -ī, n: temple

mens, mentis (-ium), f: mind, understanding, judgment, attention

nox, noctis, (-ium), f: night

ADJECTIVES

altus, -a, -um: high, lofty

medius, -a, -um: middle, mid-

pūblicus, -a, -um: public, at public expense

ūnus, -a, -um: one, only, alone (**ūnā**: at the same time)

VERBS

appellō, -āre, -āvī, -ātus: call, name

parō, -āre, -āvī, -ātus: prepare

optō, -āre, -āvī, -ātus: wish for, desire

incipiō, -ere, incēpī, inceptus: begin

sūmō, -ere, sumpsī, sumptus: take up, put on

PREPOSITIONS

ante (+ accusative): before, in front of; beforehand (as an adverb)

inter (+ accusative): between, among, during

post (+ accusative): after, behind

sub (+ ablative): under

CONJUNCTIONS AND ADVERBS

at: but

tunc: then, at that time

II. Translate the following sentences from Latin to English or English to Latin.

1. Novum templum vidēre tunc optābāmus.
2. Namque carmina dulcia mediā nocte scrībēbās.
3. Sermōnēs publicōs dē castitāte ante bellum audiēbātis.
4. Līberī aliī vērō patribus similēs erant, at aliī mātribus.
5. Hominēs nōn sōlum terram sed etiam caelum condemnant.
6. Iuvenis ad urbēs et magnās et altās veniēbam.
7. Frātrēs sorōrēsque prō patriā tantā bellum gerēbant.
8. Urbī Rōmānae praesidiō estis.
9. Without doubt, the children were beginning their pursuits.
10. After the war, we were preparing the public altar and new roads.
11. You (feminine plural) were by nature miserable.
12. The leaders wish to take up arms on behalf of the city.

The Julio-Claudian Emperors

We are fortunate to have a rich record of the Julio-Claudian dynasty, whose members descended from Augustus (his family name was Julius) and his wife, Livia (her first husband was a Claudius). Suetonius's entertaining biographies of these powerful men preserve a variety of detail from their childhoods and early education, to their appearance and dress, dining habits, and manners of death. These accounts are supplemented by Tacitus's sharp-witted and often caustic assessment of their reigns in the *Annales*. In some cases we even have the accounts of the emperors themselves: cut into stone are Augustus's autobiography (*Res Gestae*) and Claudius's address on admitting citizens from Gaul into the Senate (a copy of the speech was erected in Lugdunum [Lyon, France], his birthplace: *CIL* 13.1668).

Each of these men is fascinating in his own right. Augustus (63 BCE–CE 14), formerly called Octavian, was the sickly grandson of Julius Caesar's sister. And the great dictator had named him as his heir. After his victory over Marc Antony at Actium (on the western coast of Greece) in 31 BCE, this young man accomplished what his charismatic and brilliant great-uncle could not: the reconciliation of a civil war-torn people and peace throughout the Empire (*Pax Augusta*). Augustus derived his authority from traditional, constitutional offices and special grants of constitutional privileges from the Senate. He was *Princeps*, "the first citizen," and as such he was merely *prīmus inter parēs*, "first among equals." For the most part, he was a good-natured man who revived Roman glory, completing many of Julius Caesar's projects (including the restoration of the Senate House and a map of the world: see *NLP* 10), and erecting temples and public buildings in the names of his relatives (among others, the theater of his nephew Marcellus and the Portico of his sister Octavia, which included a public art gallery). Augustus also knew that he needed a clear plan for succession upon his death to prevent another civil war. Because he had no son of his own, he adopted nephews, grandsons, and stepsons, grooming each one in turn to assume the position of *Princeps*. When Augustus finally died, power transferred smoothly and quietly to his current heir, Tiberius.

Tiberius (reigned 14–37 CE) was Augustus's humorless stepson, Livia's firstborn. Disdaining social life in the city, Tiberius withdrew to Rhodes after significant service to Augustus in the field of battle. Suetonius and Tacitus both give a negative portrait of him, but Velleius Paterculus, who had served under Tiberius, sketched a far more positive account. Tiberius's paranoia about insurrection fueled a notorious spate of treason trials, encouraged by Tiberius's advisor, Sejanus, who had his own aspirations to the purple. Tiberius, nonetheless, was an able general and administrator, and his management of the Empire was largely efficient and without incident. This stands in stark contrast with his treatment of family. Legendary was his extreme hostility to his nephew Germanicus, favored by Augustus and the Roman people as Tiberius's heir. Tiberius's feud with Germanicus's wife, Agrippina the Elder, lasted until her suicide by starvation in 33 CE. Tiberius even refused to attend the funeral of his own mother Livia in 29 CE. He showed no favor to his own grandson Tiberius Gemellus, and only lukewarm favor to his successor, his great-nephew Gaius.

Gaius (reigned 37–41 CE) succeeded his great-uncle to the acclamation of the Roman people, who believed that the young man would pursue the legacy of his father Germanicus, an able general and promising statesman who died unexpectedly at an early age. Gaius was better known as "Caligula," so called from the *caliga*, a soldier's hob-nailed boot that the toddler wore in his father's camp. Gaius was a spoiled and coddled child, accustomed to getting his own way. His early administration was promising, until he fell ill, becoming irritable, ruthless, and irrational upon recovery. He is said to have appointed his favorite horse, Incitatus ("Rapid") as Consul. Gaius's "conquest" of Britain consisted of a challenge to the god Neptune, an order to his soldiers to gather seashells on the Gallic side of the English Channel, and a full triumph at Rome. Gaius's troops never set foot on the island. Unpopular with the elite, the Senate, and the army, he was finally assassinated by the Praetorian Guard.

Claudius (reigned 41–54 CE), Germanicus's youngest brother, was acclaimed emperor by the same Praetorian Guards who had executed Gaius. Far from the perfect Roman boy, because of his physical deformities he had been shunned by his family, left to his tutors, and excluded from public service. A scholarly man, he wrote histories of the Etruscan and Carthaginian peoples, and is the last person (so far as we know) who could read the Etruscan language. Despite his lack of administrative experience, he was an able emperor, expanding the Empire into Britain and improving infrastructure. However, he was easily manipulated by his wives (he was married four times, including to his niece, Agrippina the Younger, Gaius's sister) and by his freedmen. Agrippina persuaded Claudius to adopt her son Nero, putting him in line for succession, and she orchestrated Claudius's murder by food poisoning.

Nero (reigned 54–68 CE) resembled his uncle Gaius in many respects. He showed promise at first, thanks to the efforts of capable advisors, including his tutor and speech writer Seneca the Younger. His reign turned extravagant after the murder of his mother Agrippina the Younger, in 59 CE. Nero indulged his desire to perform, with an extensive tour of Greece, where he collected 1,800 victory crowns in competitions for music, acting, and horse racing. All the while, Nero drained the treasury, neglected public affairs, and alienated the upper classes. Meanwhile, the city was left to the whims of Tigellinus, the prefect of the Praetorian Guard and very fond of treason trials (rivaling Tiberius's prefect Sejanus in ambition and method). Other stresses likewise contributed to Nero's demise, including the revolts of Boudicca, queen of the Iceni in Britain (60 CE), and of Vindex in Gaul (68 CE). The revolt in Gaul emboldened Galba, governor of neighboring Hispania Tarraconensis, to march on Rome and vie for power, which he attained by purchasing the loyalty of the Praetorian Guard in the spring of 68 CE. In the wake of Galba's threats but lacking the nerve for suicide, Nero ordered his private secretary to kill him, thus ending the Julio-Claudian dynasty, but not its legacy.

SUGGESTIONS FOR FURTHER READING:

Barrett, Anthony A., ed. *Lives of the Caesars.* Blackwell, 2008.
Champlin, Edward, *Nero.* Harvard, 2005.
Levick, B. M. *Claudius.* Yale, 1990.
Seager, R. *Tiberius.* 2nd ed. Blackwell, 2005.
Shotter, D. *Augustus Caesar.* 2nd ed. Taylor and Francis, 2005.
Winterling, Aloys. *Caligula: A Biography.* University of California, 2011.

PASSAGES

8.1. Suetonius, *Vita Augusti* 84.2. Despite his oratorical skill, Augustus avoided extemporaneity, preferring to deliver important speeches (and even private conversations) from notes.

Sermōnēs quoque cum singulīs atque etiam cum Liviā suā graviōrēs nōn nisi scriptōs et ē libellō habēbat.

Notes: **singulī, -ae, -a**: individual, one at a time (here, a substantive); **suā**: "his own"; **graviōrēs**: "rather serious (conversations)" (accusative plural); **nisi**: unless, except; **scriptus, -a, -um**: written-out (construe with *sermōnēs*).

8.2. Ovid, *Fasti* **2.137–38.** Ovid compares Romulus's almost criminal conduct in ruling the original settlement of Rome to Augustus's absolute regal authority as *pater patriae*. Meter: elegiac couplets.

Tū breve nescioquid victae tellūris habēbās;
>   quodcumque est altō sub Iove, Caesar habet.

Notes: **tū**: here, Romulus; **nescioquid**: something or other (accusative singular neuter); **victus, -a, -um**: conquered; **tellūs, tellūris**, f: earth, ground; **quodcumque**: whatever (nominative singular neuter); **Iuppiter, Iovis**, m: Jupiter.

8.3. Vergil, *Aeneid* **8.714–18.** Venus asks her husband Vulcan to create a magical set of arms for her son Aeneas. On the shield, Vulcan has forged important scenes from Rome's history. (Such an extended description is called an *ekphrasis*.) Even though Aeneas does not understand these scenes or their importance, he marvels at Vulcan's craftsmanship. Here, Vulcan has depicted the "triple" triumphal procession Octavian would celebrate in 29 BCE in honor of his successes over Dalmatia, Actium, and Egypt. Meter: dactylic hexameter.

At Caesar, triplicī invectus Rōmāna triumphō
moenia, dīs Italīs vōtum immortāle sacrābat:
maxima ter centum tōtam dēlūbra per urbem.
Laetitiā lūdīsque viae plausūque fremēbant;
omnibus in templīs mātrum chorus, omnibus ārae.

Notes: **triplex, triplicis**: triple; **invectus, -a, -um**: carried (into), conveyed (into); **triumphus, -ī**, m: triumphal procession; **moenia, -ium**, n (plural): walls, fortifications; **Italus, -a, -um**: Italian; **vōtum, -ī**, n: vow, prayer, offering; **immortālis, -e**: immortal, everlasting; **sacrō, -āre, -āvī, -ātus**: dedicate; **maximus, -a, -um**: greatest, very great; **ter**: three times; **centum** (indeclinable): one hundred; **dēlūbrum, -ī**, n: shrine, sanctuary; **laetitia, -iae**, f: happiness, exuberance; **lūdus, -ī**, m: game, sport, public show; **plausus, -ūs**, m: applause (*plausū*: ablative singular); **fremō, -ere, fremuī, fremitus**: roar, howl; **chorus, -ī**, m: chorus.

8.4. Suetonius, *Vita Tiberii* 66.1. Lacking the charisma of Julius Caesar and Augustus, Tiberius was not popular, but he was sensitive to criticism.

Ūrēbant insuper anxiam mentem varia undique convīcia.

Notes: **ūrō, -ere, ussī, ustus**: burn, consume; **insuper**: moreover, in addition; **anxius, -a, -um**: worried, anxious; **varius, -a, -um**: varied, different, diverse; **convīcium, -iī**, n: reproach, abuse, jeer.

8.5. Tacitus, *Annales* 3.38.1. Treason trials abounded during Tiberius's reign, and the emperor seemed to delight in the court proceedings.

Nōn enim Tiberius, nōn accūsātōrēs fatiscēbant.

Notes: **accūsātor, -ōris**, m: accuser, prosecutor; **fatiscō, -ere**: become exhausted, worn out.

8.6. Suetonius, *Vita Caligulae* 31.1. Caligula perversely longed for the excitement of natural disasters.

Atque identidem exercituum caedēs, famem, pestilentiam, incendia, hiātum aliquem terrae optābat.

Notes: **identidem**: again and again; **exercitus, -ūs**, m: army (*exercituum*: genitive plural); **caedēs, -is (-ium)**, f: murder, slaughter; **famēs, -is (-ium)**, f: hunger, starvation, famine; **pestilentia, -iae**, f: plague; **incendium, -iī**, n: fire; **hiātus, -ūs**, m: chasm; **aliquem**: some (accusative singular).

8.7. Suetonius, *Vita Caligulae* 50.1. Caligula desired to be feared by his subjects to the extent that he took great pains to make himself appear physically frightful and terrifying.

Vultum vērō nātūrā horridum ac taetrum etiam ex industriā efferābat compōnens ad speculum in omnem terrōrem ac formīdinem.

Notes: **vultus, -ūs**, m: face (*vultum*: accusative singular); **horridus, -a, -um**: shaggy, disheveled, rugged; **taeter, taetra, taetrum**: revolting, monstrous; **industria, -iae**, f: industry, diligence (e.g., "on purpose"); **efferō, -āre, -āvī, -ātus**: make wild, brutalize, debauch; **compōnens (-entis)**: arranging, "contorting"; **ad speculum**: "at the mirror"; **terror, -ōris**, m: terror, alarm, dread; **formīdō, formīdinis**, f: fear, terror.

8.8. Tacitus, *Annales* 6.50.5. Caligula awaits news of Tiberius's murder and his own ascension to the throne.

Caesar in silentium fixus ā summā spē novissima expectābat.

Notes: **Caesar**: here referring to Caligula; **silentium, -iī**, n: silence; **fixus, -a, -um**: fixed, immovable; **summus, -a, -um**: highest; **spēs, spēī**, f: hope (*spē*: ablative singular); **novissimus, -a, -um**: newest, most novel, most subversive (here, a substantive); **expectō, -āre, -āvī, -ātus**: wait for, hope for.

8.9. Seneca, *Apocolocyntosis* 7.4. After his death, the emperor Claudius finds himself in heaven, as a defendant seeking the right to be a Roman god. Hercules has just interrogated Claudius about his birthplace (he was born not in Rome, but in Gaul). Like a skilled politician, Claudius avoids answering the question altogether.

Nam sī memoriā repetis, ego eram quī tibi ante templum tuum iūs dīcēbam tōtīs diēbus mense Iūliō et Augustō.

Notes: **repetō, -ere, -īvī, -ītus**: trace back, recall, recollect; **quī**: "he who" (nominative singular); **iūs dīcere**: administer justice; **tōtīs diēbus**: "on all the days"; **mensis, -is (-ium)**, m: month; **Iūlius, -a,- um**: Julian, the month named in honor of Julius Caesar; **Augustus, -a, -um**: Augustan, the month named in honor of Augustus.

8.10. Tacitus, *Annales* 12.11.1. In 47 CE, after the execution of their king, the Parthians decide to seek help from Rome to oust a vicious usurper and replace him with a Parthian prince being held at Rome as a "hostage"—a surety for the shaky peace treaty between Rome and Parthia (a common practice for warring nations). Claudius exhibits admirable diplomacy when he hosts the delegates two years later.

Incipit ōrātiōnem Caesar dē fastīgiō Rōmānō Parthōrumque obsequiīs, sēque dīvō Augustō adaequābat.

Notes: **ōrātiō, -iōnis**, f: speech, oration; **Caesar**: refers here to Claudius; **fastīgium, -iī**, n: dignity; **Parthī, -ōrum**, m (plural): Parthians, inhabitants of Parthia; **obsequium, -iī**, n: compliance, obedience, allegiance; **sē**: himself (accusative singular, here Claudius); **dīvus, -a, -um**: divine; **adaequō, -āre, -āvī, -ātus**: equal, match.

8.11. Suetonius, *Vita Neronis* 19.2. Not all of Nero's exploits were outlandish. Here, Nero plans to send an elite corps of six-foot-tall, Italian-born soldiers to the eastern reaches of the Empire.

Parābat et ad Caspiās portās expedītiōnem.

Notes: **et** = *etiam*; **Caspius, -a, -um**: Caspian (referring to the large landlocked lake in central Asia); **expedītiō, -iōnis**, f: expedition, campaign.

8.12. Suetonius, *Vita Neronis* 27.2. Suetonius recounts some of Nero's bizarre nighttime escapades.

Epulās ā mediō diē ad mediam noctem prōtrahēbat, refōtus saepius calidīs piscīnīs ac—tempore aestīvō—nivātīs.

Notes: **epula, -ae**, f: feast, banquet; **diēs, diēī**, m: day (*diē*: ablative singular); **prōtrahō, -ere, -traxī, -tractus**: drag out; **refōtus, -a, -um**: refreshed, restored; **saepius**: rather often, quite frequently; **calidus, -a, -um**: warm, hot; **piscīna, -ae**, f: swimming pool, bath; **aestīvus, -a, -um**: summery, related to summer; **nivātus, -a, -um**: cooled with snow (construe with *piscinīs*).

EXTRA PASSAGES: THE IMPERIAL FAMILY

Just as colorful as the emperors were their relatives, who ranged from the digni-fied to the scandalous. Here we meet some of the more significant imperials, men who were heirs to the throne, and women who had aspirations from the shadows. We also see that many of these outrageous characters did not live up to the Roman values of family life and austerity that Augustus tried so hard to enforce.

8.13. Suetonius, *Vita Augusti* 63.1. Augustus's daughter Julia was first married to her cousin Marcellus (the same Marcellus of *NLP* 6.3). After Marcellus's death, Augustus arranged a marriage between Julia and his lifelong friend Agrippa—who just happened to be married to one of Marcellus's sisters (as Suetonius tells us here). Despite the age difference, the marriage was happy, and the couple had five children. After Agrippa's death, Julia was then mar-ried to Augustus's dour stepson Tiberius. The marriage was so unhappy that

Julia found her comfort in drink and the company of other men, much to the shame and disappointment of her father.

Nam tunc Agrippa alteram Marcellārum habēbat et ex eā līberōs.

Notes: **alter, altera, alterum**: one of two (Marcellus had two sisters); **Marcella, -ae**, f: a Roman woman took the feminine form of her father's *nōmen*, and daughters within a family were distinguished as *māior* (elder) and *minor* (younger); **habēbat**: understand "in marriage"; **eā**: "from her (Marcella)" (ablative singular).

8.14. Juvenal, *Saturae* 6.117–19. Claudius's wife, Messalina, was notorious for her adulteries and sexual exploits. Meter: dactylic hexameter.

Sūmere nocturnōs meretrix Augusta cucullōs
ausa Palātīnō et tegetem praeferre cubīlī
linquēbat comite ancillā nōn amplius ūnā.

Notes: **nocturnus, -a, -um**: nocturnal, nightly; **meretrix, meretrīcis**, f: harlot, prostitute; **Augusta, -ae**, f: the title held by the emperor's wife (here, Messalina); **cucullus, -ī**, m: hood, hooded cloak; **ausus, -a, -um**: having dared (to); **Palātīnus, -a, -um**: pertaining to the Palatine Hill with its royal residences; **teges, tegetis**, f: crude mat; **praeferō, -ferre, -tulī, -lātus**: prefer (accusative) over (dative); **cubīle, -is**, n: bed; **linquō, -ere, līquī**: leave (with); **comes, comitis**, m/f: companion, attendant (in apposition with *ancilla*); **ancilla, -ae**, f: maidservant, female slave; **amplius**: more (than + ablative).

8.15. Suetonius, *Vita Claudii* 3.2. Born with birth defects, Claudius walked with a limp and talked with a stutter. His own mother Antonia felt no affection for her ungainly child.

Māter Antōnia portentum eum hominis dictitābat, nec absolūtum ā nātūrā, sed tantum incohātum.

Notes: **Antōnia, -iae**, f: the daughter of Marcus Antonius and Augustus's sister Octavia; **portentum, -ī**, n: monster, monstrosity; **eum**: him (accusative singular, here Claudius); **dictitō, -āre, -āvī, -ātus**: repeatedly call; **absolūtus, -a, -um**: completed, perfected; **incohātus, -a, -um**: outlined, sketched.

Future Tense

1. The **FUTURE TENSE** describes actions that will take place sometime in the future and can be translated in several ways depending upon the context. For example, *docēbunt* can mean "they will teach," "they will be teaching," and "they are about to teach." Consider the following examples:

Catullus 32.1: **Amābō, mea dulcis Ipsitilla**. <u>I shall love</u> (you), my sweet Ipsitilla.

Livy, *ab Urbe Condita* 1.58.10: **"Nec ulla deinde impudīca Lucrētiae exemplō vīvet."** "And then no unchaste woman <u>will live</u> by Lucretia's example."

Ovid, *Amores* 1.3.16: **Tū mihi, sīqua fidēs, cūra perennis eris**. If there is any loyalty, <u>you will be</u> an everlasting concern to me.

2. In Latin, first and second conjugation verbs have the same endings for the future tense. Add the personal endings that you learned in *NLP* 1 to the future signifier -**bi**-. (Note that the future signifiers for the 1st person singular and 3rd person plural are slightly different.) Study the table below.

Person	Singular	Plural
1st	-**bō**	-**bimus**
2nd	-**bis**	-**bitis**
3rd	-**bit**	-**bunt**

3. To form the future tense of first and second conjugation verbs, add the future tense endings (above) to the present stem, formed by dropping

the ending (-**āre** or -**ēre**) from the verb's infinitive. The vowel between the present stem and the future tense endings is -**ā**- for the first conjugation and -**ē**- for the second conjugation. Memorize one verb in the future tense from each of these two conjugations to serve as a model for other verbs.

FUTURE TENSE OF FIRST CONJUGATION

Person	Singular	Plural
1st	amā**bō**: I shall love	amā**bimus**: we shall love
2nd	amā**bis**: you will love	amā**bitis**: you (plural) will love
3rd	amā**bit**: he/she/it will love	amā**bunt**: they will love

FUTURE TENSE OF SECOND CONJUGATION

Person	Singular	Plural
1st	docē**bō**: I shall teach	docē**bimus**: we shall teach
2nd	docē**bis**: you will teach	docē**bitis**: you (plural) will teach
3rd	docē**bit**: he/she/it will teach	docē**bunt**: they will teach

4. In Latin, third and fourth conjugation verbs follow a slightly different pattern. Simply add the personal endings that you learned in *NLP* 1 to the future signifier -**e**-. (Note that the future signifier for the 1st person singular is slightly different.) Study the table below.

Person	Singular	Plural
1st	-am	-**ēmus**
2nd	-**ēs**	-**ētis**
3rd	-et	-ent

5. To form the future tense of third and fourth conjugation verbs, simply add the future tense endings (above) to the present stem, formed by dropping the ending (-**ere** or -**īre**) from the verb's infinitive. For third conjugation (-io) and fourth conjugation verbs, add an -**i**- between the present stem and these endings. Memorize one verb in the future tense from each of these conjugations. Consult the tables on the next page.

FUTURE TENSE OF THIRD CONJUGATION

Person	Singular	Plural
1st	mitt**am**: I shall send	mitt**ēmus**: we shall send
2nd	mitt**ēs**: you will send	mitt**ētis**: you (plural) will send
3rd	mitt**et**: he/she/it will send	mitt**ent**: they will send

FUTURE TENSE OF THIRD CONJUGATION (-IO)

Person	Singular	Plural
1st	cap**iam**: I shall take	cap**iēmus**: we shall take
2nd	cap**iēs**: you will take	cap**iētis**: you (plural) will take
3rd	cap**iet**: he/she/it will take	cap**ient**: they will take

FUTURE TENSE OF FOURTH CONJUGATION

Person	Singular	Plural
1st	aud**iam**: I shall hear	aud**iēmus**: we shall hear
2nd	aud**iēs**: you will hear	aud**iētis**: you (plural) will hear
3rd	aud**iet**: he/she/it will hear	aud**ient**: they will hear

6. It is important that you know to which conjugation a verb belongs so that you can accurately translate the verb in a Latin sentence. You may find it challenging to distinguish second conjugation verbs in the present tense from third conjugation verbs in the future tense. Consider the following examples:

Martial 1.97.4: **Tacent** omnēs. All are silent.

> *Tacent* is a second conjugation verb in the present tense.

Cicero, *ad Atticum* 2.16.2: **Quid dīcēs**? What will you say?

> *Dīcēs* is a third conjugation verb in the future tense.

Cicero, *de Amicitia* 5: **Ab hīs sermō oritur; respondet Laelius, cuius tōta disputātiō est dē amīcitiā, quam legens tē ipse cognoscēs.** From them (Gaius Fannius and Quintus Mucius) emerges a conversation; Laelius, whose entire argument—reading which you will recognize yourself—is about friendship, answers.

> *Respondet* is a second conjugation verb in the present tense; *cognoscēs*, however, is a third conjugation verb in the future tense.

7. The irregular verb "to be" conjugates as follows in the future tense.

FUTURE TENSE OF *ESSE*

Person	Singular	Plural
1st	er**ō**: I shall be	eri**mus**: we shall be
2nd	eri**s**: you will be	eri**tis**: you (plural) will be
3rd	eri**t**: he/she/it will be	eru**nt**: they will be

8. The **FUTURE IMPERATIVE** is used in commands where there is a clear reference to future time. Because English does not distinguish between present or future imperatives, you must decide whether to emphasize the "imperative" force of the verb or the "future" force of the verb in your translation. Consider the following examples:

Cicero, *in Verrem* 2.3.129: <u>**Scītōte**</u> **tantam acerbitātem istīus, tantum scelus in aratōrēs fuisse.** <u>Know</u> (or "<u>you will know</u>") that his cruelty, his (Verres') wickedness against the farmers was so great.

Adamnan, *Vita Sancti Columbae.* 2.34: **Dīcitō mihi, Columba, quō tempore prōpōnis ēnāvigāre?** <u>Tell</u> (or "<u>you will tell</u>") me, Columba, at what time do you propose to sail?

9. The future imperative is easily recognized by its distinctive endings. Study the following table.

Verb	Future Singular Imperative	Future Plural Imperative	Translation
amō, amāre	amā**tō**	amā**tōte**	Love! or You will love
doceō, docēre	docē**tō**	docē**tōte**	Teach! or You will teach
mittō, mittere	mitti**tō**	mitti**tōte**	Send! or You will send
capiō, capere	capi**tō**	capi**tōte**	Take! or You will take
audiō, audīre	audī**tō**	audī**tōte**	Listen! or You will listen
sum, esse	es**tō**	es**tōte**	Be! or So be it!

I. Required Vocabulary

NOUNS

causa, -ae, f: cause, reason, legal case
cōpia, -iae, f: abundance, (plural) troops
epistula, -ae, f: letter
glōria, -iae, f: glory, fame, ambition, renown
lacrima, -ae, f: tear
pecūnia, -iae, f: money
sententia, -iae, f: opinion, judgment

servus, -ī, m: slave

cīvis, -is (-ium), m/f: citizen
cīvitās, -ātis, f: citizenship, state, city-state
fīnis, -is (-ium), m: boundary, end, territory
lex, lēgis, f: law
nēmō, nēminis, m/f: no one
pietās, -ātis, f: responsibility, sense of duty, piety
vīs, vīris (-ium), f: force, strength, power (N.B. This noun is irregular in
    the singular: the genitive and dative singular are not attested; ac-
    cusative singular: *vim*; ablative singular: *vī*)

ADJECTIVES

cārus, -a, -um (+ dative): dear (to)

familiāris, -e: belonging to the household (used substantively to mean
    "servant, slave, friend, or intimate")

VERBS

cōgitō, -āre, -āvī, -ātus: think, reflect

respondeō, -ēre, respondī, responsus: answer, reply

cognoscō, -ere, -nōvī, -nitus: learn, understand, perceive
efficiō, -ere, -fēcī, -fectus: bring about, render, complete
trādō, -ere, trādidī, trāditus: hand over, yield

sentiō, -īre, sensī, sensus: perceive, feel

adsum, adesse, adfuī: be present, be at hand
inquit (defective verb): he/she said

CONJUNCTIONS AND ADVERBS
    autem: however, moreover, but
    maximē: most especially, certainly
    inde: from there, from then
    nōn sōlum . . . vērum etiam: not only . . . but also
    rursus or **rursum**: back, again

II. Translate the following sentences from Latin to English or English to Latin.

1. Rōmulō et Remō, familiāribus meīs, respondēbō, sed nihil hostibus nostrīs dīcam.
2. Cīvēs magnae virtūtis pecūniam nēminī trādent et pācem efficient.
3. Sine lacrimīs epistulās dulcēs nōn scrībētis.
4. Nōn sōlum dē lēgis vī vērum etiam dē cīvitātis nātūrā cōgitābāmus.
5. Ō mīlitēs, tempus locumque proeliī scītōte!
6. Neque mortem neque fortūnam cognoscis.
7. "Post bellum servus erō," inquit pater meus, "sed meum oppidum nōn relinquam!"
8. Ō amīcī, adeste animō et hominēs scelere absolvite!
9. I was entrusting the children to my wife.
10. Soon you (singular) will respond to the king about our duties.
11. You (plural) will make all the citizens clever.
12. We live here, we perceive no danger (literally: nothing of danger), and we will hand over the glory of the city to our children.

Marcus Tullius Cicero (106–43 BCE)

Forensic orator, statesman, constitutionalist, philosopher, devoted father, loyal friend: what connects these varied parts of Cicero's life is his unfaltering love for the Roman Republic. Born to an obscure family in Arpinum, some sixty miles southeast of Rome, Cicero proved that a *novus homo* could succeed in Roman political life by scaling the *cursus honōrum* in record time—he served as quaestor in 75 BCE, aedile in 69 BCE, Praetor in 66 BCE, and, finally, as Consul in 63 BCE, attaining the highest regular political office at the youngest age allowed by the Roman constitution (age forty-two for equestrians). Despite his political popularity (or perhaps because of it!), Cicero began to amass some powerful enemies who took offense at his self-proclaimed role as "defender of the Republic." In his consular election, Cicero defeated Lucius Sergius Catilina (108–62 BCE), who in turn plotted to assassinate Cicero and usurp the coveted office. When Cicero revealed his plans to the Senate on 8 November 63 BCE (*in Catilinam* I), Catiline fled to Etruria. Some of his co-conspirators, however, remained in Rome. They were arrested by the Senate, sentenced to death, and executed. Catiline himself was defeated in pitched battle in January of 62 BCE at Pistorium in northern Italy. Cicero's public antagonism toward his rival had far-reaching consequences that extended beyond the (real) threat that Catiline posed to Cicero and even to the Republic. When Publius Clodius Pulcher was accused of dressing as a woman and infiltrating the exclusively female secret rites of the *Bona Dea* in 62 BCE (held at Julius Caesar's house that particular year), Cicero produced damning evidence and exposed Clodius's fabricated alibi. Clodius managed to escape punishment (Crassus helped secure acquittal by bribing the jury). Several years later, after obtaining the position of *tribunus plebis* (an office open only to plebeians— Clodius had himself adopted into a plebeian family), Clodius retroactively enacted a law that prohibited the execution of Roman citizens without trial (which is exactly what Cicero did to Catiline's followers). As a result, Cicero was exiled and his property confiscated—a blow that struck him even harder because he believed that he had acted in the best interests of the Republic by taking action against both Catiline and Clodius.

Cicero's allies eventually secured his recall, and the great statesman was allowed to return to Rome but was barred from holding political office. As the tensions of civil war mounted, Cicero backed Pompey but received pardon from Julius Caesar after Pompey's death in Egypt. Caesar, in fact, had admired the great orator so much that he had invited Cicero to participate in the so-called First Triumvirate, the informal alliance, struck in 56 BCE, that obligated Caesar, Pompey, and Crassus to each other in matters of politics. After Caesar's assassination, Cicero began a public campaign to discredit Marc Antony. In fourteen vitriolic speeches, known collectively as the *Philippics*, he attacked Antony's character. Antony took drastic steps to punish his detractors, and his treatment of Cicero was brutal. Antony's henchmen apprehended the orator, executed him, and nailed his hands and head to the senatorial *Rostrum* in the Roman Forum.

Over the course of his stunning career, Cicero generated fifty-seven surviving legal speeches, twenty-one philosophical essays, some bad poetry, and one of the most extensive collections of correspondence from ancient Rome. In more than 900 letters, preserved by his secretary Tiro, Cicero chronicles the major events of his life—the birth of his son Marcus, his growing dissatisfaction with his wife Terentia, their subsequent divorce, his short second marriage to his much younger ward Publilia, and the premature death of his beloved daughter Tullia, who never recovered from giving birth to Cicero's grandson. These letters also record pivotal moments in the waning years of the Republic, whose destruction devastated Cicero almost more than the disintegration of his marriage and the loss of his daughter.

SUGGESTIONS FOR FURTHER READING:

Baraz, Yelena. *A Written Republic: Cicero's Philosophical Politics*. Princeton, 2012.

Everitt, Anthony. *Cicero: The Life and Times of Rome's Greatest Politician*. Random House, 2002.

May, James M., ed. *Brill's Companion to Cicero: Oratory and Rhetoric*. Brill, 2002.

Vasaly, Ann. *Representations: Images of the World in Ciceronian Oratory*. University of California, 1996.

White, Peter. *Cicero in Letters: Epistolary Relations of the Late Republic*. Oxford, 2012.

PASSAGES

9.1. Cicero, *ad Atticum* 1.2.1. In July of 65 BCE, Cicero announces the birth of his son Marcus to his dear friend Atticus.

Fīliolō mē auctum scītō, salvā Terentiā.

Notes: **fīliolus, -ī,** m: little son; **mē auctum** (*esse*): "that I have been enriched (by)"; **salvā Terentiā**: "Terentia (being) healthy" (ablative absolute).

9.2. Cicero, *ad Familiares* 14.1.5. Exiled from Rome, Cicero succumbs to depression, and the letters to his family are filled with grief and regret. Here, we read an excerpt from one such letter to his wife Terentia (written in November of 58 BCE).

Nōn queō reliqua scrībere—tanta vīs lacrimārum est—neque tē in eundem flētum addūcam.

Notes: **queō, quīre, quīvī, quītus**: be able; **reliquus, -a, -um**: remaining, rest; **eundem**: the same (accusative singular); **flētus, -ūs**, m: weeping, lamenting, crying; **addūcō, -ere, -duxī, -ductum**: lead to, induce.

9.3. Cicero, *ad Familiares* 14.7.2. In June of 49 BCE, as the political situation at Rome deteriorates into civil war, Cicero assures his wife that his powerful friends will protect their family.

Deinde conscrībam ad nostrōs familiārēs multās epistulās, quibus tē et Tulliōlam nostram dīligentissimē commendābō.

Notes: **conscrībō, -ere, -scrīpsī, -scrīptus**: compose; **quibus**: "in which (letters)" (ablative plural feminine); **Tulliōla, -ae**, f: little Tullia (for naming daughters, see *NLP* 8.13; here we have a diminutive, Cicero's tender nickname for his beloved child); **dīligentissimē**: most carefully, most industriously.

9.4. Cicero, *ad Familiares* 16.7. In December of 50 BCE, Cicero wrote a short, affectionate letter to his personal secretary, Tiro.

Nēmō nōs amat, quī tē nōn dīligit; cārus omnibus exspectātusque veniēs.

Notes: **quī**: who (nominative singular masculine); **dīligō, -ere, -lexī, -lectus**: cherish, esteem; **cārus**: in apposition with the subject; **exspectātus, -a, -um**: awaited, anticipated.

9.5. Cicero, *Philippica* 2.50. In the second *Philippic*, dating to October 44 BCE, but not delivered publicly, Cicero blames Marc Antony for the current state of political unrest and uncertainty.

Ab huius enim scelere omnium malōrum principium nātum reperiētis.

Notes: **huius**: "of this man" (genitive singular; here, Marc Antony); **principium, -iī**, n: beginning; **nātus, -a, -um**: arisen, originated, "original"; **reperiō, -īre, repperī, repertus**: find, discover.

9.6. Cicero, *Philippica* 13.45. Cicero assures Marc Antony that his long-term plans to appropriate the government are doomed because all people, even the gods, will join against him.

Omnēs tē dī, hominēs, summī, mediī, infimī, cīvēs, peregrīnī, virī, mulierēs, līberī, servī ōdērunt. Sensimus hoc nūper falsō nuntiō, vērō propediem sentiēmus.

Notes: **summus, -a, -um**: highest; **infimus, -a, -um**: lowest; **peregrīnus, -a, -um**: foreign, strange, exotic; **mulier, -ieris**, f: woman; **ōdērunt** : "they hate" (from **ōdī, -isse**: hate, detest [this verb lacks first and second principal parts]); **sensimus**: "we perceived (from)" (perfect tense of *sentiō*); **hoc**: this (accusative singular); **nūper**: recently, not long ago; **falsus, -a, -um**: deceptive, false; **nuntium, -iī**, n: message, news; **propediem**: very soon.

9.7. Cicero, *in Catilinam* 2.26. In this speech (delivered to the Senate on 9 November, 63 BCE), Cicero justifies his actions against Catiline and his debt-ridden, power-hungry compatriots. Here, Cicero calls the Roman people to arms against Catiline.

Colōnī omnēs mūnicipēsque vestrī, certiōrēs ā mē factī dē hāc nocturnā excursiōne Catilīnae, facile urbēs suās fīnēsque dēfendent.

Notes: **colōnus, -ī**, m: farmer, inhabitant (of a colony); **mūniceps, mūnicipis**, m/f: citizen (of a free town); **certiōrēs . . . factī**: "made more certain, steadfast" (nominative plural masculine); **hāc**: this (ablative singular); **nocturnus, -a, -um**: nocturnal; **excursiō, -iōnis**, f: attack, assault; **facile**: easily; **suās**: "their own"; **dēfendō, -ere, -fendī, -fēnsus**: defend, ward off.

9.8. Cicero, *pro Archia* **22.** In this speech Cicero defends the popular poet Archias, whose citizenship was called into question.

Nōs hunc Hēracliensem, multīs cīvitātibus expetītum, in hāc autem lēgibus constitūtum, dē nostrā cīvitāte ēiciēmus?

Notes: **hunc**: this man (accusative singular; here, Archias); **Hēracliensis, -e**: from Heraclea (in Sicily); **expetītus, -a, -um**: asked for, sought after; **hāc**: this (ablative singular, construe with an implied *cīvitāte*); **constitūtus, -a, -um**: settled, established; **ēiciō, -ere, -iēcī, -iectus**: cast out, eject.

9.9. Cicero, *pro Milone* **38.** In 52 BCE, Cicero's friend Milo was accused of killing their mutual enemy Clodius Pulcher, whose death fomented tremendous turmoil in Rome: the people rioted, the Senate House was burned down, and it was impossible to hold elections. Pompey restored order by bringing armed forces into the city—an unprecedented action—and his troops were quite visible during the public trial. Here, in the final words of the deeply revised and highly polished version of his defense speech (the speech as delivered was not published), Cicero appeals to Pompey's sense of probity and honesty. Despite Cicero's efforts, Milo was convicted by a vote of thirty-eight to thirteen and then exiled to Massillia on the southern coast of France.

Vestram virtūtem, iustitiam, fidem, mihi crēdite, is maximē probābit, quī in iūdicibus legendīs optimum et sapientissimum et fortissimum quemque ēlēgit.

Notes: **iustitia, -iae**, f: justice, fairness, equity; **fidēs, -eī**, f: trust, faith; **is**: he (nominative singular masculine; here, Pompey); **probō, -āre, -āvī, -ātus**: approve, prove, convince; **quī**: who (nominative singular masculine); **in iūdicibus legendīs**: "in selecting judges"; **optimus, -a, -um**: best, very good, **sapientissimus, -a, -um**: wisest, very wise; **fortissimus, -a, -um**: bravest; **quemque**: each (one), every single (man) (accusative singular masculine); **ēlēgit**: "(who) has chosen" (perfect tense).

9.10. Cicero, *pro Murena* **84.** After a passionate address to the jury, imagining that only unscrupulous men such as Catiline would vote to condemn Murena, Cicero appeals to the jury's sense of patriotism in his pleas for acquittal.

Mihi crēdite, iūdicēs, in hāc causā nōn sōlum dē L. Mūrēnae vērum etiam dē vestrā salūte sententiam ferētis.

Notes: **iūdex, iūdicis**, m: judge, juror; **hāc**: "(in) this (case)" (ablative singular feminine); **Lūcius Mūrēna, Lūciī Mūrēnae**, m: the defendant; **salūs, salūtis**, f: health, soundness; **ferētis**: "you will render."

9.11. Cicero, *de Senectute* 3. In 44 BCE, Cicero wrote this treatise as a dialogue between Cato the Elder, a conservative Roman politician of the second century BCE whose enmity for Carthage knew no bounds; Scipio Aemilianus, the adopted grandson of Scipio Africanus (Cato's political rival, who led Rome to victory against Carthage in the Second Punic War); and Scipio Aemilianus's good friend Gaius Laelius Sapiens (son of the elder Scipio's lieutenant during the Carthaginian War).

Iam enim ipsīus Catōnis sermō explicābit nostram omnem dē senectūte sententiam.

Notes: **ipsīus**: "(of Cato) himself" (genitive singular masculine); **explicō, -āre, -āvī/-uī, -ātus**: explain, set forth; **senectūs, senectūtis**, f: old age.

9.12. Cicero, *de Officiis* 2.11. In this essay, Cicero outlines the path to an honorable life for his son Marcus. In Book 2, he discusses the concepts of "expediency" and "inexpediency" in reference to the comforts and pleasures of this world.

Deōs placātōs pietās efficiet et sanctitās; proximē autem et, secundum deōs, hominēs hominibus maximē ūtilēs esse possunt.

Notes: **placātus, -a, -um**: kindly disposed, appeased, placated; **sanctitās, -ātis**, f: inviolability, sanctity; **proximē**: next; **secundum** (+ accusative): immediately after; **ūtilis, -e** (+ dative): useful; **possunt**: "they (people) are able (to)."

EXTRA PASSAGES: PLINY THE YOUNGER

Cicero's letters constitute the first large body of correspondence that survives from ancient Rome. Several generations later, Pliny the Younger also amassed a noteworthy collection of letters, which, unlike Cicero, he edited for publication during his lifetime.

9.13. Pliny the Younger, *Epistulae* 6.16.22. In this famous letter to the historian Tacitus, Pliny relates the heroic efforts of his uncle Pliny the Elder during the eruption of Mt. Vesuvius in 79 CE. (Pliny's uncle did not survive the disaster.) Here, Pliny the Younger reveals his faith in Tacitus's ability to sift the personal details of this painful letter from those fit for the historical record.

Tū potissima excerpēs; aliud est enim epistulam, aliud historiam, aliud amīcō, aliud omnibus scrībere.

Notes: **potissimus, -a, -um**: most powerful, strongest, "most suitable"; **excerpō, -ere, -cerpsī, -cerptus**: pick out, choose; **aliud . . . aliud**: "one thing (to) . . . another thing (to) . . ."; **historia, -iae**, f: account, story.

9.14. Pliny the Younger, *Epistulae* **9.33.11.** Pliny relates the perfect story for the poet Caninius Rufus to turn into a poem. In Hippo (northern Africa), local children were accustomed to swim in a lake that opened up into the sea. One child who had strayed too far was rescued by a dolphin. The dolphin then returned day after day to play with his new human friend. The boy and dolphin became quite the tourist attraction, delighting spectators who visited Hippo specifically to see the unusual twosome. Unfortunately, the city officials grew annoyed that the dolphin was "upsetting" the tranquillity of their community. So they arranged to have him killed. Pliny feels confident that Rufus's verses will do the story (and the dolphin) justice.

Haec tū quā miserātiōne, quā cōpiā dēflēbis, ornābis, attollēs!

Notes: **haec**: these things (accusative plural neuter); **quā**: "with what (pity)" (ablative singular feminine); **miserātiō, -iōnis**, f: pity, compassion; **dēfleō, -ēre,- flēvī, -flētus**: mourn, weep; **ornō, -āre, -āvī, -ātus**: equip, embellish; **attollō, -ere** (no third and fourth principal parts): raise up, lift.

9.15. Pliny the Younger, *Epistulae* **2.1.12.** Pliny writes about the death and public funeral of his guardian, Lucius Verginius Rufus, who played a critical role in suppressing the revolt against Nero led by Gaius Iulius Vindex. Rufus's troops declared him emperor after Nero's death and again after Otho's demise, but he chose instead to retire from political life. Decades later, the emperor Nerva convinced Rufus to become his co-Consul, and he died in that office. Here Pliny expresses his grief at his guardian's demise.

Vergīnium cōgitō, Vergīnium videō, Vergīnium iam vānīs imāginibus—recentibus tamen—audiō, alloquor, teneō; cui fortasse cīvēs aliquōs virtūtibus parēs et habēmus et habēbimus, glōriā nēminem.

Notes: **vānus, -a, -um**: empty, false, deceitful; **imāgō, imāginis**, f: image, form, figure; **recens (-entis)**: fresh, new; **alloquor**: "I speak to, I address"; **cui**: to whom (dative singular masculine, referring to *Vergīnius*); **fortasse**: perhaps; **aliquī, aliqua, aliquod**: some, any; **pār (paris)** (+ dative): equal (to).

LESSON 10

Fourth and Fifth Declension Nouns

1. Nouns of the fourth declension typically end in -**us** in the nominative singular and feature -u- in most of the case endings. Generally, this -u- can help you distinguish fourth declension nouns from second declension nouns. Most fourth declension nouns are either masculine (-**us**) or neuter (-**ū**). A small number are feminine, including **manus** (hand), **domus** (house), **porticus** (colonnade), and **quercus** (oak tree).

FOURTH DECLENSION NOUNS

Case	lacus, lacūs, m: lake	manus, manūs, f: hand	cornū, cornūs, n: horn
Singular			
Nominative	lac**us**	man**us**	corn**ū**
Genitive	lac**ūs**	man**ūs**	corn**ūs**
Dative	lac**uī**	man**uī**	corn**ū**
Accusative	lac**um**	man**um**	corn**ū**
Ablative	lac**ū**	man**ū**	corn**ū**
Vocative	lac**us**	man**us**	corn**ū**
Plural			
Nominative	lac**ūs**	man**ūs**	corn**ua**
Genitive	lac**uum**	man**uum**	corn**uum**
Dative	lac**ibus**	man**ibus**	corn**ibus**
Accusative	lac**ūs**	man**ūs**	corn**ua**
Ablative	lac**ibus**	man**ibus**	corn**ibus**
Vocative	lac**ūs**	man**ūs**	corn**ua**

2. For fourth declension masculine and feminine nouns, the endings for the genitive singular, nominative plural, accusative plural, and vocative plural are identical (-**ūs**). Likewise, the endings for the masculine dative and ablative plurals (-**ibus**) are identical, as well as the nominative and vocative singulars (-**us**). For fourth declension neuter nouns, all the singular endings are identical (-**ū**) with the exception of the genitive singular. The endings of the neuter nominative, accusative, and vocative plurals are also identical (-**ua**), as well as the neuter dative and ablative plurals (-**ibus**). As you learned in *NLP* 2 and 3, in instances where the ending can signify two (or more) cases, the context will help you to determine which case is being employed.

3. Nouns of the fifth declension typically end in -**ēs** in the nominative singular and feature -e- in all of the case endings. Most of these nouns are feminine. A very small number are masculine, including **diēs** (day) and **merīdiēs** (midday).

FIFTH DECLENSION NOUNS

Case	rēs, reī, f: thing, matter, situation	diēs, diēī, m: day
Singular		
Nominative	rēs	diēs
Genitive	reī	diēī
Dative	reī	diēī
Accusative	rem	diem
Ablative	rē	diē
Vocative	rēs	diēs
Plural		
Nominative	rēs	diēs
Genitive	**rērum**	diērum
Dative	**rēbus**	diēbus
Accusative	rēs	diēs
Ablative	**rēbus**	diēbus
Vocative	rēs	diēs

4. In the fifth declension, the endings for the nominative singular, vocative singular, nominative plural, accusative plural, and vocative plural are identical (-**ēs**). Likewise, the endings for the genitive and dative singulars (-**eī**) are identical, as well as the dative and ablative plurals (-**ēbus**). As with nouns in the other four declensions, you often need to use other clues in the sentence to determine the function of a noun. Case endings are just one signifier.

5. There are no adjectives with fourth or fifth declension endings. Thus, nouns of the fourth and fifth declensions will rarely have the same endings as the adjectives that modify them, but they will always match their adjectives in case, number, and gender. Consider the following examples:

Vergil, *Aeneid* 8.2: **Raucō strepuērunt cornua cantū**. The horns blared <u>with a strident song</u>.

   Both *raucō* and *cantū* have the same case, number, and gender—ablative, singular, and masculine; however, *cantū* is a noun in the fourth declension whereas *raucō* is an adjective with second declension endings.

Tacitus, *Annales* 1.6.1: **Prīmum facinus <u>novī principātūs</u> fuit Postumī Agrippae caedēs**. The first crime <u>of the new principate</u> was the murder of Postumus Agrippa.

   Both *novī* and *principātūs* have the same case, number, and gender—genitive, singular, and masculine; however, *principātūs* is a noun in the fourth declension whereas *novī* is an adjective with second declension endings.

ILS 3016: **Iovī conservātōrī <u>omnium rērum</u>** . . . To Jupiter, preserver <u>of all things</u> . . .

   Both *omnium* and *rērum* have the same case, number, and gender—genitive, plural, and feminine; however, *rērum* is a noun in the fifth declension whereas *omnium* is an adjective with third declension endings.

Suetonius, *Vita Neronis* 27.2 (*NLP* 8.12): **Epulās ā <u>mediō diē</u> ad mediam noctem prōtrahēbat**. He (Nero) dragged out the banquets <u>from the middle of the day</u> to the middle of the night.

Both *mediō* and *diē* have the same case, number, and gender—ablative, singular, and masculine; however, *diē* is a noun in the fifth declension whereas *mediō* is an adjective with second declension endings.

I. Required Vocabulary

NOUNS

insula, -ae, f: island, apartment block
silva, -ae, f: woods, forest

ōceanus, -ī, m: ocean, the sea that surrounds the earth
solum, -ī, n: land, soil
spatium, -iī, n: space

amnis, -is (-ium), m: river
collis, -is (-ium), m: hill, high ground
flūmen, flūminis, n: river, stream
frux, frūgis, f: crops, fruit
gens, gentis (-ium), f: family, clan, race
labor, -ōris, m: work, toil, effort
mons, montis (-ium), m: mountain
mōs, mōris, m: custom, habit; (plural) character
regiō, -iōnis, f: boundary, region

adflātus, -ūs, m: blowing, breathing, sea-breeze
cornū, -ūs, n: horn, wing of an army
lacus, -ūs, m: lake
manus, -ūs, f: hand, band or force (of men)
passus, -ūs, m: step, pace, "foot" (**mille passūs**: a thousand paces, mile; the English mile is 5,280 feet; the Roman mile was about 4,851 feet)
ortus, -ūs, m: rising, origin
sinus, -ūs, m: bend, curve, fold, bay; lap, bosom, embrace

diēs, diēī, m: day

rēs, reī, f: thing, object, matter, affair, circumstance

temperiēs, -iēī, f: proper mixture, mildness

ADJECTIVES

alter, altera, alterum: one of two, second, the other (**alter . . . alter**: the one . . . the other)

amoenus, -a, -um: beautiful, pleasant, charming

aprīcus, -a, -um: sunny

noxius, -a, -um: hurtful, injurious

parvus, -a, -um: small

fertilis, -e: abundant, fruitful

nōbilis, -e: distinguished, noble, famous

CONJUNCTIONS AND ADVERBS

circiter: about, approximately

ibi: there

tamquam: just as, so as, as it were, so to speak, as if

tot: so many

II. Translate the following sentences from Latin to English or English to Latin.

1. Flūmina amoena temperiemque lacuum amābimus.

2. Frūgēs collium fertilēs nōn appellātis.

3. Insulae sinūs erant diēs omnēs aprīcī.

4. Altera montis regiō adflātum amoenum, altera noxium accipiēbat.

5. In sinū parvō animālia maris meō cum patre saepe vidēbam.

6. Spatium inter silvām ac agrum circiter mille passūs est.

7. Namque rem nōbilem patriae tuae post bellum faciēs.

8. Nostrīs cum amīcīs ad lacum parvum fugere incipiēbāmus.

9. One man likes lofty mountains, the other (man) pleasant hills.

10. You (singular) know the customs of your enemies' country.

11. We now shall watch the rising of the sun in front of the Roman temples.

12. For the gods were dwelling in sunny regions between the ocean and the rivers.

The Roman Empire: Geography, Topography, and Travel

For both the Romans and Greeks, describing the world was a way of understanding the Earth, and understanding was a way of imposing control over it. The Greek approach to geography was highly theoretical: they questioned the nature of the Earth, its shape (a perfect sphere), and its size. In the third century BCE, working at the Library in Alexandria, Eratosthenes calculated the Earth's circumference at 250,000 *stadia* (a Greek unit of distance). Eratosthenes' Earth was roughly 24,662 miles (the modern estimate is 24,901 miles—remarkably close!). Alas, the accepted figure at the time was 180,000 *stadia*, a severe underestimate.

In contrast, the Romans were a practical people, and their interest in geography was likewise pragmatic. Caesar knew that uninterrupted supply lines were essential to an army's success. Armies, furthermore, benefited from topographical reconnaissance: on where best to pitch camp, set an ambush, or march in unfamiliar territory. Once a territory had been subdued, Roman governors—knowing the size of the province and the lay of the land, as well as the peculiarities of sky and soil—could then manage their territories better.

Most ancient "maps" were narrative descriptions of places and often included descriptions of topography and climate, as well as distances. However, apart from the strictly regulated Roman foot and mile, measurements were not standardized. (For example, we have at least three commonly used conversions for the Greek *stadion*.) Historians, including Pliny the Elder, often used local measurements where Roman conversions were lacking. Caesar, in fact, explains the length of the Hercynian Forest in Germany not by units of length but rather by the time it takes to travel through the forest—a common means of conveying distance.

Pictorial maps, however, did exist. Ovid shares a charming vignette of a makeshift map scratched into the sand as Ulysses explains the course of the Trojan War to Calypso (*Ars Amatoria* 2.131–38). Caesar commissioned a map of the world in 46 BCE, but it was never completed. Caesar's heir, Augustus, engaged his compatriot Agrippa to continue Caesar's work. Agrippa's map was carved into the marble walls of the Portico of Vipsania, built in his sister's honor. Unfortunately, the original map is lost, but it probably represented the entire inhabited world as known to the Romans in the 20s BCE, and it was likely erected to stress that Rome (that is to say, Augustus) had unified the whole world under the *Pax Augusta*. Displayed on a wall inside the Temple of Peace at Rome was the "Marble Plan," a map of the city of Rome engraved on 150 marble slabs, commissioned by the emperor Septimius Severus and erected during 203–211 CE. The fragmentary map (60 by 43 feet) shows ground plans of every architectural feature in the city, but it lacks geographical and political boundaries: the Tiber may have been indicated by paint. The Peutinger Map, the only extant monumental map of the Roman world, was likely based on Agrippa's map or a fourth-century CE copy of it. Drawn around 1200 CE, the Peutinger Map notes about 2,700 separate places and their associated distances.

How did ancient travelers find their destinations? Merchants might use coasting guides, or *periploi*. A *periplus* listed cities along a coast and gave details about what the area imported or exported, what tariffs to expect, and whether the people were friendly or not. But these *periploi* provided no maps, as we understand the word. Many travelers did use so-called itineraries, land versions of *periploi* that simply cataloged places and the distances between them. In the Roman world, the roads helped travelers get from one place to another: milestones often listed the cities on a route and their distances. But mostly, if you didn't know exactly where you were going, you asked for directions, as Aeneas did when he was trying to find Hesperia.

SUGGESTIONS FOR FURTHER READING:

Casson, Lionel. *Travel in the Ancient World*. Johns Hopkins, 1994.

Clarke, Katherine. *Between Geography and History: Hellenistic Constructions of the Roman World*. Oxford, 1999.

Dilke, O. A. W. *Greek and Roman Maps*. Cornell, 1985.

Dueck, Daniela. *Geography in Classical Antiquity*. Cambridge, 2012.

Irby, Georgia L. "Mapping the World: Greek Initiatives from Homer to Eratosthenes." In *Ancient Perspectives: Maps and Their Place in Mesopotamia, Egypt, Greece, and Rome*. Edited by Richard Talbert. University of Chicago and Newberry Library, 2012.

Lozovsky, Natalia. *The Earth Is Our Book: Geographical Knowledge in the Latin West ca. 400–1000*. University of Michigan, 2000.

Murphy, Trevor. *Pliny the Elder's* Natural History: *The Empire in the Encyclopedia*. Oxford, 2004.

Roller, Duane W. *Ancient Geography: The Discovery of the World in Greece and Rome*. I. B. Tauris, 2015.

PASSAGES

10.1. Pliny the Elder, *Naturalis Historia* 5.132. In his survey of the islands of the eastern Mediterranean, Pliny often gives little more than lists of toponyms (place names). However, he distinguishes Rhodes for its aesthetic appeal.

Sed pulcherrima est lībera Rhodos, circuitū CXXV aut, sī potius Isidōrō crēdimus, CIII.

Notes: **pulcherrimus, -a, -um**: most beautiful (*pulcherrima insula*); **līber, -a, -um**: free, politically independent; **Rhodos, -ī**, f: an island off the east coast of Asia Minor famous for its colossal statue of Helios; **circuitus, -ūs**, m: circumference; **CXXV**: 125 (Roman miles); **potius**: rather; **Isidōrus, -ī**, m: Isidore of Charax, who was commissioned to write a geographical survey of the east for the emperor Augustus; **CIII**: 103 (Roman miles).

10.2. Caesar, *de Bello Gallico* 6.25.1. As part of his lengthy comparison of the Gallic and Germanic peoples, Caesar launches into his description of the mysterious and exotic Hercynian Forest, where many strange animals dwell.

Huius Hercyniae silvae, quae suprā demonstrāta est, lātitūdō novem diērum iter expedītō patet.

Notes: **huius**: this (genitive singular feminine; construe with *Hercyniae silvae*); **quae**: which (nominative singular feminine); **demonstrāta est**: "(which) has been mentioned"; **lātitūdō, lātitūdinis**, f: breadth, extent; **novem**: nine; **expedītus, -a, -um**: an unencumbered (traveler); **pateō, -ēre, -uī**: extend.

10.3. Tacitus, *Germania* 5.1. The very land of Germany is unattractive and uncivilized to the Roman eye.

Terra etsī aliquantō speciē differt, in ūniversum tamen aut silvīs horrida aut palūdibus foeda.

Notes: **etsī**: although; **aliquantō**: somewhat; **speciēs, -iēī**, f: aspect, appearance; **differō, -ferre, distulī, dīlātus**: scatter, differ; **in ūniversum**: on the whole, altogether; **horridus, -a, -um**: rough, shaggy, bristly; **palūs, palūdis**, f: swamp, marsh; **foedus, -a, -um**: filthy, horrible, abominable, disgusting.

10.4. Caesar, *de Bello Gallico* 7.69.2–4. The Gallic prince Vercingetorix took his last stand against Roman occupation in September of 52 BCE at Alesia (modern Alise-Sainte-Reine), a hilltop town in central Gaul. Caesar describes the siege in great detail, including the elaborate blockade whose purpose was to prevent Gallic access to and from the town. Here, Caesar notes the topography of Alesia.

Ante id oppidum plānitiēs circiter mīlia passuum tria in longitūdinem patēbat: reliquīs ex omnibus partibus collēs— mediocrī interiectō spatiō—parī altitūdinis fastīgiō oppidum cingēbant.

Notes: **id**: this, that (accusative singular neuter, construe with *oppidum*); **plānitiēs, -iēī**, f: plateau; **mīlia passuum tria**: three miles; **longitūdō, longitūdinis**, f: length; **patēbat**: see *NLP* 10.2; **reliquus, -a, -um**: rest, remaining; **mediocrī interiectō spatiō**: "a moderate space interposed" (ablative absolute); **pār (paris)**: equal; **altitūdō, altitūdinis**, f: height; **fastīgium, -iī**, n: slope; **cingō, -ere, cīnxī, cīnctus**: encircle, surround, gird.

10.5. **Livy,** *ab Urbe Condita* **21.32.7.** Although the Carthaginians had heard reports about the Alps, the actual sight of the towering and craggy mountain range struck the troops with fear and horror as they prepared their mountainous march into northern Italy in 218 BCE. Livy judges the people from the nature of the place: both are unfinished (*informis*), and therefore uncivilized and uncultivated. Note the repetition of the prefix *in-* ("un-", "not").

Tamen ex propinquō vīsa montium altitūdō nivēsque caelō prope immixtae, tecta informia imposita rūpibus, pecora iūmentaque torrida frīgore, hominēs intōnsī et incultī, animālia inanimaque omnia rigentia gelū, cētera vīsū quam dictū foediōra terrōrem renovārunt.

Notes: **ex propinquō**: "from nearby"; **vīsus, -a, -um**: visible; **altitūdō, altitūdinis**, f: height; **nix, nivis (-ium)**, f: snow; **prope**: nearly, almost; **immixtus, -a, -um**: mixed in (with); **tectum, -ī**, n: roof, house, hut; **informis, -e**: formless, shapeless, crude; **impositus, -a, -um** (+ dative): set (on top of), clinging (to); **rūpēs, -is (-ium)**, f: rock, cliff; **pecus, pecoris**, n: cattle, herd, flock; **iūmentum, -ī**, n: mule, beast of burden; **torridus, -a, -um**: parched, shriveled, desiccated; **frīgus, frīgoris**, n: cold; **intōnsus, -a, -um**: unshaven; **incultus, -a, -um**: uncultivated, rough, unkempt; **inanimus, -a, -um**: lifeless (here, a substantive); **rigēns (-entis)**: stiff (with), rigid (from); **gelū, -ūs**, n: frost, ice, chilliness; **cēterus, -a, -um**: other, remaining, rest; **vīsū quam dictū foediōra**: "more abominable to see than to describe" (*vīsū* and *dictū*: supines, see *NLP* 36); **terror, -ōris**, m: fear, dread, alarm; **renovārunt**: (all these things) "renewed" (perfect active of *renovō, -āre, -āvī, -ātus*: renew).

10.6. Pliny the Elder, *Naturalis Historia* 5.88. Palmyra, a pleasant city in central Syria.

Palmȳra, urbs nōbilis sitū, dīvitiīs solī et aquīs amoenīs, vastō undique ambitū harēnīs inclūdit agrōs.

Notes: **situs, -ūs**, m: position; **dīvitiae, -iārum**, f (plural): riches; **vastus, -a, -um**: immeasurable, boundless; **ambitus, -ūs**, m: circuit, extent; **harēna, -ae**, f: sand, desert, seashore; **inclūdō, -ere, -clūsī, -clūsus**: enclose.

10.7. Pliny the Elder, *Naturalis Historia* 5.71. Although the Jordan valley extends almost directly to the Dead Sea, Pliny suggests that the twisting river tries to delay its final destination.

Amnis, amoenus et—quātenus locōrum situs patitur—ambitiōsus accolīsque sē praebens, velut invītus, Asphaltiten lacum dīrum nātūrā petit.

Notes: **quātenus**: to what extent; **patitur**: "it (the site) allows"; **ambitiōsus, -a, -um**: winding, twisting, eager to please; **accola, -ae**, m: neighbor, inhabitant; **sē**: itself (accusative singular masculine); **praebens (-entis)**: offering; **velut**: just as, "as if"; **invītus, -a, -um**: unwilling; **Asphaltiten**: our "Dead Sea" (Greek accusative meaning "bituminous," "full of asphalt," a flammable and unpredictable hydrocarbon); **dīrus, -a, -um**: fearful, cruel, horrible, fierce; **petō, -ere, -īvī, -ītus**: seek, aim at.

10.8. Pliny the Elder, *Naturalis Historia* 6.58. By 326 BCE, Alexander the Great turned his attention to conquering the Indian subcontinent, subjugating all the headwaters of the Indus and marching as far as the Punjab until the mutiny of his troops forced him back to the west. Here, Pliny characterizes India's climate as exotic and otherworldly.

Alia illī caelī faciēs, aliī sīderum ortūs; bīnae aestātēs in annō, bīnae messēs, mediā inter illās hieme etēsiārum flātūs; nostrā vērō brūmā lēnēs ibi aurae, mare nāvigābile.

Notes: **alia**: "different" (from Rome); **illī**: "for that place (India)" (dative singular feminine); **faciēs, -iēī**, f: form, appearance; **sīdus, sīderis**, n: star, constellation; **bīnus, -a, -um**: two by two, two each; **aestās, -ātis**, f: summer; **messis, -is (-ium)**, f: harvest; **medius, -a, -um**: middle, mid-; **illās**: them (i.e., the harvests); **hiems, hiemis**, f: winter; **etēsiae, -iārum**, m (plural): the dry Etesian winds that blow through the Mediterranean for about six weeks annually during the height of the summer heat when Sirius (the Dog Star) rises and creates dangerous sailing conditions; **flātus, -ūs**, m: blowing, blast;

brūma, -ae, f: winter, cold weather; **lēnis, -e**: soft, mild, gentle; **aura, -ae**, f: breeze, wind; **nāvigābilis, -e**: navigable.

10.9. Pliny the Elder, *Naturalis Historia* **4.89.** Pliny describes the land of the mythical Hyperboreans, who dwelled "beyond Boreas" (the north wind, inhabiting Thrace) and were celebrated in Greek mythology as a happy, carefree people living in a perfect climate.

Regiō aprīca, fēlīcī temperiē, omnī adflātū noxiō carens.

Notes: **fēlix (-īcis)**: fruitful, lucky; **carens (-entis)** (+ ablative): lacking, free from.

10.10. Pliny the Elder, *Naturalis Historia* **6.55.** As early as the principate of Augustus, the Romans engaged in trade and enjoyed diplomatic relations with the Chinese. Pliny describes these distant peoples as mild-mannered and shy, having much in common with the mythical Hyperboreans.

Aprīcīs ab omnī noxiō adflātū sēclūsa collibus, eādem, quā Hyperboreī dēgunt, temperiē.

Notes: **sēclūsus, -a, -um**: shut off (by), isolated from (construe with an understood *Serēs gens dēgit* = "Chinese people live"); **eādem**: the same (ablative singular feminine, construe with *temperiē*); **quā**: "in which," "with which"; **dēgō, -ere, dēgī**: spend time, live.

10.11. Vergil, *Aeneid* **3.389–93.** Helenus, brother of Cassandra and likewise gifted in prophecy, survives the Trojan War, eventually becoming the king of Buthrotum (in northwestern Greece), where he rules with his wife Andromache, the former bride of the Trojan hero Hector. Aeneas visits with them on his journey to Italy, and Helenus predicts how Aeneas will recognize the future site of Rome—when he comes upon a sow nursing thirty piglets. Meter: dactylic hexameter.

Cum tibi sollicitō sēcrētī ad flūminis undam
lītoreīs ingens inventa sub īlicibus sūs—
trigintā capitum fētūs ēnixa—iacēbit,
alba solō recubans, albī circum ūbera nātī,
is locus urbis erit, requiēs ea certa labōrum.

Notes: **cum**: when; **tibi**: dative of agent with *inventa*; **sollicitus, -a, -um**: worried, anxious; **sēcrētus, -a, -um**: secluded, remote; **lītoreus, -a, -um**: of the shore; **ingens**

(-entis): huge, enormous; **inventus, -a, -um**: found, discovered; **īlex, īlicis**, f: holm oak; **sūs, suis**, f: sow; **trīgintā**: thirty; **fētus, -ūs**, m: offspring, brood; **ēnixus, -a, -um**: having given birth to; **iaceō, -ēre, -uī**: lie down; **albus, -a, -um**: white; **recubans** (-antis): reclining, lying down; **circum** (+ accusative): around; **über, -eris**, n: breast, nipple; **nātus, -ī**, m: son, offspring; **is**: this, that (nominative singular masculine); **requiēs, requiētis**, f: rest, relief; **ea**: this, that (nominative singular feminine).

10.12. Pliny the Elder, *Naturalis Historia* 3.41. We now turn to the center of the Roman Empire, and here Pliny describes the virtues of Italy, to his mind the best of all possible places.

Iam vērō tōta ea vītālis ac perennis salūbritās, tālis caelī temperiēs, tam fertilēs campī, tam aprīcī collēs, tam innoxiī saltūs, tam opāca nemora, tam mūnifica silvārum genera, tot montium adflātūs, tanta frūgum vītiumque et oleārum fertilitās, tam nōbilia pecudī vellera, tam opīma taurīs colla, tot lacūs, tot amnium fontiumque übertas tōtam eam perfundens, tot maria, portūs, gremiumque terrārum commerciō patens undique et tamquam iuvandōs ad mortālēs ipsa avidē in maria procurrens!

Notes: This passage is a long series of nominatives, describing specific attributes of Italy; supply *est*; **ea**: "her" or "its" (nominative singular feminine); **vītālis, -e**: vital, life-giving; **perennis, -e**: year-round, eternal, perpetual; **salūbritās, -ātis**, f: wholesomeness; **tālis, -e**: such; **tam**: so; **campus, -ī**, m: plain, field; **innoxius, -a, -um**: harmless, innocent; **saltus, -ūs**, m: woodland with glades; **opācus, -a, -um**: shady; **nemus, nemoris**, n: wood, forest; **mūnificus, -a, -um**: bountiful, splendid; **vītis, -is (-ium)**, f: grapevine; **olea, -ae**, f: olive tree; **fertilitās, -ātis**, f: fruitfulness, fertility; **pecus, pecudis**, n: cow, sheep; **vellus, velleris**, n: fleece; **opīmus, -a, -um**: rich, splendid, fat; **taurus, -ī**, m: bull; **collum, -ī**, n: neck, throat; **fons, fontis (-ium)**, m: spring, fountain; **übertās, -ātis**, f: fruitfulness, fertility; **eam**: "her" or "it" (Italy); **perfundens** (-entis): pouring over/through; **portus, -ūs**, m: port, harbor, refuge; **gremium, -iī**, n: lap, bosom, embrace; **commercium, -iī**, n: commerce, trade routes; **patens** (-entis) (+ dative): open, accessible; **ad iuvandōs mortālēs**: "to help humankind"; **ipsa**: "she herself" (Italy itself); **avidē**: eagerly; **procurrens** (-entis): running out ahead.

EXTRA PASSAGES: ROMAN GERMANY

The Romans had long known of the peoples from the Rhine to the Danube, and came into conflict with them in the 110s BCE (by 101 BCE, Gaius Marius definitively defeated the Cimbri and Teutones who were encroaching into Roman territory). Caesar, however, was the first to describe the German people, their social structure, and their *mores* for a Roman readership (*de Bello Gallico* 6.21–28). In the ethnographic monograph *Germania*, Tacitus describes the geography, laws, and political and social structure of the various tribes known to Rome by the late first century CE. For both Caesar and Tacitus, the Germans are barbaric because of their crudeness and lack of Mediterranean civilization, but they are also noble for the simplicity of their lifestyles which, in fact, reflect the traditional Roman ideal of hard-working, simple folk.

10.13. Tacitus, *Germania* 4.2. The physical appearance of the Germans is exotic and un-Roman.

Unde habitus quoque corporum—tamquam in tantō hominum numerō—īdem omnibus: trucēs et caeruleī oculī, rutilae comae, magna corpora et tantum ad impetum valida.

Notes: supply *est*; **unde**: therefore, hence; **habitus, -ūs**, m: nature, character, attitude; **īdem**: the same (predicate nominative singular); **trux (trucis)**: rough, savage, fierce; **caeruleus, -a, -um**: blue, greenish-blue; **oculus, -ī**, m: eye; **rutilus, -a, -um**: golden red, auburn; **coma, -ae**, f: hair; **ad** (+ accusative): "for"; **impetus, -ūs**, m: attack; **validus, -a, -um**: strong, powerful.

10.14. Caesar, *de Bello Gallico* 6.23.5. The German system of government differs vastly from the orderly and "constitutional" Roman system.

In pāce nullus est commūnis magistrātus, sed principēs regiōnum atque pāgōrum inter suōs iūs dīcunt contrōversiāsque minuunt.

Notes: **pax, pācis**, f: peace; **nullus, -a, -um**: no, none, not any; **commūnis, -e**: common, general; **magistrātus, -ūs**, m: state official; **princeps, principis**, m: leader; **pāgus, -ī**, m: country district, community; **inter suōs**: "among their own people"; **iūs dīcere**: to administer justice; **contrōversia, -iae**, f: dispute, debate; **minuō, -ere, -uī, minūtus**: lessen, diminish.

10.15. Tacitus, *Germania* 11.1. The Germans have their own method of measuring time.

Nec diērum numerum, ut nōs, sed noctium computant.

Notes: **ut**: as, like; **computō, -āre, -āvī, -ātus**: reckon, calculate.

Irregular Verbs

1. There are only a few irregular verbs in Latin. You have already learned the present, imperfect, and future tenses of *esse* ("to be"). Review the charts of this important verb in *NLP* 1, 8, and 9.

PART 1: *POSSE*

2. The common irregular verb *posse* ("to be able") is a compound of *sum*. Notice how *possum* is formed by the addition of *pot-/pos-* to the forms of *sum* that you have already memorized.

PRESENT TENSE OF *POSSE*

Person	Singular	Plural
1st	pos**sum**: I am able	pos**sumus**: we are able
2nd	pot**es**: you are able	pot**estis**: you (plural) are able
3rd	pot**est**: he/she/it is able	pos**sunt**: they are able

IMPERFECT TENSE OF *POSSE*

Person	Singular	Plural
1st	pot**eram**: I was able	pot**erāmus**: we were able
2nd	pot**erās**: you were able	pot**erātis**: you (plural) were able
3rd	pot**erat**: he/she/it was able	pot**erant**: they were able

FUTURE TENSE OF *POSSE*

Person	Singular	Plural
1st	pot**erō**: I shall be able	pot**erimus**: we shall be able
2nd	pot**eris**: you will be able	pot**eritis**: you (plural) will be able
3rd	pot**erit**: he/she/it will be able	pot**erunt**: they will be able

PART 2: *VELLE, MALLE, AND NOLLE*

3. The verb *velle* ("to want") is irregular only in the present tense, but it retains the same personal endings as regular verbs. *Velle* follows the paradigm of regular third conjugation verbs in the imperfect and future tenses.

PRESENT TENSE OF *VELLE*

Person	Singular	Plural
1st	vol**ō**: I want	volu**mus**: we want
2nd	v**īs**: you want	vul**tis**: you (plural) want
3rd	vul**t**: he/she/it wants	volu**nt**: they want

IMPERFECT TENSE OF *VELLE*

Person	Singular	Plural
1st	volē**bam**: I was wanting	volē**bāmus**: we were wanting
2nd	volē**bās**: you were wanting	volē**bātis**: you (plural) were wanting
3rd	volē**bat**: he/she/it was wanting	volē**bant**: they were wanting

FUTURE TENSE OF *VELLE*

Person	Singular	Plural
1st	vol**am**: I shall want	volē**mus**: we shall want
2nd	vol**ēs**: you will want	vol**ētis**: you (plural) will want
3rd	vol**et**: he/she/it will want	vol**ent**: they will want

4. The irregular verb *malle* ("to prefer") is a compound of *velle*, formed in the present tense either by adding *mā-* to the appropriate form of *volō* (*māvīs, māvult, māvultis*) or replacing the initial "*vo-*" with "*mā-*" (*mālō, mālumus, mālunt*). *Malle* follows the paradigm of regular third conjugation verbs in the imperfect and future tenses.

PRESENT TENSE OF *MALLE*

Person	Singular	Plural
1st	mālō: I prefer	mālu**mus**: we prefer
2nd	māvīs: you prefer	māvul**tis**: you (plural) prefer
3rd	māvul**t**: he/she/it prefers	mālu**nt**: they prefer

IMPERFECT TENSE OF *MALLE*

Person	Singular	Plural
1st	mālē**bam**: I was preferring	mālē**bāmus**: we were preferring
2nd	mālē**bās**: you were preferring	mālē**bātis**: you (plural) were preferring
3rd	mālē**bat**: he/she/it was preferring	mālē**bant**: they were preferring

FUTURE TENSE OF *MALLE*

Person	Singular	Plural
1st	māl**am**: I shall prefer	mālē**mus**: we shall prefer
2nd	māl**ēs**: you will prefer	mālē**tis**: you (plural) will prefer
3rd	māl**et**: he/she/it will prefer	māl**ent**: they will prefer

5. The irregular verb *nolle* ("to not want") is another compound of *velle*, formed in the present tense either by adding *nōn* to the appropriate form of *volō* (*nōn vīs, nōn vult, nōn vultis*) or replacing the initial "v-" with an "n-" (*nōlō, nōlumus, nōlunt*). *Nolle* follows the paradigm of regular third conjugation verbs in the imperfect and future tenses.

PRESENT TENSE AND PRESENT IMPERATIVES OF *NOLLE*

Person	Singular	Plural
1st	nōl**ō**: I do not want	nōlu**mus**: we do not want
2nd	nōn v**īs**: you do not want	nōn vul**tis**: you (plural) do not want
3rd	nōn vul**t**: he/she/it does not want	nōlu**nt**: they do not want
imperative	nōl**ī**: don't (want to)!	nōl**īte**: don't (want to)!

IMPERFECT TENSE OF *NOLLE*

Person	Singular	Plural
1st	nōlē**bam**: I was not wanting	nōlē**bāmus**: we were not wanting
2nd	nōlē**bās**: you were not wanting	nōlē**bātis**: you (plural) were not wanting
3rd	nōlē**bat**: he/she/it was not wanting	nōlē**bant**: they were not wanting

FUTURE TENSE OF *NOLLE*

Person	Singular	Plural
1st	nōl**am**: I shall not want	nōlē**mus**: we shall not want
2nd	nōl**ēs**: you will not want	nōlē**tis**: you (plural) will not want
3rd	nōl**et**: he/she/it will not want	nōl**ent**: they will not want

6. In Latin, the most common way to express a **NEGATIVE IMPERATIVE** is to use the imperative of *nolle* with a complementary infinitive. Consider the following examples:

Martial 3.31.5: **Fastīdīre tamen nōlī, Rūfīne, minōrēs**. Nonetheless, Rufinus, don't disdain lesser people.

Caesar, *de Bello Gallico* 7.77.9: **Nōlīte hōs vestrō auxiliō exspoliāre**. Don't deprive these men of your help.

7. *Posse, velle, malle,* and *nolle* are frequently, but not always, construed with **COMPLEMENTARY INFINITIVES.** Consider the following examples:

Martial 2.1.1: **Ter centēna quidem poterās epigrammata ferre**. Indeed, you were able to endure three hundred epigrams.

CIL VI 10115: . . . a[n] dubitant h[ominēs] **velle imit[āre]** deum. . . . or do people hesitate to want to imitate a god.

Martial 1.3.1: **Argīlētānās māvīs habitāre tabernās**. You prefer to inhabit Argiletan taverns.

Martial 1.107.7: **In sterilēs nōlunt campōs iuga ferre iuvencī**. Oxen do not want to bear yokes into barren fields.

PART 3: *ĪRE* AND *FERRE*

8. The verb *īre* ("to go") is irregular only in the present tense, but it retains the same personal endings as regular verbs. In the imperfect and future tenses, it conjugates by adding standard first and second conjugation imperfect and future tense markers and endings to the stem ī-.

PRESENT TENSE AND PRESENT IMPERATIVES OF *ĪRE*

Person	Singular	Plural
1st	eō: I go	īmus: we go
2nd	īs: you go	ītis: you (plural) go
3rd	it: he/she/it goes	eunt: they go
imperative	ī: go!	īte: go!

IMPERFECT TENSE OF *ĪRE*

Person	Singular	Plural
1st	ībam: I was going (I went)	ībāmus: we were going (we went)
2nd	ībās: you were going (you went)	ībātis: you (plural) were going (you went)
3rd	ībat: he/she/it was going (he/she/it went)	ībant: they were going (they went)

FUTURE TENSE OF *ĪRE*

Person	Singular	Plural
1st	ībō: I shall go	ībimus: we shall go
2nd	ībis: you will go	ībitis: you (plural) will go
3rd	ībit: he/she/it will go	ībunt: they will go

9. The verb *ferre* ("to carry") is irregular only in the present tense, but it retains the same personal endings as regular verbs. *Ferre* follows the paradigm of regular third conjugation verbs in the imperfect and future tenses.

PRESENT TENSE AND PRESENT IMPERATIVES OF *FERRE*

Person	Singular	Plural
1st	fer**ō**: I carry	feri**mus**: we carry
2nd	fer**s**: you carry	fer**tis**: you (plural) carry
3rd	fer**t**: he/she/it carries	feru**nt**: they carry
imperative	fer: carry!	ferte: carry!

IMPERFECT TENSE OF *FERRE*

Person	Singular	Plural
1st	ferē**bam**: I was carrying	ferē**bāmus**: we were carrying
2nd	ferē**bās**: you were carrying	ferē**bātis**: you (plural) were carrying
3rd	ferē**bat**: he/she/it was carrying	ferē**bant**: they were carrying

FUTURE TENSE OF *FERRE*

Person	Singular	Plural
1st	fer**am**: I shall carry	fer**ēmus**: we shall carry
2nd	fer**ēs**: you will carry	fer**ētis**: you (plural) will carry
3rd	fer**et**: he/she/it will carry	fer**ent**: they will carry

I. Required Vocabulary

NOUNS

fāma, -ae, f: rumor, fame, name

ADJECTIVES

bellus, -a, -um: pretty, handsome

vērus, -a, -um: true

dīves (**dīvitis**): rich

VERBS

laudo, -āre, -āvī, -ātus: praise, commend

negō, -āre, -āvī, -ātus: deny, refuse

placeō, -ēre, -uī (+ dative): please

eō, īre, īvī or **iī, itus**: go
ferō, ferre, tulī, lātus: bring, carry, bear, endure, say
mālō, malle, māluī: prefer, choose
nōlō, nolle, nōluī: be unwilling, not want
possum, posse, potuī: be able, can
volō, velle, voluī: wish

PREPOSITIONS
trans (+ accusative): across

CONJUNCTIONS AND ADVERBS
an: or
cum: when, since, although
ecce: behold!
hodiē: today
nisi: if not, unless, except
quia: because
tandem: finally

II. Translate the following sentences from Latin to English or English to Latin.

1. Ecce! Dabāmus līberīs rem pūblicam, sed regiōnem relinquere mālēbant.
2. Poteritis negāre sermōnem, quia vēra dīcere nōlētis.
3. Eram neque nōbilis neque dīves; sum tamen nihil nisi bella.
4. Ō civēs, īte trans flūmen per agrōs ad collēs!
5. Frātrem sceleris condemnāre vīs.
6. Cicerō sine lacrimīs epistulās uxōrī scrībere nōn poterat.
7. Virtūtis causā mīles signum in proelium prō legiōne fert.
8. Ō amīce, nōlī laudāre noxia iuvenis malī carmina.
9. The leader prefers to entrust the town to a good citizen.
10. We are able to please the king with an abundance of money.
11. Carry (singular) water and guide the horses.
12. Don't (plural) go to the temple at night.

Marcus Valerius Martialis (38–104 CE)

Martial's caustic wit and sharp observations about life in Rome under the Flavian emperors have long charmed his readers. Critics, however, both ancient and modern, dismiss the epigrams as poetic experiments lacking literary weight, and they often deem Martial a flatterer who wrote merely to curry favor. The mixed reactions that his work produced perhaps allowed Martial to survive, and even thrive professionally, in a time of severe transition for Rome. Martial moved from Bilbilis, Hispania Tarraconensis to Rome around 64 CE, while Nero was still emperor and just before Seneca, Lucan, and Petronius, who were perhaps complicit in the Pisonian conspiracy against Nero in 65 CE, were forced to commit suicide. During this time, Martial escaped suspicion, honed his craft, and established a large circle of patrons, including Lucan's widow, to help support his art. In 80 CE Martial published his first collection of poems, *Liber Spectaculorum*, to commemorate the opening of the Colosseum. Around 83 CE, he published the *Xenia* and the *Apophoreta*, books of two-line poetic "gift-tags" to accompany a wide variety of presents. Over the next fifteen years, during the reigns of Titus, Domitian, and Nerva, Martial wrote eleven books of epigrams. Returning to Spain in 98 CE, the year Trajan assumed the principate, Martial published a last book of poetry. His later work indicates that he idealized his homeland, but, after reestablishing himself in Spain, he missed the excitement of Rome and grew frustrated with life outside the city. He died in Bilbilis around 104 CE.

In style, Martial's verses reflect the spirit of Catullus's short, playful poems, and at times Martial even parodies his work, making subtle and overt references to many of Catullus's best-known poems. Martial treats a broad variety of topics, crafting sympathetic portraits of pregnant animals dying in the arena, satirizing the opulence of ultra-wealthy Roman urbanites, recording the concerns of a culturally diverse population, and documenting the business of poetry as well as the art of reading in Rome. In many ways, Martial, who devoted his entire literary career to epigrams, is the definitive author of the genre. A master craftsman whose epigrams are characterized by concise grammar, skillful use of vocabulary, and nearly effortless application of meter, Martial offers satirical insight into the excesses of the upper classes at Rome in the first century CE.

SUGGESTIONS FOR FURTHER READING:

Fitzgerald, William. *Martial: The World of the Epigram.* University of Chicago, 2007.
Howell, Peter. *Martial.* Duckworth, 2009.
Rimell, Victoria. *Martial's Rome: Empire and the Ideology of Epigram.* Cambridge, 2008.
Spisak, Art L. *Martial: A Social Guide.* Duckworth, 2007.
Sullivan, J. P. *Martial the Unexpected Classic: A Literary and Historical Study.* Cambridge, 1991.
Williams, Craig. *Martial's Epigrams: A Selection.* Bolchazy-Carducci, 2011.

PASSAGES

11.1. Martial 1.5. The emperor Domitian has apparently gifted Martial (here referred to by his praenomen, Marcus) with an elaborate staged naval battle, while Martial has given Domitian only epigrams. Here, Martial imagines Domitian's reaction to the inequity of the exchange. Meter: elegiac couplets.

> Dō tibi naumachiam, tū dās epigrammata nōbīs:
> vīs, puto, cum librō, Marce, natāre tuō.

Notes: **naumachia, -iae**, f: staged naval battle; **epigramma, epigrammatis**, n: short poem, epigram; **putō, -āre, -āvī, -ātus**: think (the final -o of *putō* scans short here for the meter to work out correctly); **liber, librī**, m: book; **natō, -āre, -āvī, -ātus**: swim.

11.2. Martial 1.15.11–12. *Carpe diem!* Meter: elegiac couplets.

> Nōn est, crēde mihī, sapientis dīcere "Vīvam";
> sēra nimis vīta est crastina: vīve hodiē.

Notes: **sapiens, sapientis**, m: a wise man, philosopher; **sērus, -a, -um**: late; **nimis**: too much, excessively; **crastinus, -a, -um**: of tomorrow.

11.3. Martial 1.64. Fabulla exhibits excessive self-praise, a strikingly unattractive quality. Meter: hendecasyllabics.

> Bella es, nōvimus, et puella, vērum est,
> et dīves, quis enim potest negāre?

Sed cum tē nimium, Fabulla, laudās,
nec dīves neque bella nec puella es.

Notes: **nōvimus**: "we know" (perfect tense of *noscō, -ere, nōvī, nōtus*; translated idiomatically in present tense); **quis**: who (nominative singular); **nimium**: too much, excessively.

11.4. Martial 1.74. He was your lover, until you married him! Meter: elegiac couplets.

Moechus erat: poterās tamen hoc tū, Paula, negāre.
    Ecce vir est: numquid, Paula, negāre potes?

Notes: **moechus, -ī**, m: adulterer, lover; **hoc**: this (accusative singular neuter); **Paula, -ae**, f: a Roman woman's name meaning "a little"; **numquid**: surely not, can it be possible (that).

11.5. Martial 1.91. To Laelius, an unkind, and perhaps untalented, literary critic. Meter: elegiac couplets.

Cum tua nōn ēdās, carpis mea carmina, Laelī.
    Carpere vel nōlī nostra vel ēde tua.

Notes: **ēdās**: "you publish" (present subjunctive of *ēdō, -ere, ēdidī, ēditus*); **carpō, -ere, carpsī, carptus**: pluck, take, slander.

11.6. Martial 2.21. A kiss or a handshake? Meter: elegiac couplets.

Bāsia dās aliīs, aliīs dās, Postume, dextram.
    Dīcis "Utrum māvīs? Ēlige." Mālo manum.

Notes: **bāsium, -iī**, n: kiss; **Postumus, -ī**, m: a Roman man's name; **dexter, dextra, dextrum**: right (hand); **uter, utra, utrum**: which (of two); **ēligō, -ere, -lēgī, -lectus**: choose; the final -o of *malō* scans short here for the meter to work out correctly.

11.7. Martial 5.57. Cinna flatters himself, although he has clearly misinterpreted Martial's greeting. Meter: elegiac couplets.

Cum voco tē dōminum, nōlī tibi, Cinna, placēre:
    saepe etiam servum sīc resalūto tuum.

Notes: The final -o of *vocō* and *resalūtō* scans short here for the meter to work out correctly; **dōminus, -ī**, m: lord, master (occasionally a Roman might playfully address a favorite slave as *dōminus*); **placēre**: "to congratulate"; **resalūtō, -āre, -āvī, -ātus**: greet, hail.

11.8. Martial 5.82. Gaurus promises more than he can, or intends to, deliver. Meter: elegiac couplets.

Quid prōmittēbās mihi mīlia, Gaure, ducenta,
    sī dare nōn poterās mīlia, Gaure, decem?
An potes et nōn vīs? Rogo, nōn est turpius istud?
    Ī, tibi dispereās, Gaure: pusillus homo es.

Notes: **quid**: why; **prōmittō, -ere, -mīsī, -missus**: send forth, offer, promise; **mīlia ducenta**: two hundred thousand (sesterces); **mīlia decem**: ten thousand (sesterces); the final -o of *rogō* scans short here for the meter to work out correctly; **turpius**: rather shameful (nominative singular neuter); **istud**: that (nominative singular neuter); **tibi dispereās**: "may you destroy yourself"; **pusillus, -a, -um**: insignificant, trifling, petty.

11.9. Martial 1.61.1–2. Cities love their home-grown poets. Meter: iambic strophe.

Vērōna doctī syllabās amat vātis,
    Marōne fēlix Mantua est.

Notes: **Vērōna, -ae**, f: Catullus's hometown in northern Italy; **syllaba, -ae**, f: syllable; **vātis, -is (-ium)**, m: prophet, bard, poet; **Marō, -ōnis**, m: Vergil's cognomen (see *NLP* 1.11); **fēlix (fēlīcis)**: happy, lucky; **Mantua, -ae**, f: Vergil's hometown in northern Italy.

11.10. Martial 6.60. Just as Bilbilis loves her native son, so too does Rome, Martial's adopted city, revel in her literary immigrant—that is, almost all of Rome. Meter: elegiac couplets.

Laudat, amat, cantat nostrōs mea Rōma libellōs,
    mēque sinūs omnēs, mē manus omnis habet.
Ecce rubet quīdam, pallet, stupet, oscitat, ōdit.
    Hoc volo: nunc nōbīs carmina nostra placent.

Notes: **rubeō, -ēre**: blush; **quīdam**: a certain man (nominative singular masculine); **palleō, -ēre, -uī**: be pale; **stupeō, -ēre, -uī**: be struck senseless, be astonished; **oscitō, -āre, -āvī, -ātus**: gape; **ōdit**: "he hates" (from *odī, -isse*: hate, detest [this verb lacks first and second principal parts]); **hoc**: this (accusative singular neuter, referring to the following phrase); the final -o of *volō* scans short here for the meter to work out correctly.

11.11. Martial 11.31.1–5. In Greek mythology, Atreus and his brother were vicious enemies: Thyestes tried to cheat his brother out of the kingship by sleeping with Atreus's wife. Atreus sought a gruesome revenge by serving up Thyestes' sons to their father in a stew. (It was an old family recipe: their grandfather Tantalus had tried to trick the gods by serving up his son Pelops, father of Atreus and Thyestes, to the gods; the gods reconstituted the poor youth, who grew up to commit his own heinous crimes.) Here Martial makes light of that tragic story in his description of Caecilius's comic culinary obsession with pumpkins. Meter: hendecasyllabics.

Atreus Caecilius cucurbitārum:
sīc illās—quasi fīliōs Thyestae—
in partēs lacerat secatque mille.
Gustū prōtinus hās edēs in ipsō,
hās prīmā feret alterāque cēnā.

Notes: construe *est* as the governing verb of the first line; **Atreus**: predicate nominative (the -*eu*- in *Atreus* is a diphthong); **cucurbita, -ae**, f: gourd, pumpkin (construe with *Atreus*); **illās**: them (accusative plural feminine, referring to the pumpkins); **quasi**: like; **Thyestes, -ae**, m: Thyestes; **lacerō, -āre, -āvī, -ātus**: tear to pieces, mangle; **secō, -āre, secuī, sectus**: cut; **mille**: one thousand; **edō, esse, ēdī, ēsus**: eat; **gustus, -ūs**, m: hors d'oeuvre, first course; **prōtinus**: immediately; **hās**: them (accusative plural feminine); **ipsō**: itself, the very (ablative singular masculine); **prīmus, -a, -um**: first; (*Caecilius*) **feret**; **cēna, -ae**, f: course.

11.12. Martial, *Liber Spectaculorum* **32.** Losing to a worthy opponent is its own reward. Meter: elegiac couplets

Cēdere māiōrī virtūtis fāma secunda est.
    Illa gravis palma est, quam minor hostis habet.

Notes: **cēdō, -ere, cessī, cessus** (+ dative): yield, submit; **māior, māius**: greater (substantive); **secundus, -a, -um**: favorable, following, second; **illa**: that (nominative singular feminine); **palma, -ae**, f: palm of victory; **quam**: which (accusative singular, construe with *palma*); **minor, minus**: lesser.

EXTRA PASSAGES: GAIUS VALERIUS CATULLUS

Martial was writing within a well-established literary tradition, drawing inspiration from the playfully acerbic verses of Catullus. In the passages below, we see the universal themes of love and friendship that pervaded Catullus's poems.

11.13. Catullus 6.15–17. Catullus says that he will compose special amatory verses for Flavius. Meter: hendecasyllabics.

> Quārē, quidquid habēs bonī malīque,
> dīc nōbīs. Volo tē ac tuōs amōrēs
> ad caelum lepidō vocāre versū.

Notes: **quārē**: wherefore, therefore; **quidquid**: whatever (accusative singular); the final -o of *volō* scans short here for the meter to work out correctly; **lepidus, -a, -um**: charming, delightful; **versus, -ūs**, m: line of poetry.

11.14. Catullus 42.1–2. Catullus has loaned his writing tablets to an unnamed woman who refuses to return them. At his wits' end, Catullus appeals to the lines of poetry themselves to rally together and compel the anonymous *moecha putida* ("despicable adultress") to return the precious tablets. (See also *NLP* 4.4.) Meter: hendecasyllabics.

> Adeste, hendecasyllabī, quot estis
> omnēs undique, quotquot estis omnēs.

Notes: **hendecasyllabus, -ī**, m: hendecasyllabic, a line of poetry with eleven syllables; **quot**: how many; **quotquot**: however many.

11.15. Catullus 45.21–22. In this charming poem, Septimius and Acme swear their undying love and devotion for each other, as the god Love (*Amor*) looks on and approves their declarations. As a typical Roman man, Septimius should be motivated by military glory in remote, dangerous lands rather than romantic love for an exotic, lovestruck girl. Meter: hendecasyllabics.

> Ūnam Septimius misellus Acmēn
> māvult quam Syriās Britanniāsque.

Notes: **misellus, -a, -um**: poor, wretched; **Acmē, Acmēs**, f: a Greek woman's name meaning "pinnacle, zenith" and suggesting the young lady's physical perfection (*Acmēn*: accusative singular); **quam**: than, "over"; **Syria, -iae**, f: a Roman province in the east where Crassus campaigned in 55 BCE, seeking military conquest against the dangerous Parthians, but instead losing his life in battle; **Britannia, -iae**, f: a Roman province in the west, where Caesar campaigned in 55 and 54 BCE.

Personal, Reflexive, and Intensive Pronouns, and Pronominal Adjectives

1. Pronouns take the place of nouns and agree with the nouns to which they refer (their antecedents or referents) only in **gender** and **number**. Their case is determined according to how they function in their own sentences or clauses. In this lesson we will focus on personal, reflexive, and intensive pronouns as well as adjectives that frequently function as pronouns (pronominal adjectives). You will learn other important pronouns in *NLP* 15 and 16.

PART 1: PERSONAL PRONOUNS (THIRD PERSON)

2. You have already learned the forms for **FIRST AND SECOND PERSON PRONOUNS** in *NLP* 4. Review those tables.

3. **THIRD PERSON PRONOUNS** refer to a person (or people) about whom the narrator speaks. Latin does not really have a third person pronoun, but *is, ea, id* often serves that function. Consider the following examples:

Cicero, *pro Milone* 38 (*NLP* 9.9): **Vestram virtūtem, iustitiam, fidem, mihi crēdite, is maximē probābit.** Believe me, <u>he</u> (Pompey) will especially approve your virtue, justice, (and) loyalty.

Sallust, *Bellum Jugurthinum* 17.4: **Ea fīnīs habet ab occidente fretum nostrī maris et Ōceanī.** It (Africa) has as its boundaries from the west the narrow straits of our sea and the Ocean.

Catullus 42.10 (*NLP* 4.4): **Circumsistite eam, et reflāgitāte.** Surround her and demand back (the tablets).

4. Study the table for *is, ea, id*.

THIRD PERSON PRONOUN

Case	Masculine	Feminine	Neuter
Singular			
Nominative	is	ea	id
Genitive	eius	eius	eius
Dative	eī	eī	eī
Accusative	eum	eam	id
Ablative	eō	eā	eō
Plural			
Nominative	eī	eae	ea
Genitive	eōrum	eārum	eōrum
Dative	eīs	eīs	eīs
Accusative	eōs	eās	ea
Ablative	eīs	eīs	eīs

The forms for the nominative, genitive, and dative singulars deviate from the typical endings for first and second declension adjectives. From the accusative singular onward, however, this pronoun takes first and second declension endings attached to the stem *e-*. N.B. The accusative singular in the neuter is identical to the nominative singular in the neuter.

PART 2: REFLEXIVE PRONOUNS

5. **REFLEXIVE PRONOUNS** are used to refer back to the subject of the sentence. For first and second person subjects, the personal pronouns that you learned in *NLP* 4 serve also as the reflexive pronouns "myself" and "yourself." Consider the following examples:

Seneca, *ad Lucilium* 1.8.1: **In hōc mē recondidī.** I have concealed <u>myself</u> in this (philosophy).

    Mē is a first person singular reflexive pronoun that agrees in person and number with "I," the subject of *recondidī*.

Seneca, *ad Lucilium* 1.7.8: **Recēde in tē ipse quantum potes.** Withdraw into <u>yourself</u> as much as you yourself are able.

    Tē is a second person singular reflexive pronoun that agrees in person and number with "you," the implied subject of the imperative *recēde*.

6. For third person subjects, Latin uses a reflexive pronoun that differs from the personal pronoun. Consider the following examples:

Cicero, *de Amicitia* 98. **Omnīnō est amans suī virtus.** Virtue is altogether a lover of <u>itself</u>.

Martial 5.32. **Quadrantem Crispus tabulīs, Faustīne, suprēmīs / nōn dedit uxōrī. "Cui dedit ergō?"** <u>**Sibi**</u>. In his last will, Faustinus, Crispus did not give a quadrans ("penny") to his wife. "To whom did he give (it) then?" To <u>himself</u>.

Catullus 3.8: **Nec <u>sēsē</u> ā gremiō illīus movēbat.** Nor did it (the sparrow) move <u>itself</u> from her (Lesbia's) lap.

7. Study the table for third person reflexive pronouns.

THIRD PERSON REFLEXIVE PRONOUNS

Case and Number	
Genitive Singular and Plural	suī
Dative Singular and Plural	sibi (sibī)
Accusative Singular and Plural	sē (sēsē)
Ablative Singular and Plural	sē (sēsē)

There are no nominative forms for reflexive pronouns (a nominative cannot refer back to itself). The forms are the same for all genders, singular and plural.

N.B. It is important to distinguish this reflexive pronoun from its corresponding reflexive adjective, **suus, sua, suum**: "his, her, its, their own" (the particular definition depends on the subject of the sentence) and from the intensive pronoun **ipse, ipsa, ipsum** (see the following page).

PART 3: INTENSIVE PRONOUNS

8. **INTENSIVE PRONOUNS** are special pronouns that add extra emphasis to the antecedent/referent. They often function as adjectives. Consider the following examples:

Caesar, *de Bello Gallico* 1.1.4: **<u>Ipsī</u> in eōrum fīnibus bellum gerunt**. They <u>themselves</u> (the Helvetians) wage war in their (the Germans') borders.

Vergil, *Georgica* 4.386: **Sīc incipit <u>ipsa</u>**. Thus she <u>herself</u> (Cyrene) begins.

Cicero, *pro Cluentio* 15 (*NLP* 5.11): **Nōn <u>parietēs</u> dēnique <u>ipsōs</u>, superiōrum testēs nuptiārum!** Not, at last, the <u>very</u> <u>walls</u>, the witnesses of former nuptials!

Vegetius, *de Re Militari* 3.24 (*NLP* 7.6): **Elafantī in proeliīs magnitūdine corporum, barrītūs horrōre, <u>formae</u> <u>ipsīus</u> novitāte hominēs equōsque conturbant.** Elephants confuse men and horses in battles with the size of (their) bodies, with the fright of (their) war cry, and with the novelty of (their) <u>very</u> <u>form</u>.

9. Study the table for *ipse, ipsa, ipsum*.

INTENSIVE PRONOUNS

Case	Masculine	Feminine	Neuter
Singular			
Nominative	ipse	ipsa	ipsum
Genitive	ipsīus	ipsīus	ipsīus
Dative	ipsī	ipsī	ipsī
Accusative	ipsum	ipsam	ipsum
Ablative	ipsō	ipsā	ipsō
Plural			
Nominative	ipsī	ipsae	ipsa
Genitive	ipsōrum	ipsārum	ipsōrum
Dative	ipsīs	ipsīs	ipsīs
Accusative	ipsōs	ipsās	ipsa
Ablative	ipsīs	ipsīs	ipsīs

As with *is, ea, id* presented above, *ipse, ipsa, ipsum* has slightly unusual forms in the nominative, genitive, and dative singulars. Like *is, ea, id*, however, from the accusative singular onward, the pronoun takes first and second declension endings attached to the stem *ips-*.

PART 4: PRONOMINAL ADJECTIVES

10. Nine Latin adjectives can serve as either adjectives or pronouns (**PRONOMINAL ADJECTIVES**). You should consider this list additional required vocabulary:

alius, alia, aliud: one, other (*NLP* 6)
alter, altera, alterum: one of two, second, the other (*NLP* 10)
neuter, neutra, neutrum: neither
nullus, -a, -um: not any, none, no
sōlus, -a, -um: only, sole
tōtus, -a, -um: all, entire, complete (*NLP* 7)
ullus, -a, -um: any
ūnus, -a, -um: one (*NLP* 8) (singular only)
uter, utra, utrum: either

Consider the following examples:

Caesar, *de Bello Gallico* 6.12.1: **Alterīus factiōnis principēs erant Aeduī, alterīus Sequanī**. The leaders <u>of one</u> faction were the Aedui, (the leaders) <u>of the other</u> (faction were) the Sequani.
Alterīus is a genitive singular adjective modifying *factiōnis*.

Vergil, *Aeneid* 10.880: **Nec dīvom ullī parcimus**. Nor do we spare <u>any</u> of the gods.
Ullī functions as a dative singular pronoun.

11. These nine adjectives follow the paradigm of *is, ea, id* and *ipse, ipsa, ipsum*, as well as some other pronouns that you will learn in *NLP* 15. The forms for the genitive and dative singulars deviate from the typical endings for

first and second declension adjectives. From the accusative singular onward, however, they simply take regular first and second declension endings attached to the stem. Study the following table:

Case	Masculine	Feminine	Neuter
Singular			
Nominative	sōlus	sōla	sōlum
Genitive	sōlīus	sōlīus	sōlīus
Dative	sōlī	sōlī	sōlī
Accusative	sōlum	sōlam	sōlum
Ablative	sōlō	sōlā	sōlō
Plural			
Nominative	sōlī	sōlae	sōla
Genitive	sōlōrum	sōlārum	sōlōrum
Dative	sōlīs	sōlīs	sōlīs
Accusative	sōlōs	sōlās	sōla
Ablative	sōlīs	sōlīs	sōlīs

I. Required Vocabulary

NOUNS

līberta, -ae, f: freedwoman

lībertus, -ī, m: freedman

posterī, -ōrum, m (plural): posterity, descendants

lux, lūcis, f: light

victor, -ōris, m: conqueror, winner

PRONOUNS

ipse, ipsa, ipsum: himself, herself, itself, themselves

is, ea, id: he, she, it; this, that

ADJECTIVES

suus, sua, suum: his/her/its/their own (translation dependent upon context)

grandis, -e: large

VERBS

> **intrō, -āre, -āvī, -ātus**: enter
> **spectō, -āre, -āvī, -ātus**: observe, watch
>
> **crēscō, -ere, crēvī, crētus**: grow
> **cupiō, -ere, -īvī, -ītus**: wish, long for, desire
> **vincō, -ere, vīcī, victus**: conquer
>
> **dormiō, -īre, -īvī**: sleep

PREPOSITIONS

> **propter** (+ accusative): because of

CONJUNCTIONS AND ADVERBS

> **itaque**: and so, therefore
> **multō**: by far, by much
> **plānē**: clearly
> **vix**: scarcely, hardly

II. Translate the following sentences from Latin to English or English to Latin.

1. Ego sine līberīs meīs sōla hīc dormīre nōn cupiō.
2. Mīlitēs imperiō ducis virtūtis eius causā sēsē commendābant.
3. Nōs ipsī cum amīcīs nostrīs Rōmam intrābimus et Rōmānōrum opera magnōrum spectābimus.
4. Victor bellōrum magnōrum sibi et suae coniugī memoriam facit.
5. Ō poēta, tē carminaque dulcia tua amō, sed ea cantāre nōn possum.
6. Propter perīculum rex ipse oppidum relinquere volēbat.
7. Neque hostēs vincere neque nōbīs et legiōnī nostrae imperāre poterātis.
8. Rōmule et Reme, cīvēs dīvitēs templa grandia vōbīs brevī tempore dābunt.
9. On behalf of the Republic itself I was preparing the knights and their horses.
10. The wife desired to absolve herself from the crime.
11. Don't (singular) deny the conversation of the freedman himself.
12. Behold! You (plural) prefer to speak the truth about yourselves.

Freedmen: Upward Mobility in Rome

In Petronius's *Satyricon*, the entrance of Trimalchio's grand *pied-à-terre* in Rome is decorated with frescoes that recount this wealthy ex-slave's life, from the slave market, to his rise in business, to his promotion to *sēvir Augustālis* (see below). Rome was unique among slave-owning societies. Slaves could be freed, and these freed slaves were often completely assimilated into Roman life, with the potential to fulfill prominent and respectable roles in Roman social and religious culture. Not all ex-slaves attained the great wealth and status of the fictitious Trimalchio or his historical counterparts in the imperial court, but upward mobility was a distinct and unique possibility for Roman freedmen.

Men and women gained their freedom variously. Slaves were taxable property on whom a value was placed. Thus, a slave might be able to pay his own purchase price and freedom-tax from *pecūlia* (tips for odd jobs or a regular allowance from the household). According to their means, freedmen and freedwomen could even purchase freedom for spouses and children. An owner might free a number of slaves in his will. (In 2 BCE, Augustus decreed that no more than one hundred slaves could be manumitted in a will.) An owner might free individual slaves for any number of reasons: to show kindness to a deserving slave; to impress friends with his wealth and generosity; or to provide an incentive to other slaves to work hard in the hopes of gaining freedom. Some calculating businessmen preferred to free old and ill slaves with no resale value rather than to support them without profit. Occasionally, an owner might fall in love with a female slave, and then free her in order to marry her. Interestingly, Roman law protected freedwomen from marrying against their will, unless they were manumitted for the purpose of marriage. Slave women who had borne three children also gained their freedom as a reward for their fertility. Their children, however, remained the property of the owner. Finally, slaves might be manumitted before a trial. In 52 BCE, Cicero's friend Milo, on trial for murder, freed some or all of his slaves. The testimony of slaves was admissible only if secured under torture, and Milo feared that his slaves would be unable to endure the pain of torture and thus give incriminating (perhaps forced and false) evidence (Cicero, *pro Milone* 57).

Manumission was a simple ceremony. The owner first had to prove ownership. A Praetor then touched the slave on the top of the head with a rod, boxed the ears, and announced *hunc hominem ego volō līberum esse aiō* ("I say that I want this man to be free"). The owner spun the slave around and repeated the magic phrase. The slave then became a *libertus* (freedman), continuing his trade (baker, miller, tailor, etc.) and generally maintaining ties with his former owner that were both professional and personal, including the right of burial in the family plot. Most Roman men had three names, and *libertī* customarily took their *praenōmina* (first names) and *nōmina* (family names) from their patrons (former owners). Claudius's secretary of correspondence, Narcissus, assumed the legal name Tiberius Claudius Narcissus from the emperor's legal name, Tiberius Claudius Nero Germanicus; and Trimalchio is Gaius Pompeius Trimalchio in honor of his patron (both Narcissus and Trimalchio are Greek names, suggesting non-Roman ethnicity).

Once freed, many ex-slaves blended seamlessly into Roman society. They did have some distinction of dress. Many male *libertī* shaved their beards as a sign of their freed status (the Romans were one of the few ancient cultures whose men were clean-shaven). Freedmen proudly sported the conical freedman's cap. The toga was permitted, though not the gold ring reserved for equestrians. Although *libertī* had the right to vote, they could not hold office or intermarry with Roman elite. Nor could they attain equestrian or senatorial status, regardless of wealth. *Libertī* could, however, purchase status and respectability by underwriting or restoring public buildings and temples or by serving as *sēvirī Augustālēs*, priests of the imperial cult, who usually purchased the "appointment"—this was the highest honor for a *libertus*.

Some *libertī* rose to positions of great significance, prominence, or notoriety. From the southern Italian city of Tarentum and enslaved in 209 BCE, Livius Andronicus tutored his owner's children, and he eventually earned his freedom. According to tradition, Andronicus composed the first poem in the Latin language, a translation of the *Odyssey*, in addition to tragedy, comedy, and lyric poetry in both Latin and Greek. For this literary output, he is called the "Father of Latin Literature." Cicero's personal secretary, Tiro, is affectionately memorialized in Cicero's letters as a close friend and family member. It is telling that Cicero's profligate son, studying abroad but neglecting his studies in favor of the distractions of wine and women, appeals to Tiro to intervene on his behalf with the elder Cicero (Cicero, *ad Familiares*: 16.21). Finally, it is the freedmen in the court of the needy and malleable Claudius who were essentially running the Empire: Pallas endorsed Claudius's marriage to his own niece Agrippina but was executed in 62 CE by an ungrateful Nero, who then confiscated Pallas' vast personal fortune

(Pallas was reputed to have been wealthier than Crassus, who underwrote Caesar's extravagant career); Callistus, the secretary of petitions, determined which petitions (municipal, provincial, and individual) actually came to the emperor; Felix, as procurator of Judea, presided over the trial of Paul the Apostle. These men exercised real power, proving that it was possible, and not altogether rare, for the lowliest slave to rise nearly to the acme of Roman society in wealth and influence, if not in nobility and renown.

SUGGESTIONS FOR FURTHER READING:

Knapp, Robert. *Invisible Romans*. Harvard, 2011.
Mouritsen, Henrik. *The Freedman in the Roman World*. Cambridge, 2011.
Petersen, Lauren Hackworth. *The Freedman in Roman Art and Art History*. Cambridge, 2011.
Treggiari, Susan. *Roman Freedmen During the Late Republic*. Oxford, 2000.

PASSAGES

12.1. Cicero, *ad Familiares* 16.3.2. Here we have one of Cicero's many warm addresses to his secretary, Tiro.

> Omnēs cupimus, ego in prīmīs, quam prīmum tē vidēre, sed, mī Tīrō, valentem.

Notes: **in prīmīs**: above all, especially; **quam prīmum**: as soon as possible; **Tīrō, -ōnis**, m: Cicero's secretary; **valens (-entis)**: strong, powerful, healthy (Tiro was ill at the time).

12.2. Martial 3.46.1–4. Martial assures his friend that freedmen make better attendants than free-born citizens. Meter: elegiac couplets.

> Exigis ā nōbīs operam sine fīne togātam;
> nōn eo, lībertum sed tibi mitto meum.
> "Nōn est" inquis "idem." Multō plūs esse probābō:
> vix ego lectīcam subsequar, ille feret.

Notes: **exigō, -ere, -ēgī, -actus**: demand, collect; **opera, -ae**, f: work; **togātus, -a, -um**: togate, wearing a toga, as clients did when fulfilling obligations to their patrons; the final -o of *eō* and *mittō* scans short here for the meter to work out correctly; **inquis**: you say; **idem**: the same (accusative singular neuter); **plūs**: more; **esse**: "that it is" (indirect statement); **probō, -āre, -āvī, -ātus**: prove, convince; **lectīca, -ae**, f: litter; **subsequar**: "I shall follow"; **ille**: he, that one (nominative singular masculine).

12.3. Petronius, *Satyricon* **29.3.** Trimalchio's mural depicts his entire career, from the moment he was sold into slavery to his assumption of the position of *sēvir Augustālis*. Here, we see Trimalchio's transition from slave to craftsman, triumphantly entering Rome under the patronage of Minerva.

Erat autem vēnālicium [cum] titulīs pictīs, et ipse Trimalchiō capillātus cādūceum tenēbat, Minervāque dūcente, Rōmam intrābat.

Notes: **vēnālicium, -ī**, n: slave market; **titulus, -ī**, m: label, identification tag; **pictus, -a, -um**: painted; **capillātus, -a, -um**: long-haired; **cādūceus, -ī**, m: herald's staff, caduceus (usually associated with Mercury, a god of business and Trimalchio's divine patron); **Minervā dūcente**: "Minerva leading" (ablative absolute).

12.4. Petronius, *Satyricon* **32.3.** A conservative code of dress constrains *libertī* at Rome, and Trimalchio exults in testing these limits. At first glance, Trimalchio's second ring appears to be the gold ring reserved only for freeborn equestrians. But closer inspection reveals that appearances are deceiving, and that Trimalchio has not actually crossed any social boundaries.

Habēbat etiam in minimō digitō sinistrae manūs ānulum grandem subaurātum, extrēmō vērō articulō digitī sequentis minōrem, ut mihi vidēbātur, tōtum aureum, sed plānē ferreīs velutī stellīs ferrūminātum.

Notes: **minimus, -a, -um**: smallest (i.e., the pinky finger); **digitus, -ī**, m: finger; **sinister, sinistra, sinistrum**: left; **ānulus, -ī**, m: ring; **subaurātus, -a, -um**: gilt; **extrēmus, -a, -um**: farthest, "inmost"; **articulus, -ī**, m: joint; **sequens (-entis)**: next, following (i.e., the "ring" finger); **minor, minus**: smaller (construe with a second *ānulum*); **ut . . . vidēbātur**: "as it seemed"; **aureus, -a, -um**: golden; **ferreus, -a, -um**: of iron; **velutī**: as if; **stella, -ae**, f: star; **ferrūminātus, -a, -um**: soldered, bound.

12.5. Pliny the Younger, *Epistulae* **9.21.3.** The relationships between *libertī* and their patrons could be quite warm, even familial, and, in this letter, Sabinianus's *libertus* has played the prodigal son. Having committed some unknown offense, the anonymous *libertus* pleads with his patron's friend Pliny to intercede on his behalf. Pliny, himself fond of the young man, urges Sabinianus to excuse the young man's indiscretions, just this once.

Remitte aliquid adulescentiae ipsīus, remitte lacrimīs, remitte
indulgentiae tuae.

Notes: **remittō, -ere, -mīsī, -missus**: concede; **aliquid**: something (accusative singular
neuter); **adulescentia, -iae**, f: youthful age; **indulgentia, -iae**, f: indulgence, leniency.

12.6. Petronius, *Satyricon* **38.7.** Trimalchio's guests are not only very wealthy,
but they are also self-made, rising from nothing through the ranks of the
Roman business world.

Reliquōs autem collībertōs eius cavē contemnās. Valdē sūcossī
sunt. Vidēs illum quī in īmō īmus recumbit: hodiē sua octingenta
possidet. Dē nihilō crēvit.

Notes: **reliquus, -a, -um**: remaining, rest; **collībertus, -ī**, m: fellow *lībertus*; **cavē
contemnās**: "beware of despising"; **valdē**: very, very much; **sūcossus, -a, -um**: full of
sap, "oozing wealth"; **illum**: that man (accusative singular masculine); **quī**: who (nominative singular masculine); **īmus, -a, -um**: lowest (*in īmō*: "on the lowest [couch]"; at
Roman dinner parties, nine primary guests reclined on three couches around the
main dining table, and the seating arrangement was strictly according to social status.
Our *lībertus* here has the lowest status at the table); **recumbō, -ere, recubuī**: recline at
table; **octingentī, -ae, -a** (plural): eight hundred (million sesterces); **possideō, -ēre,
-sēdī, -sessus**: have, hold; **crēvit**: "he grew" (perfect tense of *crēscō*).

12.7. Petronius, *Satyricon* **41.3.** So many of the courses at Trimalchio's banquet
are elaborate set-ups for silly jokes, and Petronius's narrator Encolpius is
consistently perplexed. Here, we see a whole roasted boar wearing a conical freedman's cap. Once the riddle is explained, it seems perfectly logical
even to the dull-witted Encolpius.

"Plānē etiam hoc servus tuus indicāre potest: nōn enim aenigma
est, sed rēs aperta. Hic aper, cum herī summa cēna eum vindicāsset,
ā convīviīs dīmissus [est]; itaque hodiē tamquam lībertus in
convīvium revertitur."

Notes: **hoc**: this (accusative singular neuter); **indicō, -āre, -āvī, -ātus**: make known,
explain; **aenigma, aenigmatis**, n: puzzle, riddle; **apertus, -a, -um**: clear, open; **hic**: this
(nominative singular masculine); **aper, aprī**, m/f: boar; **herī**: yesterday; **summus, -a,
-um**: greatest, supreme, last; **cēna, -ae**, f: dinner, course; **vindicāsset**: "(the last course)
had liberated him (the boar)"; **convīvium, -iī**, n: banquet, assembled guests (in plural):
dīmissus est: "he was dismissed," from *dīmitto, -ere, -mīsī, -missus* (last night's guests
were too full to eat the boar course); **revertitur**: "he is returned," from *revertō, -ere,
-vertī* (yesterday's leftover boar is served at today's dinner party).

12.8. Suetonius, *Vita Augusti* 45.1. Ideally, close friendships developed between *lībertī* and their patrons. Augustus, as we see here, was not above accepting the hospitality of his freedmen.

Ipse circensēs ex amīcōrum ferē lībertōrumque cēnāculīs spectābat, interdum ex pulvīnārī et quidem cum coniuge ac līberīs sedens.

Notes: **circensēs, -um**, m (plural): races; **ferē**: almost, nearly, in general; **cēnāculum, -ī**, n: dining room; **interdum**: sometimes, occasionally; **pulvīnar, -āris**, n: imperial couch; **sedens (-entis)**: sitting.

12.9. Tacitus, *Annales* 13.13.1. Nero pursued a longstanding affair with his *līberta*, Acte, incurring the wrath of his mother, Agrippina, who felt her own influence slipping away.

Sed Agrippīna lībertam aemulam, nurum ancillam aliaque eundem in modum muliēbriter fremere.

Notes: **aemula, -ae**, f: rival (in apposition with *lībertam*); **nurus, -ūs**, f: daughter-in-law; **ancilla, -ae**, f: slave woman; **muliēbriter**: like a woman; **eundem in modum**: "in the same way"; **fremō, -ere, -uī, -itus**: grumble at, complain about (*fremere*: historical infinitive; translate as a 3rd person singular verb).

12.10. *CIL* VI 13244 = *CIL* VI 13245: Rome. Many Romans considered *lībertī* to be family members and included them in their family burial plots.

D(īs) M(anibus) M(arcus) Aurēlius Syntomus et Aurēlia Marciāne aedificium cum cepota[ph]iō et memoriam ā solō fēcērunt sibi et fīli(ī)s suīs Aurēliō Leontiō et Aurēliae Fructuōsae et līb(ertīs) līber(tābusque) posterīsque eōrum.

Notes: **Marcus Aurēlius Syntomus, Marcī Aurēliī Syntomī**, m: a Roman man's name (*Aurēlius* derives from *aurum, -ī*, n: gold—this *nōmen* becomes popular in the 2nd century CE; *Syntomus* is a Greek word meaning "short"); **Aurēlia Marciāne, Aurēliae Marciānae**, f: a Roman woman's name (*Marciāne* is a slip for *Marciāna*; the name means "daughter of Marcus"); **aedificium, -iī**, n: building, structure; **cepotaphium, -iī**, n: garden tomb; **fēcērunt**: "they (*Marcus Aurēlius Syntomus* and *Aurēlia Marciāne*) made" (perfect tense of *faciō*); **Aurēlius Leontius, Aurēliī Leontiī**, m: a Roman man's name (*Leontius* derives from *leō, leōnis*, m: lion); **Aurēlia Fructuōsa, Aurēliae Fructuōsae**, f: a Roman woman's name (*Fructuōsa* derives from *fructuōsus, -a, -um*: fruitful, fertile); **līber(tābus)** = *lībertīs* (in the feminine).

12.11. *CIL* VI 9583 [*ILS* 8341]: Rome. The family monument of a successful freedman, complete with farmhouse and gardens.

C(aius) Hostius C(aī) l(ībertus) Pamphīlus medicus hoc monumentum ēmit sibi et Nelpiae M(arcī) l(ībertae) Hymninī et līberteīs et lībertābus omnibus postereīsque eōrum. Haec est domus aeterna, hic est fundus, heīs sunt hortī, hoc est monumentum nostrum: in fronte p(edēs) XIII; in agrum p(edēs) XXIIII.

Notes: **Caius Hostius Pamphilus, Caiī Hostiī Pamphīlī**, m: a Roman man's name (Pamphilus derives from a Greek word meaning "beloved of all"); **medicus, -ī**, m: doctor; **monumentum, -ī**, n: monument, memorial; **ēmit**: "he (*Caius Hostius Pamphīlus*) bought" (perfect tense from *emō, -ere, ēmī, emptus*); **Nelpia Hymnis, Nelpiae Hymninis**, f: a woman's name; **līberteīs** = *lībertīs* (an alternate spelling that may reflect a dialect; note also **postereīs** for *posterīs* and **heīs** for *hī*); **haec**: this (nominative singular feminine); **domus, -ūs** or **-ī**, f: house, home; **aeternus, -a, -um**: eternal, everlasting; **hic**: this (nominative singular masculine); **fundus, -ī**, m: farm estate; **heīs** = *hī*: these (nominative plural masculine); **hortus, -ī**, m: garden; **hoc**: this (nominative singular neuter); **fronte**: here, "along the façade"; **in agrum pedēs**: "feet deep" (literally: "feet into the field").

12.12. *CIL* VI 11027: **Rome.** Marcus Aemilius Artema made this monument for his entire family, with one notable exception.

M(arcus) Aemilius Artēma fēcit M(arcō) Liciniō Successō frātrī bene merentī et Caeciliae Modestae coniugī suae et sibi et suīs lībertīs lībertābusq(ue) posterīsq(ue) eōrum—exceptō Hermēte līb(ertō) quem vetō propter dēlicta sua aditum ambītum.

Notes: **Marcus Aemilius Artēma, Marcī Aemiliī Artēmae**, m: a Roman man's name (*Artēma* derives from a Greek word meaning "pendant, suspension cord, buoy"); **fēcit**: "he (Marcus Aemilius Artēma) made" (perfect tense of *faciō*); **Marcus Licinius Successus, Marcī Liciniī Successī**, m: a Roman man's name; **merens (-entis)**: deserving; **Caecilia Modesta, Caeciliae Modestae**, f: a Roman woman's name (*modestus, -a, -um*: moderate, restrained); **Hermēs, Hermētis**, m: one of Marcus's freedmen; **exceptō Hermēte līb(ertō)**: "the freedman Hermes excepted" (ablative absolute); **quem**: whom (accusative singular masculine, referring back to Hermes); **vetō, -āre, vetuī, vetītus**: forbid; **dēlictum, -ī**, n: fault, offense, misdeed; **aditus, -ūs**, m: approach, entrance; **ambītum**: "to go past" (supine of *ambiō, -īre, -iī, -ītus*).

EXTRA PASSAGES: ROMAN AUTOBIOGRAPHIES

Just as many *libertī* were able to gain wealth and eminence, countless non-elite Romans recounted their own life stories in inscriptions. As we have seen in earlier lessons, these brief biographical sketches offer us valuable insight into the lives of everyday individuals throughout the Roman Empire.

12.13. *CIL* **IV 7708:** Pompeii. An election poster on a wall.

> Cn(aeum) Helvium Sabīn(um) aed(īlem) Epidius cum suīs vol(uit) et probat.

Notes: **Cnaeus Helvius Sabīnus, Cnaeī Helviī Sabīnī**, m: a Roman man's name (our candidate's *cognomen* recalls the ethnicity of the earliest Roman wives: see *NLP* 3); **aedīlis, -is (-ium)**, m: aedile, a Roman politician in charge of streets, traffic, markets, and public games; **Epidius, -iī**, m: a Roman man's name; **voluit**: "he (Epidius) wanted" (perfect tense of *volō*); **probō, -āre, -āvī, -ātus**: approve, prove.

12.14. *CIL* **VI 10125:** Rome. A loving husband honors his musically gifted wife.

> D(īs) M(anibus) Auxēsī citharoedae coniugī optimae C. Cornēlius Nēritus fēcit et sibi.

Notes: **Auxēsis, -is**, f: a Greek woman's name meaning "growth"; **citharoeda, -ae**, f: one who plays the stringed cithara and sings; **optimus, -a, -um**: best; **C(aius) Cornēlius Nēritus, C(aiī) Cornēliī Nēritī**, m: a Roman man's name (Neritus is a small Ionian island near Ithaca, where Odysseus dwelled).

12.15. *CIL* **IV 2146:** Pompeii. Pining for a beloved girlfriend.

> Vibius Restitūtus hīc sōlus dormīvit et Urbānam suam dēsīderābat.

Notes: **Vibius Restitūtus, Vibiī Restitūtī**, m: a Roman man's name; **dormīvit**: "he (Vibius Restitūtus) slept" (perfect tense of *dormiō*); **Urbāna, -ae**, f: a Roman woman's name meaning "of the city, urbane"; **dēsīderō, -āre, -āvī, -ātus**: long for, desire.

Perfect, Pluperfect, and Future Perfect Tenses

1. Three tenses form the perfect system: perfect, pluperfect, and future perfect tenses. These tenses are derived from the perfect stem, which is formed by dropping the final -**ī** from the third principal part (see *NLP* 1).

2. The **PERFECT TENSE** describes an action that has been completed in the recent past. It can be translated in several ways depending upon the context. For example, the verb *amāvimus* can be translated as "we have loved" or "we loved." Consider the following examples:

   CIL IV 2146 (*NLP* 12.15): **Vibius Restitūtus hīc sōlus <u>dormīvit</u> et Urbānam suam dēsīderābat.** Vibius Restitutus <u>slept</u> alone here, and he was desiring his Urbana.

   Horace, *Carmina* 4.7.1–4: **<u>Diffūgēre</u> nivēs, redeunt iam grāmina campīs arboribus comae.** The snows <u>have melted</u>, now the grass on the fields returns, the leaves on the trees (return).

   CIL IV 1305: **Paris hīc <u>fuit</u>.** Paris <u>was</u> (or "<u>has been</u>") here.

3. The perfect tense of all verbs, regular and irregular, is formed by adding the following endings to the perfect stem (i.e., **amāv-**, **docu-**, **mīs-**, **cēp-**, **audīv-**). These endings differ slightly from the pattern of verb endings that you have learned in previous lessons.

PERFECT TENSE ENDINGS

Person	Singular	Plural
1st	**-ī**	**-imus**
2nd	**-istī**	**-istis**
3rd	**-it**	**-ērunt/-ēre**

N.B. The alternate *-ēre* ending for the third person plural is more common in poetry than in prose. Be careful not to confuse this ending with the infinitive ending for the second conjugation.

PERFECT TENSE OF PARADIGM VERBS

	1st Conj.	2nd Conj.	3rd Conj.	3rd Conj. (-io)	4th Conj.
Singular					
1st	amāvī: I have loved	docuī: I have taught	mīsī: I have sent	cēpī: I have taken	audīvī: I have heard
2nd	amāvistī: you have loved	docuistī: you have taught	mīsistī: you have sent	cēpistī: you have taken	audīvistī: you have heard
3rd	amāvit: he/she/it has loved	docuit: he/she/it has taught	mīsit: he/she/it has sent	cēpit: he/she/it has taken	audīvit: he/she/it has heard
Plural					
1st	amāvimus: we have loved	docuimus: we have taught	mīsimus: we have sent	cēpimus: we have taken	audīvimus: we have heard
2nd	amāvistis: you have loved	docuistis: you have taught	mīsistis: you have sent	cēpistis: you have taken	audīvistis: you have heard
3rd	amāvērunt/ amāvēre: they have loved	docuērunt/ docuēre: they have taught	mīsērunt/ mīsēre: they have sent	cēpērunt/ cēpēre: they have taken	audīvērunt/ audīvēre: they have heard

N.B. the perfect stems for the irregular verbs:

sum: **fu-**   *nōlō*: **nōlu-**
possum: **potu-**   *eō*: **iv-** or **ī-**
volō: **volu-**   *ferō*: **tul-**
mālō: **mālu-**

4. The **PLUPERFECT TENSE** describes an action that has been completed at some point in the past before another action was completed. For example, the verb *audīverant* is translated "they had heard." Consider the following examples:

Caesar, *de Bello Civili* 1.26.1: **Contra haec Pompēius nāvēs magnās onerāriās, quās in portū Brundisinō <u>dēprehenderat</u>, adornābat.** In response to these things, Pompey was equipping large transport ships, which <u>he had intercepted</u> in the harbor of Brundisium.

Vergil, *Aeneid* 8.642–43: **Citae Mettum in dīversa quadrīgae <u>distulerant</u>.** Swift chariots <u>had torn</u> Mettus <u>apart</u> in different directions.

Vitruvius, *de Architectura* 10.16.3: **Diognētus enim <u>fuerat</u> Rhodius architectus.** For Diognetus <u>had been</u> an architect from Rhodes.

5. The pluperfect tense is formed by adding the following endings to the perfect stem. All four conjugations as well as irregular verbs follow this pattern (N.B. the pluperfect endings resemble the imperfect tense of *esse*).

PLUPERFECT TENSE ENDINGS

Person	Singular	Plural
1st	-eram	-erāmus
2nd	-erās	-erātis
3rd	-erat	-erant

PLUPERFECT TENSE OF PARADIGM VERBS

	1st Conj.	2nd Conj.	3rd Conj.	3rd Conj. (-io)	4th Conj.
Singular					
1st	amāveram: I had loved	docueram: I had taught	mīseram: I had sent	cēperam: I had taken	audīveram: I had heard
2nd	amāverās: you had loved	docuerās: you had taught	mīserās: you had sent	cēperās: you had taken	audīverās: you had heard
3rd	amāverat: he/she/it had loved	docuerat: he/she/it had taught	mīserat: he/she/it had sent	cēperat: he/she/it had taken	audīverat: he/she/it had heard
Plural					
1st	amāverāmus: we had loved	docuerāmus: we had taught	mīserāmus: we had sent	cēperāmus: we had taken	audīverāmus: we had heard
2nd	amāverātis: you had loved	docuerātis: you had taught	mīserātis: you had sent	cēperātis: you had taken	audīverātis: you had heard
3rd	amāverant: they had loved	docuerant: they had taught	mīserant: they had sent	cēperant: they had taken	audīverant: they had heard

6. The **FUTURE PERFECT TENSE** describes an action that will be completed before another action can occur. For example, the verb *docueritis* is translated "you (plural) will have taught." Consider the following examples:

Ovid, *Amores* 1.3.4: **Audīerit nostrās tot Cytherēa precēs!** Venus <u>will have heard</u> so many of our prayers!

Horace, *Carmen* 1.11.7–8: **Dum loquimur, <u>fūgerit</u> invida aetās: carpe diem!** While we talk, envious time <u>will have fled</u>: seize the day!

Livy, *ab Urbe Condita* 1.58.2: **"Tacē, Lucrētia,"** inquit, **"Sextus Tarquinius sum; ferrum in manū est; moriēre, sī <u>ēmīseris</u> vōcem."** "Be quiet, Lucretia," he said, "I am Sextus Tarquinius; there is a sword in (my) hand; you will die, if <u>you will have uttered</u> a sound."

7. The future perfect tense is formed by adding the following endings to the perfect stem. All four conjugations as well as irregular verbs follow this pattern. (N.B. The future perfect endings resemble the future tense of *esse*, except in the 3rd person plural.)

FUTURE PERFECT TENSE ENDINGS

Person	Singular	Plural
1st	-erō	-erimus
2nd	-eris	-eritis
3rd	-erit	-erint

FUTURE PERFECT TENSE OF PARADIGM VERBS

	1st Conj.	2nd Conj.	3rd Conj.	3rd Conj. (-io)	4th Conj.
Singular					
1st	amāverō: I shall have loved	docuerō: I shall have taught	mīserō: I shall have sent	cēperō: I shall have taken	audīverō: I shall have heard
2nd	amāveris: you will have loved	docueris: you will have taught	mīseris: you will have sent	cēperis: you will have taken	audīveris: you will have heard
3rd	amāverit: he/she/it will have loved	docuerit: he/she/it will have taught	mīserit: he/she/it will have sent	cēperit: he/she/it will have taken	audīverit: he/she/it will have heard
Plural					
1st	amāverimus: we shall have loved	docuerimus: we shall have taught	mīserimus: we shall have sent	cēperimus: we shall have taken	audīverimus: we shall have heard
2nd	amāveritis: you will have loved	docueritis: you will have taught	mīseritis: you will have sent	cēperitis: you will have taken	audīveritis: you will have heard
3rd	amāverint: they will have loved	docuerint: they will have taught	mīserint: they will have sent	cēperint: they will have taken	audīverint: they will have heard

8. In addition to the present tense infinitive that you learned in *NLP* 1, Latin also has a perfect tense infinitive. Consider the following examples:

Ovid, *Amores* 1.1.3–4: **<u>Rīsisse</u> Cupīdō / dīcitur atque ūnum <u>surripuisse</u> pedem.** Cupid is said <u>to have laughed</u> and <u>to have stolen</u> one foot.

Ovid, *Fasti* 4.321: **Casta negor: sī tū damnās, <u>meruisse</u> fatēbor.** I am not said (to be) chaste: if you condemn (me), I will confess <u>to have earned</u> (it).

9. To form the perfect infinitive, add **-isse** to the perfect stem.

PERFECT INFINITIVE

1st Conj.	2nd Conj.	3rd Conj.	3rd Conj. (-io)	4th Conj.
amā**visse**: to have loved	docu**isse**: to have taught	mī**sisse**: to have sent	cē**pisse**: to have taken	audī**visse**: to have heard

I. Required Vocabulary

NOUNS

umbra, -ae, f: shade, shadow

villa, -ae, f: country house, estate

domus, -ī or **-ūs**, f: house, home

fīlius, -iī, m: son

lectus, -ī, m: bed, couch, sofa

oculus, -ī, m: eye

tectum, -ī, n: roof, building, house

xystus, -ī, m: open colonnade, walk planted with trees, promenade

ars, artis (-ium), f: skill

canis, -is, m/f: dog

honor, -ōris, m: honor, glory, mark of respect or distinction

penātēs, -ium, m (plural): the gods of the home, hearth, or family line

ADJECTIVES

amplus, -a, -um: large, spacious

laetus, -a, -um: glad, joyful, happy

proximus, -a, -um: closest

ingens (-entis): huge, enormous

VERBS

cēnō, -āre, -āvī, -ātus: dine, eat

caveō, -ēre, cāvī, cautus: be on guard, beware

iubeō, -ēre, iussī, iussus: order, command

cadō, -ere, cecidī, cāsus: fall, be killed, abate
claudō, -ere, clausī, clausus: close, shut
contingō, -ere, -tigī, -tactum: touch
dūcō, -ere, duxī, ductus: lead; think, consider

PREPOSITIONS

apud (+ accusative): at, among, in the case of, at the house of
ob (+ accusative): against, on account of
super (+ accusative): above

CONJUNCTIONS AND ADVERBS

dum: while, as long as, provided that
-ne: introduces a question that expects a positive answer
prīmum or **prīmō**: at first, for the first time
tam: so
ubi: where, when

II. Translate the following sentences from Latin to English or English to Latin.

1. Vēnistisne domum ad vestrōs fīliōs penātēsque?
2. In tuā villā fuī ubi tua bona mihi dēdistī.
3. Oculōs eōs claudere iubēbam.
4. Cēnābimus bene, mī amīce, apud mē paucīs diēbus.
5. Cavē canem ingentem et ignem amplum.
6. Labor est duxisse tam multās legiōnēs.
7. Rōmam, decus posterōrum, spectāre cupīverāmus.
8. Māter et pater līberōs vidēbunt, sī templum intrāverint.
9. You (singular) have praised the skills of the leader and the glory of the horses.
10. We shall have sent sweet letters to the freedmen and freedwomen.
11. Had the kings conquered great cities?
12. While it was night, I was happy.

The Roman Home

The wealthiest Romans frequently owned several homes: *pieds-à-terre* in the city, country estates in the hills near Rome, or vacation manors on the Bay of Naples. Cicero owned property at Tusculum in the Alban hills and at Formiae, south of Rome. Horace was always grateful to his patron Maecenas for the Sabine farm, his retreat from the hustle and bustle of city life. Augustus's imperial abode on the Palatine Hill (whence our word "palace") was modest, by the standards of his descendants. Hadrian's sumptuous villa at Tivoli continues to attract visitors.

Although details varied, there was a template. Vitruvius, in fact, describes the ideal Roman house, giving ratios and precise measurements for standard rooms (*de Architectura* 6.3). An elite Roman house included an atrium: where a family displayed the wax masks of their ancestors; where visitors were greeted; and where rainwater was collected through the *compluvium* in the roof into an *impluvium* (sunken basin) in the floor. Along the sides of the atrium were smaller, less grand rooms, serving all the usual functions: bedrooms (*cubicula*), offices (*tablīna*), and dining rooms (*trīclīnia*). The atrium often looked out onto a walled, open-air peristyle garden, where the household staff maintained plants for ornament and food (fruit and nut trees). It is here that a kitchen and oven room might be placed (the threat of fire was perennial). The garden usually included a *piscīna* (pool) for decoration, fish, or even just cooling one's feet on a hot day. Along the columned, covered peristyle, there were often other rooms: summer *trīclīnia* and *cubicula*, for example. The wealthiest abodes even included private baths and flush toilets, connected to the city's water grid. Such villas are found throughout the Roman Empire: in the city of Rome, in the resort towns of Campania on the Bay of Naples, and in Fishbourne in West Sussex, England, where Cogidubnus showed his loyalty to Rome by mimicking the architecture of his conquerors, a less than practical choice in the cold, wet climate of Britain. Such homes were richly decorated. Floors were adorned with mosaics, from simple geometric "Greek-key" borders to elaborate pastiches from history and mythology, still lifes, and animals. Walls were colorfully painted with geometric designs, scenes from mythology, and fantastical landscapes. The remains from Pompeii and surrounding towns have also yielded a rich cache of furniture: window treatments, tables, chairs, couches, beds, and even cribs.

Most Romans inhabited modest apartments in the city, similarly but less elaborately adorned, multistory *insulae*. Many apartment blocks at Rome and Pompeii were occupied by shops on the first floor, and dwellings on subsequent stories (up to five are attested). Juvenal complains of thin walls and noisy neighbors, the arduous hike to the third floor, slum lords, and high rents (*Satura* 3.193–225), and Martial's apartment was dank and cold, with a single ill-fitting window (8.14). If cooking occurred at all, it was done over a brazier, and residents used chamber pots at home.

Just as important as the physical space in these dwellings were the religious and symbolic accoutrements. Many homes, even modest ones, sported a *larārium*, a shrine for the *larēs*, the ancestral guardians who protected the members of the household. Also important were the *penātēs* who protected the inner part of the house, especially the food stores. Iconographically, the *penātēs* are often depicted as serpents. Together the *larēs* and *penātēs* come to symbolize the home. As a refugee from Troy, Aeneas diligently cultivated and protected his own *larēs* and *penātēs*, which eventually became the "household" gods for the entire state of Rome.

SUGGESTIONS FOR FURTHER READING:

Clarke, John R. *The Houses of Roman Italy, 100 B.C.–A.D. 250: Ritual, Space, and Decoration*. University of California, 1991.

Connolly, Peter and Hazel Dodge. *The Ancient City: Life in Classical Athens and Rome*. Oxford, 2000.

Hales, Shelley. *The Roman House and Social Identity*. Cambridge, 2003.

Nevett, Lisa C. *Domestic Space in Antiquity*. Cambridge, 2010.

Pappalardo, Umberto, Rosaria Ciardiello, and Luciano Pedicini. *Greek and Roman Mosaics*. Abbeville, 2012.

Wallace-Hadrill, Andrew. *Houses and Society in Pompeii and Herculaneum*. Princeton, 1996.

PASSAGES

13.1. Petronius, *Satyricon* 38. For rent.

Itaque proximē cum hōc titulō proscripsit: C. POMPĒIUS DIOGENĒS EX KALENDĪS IŪLIĪS CĒNĀCVLUM LOCAT; IPSE ENIM DOMVM ĒMIT.

Notes: **proximē**: just recently; **hōc**: "this" (ablative singular masculine); **titulus, -ī**, m: inscription, label; **proscrībō, -ere, -scripsī, -scriptus**: publish, make known publicly (construe Diogenes as the subject); **C(aius) Pompēius Diogenēs, C(aiī) Pompēiī Diogenis**, m: a Roman man's name; **ex** (+ ablative): here "after"; **kalendae, -ārum**, f (plural): Kalends (see Appendix D); **Iūlius, -a, -um**: Julian, here, "of July"; **cēnāculum, -ī**, n: attic apartment; **locō, -āre, -āvī, -ātus**: rent, lease; **emō, -ere, ēmī, emptus**: buy, purchase.

13.2. *CIL* **VIII 24106** [*ILS* **9367**]: El Mraissa/Carpis, Africa Proconsularis. A local magistrate underwrites the improvements and upkeep of an elaborate public bath.

D(ecimus) Laelius D(ecimī) f(īlius) Balbus q(uaestor) prō pr(aetōre) assa, dēstrictār(ium), sōlāriumque faciundu(m) coerāv(it).

Notes: **Decimus Laelius Balbus, Decimī Laeliī Balbī**, m: a Roman man's name; **quaestor, -ōris**, m: a magistrate who oversaw the state finances at Rome; **prō praetōre**: "acting with the authority of a Praetor," a magistrate who oversaw the defense of the city of Rome; **assa, -ōrum**, n (plural): cabin for steam bath; **dēstrictārium, -iī**, n: scraping room; **sōlārium, -iī**, n: sun terrace; **faciundum coerāvit**: "(he) took care that [three things in the accusative case] be built"; **coerō, -āre, -āvī, -ātus**: take care of, care for (an archaic spelling of *cūrō, -āre, -āvī, -ātus*).

13.3. *CIL* **III 7960** [*ILS* **5548**]: Dacia (Romania). This father and son team have underwritten public buildings, and the autobiographical testimony of their eugertism includes some specific and unusual architectural terms.

Tib(erius) Cl(audius) Ianuārius Aug(ustālis) col(ōniae) patr(ōnus) dec(uriae) I pictūram, porticūs, et accubitum; item Cl(audius) Vērus fīlius eius ob honōrem duplī prōporticum et culīnam et frontālem ex suō fēcērunt.

Notes: **Tiberius Claudius Ianuārius, Tiberiī Claudiī Ianuāriī**, m: a Roman man's name; **Augustālis, -is**, m: Augustan priest; **colōnia, -iae**, f: colony; **patrōnus, -ī**, m: protector, defender, patron; **decuriae I** = *decuriae prīmae*; **decuria, -iae**, f: an administrative body of ten men; **pictūra, -ae**, f: painting, picture; **porticus, -ūs**, f: portico, colonnade; **accubitus, -ūs**, m: bench; **item**: likewise; **Claudius Vērus, Claudiī Vērī**, m: a Roman man's name; **duplus, -a, -um**: double (*duplī*: "worth double," genitive of value); **prōporticus, -ūs**, f: entrance to columned hall; **culīna, -ae**, f: kitchen; **frontālis, -is**, m: front side of building near street; **ex suō**: "from their own resources"; "at their own expense."

13.4. Pliny the Younger, *Epistulae* **2.17.18.** Like other Romans of his class, Pliny is proud of his country villa at Laurentinum, just seventeen miles south of the city. It offered a quick respite from the hustle and bustle of city living, and it boasted easy access and magnificent views. Pliny describes each room of the spacious yet frugal house, its grounds, and gardens. Running water is the only amenity that is lacking. Here, Pliny recounts one particular spot on the grounds, a refreshing getaway at any time of day.

Nam ante merīdiem xystum, post merīdiem gestātiōnis hortīque proximam partem umbra sua temperat, quae, ut diēs crēvit dēcrēvitve, modo brevior, modo longior, hāc vel illā cadit.

Notes: **merīdiēs, -iēī,** m: noon, midday; **gestātiō, -iōnis,** f: promenade; **hortus, -ī,** m: garden, park; **temperō, -āre, -āvī, -ātus:** regulate, make mild; **quae:** which (nominative singular feminine); **ut:** as; **dēcrēscō, -ere, -crēvī, -crētus:** decrease, diminish, fade; **-ve:** or (enclitic conjunction like -*que*) **brevior, -ius:** shorter; **longior, -ius:** longer; **hāc vel illā:** "this way or that."

13.5. Martial 3.52. Although homeowners' insurance *per sē* was unknown in imperial times, friends and clients contributed money and valuables to neighbors who had lost their homes to fire (see Juvenal, *Saturae* 3.212–22). Here, Tongilianus takes advantage of this practice, like someone defrauding an insurance company. Meter: elegiac couplets.

Empta domus fuerat tibi, Tongiliāne, ducentīs:
    abstulit hanc nimium cāsus in urbe frequens.
Conlātum est deciens. Rogo, nōn potes ipse vidērī
    incendisse tuam, Tongiliāne, domum?

Notes: **emptus, -a, -um:** bought; **tibi:** dative of agent with *empta*; **Tongiliānus, -ī,** m: a Roman man's name; **ducentīs:** for 200,000 sesterces; **auferō, -ferre, abstulī, ablātus:** take away, remove; **hanc:** this (accusative singular feminine, modifying an implied *domum*); **nimium:** excessively, too; **cāsus, -ūs,** m: chance, accident; **frequens (-entis):** constant, repeated; **conlātum est:** "it has been collected"; **deciens:** (for) ten times (the value); the final -o in *rogo* scans short for the meter to work out correctly; **vidērī:** "to appear" (present passive infinitive of *video*); **incendō, -ere, -cendī, -census:** set fire (to).

13.6. Catullus 9.1–5. Catullus rejoices that his friend Veranius has arrived home safely after a tour of duty in Spain. Meter: hendecasyllabics.

Verānī, omnibus ē meīs amīcīs
antistans mihi mīlibus trecentīs,

vēnistīne domum ad tuōs penātēs
frātrēsque ūnanimōs anumque mātrem?
Vēnistī. Ō mihi nuntiī beātī!

Notes: **Verānius, -iī**, m: a Roman man's name; **antistans (-antis)** (+ dative): standing
out, surpassing, excelling; **trecentī, -ae, -a** (plural): three hundred; **ūnanimus, -a,
-um**: like-minded, harmonious; **anus, -ūs**, f: old woman; **nuntius, -iī**, m: messenger,
message, news; **beātus, -a, -um**: happy, blessed, prosperous.

13.7. Ovid, *Metamorphoses* **8.637–39.** Disguised as poor travelers, Jupiter and
Mercury come to earth to test the generosity of humanity. The gods receive
hospitality only from the very impoverished Baucis and Philemon, who
offer their divine guests everything they have—they even attempt to
slaughter their pet goose to enhance the feast (only by the petition of the
gods themselves is the pet spared). To reward their generous hosts, Jupiter
and Mercury offer the pair one wish each. Baucis and Philemon declare
their desire to serve as priests of the gods for the remainder of their lives
and then to die at the same time. The gods do better than their word: the
hut is transformed into a beautiful marble palace, and, at the moment of
death, the loving couple are changed into a linden and an oak tree, sharing
a single trunk and eternal life. Here, Jupiter and Mercury have to duck to
enter the humble threshold. Meter: dactylic hexameter.

Ergō ubi caelicolae parvōs tetigēre penātēs
summissōque humilēs intrārunt vertice postēs,
membra senex positō iussit relevāre sedīlī.

Notes: **caelicola, -ae**, m: heaven-dweller, god, "Olympian"; **tangō, -ere, tetigī, tactus**:
touch; **penātēs**: referring not to the household gods but rather to the house that they
protect (an example of metonymy); **summissus, -a, -um**: lowered; **humilis, -e**: low,
humble, poor; **intrā(vē)runt** (the form has been syncopated for the meter to work out
correctly); **vertex, -icis**, m: the crown of the head, head, summit; **postis, -is (-ium)**, m:
doorpost; **membrum, -ī**, n: limb; **senex, senis**, m: old man; **positus, -a, -um**: placed,
"provided"; **relevō, -āre, -āvī, -ātus**: lift, raise, relieve; **sedīle, -is (-ium)**, n: seat, bench.

13.8. Vergil, *Aeneid* **3.147–52.** The *penātēs*, representing the collective household gods of the Trojan exiles, appear to Aeneas in a dream, reminding him
of another *terra antīqua*, the homeland of the Trojan king Dardanus, who
hailed from a land called "Hesperia" by the Greeks, and "Italia" by the

current inhabitants. It is the *penātēs* who finally set Aeneas in the right direction. Here Aeneas describes the dream. Meter: dactylic hexameter.

Nox erat et terrīs animālia somnus habēbat.
Effigiēs sacrae dīvum Phrygiīque penātēs—
quōs mēcum ā Trōiā mediīsque ex ignibus urbis
extuleram—vīsī ante oculōs astāre iacentis
in somnīs multō manifestī lūmine, quā sē
plēna per insertās fundēbat lūna fenestrās.

Notes: **somnus, -ī,** m: sleep, slumber, (plural) dreams; **effigiēs, -iēī,** f: image, likeness; **dīvum** = *deōrum*; **Phrygius, -a, -um:** Phrygian, referring to an ancient kingdom in western Turkey near Troy; **quōs:** whom (accusative plural masculine, construe with *effigiēs* and *penātēs*); **efferō, -ferre, extulī, ēlātus:** bring out, carry out, bear; **vīsī** (*sunt*): "(the images and household gods) seemed to"; **astāre** = *adstāre*; **adstō, -āre, -stitī:** stand by, stand up; **iacens (-entis):** lying (construe with an understood *meī*); **manifestus, -a, -um:** clear, conspicuous, notable (modifies *penātēs*); **lūmen, lūminis,** n: light; **quā:** where; **plēnus, -a, -um:** full; **insertus, -a, -um:** planted, inserted, "inset"; **fundō, -ere, fūdī, fūsus:** pour, scatter; **lūna, -ae,** f: moon; **fenestra, -ae,** f: window.

13.9. Statius, *Silvae* 1.3.47–49. Here, Statius describes the rich interior decorations of Manilius Vopiscus's well-appointed Tiburtine villa, a pleasant escape from the burning summer heat of the city. Meter: dactylic hexameter.

Vīdī artēs veterumque manūs variīsque metalla
vīva modīs. Labor est aurī memorāre figūrās
aut ebur aut dignās digitīs contingere gemmās.

Notes: **vetus (veteris):** old (*veterum manūs*: "antiques"; literally: "hands of old [masters]"); **varius, -a, -um:** changing, various, varied; **metallum, -ī,** n: metal (Statius is describing metal-cast statues); **vīvus, -a, -um:** living, alive; **aurum, -ī,** n: gold; **memorō, -āre, -āvī, -ātus:** remember, recount, mention; **figūra, -ae,** f: shape, image, beauty; **ebur, eboris,** n: ivory; **dignus, -a, -um** (+ infinitive): worthy (to); **digitus, -ī,** m: finger; **gemma, -ae,** f: jewel, precious stone.

13.10. Suetonius, *Vita Augusti* 72.3. Despite his authority and power, Augustus was a modest man who eschewed extravagance. His own daily habits of dress and dining were simple, and he criticized his relatives for their extravagant homes.

Ampla et operōsa praetōria gravābātur. Et neptis quidem suae
Iūliae, profūsē ab eā exstructa, etiam dīruit ad solum.

Notes: **operōsus, -a, -um**: laborious, industrious, elaborate; **praetōrium, -iī, n**: mansion, palace; **gravābātur**: "he was vexed at"; understand another *praetōria* at the beginning of the second sentence (serving as the direct object of *dīruit*); **neptis, -is (-ium)**, f: granddaughter; **Iūlia, -iae**, f: a Roman woman's name, the feminine version of the *nomen Iūlius*, to which family Julius Caesar and his grand-nephew Augustus belonged; **profūsē**: excessively, lavishly, extravagantly; **exstructus, -a, -um**: built up; **dīruō, -ere, -uī, -utus**: destroy, demolish, pull to pieces.

13.11. Ovid, *Tristia* 1.3.43–46. Exiled to dismal and remote Tomis, Ovid is about to leave Rome, and his lamenting wife prays to the household gods. Meter: elegiac couplets.

Illa etiam ante larēs passīs adstrāta capillīs
    contigit extinctōs ōre tremente focōs,
multaque in āversōs effūdit verba penātēs
    prō dēplōrātō nōn valitūra virō.

Notes: **illa**: she (Ovid's wife); **lar, laris, m**: the god who protects the Roman home; **passīs capillīs**: "her hair disheveled" (ablative absolute); **adstrātus, -a, -um**: prostrated, frazzled; **extinctus, -a, -um**: quenched, destroyed; **ōs, ōris, n**: mouth; **tremens (-entis)**: trembling, shuddering; **focus, -ī, m**: fireplace, hearth; **āversus, -a, -um**: turned away, hostile; **effundō, -ere, -fūdī, -fūsus**: pour out; **dēplōrātus, -a, -um**: miserable, hopeless; **valitūrus, -a, -um**: prevailing, powerful.

13.12. Petronius, *Satyricon* 29. Just about to enter Trimalchio's extravagant *pied-à-terre* in Rome, the *Satyricon's* narrator, Encolpius, spies a guard dog, who turns out not to be real but rather just a convincing fresco. It was common enough for Roman homes to have such talismans to scare off intruders.

Cēterum ego dum omnia stupeō, paene resupīnātus crūra mea frēgī. Ad sinistram enim intrantibus nōn longē ab ostiāriī cellā canis ingens, catēnā vinctus, in pariete erat pictus, superque quadrātā litterā scriptum: CAVĒ CANEM. Et collēgae quidem meī rīsērunt.

Notes: **cēterum**: in addition, however, but; **stupeō, -ēre, -uī**: be stunned at, be amazed at, gape; **paene**: almost (construe with *frēgī*); **resupīnātus, -a, -um**: thrown back; **crūs, crūris**, n: shin, leg; **frangō, -ere, frēgī, fractus**: break, shatter; **sinister, sinistra, sinistrum**: left; **intrans (-antis)**, m: one entering, **longē**: far off, distant; **ostiārius, -iī**, m: porter, doorkeeper; **cella, -ae**, f: room; **catēna, -ae**, f: chain; **vinctus, -a, -um**: bound, tied up; **pariēs, -ietis**, f: wall; **pictus, -a, -um**: painted; **superque**: construe with an understood *canem*; **quadrātus, -a, -um**: squared, square; **littera, -ae**, f: letter; **scriptum, -ī**, n: inscription, something written; **collēga, -ae**, m/f: companion, associate; **rīdeō, -ēre, rīsī, rīsus**: laugh.

EXTRA PASSAGES: HOSPITALITY

Just as important as the material and symbolic comforts of the home was the strict code of hospitality (*hospitium* in Latin, *xenia* in Greek). This code established an unbreakable bond of friendship that, if violated, incurred the unrelenting wrath of the gods. (At Troy, when the Greek hero Diomedes and the Trojan ally Glaucus, meeting in single combat, discover the bond of *xenia* shared by their ancestors, they acknowledge that they cannot fight each other.) *Xenia* requires that hosts extend hospitality to traveling friends, relatives, and even strangers, and that they treat their guests well, providing food, entertainment, and a safe place to sleep. In turn, guests must not betray their hosts in any way: they must not steal, kill, or kidnap wives (this was the heinous crime committed by Paris against the Greeks that sparked the Trojan War). The obligations are reciprocal and descend to the heirs. We see this code celebrated in Roman literature, and the elaborate institutionalized Roman dinner party derives from the same mandate of *xenia* that finds its roots in the Homeric code.

13.13. Ovid, *Metamorphoses* 8.628–30. Jupiter and Mercury, disguised as travelers, finally receive hospitality in the humble home of Baucis and Philemon (see *NLP* 13.7). Meter: dactylic hexameter.

> Mille domōs adiēre, locum requiemque petentēs;
> mille domōs clausēre serae. Tamen ūna recēpit,
> parva quidem, stipulīs et cannā tecta palustrī.

Notes: **mille**: one thousand; **adeō, -īre, -iī** or **-īvī, -itus**: go to, approach; **requiēs, -iētis**, f: rest, respite, relaxation (*requiem = requiētem*); **petens (-entis)**: seeking; **sera, -ae** f: bolt (of a door); **ūna** (*domus*); **recipiō, -ere, -cēpī, -ceptus**: take back, receive; **stipula, -ae**, f: stalk, stubble, straw; **canna, -ae**, f: reed, cane; **paluster, palustris, palustre**: marshy, swampy, fenny.

13.14. Catullus 13.1–5. Catullus issues a strange invitation to his friend Fabullus—he will enjoy a great party at Catullus's house as long as he brings everything! Meter: hendecasyllabics.

> Cēnābis bene, mī Fabulle, apud mē
> paucīs, sī tibi dī favent, diēbus,
> sī tēcum attuleris bonam atque magnam
> cēnam, nōn sine candidā puellā
> et vīnō et sale et omnibus cachinnīs.

Notes: **paucī, -ae, -a**: few; **faveō, -ēre, fāvī, fautus** (+ dative): favor, support; **afferō, -ferre, attulī, allātus**: bring, carry, introduce; **cēna, -ae**, f: dinner; **candidus, -a, -um**: bright, shining, pretty; **sāl, salis**, m: salt, wit, humor; **cachinnus, -ī**, m: laughter.

13.15. *CIL* IV 4957: Pompeii. A guest's unfortunate accident.

> Minximus in lectō—fateor—peccāvimus, hospes! Sī dīcēs quārē,
> nulla matella fuit.

Notes: **mingō, -ere, minxī, minctus**: urinate; **fateor**: "I confess"; **peccō, -āre, -āvī, -ātus**: err, make a mistake; **hospes, hospitis**, m/f: host, guest; **quārē**: wherefore, why; **matella, -ae**, f: pot, vessel, chamber pot.

LESSON 14

Numbers

1. In Latin, **CARDINAL NUMBERS** ("one," "two," etc.) are mostly indeclinable adjectives (the common exceptions are 1, 2, 3, 500). Ordinal numbers ("first," "second," etc.) are regular first and second declension adjectives. Study the following table:

	Cardinal	Ordinal
1 (I)	ūnus, -a, -um	prīmus, -a, -um
2 (II)	duo, duae, duo	secundus, -a, -um
3 (III)	trēs, tria	tertius, -a, -um
4 (IV, IIII)	quattuor	quartus, -a, -um
5 (V)	quinque	quintus, -a, -um
6 (VI)	sex	sextus, -a, -um
7 (VII)	septem	septimus, -a, -um
8 (VIII)	octō	octāvus, -a, -um
9 (IX)	novem	nōnus, -a, -um
10 (X)	decem	decimus, -a, -um
11 (XI)	undecim	undecimus, -a, -um
12 (XII)	duodecim	duodecimus, -a, -um
13 (XIII)	tredecim	tertius decimus, -a, -um
14 (XIV)	quattuordecim	quartus decimus, -a, -um
15 (XV)	quindecim	quintus decimus, -a, -um
16 (XVI)	sēdecim	sextus decimus, -a, -um
17 (XVII)	septendecim	septimus decimus, -a, -um
18 (XVIII)	duodēvīgintī	duodēvīcēsimus, -a, -um
19 (XIX)	undēvīgintī	undēvīcēsimus, -a, -um
20 (XX)	vīgintī	vīcēsimus, -a, -um
21 (XXI)	vīgintī et ūnus	ūnus, -a, -um et vīcesimus, -a, -um
27 (XXVII)	vīgintī et septem	vīcēsimus, -a, -um septimus, -a, -um

28 (XXVIII)	duodētrīgintā	duodētrīcesimus, -a, -um
29 (XXIX)	undētrīgintā	undētrīcesimus, -a, -um
30 (XXX)	trīgintā	trīcēsimus, -a, -um
40 (XL)	quadrāgintā	quadrāgēsimus, -a, -um
50 (L)	quinquāgintā	quinquāgēsimus, -a, -um
60 (LX)	sexāgintā	sexāgēsimus, -a, -um
70 (LXX)	septuāgintā	septuāgēsimus, -a, -um
80 (LXXX)	octōgintā	octōgēsimus, -a, -um
90 (XC)	nōnāgintā	nōnāgēsimus, -a, -um
100 (C)	centum	centēsimus, -a, -um
500 (D)	quingentī, -ae -a	quingentēsimus, -a, -um
1000 (M)	mille	millēsimus, -a, -um

2. The cardinal numbers "one" (singular only, a pronominal adjective following the paradigm in *NLP* 12), "two" (plural only), and "three" (plural only) have slightly irregular declensions:

Case	Masculine	Feminine	Neuter
Nominative	ūn**us**	ūn**a**	ūn**um**
Genitive	ūn**īus**	ūn**īus**	ūn**īus**
Dative	ūn**ī**	ūn**ī**	ūn**ī**
Accusative	ūn**um**	ūn**am**	ūn**um**
Ablative	ūn**ō**	ūn**ā**	ūn**ō**

Case	Masculine	Feminine	Neuter
Nominative	duo	du**ae**	duo
Genitive	du**ōrum**	du**ārum**	du**ōrum**
Dative	du**ōbus**	du**ābus**	du**ōbus**
Accusative	du**ōs**/duo	du**ās**	duo
Ablative	du**ōbus**	du**ābus**	du**ōbus**

Case	Masculine	Feminine	Neuter
Nominative	tr**ēs**	tr**ēs**	tr**ia**
Genitive	tr**ium**	tr**ium**	tr**ium**
Dative	tr**ibus**	tr**ibus**	tr**ibus**
Accusative	tr**ēs**/tr**īs**	tr**ēs**/tr**īs**	tr**ia**
Ablative	tr**ibus**	tr**ibus**	tr**ibus**

3. **Mille** is indeclinable when it means "a thousand." In certain plural expressions, however, it declines as a neuter third declension i-stem noun and is completed by a partitive genitive.

Ovid, *Metamorphoses* 8.628 (*NLP* 13.13): <u>**Mille domōs**</u> **adiēre**. They (Mercury and Jupiter) entered <u>a thousand homes</u>.

Caesar, *de Bello Gallico* 7.90.2 (*NLP* 7.11): **Captīvōrum circiter** <u>**vīgintī mīlia**</u> **Aeduīs Arvernīsque reddit**. He (Caesar) returns approximately <u>20,000</u> (of) captives to the Aedui and Arverni.

I. Required Vocabulary

NOUNS

bestia, -iae, f: wild beast
palma, -ae, f: palm, hand, palm branch, palm tree, victory wreath

amphitheātrum, -ī, n: amphitheater
praemium, -iī, n: prize, reward
spectāculum, -ī, n: spectacle, performance, show

agitātor, -ōris, m: driver, charioteer
classis, -is (-ium), f: fleet
factiō, -iōnis, f: band, group, team
gladiātor, -ōris, m: gladiator
mūnus, mūneris, n: duty, gift, show, performance, spectacle, function
nepōs, nepōtis, m: grandson, descendant
princeps, principis, m: leader, chief, emperor
vēnātiō, -iōnis, f: staged hunt
vulnus, vulneris, n: wound

ADJECTIVES

aequus, -a, -um: equal, fair, evenly matched (*in aequō*: on level ground)
albus, -a, -um: white
ambō, ambae, ambō: both, two (*ambō* declines like *duo*)
extrēmus, -a, -um: last, uttermost, lengthy, furthest

prasinus, -a, -um: green
russātus, -a, -um: red
venetus, -a, -um: blue

nāvālis, -e: naval
par (paris): equal, pair

VERBS
pugnō, -āre, -āvī, -ātus: fight

CONJUNCTIONS AND ADVERBS
bis: two times
ter: three times
viciens: twenty times

II. Translate the following sentences from Latin to English or English to Latin.

1. Agitātor factiōnis russātae XXX annōs vixit.
2. LIV annōs vixerimus.
3. In amphitheātrō pugnāvērunt gladiātōrum circiter tria mīlia.
4. Ter vēnātiōnēs meō nōmine populō dedī.
5. Bis equīs meīs vīcī in factiōne venetā.
6. Caesar centum praemia agitātōrī mīsit.
7. Quintō diē vīgintī bestiās cēpistī.
8. Septuāgintā gladiātōrēs fūgērunt.
9. Twice you (singular) gave prizes to the charioteers.
10. The horses had lived for twenty years.
11. Approximately one thousand gladiators will fight.
12. Three times we won on the blue team.

Roman Entertainment

Entertainment at Rome was multifaceted and rich, including theater, athletic competitions, battle reenactments, and chariot races. Formal plays were performed only at set times during the year in conjunction with religious festivals. From 240 BCE onward, plays were included every September in the annual *Lūdī Rōmānī* (established in 336 BCE to honor the foundation of Rome). Plays were also put on in honor of Ceres, Apollo, and the Magna Mater (the Great Mother Cybele, whose strange cult was imported from Phrygia; see *NLP* 36). In addition to formally scripted drama, male and female actors produced mimes (short, crude comic sketches) as early as 212 BCE, and pantomimes (short, one-performer pieces combining acting, singing, and dancing), which became popular in the Empire. The first permanent theater in Rome, the Theater of Pompey, was constructed in 55 BCE, with a seating capacity of about 10,000. Pompey the Great commissioned this theater to commemorate his triple military triumph in 61 BCE and his successes in the East. To avoid censure (the Romans were wary of building a permanent theater), the building included a temple of Venus Victrix and was thus a consecrated religious site. Under Augustus, legislation formally restricted the social and political rights of actors and actresses and categorized them as "scandalous" and of "ill repute."

Roman audiences also enjoyed brutal and bloody staged combats. Gladiators were trained in special styles and armed with particular implements: the *retiāriī* (net fighters) fought at a distance with a trident while trying to ensnare competitors in a net; *murmillōnēs* (from the Greek word *mormullos*, referring to a species of fish) and Samnites were both heavily armed with visored helmets, short swords, and oblong shields; the lightly protected *secūtor* (chaser) parried with a short sword or dagger; the lightly protected *Thrax* (Thracian) fought with a round shield and curved sword (scimitar) characteristic of eastern fighters. Gladiators were matched against different types (e.g., *retiārius* against *murmillō*), and were largely drawn from prisoners of war, condemned criminals, and slaves (such as Spartacus, a Thracian slave who led a revolt against Rome 73–71 BCE; see *NLP* 15). Gladiators trained under *lanistae* (often retired gladiators themselves) at schools, especially at Rome, Capua, and Pompeii (abuses at the Capuan school spurred the Spartacus revolt). Amphitheaters, from Isca Augusta (Caerleon, Wales) to Augusta Trevorum

(Trier, Germany) to Utica (Tunisia, northern Africa) to Turkey, provided the venue for gladiatorial combats. The most famous and largest of these buildings was the Flavian Amphitheater in Rome (the Colosseum), completed in 80 CE and accommodating about 50,000 spectators. The inaugural games in 80 CE, lasting 100 days, are celebrated in Martial's *Liber Spectaculorum*. The Flavian amphitheater is a technological marvel with an imperial box (now completely lost), vaulted passageways, and an elaborate system of lifts and trap doors whence animals were sent into the arena.

Even more popular than the bloody gladiatorial games were the chariot races. At Rome the Circus Maximus, seating up to 250,000 spectators, consisted of a long oval track divided by a central barrier (*spīna*), at the ends of which were turning posts (*mētae*). The *spīna* was decorated with monuments, including Augustus's obelisk, and lap markers (often in the shape of dolphins) to track the seven laps required for a race. Teams of four, six, eight, or twelve horses raced by colors that signified their stables—red, white, green, or blue. In the later Empire, these stables served as political factions and sponsored candidates for public office. Bets were placed on the color, not the driver. Crews stood at the ready to clear the tracks of frequent mid-race accidents. Circus facilities included fan clubs, food stands, astrologers, and betting booths. Like gladiators, charioteers were usually slaves or ex-slaves, but they could become quite popular, and fans closely followed their careers, which were proudly recorded on their tombstones.

SUGGESTIONS FOR FURTHER READING:

Boatwright, Mary. "Theaters in the Roman Empire." *Biblical Archaeologist* 53.4 (1990): 184–92.

Fagan, Garrett G. *The Lure of the Arena: Social Psychology and the Crowd at the Roman Games*. Cambridge, 2011.

Humphries, John. *Roman Circuses: Arenas for Chariot Racing*. University of California, 1986.

Kyle, Donald. *Sport and Spectacle in the Ancient World*. Wiley-Blackwell, 2006.

Mahoney, Anne. *Roman Sports and Spectacle: A Sourcebook*. Focus, 2001.

Moore, Timothy. *Roman Theatre*. Cambridge, 2012.

PASSAGES

14.1. *CIL* **VI 10111:** Rome. Marble tablet commemorating the short life of an actress.

Luria prīvāta mīma v(ixit) a(nnōs) XIX. Bleptus fēcit.

Notes: **Luria, -iae,** f: a woman's name; **prīvātus, -a, -um:** private; **mīma, -ae,** f: comic actress; **Bleptus, -ī,** m: a man's name; the direct object of *fēcit* is an understood *hoc* ("this"), whose antecedent is the tablet.

14.2. *CIL* **VI 10123:** Rome. Marble tablet commemorating the long life of a singer.

C. Asinius Nymphius citharoedus vix(it) an(nōs) LXXVI.

Notes: **C(āius) Asinius Nymphius, C(āiī) Asiniī Nymphiī,** m: a man's name; **citharoedus, -ī,** m: singer to the cithara, a type of Greek lyre.

14.3. *CIL* **VI 10114:** Rome. Marble statue base with a dedication to an actor.

M(arcus) Ulpius Aug(ustī) līb(ertus) Apolaustus maximus pantomīmōrum corōnātus adversus histriōnēs et omnēs scaenicōs artificēs XII.

Notes: **Marcus Ulpius Apolaustus, Marcī Ulpiī Apolaustī,** m: an actor; **Augustus, -ī:** the emperor of Rome (here, Trajan who reigned 98–117 CE); **maximus, -a, -um:** greatest; **pantomīmus, -ī,** m: type of actor; **corōnātus** (*est*): "he was crowned" (perfect passive of *corōnō, -āre, -āvī, -ātus:* crown); **adversus** (+ accusative): in comparison with, in competition with; **histriō, -iōnis,** m: actor; **scaenicus, -a, -um:** theatrical, of the stage; **artifex, artificis,** m: craftsman, artist, performer; **XII:** twelve (times).

14.4. Martial 5.25.1–2. As censor the emperor Domitian (reigned 81–96 CE) reactivated the custom of reserving specific seats in the theater for equestrians with full property qualifications. Here, poor Chaerestratus is forced to switch his seat several times to evade the watchful eye of Leitus, the apparent enforcer of the seating codes. Meter: elegiac couplets.

"Quadringenta tibī nōn sunt, Chaerestrate: surge,
    Lēitus ecce venit: stā, fuge, curre, latē."

Notes: **quadringenta** (*mīlia sestertium*): four hundred (thousand sesterces);
Chaerestratus, -ī, m: a man's name; **surgō, -ere, surrexī, surrectus**: rise, get up;
Lēitus, -ī, m: a man's name; **stō, -āre, stetī, stātus**: stand (up); **currō, -ere, cucurrī,
cursus**: run; **lateō, -ēre, -uī**: hide.

14.5. Augustus, *Res Gestae* **22.1.** Augustus catalogues the gladiatorial combats
that he provided for the Roman people.

Ter mūnus gladiātōrium dedī meō nōmine et quinquiens fīliōrum
meōrum aut nepōtum nōmine, quibus mūneribus dēpugnāvērunt
hominum circiter decem millia.

Notes: **gladiātōrius, -a, -um**: gladiatorial; **quinquiens**: five times; **quibus mūneribus**:
"in which performances"; **dēpugnō, -āre, -āvī, -ātus**: fight hard; **millia** = *mīlia*.

14.6. Augustus, *Res Gestae* **22.3.** Augustus lists the *vēnātiōnēs* (staged beast
hunts) that he sponsored. In these spectacles, *vēnātōrēs* (hunters) hunted
wild animals with bows and arrows. (The emperor Commodus [ruled 177–
192 CE] even participated from the safety of the imperial box!)

Vēnātiōnēs bestiārum Āfricānārum meō nōmine aut fīliōrum
meōrum et nepōtum in circō aut in forō aut in amphitheātrīs
populō dedī sexiens et vīciens, quibus confecta sunt bestiārum
circiter tria millia et quingentae.

Notes: **Āfricānus, -a, -um**: African; **circus, -ī, m**: circus, racetrack; **forum, -ī, n**:
forum, marketplace; **sexiens**: six times; **quibus**: "in which" (ablative plural); **conficio,
-ere, -fēcī, -fectus**: kill (*confecta sunt*: "[3,500 beasts] were killed"); **millia** = *mīlia*.

14.7. *CIL* **IV 9979:** Pompeii. An advertisement for gladiatorial combat on November 4–7.

Vēn(ātōrum) et glad(iātōrum) par(ia) XX M(arcī) Tullī pugn(ābunt)
Pom(pēiīs) (ē) pr(īdiē) Nōn(ās) Novembrēs (ad) VII Īdūs
Nov(embrēs).

Notes: **vēnātor, -ōris, m**: hunter; **Marcus Tullius, Marcī Tullī, m**: a man's name, recalling the famous orator; **Pompēiī, -ōrum, m** (plural): Pompeii (*Pompēiīs*: locative); **prīdiē**:
on the day before (an accusative or genitive follows *prīdiē*); **Nōnae, -ārum, f** (plural): the
Nones (see Appendix D); **Novembris, -e**: of November; **Īdūs, -uum, f** (plural): the Ides.

14.8. Martial, *Liber Spectaculorum* **29.7–12.** Martial commemorates the extraordinary fight between the gladiators Priscus and Verus that marked the opening of the Colosseum in Rome. Both men fought with equal valor, and Titus declared them both victors. Meter: elegiac couplets.

> Inventus tamen est fīnis discrīminis aequī:
> pugnāvēre parēs, subcubuēre parēs.
> Mīsit utrīque rudēs et palmās Caesar utrīque:
> hoc pretium virtūs ingeniōsa tulit.
> Contigit hoc nullō nisi tē sub principe, Caesar:
> cum duo pugnārent, victor uterque fuit.

Notes: **inventus** (*est*): "(an end) was found"; **discrīmen, discrīminis,** n: division, difference, decisive battle; **subcumbō, -ere, -cubuī, -cubitus:** fall back, yield; **uterque, utraque, utrumque:** each (of two), both (dative singular); **rudis, -is (-ium),** f: wooden victory sword for a retiring gladiator; **Caesar, -aris,** m: title for Augustus and the subsequent emperors (here, Titus); **hoc:** "this" (accusative singular neuter, construe with *pretium*); **pretium, -iī,** n: price, reward; **ingeniōsus, -a, -um:** clever, talented; **hoc:** this (nominative singular neuter); **cum duo pugnārent:** "although the two fought."

14.9. Augustus, *Res Gestae* **23.** Augustus recalls the mock naval battle that he staged for the Roman people. Held in the very large grove of the Caesars, it involved thirty ships and approximately three thousand men. Julius Caesar was the first to produce one of these spectacles in 46 BCE, on the left bank of the Tiber. Claudius's extravagant naval battle on the Fucine Lake in 52 CE included 19,000 combatants (prisoners of war and condemned criminals).

> Nāvālis proelī spectāclum populō dedī trans Tiberim in quō locō nunc nemus est Caesarum—cavātō solō in longitūdinem mille et octingentōs pedēs, in lātitūdinem mille et ducentī—in quō trīgintā rostrātae nāvēs trirēmēs aut birēmēs, plūrēs autem minōrēs inter sē conflixērunt; quibus in classibus pugnāvērunt praeter rēmigēs millia hominum tria circiter.

Notes: **proelī** = *proeliī*; **Tiberis, -is,** m: Tiber River; **in quō locō:** "in which place"; **nemus, nemoris,** n: grove; **cavātō solō:** "the ground having been excavated" (ablative absolute); **longitūdō, longitūdinis,** f: length; **octingentī, -ae, -a:** eight hundred; **pēs, pedis,** m: foot; **lātitūdō, lātitūdinis,** f: width; **ducentī, -ae, -a:** two hundred; **in quō** (*nemore*): "in which (grove)"; **rostrātus, -a, -um**: beaked (with a tapering bow, like the beak of a bird); **nāvis, -is (-ium)**, f: ship; **trirēmis, -is (-ium)**, f: trireme; **birēmis, -is (-ium)**, f: bireme; **plūs (plūris)**: several, many, more; **minor, minus**: lesser, subordinate; **conflīgo, -ere, -flīxī, -flictus**: knock together, battle, fight; *quibus in classibus*: "in which fleets"; **praeter** (+ accusative): in addition to, besides; **rēmex, rēmigis**, m: rower; **millia** = *mīlia*.

14.10. **Juvenal,** *Saturae* **10.78–81.** Juvenal laments that people care not for politics, but for entertainment. Meter: dactylic hexameter.

> Nam quī dabat ōlim
> imperium, fascēs, legiōnēs, omnia, nunc sē
> continet atque duās tantum rēs anxius optat,
> pānem et circensēs.

Notes: **quī**: "he who" (nominative singular masculine, referring to a Roman citizen eligible to vote and stand for office); **ōlim**: once; **fascēs, -ium**, m (plural): bundle of rods with an axe-head that symbolizes the absolute authority high-ranking Roman politicians have over fellow citizens; **contineō, -ēre, -tinuī, -tentus**: hold back, detain, keep in hand; **anxius, -a, -um**: worried, anxious; **pānis, -is (-ium)**, m: bread; **circensēs, -ium**, m (plural): races, circuses.

14.11. **Tacitus,** *Annales* **14.17.1–2.** In 59 CE, Nucerian and Pompeian spectators rioted at a gladiatorial event.

> Ergō dēportātī sunt in urbem multī ē Nūcerīnīs—truncō per vulnera corpore—ac plērīque līberōrum aut parentum mortēs dēflēbant. Cuius reī iūdicium princeps senātuī, senātus consulibus permīsit. Et—rursus rē ad patrēs relātā—prohibitī pūblicē in decem annōs eius modī coetū Pompēiānī.

Notes: **dēportātī sunt**: "(many) were carried away"; **Nūcerīnus, -a, -um**: of Nuceria, a town in Campania; **truncō . . . corpore**: "the body having been maimed" (ablative absolute); **plērusque, plēraque, plērumque**: a good many, most; **parens, -entis**, m/f: parent; **dēfleō, -ēre, -flēvī, -fletus**: lament, mourn; **cuius reī**: "of which matter"; **iūdicium, -iī**, n: judgment, investigation; **senātus, -ūs**, m: senate; **consul, consulis**, m: Consul; **permittō, -ere, -mīsī, -missus**: entrust, surrender, relinquish; **rē . . . relātā**: "after the matter had been reported" (ablative absolute); **patrēs, -um**, m (plural): senators; **prohibitī** (*sunt*): "(the people of Pompeii) were prohibited (from)" (perfect passive of *prohibeō, -ēre, -uī, -itus*: restrain, prohibit); **pūblicē**: publicly, officially; **coetus, -ūs**, m: assembly, gathering; **Pompēiānus, -a, -um**: of Pompeii.

14.12. *CIL* VI 10063: **Rome.** A tombstone for a famous charioteer of the "red team," who, it seems, even won a few victories for the other three stables.

D(īs) m(ānibus) Musclōsō a(gitātōri) f(actiōnis) r(ussatae) nāt(iōne)
Tuscus.
Vīc(it) pal(mās) DCLXXXII:
a(lbā factiōne) III
p(rasinā factiōne) V
v(enetā factiōne) II
r(ussātā factiōne) DCLXXII.
Āpulēia Verēcundia coniunx m(arītō) c(ārissimō) p(osuit).

Notes: **Musclōsus, -ī,** m: a charioteer; **nātiō, -iōnis,** f: tribe, race, people; **Tuscus, -a, -um**: Etruscan (a cutter's slip, *Tuscus* should be *Tuscō* to agree with *Musclōsō*); **Āpulēia Verēcundia, Āpulēiae Verēcundiae,** f: a woman's name (*Verēcundia*: from *verēcundia, -iae,* f: modesty, decency); **marītus, -ī,** m: husband; **cārissimus, -a, -um**: dearest, most cherished; the direct object of *posuit* is *hoc* (see *NLP* 14.1), whose antecedent is the tombstone.

EXTRA PASSAGES: GAMES
IN VERGIL'S *AENEID* BOOK 5

In Book 5 of Vergil's *Aeneid*, Aeneas holds athletic games to honor the first anniversary of his father's death. The Trojans compete in several events: boat race, foot race, boxing match, and archery contest. As the games unfold, we finally see Aeneas emerge as "leader," not the storm-tossed, love-struck adventurer of Books 1–4: with ease he settles the petty squabbles of his men, in some cases awarding prizes to both winners and losers. By the end of Book 5, Aeneas uses these same skills to address the concerns of the Trojan women, who have grown frustrated at the long journey and set fire to the ships.

14.13. Vergil, *Aeneid* **5.114–15.** The boat race. Meter: dactylic hexameter.

Prīma parēs ineunt gravibus certāmina rēmīs,
quattuor ex omnī dēlectae classe carīnae.

Notes: **ineō, -īre, -iī, -itus**: enter; **certāmen, -inis,** n: contest; **rēmus, -ī,** m: oar; **dēlectus, -a, -um**: chosen; **carīna, -ae,** f: keel, ship.

14.14. Vergil, *Aeneid* **5.258–62.** Despite coming in second in the boat race, Mnestheus receives a stunning gold breastplate that Aeneas himself had claimed as spoils during the Trojan War. Meter: dactylic hexameter.

At quī deinde locum tenuit virtūte secundum,
lēvibus huic hāmīs consertam aurōque trilīcem
lōrīcam, quam Dēmoleō dētraxerat ipse
victor apud rapidum Simoenta sub Īliō altō,
dōnat habēre, virō decus et tūtāmen in armīs.

Notes: **quī**: "he (Mnestheus) who" (nominative singular masculine); **lēvis, -e**: smooth; **huic**: "to this man (Mnestheus)" (dative singular masculine); **hāmus, -ī**, m: hook; **consertus, -a, -um**: joined, fitted (with); **aurum, -ī**, n: gold; **trilix, trilīcis**: three-ply; **lōrīca, -ae**, f: breastplate; **quam**: "which" (accusative singular); **dōnō, -āre, -āvī, -ātus**: grant, bestow; **Dēmoleos, -ī**, m: a Greek warrior; **dētrahō, -ere, -traxī, -tractus**: remove, rob, strip away; **ipse**: Aeneas; **rapidus, -a, -um**: rapid, swift; **Simoīs, -entis**, m: river in Troy (*Simoenta*: Greek accusative); **Īlium, -iī**, n: Troy; **tūtāmen, tūtāminis**, n: protection.

14.15. Vergil, *Aeneid* **5.424–25.** The youthful Dares and the veteran Entellus have just agreed to the terms of the boxing match. Aeneas sees to it that the match will be as equitable as possible. Meter: dactylic hexameter.

Tum satus Anchīsā caestūs pater extulit aequōs
et paribus palmās ambōrum innexuit armīs.

Notes: **tum**: then; **satus, -a, -um**: sown, born (from) (+ ablative); **Anchīsēs, -ae**, m: father of Aeneas; **caestus, -ūs**, m: boxing glove; **efferō, efferre, extulī, ēlātus**; carry out, bring out; **innectō, -ere, -nexuī, -nexus**: entwine, tie, fasten together.

Demonstrative and Indefinite Pronouns

1. As you learned in *NLP* 4 and 12, pronouns take the place of nouns and agree with their antecedents in gender and number only. Their case is determined according to how they function in their own sentences or clauses. In this lesson we will focus on demonstrative and indefinite pronouns. You will learn other important pronouns in *NLP* 16.

PART 1: DEMONSTRATIVE PRONOUNS

2. **DEMONSTRATIVE PRONOUNS** indicate a specific person or thing in reference to the speaker or narrator. In Latin, there are five basic demonstrative pronouns:

   hic, haec, hoc: this/these person(s)/thing(s)
   ille, illa, illud: that/those person(s)/thing(s)
   iste, ista, istud: that/those person(s)/thing(s) of yours
   is, ea, id: this/these person(s)/thing(s) *or* that/those person(s)/thing(s)
   īdem, eadem, idem: the same person(s)/thing(s)

3. **HIC, HAEC, HOC** is used to refer to a person or object that is close to the speaker or narrator. Consider the following examples:

   Ovid, *Metamorphoses* 14.849–50: **<u>Hanc</u> manibus nōtīs Rōmānae conditor urbis / excipit.** He (Romulus), the founder of the Roman city, receives <u>this woman</u> (Hersilia, his wife) with familiar hands.

Caesar, *de Bello Gallico* 1.1.3: **Hōrum omnium fortissimī sunt Belgae**. <u>Of all these men</u>, the Belgians are the strongest.

Hic, haec, hoc can also function as an adjective:

Martial, *Liber Spectaculorum* 29.10 (*NLP* 14.8): **Hoc pretium virtūs ingeniōsa tulit**. Clever talent carried <u>this reward</u>.

Pliny the Elder, *Naturalis Historia* 3.60: **Haec lītora fontibus calidīs rigantur**. <u>These shores</u> are moistened by warm springs.

4. Study the table for *hic, haec, hoc.*

Case	Masculine	Feminine	Neuter
Singular			
Nominative	hic	haec	hoc
Genitive	hu**ius**	hu**ius**	hu**ius**
Dative	hu**ic**	hu**ic**	hu**ic**
Accusative	hu**nc**	ha**nc**	hoc
Ablative	hōc	hāc	hōc
Plural			
Nominative	hī	hae	haec
Genitive	hō**rum**	hā**rum**	hō**rum**
Dative	hīs	hīs	hīs
Accusative	hōs	hās	haec
Ablative	hīs	hīs	hīs

The singular forms of this pronoun are highly irregular; however, in the plural, the pronoun simply takes regular first and second declension endings attached to the stem *h-*.

5. **ILLE, ILLA, ILLUD** is used to refer to a person or object that is at some distance from the speaker or narrator. Consider the following examples:

Ovid, *Ars Amatoria* 1.124: **Haec queritur, stupet haec; haec manet, <u>illa</u> fugit**. This (Sabine) woman laments, this woman stands dumbstruck; this woman stays, <u>that woman</u> flees.

Martial 1.33.4: **<u>Ille</u> dolet vērē quī sine teste dolet**. <u>That man</u>, who grieves without a witness, grieves truly.

Ille, illa, illud can also function as an adjective:

Martial, *Liber Spectaculorum* 32.2 (*NLP* 11.12): **<u>Illa</u> gravis <u>palma</u> est, quam minor hostis habet**. <u>That reward</u> is weighty which a lesser enemy holds.

Ovid, *Amores* 1.1.25: **Certās habuit <u>puer ille</u> sagittās**. <u>That boy</u> (Cupid) had sure arrows.

6. Study the table for *ille, illa, illud.*

Case	Masculine	Feminine	Neuter
Singular			
Nominative	ille	illa	illud
Genitive	illīus	illīus	illīus
Dative	illī	illī	illī
Accusative	illum	illam	illud
Ablative	illō	illā	illō
Plural			
Nominative	illī	illae	illa
Genitive	illōrum	illārum	illōrum
Dative	illīs	illīs	illīs
Accusative	illōs	illās	illa
Ablative	illīs	illīs	illīs

Ille, illa, illud has slightly unusual forms in the nominative, genitive, dative, and accusative singulars, but these endings follow the paradigm that you have already learned for *is, ea, id* in *NLP* 12. From the ablative singular onward, the pronoun takes regular first and second declension endings attached to the stem *ill-*.

7. *Hic, haec, hoc* and *ille, illa, illud* can also be translated respectively as "the latter" and "the former" (the "latter" indicating the one "close by" and the "former" indicating the one "farther away"). Consider the following examples:

Martial 5.43: **Thāis habet nigrōs, niveōs Laecānia dentēs. / Quae ratiō est? Emptōs <u>haec</u> habet, <u>illa</u> suōs**. Thais has black teeth, Laecania white ones. What is the reason? <u>The latter</u> has "bought" ones, <u>the former</u> her own.

Tacitus, *Annales* 1.9.4: **Postquam <u>hic</u> sōcordiā senuerit, <u>ille</u> per libīdinēs pessum datus sit** . . . After <u>the latter</u> (Lepidus) grew old from inactivity (and) <u>the former</u> (Antony) was destroyed to the ground by lust . . .

8. **ISTE, ISTA, ISTUD** is used to refer to a person or object at some distance from the speaker or narrator. It often has a pejorative connotation. Consider the following examples:

Ovid, *Metamorphoses* 4.336: **"Dēsinis, an fugiō tēcumque" ait "<u>ista</u> relinquō!"** He (Hermaphroditus) said: "You (Salmacis) stop or I flee and leave <u>those things of yours</u> with you!"

Ovid, *Metamorphoses* 10.329: **Fēlīcēs, quibus <u>ista</u> licent!** Happy are those for whom <u>those things</u> are allowed!

Iste, ista, istud can also function as an adjective:

Ovid, *Ars Amatoria* 1.218: **Diffundetque animōs omnibus <u>ista diēs</u>**. And <u>that day</u> will gladden everyone's spirits.

Martial 5.58.2: **Dīc mihi, <u>crās istud</u>, Postume, quandō venit?** Tell me, Postumus, when does <u>that tomorrow</u> come?

9. The declension of *iste, ista, istud* is identical to that of *ille, illa, illud*. Simply change the stem from *ill-* to *ist-*.

10. In *NLP* 12, you learned the pronoun **IS, EA, ID**. This word also functions as a demonstrative pronoun and refers to a person or object that is either near to ("this/these") or at some distance from ("that/those") the speaker or narrator. You must use the context to determine the best translation of this word, and often more than one meaning could prevail.

Livy, *ab Urbe Condita* 1.3.6: **<u>Is</u> Aenēam Silvium creat; <u>is</u> deinde Latīnum Silvium**. <u>This/That man</u> (Silvius, son of Ascanius) bears Aeneas Silvius; next, <u>this/that man</u> (Aeneas Silvius) bears Latinus Silvius.

Suetonius, *Vita Augusti* 63 (*NLP* 8.13): **Nam tunc Agrippa alteram Marcellārum habēbat et <u>ex eā</u> līberōs**. For then Agrippa had one of the two Marcellas (they were sisters) and children <u>from this/that woman</u>.

Just as *hic, haec, hoc* and *ille, illa, illud* can also function as adjectives, so too can *is, ea, id*:

Vergil, *Aeneid* 2.17: **Vōtum prō reditū simulant; ea fāma vagātur**. They (the Greeks) represent (the giant horse) as an offering for their return; <u>that rumor</u> spreads.

Pliny the Elder, *Naturalis Historia* 4.89: **Pōne eōs montēs ultrāque Aquilōnem gens fēlix**. Behind <u>those mountains</u> and beyond the North Wind (is) a happy population.

11. **ĪDEM, EADEM, IDEM** indicates identical person(s) or object(s) and is translated as "the same." Consider the following examples:

Catullus 22.3: **Īdemque longē plūrimōs facit versūs**. And <u>the same man</u> for a long time makes very many verses.

Pliny the Elder, *Naturalis Historia* 2.210 (*NLP* 16.4): **In eōdem et relicta sacrificia nōn putrescunt**. <u>In the same (spot)</u> (i.e, a shrine to Minerva), the offerings left behind also do not decay.

Like the other demonstratives, *īdem, eadem, idem* can also function as an adjective:

Augustus, *Res Gestae* 26.5: **Ductī sunt duo exercitūs eōdem ferē tempore in Aethiopiam et in Ārabiam**. Two armies were led <u>at</u> approximately <u>the same time</u> into Ethiopia and into Arabia.

Livy, *ab Urbe Condita* 1.58.5: **Lucrētia maesta tantō malō nuntium Rōmam eundem ad patrem Ardeamque ad virum mittit**. Lucretia, distraught from so great an evil, sends <u>the same message</u> to Rome to her father and to Ardea to her husband.

12. *Īdem, eadem, idem* is declined almost exactly as the pronoun *is, ea, id* with the addition of *-dem* at the end of each form (see table on p. 199). Notice that, in the accusative masculine singular and the accusative feminine singular,

eum switches to *eun-* and *eam* to *ean-* to harmonize with the following "d."
In the genitive plural, *eōrum* switches to *eōrun-* and *eārum* to *eārun-*.

Case	Masculine	Feminine	Neuter
Singular			
Nominative	īdem	eadem	idem
Genitive	eiusdem	eiusdem	eiusdem
Dative	eīdem	eīdem	eīdem
Accusative	eundem	eandem	idem
Ablative	eōdem	eādem	eōdem
Plural			
Nominative	eīdem *or* iīdem	eaedem	eadem
Genitive	eōrundem	eārundem	eōrundem
Dative	eīsdem *or* īsdem	eīsdem *or* īsdem	eīsdem *or* īsdem
Accusative	eōsdem	eāsdem	eadem
Ablative	eīsdem *or* īsdem	eīsdem *or* īsdem	eīsdem *or* īsdem

PART 2: INDEFINITE PRONOUNS

13. **INDEFINITE PRONOUNS** refer to unspecified persons or things. In Latin, there are two basic indefinite pronouns:

aliquis, aliqua, aliquid: someone, something
quīdam, quaedam, quiddam: a certain person(s) / things(s)

Consider the following examples:

Catullus 1.3–4: **Namque tū solēbās / meās esse <u>aliquid</u> putāre nūgās.** For you were accustomed to think that my trifles were <u>something</u>.

Pliny the Younger, *Epistulae* 9.21.3 (*NLP* 12.7): **Remitte <u>aliquid</u> adulescentiae ipsius.** Concede <u>something</u> to the youth of that very man.

Martial 6.60.3 (*NLP* 11.10): **Ecce rubet <u>quīdam</u>, pallet, stupet, oscitat, ōdit.** Behold, <u>a certain man</u> blushes, grows pale, is struck senseless, stands agape, (and) hates.

Frontinus, *de Aquaeductu Urbis Romae* 1.18: **Inde fluunt quaedam altiōribus locīs et quaedam ērigī in ēminentiōra nōn possunt.** Then certain ones (i.e., waters) flow on higher places and certain ones are not able to be raised up to rather high spots.

14. Study the table for *aliquis, aliqua, aliquid.*

Case	Masculine	Feminine	Neuter
Singular			
Nominative	aliquis	aliqua	aliquid
Genitive	alicuius	alicuius	alicuius
Dative	alicui	alicui	alicui
Accusative	aliquem	aliquam	aliquid
Ablative	aliquō	aliquā	aliquō
Plural			
Nominative	aliquī	aliquae	aliqua
Genitive	aliquōrum	aliquārum	aliquōrum
Dative	aliquibus	aliquibus	aliquibus
Accusative	aliquōs	aliquās	aliqua
Ablative	aliquibus	aliquibus	aliquibus

Aliquis, aliqua, aliquid has slightly unusual forms in the nominative, genitive, dative, and accusative singulars and in the dative and ablative plurals. The other forms of the pronoun, however, take regular first and second declension endings attached to the stem *aliqu-*.

15. After *sī, nisi, num,* and *nē,* the *ali-* drops off the pronoun and the translation often shifts to "anyone" or "anything." Consider the following examples:

Martial 1.33.2: **Sī quis adest, iussae prōsiliunt lacrimae.** If anyone is present, commanded tears shoot out.

Tacitus, *Annales* 2.15.2: **Classem quippe et āvia Ōceanī quaesīta nē quis venientibus occurrerent.** The fleet, to be sure, and the pathless tracks of Ocean (were) procured lest anyone attack them as they came.

16. Study the table for *quīdam, quaedam, quiddam.*

Case	Masculine	Feminine	Neuter
Singular			
Nominative	quīdam	quaedam	quiddam
Genitive	cuiusdam	cuiusdam	cuiusdam
Dative	cuidam	cuidam	cuidam
Accusative	quendam	quandam	quiddam
Ablative	quōdam	quādam	quōdam
Plural			
Nominative	quīdam	quaedam	quaedam
Genitive	quōrundam	quārundam	quōrundam
Dative	quibusdam	quibusdam	quibusdam
Accusative	quōsdam	quāsdam	quaedam
Ablative	quibusdam	quibusdam	quibusdam

Quīdam, quaedam, quiddam use the indeclinable suffix -*dam* in the same way as the pronoun *idem, eadem, idem* uses -*dem*. In addition, the pronoun largely follows the paradigm of *aliquis, aliqua, aliquid* even though the nominative singulars differ. Notice also that, in the accusative masculine singular and the accusative feminine singular, *quem* switches to *quen-* and *quam* to *quan-* to harmonize with the following "d." In the genitive plural, *quōrum* switches to *quōrun-* and *quārum* to *quārun-*.

17. Both of these indefinite pronouns can also function as adjectives:

Suetonius, *Vita Caligulae* 31 (*NLP* 8.6): **Hiātum aliquem terrae optābat.** He (Caligula) wished for <u>some opening</u> of the earth.

Pliny the Younger, *Epistulae* 2.1.12 (*NLP* 9.15): **Cui fortasse <u>cīvēs aliquōs</u> virtūtibus parēs et habēmus.** To whom perhaps we also have <u>some citizens</u> equal in virtues.

Livy, *ab Urbe Condita* 1.3.6: **Silvius deinde regnat, Ascaniī fīlius, <u>cāsū quōdam</u> in silvīs nātus.** Silvius, the son of Ascanius, reigns next, born <u>by a certain misfortune</u> in the woods.

Tacitus, *Agricola* 12: **In pedite rōbur; <u>quaedam nātiōnēs</u> et currū proeliantur.** (There is) strength in the infantry; <u>certain nations</u> also battle with the chariot.

18. Although the forms for indefinite pronouns and adjectives are almost identical, there are some differences in the masculine and neuter singular forms:

aliquis (nominative masculine singular) becomes *aliquī*
aliquid (nominative neuter singular) becomes *aliquod*
aliquid (accusative neuter singular) becomes *aliquod*
quiddam (nominative neuter singular) becomes *quoddam*
quiddam (accusative neuter singular) becomes *quoddam*

I. Required Vocabulary

NOUNS

familia, -iae, f: household, household slave, band of household slaves, family

dominus, -ī, m: household master, lord
geminus, -ī, m: twin
nātus, -ī, m: son

nāvis, -is (-ium), f: ship

PRONOUNS

aliquis, aliqua, aliquid: someone, something; anyone, anything (pronoun)
hic, haec, hoc: this, these
īdem, eadem, idem: the same
ille, illa, illud: that, those
iste, ista, istud: that (of yours), those (of yours)
quīdam, quaedam, quiddam: a certain one, a certain thing (pronoun)

ADJECTIVES

aliquī, aliqua, aliquod: some, any
quīdam, quaedam, quoddam: a certain
turpis, -e: disgraceful, shameful, ugly

VERBS

rīdeō, -ēre, rīsī, rīsus: laugh, laugh at

dīligō, -ere, -lexī, -lectus: cherish, esteem

pōnō, -ere, posuī, positus: put, place, put aside, consider (**castra pōnere**: to pitch camp)

intellegō, -ere, -lexī, -lectus: understand

reddō, -ere, reddidī, redditus: return, give back

abeō, -īre, -īvī or **-iī, -ītus**: go away

PREPOSITIONS

circā (+ accusative): around, about (*circā* can also be used alone as an adverb)

CONJUNCTIONS AND ADVERBS

em: here; often followed by the dative case (*em tibi* = "here you are!")

interim: meanwhile

numquam: never

tum: then

utrum . . . an: whether . . . or

II. Translate the following sentences from Latin to English or English to Latin.

1. Interim rīdēbāmus illās quia putābant turpe cum gladiātōribus cēnāre.
2. Ō amīcī, ubi iste est servus bonus?
3. In nāvēs quōsdam numquam ducētis.
4. Caesar inter aliqua flūmina castra posuit.
5. Idem est nōmen duābus sorōribus.
6. Eō annō lēgiō mea cum urbe tuā bellum gesserat.
7. Pater geminum alterum amāvit, māter alterum.
8. Haec familia cum dominō malō pugnābit.
9. I had laughed at those soldiers because they never understood me.
10. Whether slaves or free, all citizens cherish the same things.
11. Will you (singular) mention your crime to anyone?
12. Those freedmen no longer trusted these freedwomen.

Slavery in Rome

As Rome expanded and grew more powerful, so too did its slave population increase. Contributing to this increase, though in small numbers, were piracy (a common trope in Plautus), the exposure of unwanted children (exposed girls were usually raised in brothels), and debt slavery (even Roman citizens could become slaves into the fourth century BCE). From the third century BCE onward, wars of expansion and rebellious provinces were a major source of slaves: Caesar is reputed to have sent over a million slaves to Rome from his campaigns in Gaul; the entire population of Judea was sold into slavery after Titus's victory over Jerusalem in 70 CE. Especially prized among Romans were the "exotic" blond-haired Gallic and Germanic slaves. Once the borders of the Empire became stable, home-born slaves fueled the workforce and marketplace, and owners occasionally rewarded particularly fertile slave women with freedom.

The largest slave markets existed at Rome and Delos, but slaves were auctioned throughout the Empire. Slaves were exhibited with neck placards listing their country of origin, age, physical and intellectual achievements or debilities, and their guiltlessness of crimes. Particularly accomplished, and therefore expensive, slaves were shown only to the wealthiest buyers. In this way, prisoners of war were sold (dealers would follow the army), as were the children of estate slaves (epitaphs reveal that family members resented separation from spouses and children). Sales were sealed with contracts that named the slave and conditions of sale, often non-returnable except in the case of epilepsy. Those who might need a slave for a limited period of time but could not afford full-time upkeep would rent them instead.

Private slaves performed all manner of duties, serving as agricultural workers, cooks, tailors, chambermaids, litter bearers, valets, secretaries, physicians, tutors, and overseers. Cato the Elder (*de Agricultura*) and Columella (*de Re Rustica*) both give advice to the private estate owner on how to select and care for household and farm slaves. The stingy Cato (2.56–59) even prescribes food and wine rations, and he mandates that slaves be given only one tunic, one cloak, and sturdy wooden shoes every other year! Cato also refused to employ slaves as tutors for his son, thinking it beneath Roman dignity that such an important task—the education of a Roman child—be relegated to a slave. Likewise, some Romans felt resentment toward slaves (and *lībertī*) who took jobs that might otherwise have gone to Roman citizens.

In some estates hundreds (even thousands) of slaves were kept, especially at the huge plantations (*latifundia*) in southern Italy, Sicily, Egypt, and Spain where much of the city's food was grown. Such large estates inspired real fear of revolt. Yet large-scale organized revolts were rare. The most noteworthy revolt occurred in 73–71 BCE, led by Spartacus in reaction to abuses at the gladiatorial training school in Capua. Many gladiators were slaves, and wealthy Romans of the late Republic kept scores of gladiator slaves to entertain friends and family, to serve as personal bodyguards, and to intimidate political rivals.

The state also owned slaves. One crew served the imperial household. Another crew fulfilled many tasks for the upkeep of the city. They served as lictors and jailors, and they helped maintain public infrastructure, including the aqueducts (see *NLP* 17). Slaves worked as overseers, pavers, and plasterers. Groups of slaves were also stationed at reservoirs and public baths to deal with sudden emergencies. According to Frontinus (*de Aquaeductu Urbis Romae* 2.116), they even received wages for their work.

The quality of a slave's life depended on the owner: some were generous, as Cicero was to his secretary, Tiro; others were diabolical, as was Larcius Macedo, whose cruelty prompted the household slaves to attack (Macedo died of his wounds, but only after many of the slaves had been caught and executed). In Plautus, it is a common threat to send misbehaving slaves to work in the fields. The worst fate for a slave, however, was relegation to the mines or mills, where the work was both physically demanding and demeaning. Spartacus was "promoted" from the Thracian silver mines before his storied career as a gladiator. Apuleius vividly describes the horrendous working conditions in a flour mill (*Metamorphoses* 9.12). It is no surprise, therefore, that slaves would try to run away. Those who were caught and returned might be fitted with collars identifying the crime (running away) and owner, or they might be branded with the letter "F" (*fūgī*).

SUGGESTIONS FOR FURTHER READING:

Bell, Sinclair and Teresa Ramsby, eds. *Free at Last: The Impact of Freed Slaves on the Roman Empire*. Bristol Classical Press, 2012.

Bradley, Keith. *Slavery and Society at Rome.* Cambridge, 1994.

Bradley, Keith and Paul Cartledge, eds. *The Cambridge World History of Slavery. Volume 1: The Ancient Mediterranean World.* Cambridge, 2011.

Garnsey, Peter. *Ideas of Slavery from Aristotle to Augustus.* Cambridge, 1996.

Harper, Kyle. *Slavery in the Late Roman World AD 275–425.* Cambridge, 2011.

Joshel, Sandra R. *Slavery in the Roman World.* Cambridge, 2010.

Watson, Alan. *Roman Slave Law.* Johns Hopkins, 1987.

PASSAGES

15.1. Seneca the Younger, *Epistulae* **47.1.** Seneca the Younger subscribed to radical Stoic views about humanity and slavery—that all people were equally citizens of the universe. Like other Stoics of his time, Seneca, at least on paper, believed that slaves should be treated with compassion. Nonetheless, he was a wealthy Roman who owned many slaves and had no intention of freeing them. Here, Seneca's friend Lucilius lives on good terms with his own slaves.

Libenter ex iīs, quī ā tē veniunt, cognōvī familiāriter tē cum servīs tuīs vīvere: hoc prūdentiam tuam, hoc ērudītiōnem decet. "Servī sunt." Immō hominēs. "Servī sunt." Immō contubernālēs. "Servī sunt." Immō humilēs amīcī.

Notes: **libenter**: willingly, gladly; **ex iīs** = *ex eīs*; **quī**: who (nominative plural masculine); **familiāriter**: on friendly terms; **tē . . . vīvere**: "that you live"; **prūdentia, -iae**, f: discretion, sagacity, judgment; **ērudītiō, -iōnis**, f: instruction, knowledge; **decet, -ēre, decuit**: befit, suit; **immō**: rather, on the contrary; **contubernālis, -is**, m/f: tent-mate, companion; **humilis, -e**: humble, poor.

15.2. Seneca the Younger, *Epistulae* **47.2.** Some Romans remained indifferent toward their slaves.

Itaque rīdeō istōs quī turpe existimant cum servō suō cēnāre.

Notes: **quī**: see *NLP* 15.1; **existimō, -āre, -āvī, -ātus**: think (it), believe.

15.3. Seneca the Younger, *Epistulae* **47.13.** Slaves should be treated equitably.

Vīve cum servō clēmenter, cōmiter quoque, et in sermōnem illum admitte et in consilium et in convictum.

Notes: **clēmenter**: mercifully, mildly; **cōmiter**: courteously; **admittō, -ere, -mīsī, -missus**: receive, grant, permit; **convictus, -ūs**, m: association, entertainment, feast.

15.4. Plautus, *Pseudolus* **161–62.** Pseudolus ("False One" or "Liar") is a clever and conniving slave, attempting to help his young master (Calidorus, "Lusty Fellow") obtain a prostitute (Phoenicium, "the girl from Phoenicia") with whom Calidorus has fallen in love. Phoenicium's owner, the pimp Ballio (Mr. "Pimp"), preparing to entertain some important clients, barks orders to his slaves.

"Habēs quod faciās: properā, abī intrō.
Tū estō lectisterniātor. Tū argentum ēluitō, idem exstruitō."

Notes: **quod faciās**: "what you should do"; **properō, -āre, -āvī, -ātus**: hurry; **intrō**: within, inside; **lectisterniātor, -ōris**, m: the slave who arranges the couches around a dining table; **argentum, -ī**, n: silver, silverware, money; **ēluō, -ere, -luī, -lūtus**: wash clean; **idem**: likewise, also; **exstruō, -ere, -strūxī, -structus**: heap, pile up.

15.5. Petronius, *Satyricon* **97.1.** After leaving Trimalchio's banquet, Encolpius and Ascyltus vie for the affections of the pretty slave boy Giton. Hiding in an inn, Encolpius cleverly orders poor little Giton to hang from the bottom of a mattress to evade Ascyltus's search. Here, Ascyltus proclaims a reward for Giton's return.

"Puer in balneō paulō ante aberrāvit, annōrum circā XVI, crispus, mollis, formōsus, nōmine Giton. Sī quis eum reddere aut commonstrāre voluerit, accipiet nummōs mille."

Notes: **balneum, -ī**, n: bath house; **paulō**: a little; **aberrō, -āre, -āvī**: wander away; **crispus, -a, -um**: curly-headed; **mollis, -e**: soft, gentle; **formōsus, -a, -um**: beautiful (full of *forma*); **quis** = *aliquis*; **commonstrō, -āre, -āvī, -ātus**: show, point out; **nummus, -ī**, m: coin.

15.6. Plautus, *Pseudolus* 496–501. The harshest punishment for a misbehaving slave was work in the mines or mills. After being caught in an elaborate scheme to defraud Simo (Calidorus's father, "Mr. Snub-nose"), Pseudolus defends his subterfuge.

Pseudolus: Dēsiste, rectē ego meam rem sapiō, Calliphō;
peccāta mea sunt. Animum advorte nunciam.
Quāpropter tē expertem amōris nātī habuerim?
Pistrīnum in mundō scībam, sī dixem, mihi.
Simo: Nōn ā mē scībās pistrīnum in mundō tibi,
cum ea mussitābās? **Pseudolus:** Scībam.

Notes: **dēsistō, -ere, -stitī, -stitus**: stop, withdraw; **rectē**: rightly, correctly; **sapiō, -ere, -īvī or -iī**: taste, discern; **Calliphō, -ōnis**, m: a Greek man's name, meaning "sweet talker" (the neighbor and friend of Pseudolus's master Simo); **peccātum, -ī**, n: error, mistake, fault; **advorte**: an archaic spelling of *adverte* from *advertō, -ere, -vertī, -versus*: turn towards, direct attention to; **nunciam**: here and now, now at last; **quāpropter**: for what reason, why; **expers (-tis)** (+ genitive): having no part (in), ignorant (of); **habuerim**: "should I consider?" (perfect subjunctive); **pistrīnum, -ī**, n: mill; **in mundō**: in store, ready; **scībam** = *sciēbam*; **sī dixem** = *sī dixeram*: "if I had spoken"; **scībās** = *sciēbās*; **mussitō, -āre, -āvī, -ātus**: continue to keep quiet (about).

15.7. Livy, *ab Urbe Condita* 8.15.7–8. The Vestal Virgins, chosen only from aristocratic families, were a prestigious priesthood of six aristocratic women who tended the flame in Vesta's temple and prepared the meal for state sacrifices. It was an honor to the girl's family, and the position invested those chosen with social and financial authority as well as autonomy otherwise not enjoyed by Roman women. If the requisite oath of chastity was broken, the traditional punishment was burial alive. In 337 BCE, the fashionable Vestal Minucia incurred suspicion and was ordered not to free any of her slaves before the trial (see *NLP* 12 for the testimony of slaves in court).

Eō annō Minucia Vestālis, suspecta prīmō propter mundiōrem iustō cultum, insimulāta deinde apud pontificēs ab indice servō, cum dēcrētō eōrum iussa esset sacrīs abstinēre familiamque in potestāte habēre—factō iudiciō—vīva sub terram ad portam Collīnam dextrā viam strātam dēfossa Scelerātō Campō; crēdō ab incestō id eī locō nōmen factum.

Notes: **Vestālis, -e**: Vestal (Virgin); **suspectus, -a, -um**: suspected; **mundior, -ius**: neater (than), more elegant (than) (+ ablative); **iustum, -ī**, n: justice, what is right; **cultus, -ūs**, m: refinement, dress; **insimulātus, -a, -um**: accused, charged; **pontifex, -icis**, m: priest; **index, indicis**, n: informer, spy; **cum . . . iussa esset**: "when she had been ordered"; **dēcrētum, -ī**, n: decree, decision; **sacra, -ōrum**, n (plural): rites, worship; **abstineō, -ēre, -tinuī, -tentus**: withhold (from), keep away (from); **potestās, -ātis**, f: power, control; **factō iudiciō**: "a judgment having been made" (ablative absolute); **vīvus, -a, -um**: living; **Porta Collīna, Portae Collīnae**, f: one of the city gates, near the Quirinal Hill; **dextrā** (+ accusative): to the right of; **strātus, -a, -um**: paved; **dēfossa est**: "she was buried"; **Scelerātus Campus, Scelerātī Campī**, m: Polluted Field, near the *Porta Collīna* and where convicted Vestals were buried alive; **credō . . . factum (esse)**: "I believe that (the name) was made" (indirect statement); **incestum, -ī**, n: sin, defilement.

15.8. Sallust, *Historiae Fragmenta* **3.64.** Varinius was one of the senatorial generals in command against Spartacus's highly disciplined slave army in 73–72 BCE. Here Varinius establishes a fortified camp near the slave camps. Within days, however, the well-organized slave army would demolish Varinius and his inexperienced troops.

Et tamen interim cum volentibus, numerō quattuor [mīlium, iuxtā illōs castra pōni]t va[llō, fossā, per]magnīs operibus commūnīta.

Notes: **volens (-entis)**: willing (here *volentibus* is used substantively: "[with] those willing"); **iuxtā** (+ accusative): close by, near; **illōs**: the slaves; **vallum, -ī**, n: wall, rampart, entrenchment, line of palisades, stakes; **fossa, -ae**, f: ditch, trench; **permagnus, -a, -um**: very great; **commūnītus, -a, -um**: fortified.

15.9. Cicero, *in Verrem* **2.3.8.** The former governor of Sicily, Gaius Verres, is on trial for extravagant (and blatant) extortion during his term as governor (73–70 BCE). The people of Sicily had, in fact, asked Cicero to represent them against Verres. Here, Cicero accuses the former governor of currying favor with the household slaves to gain introductions to the leading men in Sicily (who may also have owned valuable art collections).

Huic hominī sī cuius domus patet, utrum ea patēre an hiāre ac poscere aliquid vidētur, hunc vestrī iānitōrēs, hunc cubiculāriī dīligunt; hunc lībertī vestrī, hunc servī ancillaeque amant.

Notes: **pateō, -ēre, patuī**: lie open, extend, spread; **hiō, -āre**: gape; **poscō, -ere, popōscī**: demand, claim; **vidētur**: "it (the house) seems"; **iānitor, -ōris**, m: porter, doorman; **cubiculārius, -iī**, m: chamber servant; **ancilla, -ae**, f: female slave.

15.10. Varro, *de Agricultura* 1.17.1. In this handbook, Varro addresses both practical and theoretical aspects of managing an estate. In discussing how a farm is cultivated, Varro considers the classes of people who perform the actual work: slaves, free men, hired labor, family members. Varro here alludes to the Aristotelian interpretation of slaves as "living tools" (*Nichomachean Ethics* 8.11 [1161b3–4]), literally objectifying this large class of ancient men and women.

Quās rēs aliī dīvidunt in duās partēs, in hominēs et adminicula hominum, sine quibus rēbus colere nōn possunt; aliī in trēs partēs—instrūmentī genus vōcāle et sēmivōcāle et mūtum: vōcāle, in quō sunt servī, sēmivōcāle, in quō sunt bovēs, mūtum, in quō sunt plaustra.

Notes: **quās rēs**: "these matters" (i.e., the means by which the land is tilled); **dīvidō, -ere, -vīsī, -vīsus**: divide, separate; **adminiculum, -ī**, n: aid, prop, support; **sine quibus rēbus**: "without which things"; **instrūmentum, -ī**, n: equipment, tool; **vōcālis, -e**: vocal, speaking; **sēmivōcālis, -e**: semivocal; **mūtus, -a, -um**: inarticulate; **quō**: "in which" (ablative singular neuter); **bōs, bovis**, m: ox; **plaustrum, -ī**, n: wagon.

15.11. Frontinus, *de Aquaeductu Urbis Romae* 2.98. An important statesman at Rome in the late first century CE, Frontinus held several administrative posts, including Commissioner of the Aqueducts (*Cūrātor Aquārum*) in 95 CE. As *Cūrātor Aquārum*, he produced a handbook describing the history, maintenance, and legal aspects of this vital water system. Here, Frontinus describes the public slaves who maintain the aqueducts. This group originated from a private band established by Agrippa, who himself had also served as *Cūrātor Aquārum* under Augustus.

Habuit et familiam propriam aquārum, quae tuērētur ductūs atque castella et lacūs. Hanc Augustus hērēditāte ab eō sibi relictam pūblicāvit.

Notes: construe Agrippa as the subject of *habuit*; **proprius, -a, -um**: one's own; **quae tuērētur**: "who were to watch over" or "who were to maintain"; **ductus, -ūs**, m: duct, channel, conduit; **castellum, -ī**, n: shelter, basin; **hērēditās, -ātis**, f: inheritance; **ab eō**: "by him (Agrippa)"; **sibi**: Augustus; **relictus, -a, -um**: left, bequeathed; **pūblicō, -āre, -āvī, -ātus**: appropriate, make public.

15.12. Tacitus, *Annales* 12.1.2. We recall from *NLP* 12 that slaves could gain freedom, and those *lībertīnī* often continued to serve their former owners in the same capacities as before. After the death (or execution) of Claudius's unfaithful wife Messalina, the courtly *lībertīnī* Pallas and Callistus suggested candidates for the emperor's new wife. The contenders included Claudius's notorious niece Iulia Agrippina and Lollia Paulina, the former wife of Claudius's nephew and predecessor, Gaius Caligula.

> Sed maximē ambigēbātur inter Lolliam Paulīnam M. Lolliī consulāris et Iūliam Agrippīnam Germānicō genitam: huic Pallas, illī Callistus fautōrēs aderant.

Notes: **ambigēbātur**: "there was hesitation"; **Lollia Paulīna, Lolliae Paulīnae**, f: the daughter of Lollius Paulinus; **Marcus Lollius, Marcī Lolliī**, m: a Roman man's name; **consulāris, -is (-ium)**, m: former Consul; **Iūlia Agrippīna, Iūliae Agrippīnae**, f: a Roman woman's name; **Germānicus, -ī**, m: Claudius's older brother, who died in 19 CE (ablative of source); **genitus, -a, -um**: born from; **Pallas** and **Callistus**: see *NLP* 12; **fautor, -ōris**, m: patron, promoter; **adeō, -īre, -iī, -itus**: approach.

EXTRA PASSAGES: TITUS MACCIUS PLAUTUS

Born around 250 BCE in central Italy, the comic playwright Plautus is the earliest Roman author whose works come down to us intact. We have twenty full plays and fragments of another thirty or so. Plautine comedy draws from the stock characters (the grouchy old man, the young lovers, the clever slave, etc.) of Greek New Comedy and its traditional plots: boy falls in love with girl (often a prostitute); boy and clever slave deceive boy's father; prostitute turns out to be free-born; and the happy couple marries. Into these conventions and formulaic plots, Plautus weaves together Latin puns, farce, and slapstick humor, creating something new and distinctly Roman. Plautus's most popular scripts include *Pseudolus*, *Miles Gloriosus*, and *Menaechmi*. Burt Shevelove and Stephen Sondheim blended the characters and plots of the first two to create the popular musical *A Funny Thing Happened on the Way to the Forum* (1962). Below are selections from the *Menaechmi*, which has also taken a prime place in the history of comic theater: Shakespeare reinvented it as *Comedy of Errors*, and, more recently, Richard Rodgers, Lorenz Hart, and George Abbott took it as the model for a musical rendition, *The Boys from Syracuse* (1938).

15.13. Plautus, *Menaechmi* 26–28. In the prologue of this play, the audience learns that, long ago, the father of twins went on a business trip to Tarentum, taking one of the twins with him and leaving the other at home with his mother.

> Impōnit geminum alterum in nāvem pater,
> Tarentum āvexit sēcum ad mercātum simul,
> illum reliquit alterum apud mātrem domī.

> Notes: **impōnō, -ere, -posuī, -positus**: place on, station; **Tarentum, -ī, n**: Tarentum, a coastal town in southern Italy; **āvehō, -ere, -vexī, -vectus**: carry away; **ad mercātum**: "to trade" (supine); **simul**: together, at the same time.

15.14. Plautus, *Menaechmi* 40–41. After losing his son in Tarentum (a merchant carried him off to Epidamnus), the father died from the grief. Back at home, the grandfather changed the name of the "surviving" twin to that of his lost brother.

> Immūtat nōmen avos huic geminō alterī;
> ita illum dīlexit, quī subruptust, alterum.

> Notes: **immūtō, -āre, -āvī, -ātus**: change; **avos** = *avus* from *avus, -ī, m*: grandfather; **quī**: see *NLP* 15.1; **subruptust** = *subruptus est*: "(who) was stolen."

15.15. Plautus, *Menaechmi* 48. This name change sets up the play's confusion (and humor): friends and family cannot distinguish one identical twin from the other.

> Idem est ambōbus nōmen geminīs frātribus.

Relative Pronouns, Relative Clauses, and Interrogative Pronouns

1. A **RELATIVE CLAUSE** provides more information about a particular noun—its **ANTECEDENT**—in a given sentence. Relative clauses are introduced by **RELATIVE PRONOUNS**. Consider the following examples:

Martial 1.8.6: **Hunc volō, laudārī quī sine morte potest**. I want <u>this man</u>, <u>who is able to be praised without death</u>.

> The relative clause, introduced by the relative pronoun *quī,* gives us more information about "this man."

Frontinus, *de Aquaeductu Urbis Romae* 2.126: **Arborēs magis nocent, quārum rādīcibus concamerātiōnēs et latera solvuntur**. <u>Trees</u> are more harmful, <u>by whose roots the coverings and sides are burst</u>.

> The relative clause, introduced by the relative pronoun *quārum,* gives us more information about "trees."

Augustus, *Res Gestae* 26.1: **Omnium prōvinciārum populī Rōmānī quibus fīnitimae fuerunt gentēs quae nōn parērent imperiō nostrō fīnēs auxī**. I increased the borders <u>of all the provinces</u> of the Roman people <u>to which there were neighboring</u> <u>*tribes, which were not obeying our command*</u>.

> The first relative clause, introduced by the relative pronoun *quibus,* gives us more information about "all the provinces"; the second, introduced by the relative pronoun *quae,* about the "tribes."

Caesar, *de Bello Gallico* 7.71.6: **Cōpiās omnēs, quās prō oppidō collocāverat, in oppidum recipit**. He (Caesar) receives into the town <u>all the troops,</u> <u>which</u> <u>he had gathered in front of the town</u>.

The relative clause, introduced by the relative pronoun *quās,* gives us more information about "all the troops."

Caesar, *de Bello Gallico* 1.21.3: **Ipse de quartā vigiliā <u>eōdem itinere</u> quō hostēs ierant ad eōs contendit**. From the fourth watch he himself (Caesar) hurried toward them <u>on the same path</u> <u>by which the enemy had gone</u>.

The relative clause, introduced by the relative pronoun *quō,* gives us more information about the enemy's "path."

2. The following table provides the forms of the **RELATIVE PRONOUN**. The forms of this pronoun are almost identical to the forms of the indefinite adjective *quīdam, quaedam, quoddam* ("a certain") that you learned in *NLP* 15, once the indeclinable suffix -*dam* has been dropped from each form.

RELATIVE PRONOUN

Case	Masculine	Feminine	Neuter
Singular			
Nominative	quī	quae	quod
Genitive	cuius	cuius	cuius
Dative	cui	cui	cui
Accusative	quem	quam	quod
Ablative	quō	quā	quō
Plural			
Nominative	quī	quae	quae
Genitive	quōrum	quārum	quōrum
Dative	quibus	quibus	quibus
Accusative	quōs	quās	quae
Ablative	quibus	quibus	quibus

3. Like other pronouns, a **RELATIVE PRONOUN AGREES WITH ITS ANTECEDENT** in **gender** and **number**. Its case is determined by the grammatical function that it serves in its own clause. Consider the following examples:

Catullus 22.1–2: **<u>Suffēnus iste</u>, Vāre, <u>quem</u> probē nostī, / homo est venustus et dicax et urbānus.** That Suffenus, Varus, <u>whom</u> you know well, is a charming and talkative and sophisticated man.

> *Quem* and its antecedent *Suffēnus* are both masculine and singular. *Quem* is in the accusative case, functioning as a direct object of *nostī*.

Caesar, *de Bello Gallico* 7.71.6: **<u>Pecus</u>, <u>cuius</u> magna erat cōpia ā Mandūbiīs compulsa, virītim distribuit.** He individually distributed the <u>cattle</u>, <u>whose</u> great abundance had been rounded up by the Mandubii.

> *Cuius* and its antecedent *pecus* are both neuter and singular. *Cuius* is in the genitive case, functioning as a partitive genitive with *cōpia*.

Frontinus, *de Aquaeductu Urbis Romae* 2.115: **Longa ac dīversa sunt <u>spatia</u>, per quae fistulae tōtā meant urbe latentēs sub silice.** Long and varied are the <u>spaces</u> through <u>which</u> the pipes, hiding under the rock, wander in the whole city.

> *Quae* and its antecedent *spatia,* are both neuter and plural. *Quae* is in the accusative case, functioning as the object of the preposition *per*.

4. The antecedent of a relative pronoun can appear as part of the relative clause. It then stands in apposition to the relative pronoun, which behaves like an adjective:

Caesar, *de Bello Gallico* 3.18.6: **. . . inopia cibāriōrum, <u>cui</u> <u>reī</u> parum diligenter ab iīs erat prōvīsum. . . .** the lack of rations, for <u>which</u> <u>situation</u> there had been too little attention from them.

> *Reī* is technically the antecedent of *cui*, but it has been drawn into the relative clause and stands in apposition to the relative pronoun. Both *rēī* and *cui* refer back to the reasons why Sabinus hesitated to attack the Gauls.

Vergil, *Aeneid* 4.261–64: **Illī stēllātus iaspide fulvā / ensis erat Tyriōque ardēbat mūrice laena / dēmissa ex umerīs, dīvēs <u>quae</u> <u>mūnera</u> Dīdō / fēcerat.**

> His sword was studded with tawny jasper and the cloak draped from his shoulders was burning with Tyrian scarlet, <u>which</u> <u>gifts</u> wealthy Dido had made.

Mūnera is technically the antecedent of *quae*, but it has been drawn into the relative clause and stands in apposition to the relative pronoun. Both *mūnera* and *quae* refer back to the sword and the cloak which Dido had given to Aeneas.

5. Relative pronouns can be easily confused with **INTERROGATIVE PRONOUNS**, which are used to introduce "who" or "what" questions. Both types of pronouns have similar forms, and often only context will determine which pronoun is being employed. Consider the following examples and note the interrogative pronoun that begins each sentence:

Catullus 9.11: **Quid mē laetius est beātiusve?** <u>What</u> is happier or more blessed than me?

Catullus 8.17: **Quem nunc amābis? Cuius esse dīcēris?** <u>Whom</u> now will you love? <u>Whose</u> will you be said to be?

6. Study the following table for the interrogative pronoun. Note that it differs from the relative pronoun in the nominative singular and accusative singular but it is identical to the relative pronoun in its plural forms.

INTERROGATIVE PRONOUN

Case	Masculine	Feminine	Neuter
Singular			
Nominative	quis	quis	quid
Genitive	cu**ius**	cu**ius**	cu**ius**
Dative	cui	cui	cui
Accusative	quem	quem	quid
Ablative	quō	quā	quō
Plural			
Nominative	quī	quae	quae
Genitive	qu**ōrum**	qu**ārum**	qu**ōrum**
Dative	qu**ibus**	qu**ibus**	qu**ibus**
Accusative	qu**ōs**	qu**ās**	quae
Ablative	qu**ibus**	qu**ibus**	qu**ibus**

I. Required Vocabulary

NOUNS

īra, -ae, f: wrath, anger

lūna, -ae, f: moon

stella, -ae, f: star

nūbila, -ōrum, n (plural): clouds

superī, -ōrum, m (plural): gods

saxum, -ī, n: rock, cliff

ventus, -ī, m: wind

āēr, āeris, m: air, atmosphere

imber, imbris (-ium), m: shower, storm

nemus, nemoris, n: grove, forest

orbis, -is (-ium) m: circle, disk; globe, earth, world

sanguis, sanguinis, m: blood

sīdus, sīderis, n: star, constellation, planet

tempestas, -ātis, f: period of time, season; bad weather, storm

PRONOUNS

quī, quae, quod: who, what

quis, quid: who? what?

ADJECTIVES

paucī, -ae, -a (plural): few

uterque, utraque, utrumque: each (of two), both

vīcīnus, -a, -um: neighboring, near (used substantively as "neighbors")

VERBS

iaceō, -ēre, iacuī: lie down

fallō, -ere, fefellī, falsus: deceive, cheat, be mistaken

inpluō, -ere, -uī: rain

metuō, -ere, -uī, -ūtus: to fear, to dread

noscō, -ere, nōvī, nōtus: learn, get to know

recipiō, -ere, -cēpi, -ceptus: take back, receive

redeō, -īre, -iī or īvī, -itus: go back, return

CONJUNCTIONS AND ADVERBS
    adhūc: thus far, to this point, still
    cēterum: in addition, however
    hinc: from here; **hinc . . . hinc**: here and there
    ideō: therefore, for this reason
    item: likewise

II. Translate the following sentences from Latin to English or English to Latin.

1. Poētae quī adhūc tempestātēs metuunt sīdera nōn noscunt.
2. Imbribus quōs populī Rōmānī optāvēre agrī crescēbant.
3. Item mīlitēs quōrum īra magna erat urbēs cīvium vīcīnōrum cēperant.
4. Uxor laeta est cui vir crēdidit.
5. Ō mātrēs, dīligite līberōs quibus orbem dedistis.
6. Itaque mare cuius undae propter ventōs crescēbant spectābāmus.
7. Eō tempore illīs in regiōnibus in quibus habitāvistī numquam inpluit.
8. Dī hominibus signa quibus agrōs colere noscunt mittunt.
9. The stars which fall from the sky still please me.
10. The soldiers pitched camp near the rocks on which the king was lying.
11. That man whose city is great is able to wage war on his neighbors.
12. We saw the light of the moon in the grove through which few men went.

Meteorology

"Meteorology" is a Greek term that refers to the study of *meteōria*, "things high up," but the ancient science differed greatly from the modern study of the atmosphere. The Greeks and Romans lacked the tools to take accurate measurements of temperature and barometric pressure, nor did they seek to predict weather. The scope of ancient meteorology is far broader and included such things as comets, precipitation, rainbows (and even moonbows), winds as well as phenomena that were not so "high up"—volcanic eruptions, for example, and earthquakes, which were thought to be caused by winds. Although in myth and poetry Jupiter was responsible for thunder and lightning and Neptune caused earthquakes, natural philosophers believed that meteorological phenomena could be explained rationally. Lucretius (*de Rerum Natura*), among others, argued that the physical world worked according to orderly, unchanging laws. Capricious gods do not cause bad weather; physics does.

From Homer onward, weather phenomena were observed, described, and explicated both fancifully and rationally by poets, natural philosophers, physicians, astrologers, and farmers. Aristotle and his student Theophrastus wrote books on meteorology in Greek. Among other things, Aristotle theorized that rainbows occur when sunlight is reflected at fixed angles from clouds. These optical wonders can be seen during the day (rainbows) or, rarely, at night under a full moon (moonbows, as indeed they can). He also explained comets, meteors, the aurora borealis and even the Milky Way as phenomena of the upper atmosphere, caused by hot, dry exhalations from the air that accreted and occasionally burst into flame. (Only in the sixteenth century was this theory refuted when comets were accepted as celestial, not atmospheric, phenomena.)

In Latin, Seneca the Younger (*Naturales Quaestiones*) and Pliny the Elder (*Naturalis Historia*, Book 2) treated meteorology at length. Pliny even tackled the problem of trying to predict the weather (*Naturalis Historia*, Book 18), which was more often seen as prognostic than as predictable. Astrologers and physicians thus deemed meteorological phenomena significant indicators of health and fortune. The Latin medical writer Celsus observed that some diseases prevailed at certain times of the year and under certain weather conditions.

Historians and physicians also saw connections between climate and the character and health of different peoples. According to the author of the Hippocratic *Airs, Waters, Places*, people tended to mirror their physical environments: in the harsh, fluctuating and rocky regions of northern Europe, the people were naturally hardy and adaptable; the mild environs of Asia encouraged pleasure, not courage, in the inhabitants. According to Herodotus, Egyptians were the healthiest people because their climate lacked seasonal variation. To Strabo, the mild, temperate, yet varied climate of Rome facilitated her rise on the world stage (Roman winters are mild and wet, summers are warm to hot and dry).

SUGGESTIONS FOR FURTHER READING:

Kahn, Charles H. *Anaximander and the Origins of Greek Cosmology*. Columbia, 1960. repr. Hackett, 1994.

Lehoux, Daryn. *Astronomy, Weather and Calendars in the Ancient World: Parapegmata and Related Texts in Classical and Near-Eastern Societies*. Cambridge, 2007.

Taub, Liba. *Ancient Meteorology*. Routledge, 2003.

PASSAGES

16.1. Vegetius, *de Re Militari* 4.41. In his handbook on the Roman army, Vegetius discusses things of importance to a commander in the camp or on campaign, including weather conditions. Here, Vegetius explains how colors can presage fair weather or storms.

Rubicundus color ventōs, caeruleus indicat pluviās, ex utrōque commixtus nimbōs et furentēs procellās. Laetus orbis ac lūcidus serēnitātem nāvigiīs reprōmittit, quam gestat in vultū.

Notes: **rubicundus, -a, -um**: red, ruddy; **caeruleus, -a, -um**: blue; **indicō, -āre, -āvī, -ātus**: point out, show, make known; **pluvia, -iae**, f: rain; **commixtus, -a, -um**: combined, intermingled; **nimbus, -ī**, m: rainstorm, cloud; **furens (-entis)**: raging; **procella, -ae**, f: storm, gale; **orbis** (*lūnae*); **lūcidus, -a, -um**: clear, bright, full of light; **serēnitās, -ātis**, f: fair weather; **nāvigium, -iī**, n: ship, vessel; **reprōmittō, -ere, -mīsī, -missus**: promise, guarantee; **gestō, -āre**: carry, bear; **vultus, -ūs**, m: look, expression, face.

16.2. Seneca the Younger, *Naturales Quaestiones* 1.1.12. Seneca the Younger's literary output includes a treatise on natural philosophy (i.e., science), wherein he discusses all manner of natural phenomena. Here he describes the signs of coming storms and where to find them. He also alludes to the perennially superstitious nature of sailors.

Argūmentum tempestātis nautae putant, cum multae transvolant stellae. Quod sī ventōrum signum est, ibi est unde ventī sunt: id est in āere, quī medius inter lūnam terrāsque est.

Notes: **argūmentum, -ī**, n: proof, subject; **nauta, -ae**, m: sailor; **transvolō, -āre, -āvī, -ātus**: fly across (the sky), hasten across (e.g., a meteor shower); **quod sī**: but if; **unde**: from where.

16.3. Seneca the Younger, *Naturales Quaestiones* 2.12.6. Seneca explains why we see lightning before we hear thunder.

Cēterum illa vīs expressī spīritūs ignis est quī fulgurātiōnis nōmen habet, levī impetū accensus et vānus. Ante autem vidēmus fulgōrem quam sonum audīmus, quia oculōrum vēlōcior sensus est et multum aurēs antecēdit.

Notes: **expressus, -a, -um**: squeezed out, pressed out; **spīritus, -ūs**, m: breath, spirit; **fulgurātiō, -iōnis**, f: flash of lightning; **impetus, -ūs**, m: attack; **accensus, -a, -um**: kindled, illuminated; **vānus, -a, -um**: empty, void; **ante . . . quam**: before (*tmesis*); **fulgor, -ōris**, m: lightning, brightness; **sonus, -ī**, m: noise; **vēlōcior**: rather swift; **sensus, -ūs**, m: feeling, emotion, perception; **multum**: much, by much; **auris, -is** (-**ium**), f: ear; **antecēdō, -ere, -cessī, -cessus**: go before, surpass.

16.4. Pliny the Elder, *Naturalis Historia* 2.210. Two temple precincts where rain never falls.

Celebre fānum habet Veneris Paphos, in cuius quandam āream nōn inpluit, item in Neā, oppidō Trōadis, circā simulācrum Minervae; in eōdem et relicta sacrificia nōn putrescunt.

Notes: **celeber, celebris, celebre**: celebrated, famous; **fānum, -ī**, n: consecrated place, holy place, temple precinct; **Venus, Veneris**, f: the Roman goddess of beauty and sex; **Paphos, -ī**, m: a town in Cyprus sacred to Venus; **ārea, -ae**, f: open space, courtyard; **Nea, -ae**, f: a tiny maritime town which was one of the "twin" townlets that made up Didyma (Strabo 3.5.3); **Trōas, Trōadis**, m: the Troad, the territory around Troy; **simulācrum, -ī**, n: likeness, statue; **eōdem** (*locō*); **relictus, -a, -um**: left behind; **sacrificium, -iī**, n: sacrificial offering; **putrescō, -ere**: become rotten, decay.

16.5. Seneca the Younger, *Naturales Quaestiones* 1.3.6. The reflective properties of raindrops.

Ergō stillicidia illa infīnīta, quae imber cadens dēfert, totidem specula sunt, totidem sōlis faciēs habent.

Notes: **stillicidium, -iī**, n: raindrop; **infīnītus, -a, -um**: unbounded, countless; **cadens** (-**entis**): falling; **dēferō, -ferre, -tulī, -lātus**: carry down, bring down; **totidem**: so many; **speculum, -ī**, n: mirror; **faciēs, -iēī**, f: form, appearance.

16.6. Ovid, *Metamorphoses* 6.63–66. Foolish Arachne dared to compare her weaving skills to Minerva's. The goddess challenged the girl to a competition. Ovid's description of the contest begins with a stunning simile that compares the act of weaving, with all its colorful threads, to a rainbow. In the end, angered by the flawlessness of Arachne's tapestry (and its poorly chosen theme—divine peccadillos), Minerva destroys the girl, but then relents, turning her into a spider so she can continue to weave forever. Meter: dactylic hexameter.

> Quālis ab imbre solet percussīs sōlibus arcus
> inficere ingentī longum curvāmine caelum;
> in quō dīversī niteant cum mille colōrēs
> transitus ipse tamen spectantia lūmina fallit.

Notes: **quālis, -e**: of what sort, just as; **soleō, -ēre, solitus sum**: be accustomed to; **percussīs sōlibus**: "suns having been stricken" (ablative absolute); **arcus, -ūs**, m: arch, bow; **inficiō, -ere, -fēcī, -fectus**: corrupt, poison, dye, stain; **curvāmen, curvāminis**, n: arc, curve, bend; **dīversus, -a, -um**: separate, diverse; **niteō, -ēre, nituī**: shine, glitter, bloom (*niteant*: present subjunctive); **transitus, -ūs**, m: passing over, transit, transition; **spectans (-antis)**: watching; **lūmen, lūminis**, n: light, (in plural) eyes.

16.7. Pliny the Younger, *Epistulae* 6.20.13. Pliny and his family were at the Bay of Naples in 79 CE when Vesuvius erupted, and his uncle Pliny the Elder lost his life on a rescue mission. The Younger Pliny survived, and here he describes his own harrowing escape.

> Iam cinis, adhūc tamen rārus. Respiciō: densa cālīgō tergīs imminēbat, quae nōs torrentis modō infūsa terrae sequēbātur.

Notes: **cinis, cineris**, m/f: ash, ember; **rārus, -a, -um**: thin, scattered; **respiciō, -ere, -spēxi, -spectus**: look back, regard, consider; **densus, -a, -um**: thick, close; **cālīgō, cālīginis**, f: fog, mist, vapor; **tergum, -ī**, n: back; **immineō, -ēre** (+ dative): overhang, threaten; **torrens (-entis)**: rushing, burning (here, a substantive: "flood"); **modō**: "in the manner of"; **infūsus, -a, -um**: pouring over (+ dative); **sequēbātur**: "(which) was following."

16.8. Pliny the Elder, *Naturalis Historia* 3.94. Pliny is here detailing the characteristics of the Aeolian islands. He has already described Lipari and the "Holy Island," and is now tackling Strongyle, where some islanders were able to foretell the weather, especially wind patterns, from the smoke of a volcano.

Tertia Strongylē, ā Liparā ad exortum sōlis vergens, in quā regnāvit Aeolus; quae ā Liparā liquidiōre tantum flammā differt, ē cuius fūmō, quīnam flātūrī sint ventī in trīduō, praedīcere incolae trāduntur.

Notes: **tertia** (*insula est*); **Strongylē, -ēs,** f: modern Stromboli, a small island with one of the three active volcanoes in Italy; **Liparē, -ēs,** f: Lipari, the largest of the Aeolian islands off the northern coast of Sicily; **exortus, -a, -um:** rising (substantive); **vergens (-entis):** sloping, inclining, extending; **regnō, -āre, -āvī, -ātus:** rule; **Aeolus, -ī,** m: the king of the winds; **liquidior, -ius:** rather clear; **flamma, -ae,** f: flame; **differō, -ferre, distulī, dīlātus:** differ; **fūmus, -ī,** m: smoke, steam, vapor; **quīnam . . . trīduō:** "which winds might blow within three days" (indirect question following *praedīcere*); **praedīcō, -ere, -dīxī, -dictus:** foretell, predict; **incola, -ae,** m: inhabitant; **trāduntur:** "(the inhabitants) are said (to)."

16.9. Caesar, *de Bello Gallico* 3.8.1. In 56 BCE, Caesar battled the Venetii (inhabiting Gallia Lugdunensis, modern Brittany) who enjoyed decided military and economic advantages because of their precise knowledge of the English Channel (where the tides and currents were much greater than on the relatively calm waters of the Mediterranean) and the weather that affected sailors there.

Huius est cīvitātis longē amplissima auctōritās omnis ōrae maritimae regiōnum eārum, quod et nāvēs habent Venetī plūrimās—quibus in Britanniam nāvigāre consuērunt—et scientiā atque ūsū rērum nauticārum cēterōs antecēdunt.

Notes: **longē:** by far; **amplissimus, -a, -um:** most important, most influential; **auctōritās, -ātis,** f: influence, authority, control; **ōra, -ae,** f: edge, border, coast; **maritimus, -a, -um:** maritime, of the sea; **Venetī, -ōrum,** m (plural): a Gallic tribe (construe as the subject of the remaining verbs in the passage); **plūrimus, -a, -um:** very many; **Britannia, -iae,** f: Britain; **navigō, -āre, -āvī, -ātus:** sail, voyage; **consuescō, -ere, -suēvī, -suētus:** be accustomed to (*consuērunt = consuēvērunt*); **scientia, -iae,** f: knowledge; **ūsus, -ūs,** m: experience, use; **nauticus, -a, -um:** nautical, naval; **cēterus, -a, -um:** the other(s); **antecēdō, -ere, -cessī, -cessus:** surpass.

16.10. Caesar, *de Bello Gallico* 4.34.4. A terrible British storm in 55 BCE.

Secūtae sunt continuōs complūrēs diēs tempestātēs, quae et nostrōs
in castrīs continērent et hostem ā pugnā prohibērent.

Notes: **secūtae sunt**: "(storms) followed"; **continuus, -a, -um**: incessant, uninterrupted;
complūrēs, -a (plural): several; **continērent**: "(which) held back" (imperfect subjunctive);
pugna, -ae, f: battle, fight; **prohibērent**: "(which) prevented" (imperfect subjunctive).

16.11. Vergil, *Aeneid* 1.108–12. In her efforts to delay the founding of Rome, Juno
arranges for Aeolus, the god of the winds, to send a storm to throw the
Trojans off their course. The squall is described in vivid detail. Meter: dactylic hexameter.

Trīs Notus abreptās in saxa latentia torquet
(saxa vocant Italī mediīs quae in fluctibus "Ārās,"
dorsum immāne marī summō); trīs Eurus ab altō
in brevia et Syrtīs urget—miserābile vīsū—
inlīditque vadīs atque aggere cingit harēnae.

Notes: **trīs** (*nāvēs*): three (ships); **Notus, -ī**, m: south wind; **abreptus, -a, -um**: snatched
away; **latens (-entis)**: lurking, concealed; **torqueō, -ēre, torsī, tortus**: twist, whirl; **fluctus,
-ūs**, m: wave, billow; **āra, -ae**, f: altar; **dorsum, -ī**, n: back, ridge, reef; **immānis, -e**: huge,
monstrous, savage; **summus, -a, -um**: highest, deepest; **Eurus, -ī**, m: east wind; **altum**
(substantive); **in brevia**: "against the shallows"; **syrtis, -is (-ium)**, f: sand bar (also the name
of two shallow, sandy gulfs off the coast of Libya); **urgeō, -ēre, ursī**: drive, force, press;
miserābile vīsū: "miserable to see" (*vīsū*: supine, see *NLP* 36); **inlīdō, -ere, -līsī, -līsus**:
dash against (+ dative); **vadum, -ī**, n: shallow, shoal, depth; **agger, aggeris**, m: mound,
wall, bank; **cingō, -ere, cinxī, cinctus**: encircle, surround, gird; **harēna, -ae**, f: sand, beach.

16.12. Ovid, *Metamorphoses* 7.197–200. The semi-divine Medea promises to add
years to the life of Jason's aged father. As she prepares to perform her
witchcraft, she calls on the forces of nature (and weather), which she is able
to control with her chants. Meter: dactylic hexameter.

"Auraeque et ventī montēsque amnēsque lacūsque,
dīque omnēs nemorum, dīque omnēs noctis, adeste,
quōrum ope, cum voluī, rīpīs mīrantibus amnēs
in fontēs rediēre suōs."

Notes: **aura, -ae**, f: breeze; **ops, opis**, f: power, help; **rīpīs mīrantibus**: "the riverbanks being amazed" (ablative absolute); **fons, fontis (-ium)**, f: spring, fountain.

EXTRA PASSAGES: ASTRONOMY

Despite the fact that the Greeks and Romans were staunch geocentrists (heliocentrism, the idea that the Earth orbits the sun, was proposed by Aristarchus of Samos c. 200 BCE and flatly rejected on religious grounds), they had a sophisticated knowledge of both observational and theoretical astronomy. They observed all the objects in the sky: sun, moon, planets, comets, constellations. And they devised complicated geometric explanations to account for the perceived anomalies in celestial motions—why, for example, the planet Mars sometimes travels in one direction, sometimes the other. They also employed astral data in computing latitudes, they predicted solar and lunar eclipses with accuracy, and they investigated many aspects of mathematical astronomy, including the relative sizes of the sun and moon. Long enduring, however, was the notion that the stars were divine, occupying a sphere around the Earth comprised of Aristotle's perfect fifth element (aither or quintessence). To the Roman imagination, celestial bodies had the power to affect events on Earth or to serve as messages from the gods.

16.13. Pliny the Elder, *Naturalis Historia* 2.92. The ancients believed that comets, portending political disaster, were sent by the gods as signs of divine displeasure.

Sed comētēs numquam in occāsūrā parte caelī est, terrificum magnā ex parte sīdus atque nōn leviter piātum, ut cīvīlī mōtū—Octaviō consule—iterumque Pompēī et Caesaris bellō, in nostrō vērō aevō circā venēficium, quō Claudius Caesar imperium reliquit Domitiō Nerōnī, ac deinde principātū eius adsiduum prope ac saevum.

Notes: **comētēs, -ae**, m: comet; **occāsūrus, -a, -um**: western; **terrificus, -a, -um**: frightful, terrible; **leviter**: softly, lightly, easily; **piātus, -a, -um**: appeased; **ut**: as, when; **cīvīlis, -e**: civil, civic, relating to the state; **mōtus, -ūs**, m: motion, rebellion, riot; **Octaviō consule**: "when Octavian was consul" (ablative absolute; 43 BCE; Octavian, the great-nephew and heir of Julius Caesar, was later called Augustus); **iterum**: again, a second time; **Pompēius, ī**, m: Pompey the Great (the civil war between Pompey and Caesar lasted from 49 BCE, when Caesar famously crossed the Rubicon, the river marking the northern extent of Italy, until the defeat of Pompey at Pharsalus in Greece in 48 BCE); **aevum, -ī**, n: lifetime; **venēficium, -iī**, n: preparation of poison, magic, sorcery ("the time of the poisoning"—it was rumored and widely believed that Claudius's niece-wife Agrippina poisoned her husband with a dish of mushrooms to expedite the ascension of her son Nero to the throne); **Domitius Nero, Domitiī Nerōnis**, m: Nero, whose father was Gnaeus Domitius Ahenobarbus; **principātus, -ūs**, m: principate, rule; **adsiduus, -a, -um**: constant (here modifying *sīdus*); **prope**: nearly; **saevus, -a, -um**: fierce, raging, wrathful.

16.14. Manilius, *Astronomica* 1.267–70. Manilius describes the zodiac signs of Libra and Scorpio and Scorpio's interplay with Centaur, a nearby constellation that represents a composite mythological beast (half horse, half man) who is almost always shown as an archer. Meter: dactylic hexameter.

Aequātō tum Lībra diē cum tempore noctis
attrahit ardentī fulgentem Scorpion astrō,
in cuius caudam contentō dīrigit arcū
mixtus equō volucrem missūrus iamque sagittam.

Notes: **aequātō diē cum tempore noctis**: "the day equaled with the duration of night" (ablative absolute; the Sun enters Libra during the autumnal equinox); **Lībra, -ae**, f: balance, scales (because of its proximity to Scorpio, Libra was once identified as the "scales" (*chelae*) of Scorpio but later came to represent the ideal of justice. Libra was both the moon sign for the city of Rome and Augustus's ascendant); **attrahō, -ere, -traxī, -tractus**: draw to, attract; **ardens (-entis)**: burning, glowing; **fulgens (-entis)**: flashing, shining (Antares, "the heart of Scorpio," the brightest star in the constellation); **Scorpiō, -iōnis**, m: Scorpio (*Scorpion*: Greek accusative), a poisonous creature, and a dangerous sign in the Roman zodiac (also Tiberius's sun sign); **astrum, -ī**, n: star, constellation (Antares, the brightest star in Scorpio); **cauda, -ae**, f: tail; **contentus, -a, -um**: stretched, taut; **dīrigō, -ere, -rexī, -rectus**: direct, guide, point; **mixtus, -a, -um**: mixed, mingled (that is, Sagittarius the half-horse Centaur, who seems to aim his bow directly at Scorpio's tail); **volucer, volucris, volucre**: flying, winged, swift; **missūrus, -a, -um**: about to volley/shoot; **sagitta, -ae**, f: arrow.

16.15. **Ovid, *Metamorphoses* 2.171–75.** Once Phaethon takes the reins of his father's chariot, the divine horses sense the boy's hesitation and they run wild in the heavens (see *NLP* 2.8). Ovid here describes the constellations of the zodiac as they try to escape the onslaught of the out-of-control vehicle. The constellations find themselves out of place and the celestial sphere is thrown into chaos. Meter: dactylic hexameter.

> Tum prīmum radiīs gelidī caluēre Triōnēs
> et vetitō frustrā temptārunt aequore tingī;
> quaeque polō posita est glaciālī proxima Serpens,
> frīgore pigra prius nec formīdābilis ullī,
> incaluit sumpsitque novās fervōribus īrās.

Notes: **radius, -iī**, m: staff, rod, ray (of the sun), beam of light; **gelidus, -a, -um**: cold, icy, frosty; **caleō, -ēre, -uī**: be warm, grow hot, glow; **Triōnēs, -um**, m (plural): the plowing oxen, the seven stars known together as the constellations of Ursa Major and Ursa Minor, which—from earliest times—indicated north (and, consequently, the cold regions); **vetitus, -a, -um**: forbidden (Ursa Major always wobbles around the North Pole and, unlike other constellations, does not seem to traverse the night sky, so it never "rises" or "sets" into the Ocean); **frustrā**: in vain; **temptō, -āre, -āvī, -ātus**: try, test; **temptārunt** = *temptāvērunt*; **aequor, -oris**, n: level surface, sea, plain; **tingī**: "to be dipped in"; **polus, -ī**, m: pole, axis; **posita est**: "(which) has been (traditionally) placed/positioned"; **glaciālis, -e**: icy; **Serpens, -entis**, m/f: serpent, snake (here, feminine); **frīgus, frīgoris**, n: cold, coolness; **piger, pigra, pigrum**: sluggish, slow; **prius**: previously, before; **formīdābilis, -e**: fearful, terrifying; **ullus, -a, -um**: any; **incalescō, -ere, -caluī**: grow hot; **fervor, -ōris**, m: heat, boiling, passion.

Passive Verbs: Present, Imperfect, and Future Tenses

1. The verbs that you have learned since *NLP* 1 have all been in the active voice (where the subject performs the action of the verb). In this Lesson, we will learn about verbs in the passive voice (where the subject is acted upon). Consider the following examples:

   CIL IV 807: **Hospitium. Hīc <u>locātur</u> trīclīnium cum tribus lectīs et comm(odīs)**. Lodging. Here a dining room <u>is placed</u> with three couches and furnishings.

   Vegetius, *de Re Militari* 2.23: **Veterēs autem et ērudītī sine intermissiōne semel in diē <u>exercēbantur</u> armīs**. Veterans, however, and skilled men <u>were being trained</u> in weapons without interruption once a day.

   Catullus 8.14: **At tū dolēbis, cum <u>rogāberis</u> nulla**. But you will feel pain when <u>you will be asked</u> not at all.

2. In this Lesson, we will focus on three tenses of the passive voice: present, imperfect, and future. To form these verbs, you will follow the same basic patterns that you learned in *NLP* 1, 8, and 9. The personal endings for the active voice that you learned in *NLP* 1 will be replaced by a new set of personal endings for the passive voice. Study the following table:

Person	Singular	Plural
1st	**-r**	**-mur**
2nd	**-ris/-re**	**-minī**
3rd	**-tur**	**-ntur**

N.B. Verbs with three principal parts are generally intransitive (i.e., they cannot take a direct object in Latin). These verbs do not usually appear in the passive voice.

3. To form the **PRESENT PASSIVE**, drop the personal endings for the active voice from the present tense forms that you learned in *NLP* 1 and add the personal endings for the passive voice learned above. N.B. The **first person singular** is formed a bit differently: add the passive ending -r directly to the active form (but drop the macron).

PRESENT PASSIVE OF PARADIGM VERBS

		1st Conj.	2nd Conj.	3rd Conj.	3rd Conj. (-io)	4th Conj.
Singular						
1st		amor: I am loved	doceor: I am taught	mittor: I am sent	capior: I am taken	audior: I am heard
2nd		amāris/ amāre: you are loved	docēris/ docēre: you are taught	mitteris/ mittere: you are sent	caperis/ capere: you are taken	audīris/ audīre: you are heard
3rd		amātur: he/she/it is loved	docētur: he/she/it is taught	mittitur: he/she/it is sent	capitur: he/she/it is taken	audītur: he/she/it is heard
Plural						
1st		amāmur: we are loved	docēmur: we are taught	mittimur: we are sent	capimur: we are taken	audīmur: we are heard
2nd		amāminī: you (plural) are loved	docēminī: you (plural) are taught	mittiminī: you (plural) are sent	capiminī: you (plural) are taken	audīminī: you (plural) are heard
3rd		amantur: they are loved	docentur: they are taught	mittuntur: they are sent	capiuntur: they are taken	audiuntur: they are heard

N.B. The vowel signifier for the **second person singular** of the third conjugation (regular and -io) is **-e-**, not **-i-**.

4. Study the table on the following page for the present passive system of the irregular verb *ferō*. (In the imperfect and future passive, *ferō* behaves like a regular third conjugation verb.)

Person	Singular	Plural
1st	fero**r**: I am carried	feri**mur**: we are carried
2nd	fer**ris**/fer**re**: you are carried	feri**minī**: you (plural) are carried
3rd	fer**tur**: he/she/it is carried	feru**ntur**: they are carried

5. To form the **IMPERFECT PASSIVE,** drop the personal endings for the active voice from the imperfect tense forms that you learned in *NLP 8* and add the personal endings for the passive voice learned above.

IMPERFECT PASSIVE OF PARADIGM VERBS

	1st Conj.	2nd Conj.	3rd Conj.	3rd Conj. (-io)	4th Conj.
Singular					
1st	amā**bar**: I was (being) loved	docē**bar**: I was (being) taught	mittē**bar**: I was (being) sent	capiē**bar**: I was (being) taken	audiē**bar**: I was (being) heard
2nd	amā**bāris**/ amā**bāre**: you were (being) loved	docē**bāris**/ docē**bāre**: you were (being) taught	mittē**bāris**/ mittē**bāre**: you were (being) sent	capiē**bāris**/ capiē**bāre**: you were (being) taken	audiē**bāris**/ audiē**bāre**: you were (being) heard
3rd	amā**bātur**: he/she/it was (being) loved	docē**bātur**: he/she/it was (being) taught	mittē**bātur**: he/she/it was (being) sent	capiē**bātur**: he/she/it was (being) taken	audiē**bātur**: he/she/it was (being) heard
Plural					
1st	amā**bāmur**: we were (being) loved	docē**bāmur**: we were (being) taught	mittē**bāmur**: we were (being) sent	capiē**bāmur**: we were (being) taken	audiē**bāmur**: we were (being) heard
2nd	amā**bāminī**: you (plural) were (being) loved	docē**bāminī**: you (plural) were (being) taught	mittē**bāminī**: you (plural) were (being) sent	capiē**bāminī**: you (plural) were (being) taken	audiē**bāminī**: you (plural) were (being) heard
3rd	amā**bantur**: they were (being) loved	docē**bantur**: they were (being) taught	mittē**bantur**: they were (being) sent	capiē**bantur**: they were (being) taken	audiē**bantur**: they were (being) heard

6. To form the **FUTURE PASSIVE**, drop the personal endings for the active voice from the future tense forms that you learned in *NLP 9* and add the

personal endings for the passive voice learned above. N.B. The future signifier for the **second person singular** of the first and second conjugations is -**be**, not -**bi**.

FUTURE PASSIVE OF PARADIGM VERBS

	1st Conj.	2nd Conj.	3rd Conj.	3rd Conj. (-io)	4th Conj.
Singular					
1st	amā**bor**: I shall be loved	docē**bor**: I shall be taught	mitt**ar**: I shall be sent	capi**ar**: I shall be taken	audi**ar**: I shall be heard
2nd	amā**beris**/ amā**bere**: you will be loved	docē**beris**/ docē**bere**: you will be taught	mitt**ēris**/ mitt**ēre**: you will be sent	capi**ēris**/ capi**ēre**: you will be taken	audi**ēris**/ audi**ēre**: you will be heard
3rd	amā**bitur**: he/she/it will be loved	docē**bitur**: he/she/it will be taught	mitt**ētur**: he/she/it will be sent	capi**ētur**: he/she/it will be taken	audi**ētur**: he/she/it will be heard
Plural					
1st	amā**bimur**: we shall be loved	docē**bimur**: we shall be taught	mitt**ēmur**: we shall be sent	capi**ēmur**: we shall be taken	audi**ēmur**: we shall be heard
2nd	amā**biminī**: you (plural) will be loved	docē**biminī**: you (plural) will be taught	mitt**ēminī**: you (plural) will be sent	capi**ēminī**: you (plural) will be taken	audi**ēminī**: you (plural) will be heard
3rd	amā**buntur**: they will be loved	docē**buntur**: they will be taught	mitt**entur**: they will be sent	capi**entur**: they will be taken	audi**entur**: they will be heard

7. Infinitives can also be passive. Consider the following examples:

Pliny the Younger, *Epistulae* 3.21.6: **Quid hominī potest <u>darī</u> māius quam glōria et laus et aeternitās?** What is able <u>to be given</u> to a man greater than glory and praise and immortality?

Tacitus, *Annales* 1.3.2: **Principēs iuventūtis <u>appellārī</u>, <u>dēstinārī</u> consulēs speciē recūsantis flagrantissimē cupīverat.** With the appearance of refusing very passionately, he (Augustus) had desired (his grandsons) <u>to be called</u> leaders of the youth, <u>to be destined</u> as consuls.

8. The following table provides the forms for the present passive infinitives. In the first, second, and fourth conjugations, the final **-e** on the present active infinitive is replaced with **-ī**. In the third conjugation (regular and **-io**), the final **-ere** on the present active infinitive is replaced with **-ī**. (N.B. It is very easy to confuse the present passive infinitive of a third conjugation verb with the first person singular perfect active of the same verb. Cf. *mittī* and *mīsī*, *capī* and *cēpī*.)

Present Active Infinitive	Present Passive Infinitive
am**ā**re: to love	amā**rī**: to be loved
doc**ē**re: to teach	docē**rī**: to be taught
mitt**ere**: to send	mitt**ī**: to be sent
cap**ere**: to take	cap**ī**: to be taken
aud**ī**re: to hear	audī**rī**: to be heard

9. Imperatives can also be passive. Consider the following examples:

Ovid, *Metamorphoses* 7.47–48: **Accingere et omnem / pelle moram.** Be equipped and cast aside every delay.

Ovid, *Metamorphoses* 9.176–78: **"Clādibus," exclāmat "Sāturnia, pascere nostrīs: / pascere, et hanc pestem spectā, crūdēlis, ab altō / corque ferum satiā."** Be sated by my ruin," he (Hercules) shouts, "O Juno, be sated and look at this destruction, O cruel one, from (your) height, and satisfy (your) wild heart."

10. The following table provides the forms for the passive imperatives. N.B. The singular imperative is identical to one variant of the second person singular present passive form (which also resembles the present active infinitive), and the plural imperative is identical to the second person plural present passive form.

Verb	Singular Passive Imperative	Plural Passive Imperative	Translation
amō, amāre	am**ā**re	amā**minī**	Be loved!
doceō, docēre	doc**ē**re	docē**minī**	Be taught!
mittō, mittere	mitt**ere**	mitti**minī**	Be sent!
capiō, capere	cap**ere**	capi**minī**	Be taken!
audiō, audīre	aud**ī**re	audī**minī**	Be heard!

11. Passive verbs are often complemented by an ablative of personal agent. This ablative construction indicates by whom the action of the verb is performed. The "by" of this construction is expressed with the Latin preposition *ā/ab* and the object of this preposition is usually a person or animal. Consider the following examples:

Cicero, *in Catilinam* 3.6: **Dūcuntur et <u>ab illīs</u> gladiī et <u>ā nostrīs</u>.** Swords are drawn <u>both by them </u>(Catiline's supporters) and <u>by our people</u>.

Pliny the Elder, *Naturalis Historia* 21.19: **Est et quae "Graeca" appellātur <u>ā nostrīs</u>, <u>ā Graecīs</u> "lychnis."** There is also (a rose) which is called "Greek" <u>by our people</u>, "shining" <u>by the Greeks</u>.

12. Passive verbs can also be complemented by an ablative of means or instrument (see *NLP* 7). The "by" of this construction is not expressed with a Latin preposition (it is understood with the ablative ending), and the noun in the ablative case is usually a thing or physical object. Consider the following examples:

Tacitus, *Germania* 1.1: **Germānia omnis ā Gallīs Raetīsque et Pannoniīs <u>Rhēnō et Dānuviō flūminibus</u>, ā Sarmatīs Dacīsque <u>mūtuō metū aut montibus</u> sēparātur.** All Germany is separated from the Gauls and Raetians and Pannonians <u>by the Rhine and Danube rivers</u>, from the Sarmatians and Dacians <u>by mutual fear or mountains</u>.

Caesar, *de Bello Gallico* 6.21.2: **Deōrum numerō eōs sōlōs dūcunt, quōs cernunt et <u>quōrum</u> apertē <u>opibus</u> iuvantur: Sōlem et Vulcānum et Lūnam.** In the number of the gods, they consider only those whom they discern and <u>by whose resources</u> they are openly helped: the Sun, Vulcan, and the Moon.

I. Required Vocabulary

NOUNS

culpa, -ae, f: blame, fault

piscīna, -ae, f: fishpond

auxilium, -iī, n: aid, help
liber, librī, m: book
milliārium, -iī, n: milestone
rīvus, -ī, m: stream
vitium, -iī, n: fault, vice

fons, fontis (-ium), m: spring, fountain
imperātor, -ōris, m: commander-in-chief, emperor, victorious general

arcus, -ūs, m: arch, vault, bow

speciēs, -iēī, f: appearance, kind, type

ADJECTIVES
dignus, -a, -um (+ ablative): worthy
iustus, -a, -um: just

vetus (veteris): old, ancient

VERBS
dēbeō, -ēre, -uī, -itus: owe, ought to
noceō, -ēre, -uī: hurt, harm, injure
timeō, -ēre, -uī: fear, dread

āmittō, -ere, -mīsī, -missus: send away, let go, lose
dīdūcō, -ere, -duxī, -ductus: draw apart, separate
exigō, -ere, -ēgī, -actus: demand, discover
petō, -ere, -īvī/iī, -ītus: seek, demand, ask, beg
solvō, -ere, solvī, solūtus: break, weaken, loosen, relax

inveniō, -īre, -vēnī, -ventus: come upon, find, meet, discover
perveniō, -īre, -vēnī, -ventus: come to, reach, arrive at

PREPOSITIONS
extrā (+ accusative): beyond, outside

CONJUNCTIONS AND ADVERBS

magis: more, to a greater extent

sīcut: as, just as

II. Translate the following sentences from Latin to English or English to Latin.

1. Utraque autem familia in dignās officiōrum speciēs dīdūcēbātur.
2. Ō hostēs, sceleribus vestrīs nocēmur!
3. Aquae duo genera ā cīvibus Rōmānīs exiguntur.
4. Post millārium XX viam quae Appia vocātur vidēbāmus.
5. Ipse pervēnī ad templum vetus cuius arcūs solvēbantur.
6. Extrā piscīnam fons magnus invenīrī debet.
7. Rēgēs magis nocent et ā nostrīs timentur.
8. Propter vitia eōrum librī poētārum nōn recipientur.
9. Water was (being) demanded by the mothers on behalf of the children.
10. The horns of the animals will not be feared by the Roman legions.
11. O temple, you ought to be cherished.
12. In the neighboring grove, our horses were injured by rocks.

The Roman Water Supply and Aqueducts

Humans have been fabricating aquifer systems for millennia, at the very least from the Bronze Age in Crete, when rudimentary aqueducts were constructed at Knossos. In the sixth century BCE at Athens, clay pipes brought water into the city from extramural springs through underground tunnels—a Persian invention that spread quickly through the Mediterranean world. At the same time, a 3,400-foot rock-hewn tunnel was constructed on Samos—a remarkable feat of engineering in its day. Aqueduct systems became steadily more elaborate over the years. By the second century BCE, at Pergamum in western Turkey, water was being siphoned into the city from a spring 15.5 miles away. There, pipes of various materials followed the contours of the terrain, descending about 600 feet over a valley before rising another thousand feet to deposit the water in a basin on top of the city's citadel.

The Pergamum aqueduct may have inspired the first full-scale aqueduct at Rome, the *Aqua Marcia*. Roman initiatives in hydraulic engineering were also influenced by their neighbors, the Etruscans, who had developed a network of drains to manage excess moisture along their west-facing coast. Built in 144–140 BCE, underwritten by spoils from campaigns against Carthage (146 BCE) and Corinth, and renowned for the purity of its water, the *Aqua Marcia* incorporated both subterranean and elevated features. The longest of the eleven aqueducts that served the city, the *Aqua Marcia* extended nearly 57 miles from the Anio valley (to the northeast of Rome), and it supplied over 49.5 million gallons of water a day in the late first century CE.

Wherever the Romans went, aqueducts were built, often as tokens of imperial or private benefaction to supply agricultural and municipal needs and luxury demands, including public baths, fountains, and latrines. In Rome alone there were 144 public latrines and more than 800 public baths. Most aqueducts were limited to a height of 70 feet, but, where greater elevation was mandated, massive pillars, narrow arches, and double tiers were employed, as at Segovia in Spain, where that spectacular aqueduct still brings water into the city. Sporting an additional tier of smaller arches on top, the Pont du Gard aqueduct at Nîmes towers 180 feet above the river. Stone slabs above the channel protect the water from sun and pollution.

At Rome, water was managed with an extensive system of lead pipes underneath the city streets (pipes were standardized by the late first century BCE). Taps and valves enabled the continuous supply of running water to be rerouted or diverted as repairs became necessary. Branch pipes led from the main line at intervals to supply public and private buildings. Most homes lacked running water, and householders continued to collect water at fountains or through their *impluvia*. There were fees for private access to the water system, and this, inevitably, led to hacking, for which there were stiff fines (10,000 sesterces!).

In 97 CE, the emperor Nerva appointed Sextus Iulius Frontinus *Cūrātor Aquārum* (supervisor of the water supply). Lacking a handbook to guide his work and wanting to prove that he was no mere rubber-stamping bureaucrat, Frontinus wrote his own, *de Aquaeductu Urbis Romae*. He consulted technical reports, official plans, and senatorial decrees. In two books, replete with fascinating details about the history of Roman aqueducts, the slaves who maintained the system, and the day-to-day administration and maintenance of the aqueduct system, the treatise is a model of Roman efficiency and practicality. Of the aqueducts, Frontinus himself declares: *Tot aquārum tam multīs necessāriīs mōlibus pȳramidas vidēlicet ōtiōsās comparēs aut cētera inertia sed fāmā celebrāta opera Graecōrum* ("Compare the pyramids, clearly idle, or other works of the Greeks, sluggish but famous, with these numerous and indispensable monuments of so much water!" *de Aquaeductu Urbis Romae* 1.16).

SUGGESTIONS FOR FURTHER READING:

Aicher, Peter J. *Guide to the Aqueducts of Ancient Rome.* Bolchazy-Carducci, 1995.
Evans, Harry B. *Water Distribution in Ancient Rome: The Evidence of Frontinus.* University of Michigan, 1997.
Hodge, A. Trevor. *Roman Aqueducts and Water Supply.* 2nd ed. Duckworth, 2002.
Landels, J.G. *Engineering in the Ancient World.* University of California, 2000.
Oleson, John Peter, ed. *The Oxford Handbook of Engineering and Technology in the Classical World.* Oxford, 2008.
Wikander, Örjan, ed. *Handbook of Ancient Water Technology.* Brill, 2000.

PASSAGES

17.1. Augustus, *Res Gestae* **20.2.** Augustus underwrote many projects to improve urban infrastructure, including the aqueduct system.

Rīvōs Aquārum complūribus locīs vetustāte lābentēs refēcī, et Aquam quae Marcia appellātur duplicāvī fonte novō in rīvum eius inmissō.

Notes: **complūrēs, -a** (plural): several; **vetustās, -ātis**, f: age; **lābens** (**-entis**): slipping, falling; **reficiō, -ere, -fēcī, -fectus**: restore, repair; **duplicō, -āre, -āvī, -ātus**: lengthen, increase; **inmissus, -a, -um**: sent (into).

17.2. **Frontinus,** *de Aquaeductu Urbis Romae* **1.4.** Nine aqueducts were actively supplying the city in Frontinus's day.

Nunc autem in urbem influunt Aqua Appia, Aniō Vetus, Marcia, Tepula, Iūlia, Virgō, Alsietīna, quae eadem vocātur Augusta, Claudia, Aniō Novus.

Notes: **influō, -ere, -fluxī, -fluxus:** flow (into); **Appius, -a, -um:** Appian (*Aqua Appia:* the first Roman aqueduct, constructed in 312 BCE by Appius Claudius Caecus, who was also responsible for the Via Appia); **Aniō, Aniēnis,** m: Anio, a tributary of the Tibur; **Tepulus, -a, -um:** warm (the source of the *Aqua Tepula* was in the Alban hills, about eleven miles from Rome; Frontinus tells us that its tepid waters, as implied by its name, were not fit to drink); **Iūlius, -a, -um:** Julian (*Aqua Iūlia:* built by Agrippa in 33 BCE); **(Aqua) Virgō:** completed by Agrippa in 19 BCE, and named, according to legend, for a young Roman girl who led thirsty soldiers to the spring that would eventually supply this aqueduct; **(Aqua) Alsietīnus, -a, -um:** completed in 2 BCE, its source was the *lacus Alsietīnus* some twenty miles west of Rome; **Claudius, -a, -um:** Claudian (*Aqua Claudia:* begun under the emperor Caligula in 38 CE and completed by his uncle Claudius by 52 CE).

17.3. **Juvenal,** *Saturae* **3.10–11.** Preparing to leave Rome and escape the anxieties of life in the big city, Juvenal's unnamed friend looks at a once majestic aqueduct, now leaky and decrepit. Meter: dactylic hexameter.

Sed dum tōta domus raedā compōnitur ūnā,
substitit ad veterēs arcūs madidamque Capēnam.

Notes: **raeda, -ae,** f: wagon, a heavy-duty four-wheeled vehicle for long distance travel; **compōnō, -ere, -posuī, -positus:** place, bring together; **subsistō, -ere, -stitī:** stop, halt; **madidus, -a, -um:** wet, moist; **Capēna, -ae,** f: the *Aqua Capena*, an extension of the *Aqua Marcia* underwritten by Domitian.

17.4. **CIL VI 1256: Rome.** This monumental inscription, displayed prominently on the Porta Praenestina (Porta Maggiore), Rome's eastern gate, records Claudius's expansion of the aqueduct system in 52 CE, which included work on the *Aqua Claudia* and the *Anio Novus*.

Ti(berius) Claudius Drūsī f(īlius) Caisar Augustus Germānicus Pontif(ex) Maxim(us), tribūniciā potestāte XII, co(n)s(ul) V, imperātor XXVII, pater patriae, Aquās Claudiam ex fontibus—quī vocābantur Caeruleus et Curtius—ā milliāriō XXXXV, item Aniēnem Novam ā milliāriō LXII suā impensā in urbem perducendās cūrāvit.

Notes: **Tiberius Claudius Caisar Augustus Germānicus, Tiberiī Claudiī Caisaris Augustī Germānicī**, m: the emperor Claudius (ruled 41–54 CE); **Drūsus, -ī**, m: son of Livia, brother of Tiberius; **pontifex maximus, pontificis maximī**, m: the chief priest at Rome, responsible for the oversight of all priestly colleges (from Augustus onward, this office was among the emperor's prerogatives); **tribūnicia potestās, tribūniciae potestātis**, f: tribunician authority, held by those elected officials whose charge was the welfare of the plebeian class. The office, open only to plebeians, carried with it the very powerful right to convoke the Senate and veto any acts of the other magistrates. Most emperors were born into the patrician class, and from Augustus onward, *tribūnicia potestās* was among the imperial prerogatives; **XII**: Claudius held this authority for 12 years by the time of the inscription's dedication (construe V and XXVII similarly); **Caeruleus, -a, -um**: blue, caerulean; **Curtius, -a, -um**: Curtian, of the Curtii, an ancient Roman *gens* (these two springs were located 300 paces from the thirty-eighth milestone of the Via Sublacensis, only 100 paces from the sources of the *Aqua Marcia*); **impensa, -ae**, f: expense; **perducendās**: "that (aqueducts) be brought in"; **cūrō, -āre, -āvī, -ātus**: provide for, undertake.

17.5. **Frontinus,** *de Aquaeductu Urbis Romae* **1.15.4–5.** Several sources of water feed the Anio Novus.

Iungitur eī rīvus Herculāneus oriens eādem viā ad mil(l)iārium trīcēsimum octāvum ē regiōne fontium Claudiae trans flūmen viamque. Nātūrā est pūrissimus, sed mixtus grātiam splendōris suī āmittit.

Notes: **iungō, -ere, iunxi, iunctus**: join, unite, harness; **eī**: the *Novus Anio*; **Herculāneus, -a, -um**: of Hercules; **oriens (-ientis)**: rising (from); **(Aquae) Claudiae; trans** (+ accusative): across; **pūrissimus, -a, -um**: cleanest, most pure; **mixtus, -a, -um**: mixed (e.g., when the waters of the Herculanean stream mingle with those of the *Novus Anio*); **grātia, -iae**, f: pleasantness; **splendor, -ōris**, m: brilliance, magnificence.

17.6. **Frontinus,** *de Aquaeductu Urbis Romae* **1.20.** Pipes distributed water underneath the city streets.

Fīniuntur arcūs eārum post hortōs Pallantiānōs et inde in ūsum urbis fistulīs dīdūcuntur.

Notes: **fīniō, -īre, -īvī, -ītus**: bound, limit, enclose; **eārum**: the *Aquae Anio* and *Claudia*; **hortus, -ī**, m: garden; **Pallantiānus, -a, -um**: of Pallas, Claudius's freedman (these spectacular gardens were laid out on the Esquiline Hill); **ūsus, -ūs**, m: use, enjoyment; **fistula, -ae**, f: tube, pipe.

17.7. Frontinus, *de Aquaeductu Urbis Romae* 1.26. Even in antiquity, pipe gauges were standardized.

Omnis autem modulus colligitur aut diamētrō aut perimētrō aut āreae mensūrā, ex quibus et capācitās appāret.

Notes: **modulus, -ī,** m: efflux tube; **colligō, -ere, -lēgī, -lectus:** collect, "gauge"; **diamēter, -trī,** m: diameter; **perimēter, -trī,** m: circumference; **ārea, āreae,** f: area, open space; **mensūra, -ae,** f: proportion, measure; **capācitās, -ātis,** f: capacity, breadth; **appāreō, -ēre, -uī, -itus:** appear, become evident.

17.8. Frontinus, *de Aquaeductu Urbis Romae* 2.117. At Rome, two gangs of slaves were charged with the daily maintenance of the aqueducts. One belonged to the state, the other to the emperor. Within each group, individual slaves specialized in the many tasks necessary to keep the water flowing into the city at a steady and predictable rate.

Utraque autem familia in aliquot ministeriōrum speciēs dīdūcitur: vīlicōs, castellāriōs, circitōrēs, silicāriōs, tectōrēs, aliōsque opificēs.

Notes: **aliquot** (indeclinable): some, several; **ministerium, -iī,** n: employment, service; **vīlicus, -ī,** m: overseer; **castellārius, -iī,** m: reservoir keeper; **circitor, -ōris,** m: inspector; **silicārius, -iī,** m: paver; **tector, -ōris,** m: plasterer; **opifex, -icis,** m: craftsman.

17.9. Frontinus, *de Aquaeductu Urbis Romae* 2.120. The aqueducts required regular attention, maintenance, and repairs for many reasons, both natural and manmade.

Nascuntur opera ex hīs causīs: aut impotentiā possessōrum quid corrumpitur aut vetustāte aut vī tempestātium aut culpā male factī operis, quod saepius accidit in recentibus.

Notes: **opera nascuntur:** "necessity of repairs arises"; **impotentia, -iae,** f: lack of self-restraint, lawlessness; **possessor, -ōris,** m: owner (whose property abuts the aqueduct); **quid** = *aliquid*; **corrumpō, -ere, -rūpī, -ruptus:** break, destroy; **vetustās, -ātis,** f: age, antiquity, long duration; **male:** badly, poorly; **factus, -a, -um:** done, completed; **saepius:** rather frequently; **accidō, -ere, -cīdī:** happen; **recentibus:** "in recent times."

17.10. Frontinus, *de Aquaeductu Urbis Romae* 2.126. Trees could potentially do great harm to aqueduct infrastructure.

Arborēs magis nocent, quārum rādīcibus concamerātiōnēs et latera solvuntur.

Notes: **arbor, -oris**, f: tree; **rādix, -īcis**, f: root; **concamerātiō, -iōnis**, f: vaulted roof; **latus, lateris**, n: side.

17.11. Vitruvius, *de Architectura* 8.3.15. Some water sources were poisonous, and precautions were taken to protect the locals.

Etiamque inveniuntur aquae genera mortifera, quae per maleficum sūcum terrae percurrentia recipiunt in sē vim venēnātam, utī fuisse dīcitur Terracīnae fons, quī vocābātur Neptūnius. Ex quō quī biberant inprūdentēs vītā prīvābantur; quāpropter antīquī eum obstruxisse dīcuntur.

Notes: **mortifer, -fera, -ferum**: deadly, fatal; **maleficus, -a, -um**: evil-doing, harmful, injurious; **sūcus, -ī**, m: sap; **percurrens (-entis)**: running through; **venēnātus, -a, -um**: poisonous; **utī**: as, just like; **Terracīna, -ae**, f: a town about 45 miles southeast of Rome on the Appian Way; **Neptūnius, -a, -um**: of Neptune (this spring contained arsenic, one of several mineral springs by the coast); **bibō, -ere, bibī, bibitus**: drink; **inprūdens (-entis)**: unaware, ignorant, rash; **prīvō, -āre, -āvī, -ātus**: strip, deprive of; **quāpropter**: wherefore; **antīquus, -a, -um**: ancient, old; **obstruō, -ere, -struxī, -structus**: block, stop.

17.12. Pliny the Younger, *Epistulae* 10.90.1. Before consulting Trajan, Pliny investigated the costs and feasibility of an aqueduct at Sinope, including the location and quality of a source of water.

Sinōpensēs, domine, aquā dēficiuntur, quae vidētur et bona et cōpiōsa ab sextō decimō mīliāriō posse perdūcī.

Notes: **Sinōpensēs, -ium**, m (plural): the people of Sinope, a seaport town on the southern coast of the Black Sea; **dēficiō, -ere, -fēcī, -fectus**: fail, run short; **cōpiōsus, -a, -um**: plentiful, abundant; **mīliāriō** = *milliāriō*.

EXTRA PASSAGES: SPRINGS, FOUNTAINS AND BATHS

Both natural and artificial sources of water provided pleasure to the Romans, who found just as much delight in springs and fountains in the countryside as they did in the luxurious baths of the city.

17.13. Horace, *Carmina* 3.13.1–5. Horace immortalizes his Bandusian spring, one of the refreshingly cool springs on his beloved Sabine farm. This ode has long been admired as a masterpiece of Latin poetry. Meter: fourth Asclepiadean.

Ō fons Bandusiae splendidiŏr vitrō,
dulcī digne merō nōn sine flōribus,
crās dōnāberis haedō,
      cui frons turgida cornibus
prīmīs et venerem et proelia dēstinat.

Notes: **Bandusia, -iae**, f: the site of this famous spring, possibly near Venusia in Apulia, southeastern Italy; **splendidiŏr, -ius** (+ ablative): brighter (than), clearer (than), more brilliant (than); **vitrum, -ī**, n: glass; **merum, -ī**, n: undiluted wine; **flōs, flŏris**, m: flower, blossom; **crās**: tomorrow; **dōnō, -āre, -āvī, -ātus**: give, present with; **haedus, -ī**, m: kid, young goat; **turgidus, -a, -um**: swollen (with), budding (with); **venus, veneris**, f: charm, love; **dēstinō, -āre, -āvī, -ātus**: fix upon, settle, appoint.

17.14. Tacitus, *Agricola* 21.2. The Britons were so eager to please Agricola, their even-handed Roman governor (77–85 CE), that they embraced Roman culture, but, like the Romans, they began to overindulge in the luxuries of city living, including the baths.

Inde etiam habitūs nostrī honor et frequens toga; paulātimque discessum ad dēlēnīmenta vitiōrum: porticūs et balinea et convīviōrum ēlegantiam. Idque apud imperītōs "hūmānitās" vocābātur, cum pars servitūtis esset.

Notes: **habitus, -ūs**, m: style; **frequens (-entis)**: usual, common; **paulātim**: gradually, little by little; **discessum** (*est*): "there was a departure"; **dēlēnīmentum, -ī**, n: charm; **porticus, -ūs**, m: colonnade, gallery; **balineum, -ī**, n: bath; **convīvium, -iī**, n: feast, banquet; **ēlegantia, -iae**, f: refinement, grace; **imperītus, -a, -um**: unskilled, inexperienced, ignorant; **hūmānitās, -ātis**, f: culture, refinement; **cum . . . esset**: "although it was (part)"; **servitūs, -ūtis**, f: slavery, servitude.

17.15. Martial 3.44.12–18. Wherever he goes (even into the baths, where he expects a little privacy!), Martial is absolutely unable to avoid Ligurnius's bad recitations of his bad poetry. Meter: hendecasyllabics.

> In thermās fugiō: sonās ad aurem.
> Piscīnam petō: nōn licet natāre.
> Ad cēnam properō: tenēs euntem.
> Ad cēnam veniō: fugās edentem.
> Lassus dormio: suscitās iacentem.
> Vīs, quantum faciās malī, vidēre?
> Vir iustus, probus, innocens timēris.

Notes: **thermae, -ārum**, f (plural): warm baths; **sonō, -āre, sonuī, sonitus**: resound, echo harshly; **auris, -is (-ium)**, f: ear; **licet, -ēre, licuit** (+ dative): it is permitted; the final -o in *peto* and *dormio* scans short for the meter to work out correctly; **natō, -āre, -āvī, -ātus**: swim; **cēna, -ae**, f: dinner; **properō, -āre, -āvī, -ātus**: hurry; **(mē) euntem**: "(me) going"; **fugō, -āre, -āvī, -ātus**: put to flight, chase away; **(me) edentem**: "(me) eating"; **lassus, -a, -um**: tired, exhausted; **suscitō, -āre, -āvī, -atus**: stir, rouse, wake up; **(me) iacentem**: "(me) lying down"; **quantum faciās malī**: "how much evil you can do"; **probus, -a, -um**: good, excellent, fine; **innocens (-entis)**: harmless, blameless.

Passive Verbs: Perfect, Pluperfect, and Future Perfect Tenses

1. As we learned in *NLP* 13, three tenses form the **PERFECT SYSTEM**: perfect, pluperfect, and future perfect. In this lesson, you will learn the forms of these tenses in the passive voice, all of which are derived from the fourth principal part in combination with a form of *esse*. Just as they did for the active forms of the perfect system, all four conjugations follow the same pattern.

2. The passive forms of the perfect system are all two-word verb phrases: the fourth principal part acts as an adjective (**-us, -a, -um**) in agreement with its subject and declines accordingly; the second word of the verb form is a form of *esse*. Consider the following examples:

Sallust, *Bellum Catilinae* 1.2: **Sed nostra omnis <u>vīs</u> in animō et corpore <u>sita est</u>**. But all our <u>strength</u> <u>has been placed</u> in the spirit and body.
  Sita is nominative, singular, feminine, agreeing with *vīs*, the subject of *sita est*.

Tacitus, *Annales*, 2.41.2: **Bellumque, quia conficere <u>prohibitus erat</u>, prō confectō accipiēbātur**. And the war was accepted as resolved because <u>he</u> (Germanicus) <u>had been prevented</u> from completing (it).
  Prohibitus is nominative, singular, masculine, agreeing with Germanicus, the understood subject of *prohibitus erat*.

Sallust, *Bellum Catilinae* 51.25: **At enim quis reprehendet, <u>quod</u> in parricīdās reī pūblicae <u>decrētum erit</u>?** For who will censure <u>what</u> <u>will have been decreed</u> against parricides of the state?

Decrētum is nominative, singular, neuter, agreeing with *quod*, the subject of *decrētum erit*.

3. The **PERFECT PASSIVE** is formed with the fourth principal part, declined to agree with the subject, and the **present tense** of *esse*. Study the following table:

PERFECT PASSIVE OF PARADIGM VERBS

	1st Conj.	2nd Conj.	3rd Conj.	3rd Conj. (-io)	4th Conj.
Singular					
1st	amātus, -a, -um sum: I have been loved	doctus, -a, -um sum: I have been taught	missus, -a, -um sum: I have been sent	captus, -a, -um sum: I have been taken	audītus, -a, -um sum: I have been heard
2nd	amātus, -a, -um es: you have been loved	doctus, -a, -um es: you have been taught	missus, -a, -um es: you have been sent	captus, -a, -um es: you have been taken	audītus, -a, -um es: you have been heard
3rd	amātus, -a, -um est: he/she/it has been loved	doctus, -a, -um est: he/she/it has been taught	missus, -a, -um est: he/she/it has been sent	captus, -a, -um est: he/she/it has been taken	audītus, -a, -um est: he/she/it has been heard
Plural					
1st	amātī, -ae, -a sumus: we have been loved	doctī, -ae, -a sumus: we have been taught	missī, -ae, -a sumus: we have been sent	captī, -ae, -a sumus: we have been taken	audītī, -ae, -a sumus: we have been heard
2nd	amātī, -ae, -a estis: you have been loved	doctī, -ae, -a estis: you have been taught	missī, -ae, -a estis: you have been sent	captī, -ae, -a estis: you have been taken	audītī, -ae, -a estis: you have been heard
3rd	amātī, -ae, -a sunt: they have been loved	doctī, -ae, -a sunt: they have been taught	missī, -ae, -a sunt: they have been sent	captī, -ae, -a sunt: they have been taken	audītī, -ae, -a sunt: they have been heard

4. The **PLUPERFECT PASSIVE** is formed with the fourth principal part, declined to agree with the subject, and the **imperfect tense** of *esse*. Study the following table:

PLUPERFECT PASSIVE OF PARADIGM VERBS

	1st Conj.	2nd Conj.	3rd Conj.	3rd Conj. (-io)	4th Conj.
Singular					
1st	amātus, -a, -um **eram:** I had been loved	doctus, -a, -um **eram:** I had been taught	missus, -a, -um **eram:** I had been sent	captus, -a, -um **eram:** I had been taken	audītus, -a, -um **eram:** I had been heard
2nd	amātus, -a, -um **erās:** you had been loved	doctus, -a, -um **erās:** you had been taught	missus, -a, -um **erās:** you had been sent	captus, -a, -um **erās:** you had been taken	audītus, -a, -um **erās:** you had been heard
3rd	amātus, -a, -um **erat:** he/she/it had been loved	doctus, -a, -um **erat:** he/she/it had been taught	missus, -a, -um **erat:** he/she/it had been sent	captus, -a, -um **erat:** he/she/it had been taken	audītus, -a, -um **erat:** he/she/it had been heard
Plural					
1st	amātī, -ae, -a **erāmus:** we had been loved	doctī, -ae, -a **erāmus:** we had been taught	missī, -ae, -a **erāmus:** we had been sent	captī, -ae, -a **erāmus:** we had been taken	audītī, -ae, -a **erāmus:** we had been heard
2nd	amātī, -ae, -a **erātis:** you had been loved	doctī, -ae, -a **erātis:** you had been taught	missī, -ae, -a **erātis:** you had been sent	captī, -ae, -a **erātis:** you had been taken	audītī, -ae, -a **erātis:** you had been heard
3rd	amātī, -ae, -a **erant:** they had been loved	doctī, -ae, -a **erant:** they had been taught	missī, -ae, -a **erant:** they had been sent	captī, -ae, -a **erant:** they had been taken	audītī, -ae, -a **erant:** they had been heard

5. The **FUTURE PERFECT PASSIVE** is formed with the fourth principal part, declined to agree with the subject, and the **future tense** of *esse*. Study the table on the following page.

FUTURE PERFECT PASSIVE OF PARADIGM VERBS

	1st Conj.	2nd Conj.	3rd Conj.	3rd Conj. (-io)	4th Conj.
Singular					
1st	amātus, -a, -um **erō:** I shall have been loved	doctus, -a, -um **erō:** I shall have been taught	missus, -a, -um **erō:** I shall have been sent	captus, -a, -um **erō:** I shall have been taken	audītus, -a, -um **erō:** I shall have been heard
2nd	amātus, -a, -um **eris:** you will have been loved	doctus, -a, -um **eris:** you will have been taught	missus, -a, -um **eris:** you will have been sent	captus, -a, -um **eris:** you will have been taken	audītus, -a, -um **eris:** you will have been heard
3rd	amātus, -a, -um **erit:** he/she/it will have been loved	doctus, -a, -um **erit:** he/she/it will have been taught	missus, -a, -um **erit:** he/she/it will have been sent	captus, -a, -um **erit:** he/she/it will have been taken	audītus, -a, -um **erit:** he/she/it will have been heard
Plural					
1st	amātī, -ae, -a **erimus:** we shall have been loved	doctī, -ae, -a **erimus:** we shall have been taught	missī, -ae, -a **erimus:** we shall have been sent	captī, -ae, -a **erimus:** we shall have been taken	audītī, -ae, -a **erimus:** we shall have been heard
2nd	amātī, -ae, -a **eritis:** you will have been loved	doctī, -ae, -a **eritis:** you will have been taught	missī, -ae, -a **eritis:** you will have been sent	captī, -ae, -a **eritis:** you will have been taken	audītī, -ae, -a **eritis:** you will have been heard
3rd	amātī, -ae, -a **erunt:** they will have been loved	doctī, -ae, -a **erunt:** they will have been taught	missī, -ae, -a **erunt:** they will have been sent	captī, -ae, -a **erunt:** they will have been taken	audītī, -ae, -a **erunt:** they will have been heard

6. Just as the present passive system has a present passive infinitive, the perfect passive system has a perfect passive infinitive. Consider the following examples:

Ovid, *Metamorphoses* 9.25–26: **Ēlige, <u>fictum / esse</u> Iovem mālīs, an tē per dēdecus ortum?** Choose, would you prefer Jove <u>to have been invented</u> or yourself to have been born through disgrace?

Cicero, *in Catilinam* 5: **Vērum ego hoc, quod iam prīdem <u>factum esse</u> oportuit, certā dē causā nōndum addūcor ut faciam.** But I am not yet compelled from a certain reason to do this which ought <u>to have been done</u> already in time past.

7. The **PERFECT PASSIVE INFINITIVE** is formed with the fourth principal part, declined to agree with its subject, and the **infinitive *esse***. Study the following table:

PERFECT PASSIVE INFINITIVE

1st Conj.	2nd Conj.	3rd Conj.	3rd Conj. (-io)	4th Conj.
amātus, -a, -um esse: to have been loved	doctus, -a, -um esse: to have been taught	missus, -a, -um esse: to have been sent	captus, -a, -um esse: to have been captured	audītus, -a, -um esse: to have been heard

8. Remember, as you learned in *NLP* 17, that passive verbs are often complemented by an ablative of personal agent or an ablative of means. Consider the following examples:

Catullus 87.2: **. . . quantum <u>ā mē</u> Lesbia amāta mea est**. . . . as much as my Lesbia has been loved <u>by me</u>.

Ā mē is an ablative of personal agent.

Ovid, *Metamorphoses* 1.530: **Auctaque forma <u>fugā</u> est**. And her (Daphne's) beauty was augmented <u>by (her) flight</u>.

Fugā is an ablative of means.

I. Required Vocabulary

NOUNS

littera, -ae, f: letter of the alphabet; in plural: dispatch, epistle

initium, -iī, n: beginning

auctor, -ōris, m: originator, proposer, founder

aedēs, -is (-ium), f: temple, shrine; room, house, home

auctōritās, -ātis, f: responsibility, authority

imāgō, imāginis, f: image, likeness, copy

pax, pācis, f: peace, harmony
potestās, -ātis, f: power, control, authority

currus, -ūs, m: chariot
exercitus, -ūs, m: army
metus, -ūs, m: fear, dread
senātus, -ūs, m: Senate

aciēs, -iēī, f: edge, battleline, battle

PRONOUNS
quisquam, quicquam / quidquam: any (single) person, anyone at all

ADJECTIVES
antīquus, -a, -um: ancient, old
aureus, -a, -um: golden
cēterus, -a, -um: other, the rest
dīvus, -a, -um: divine, deified

plūs (plūris): more

VERBS
mūtō, -āre, -āvī, -ātus: change, alter, shift

caedō, -ere, cecīdī, caesus: cut down, strike, beat, kill
contemnō, -ere, -tempsī, -temptus: despise
iaciō, -ere, iēcī, iactus: throw, hurl
indīcō, -ere, -dixī, -dictus: declare, point out
sinō, -ere, sīvī, situs: allow, leave; place, lay down, bury

dēferō, -ferre, -tulī, -lātus: bring down, hand over

CONJUNCTIONS AND ADVERBS
ferē: nearly, almost
mox: soon
posteā: afterwards
quasi: as if
quondam: once, formerly

II. Translate the following sentences from
Latin to English or English to Latin.

1. Ductī erant in urbem meam imperātor maximus et exercitūs.
2. Imāginēs meī ā populīs Rōmānīs multōs annōs habitae sunt.
3. Senātus Iulium Caesarem dīvum hīc sinī iubet.
4. Hostis indictus es et tuum nōmen contemptum est.
5. Saxa ingentia ad mīlitēs iacta sunt et aliquī ab aciē ad nāvēs fūgērunt.
6. Currus aureus in aede meā positus erit.
7. Cēterum gestae erant rēs et auctor turpis rīsus est.
8. In bellī initiō pauca oppida caesa sunt et pax in metum auctōritāte Rōmānā mūtāta est.
9. The command of the cities had been sought by the fierce kings.
10. The Roman army ought to have been despised by you (plural).
11. The emperor has been killed by rocks, and we have been separated into three camps.
12. For almost ten years peace has been cherished by the citizens.

Imperium *and Empire*

Roman imperial aspirations date from the city's earliest days, from Romulus's abduction and rape of the Sabine women, which resulted in an alliance between the Romans and their Sabine neighbors, to the wars of expansion into central Italy against the Etruscans and Samnites (sixth to early third century BCE), to wars for control of the western Mediterranean against the Carthaginians (third and second centuries BCE). Rome was a fighting nation, and her nobility earned glory and renown from successes in the field of battle. In the context of a healthy Republic, when troops were drawn strictly from landowning citizens, military glory enhanced the political careers of Cincinnatus, Cato the Elder and Scipio Africanus (heroes of the second Punic War), and others. This changed with the army reforms of Gaius Marius (see *NLP* 7). By eliminating the requirement that Roman soldiers own land, Marius created a standing professional army whose allegiance was no longer to the state, but rather to the successful commander who secured for his men regular wages, terms of service, a percentage of war booty, and—perhaps most importantly—a grant of land for retired men. This new culture propelled the political careers and imperial aspirations of Marius, Sulla, Pompey, Crassus, Julius Caesar, his nephew Octavian (Augustus), and Marc Antony. This trajectory was a significant factor in Rome's conversion from Republic to Empire. The right to lead an army was among the special prerogatives of the highest elected officials in republican Rome (Praetor, Consul, Dictator): a victorious general was acclaimed "*imperātor*" by his troops; and grand triumphal parades, awarded by senatorial vote, were the public expressions of thanksgiving to returning generals.

Augustus had declared the Republic "restored" in 27 BCE, but his authority was clearly greater than that of any previous Roman magistrate. Among other things, Augustus retained control over the standing army. He distributed the legions throughout the frontier provinces, many days' march from the city and where they could not easily threaten the safety of the *imperātor* or figure into the bloody political games that were so prevalent in the final decades of the Republic. This connection between the *imperātor* and his army, in fact, would always drive the emperorship. Although Germanicus's young son Gaius Caligula ("Little Boot" after the army garb he wore as a toddler) was the darling of the army in Germany, as an adult he had no experience in the field but craved the glory of triumph. Caligula exaggerated the surrender of a British prince (claiming that all of Britain had capitulated to him), fabricated battles on the Rhine against his own German guardsmen, and—abandoning a poorly planned invasion of Britain in 40 CE—declared victory over Neptune (like Caesar's troops nearly a century before, Caligula's had probably threatened to mutiny before crossing the foreboding English Channel). Caligula ordered his troops to "gather the spoils of the ocean" (seashells: Suetonius, *de Vita Gaii* 46), and he marched back to Rome, where he celebrated his unmerited triumph. Three years later and perhaps with greater sincerity, Claudius, eschewing the Senate's vote of (unearned) triumphal regalia, sought credibility with the army by an invasion of Britain "of which no one had attempted a conquest" since Julius Caesar's expeditions of 55/54 BCE (Suetonius, *de Vita Claudii* 17). Claudius, in fact, did visit the island, receiving the surrender of "eleven kings without any loss" and participating as a conquering general in the final march on Camulodunum (Colchester)—possibly even with war elephants.

The virtual calm during Hadrian's reign (117–138 CE) as well as his lack of military experience, in part inspired an extensive public works program throughout the Empire, including aqueducts, temple restoration, and the walls in Britain and Germany (rebellion was less likely fomented when the army was kept occupied).

Just as Tiberius controlled the city through the elite imperial bodyguard, the Praetorian Guard, other emperors would find this branch of service the key to securing or losing power. Caligula was executed by a Praetorian guardsman (Cassius Chaerea), and his uncle Claudius, Germanicus's youngest brother, was declared emperor by those very same troops. The Praetorians also ensured Nero's ascension but deserted him in the end. The Guard remained loyal to the pragmatic Vespasian (who reduced their numbers), to his cruel son Domitian (who increased their pay), and even to Commodus, Marcus Aurelius's vicious son, who was slain by an imperial freedman. After Domitian's death in 96 CE, the Guard refused to endorse the Senate's choice for emperor, the elderly Nerva (96–98 CE), unless he adopted and named as his successor the popular and capable Trajan (98–117 CE), the Spanish-born general of the German legions.

From the death of Augustus, it became imperial practice for the ascending emperor to pay donatives to the troops, partly to secure their loyalty. Galba's refusal of this bequest to the Praetorians in 68 CE after Nero's suicide cost him both their support and the emperorship. The Praetorian Guard duly executed the stingy Galba, transferred their allegiance to Otho, and fought fiercely on his behalf at the very bloody battle of Cremona in 69 CE. They remained loyal to the deceased emperor, eventually executing Otho's successor, the gluttonous Vitellius. By the late second century, the donative was so perfunctory that the Praetorian Guard dared to hold an auction of the Empire. In 193 CE, after the Praetorians assassinated Commodus's successor Pertinax (ruled January to March 193 CE) for defiantly attempting to impose discipline on the corps, the wealthy Didius Julianus purchased the emperorship and the loyalties of the Praetorians for 6,250 drachmas per guardsman (outbidding Pertinax's father-in-law Sulpicianus who offered a meager 5,000 drachmas per guardsman!) but was soon abandoned by them, ushering in a new period of civil war. By the third century, the Praetorian Guard and other branches of the army were so strong that, succumbing to the combined pressures of civil war, disease, economic depression, and wars on two simultaneous fronts, Rome fell into a period of military anarchy. From 235 to 284 CE, the emperorship was claimed by twenty-two legitimate emperors and forty usurpers who rose from the army's ranks. Of these sixty or so men, only two died in battle against foreign enemies (Gordian III, 244 CE; Decius, 251 CE), one was struck by lightning (Carus, 283 CE), one died from the plague (Gothicus, 270 CE), and a fifth was tortured to death by the Sassanids (Valerian, 260 CE). The rest either died in battle against rivals or were assassinated by their own troops.

SUGGESTIONS FOR FURTHER READING:

Beard, Mary. *The Roman Triumph*. Harvard, 2007.
Bingham, Sandra J. *The Praetorian Guard: A History of Rome's Elite Special Forces*. I. B. Tauris. 2013.
Gruen, Erich S. "Augustus and the Making of the Principate." In *The Cambridge Companion to the Age of Augustus*, edited by Karl Galinsky, 33–51. Cambridge, 2005.
Hekster, Olivier. *Rome and Its Empire, AD 193–284*. Debates and Documents in Ancient History. University of Edinburgh, 2008.
Morgan, Gwyn. *69 A.D.: The Year of the Four Emperors*. Oxford, 2006.
Southern, Patricia. *The Roman Empire from Severus to Constantine*. Routledge, 2001.
Syme, Ronald. *The Roman Revolution*. Oxford, 1931.

PASSAGES

18.1. Augustus, *Res Gestae* **4.3.** In August 29 BCE, Augustus celebrated three military triumphs, for victories in Dalmatia, Actium, and Egypt. Augustus here shows how these parades personified the Roman (imperial) subjugation of enemy states.

In triumphīs meīs ductī sunt ante currum meum rēgēs aut rēgum līberī novem.

Notes: **triumphus, -ī**, m: triumphal parade, triumph.

18.2. Augustus, *Res Gestae* **26.5.** As emperor, Augustus's authority as commander-in-chief extended into the Middle East and Africa.

Meō iussū et auspiciō ductī sunt duo exercitūs eōdem ferē tempore in Aethiopiam et in Ārabiam (quae appellātur Eudaemon), magnaeque hostium gentis utriusque cōpiae caesae sunt in aciē et complūra oppida capta.

Notes: **iussū**: by order; **auspicium, -iī**, n: guidance, protection; **Aethiopia, -iae**, f: a kingdom extending from the upper Nile into the regions south of the Sahara; **Eudaemon (-onis)**: of good omen, blessed (a Greek adjective: here it refers to the province of *Ārabia Fēlix*, extending into the southern portion of the Arabian Peninsula); **complūrēs, -a** (plural): several; **capta** (*sunt*).

18.3. Augustus, *Res Gestae* **31.1.** As emperor, Augustus extended Roman diplomatic ties farther than any of his predecessors.

Ad mē ex Indiā rēgum lēgātiōnēs saepe missae sunt, nōn vīsae ante id tempus apud quemquam Rōmānōrum dūcem.

Notes: **India, -iae**, f: Alexander the Great had campaigned in the Indian subcontinent in 327/6 BCE, reaching as far as the Punjab until his mutinous troops forced retreat; **lēgātiō, -iōnis**, f: envoy; **vīsus, -a, -um**: seen.

18.4. Augustus, *Res Gestae* **34.2–3.** The Senate awarded Augustus with many imperial accolades.

Quō prō meritō meō, senātūs consultō, "Augustus" appellātus sum, et laureīs postēs aedium meārum vestītī pūblicē, corōnaque cīvica super iānuam meam fixa est, et clupeus aureus in cūriā Iūliā positus.

Notes: **meritum, -ī**, n: benefit, service; **consultum, -ī**, n: decree; **laurea, -ae**, f: laurel, sacred to Augustus's patron god Apollo, and a symbol of victory; **postis, -is (-ium)**, m: doorpost; **vestiō, -īre, -īvī, -ītus**: dress, adorn, clothe; **vestītī** (*sunt*); **pūblicē**: publicly; **corōna, -ae**, f: garland, wreath, crown; **cīvicus, -a, -um**: civic (the *corōna cīvica*, of oak, was awarded to a Roman who had saved the life of a fellow citizen during battle); **iānua, -ae**, f: door; **fīgō, -ere, fixī, fixus**: fasten, attach, fix; **clupeus** = *clipeus, -ī*, m: a large round shield carried by Roman soldiers; **cūria Iūlia, cūriae Iūliae**, f: the Senate House, whose construction began under Caesar in 44 BCE just before his assassination, not completed until 29 BCE, when it was dedicated by Augustus; **positus** (*est*).

18.5. Suetonius, *Vita Caligulae* 44.2. With his typical bravura, Caligula decides to "conquer" Britain, but never crosses the Channel. Upon returning to the city, he celebrated a grand (and unearned) triumph.

Quasi ūniversa trādita insula, magnificās Rōmam litterās mīsit.

Notes: **ūniversus, -a, -um**: entire; **trādita** (*erat*); **magnificus, -a, -um**: grand, splendid, boastful.

18.6. Tacitus, *Annales* 13.41.4. Rome's Parthian War (58–63 CE) was spearheaded by a brilliant Roman general Gnaius Domitius Corbulo. Although the emperor Nero never took to the field, after Corbulo's successes in 58 CE against Parthia's ally, the Armenian king Tiridates, the emperor received senatorial credit for the victory.

Ob haec consalūtātus imperātor Nero, et, senātūs consultō, supplicātiōnēs habitae, statuaeque et arcūs et continuī consulātūs principī.

Notes: **haec**: Corbulo's successes against Tiridates; **consalūtō, -āre, -āvī, -ātus**: greet, hail; **consalūtātus** (*est*); **imperātor**: appositive; **supplicātiō, -iōnis**, f: thanksgiving, religious festival, supplication; **habitae** (*sunt*); **statua, -ae**, f: statue; **continuus, -a, -um**: uninterrupted, successive; **consulātus, -ūs**, m: consulship; supply *decrētī sunt* ("they were decreed") as the verb governing this clause.

18.7. Tacitus, *Historiae* 1.64.1. After Nero's suicide in 68 CE, Rome plunged into civil war, and a series of candidates assumed the throne in 69 CE, the "Year of the Four Emperors." By January, Otho had ousted the aged Galba. But the gluttonous Vitellius rallied legions in Germany to make his own bid. As the legions aligned themselves with one candidate or another, so too did most of the provinces, although, as we learn here, it was often difficult to choose among the candidates.

Gallīs cunctātiō exempta est: in Othōnem ac Vitellium odium pār, ex Vitelliō et metus.

Notes: **Gallī, -ōrum**, m (plural): the people of Gaul; **cunctātiō, -iōnis**, f: delay, hesitation; **eximō, -ere, -ēmī, -emptus**: take away, remove; **Othō, -ōnis**, m: 32–69 CE, an extravagant noble among Nero's coterie until 58 CE, when he was forced to divorce his beautiful wife Poppaea Sabina, who then married Nero; **Vitellius, -iī**, m: he reigned from April 16 to December 22, when he was executed by Vespasian's forces in Rome; **odium, -iī**, n: hatred.

18.8. Pliny the Younger, *Epistulae* 9.19.1. In 67 CE, Vindex, a noble from Gallia Aquitania, led a revolt against Nero in opposition to the imperial tax policy. Upon Nero's demise, Vindex declared allegiance to Galba, governor of Hispania Tarraconensis, hoping to gain his support. Verginius Rufus ("Red"), however, with troops in Germania Superior, defeated and killed Vindex, and, remarkably, he declined the crown when his troops declared their support. For this, Rufus was so widely admired that he received a state funeral when he died in 97 CE. His epitaph is recorded by Pliny, his ward and neighbor.

Hīc situs est Rūfus, pulsō quī Vindice quondam imperium asseruit nōn sibi sed patriae.

Notes: **pulsō ... Vindice**: "Vindex having been defeated" (ablative absolute); **asserviō, -īre, -uī / īvī**: devote, assist, help.

18.9. Tacitus, *Historiae* 2.76.2. After the ascension of Vitellius, Vespasian, commander of the Roman armies in the East, contemplates his own imperial aspirations and the dangers of civil war. With growing support from the eastern troops, the current governor of Syria, Gaius Licinius Mucianus, urges Vespasian to make a bid for the sake of the state and his own good name.

"Ego tē, Vespasiāne, ad imperium vocō; quam salūtāre Reī pūblicae, quam tibi magnificum, iuxtā deōs in tuā manū positum est."

Notes: **quam ... quam**: as ... as; **salūtāris, -e**: healthful, advantageous; **magnificus, -a, um**: see *NLP* 18.5; **iuxtā** (+ accusative): close to, near to; **positum est**: understand *imperium* as the subject.

18.10. Suetonius, *Vita Vespasiani* 4.5. In 69 CE, while Rome was distracted by civil war, several provinces, including Judea, took the opportunity to revolt from Roman authority. The political situation in the East was particularly delicate, and it was important to choose an able commander who would neither abuse his position nor have imperial aspirations, especially given the prophecy that the next world leader would come from the East. Accordingly, Vespasian was chosen to quell the uprising in Judea.

Ipse potissimus dēlectus est, ut et industriae expertae nec metuendus ullō modō ob humilitātem generis ac nōminis.

Notes: **potissimus, -a, -um**: best, most powerful; **dēligō, -ere, -lēgī, -lectus**: pick, choose, select; **ut**: as; **industria, -iae**, f: diligence, industry; **expertus, -a, -um**: tested, proven, experienced; **metuendus, -a, -um**: to be feared; **humilitās, -ātis**, f: obscurity, insignificance.

18.11. *Scriptores Historiae Augustae: Vita Hadriani* **17.10.** This strange collection of imperial biographies (composed around 300 CE), meant to pick up where Suetonius left off, includes some thirty biographies of emperors from Hadrian (ruled 117–138 CE) to Numerianus (assassinated in 284 CE). It is marred by historical inaccuracies and references to inauthentic documents, and scholars have hotly debated its nature and purpose, concluding that it might be historical fiction or even satire. Nonetheless, much of the history is genuine, and it often provides our only written source for this period. We see here that foreign diplomacy remained an abiding concern for the emperors, and Hadrian's relationship with foreign rulers varied greatly.

Rēgibus multīs plūrimum dētulit, ā plērīsque vērō etiam pācem redēmit, ā nōnnullīs contemptus est.

Notes: **plūrimum, -ī**, n: the most; **plērusque, plēraque, plērumque**: very many, a large part; **redimō, -ere, -ēmī, -emptus**: buy, procure, obtain; **nōnnullus, -a, -um**: some.

18.12. *Scriptores Historiae Augustae: Vita Marci Aurelii* **9.1–2.** From the Republic onward, victorious generals took on honorific names from the peoples they conquered (Scipio who vanquished Carthage in the Second Punic War was known as Africanus; Claudius's son was called Brittanicus in honor of the conquest of that island). It was humility for emperors to decline honorifics, but grace to accept them later, despite the fact that they rarely saw military action.

Gestae sunt rēs in Armeniā prosperē per Statium Priscum Artaxatīs captīs, dēlātumque Armeniācum nōmen utrīque principum. Quod Marcus per verēcundiam prīmō recūsāvit, posteā tamen recēpit.

Notes: **Armenia, -iae**, f: a mountain kingdom north of Syria over whose lands Rome and Parthia battled in 163 CE; **prosperē**: favorably; **Statius Priscus, Statiī Priscī**, m: a capable administrator who was appointed governor of several contentious provinces, including Britain (161–163 CE); he was sent to Cappadocia in 163 CE, where he ably defended Roman interests against Vologessus; **Artaxata, -ōrum**, n (plural): the capital of Armenia; **Artaxatīs captīs**: "Artaxata having been captured" (ablative absolute); **dēlātum** (*est*); **Armeniācus, -a, -um**: Armenian, vanquisher of Armenia (neither emperor had seen combat: the title appears on Verus's coins; Marcus Aurelius assumed the title in 164 CE); **verēcundia, -iae**, f: modesty, respect; **prīmō**: at first; **recūsō, -āre, -āvi, -ātus**: refuse, object to.

EXTRA PASSAGES: VESPASIAN

Of humble, modest origins (his ancestors were tax collectors), Vespasian was a charismatic, capable, efficient, generous emperor, who supported the arts and enjoyed off-color jokes. His final words were reputedly "*Vae, inquit, putō, deus fiō*" ("Alas," he said, "I think I am becoming a god!") in reference to the Roman practice of deifying "good" emperors. His successful military career began in the 40s CE in Britain, followed by a consulship (51 CE), and eventually the governorship of Africa (63 CE), where, instead of extorting the provincials, he managed to earn their respect and friendship. Vespasian achieved further success in Judea during his appointment to quell that mutinous province, and he earned the unwavering respect and loyalty of his troops, despite his reputation as a strict disciplinarian. With encouragement from the governor of Syria and his lieutenants, Vespasian made his own bid for emperorship against Vitellius in 69 CE. Eventually successful, Vespasian restored peace to a war-torn Empire, ruling with his son, the equally capable Titus, until his death in 79 CE.

18.13. Tacitus, *Historiae* 1.50. Like many other writers, Tacitus believed that power corrupts and that Vespasian's imperial predecessors had quickly degenerated into excess and profligacy. Vespasian restored some dignity to the office.

Sōlusque omnium ante sē principum in melius mūtātus est.

Notes: **in melius**: "for the better."

18.14. Tacitus, *Agricola* 13.3. When Claudius launched his invasion of Britain in 43 CE—the first successful foray to the island since Julius Caesar in 55–54 BCE—the future emperor Vespasian was among the participating officers.

Dīvus Claudius auctor iterātī operis, transvectīs legiōnibus auxiliīsque et adsumptō in partem rērum Vespasiānō, quod initium ventūrae mox fortūnae fuit: domitae gentēs, captī rēges et monstrātus fātīs Vespasiānus.

Notes: **iterātus, -a, -um**: repeated, renewed, revised; **operis**: i.e., the British campaign; **transvectīs . . . auxiliīs**: "legions and auxiliary troops having been transported across" (ablative absolute); **adsumptō . . . Vespasiānō**: "Vespasian having been brought" (ablative absolute); **quod**: "a thing which"; **ventūrus, -a, -um**: about to come; **domō, -āre, -uī, -itus**: tame, subdue; **domitae** (*sunt*); **captī** (*sunt*); **monstrō, -āre, -āvī, -ātus**: show; **monstrātus** (*est*).

18.15. Suetonius, *Vita Vespasiani* 7.3. Vespasian finds himself uncomfortable in his new role as emperor, but the gods seem to favor him. In addition, as we read here, Vespasian's rise to greatness seems to have been predicted not only by messianic prophecies but also by ancient Tegean artists.

Per idem tempus Tegeae in Arcadiā instinctū vāticinantium effossa sunt sacrātō locō vāsa operis antīquī, atque in iīs assimilis Vespasiānō imāgo.

Notes: **Tegea, -ae**, f: in the Peloponnese, north of Sparta, the site of an important shrine of Athena; **Tegeae**: locative; **Arcadia, -iae**, f: a region in the central Peloponnese in Greece; **instinctus, -ūs**, m: instigation, incitement, prompting; **vāticinans, -antis**, m: soothsayer; **effodiō, -ere, -fōdī, -fossus**: dig out, excavate; **sacrātus, -a, -um**: consecrated, sacred; **vās, vāsis**, n: vase, vessel; **assimilis, -e**: very similar.

Comparatives and Superlatives of Adjectives and Adverbs

1. As they do in English, Latin adjectives have degree: positive ("big, good, learned"), comparative ("bigger, better, more learned"), and superlative ("biggest, best, most learned").

PART 1: COMPARATIVE ADJECTIVES

2. **POSITIVE ADJECTIVES** are the basic adjectives that you already learned in *NLP* 2 and 3. They follow either a first and second declension paradigm (*bonus, -a, -um*: good) or a third declension paradigm (*brevis, -e*: short).

3. **COMPARATIVE ADJECTIVES** indicate a quality that is intensified but not the greatest. Consider the following examples:

Caesar, *de Bello Gallico* 1.24.3: **Eum ab iīs quī in <u>superiōre</u> aciē constiterant mūnīrī iussit**. He ordered it to be guarded by those who had made their stand on a <u>rather high</u> point.

Ovid, *Metamorphoses* 10.150–51: **Cecinī plectrō <u>graviōre</u> Gigantās / sparsaque Phlegraeīs victrīcia fulmina campīs**. With a <u>rather heavy</u> plectrum I sang about Giants and the vanquishing thunderbolts scattered on the plains of Phlegra.

4. **COMPARATIVE ADJECTIVES** can also indicate a qualitative difference between two nouns. In this case, the comparative adjective is often followed by an **ABLATIVE OF COMPARISON**. Consider the following examples:

Aberdeen Bestiary 18r: **Nihil sagātius canibus.** Nothing (is) <u>wiser</u> than <u>dogs</u>.
>   *Sagātius* is a comparative adjective followed by the ablative of comparison *canibus.*

CIL V 5320.4–8: **Vīta brevis longō melior mortālibus aevō.** A short life (is) <u>better</u> for mortals than a <u>long lifetime</u>.
>   *Melior* is a comparative adjective followed by the ablative of comparison *longō aevō.*

5. A comparative adjective can be followed by *quam* plus the noun to which the first noun is being compared. Both nouns will appear in the **same case** and fulfill the **same syntactic function**. Consider the following examples:

Caesar, *de Bello Gallico* 1.52.7: . . . **expedītior erat QUAM iī quī inter aciem versābantur.** . . . <u>he</u> (Caesar) was <u>less encumbered</u> THAN <u>those</u> who were maneuvering within the battle line.
>   *Quam* follows the comparative adjective *expedītior* which compares Caesar (understood from *erat*) and *iī*, both nominative subjects.

Tacitus, *Annales* 1.11.2: **Plūs in ōrātiōne tālī dignitātis QUAM fideī erat.** There was <u>more dignity</u> THAN <u>credibility</u> in such a speech.
>   *Quam* follows the comparative substantive adjective *plūs* which compares *dignitātis* and *fideī*, both partitive genitives.

Sallust, *Bellum Catilinae* 19.1: **Equōrum māior cōpia nōbīs QUAM illīs est.** The supply of horses is <u>greater</u> <u>for us</u> THAN <u>for them</u>.
>   *Quam* follows the comparative adjective *māior* which compares *nōbis* and *illīs*, both datives of possession.

6. Most **COMPARATIVE ADJECTIVES** are formed by adding **-ior** to the stem of the positive adjective. Note that the neuter nominative singular of the comparative ends in **-ius** (and should not be confused with the masculine

nominative singular of the second declension positive adjective). Study the following table:

Positive	Comparative
doctus, -a, -um	doctior, doctius
brevis, -e	brevior, brevius
sapiens (-ientis)	sapientior, sapientius

7. All comparative adjectives follow the third declension adjective paradigm that you learned in *NLP* 3. As the table below indicates, the ablative singular of a comparative adjective can end in -ī or -e. N.B. The genitive plural does **not** take the i-stem ending.

Case	Masculine	Feminine	Neuter
Singular			
Nominative	brev**ior**	brev**ior**	brev**ius**
Genitive	brev**iōris**	brev**iōris**	brev**iōris**
Dative	brev**iōrī**	brev**iōrī**	brev**iōrī**
Accusative	brev**iōrem**	brev**iōrem**	brev**ius**
Ablative	brev**iōre** / brev**iōrī**	brev**iōre** / brev**iōrī**	brev**iōre** / brev**iōrī**
Vocative	brev**ior**	brev**ior**	brev**ius**
Plural			
Nominative	brev**iōrēs**	brev**iōrēs**	brev**iōra**
Genitive	brev**iōrum**	brev**iōrum**	brev**iōrum**
Dative	brev**iōribus**	brev**iōribus**	brev**iōribus**
Accusative	brev**iōrēs** / brev**iōrīs**	brev**iōrēs** / brev**iōrīs**	brev**iōra**
Ablative	brev**iōribus**	brev**iōribus**	brev**iōribus**
Vocative	brev**iōrēs**	brev**iōrēs**	brev**iōra**

PART 2: SUPERLATIVE ADJECTIVES

8. **SUPERLATIVE ADJECTIVES** indicate a heightened degree of a quality. Consider the following examples:

Ovid, *Metamorphoses* 3.50: **Fēcerat exiguās iam sōl <u>altissimus</u> umbrās.** The <u>highest</u> sun (i.e., at its zenith) had already made the shadows short.

Aberdeen Bestiary 8v: **Pardus est genus varium ac <u>vēlōcissimum</u>.** The pard is a variegated type and <u>very swift</u>.

9. **SUPERLATIVE ADJECTIVES** can also indicate a comparison among three or more nouns. These superlatives are often followed by a **PARTITIVE GENITIVE.** Consider the following examples:

Vergil, *Aeneid* 1.343–44: **Huic coniunx Sȳchaeus erat, <u>dītissimus agrī</u> / <u>Phoenicum</u>.** Her spouse was Sychaeus, the <u>richest</u> in land <u>of the Phoenicians</u>. The partitive genitive *Phoenicum* names the group of which Sychaeus was the richest.

Catullus 49.4–5: **Grātiās tibi maximās Catullus / agit <u>pessimus</u> <u>omnium</u> poēta.** Catullus, the <u>worst</u> poet <u>of all</u>, gives the greatest thanks to you. The partitive genitive *omnium* names the group of which Catullus is the worst.

10. When a superlative adjective appears with *quam*, the expression is translated "as _____ as possible." Consider the following examples:

Sallust, *Bellum Jugurthinum* 17.7: **<u>Quam paucissumīs</u> dīcam.** I will speak with <u>as few (words) as possible</u>.

Caesar, *de Bello Gallico* 1.9.3: **<u>Quam plūrimās</u> cīvitātēs suō beneficiō habēre obstrictās volēbat.** He wanted to have <u>as many states as possible</u> bound to his service.

11. Most **SUPERLATIVE ADJECTIVES** are formed by adding -**issimus**, -**a**, -**um** to the stem of the positive adjective. Study the following table:

Positive	Superlative
doctus, -a, -um	doct**issimus**, -**a**, -**um**
brevis, -e	brev**issimus**, -**a**, -**um**
sapiens (-ientis)	sapient**issimus**, -**a**, -**um**

12. The superlative forms of all adjectives follow the paradigm for first and second declension adjectives. Study the following table:

Case	Masculine	Feminine	Neuter
Singular			
Nominative	brev**issimus**	brev**issima**	brev**issimum**
Genitive	brev**issimī**	brev**issimae**	brev**issimī**
Dative	brev**issimō**	brev**issimae**	brev**issimō**
Accusative	brev**issimum**	brev**issimam**	brev**issimum**
Ablative	brev**issimō**	brev**issimā**	brev**issimō**
Vocative	brev**issime**	brev**issima**	brev**issimum**
Plural			
Nominative	brev**issimī**	brev**issimae**	brev**issima**
Genitive	brev**issimōrum**	brev**issimārum**	brev**issimōrum**
Dative	brev**issimīs**	brev**issimīs**	brev**issimīs**
Accusative	brev**issimōs**	brev**issimās**	brev**issima**
Ablative	brev**issimīs**	brev**issimīs**	brev**issimīs**
Vocative	brev**issimī**	brev**issimae**	brev**issima**

13. Irregular adjectives decline exactly as do regular adjectives in the comparative and superlative forms. Only their basic formation is different—in most cases, the stem of the positive adjective changes dramatically. The nominative singular forms of these irregular adjectives must be memorized. Study the following table:

Positive	Comparative	Superlative
bonus, -a, -um (good)	melior, melius (better)	optimus, -a, -um (best)
magnus, -a, -um (big)	māior, māius (bigger)	maximus, -a, -um (biggest)
malus, -a, -um (bad)	pēior, pēius (worse)	pessimus, -a, -um (worst)
multus, -a, -um (much)	--, plūs (more)	plūrimus, -a, -um (most)
parvus, -a, -um (small)	minor, minus (smaller)	minimus, -a, -um (smallest)
superus, -a, -um (high)	superior, superius (higher)	summus, -a, -um suprēmus, -a, -um (highest)

N.B. You should consider these irregular forms as additional required vocabulary.

14. Adjectives whose nominative singular masculine ends in -**er** in the positive degree will form their superlatives by adding -**rimus, -a, -um** directly to the nominative singular masculine, regardless of the adjective's stem. (N.B. The comparative forms of these adjectives are completely regular.) Study the following table:

Positive	Comparative	Superlative
līber, lībera, līberum (free)	līberior, līberius	līber**rimus, -a, -um**
sacer, sacra, sacrum (sacred)	sacrior, sacrius	sacer**rimus, -a, -um**
pulcher, pulchra, pulchrum (beautiful)	pulchrior, pulchrius	pulcher**rimus, -a, -um**
ācer, acris, acre (sharp, fierce)	acrior, acrius	ācer**rimus, -a, -um**
celer, celeris, celere (swift)	celerior, celerius	celer**rimus, -a, -um**

15. The following six adjectives have nominative singular masculine forms that end in -**lis** in the positive degree. Their superlatives are formed by adding -**limus, -a, -um** to the stem of the positive adjective. (N.B. The comparative forms of these adjectives are completely regular.). Study the following table:

Positive	Comparative	Superlative
facilis, -e (easy)	facilior, facilius	facil**limus, -a, -um**
difficilis, -e (difficult)	difficilior, difficilius	difficil**limus, -a, -um**
similis, -e (similar)	similior, similius	simil**limus, -a, -um**
dissimilis, -e (dissimilar)	dissimilior, dissimilius	dissimil**limus, -a, -um**
gracilis, -e (graceful)	gracilior, gracilius	gracil**limus, -a, -um**
humilis, -e (low, humble)	humilior, humilius	humil**limus, -a, -um**

PART 3: COMPARISON OF ADVERBS

16. In Latin, adverbs are indeclinable. You have memorized many adverbs as part of the required vocabulary lists (e.g., *saepe, nunc, hīc*). Other adverbs are formed from adjectives and thus can have degrees ("fiercely, more fiercely, most fiercely"; "badly, worse, worst"). Consider the following examples:

    Martial 1.77.2: **Parcē bibit Charinus**. Charinus drinks <u>sparingly</u>.
    Parcē is a positive adverb from the Latin adjective *parcus, -a, -um*: sparing.

    Martial 3.4.5: **Breviter tū multa fatēre**. You confess many things <u>quickly</u>.
    Breviter is a positive adverb from the Latin adjective *brevis, -e*: short, quick.

    Catullus 14.1 (*NLP* 13.14): **Cēnābis bene, mī Fabulle, apud mē**. You will dine <u>well</u>, my Fabullus, at my house.
    Bene is an irregular positive adverb from the Latin adjective *bonus, -a, -um*: good.

    Martial 3.17.3: **Sed magis ardēbat Sabidī gula**. But Sabidius's appetite was burning <u>all the more</u>.
    Magis is an irregular positive adverb from the Latin adjective *magnus, -a, -um*: great.

    Caesar, *de Bello Gallico* 5.43.4: **Tum omnēs ācerrimē fortissimēque pugnārent**. Then they all would fight <u>most vigorously</u> and <u>most bravely</u>.
    Ācerrimē is a superlative adverb from the Latin adjective *ācer, acris, acre*: sharp; *fortissimē* is a regular superlative adverb from the Latin adjective *fortis, -e*.

17. **POSITIVE ADVERBS** are usually (but not always) formed by adding -ē to the stem of a first and second declension adjective, or by adding -**iter** to the stem of a third declension adjective. **COMPARATIVE ADVERBS** are identical to the nominative singular neuter of the comparative form of the corresponding adjective. **SUPERLATIVE ADVERBS** are formed by adding -ē to the stem of the superlative form of the corresponding adjective.

Positive Adjective	Positive Adverb	Comparative Adverb	Superlative Adverb
doctus, -a, -um	doctē	doct**ius**	doct**issimē**
brevis, -e	breviter	brev**ius**	brev**issimē**
pulcher, pulchra, pulchrum	pulchrē	pulchr**ius**	pulch**errimē**
ācer, acris, acre	acriter	acr**ius**	āc**errimē**
facilis, -e	faciliter	facil**ius**	fac**illimē**

18. The following adverbs are irregular (like their corresponding adjectives). Note that the comparative adverbs are identical to the nominative singular neuter of the comparative form of the corresponding adjective, and that the superlative adverbs are formed by adding **-ē** to the stem of the superlative form of the corresponding adjective:

Positive Adjective	Positive Adverb	Comparative Adverb	Superlative Adverb
bonus, -a, -um	bene (well)	melius (better)	optimē (best)
magnus, -a, -um	magnopere (greatly)	magis (more)	maximē (most)
malus, -a, -um	malē (badly)	pēius (worse)	pessimē (worst)
multus, -a, -um	multum (much)	plūs (more)	plūrimē (most)
parvus, -a, -um	parum (little)	minus (less)	minimē (least)

N.B. You should consider these irregular forms as additional required vocabulary.

19. As with superlative adjectives, when a superlative adverb appears with *quam*, the expression is translated "as _____ as possible." Consider the following examples:

Sallust, *Bellum Jugurthinum* 25.5: . . . **quam ocissimē ad prōvinciam accēdat**. . . . (requesting that) he come to the province <u>as quickly as possible</u>.

Caesar, *de Bello Gallico* 1.37.4: **Itaque rē frūmentāriā, quam celerrimē potuit, comparātā magnīs itineribus ad Ariovistum contendit**. And so after the grain supply was secured, <u>as quickly as</u> he was able, he hurried to Ariovistus in long marches.

20. Comparative adjectives and adverbs (and implicit expressions of comparison) can be followed by an **ABLATIVE OF DEGREE OF DIFFERENCE** (most often *multō*: "by much" or *paulō*: "by a little bit"). Consider the following examples:

Catullus 72.6: **Multō mī tamen es vīlior et levior.** To me, however, you (Lesbia) are cheaper and more trivial <u>by much</u> (much cheaper and more trivial).

Caesar, *de Bello Gallico* 6.27.1: **Magnitūdine <u>paulō</u> antecēdunt.** They excel in size <u>by a little bit</u>.

I. Required Vocabulary

NOUNS

bēlua, -ae, f: beast, large animal
iniūria, -iae, f: injury, wrong, injustice

tēlum, -ī, n: missile, dart, javelin, spear

avis, -is (-ium), f: bird
latus, lateris, n: side, flank
lītus, lītoris, n: sea-shore, beach
magnitūdō, magnitūdinis, f: size, bulk, greatness
pectus, pectoris, n: breast, heart, soul

fluctus, -ūs, m: wave
ūsus, -ūs, m: practice, skill, exercise, use, need

ADJECTIVES

grātus, -a, -um (+ dative): pleasing, welcome, agreeable
līber, lībera, līberum: free
pius, pia, pium: dutiful, devoted, affectionate
pulcher, pulchra, pulchrum: pretty
reliquus, -a, -um: remaining, left
singulus, -a, -um: single, separate, one at a time

superus, -a, -um: high
tūtus, -a, -um: safe, protected, secure

ācer, acris, acre: sharp, vigorous, brave, bitter
celer, celeris, celere: quick, fast, rapid, swift
dissimilis, -e: dissimilar
facilis, -e: easy
fortis, -e: brave
gracilis, -e: graceful
humilis, -e: low, humble
quālis, -e (+ dative): of what sort / kind as, just like

VERBS

impleō, -ēre, -ēvī, -ētus: fill in / up, complete

discō, -ere, didicī: learn, get to know
rapiō, -ere, -uī, raptus: tear away, seize, snatch
regō, -ere, rexī, rectus: rule, guide
suscipiō, -ere, -cēpī, -ceptus: accept, receive, maintain, undertake

CONJUNCTIONS AND ADVERBS

hūc: here, to this place
iterum: again
longē: by far
quam: than
quamvīs: although, however much
quoniam: since, because
semper: always, every time
unde: from where, whence

II. Translate the following sentences from Latin to English or English to Latin.

1. Tunc dulciōra carmina ā poētīs Rōmānīs cantāta erant.
2. Quaedam animālia celerius quam hominēs fugiunt.
3. Mīlitēs hostem semper quam fortissimē pugnābant.

4. Illī gladiātōrēs māiōrēs multō hīs sunt.

5. Quamvīs iniūriās plūrimās fēceritis, tamen virtūtem discētis.

6. Patriam nostram amāmus, maximam omnium cīvitātum.

7. Templa eadem dīs grātissima dōnīs quam sacerrimīs implēveris.

8. Ad lītus amoenius habitāre mālumus.

9. The army seized its own camp from the enemy as quickly as possible.

10. The citizens had been guided rather safely by the kings.

11. The soldiers will not be harmed since they will soon have the best weapons.

12. Dogs are more clever than certain types of birds.

Animals in the Roman World

Widely represented in art and literature, animals were an important and visible aspect of Greek and Roman society. Part of the standard hero's quest was the hunt of a wild and dangerous animal—a lion or boar in the case of Heracles, Meleager, or Theseus—and this aspect of animal lore inspired the popular staged beast hunts in the arena (see *NLP* 14). Animals were also associated with specific gods, who in turn protected their sacred animals and accepted them as sacrifices: Jupiter, god of bulls, was worshipped with bull sacrifice; Neptune, the father of horses, received offerings of horses by drowning. For the Romans, animals provided a key to revealing the will of the gods whether through augury (examining the flight patterns of birds, their pitch, height, or numbers—recall the rival signs observed by Romulus and Remus in *NLP* 3.4) or through *haruspicium*, wherein the livers of sacrificial animals were examined for signs from the gods. Before any important state business, magistrates looked for such signs; for this purpose the state even kept chickens whose eating patterns were thought to reveal whether the gods approved a state decision. About to engage the Carthaginians in a naval battle off Sicily in 249 BCE, Publius Claudius Pulcher took the auspices from the sacred chickens, but they refused to eat—indicating divine disapproval for the battle. Claudius threw the chickens into the sea, saying "If they won't eat, let them drink." He lost the battle.

Animals were also kept as pets. Artwork shows children with goats, sheep, Maltese dogs, and cats (cats were sacred in Egypt, and their export was illegal until the time of Augustus, but cats soon became common pets). Martial (7.87) mentions exotic long-eared (fennec) foxes and ichneumons. Ferrets were also kept as mousers, as were snakes. Dogs were always admired for their loyalty: Odysseus's dog, Argos, died at the sight of his master finally returning home (*Odyssey* 17.300–27); Ovid gives the names of Actaeon's thirty-five hunting dogs (*Metamorphoses* 3.206–27); and beloved dogs were commemorated with funerary epitaphs. Horses, too, were cherished companions: the immortal horses of Achilles mourned for their deceased master (*Iliad* 17.426–56), as did Pallas' horse Aethon (*NLP* 7.13). Alexander and Caesar both had remarkable polydactyl horses (Suetonius, *de Vita Caesaris* 61), at least according to legend. Caligula elevated his horse Incitatus to the consulship (Suetonius, *de Vita Gaii* 55). Nightingales and blackbirds were popular songbirds, kept in cages; the exotic parrot charmed even the humorless Domitian; and Catullus immortalized Lesbia's pet sparrow (Catullus 2 and 3). Geese were also significant as companions (the humble Baucis and Philemon were willing to sacrifice their beloved pet goose to honor the gods, *Metamorphoses* 8.684–87) and as watch animals (Juno's sacred Capitolian geese warned the slumbering Romans and their somnolent canines of the imminent Gallic attack on the city in 390 BCE).

Aristotle, the first to study animals methodically, devised a taxonomy that prevailed until the Renaissance. Although his work profited from the observations of others and he was fully committed to obtaining information through autopsy, he was perhaps the first scientist to engage in dissection systematically. Identifying more than 500 species of mammals and birds, 120 varieties of fish, and 60 types of insects, he categorized animals according to the presence or absence of various features (claws, beaks, feathers, scales); what they ate; whether they were land- or sea-dwelling. He divided animals into two categories: blooded (viviparous and oviparous quadrupeds, marine mammals, birds, fish) and bloodless (mollusks, crustacea, testacea, insects). Several centuries later, Pliny the Elder devoted four books of his *Naturalis Historia* to animals, including colorful anecdotes bespeaking their entertainment value. In the second century CE, Aelian was the first thinker since Aristotle to treat the entire animal world systematically in his *On the Nature of Animals*, wherein ethical anecdotes about animals were presented as proof of divine providence.

Philosophers debated ethical questions surrounding the human treatment of animals. Pythagoras and Empedocles believed that the immortal soul could be transferred between life forms after death (human, animal, or even plant), and so they advocated against eating animals because they were, literally, related to human beings. Although Aristotle conceded that animals deserve praise or censure for their voluntary acts, he maintained that we owe them no justice because they lack reason and speech. The Stoics went even further, denying that animals were capable of memory, emotion, forethought, intention, or voluntary action. Although such views prevailed in philosophy, Aristotle's student Theophrastus argued that killing non-dangerous animals was an act of injustice. Compassion and sympathy, however, were rare. Arguing that animals were capable of reason, Plutarch was almost unique in his concern over animal suffering and mistreatment and in ascribing reason (and a rational soul) to animals; dominant Aristotelian and Stoic ideals influenced the Christian view that animals are not ensouled.

Finally, animals were utilized to explore human character and morality. Anthropomorphism found its fullest expression in the popular fables of Aesop. With the richly illustrated medieval bestiaries (the British-produced *Aberdeen Bestiary* is one of the finest examples of the type), we have the acme of this tradition: animals (real and imaginary) are employed as Christianizing metaphors to explore and explain human society and foibles. The author tells us that the *Bestiary*'s purpose is "to improve the minds of ordinary people, in such a way that the soul will at least perceive physically things which it has difficulty grasping mentally: that what they have difficulty comprehending with their ears, they will perceive with their eyes" (25v). This sentiment provides an ancient analogue to the French anthropologist Claude Lévi-Strauss, who famously said "animals are good to think [with]" (*Totemism*; London, 1964, p. 89).

SUGGESTIONS FOR FURTHER READING:

The Aberdeen Bestiary Project: *http://www.abdn.ac.uk/bestiary*
Gilhus, Ingvild Saelid. *Animals, Gods and Humans: Changing Attitudes to Animals in Greek, Roman and Early Christian Ideas*. Routledge, 2006.

Newmeyer, Stephen T. *Animals, Rights and Reason in Plutarch and Modern Ethics.* Routledge, 2006.

Newmeyer, Stephen T. *Animals in Greek and Roman Thought: A Sourcebook.* Routledge, 2011.

Sorabji, R. *Animal Minds and Human Morals: The Origins of the Western Debate.* Cornell, 1993.

Toynbee, J. M. C. *Animals in Roman Life and Art.* Cornell, 1973.

PASSAGES

19.1. Pliny the Elder, *Naturalis Historia* 9.128. True purple dye, a highly prized luxury commodity, came only from certain types of snails, including the murex and closely related purple sea snail.

Conchae omnēs celerrimē crēscunt, praecipuē purpurae: annō magnitūdinem implent.

Notes: **concha, -ae**, f: shellfish, mussel; **praecipuē**: especially; **purpura, -ae**, f: purple shellfish.

19.2. Pliny the Elder, *Naturalis Historia* 8.89. The Greeks and Romans have always been fascinated by the strange creatures of Egypt, and the Greek historian Herodotus (484–425 BCE) reported some bizarre "facts" about the crocodile, including its porcine eyes, tusks proportional to its body mass, lack of a tongue, and inability to move its lower jaw. By Pliny's day Egyptian motifs were fashionable in public and private artwork. Augustan-era public art, in particular, utilized crocodile imagery to symbolize Augustus's conquest of Cleopatra at Actium in 31 BCE.

Nec aliud animal ex minōre orīgine in māiōrem crēscit magnitūdinem.

Notes: **orīgō, orīginis**, f: origin, source, beginning.

19.3. **Pliny the Elder,** *Naturalis Historia* **8.95.** Pliny's description of the hippopotamus relies closely on Herodotus's (2.71). Pliny is not known to have gone to Egypt, and it is unlikely that he ever saw such an animal.

Māior altitūdine in eōdem Nīlō bēlua hippopotamus ēditur, ungulīs bīnīs quālēs būbus, dorsō equī et iubā et hinnītū, rostrō resīmō, caudā et dentibus aprōrum aduncīs, sed minus noxiīs.

Notes: **altitūdō, altitūdinis,** f: height, depth; **Nīlus, -ī,** m: the Nile River; **hippopotamus, -ī,** m: river horse, hippopotamus; **ēdō, -ere, ēdidī, ēditus:** bring forth, produce; **ungula, -ae,** f: hoof, claw; **bīnī, -ae, -a** (plural): two apiece, "cloven" (the hippopotamus foot is divided into four toes, hence "cloven times two"); **bōs, bovis,** m / f: ox, bull, cow (*bubus:* archaic dative plural); **dorsum, -ī,** n: back, ridge; **iuba, -ae,** f: mane, crest; **hinnītus, -ūs,** m: neighing, whinny (onomatopoeic word); **rostrum, -ī,** n: snout; **resīmus, -a, -um:** bent backwards, turned up; **cauda, -ae,** f: tail; **dens, dentis** (-ium), m: tooth; **aper, aprī,** m: wild boar; **aduncus, -a, -um:** bent inwards, crooked.

19.4. **Pliny the Elder,** *Naturalis Historia* **8.139.** In the context of hibernating animals, Pliny describes how tenaciously snails stay put in the cold winter months. Here he refers to the snail's practice of estivation, whereby, after retreating into their shells, they cling to a safe surface when the summer grows too warm or dry.

Illae quidem iterum et aestātibus, adhaerentēs maximē saxīs aut, etiam iniūriā resupīnātae āvolsaeque, nōn tamen exeuntēs.

Notes: **illae . . . iterum:** "indeed they (hibernate) again"; **illae** (*cochleae*): "those (snails)"; **aestās, -ātis,** f: summer; **adhaerens** (-entis): clinging (to); **resupīnātus, -a, -um:** prostrate, thrown back; **āvolsus, -a, -um:** wrenched away; **exeuns** (-euntis): leaving (from their shells).

19.5. **Pliny the Elder,** *Naturalis Historia* **9.7.** Dolphins were sacred to Apollo, Dionysus, and Neptune, and there are many stories of dolphins showing kindness to human beings, either saving them from shipwreck or befriending them. Aelian relates the tale of a dolphin who committed suicide after his best (human) friend died, and Propertius recounts a dream in which a dolphin saved his beloved Cynthia after a shipwreck (2.26a).

Vēlōcissimum omnium animālium, nōn sōlum marīnōrum, est delphīnus, ōcior volucre, acrior tēlō.

Notes: **vēlox (vēlōcis):** swift, rapid, quick; **marīnus, -a, -um:** of the sea, marine; **delphīnus, -ī,** m: dolphin; **ōcior, -ius:** quicker, swifter (comparative of a Greek adjective whose positive form is not attested in Latin); **volucer, -cris, -cre:** flying, winged.

19.6. *Aberdeen Bestiary 77r.* The tortoise inspired a brilliant Roman military technique—the *testūdō*, wherein soldiers held their shields defensively: the front line held their shields in front, the men on the sides held their shields out to the side, and soldiers within the formation held their shields overhead; this was, essentially, an ancient "tank." Here, we read how tortoises also inspire maritime superstition.

Trādunt aliquī quod incrēdibile est: tardius īre nāvigia, testūdinis pedem dextrum vehentia.

Notes: **incrēdibilis, -e**: unbelievable, incredible, extraordinary; **tardus, -a, -um**: slow, tardy; **īre nāvigia**: "that ships go" (indirect statement); **testūdō, testūdinis**, f: turtle, tortoise; **pēs, pedis**, m: foot; **dexter, dextra, dextrum**: right; **vehens (-entis)**: carrying.

19.7. *Aberdeen Bestiary 59r.* Sailors interpret signs from birds according to sympathetic magic: what the bird does (or does not do) presages what will (or will not) happen to the ship.

Cignus in auspiciīs semper lētissimus āles. Hunc optant naute quia sē nōn mergit in undīs.

Notes: **cignus** = *cygnus, -ī,* m: swan; **auspicium, -iī**, n: divination (by observing birds); **lētissimus** = *laetissimus;* **āles, ālitis (-ium)**, m / f: bird; **naute** = *nautae* from *nauta, -ae,* m: sailor; **mergō, -ere, mersī, mersus**: dip, plunge, sink (i.e., the swan does not "drown" or sink).

19.8. *Aberdeen Bestiary 46r.* Cranes are social birds, concerned with the well-being of each member of the flock. Thought to possess the ideals of devotion, energy, and vigilance, cranes were much admired for their military discipline, as we see here when they change their watch-guards.

At illa, volens suscipere sortem, nec ūsū nostrō invīta et pigrior sompnō renuntiat, sed impigrē suīs excutitur strātīs.

Notes: **illa**: "that (crane)"; **volens (-entis)**: wanting, wishing; **sors, sortis**, f: lot, duty; **invītus, -a, -um**: reluctant, unwilling; **piger, pigra, pigrum**: sluggish, lazy; **sompnō** = *somnō* from *somnus, -ī,* m: sleep, slumber; **renuntiō, -āre, -āvī, -ātus**: report, announce (a new watch); **impiger, impigra, impigrum**: diligent, active; **excutiō, -ere, -cussī, -cussus**: shake from; **strātum, -ī**, n: cover, blanket.

19.9. *Aberdeen Bestiary* **47r.** The ibis is a wading bird sacred to the Egyptian god of medicine, Thoth. Here, we learn how the ibis finds food for its young.

Hēc serpentum ōvīs ūtitur et morticīnīs, et ex eīs grātissimum cibum pullīs suīs reportat.

Notes: **hēc** = *haec* (the ibis); **serpens, -entis (-ium)**, m / f: snake, serpent; **ōvum, -ī**, n: egg; **ūtitur**: "(it) feeds on" (+ ablative); **morticīnus, -a, -um**: dead, carrion; **cibum, -ī**, n: food, nourishment; **pullus, -ī**, m: young animal, chick; **reportō, -āre, -āvī, -ātus**: bring back, carry back.

19.10. *Aberdeen Bestiary* **77v.** Frogs were usually thought to chatter nonsensically, but Pliny and Aelian both mention the mute frogs of Seriphos, who recover their voices when transported elsewhere. Countless visitors to Seriphos have debunked the legend of the mute frogs, and we do not know to what species these "mute" frogs might have belonged.

Ex quibus, quēdam "aquāticē" dīcuntur; quēdam "palustrēs"; quīdam "rubētē" ob id quod in vepribus vīvunt; "grandiōrēs" cēterīs. Aliē "calamītēs" vocantur quoniam inter arundinēs fruticēsque vīvunt, minimē omnium et viridissimē, mūtē, et sine vōce sunt.

Notes: **quibus** *(rānīs from rāna, -ae,* f: frog); **quēdam** = *quaedam*; **aquāticē** = *aquāticae, from aquāticus, -a, -um*: aquatic, living in water; **paluster, palustris, palustre**: marshy, boggy; **quīdam**: a slip for *quēdam*; **rubētē** = *rubētae, from rubēta, -ae,* f: a species of toad dwelling in bramble bushes; **veprēs, -is (-ium)**, m: thorn bush, bramble bush; **grandis, -e**: full grown, great, large; **aliē** = *aliae*; **calamītēs, -is**, m: small, green frog; **arundinēs** = *harundinēs, from harundō, harundinis,* f: reed; **frutex, fruticis**, f: shrub, bush; **minimē** = *minimae*; **viridissimē** = *viridissimae, from viridis, -e*: green, young, blooming; **mūtē** = *mūtae, from mūtus, -a, -um*: inarticulate, unable to speak.

19.11. Pliny the Elder, *Naturalis Historia* **9.81.** Color-changing fishes.

Mūtant colōrem candidum mēnae et fiunt aestāte nigriōrēs.

Notes: **candidus, -a, -um**: shining, bright; **mēna, -ae,** f: small fish, sprat; **fiō, fierī**: become; **aestāte**: see *NLP* 19.4; **niger, nigra, nigrum**: black, dark.

19.12. Ovid, *Metamorphoses* 13.962–63. Not all the sea creatures capturing the Roman imagination are known to modern biology. Glaucus was a fisherman, marveling at fish leaping from his net onto the grass and then returning to the deep. After searching for some magical herb in the grass that could explain the strange behavior of the fish, Glaucus ate the foliage and then felt an irresistible urge to head for the water. Jumping into the sea, he was transformed into a merman, as Glaucus himself vividly recounts here. Meter: dactylic hexameter.

"Ingentēsque umerōs et caerula bracchia vīdī
crūraque pinnigerō curvāta novissima pisce."

Notes: **umerus, -ī**, m: shoulder; **caerulus, -a, -um**: blue, greenish-blue; **bracchium, -iī**, n: arm; **crūs, crūris**, n: leg, shin; **pinniger, pinnigera, pinnigerum**: winged, with fins; **curvātus, -a, -um**: curved; **piscis, -is (-ium)**, m: fish.

EXTRA PASSAGES: BODIES OF WATER

You may have noticed that all the animals featured in the passages above are either aquatic or amphibious. The culture of the ancient Mediterranean was maritime. Seas, rivers, lakes, and other bodies of water defined not only the coastlines and islands, but also shaped mythology, warfare, and economics (it was far cheaper to ship goods by sea than by land). The sea was the origin of life, according to Hesiod, and it marked the boundaries of the inhabitable world to the extent that even in the first century CE Roman soldiers mutinied before crossing the English Channel to invade Britain.

19.13. Pliny the Elder, *Naturalis Historia* 2.212. Despite the low amplitude of the tides in the Mediterranean (exposed to the Atlantic by only a narrow passageway), the ancients were aware of them and curious about them. From early on they recognized a correlation between tides and the phases of the moon.

Et dē aquārum nātūrā complūra dicta sunt, sed aestūs marī accēdere ac reciprocāre, maximē mīrum plūribus quidem modīs. Vērum causa in sōle lūnāque.

Notes: **complūrēs, -a**: several, many; **aestus, -ūs**, m: tide, spray; **accēdere**: "(that the tides) rise" (indirect statement); **reciprocāre**: "(that the tides) fall" (indirect statement); **mīrus, -a, -um**: wonderful, astonishing, mysterious; **vērum**: but.

19.14. Vergil *Aeneid* **3.73–79.** Delos was one of Apollo's sacred islands, where he and his twin sister Diana were born. Juno, always the jealous wife, was furious with Latona, who had been raped by Jupiter and then became pregnant with the twins. Juno threatened that no land that "saw the light of day" would give her refuge. Latona searched long and hard, appealing to *polis* after *polis*, island after island, all fearful of Juno's threats. Eventually, Latona made a bargain with Delos, a poor and rocky "floating island" bobbing about in the Aegean, sometimes submerged, so not always seeing "the light of day." Latona promised fame and wealth in exchange for a place to give birth to her twins. True to his mother's word, Apollo did not destroy the island but instead made it the center of an important cult. Here, Aeneas describes it as a welcome haven from his arduous sea voyage. Meter: dactylic hexameter.

"Sacra marī colitur mediō grātissima tellus
Nēreïdum mātrī et Neptūno Aegaeō,
quam pius Arquitenens—ōrās et lītora circum
errantem—Myconō ē celsā Gyarōque revinxit,
immōtamque colī dedit et contemnere ventōs.
Hūc feror; haec fessōs tūtō placidissima portū
accipit."

Notes: **tellūs, tellūris**, f: earth, land; **Nēreïs, Nēreïdis**, f: sea-nymph, daughter of Nereus and Doris; **Neptūnus, -ī**, m: the Roman god of the sea; **Aegaeus, -a, -um**: Aegean, the body of water between Greece and Turkey; **pius, -a, -um**: dutiful, devoted, affectionate; **Arquitenens, -entis**, m: the archer (Apollo); **ōra, -ae**, f: coast, edge, boundary; **lītus, lītoris**, n: seashore, beach; **circum** (+ accusative): around (the object need not appear directly after the preposition, especially in poetry); **errans (-antis)**: wandering, floating; **Myconus, -ī**, f: a low-lying island in the Cyclades in the Aegean; **celsus, -a, -um**: lofty, high, upraised; **Gyarus, -ī**, f: another island in the northern Cyclades, proverbially desolate (in the early Empire a place of exile for the emperor's political enemies); **revinciō, -īre, -vīnxī, -vinctus**: tie, bind fast, moor; **immōtus, -a, -um**: fixed, unmoving, stationary; **haec** (*insula*); **fessus, -a, -um**: tired, exhausted, weary; **fessōs** (*nōs*); **placidus, -a, -um**: calm, peaceful, quiet; **portus, -ūs**, m: harbor, port, haven.

19.15. Ovid, *Metamorphoses* **1.309–12.** In the wake of the great flood sent by Jupiter to destroy the human race that had turned against the gods, Ovid imagines chaos also ensuing within the animal world: terrestrial animals suddenly find themselves battling the great deluge, aquatic animals are thrust into strange and unfamiliar surroundings, and natural enemies are swimming together—for their very lives! Meter: dactylic hexameter.

Obruerat tumulōs inmensa licentia pontī,
pulsābantque novī montāna cacūmina fluctūs.
Maxima pars undā rapitur; quibus unda pepercit,
illōs longa domant inopī iēiūnia victū.

Notes: **obruō, -ere, -ruī, -rutus**: cover, bury, collapse, fall; **tumulus, -ī**, m: hillock, mound; **inmensus, -a, -um**: vast, boundless, immeasurable; **licentia, -iae**, f: freedom, liberty, licentiousness; **pontus, -ī**, m: sea; **pulsō, -āre, -āvī, -ātus**: beat, strike; **montanus, -a, -um**: of a mountain, mountainous; **cacūmen, cacūminis**, n: summit, zenith, top, tip, extreme point; **parcō, -ere, pepercī, parsus**: spare, economize; **domō, -āre, -uī, -itus**: tame, subdue, break in; **inops (inopis)**: meager; **iēiunium, -iī**, n: abstinence, fast; **victus, -ūs**, m: way of living, support, nourishment, food.

Impersonal Verbs and Fiō

PART 1: IMPERSONAL VERBS

1. In Latin some verbs occur only in the third person singular active (all tenses). Typically, they are completed by an infinitive. Because they do not have a personal subject, they are known as **IMPERSONAL VERBS**. Below are some of the most common impersonal verbs. You should consider this list additional required vocabulary.

accidit, -ere, accidit: it happens
constat, -āre, constitit / constātum est: it is agreed, it is well-known
decet, -ēre, -uit: it is proper, it is seemly, it is fitting
libet, -ēre, -uit / libitum est: it pleases
licet, -ere, -uit / licitum est: it is permitted
miseret, -ēre, -uit / miseritum est: it distresses, it induces pity
necesse est: it is necessary
oportet, -ēre, -uit: it is fitting
paenitet, -ēre: it causes regret
piget, -ēre, -uit: it displeases
placet, -ēre, -uit / placitum est: it pleases, it is agreeable
prōdest, -esse, -fuit: it is useful, it is advantageous, it benefits
pudet, -ere, -uit / puditum est: it shames, it disgraces
refert, -ferre, -tulit: it matters
taedet, -ēre, -uit / taesum est: it bores, it disgusts

2. Latin uses these impersonal verbs more frequently than English. Consider the examples on the following page.

Horace, *Carmina* 1.4.9–10: **Nunc <u>decet</u> aut viridī nitidum caput impedīre myrtō / aut flōre**. Now <u>it is proper</u> to wreathe (your) shining head either with green myrtle or with a flower.

Ovid, *Metamorphoses* 9.631: **<u>Libet</u> temptāre**. <u>It is pleasing</u> to try.

Cicero, *ad Atticum* 2.10: **Lūdōs Antī spectāre nōn <u>placet</u>**. <u>It is</u> not <u>pleasing</u> to watch the games at Antium.

Cicero, *ad Atticum* 14.1.2: **Magnī <u>refert</u> hic quid velit**. <u>It matters</u> a great deal what this man (Brutus) wants.

Vergil, *Aeneid* 3.478: **Et tamen hanc pelagō praeterlābāre <u>necesse est</u>**. And nonetheless <u>it is necessary</u> to sail past this (coast) on the sea.

3. Impersonal verbs that express emotion are construed with a **PERSONAL DIRECT OBJECT IN THE ACCUSATIVE CASE**. It may prove difficult to provide good literal translations of these expressions. Consider the following examples:

Cicero, *Philippica* 2.69: **<u>Mē</u> quidem <u>miseret</u> parietum ipsōrum atque tectōrum**. Indeed <u>it pities</u> <u>**me**</u> of the very walls and roofs (i.e., I pity the very walls and roofs).

Sallust, *Bellum Jugurthinum* 4.9: **Vērum ego līberius altiusque prōcessī, dum <u>mē</u> cīvitātis mōrum <u>piget</u> <u>taedet</u>que**. But I have proceeded rather freely and rather far while it <u>displeases and disgusts</u> <u>**me**</u> of the customs of the state (i.e., The customs of the state displease and disgust me).

Tertullian, *Apology* 1.12: **<u>Nēminem</u> <u>pudet</u>, <u>nēminem</u> <u>paenitet</u>**. <u>It shames **no one**</u>, <u>it causes regret to</u> **no one**.

4. Many impersonal verbs are construed with an **INFINITIVE** or infinitive clause as their subject. In such expressions, if the infinitive has its own

subject, it must be rendered in the accusative case. Consider the following examples:

Cicero, *ad Atticum* 1.12: **Pompēium nōbīs amīcissimum constat esse**. <u>It is agreed</u> that **<u>Pompey is very friendly to us</u>**.

Cicero, *de Domo* 10.26: **Nōn <u>licuit</u> dē salūte populī Rōmānī sententiam <u>dīcere</u>**. <u>It was</u> not <u>permitted</u> **<u>to speak</u>** an opinion about the safety of the Roman people.

Cicero, *Divination in Caecilium* 29: **Deinde <u>accūsātōrem firmum vērumque esse</u> oportet**. Then <u>it is fitting</u> **<u>that an accuser be steadfast and truthful</u>**.

5. Other impersonal verbs are construed with a **DATIVE OF REFERENCE** (see *NLP* 6) and an **INFINITIVE** or infinitive clause as their subject. Consider the following examples:

Cicero, *ad Atticum* 1.16.18: **Libet *mihi* <u>facere</u> in Arpīnātī**. <u>It is pleasing</u> *for me* <u>to do</u> (this) at Arpinatum.

Cicero, *in Verrem* 2.4.44: ***Cn. Calidiō*, equitī Rōmānō, per omnīs aliōs praetōrēs <u>licuit</u> <u>habēre</u> argentum bene factum**. By all other Praetors, <u>it was permitted</u> *for Cnaeus Calidus*, a Roman equestrian, <u>to have</u> finely made silver.

Cicero, *in Verrem* 2.2.31: **Nōn <u>necesse erit</u> *L. Octāviō* iūdicī <u>cōgere</u>, P. Servilium Q. Catulō fundum restituere?** <u>Will it</u> not <u>be necessary</u> *for Lucius Octavius* as judge <u>to compel</u> Publius Servilius to restore the estate to Quintus Catulus?

6. Some impersonal verbs are complemented just by a **DATIVE OF REFERENCE** (see *NLP* 6). Consider the following examples:

Cicero, *Divinatio in Caecilium* 51: **<u>Mihi</u> quam multīs custōdibus <u>opus erit</u>?** How many guards will <u>I</u> <u>have need</u> of?
     Mihi is a dative of reference with the impersonal verb *opus est*.

Caesar, *de Bello Gallico* 1.34.2: **Sī quid <u>ipsī</u> ā Caesare <u>opus esset</u>** . . . If <u>there</u> <u>were</u> any <u>need</u> by Caesar <u>for him</u> (Ariovistus) . . . (i.e, "If Caesar had any need for him . . . ")

    Ipsī is a dative of reference with the impersonal verb *opus esset*.

7.   Latin often uses impersonal expressions to describe natural phenomena. Consider the following examples:

Ovid, *Metamorphoses* 1.572–73: **Summīsque adspergine silvīs / inpluit**. And in the highest woods <u>it rains</u> with spray.

Terence, *Heauton Timorumenos* 248: **Et <u>vesperāscit</u>, et nōn nōvērunt viam**. It <u>grows late</u>, and they did not know the way.

8.   Verbs of motion can be used impersonally in the passive voice. Consider the following examples of common **IMPERSONAL PASSIVES**:

Sallust, *Bellum Iugurthinum* 107: **Deinde paucīs diēbus, quō īre intenderant, <u>perventum est</u>**. Then in a few days <u>they arrived</u> (literally: "there was an arriving") to where they had aimed to go.

Cicero, *Philippica* 8.6.1: **<u>Pugnātur</u> ācerrimē**. <u>The fighting is</u> very fierce (literally: "it is being fought very fiercely").

Vergil, *Aeneid* 9.641: **Sīc <u>itur</u> ad astra**. <u>Thus they go</u> to the stars (literally: "there is a going to the stars).

N.B. *Itur* is the third person singular passive of *eō, īre, īvī, itūrus*. You should consider this form as additional required vocabulary.

PART 2: FIŌ

9.   In *NLP* 17 and 18, you learned how to form the passive voice of regular verbs from all four conjugations. Most irregular verbs do not have a passive voice (*esse, posse, īre, velle, nolle, malle*). Latin employs the irregular

verb **FĪŌ, FIERĪ, FACTUS SUM** to express the passive voice of *faciō*. **FĪŌ** behaves like a normal third conjugation -io verb in the present, imperfect, and future tenses. The perfect system of *fīō* is identical to the perfect passive forms of *faciō* (e.g., *factum est*). Study the following tables:

PRESENT TENSE OF FĪŌ

Person	Singular	Plural
1st	fīō: I become, I am made	fī**mus**: we become, we are made
2nd	fīs: you become, you are made	fī**tis**: you (plural) become, you (plural) are made
3rd	fit: he / she / it becomes, he / she / it is made	fī**unt**: they become, they are made

IMPERFECT TENSE OF FĪŌ

Person	Singular	Plural
1st	fīē**bam**: I became, I was made	fīē**bāmus**: we became, we were made
2nd	fīē**bās**: you became, you were made	fīē**bātis**: you (plural) became, you (plural) were made
3rd	fīē**bat**: he / she / it became, he / she / it was made	fīē**bant**: they became, they were made

FUTURE TENSE OF FĪŌ

Person	Singular	Plural
1st	fīa**m**: I shall become, I shall be made	fīē**mus**: we shall become, we shall be made
2nd	fīē**s**: you will become, you will be made	fīē**tis**: you (plural) will become, you (plural) will be made
3rd	fīe**t**: he / she / it will become, he / she / it will be made	fīe**nt**: they will become, they will be made

10. Like *sum*, *fīō* can function as a linking verb. Consider the following examples:

Cicero, *in Catilinam* 1.2: <u>**Fit** pūblicī consilī **particeps**</u>. He (Catiline) <u>becomes</u> a <u>participant</u> in the public deliberation.

Sallust, *Bellum Catilinae* 10.6: **Imperium ex iustissumō atque optumō crūdēle intolerandum factum (est)**. The rule, from the most just and best, became <u>cruel</u> (and) <u>intolerable</u>.

11. *Fiō* can also be used intransitively. In these instances, *fiō* is best translated as "happen" or "occur." Consider the following examples:

Caesar, *de Bello Gallico* 7.67.7: **Omnibus locīs fit caedēs**. Slaughter <u>happens</u> in all places.

Livy, *ab Urbe Condita* 1.48.2: **Concursus populī fiēbat in cūriam**. There <u>occurred</u> a rush of people into the Senate House.

Cicero, *ad Atticum* 6.1: **Sed quid iīs fīet, sī hūc Paulus vēnerit?** But what <u>will happen</u> to them if Paulus will have come here?

I. Required Vocabulary

NOUNS

dīvitiae, -iārum, f (plural): riches, wealth

flamma, -ae, f: flame, blaze, torch

grātia, -iae, f: favor, esteem, regard (**grātiās agere**: to give thanks)

dōnum, -ī, n: gift

sacerdōtium, -iī, n: priesthood

vestīgium, -iī, n: track, trace, mark

crīmen, crīminis, n: crime, guilt, charge

fās, n (indeclinable): in accord with divine law

māiōr, -ōris, m/f: ancestor (from comparative adjective of *magnus*: "the greater ones")

moenia, -ium, n (plural): walls, fortifications

parens, -entis, m/f: parent

praetor, -ōris, m: leader, military leader, magistrate at Rome with the constitutional authority to lead an army

spīritus, -ūs, m: breath, spirit, soul

fidēs, -ēī, f: faith, trust

PRONOUNS

quisque, quaeque, quidque: each

ADJECTIVES

audax (audācis): bold, daring, courageous, foolhardy
tālis, -e: of such a kind

VERBS

servō, -āre, -āvī, -ātus: observe, watch over, keep, protect

sustineō, -ēre, -uī, -tentus: hold back, support, sustain
valeō, -ēre, -uī: be strong, be able, fare well, prevail

pergō, -ere, perrexī, perrectus: continue, proceed, go on with
poscō, -ere, poposcī: demand, inquire
tangō, -ere, tetigī, tactus: touch, reach, border on, affect

fiō, fierī, factus sum: become

coepī, -isse, coeptus (defective verb appearing only in the perfect
    system): begin
meminī, -isse (+ genitive: defective verb appearing only in the perfect
    system): remember, recall

CONJUNCTIONS AND ADVERBS

praeter (+ accusative): beyond, except, in addition to, in front of
plērumque: for the most part, commonly, generally
postquam: after, when
quandō: when

II. Translate the following sentences from Latin to English or English to Latin.

1. Patriam quoque parentēs nostrōs servāre oportet.
2. Virtūtem plērumque ab hostibus audāciōribus petī nōn decet.
3. Spīritus poētae cuius carmina amoena erant sanctissimus fit.
4. Nam mē crīminis tuī meminisse pudet taedetque.
5. Nunc vestigia animālium quōrum imāginēs in aedibus deōrum vīsae sunt discere libet.

6. Quandō inpluit, praeter urbis moenia pergere nōn licuit.

7. Itur in nemus antiquum.

8. Mōrēs senātūs populīque Rōmānī sustinēre Cicerōnī placuit.

9. It displeases me to see very bold children.

10. It is fitting that faith prevails among all the citizens.

11. It is in accord with divine law to worship the gods here in the temples.

12. I pity these city walls.

Carthage

According to tradition, Carthage ("New Town") was founded by the Phoenician Queen Dido of Tyre (southern Lebanon) in 814/13 BCE, on a longitude just west of Rome. Archaeology, however, dates the city's beginnings to the mid-eighth century, contemporary with Rome's founding. The city itself was well situated between good harbors on the coast of northeastern Tunisia and fertile lands where agriculture flourished, and it soon became the most important maritime trade center in the western Mediterranean, facilitating the exchange of agricultural produce, raw materials, and luxury goods between Iberia, Italy, and Greece. Carthage was also a center of exploration and colonization. Around 500 BCE, the Carthaginian navigator Hanno set sail through the Pillars of Hercules (Straits of Gibraltar) to sail around Africa. The expedition turned back at Mount Cameroun on the excuse that they had run out of supplies, but not before the adventurers had captured a "gorilla," whose hide remained on display in Carthage for centuries. Attempts to colonize the western Mediterranean were more successful. From c. 600 BCE Carthage prevailed against Greek and Etruscan interests in Sardinia, Corsica, Sicily, and Spain, but it refrained from interfering in Italy.

Treaties between Rome and Carthage were struck in 508 BCE and 348 BCE. In 280 BCE, the Carthaginian fleet even came to the aid of Rome against the Greek general Pyrrhus's incursion into southern Italy. By 264 BCE, however, as tensions over the hegemony of the western Mediterranean grew, interference in Sicilian politics brought Rome and Carthage into direct conflict. The Mamertines, mercenaries from Campania, seized Messina (on the northwest tip of Sicily, just opposite Italy's "toe"), and they soon clashed with Hiero of Syracuse, who sought to expand his own holdings in Sicily. The Mamertines appealed to both Carthage and Rome for help. The Carthaginians quickly agreed, provided they be allowed to place a garrison in Messina. The Mamertines, however, renewed their appeal to Rome (perhaps expecting the Romans to be more reliable), and Rome sent an armed expedition to their aid, thus precipitating the First Punic War (264–241 BCE).

After a drawn-out campaign fought mostly at sea, Rome eventually emerged victorious. Carthage was obliged to evacuate Sicily and its island holdings west of Italy. An onerous indemnity of 23,000 talents was also imposed. Finding it difficult to pay such an amount, Carthaginian generals then turned to Spain, expanding their holdings and influence as far north as the Ebro River. The Carthaginian attack on Saguntum, a Roman ally, in turn, sparked the Second Punic War (218–201 BCE), which is vividly recounted by Livy and Polybius. Carthage's masterful general and tactician Hannibal was well matched by the equally brilliant Scipio Africanus. After the Romans inflicted a devastating loss on Carthage, the Carthaginians ceded all their territory (except for the city itself and immediate suburbs), all war vessels (except for ten triremes—hardly a sufficient military threat), and all their war elephants. Carthage was again burdened with another oppressive indemnity (10,000 talents total, to be paid over fifty years) and was further hamstrung in that all border disputes were to be arbitrated by the Roman Senate. Rome almost invariably decided in favor of Carthage's belligerent Numidian neighbors, who engaged in frequent border skirmishes.

By 151 BCE, the indemnity was fully paid. Carthage, which had considered the terms of its treaty with Rome fulfilled, raised a military expedition to repel yet another Numidian incursion and suffered yet another defeat, which sparked the Third Punic War (149–146 BCE) despite desperate efforts at diplomacy. Capitulating to Roman demands (hostages and the relinquishment of weapons), Carthage decided on war when Rome threatened to burn the city. Scipio Aemilianus, the adopted grandson of the Roman hero of the Second Punic War, eventually assaulted the city, overwhelming the starving inhabitants, who fought valiantly. The city was burned, and the surviving inhabitants were sold into slavery. The tradition that the fields were salted is almost certainly apocryphal, but a ceremonial plowing ritual is probable. Cato the Elder who served as a junior officer in the Second Punic War and who ended many of his senatorial speeches with the tagline *Carthāgō delenda est* ("Carthage must be destroyed") may have inspired such a legend.

The site was eventually refounded by Augustus, completing another of Caesar's many plans, and built up as a Roman city with a forum, basilica (the largest outside Rome), theater, circus, amphitheater, and the monumental Baths of Antoninus, whose stunning remains face the sea, supplied by the equally impressive Zaghouan aqueduct (82 miles, the longest known in antiquity, underwritten by Hadrian, c. 128 CE). By 40 CE, Carthage was appointed the capital of the province of Africa, thriving again as a mercantile and intellectual hub. The city's culture was a *koine* of Punic, Roman, and Greek. Particularly impressive are the richly detailed and varied mosaics from private homes and public spaces. Carthaginian religion was also syncretic, with annual tributes to Melqart ("King of the City," assimilated to Heracles), and the ancient Ba'al ("Master") Hammon and his consort Tanit ("Serpent Lady"), who were appeased only by child sacrifice. Scholars are divided over whether such human sacrifice occurred, but archaeology and Near Eastern sources strongly suggest that leading citizens were obliged to offer child sacrifices (or animal substitutes) to appease their gods. In late antiquity, Carthage became a stronghold of orthodox Christianity.

SUGGESTIONS FOR FURTHER READING:

Ben Khader, Aïcha Ben Abed. *Tunisian Mosaics: Treasures from Roman Africa.* Translated from the French by Sharon Grevet. Getty, 2006.

Brown, Shelby. *Late Carthaginian Child Sacrifice and Sacrificial Monuments in Their Mediterranean Context.* Academic Press, 1991.

Hoyos, Dexter. *The Carthaginians.* Routledge, 2010.

Lancel, Serge. *Carthage: A History.* Translated by Antonia Neville. Blackwell, 1995.

Lazenby, J. F. *Hannibal's War: A Military History of the Second Punic War.* University of Oklahoma, 1998.

Rives, J. B. *Religion and Authority in Roman Carthage from Augustus to Constantine.* Oxford, 1995.

PASSAGES

20.1. Livy, *ab Urbe Condita* 21.3.4. After the death of Hamilcar Barca in battle (228 BCE), the Carthaginian military leadership in Spain was taken up by his son-in-law Hasdrubal. Hasdrubal had requested that Hamilcar Barca's young son, Hannibal, accompany the army on campaign. The friends of

Hannibal's father approved the request, eager that the young man see active service and hoping that Hannibal would eventually take his father's place, but his father's enemies were hoping to weaken the Barca family and their political supporters. Hanno, leader of the anti-Barca party, here urges that Hannibal stay at home and not train under Hasdrubal, as Hasdrubal's intentions were not entirely honorable.

Nōs tamen minimē decet iuventūtem nostram prō mīlitārī rudīmentō adsuēfacere libīdinī praetōrum.

Notes: **iuventus, iuventūtis**, f: youth, young man in the prime of life; **mīlitāris, -e**: military, of a soldier; **rudīmentum, -ī**, n: trial, basic training; **adsuēfaciō, -ere, -fēcī, -factus**: accustom to, habituate, make accustomed to; **libīdō, libīdinis**, f: violent desire, appetite, obscene passion.

20.2. Livy, *ab Urbe Condita* 21.4.1. Like Rome, Carthage was governed by a Senate that was responsible for assigning military commissions. When the Carthaginian Senate debates which general should have command in Spain in 222 BCE, Hanno or Hannibal, Hannibal proves more popular with both the people and the troops who remember his father Hamilcar's military successes. The Senate votes in favor of the war hero's son.

Paucī ac fermē optimus quisque Hannōnī adsentiēbantur; sed, ut plērumque fit, māior pars meliōrem vīcit.

Notes: **fermē**: almost, nearly; **Hannō, -ōnis**, m: opponent of the Barca family mentioned in the previous passage; **adsentiēbantur**: "(they) supported" (deponent); **ut**: as.

20.3. Livy, *ab Urbe Condita* 21.23.4. By the spring 218 BCE, Hannibal and his massed troops begin their northward march through the Pyrenees. The men, however, remain ignorant of their ultimate mission. There is much speculation, and the foreign allies strongly (and rightly) suspect that Hannibal's goal is the invasion of Italy. The only way to reach Italy, after crossing the Pyrenees into Gaul, is along a treacherous pass through the Alps, which were considered impassable. Livy describes the less than enthusiastic reaction of Hannibal's Spanish allies.

Postquam per Pyrēnaeum saltum trādūcī exercitus est coeptus rūmorque per barbarōs manāvit certior dē bellō Rōmānō, tria

mīlia inde Carpetānōrum peditum iter āvertērunt. Cōnstābat nōn
tam bellō mōtōs quam longinquitāte viae īnsuperābilīque Alpium
trānsitū.

Notes: **Pyrēnaeus, -a, -um**: belonging to the Pyrenees, the mountain range between
Spain and Gaul; **saltus, -ūs**, m: pass through a mountain, forest, ravine; **trādūcō, -ere,
-dūxī, -ductus**: lead across, carry across, transfer; **rūmor, -ōris**, m: report, rumor;
barbarus, -ī, m: stranger, foreigner, uncivilized person; **manō, -āre, -āvī, -ātus**: flow,
drip; **Carpetānī, -ōrum**, m (plural): a Spanish tribe in central Spain whose major
town was Toletum (Toledo); **pedes, -itis**, m: foot soldier, infantry; **āvertō, -ere, -vertī,
-versus**: turn away, "desert"; **tam . . . quam**: so much . . . as; **mōtōs**: "that they were
terrified"; **longinquitās, -ātis**, f: length, distance, remoteness; **īnsuperābilis, -e**: in-
surmountable, impassable, unconquerable; **Alpēs, -ium**, f (plural): the Alps (perhaps
etymologically related to *albus, -a, -um*); **trānsitus, -ūs**, m: crossing, transit.

20.4. Livy, *ab Urbe Condita* 21.38.1. We do not know which pass Hannibal took
through the Alps into Italy. However, in 1959, two Cambridge students bor-
rowed an elephant from the Turin zoo ("Jumbo"), in an attempt to retrace
Hannibal's route, hiking from Montmelian, France, through the Col du
Mont Cenis (the pass favored by Napoléon Bonaparte who studied ancient
military strategy), into Susa, in Italy (an account was published: John Hoyte,
Trunk Road for Hannibal: With an Elephant Over the Alps. London, 1960).

Hōc maximē modō in Italiam perventum est quīntō mēnse ā
Carthāgine Novā, ut quīdam auctōrēs sunt, quīntō decimō diē
Alpibus superātīs.

Notes: **mēnsis, -is (-ium)**, m: month; **Carthāgō Nova, Carthāginis Novae**, f: a Carthaginian colony in southern Spain (modern Cartagena); **ut**: see *NLP* 20.2; **sunt**:
"(certain authors) report"; **Alpibus superātīs**: "the Alps having been conquered"
(ablative absolute).

20.5. Vergil, *Aeneid* 4.335–36. According to tradition, the animosity between
Carthage and Rome dates back to the ill-starred love affair between the
Trojan hero Aeneas and the Carthaginian queen Dido. After learning of
Aeneas' plans to leave Carthage, Dido savagely reproaches him for trying
to abandon her without even a word. She appeals to the kindnesses she
has shown his men and the pledges that she and Aeneas have exchanged.

Aeneas' reply is characteristically Roman: sober and legalistic. Meter: dactylic hexameter.

"Nec mē meminisse pigēbit Elissae
dum memor ipse meī, dum spīritus hōs regit artūs."

Notes: **Elissa, -ae**, f: Dido; **memor, -oris** (+ genitive): mindful; **artus, -ūs**, m: joint, limb, body.

20.6. Vergil, *Aeneid* 4.550–52. After Aeneas tries to explain that the gods have urged him to return to his mission, Dido continues her tirade. Here she reproaches herself for not having kept faith with her first husband, Sychaeus. Meter: dactylic hexameter.

"Nōn licuit thalamī expertem sine crīmine vītam
dēgere mōre ferae, tālīs nec tangere cūrās;
nōn servāta fidēs cinerī prōmissa Sychaeō."

Notes: **thalamus, -ī**, m: bridal chamber, bedroom; **expers (expertis)** (+ genitive): free (of / from); **dēgō, -ere, dēgī**: spend, live; **fera, -ae**, f: wild beast; **cinis, cineris**, m: ember, ashes; **servāta** (*est*); **prōmissus, -a, -um**: promised; **Sychaeus, -eī**, m: Dido's husband, murdered by her brother before she fled to Carthage.

20.7. Vergil, *Aeneid* 4.612–18. As the Trojan fleet departs, Dido's frenzy increases and she calls down vicious curses on Aeneas before she commits suicide. Her final and most virulent curse, that there be no love between their peoples and no treaties, is eventually realized through the Punic Wars of the third and second centuries BCE. Meter: dactylic hexameter.

"Sī tangere portūs
infandum caput ac terrīs adnāre necesse est,
et sīc fāta Iovis poscunt, hic terminus haeret,
at bellō audācis populī vexātus et armīs,
fīnibus extorris, complexū āvulsus Iūlī,
auxilium implōret videatque indigna suōrum
fūnera."

Notes: **portus, -ūs**, m: harbor, port, haven; **infandus, -a, -um**: unspeakable, abominable; **adnō, -nāre, -nāvī** (+ dative): swim / float towards; **Iuppiter, Iovis**, m: the chief god of the Romans; **poscō, -ere, poposcī**: demand, inquire; **terminus, -ī**, m: end, goal, limit; **haereō, -ēre, haesī, haesus**: cling, stick, adhere; **vexātus, -a, -um**: agitated, harassed, annoyed; **extorris, -e**: foreign, banished, exiled; **complexus, -ūs**, m: embrace, grasp; **āvulsus, -a, -um**: torn from; **Iūlus, -ī**, m: Aeneas' son Ascanius, who became known as Iulus after the fall of Troy; **implōret videatque**: "let him beg (for help) and let him see" (present subjunctives); **indignus, -a, -um**: unworthy, undeserved; **fūnus, fūneris**, n: burial, death, disaster.

20.8. Ovid, *Heroides* 7.167–68. Ovid's Dido is more elegant, restrained, and feminine than Vergil's. She appeals to notions of Roman *pietas* as well as her own strongly developed sense of honor, blaming herself for falling in love with a man who would not return her affection. Despite her protestations, Dido still loves Aeneas deeply and begs him to take her with him. Meter: elegiac couplets.

> Sī pudet uxōris, nōn nupta sed hospita dīcar;
> > dum tua sit Dīdō, quidlibet esse feret.

Notes: **nupta, -ae**, f: bride; **hospita, -ae**, f: hostess, stranger; **dum sit**: "so long as (Dido) exists"; **Dīdō, Dīdūs**, f: the founder of Carthage; **quidlibet esse**: "whatever is to be".

20.9. Ovid, *Fasti* 3.651–54. After Dido's suicide, her sister Anna finds her way to Italy, where she is taken in by Aeneas. Aeneas' wife, Lavinia, resents her husband's attentions to the Sidonian lady and plots Anna's demise. Warned by her sister's ghost, Anna flees the palace, finding refuge with a local river god, while Aeneas' men pursue her. Here we meet Anna, transformed, addressing the men. She will be worshipped at Rome as Anna Perenna on the Ides of March, in an annual festival on the banks of the Tibur, where revelers imbibe as many cups of wine as years they hope yet to live. It is no wonder that Caesar's enemies chose this day for the assassination, when his supporters would have been otherwise engaged. Meter: elegiac couplets.

> Ventum erat ad rīpās: inerant vestīgia rīpīs;
> > sustinuit tacitās conscius amnis aquās.
> Ipsa loquī vīsa est, "Placidī sum nympha Numīcī:
> > amne perenne latens Anna Perenna vocor."

Notes: **rīpa, -ae**, f: riverbank; **insum, -esse, -fuī, -futūrus**: be in, be on; **tacitus, -a, -um**: silent, mute; **conscius, -a, -um**: aware, privy, witnessing; **loquī**: "to speak" (deponent); **placidus, -a, -um**: quiet, still, gentle; **nympha, -ae**, f: a goddess of springs and fountains; **Numīcius, -iī**, m: a small river in Latium, near Lavinium, where Aeneas was buried. The eponymous river god cleansed Aeneas of his mortality, to be worshipped as Jupiter Indigēs (*Numīcī = Numīciī*); **perennis, -e**: everlasting, through the year (*perenne = perennī*); **latens (-entis)**: hiding (in); **Anna, -ae**, f: a name etymologically related to *annus*; **perennus, -a, -um**: lasting, durable, perennial.

20.10. Sallust, *Bellum Jugurthinum* 14.24–25. Border skirmishes between Carthage and its neighbors created further challenges for Rome. After the death of Micipsa in 118 BCE, his son Hiempsal took the throne but was soon murdered by the agents of his adopted brother Jugurtha. Numidia braced for civil war as Adherbal, another son of Micipsa, and Jugurtha rallied their troops. Each prince appealed to Rome for support. After reminding the Romans of Numidia's long-standing loyalty to Roman interests, Adherbal here appeals to the Roman sense of justice.

"Nunc neque vīvere libet neque morī licet sine dēdecore. Patrēs conscriptī, per vōs, per līberōs atque parentīs vestrōs, per māiestātem populī Rōmānī, subvenīte mihi miserō, īte obviam iniūriae, nōlīte patī regnum Numidiae, quod vestrum est, per scelus et sanguinem familiae nostrae tābescere."

Notes: **morī**: "to die" (deponent infinitive); **dēdecus, dēdecoris**, n: dishonor, disgrace, shame; **pater conscriptus, patris conscriptī**, m: senator; **māiestās, -ātis**, f: dignity, grandeur, greatness; **subveniō, -īre, -vēnī, -ventus**: come to aid, come to relieve; **īre obviam** (+ dative): to go to meet, to face up to; **nōlīte patī**: "do not allow" (*patī*: deponent infinitive); **Numidia, -iae**, f: an ancient kingdom in northern Africa west of Carthage; **tābescō, -ere, tābuī**: melt, waste away.

20.11. Sallust, *Bellum Jugurthinum* 85.38. Before Marius returned to campaign in Numidia, he called a public assembly both to annoy the Senate (who feared his popularity with the mob) and to recruit soldiers. Marius refers to the stark contrast between the hardworking, disciplined men of Rome's glorious past and the current leadership given more to luxury than virtue. Claiming not to "know the proper arrangements for a smart dinner party," Marius here implicitly contrasts his future soldiers with the Senators.

"Māiōrēs eōrum omnia quae licēbat illīs relīquēre: dīvitiās, imāginēs, memoriam suī praeclāram; virtūtem nōn relīquēre, neque poterant: ea sōla neque datur dōnō neque accipitur."

Notes: **imāginēs**: referring to the wax masks of the ancestors (see *NLP* 13); **praeclārus, -a, -um**: excellent, distinguished.

20.12. Sallust, *Bellum Jugurthinum* 102.9. After a final bloody battle, disastrous for both sides, Bocchus (Jugurtha's father-in-law and onetime ally) negotiated a peace with Rome, handing Jugurtha to the Romans. Chosen as the envoy to accept Bocchus's plea bargain is Sulla, who would later fight against Marius in civil war at Rome in the 80s BCE. Sulla here addresses a former enemy as a current friend in a spirit of understanding and forgiveness.

"Sed quoniam hūmānārum rērum Fortūna plēraque regit, cui scīlicet placuit et vim et grātiam nostram tē experīrī, nunc, quandō per illam licet, festīnā atque, utī coepistī, perge."

Notes: **plērusque, plēraque, plērumque**: very many, a large part, the most; **scīlicet**: evidently, certainly; **experīrī**: "to experience" (deponent infinitive); **festīnō, -āre, -āvī, -ātus**: hasten, hurry; **utī**: as.

EXTRA PASSAGES: NORTH AFRICAN CHRISTIAN WRITERS

In the Christian era, Carthage became a center of Christian thought. The scant archaeological remains from this era include several basilicas. Two of the most important early Christian writers were from North Africa. Born at Carthage and called "the Father of Latin Christianity," Tertullian (160–225 CE) was the first to produce a significant collection of Christian writings in Latin (the field had been dominated by Greek authors, including Clement, Origen, and Cyril, all from Alexandria). Tertullian advocated a life of discipline, self-denial, and austerity as the path to God. In the next century, Augustine (354–430 CE) was born at Hippo (in modern Algeria) to a Christian mother and "pagan" father. After receiving a classical education in rhetoric at Carthage, he converted to Christianity as an adult and was baptized in 387 CE. Deeply influenced by Aristotle, Vergil, Cicero, and Neoplatonism, Augustine succeeded in infusing classical philosophical thought into Christian dogma.

20.13. Augustine, *Confessiones* 1.7.12. In this autobiographical work, Augustine explores his own path to God, from his less than pious youth to conversion. Here, he contemplates his own infancy, dismissing it as a period of life lacking in awareness.

Piget mē adnumerāre huic vītae meae quam vīvō in hōc saeculō.

Notes: **adnumerō, -āre, -āvī, -ātus**: add (something) to (here construe Augustine's infancy as the object of *adnumerāre*); **saeculum, -ī**, n: age, generation.

20.14. **Tertullian,** *Apologeticus* **34.3.** In the eastern Mediterranean it was common to worship powerful leaders as living gods. This practice eventually found its way to Rome, and well-loved leaders (starting with Caesar and Augustus) were deified by a simple vote of the Senate. Emperor worship eventually came to include paying homage to living leaders, with offerings of incense to the protective spirit of the sitting emperor; refusal to do so was considered treason. Tertullian here criticizes this imperial demand.

Estō religiōsus in deum, quī vīs illum propitium imperatōrī! Dēsine alium deum crēdere atque ita et hunc deum dīcere, cui deō opus est!

Notes: **religiōsus, -a, -um**: scrupulous, strict in religious observance; **propitius, -a, -um**: favorable (to), gracious (to) (construe with an understood *esse*); **dēsinō, -ere, -sīvī, -situs** (+ infinitive): cease (to), stop (from), desist (from); **crēdere**: here governing an accusative direct object (not the expected dative object); **opus est**: there is a need (for).

20.15. **Tertullian,** *ad Uxorem* **1.7.5.** Tertullian wrote his wife two letters about marriage, the evils of remarriage, and the problems of marrying outside the faith. He represents widowhood as an opportunity for continence, moderation, and physical purity. The church lauded the Roman ideal of the *ūnivīra* (the woman who has been married only once, to one man), and the corresponding ideal of the "*ūnifēminus.*" Here we learn that the demands of ritual purity on the Pontifex Maximus also forbade remarriage.

Rēgem saeculī, Pontificem Maximum, rursus nūbere nefās est.

Notes: **saeculī**: see *NLP* 20.13; **pontifex maximus, pontificis maximī**, m: the elected priest at Rome who oversaw all religious activity in the city, served for life, and held great political authority (among the prerogatives of the emperor from Augustus onward); **nūbō, -ere, nupsī, nuptus**: cover, veil, marry; **nefās**, n (indeclinable): not in accord with divine law, wicked, evil.

Deponent Verbs

1. In Latin, some verbs have passive endings but active meanings. These verbs are **DEPONENT**. Study the following examples:

Martial 5.83: **<u>Insequeris</u>, fugiō; fugis, <u>insequor</u>.** <u>You pursue</u>, I flee; you flee, <u>I pursue</u>.

Tacitus, *Annales* 1.7.5: **Mīles in forum, mīles in cūriam <u>comitābātur</u>.** The soldiery <u>accompanied</u> (Tiberius) into the forum, the soldiery (accompanied him) into the Senate House.

Livy, *ab Urbe Condita* 1.58.2: **"Sextus Tarquinius sum; ferrum in manū est; <u>moriēre</u>, sī ēmīseris vōcem."** "I am Sextus Tarquinius. There is a sword in my hand. You <u>will die</u>, if you (will have) uttered a cry."

Vergil, *Aeneid* 9.5: **Ad quem sīc roseō Thaumantias ōre <u>locūta est</u>.** The daughter of Thaumas <u>spoke</u> to him thus from her rosy mouth.

Vergil, *Aeneid* 8.520: **Vix ea <u>fātus erat</u>.** Scarcely <u>had he spoken</u> these things.

Ovid, *Metamorphoses* 15.448–49: **Quō cum tellus <u>erit ūsa</u>, <u>fruentur</u>/aetheriae sēdēs, caelumque erit exitus illī.** When the earth <u>will have used</u> him (Caesar), the heavenly seats <u>will enjoy</u> him, and the sky will be his destination.

2. The only way to know whether a verb with passive endings is regular or deponent is to learn the verb's principal parts. Deponent verbs have **UNIQUE DICTIONARY ENTRIES** with **THREE** (not four) principal parts (1st singular present, present infinitive, and 1st singular perfect), all of which are **PASSIVE** in form.

Below are the principal parts for the paradigm deponent verbs:

cōnor, cōnārī, cōnātus sum: try (1st conjugation)
polliceor, pollicērī, pollicitus sum: promise (2nd conjugation)
loquor, loquī, locūtus sum: speak (3rd conjugation)
ingredior, ingredī, ingressus sum: enter (3rd conjugation -io)
orior, orīrī, ortus sum: rise (4th conjugation)

N.B. As with regular verbs, you identify the conjugation of a deponent verb from the second principal part—the **passive** form of the present infinitive (see *NLP* 17).

3. For the **PRESENT, IMPERFECT, AND FUTURE TENSES** of deponent verbs, you will use the same passive forms that you learned in *NLP* 17. Review the tables below, keeping in mind that you do not need to memorize any new forms. Rather, you must recognize that these verbs look passive but translate as if they are active.

PRESENT DEPONENT TENSE

	1st Conj.	2nd Conj.	3rd Conj.	3rd Conj. (-io)	4th Conj.
Singular					
1st	cōnor: I try	polliceor: I promise	loquor: I speak	ingredior: I enter	orior: I rise
2nd	cōnāris / cōnāre: you try	pollicēris / pollicēre: you promise	loqueris / loquere: you speak	ingrederis / ingredere: you enter	orīris / orīre: you rise
3rd	cōnātur: he / she / it tries	pollicētur: he / she / it promises	loquitur: he / she / it speaks	ingreditur: he / she / it enters	orītur: he / she / it rises
Plural					
1st	cōnāmur: we try	pollicēmur: we promise	loquimur: we speak	ingredimur: we enter	orīmur: we rise
2nd	cōnāminī: you try	pollicēminī: you promise	loquiminī: you speak	ingrediminī: you enter	orīminī: you rise
3rd	cōnantur: they try	pollicentur: they promise	loquuntur: they speak	ingrediuntur: they enter	oriuntur: they rise

IMPERFECT DEPONENT TENSE

	1st Conj.	2nd Conj.	3rd Conj.	3rd Conj. (-io)	4th Conj.
Singular					
1st	cōnābar: I was trying	pollicēbar: I was promising	loquēbar: I was speaking	ingrediēbar: I was entering	oriēbar: I was rising
2nd	cōnābāris / cōnābāre: you were trying	pollicēbāris / pollicēbāre: you were promising	loquēbāris / loquēbāre: you were speaking	ingrediēbāris / ingrediēbāre: you were entering	oriēbāris / oriēbāre: you were rising
3rd	cōnābātur: he / she / it was trying	pollicēbātur: he / she / it was promising	loquēbātur: he / she / it was speaking	ingrediēbātur: he / she / it was entering	oriēbātur: he / she / it was rising
Plural					
1st	cōnābāmur: we were trying	pollicēbāmur: we were promising	loquēbāmur: we were speaking	ingrediēbāmur: we were entering	oriēbāmur: we were rising
2nd	cōnābāminī: you were trying	pollicēbāminī: you were promising	loquēbāminī: you were speaking	ingrediēbāminī: you were entering	oriēbāminī: you were rising
3rd	cōnābantur: they were trying	pollicēbantur: they were promising	loquēbantur: they were speaking	ingrediēbantur: they were entering	oriēbantur: they were rising

FUTURE DEPONENT TENSE

	1st Conj.	2nd Conj.	3rd Conj.	3rd Conj. (-io)	4th Conj.
Singular					
1st	cōnābor: I shall try	pollicēbor: I shall promise	loquar: I shall speak	ingrediar: I shall enter	oriar: I shall rise
2nd	cōnāberis / cōnābere: you will try	pollicēberis / pollicēbere: you will promise	loquēris / loquēre: you will speak	ingrediēris / ingrediēre: you will enter	oriēris / oriēre: you will rise
3rd	cōnābitur: he / she / it will try	pollicēbitur: he / she / it will promise	loquētur: he / she / it will speak	ingrediētur: he / she / it will enter	oriētur: he / she / it will rise

(continued)

	1st Conj.	2nd Conj.	3rd Conj.	3rd Conj. (-io)	4th Conj.
Plural					
1st	cōnābimur: we shall try	pollicēbimur: we shall promise	loquēmur: we shall speak	ingrediēmur: we shall enter	oriēmur: we shall rise
2nd	cōnābiminī: you will try	pollicēbiminī: you will promise	loquēminī: you will speak	ingrediēminī: you will enter	oriēminī: you will rise
3rd	cōnābuntur: they will try	pollicēbuntur: they will promise	loquentur: they will speak	ingredientur: they will enter	orientur: they will rise

4. For the **PERFECT, PLUPERFECT, AND FUTURE PERFECT TENSES** of deponent verbs, you will use the same passive forms that you learned in *NLP* 18. Again, there are no new forms to memorize. Focus instead on the active meanings of these "passive-looking" verbs.

PERFECT DEPONENT TENSE

	1st Conj.	2nd Conj.	3rd Conj.	3rd Conj. (-io)	4th Conj.
Singular					
1st	cōnātus, -a, -um **sum**: I have tried	pollicitus, -a, -um **sum**: I have promised	locūtus, -a, -um **sum**: I have spoken	ingressus, -a, -um **sum**: I have entered	ortus, -a, -um **sum**: I have risen
2nd	cōnātus, -a, -um **es**: you have tried	pollicitus, -a, -um **es**: you have promised	locūtus, -a, -um **es**: you have spoken	ingressus, -a, -um **es**: you have entered	ortus, -a, -um **es**: you have risen
3rd	cōnātus, -a, -um **est**: he/she/it has tried	pollicitus, -a, -um **est**: he/she/it has promised	locūtus, -a, -um **est**: he/she/it has spoken	ingressus, -a, -um **est**: he/she/it has entered	ortus, -a, -um **est**: he/she/it has risen
Plural					
1st	cōnātī, -ae, -a **sumus**: we have tried	pollicitī, -ae, -a **sumus**: we have promised	locūtī, -ae, -a **sumus**: we have spoken	ingressī, -ae, -a **sumus**: we have entered	ortī, -ae, -a **sumus**: we have risen
2nd	cōnātī, -ae, -a **estis**: you have tried	pollicitī, -ae, -a **estis**: you have promised	locūtī, -ae, -a **estis**: you have spoken	ingressī, -ae, -a **estis**: you have entered	ortī, -ae, -a **estis**: you have risen
3rd	cōnātī, -ae, -a **sunt**: they have tried	pollicitī, -ae, -a **sunt**: they have promised	locūtī, -ae, -a **sunt**: they have spoken	ingressī, -ae, -a **sunt**: they have entered	ortī, -ae, -a **sunt**: they have risen

PLUPERFECT DEPONENT TENSE

	1st Conj.	2nd Conj.	3rd Conj.	3rd Conj. -io	4th Conj.
Singular					
1st	cōnātus, -a, -um **eram:** I had tried	pollicitus, -a, -um **eram:** I had promised	locūtus, -a, -um **eram:** I had spoken	ingressus, -a, -um **eram:** I had entered	ortus, -a, -um **eram:** I had risen
2nd	cōnātus, -a, -um **erās:** you had tried	pollicitus, -a, -um **erās:** you had promised	locūtus, -a, -um **erās:** you had spoken	ingressus, -a, -um **erās:** you had entered	ortus, -a, -um **erās:** you had risen
3rd	cōnātus, -a, -um **erat:** he/she/it had tried	pollicitus, -a, -um **erat:** he/she/it had promised	locūtus, -a, -um **erat:** he/she/it had spoken	ingressus, -a, -um **erat:** he/she/it had entered	ortus, -a, -um **erat:** he/she/it had risen
Plural					
1st	cōnātī, -ae, -a **erāmus:** we had tried	pollicitī, -ae, -a **erāmus:** we had promised	locūtī, -ae, -a **erāmus:** we had spoken	ingressī, -ae, -a **erāmus:** we had entered	ortī, -ae, -a **erāmus:** we had risen
2nd	cōnātī, -ae, -a **erātis:** you had tried	pollicitī, -ae, -a **erātis:** you had promised	locūtī, -ae, -a **erātis:** you had spoken	ingressī, -ae, -a **erātis:** you had entered	ortī, -ae, -a **erātis:** you had risen
3rd	cōnātī, -ae, -a **erant:** they had tried	pollicitī, -ae, -a **erant:** they had promised	locūtī, -ae, -a **erant:** they had spoken	ingressī, -ae, -a **erant:** they had entered	ortī, -ae, -a **erant:** they had risen

FUTURE PERFECT DEPONENT TENSE

	1st Conj.	2nd Conj.	3rd Conj.	3rd Conj. -io	4th Conj.
Singular					
1st	cōnātus, -a, -um **erō:** I shall have tried	pollicitus, -a, -um **erō:** I shall have promised	locūtus, -a, -um **erō:** I shall have spoken	ingressus, -a, -um **erō:** I shall have entered	ortus, -a, -um **erō:** I shall have risen
2nd	cōnātus, -a, -um **eris:** you will have tried	pollicitus, -a, -um **eris:** you will have promised	locūtus, -a, -um **eris:** you will have spoken	ingressus, -a, -um **eris:** you will have entered	ortus, -a, -um **eris:** you will have risen
3rd	cōnātus, -a, -um **erit:** he/she/it will have tried	pollicitus, -a, -um **erit:** he/she/it will have promised	locūtus, -a, -um **erit:** he/she/it will have spoken	ingressus, -a, -um **erit:** he/she/it will have entered	ortus, -a, -um **erit:** he/she/it will have risen

(continued)

	1st Conj.	2nd Conj.	3rd Conj.	3rd Conj. -io	4th Conj.
Plural					
1st	cōnātī, -ae, -a **erimus:** we shall have tried	pollicitī, -ae, -a **erimus:** we shall have promised	locūtī, -ae, -a **erimus:** we shall have spoken	ingressī, -ae, -a **erimus:** we shall have entered	ortī, -ae, -a **erimus:** we shall have risen
2nd	cōnātī, -ae, -a **eritis:** you will have tried	pollicitī, -ae, -a **eritis:** you will have promised	locūtī, -ae, -a **eritis:** you will have spoken	ingressī, -ae, -a **eritis:** you will have entered	ortī, -ae, -a **eritis:** you will have risen
3rd	cōnātī, -ae, -a **erunt:** they will have tried	pollicitī, -ae, -a **erunt:** they will have promised	locūtī, -ae, -a **erunt:** they will have spoken	ingressī, -ae, -a **erunt:** they will have entered	ortī, -ae, -a **erunt:** they will have risen

5. Deponent infinitives are formed in exactly the same way as the passive infinitives of regular verbs (see *NLP* 17 and 18). Again, there are no new forms to memorize. Focus instead on the active meanings of these "passive-looking" infinitives. Study the following table:

INFINITIVES OF DEPONENT VERBS

	1st Conj.	2nd Conj.	3rd Conj.	3rd Conj. -io	4th Conj.
Present Deponent	cōnārī: to try	pollicērī: to promise	loquī: to speak	ingredī: to enter	orīrī: to rise
Perfect Deponent	cōnātus, -a, -um **esse:** to have tried	pollicitus, -a, -um **esse:** to have promised	locūtus, -a, -um **esse:** to have spoken	ingressus, -a, -um **esse:** to have entered	ortus, -a, -um **esse:** to have risen

6. Deponent imperatives are formed in exactly the same way as the passive imperatives of regular verbs (see *NLP* 17). Again, there are no new forms to memorize. Focus instead on the active meanings of these "passive-looking" imperatives. Study the following table:

PRESENT IMPERATIVE OF DEPONENT VERBS

	1st Conj.	2nd Conj.	3rd Conj.	3rd Conj. (-io)	4th Conj.
Singular	cōnā**re:** try!	pollicē**re:** promise!	loque**re:** speak!	ingrede**re:** enter!	orī**re:** rise!
Plural	cōnā**minī:** try!	pollicē**minī:** promise!	loqui**minī:** speak!	ingredi**minī:** enter!	orī**minī:** rise!

7. A few deponent verbs complete their meaning with an ablative of means. These ablative expressions usually translate into English as if they were direct objects. Consider the following examples:

Vergil, *Aeneid* 6.885–86: **Fungar <u>inānī/mūnere</u>**. <u>I shall perform</u> <u>a futile service</u>.

Caesar, *de Bello Gallico* 1.26.4: **<u>Impedīmentīs castrīsque</u> nostrī <u>potītī sunt</u>**. Our men <u>acquired</u> <u>the baggage and the camp</u>.

Catullus 12.1–2: **Marrucīne Asinī, <u>manū sinistrā</u>/nōn belle <u>ūteris</u>, in iocō atque vīnō.** Marrucinus Asinius, <u>you do not use</u> <u>your left hand</u> well in joke and in wine.

There are five common deponent verbs that fit this profile:

> **fruor, -ī, fructus sum**: enjoy
> **fungor, -ī, functus sum**: perform
> **potior, -īrī, potitus sum**: acquire
> **ūtor, -ī, usus sum**: use
> **vescor, -ī**: eat

8. Some verbs are classified as **SEMI-DEPONENT** with **active** forms and meanings in the present, imperfect, and future tenses, but with **passive** forms and active meanings in the perfect, pluperfect, and future perfect tenses. Like regular deponent verbs, semi-deponents have three principal parts (1st singular present, infinitive, and 1st singular perfect). The first two principal parts are active in form, and the third is passive in form. Below are three very common semi-deponent verbs.

> **audeō, -ēre, ausus sum**: dare
> **gaudeō, -ēre, gāvīsus sum**: rejoice, delight in
> **soleō, -ēre, solitus sum**: be accustomed

9. These semi-deponent verbs can sometimes cause confusion because it is easy to forget that the passive forms of the perfect system have active meanings. Study the following examples:

Catullus 1.5–6: **Cum <u>ausus es</u> ūnus Ītalōrum / omne aevum tribus explicāre cartīs** ... When you alone of the Italians <u>dared</u> to unfold the entire age in three books ...

Cicero, *ad Familiares* 11.13.4: **<u>Gāvīsus sum</u>**. <u>I rejoiced</u>.

Sallust, *Bellum Jugurthinum* 4.7: **Etiam hominēs novī, quī antea per virtūtem <u>solitī erant</u> nōbilitātem antevenīre** ... Even new men, who previously <u>had been accustomed</u> to outstrip their renown through virtue ...

I. Required Vocabulary

NOUNS

prōvincia, -iae, f: command, province, the backwoods

vulgus, -ī, n: the people, the public, the crowd

ardor, -ōris, m: passion, eagerness
sēdēs, -is (-ium), f: seat, base, home

ADJECTIVES

fessus, -a, -um: tired, weary, worn out, exhausted

VERBS

audeō, -ēre, ausus sum: dare
gaudeō, -ēre, gāvīsus sum: rejoice, delight in
soleō, -ēre, solitus sum: be accustomed

cōnor, -ārī, cōnātus sum: try
mīror, -ārī, mīrātus sum: wonder (at), marvel (at)

polliceor, -ērī, pollicitus sum: offer, promise
reor, rērī, ratus sum: think, suppose, judge, consider

dēgredior, -gredī, dēgressus sum: step down, depart for
    ingredior, -gredī, ingressus sum: enter
    regredior, -gredī, regressus sum: step back, retreat
    transgredior, -gredī, transgressus sum: cross over, pass over to
loquor, loquī, locūtus sum: speak, mention, say, address
    adloquor, -loquī, adlocūtus sum: speak, address
oblīviscor, -ī, oblītus sum (+ genitive): forget
proficiscor, proficiscī, profectus sum: set out, depart
sequor, sequī, secūtus sum: follow, accompany, attend, yield, aim at
    consequor, -sequī, consecūtus sum: follow, go after
    prōsequor, -sequī, prōsecūtus sum: follow, accompany, attend
ulciscor, -ī, ultus sum: avenge, take vengeance, punish
ūtor, -ī, ūsus sum (+ ablative): use

orior, -īrī, ortus sum: rise, begin, spring forth (from)

CONJUNCTIONS AND ADVERBS
    igitur: therefore
    ōlim: once
    statim: immediately

II. Translate the following sentences from Latin to English or English to Latin.

1. Mātrēs patrēsque crīmina līberōrum audācia mīrantur.
2. Imperātor mīlitēs post proelium statim locūtus est.
3. Parentēs grātiās ēgērunt quod ipsī ante moenia nōn caesī erant.
4. Vulgus rēgem acrem ulciscētur.
5. Cīvēs inter flūmina et per montēs regrediēbantur.
6. Dīvitiīs et dōnīs numquam ūsī estis.
7. Flammae in castra transgressae sunt, et dūcēs rem gravem rēbantur.
8. Urbis sanctae oblīviscēmur.
9. Today we shall set out to the greatest temples.
10. On account of his oration, the soldiers had followed their general.
11. Caesar shall have addressed the legions in the provinces.
12. Certain kings were being killed in front of the ancient city.

Tacitus the Biographer:
Germanicus, Corbulo, and Agricola

Tacitus lived in a time when the emperor, for good or bad, held absolute power at Rome. Long gone were the days of open debate in the Senate, long gone the time when the *populī Rōmānī* (or at least a small slice of the landed *populī Rōmānī*) chose their own leaders, and when good men could advance from the lowest ranks to the highest echelons of honor, when brave men were recognized and honored for their achievements as a matter of course (after Augustus took power, the triumphal parade, once the right of any successful general in the field, became strictly an imperial prerogative). Even under the peaceful, benign regimes of emperors like Nerva and Trajan, Tacitus remained a staunch republican, advocating the ideals of that bygone era over the current system of absolutism. In his portrayals of Germanicus, Corbulo, and Agricola, Tacitus gives us biographies of three charismatic Romans, all more popular and more militarily successful than their emperors, and each, as a result, incurring imperial jealousy and enmity.

To protect his legacy, Augustus took steps to secure the succession for the next two generations, forcing his adopted son Tiberius to adopt in turn Germanicus, the son of Tiberius's popular brother Drusus (who may have harbored republican sympathies). No doubt this adoption was the source of some resentment in the aging Tiberius, whose own considerable accomplishments as both a soldier and statesman were overlooked, then as now. Tacitus's Germanicus was, of course, a literary construct whose traits were selected from the historical Germanicus. In quelling the mutiny that arose after Augustus's death, Germanicus's behavior was often rash. In the East the young man deliberately disregarded imperial mandates—for instance, he visited Egypt without Tiberius's permission, perhaps to enhance his own popularity. Tiberius's approval ratings plummeted after Germanicus's death by poison, perhaps under orders from Tiberius himself. And Tacitus makes it quite clear that the *princeps* feared the popularity and increasing power of his nephew, sufficient cause for his surreptitious execution.

Gnaeus Domitius Corbulo (c. 1–66 CE), like Germanicus, enjoyed military success in Germany, where he defeated the Chauci in 47 CE (under Claudius). Corbulo's reputation and popularity were secured under Nero when he obtained the command in Cappadocia to protect Roman interests in Armenia against Parthian incursion, eventually brokering a treaty with Parthia. Corbulo traveled in powerful circles: his half sister Caesonia was Gaius Caligula's wife, and his younger daughter, Domitia Longina, married the future emperor Domitian (in 71 CE). His son-in-law, Annius Vinicianus, was implicated in a conspiracy against Nero in 66 CE at Beneventum. Perhaps out of jealousy of Corbulo's accomplishments, fear of his popularity, or even his implication in the Pisonian conspiracy of 66 CE, Nero ordered his general to commit suicide. Corbulo's own (lost) memoirs informed the accounts of Tacitus and Cassius Dio.

Tacitus memorialized his own father-in-law, Gnaeus Julius Agricola (40–93 CE), who gained renown in Britain, first during the revolt of Boudicca (60–61 CE) and then as governor (77–84 CE), after supporting the Flavian imperial cause in 69/70 CE. Agricola is known almost exclusively from Tacitus's biography, which celebrates the man's prowess as a soldier, statesman, and diplomat. In Britain, Agricola pacified bellicose territories and extended Roman authority into southern Scotland. His circumnavigation proved, after centuries of debate, that Britain was an island. Recalled to Rome in 84 CE, Agricola was denied further appointments, presumably because of Domitian's jealousy of Agricola's successes in contrast with his own failures against the Dacians, as Tacitus implies.

SUGGESTIONS FOR FURTHER READING:

Gilmartin, Kristine. "Corbulo's Campaign in the East." *Historia* 22 (1973): 583–626.

Martin, Ronald H. "Tacitus on Agricola: Truth and Stereotype." In *Form and Fabric: Studies in Rome's Material Past in Honour of B. R. Hartley*, edited by Joanna Bird and Brian Hartley, 9–12. Oxford, 1998.

Pelling, Christopher. "Tacitus and Germanicus." In *Oxford Readings in Classical Studies: Tacitus*, edited by Rhiannon Ash, 281–313. Oxford, 2012.

Powell, Lindsay. *Germanicus: The Magnificent Life and Mysterious Death of Rome's Most Popular General*. Pen and Sword, 2013.

Syme, Ronald. *Tacitus*. 2 vols. Oxford, 1958.

Syme, Ronald. "Domitius Corbulo." *Journal of Roman Studies* 60 (1970): 37–39.

PASSAGES

21.1. Tacitus, *Annales* 1.49.4. After the mutinies that followed Tiberius's ascension, Germanicus played into the affections that his men felt for him, and which he clearly enjoyed.

Sequitur ardōrem mīlitum Caesar.

Notes: **Caesar, -aris,** m: here, Germanicus.

21.2. Tacitus, *Annales* 1.58.5. In 9 CE, Arminius, chief of the Cherusci in Germany, annihilated three Roman legions under the command of Publius Quinctilius Varus. This defeat, in the thickly wooded Teutoberg Forest, was humiliating. The Romans had a long memory, and Germanicus engaged the Cherusci in two punitive battles. After Germanicus's first victory over Arminius, 15 CE, he shows generosity towards Arminius's father-in-law, Segestes, a pro-Roman Cherusci noble.

Caesar clēmentī responsō līberīs propinquīsque eius incolumitātem, ipsī sēdem vetere in prōvinciā pollicētur.

Notes: **clēmens (-entis):** kind, merciful, mild; **responsum, -ī,** n: answer, reply, response; **propinquus, -ī,** m: relative; **incolumitās, -ātis,** f: safety, preservation.

21.3. Tacitus, *Annales* 2.69.2. Hoping to separate Germanicus from his loyal troops in Gaul and Germany, Tiberius sent the popular general to command the eastern province of Asia in 18 CE. In the following year, Germanicus fell mysteriously ill. Here, the Syrian governor Gnaeus Calpurnius Piso, with whom Germanicus had been feuding, comes to visit the ailing Caesar. Soon afterward, Germanicus dies, and there is much speculation that Piso may have somehow caused the death.

Tum Seleuciam dēgreditur, opperiens aegritūdinem, quae rursum Germānicō acciderat.

Notes: **Seleucia, -iae,** f: Selucia Pieria, the port at Antioch in Turkey; **opperiens (-ientis):** awaiting; **aegritūdō, aegritūdinis,** f: sickness, illness; **accidō, -ere, accidī** (+ dative): happen, befall.

21.4. Tacitus, *Annales* **2.71.1.** Knowing that he is about to die, Germanicus launches into his final address to friends and family, blaming Plancina and her husband Piso for his untimely demise and making an entreaty for justice and vengeance against Tiberius's agents.

Caesar paulisper ad spem ērectus, dein—fessō corpore—ubi fīnis aderat, adsistentīs amīcōs in hunc modum adloquitur.

Notes: **paulisper**: for a little while; **spēs, speī**, f: hope; **ērectus, -a, -um**: raised, encouraged; **fessō corpore**: "his body exhausted" (ablative absolute); **adsistens (-entis)**: standing by.

21.5. Tacitus, *Agricola* **7.5.** In 69 CE, Otho's forces were plundering northwestern Italy, where Agricola's mother lived. The troops murdered Agricola's mother and looted the family estate. Just as Agricola was seeing to funeral arrangements, he heard the happy news that there was now a worthy candidate, Vespasian (whom we met in *NLP* 18.13–15) vying for supreme rule at Rome.

Igitur ad sollemnia pietātis profectus Agricola, nuntiō adfectātī ā Vespasiānō imperiī dēprehensus ac statim in partīs transgressus est.

Notes: **sollemne, -is**, n: religious rite, sacrifice, formality; **profectus** (*est*); **nuntium, -iī**, n: message, news; **adfectātus, -a, -um**: grasped, aimed at; **dēprehensus** (*est*); **dēprehendō, -ere, dēprehendī, dēprehensus**: intercept; **in partīs**: "to the political party / side (of Vespasian)."

21.6. Tacitus, *Agricola* **18.6.** Agricola served as governor of the bellicose province of Britain during 77–85 CE, an unusually lengthy term of office (governors typically served three to five years). He campaigned extensively, subduing militant tribes in Wales, northern England, and Caledonia (at the famous battle of Mons Graupius in 83 CE). Despite his great successes, he conducted his office with restraint and modesty.

Nē laureātīs quidem gesta prōsecūtus est, sed ipsā dissimulātiōne fāmae fāmam auxit.

Notes: **nē . . . quidem**: not even; **laureātīs** (*litterīs*); **laureātus, -a, -um**: crowned with laurel (the Romans customarily crowned dispatches announcing victories with laurel); **gestum, -ī**, n: deed, accomplishment, exploit, success; **dissimulātiō, -iōnis**, f: concealment, disguise; **augeō, -ēre, auxī, auctus**: increase, enlarge, enrich.

21.7. Tacitus, *Agricola* **35.1.** As Caledonian and Roman troops are on the verge of battle at Mons Graupius (an unidentified site in northeastern Scotland), each leader addresses his troops. Maintaining that the massed Caledonian forces (30,000 strong) are merely a worn-out remnant of the brave foes that the Roman troops have already faced, Agricola praises his soldiers for their courage in battle. Here, we witness the enthusiastic reaction to Agricola's rousing pep talk.

Et adloquente adhūc Agricolā mīlitum ardor ēminēbat, et fīnem ōrātiōnis ingens alacritās consecūta est, statimque ad arma discursum.

Notes: **adloquente Agricolā**: "Agricola speaking" (ablative absolute); **ēmineō, -ēre, -uī**: stand out, be conspicuous; **ōrātiō, -iōnis**, f: speech; **alacritās, -ātis**, f: quickness, eagerness; **discursum** (*est*) (impersonal passive); **discurrō, -ere, -cucurri, -cursus**: rush, run to and fro.

21.8. Tacitus, *Agricola* **36.1.** Tacitus offers a lively account of the opening skirmish at Mons Graupius.

Ac prīmō congressū ēminus certābātur; simulque constantiā, simul arte Britannī ingentibus gladiīs et brevibus caetrīs missilia nostrōrum vītāre vel excutere, atque ipsī magnam vim tēlōrum superfundere, dōnec Agricola quattuor Batavōrum cohortīs ac Tungrōrum duās cohortātus est, ut rem ad mūcrōnēs ac manūs addūcerent.

Notes: **congressus, -ūs**, m: meeting, encounter, combat; **ēminus**: from a distance, from afar; **certō, -āre, -āvī, -ātus**: contend, struggle (impersonal passive); **simul**: at the same time; **constantia, -iae**, f: steadiness, firmness, uniformity; **Britannus, -ī**, m: Briton; **gladius, -iī**, m: sword; **caetra, -ae**, f: short Spanish shield; **missilia, -ium**, n (plural): missiles, projectiles; **vītō, -āre, -āvī, -ātus**: avoid, shun (historical infinitive, translate as a third person plural verb with a nominative plural subject); **excutiō, -ere, -cussī, -cussus**: shake off, throw off (historical infinitive); **superfundō, -ere, -fūdī, -fūsus**: pour out, shower down (historical infinitive); **dōnec**: up to the time when, until; **Batavus, -ī**, m: an auxiliary soldier from Batavia (modern Holland), renowned for their bravery and not required to pay taxes or tribute to Rome; **cohors, cohortis (-ium)**, f: troop, company, cohort; **Tungrus, -ī**, m: an auxiliary soldier from the Tungrian tribe of Gaul (modern Belgium); **cohortor, -ī, cohortātus est**: encourage, excite, exhort; **ut rem . . . addūcerent**: "to bring the situation"; **mūcro, -ōnis**, m: point of a sword, sword; **manūs**: hand-to-hand combat.

21.9. Tacitus, *Agricola* **43.1.** Tacitus equivocates on the cause of Agricola's death (he was only fifty-four), whether from natural causes or on Domitian's orders. He is, however, unequivocal about the universal outpouring of grief over the death of his father-in-law.

> Vulgus quoque et hīc aliud agens populus et ventitāvēre ad domum et per fora et circulōs locūtī sunt; nec quisquam audītā morte Agricolae aut laetātus est aut statim oblītus.

Notes: **agens (-entis)**: doing, being busy with; **ventitō, -āre, -āvī, -ātus**: come often, keep coming; **forum, -ī**, n: forum, open square, marketplace; **circulus, -ī**, m: circle, circuit, conversational group; **audītā morte**: "(news of) his death having been heard" (ablative absolute); **laetor, -ārī, laetus sum**: rejoice, be glad; **oblītus** (*est*).

21.10. Tacitus, *Annales* **13.34.2.** The Parthian Empire (northeastern Iran), along the Silk Road, came into conflict with Rome as it expanded westward. Pompey actively campaigned in the region, and Crassus lost his life in battle at Carrhae in 53 BCE against a much smaller but well-trained and organized corps of mounted archers. Worse, he lost the legionary standards. The conflict was never resolved. In 58 CE, Corbulo is sent to deal with matters in the East.

> Corbulō dignum magnitūdine populī Rōmānī rēbātur parta ōlim ā Lūcullō Pompēiōque recipere.

Notes: **Corbulō, -ōnis**, m: powerful Roman commander under Nero; **partum, -ī**, n: gain, acquisition, "territory acquired"; **Lūcullus, -ī**, m: Lucius Lucinius Lucullus, Sulla's ally during the civil wars between Sulla and Marius in the 80s BCE, served as quaestor (88–80 BCE), and campaigned against Mithridates VI in Pontus (73–67 BCE); **Pompēius, -iī**, m: Pompey the Great, who took over Lucullus's command, eradicating pirates in the eastern Mediterranean, vanquishing Mithridates VI, the king of Pontus who had been at war with Rome since 89 BCE. Pompey's pacification of the East (including Parthia) resulted in a continuous band of Roman provinces and a 70 percent increase in tribute. These new provinces and allied client kingships, however, owed their allegiance to Pompey, rather than to the Roman state, and they supported Pompey in the 40s BCE against Caesar.

21.11. Tacitus, *Annales* 14.23.3. In 60 CE, after destroying one Parthian town and proceeding westward to attack another, Corbulo was ambushed by the Mardi, a tribe inhabiting the mountains of central Parthia.

> Quōs Corbulō immissīs Hibērīs vastāvit hostīlemque audāciam externō sanguine ultus est.

Notes: **quōs**: the Mardi; **immissīs Hibērīs**: "Iberian troops having been sent in" (ablative absolute); **vastō, -āre, -āvī, -ātus**: empty, ravage, devastate; **hostīlis, -e**: hostile, enemy, unfriendly; **audācia, -iae**, f: courage, boldness, daring; **externus, -a, -um**: external, foreign, strange.

21.12. Tacitus, *Annales* 13.35.4. Although a generous, charismatic leader, Corbulo was also a strict disciplinarian, enforcing severe punishments for desertion (a common problem because of the harsh Parthian climate and grueling campaigns) and swift and irrevocable sanctions for the worst military crime, that of losing the legionary standards in battle.

> Nec enim, ut in aliīs exercitibus, prīmum alterumque dēlictum venia prōsequēbātur, sed quī signa reliquerat, statim capite poenās luēbat.

Notes: **dēlictum, -ī**, n: misdeed, offense, fault, crime; **venia, -iae**, f: grace, indulgence, favor; **capite**: synecdoche for "life"; **poena, -ae**, f: fine, punishment, penalty; **luō, -ere, luī**: loose, expiate, atone for, pay (*poenās luere*: pay the penalty, suffer punishment).

EXTRA PASSAGES: POETIC BIOGRAPHIES

Just as Tacitus painted complex portraits of Germanicus, Agricola, and Corbulo, poets, too, despite different goals and literary constraints, composed engaging portraits of famous and important Roman political figures.

21.13. Vergil, *Aeneid* 8.685–88. Venus asks her husband Vulcan to craft a wondrous set of armor that will help protect her son Aeneas in battle. Vulcan obliges and forges the entire history of Rome on Aeneas' shield. Here we read a biography of Marc Antony, defeated by Augustus in the Battle of Actium. Meter: dactylic hexameter.

Hinc ope barbaricā variīsque Antōnius armīs,
victor ab Aurōrae populīs et lītore rubrō,
Aegyptum vīrīsque Orientis et ultima sēcum
Bactra vehit, sequiturque (nefās) Aegyptia coniunx.

Notes: **ops, opis**, f: power, might, influence; **barbaricus, -a, -um**: foreign, barbarian; **varius, -a, -um**: varied, composed of different colors; **Aurōra, -ae**, f: the goddess Dawn, here associated with the East; **ruber, rubra, rubrum**: red; **Aegyptus, -ī**, f: Egypt; **Oriens, -ientis**, m: the East; **ultimus, -a, -um**: farthest, most distant; **Bactra, -ōrum**, n (plural): Bactra (Persia); **vehō, -ere, vexī, vectus**: carry, transport; **nefās**, n (indeclinable): not in accord with divine law, wicked, evil; **Aegyptius, -a, -um**: Egyptian.

21.14. Propertius, *Elegiae* **4.6.59–60.** The deified Julius Caesar proudly observes Augustus's victory at the battle of Actium. Meter: elegiac couplets.

At pater Īdaliō mīrātur Caesar ab astrō:
    "Sum deus; est nostrī sanguinis ista fidēs."

Notes: **Īdalius, -a, -um**: belonging to Idalium, a city in Cyprus, sacred to Venus, Caesar's divine ancestress; **astrum, -ī**, n: star, constellation (After Caesar's assassination, a comet appearing in the night sky was believed to be a sign of his divinity. This seven-night phenomenon was widely referred to in contemporary literature as the *sidus Iulium* (Julian star) or *Caesaris astrum* (star of Caesar). Modern astronomers have confirmed comet C/-43 K1 for the month of July in 44 BCE); **ista**: Augustus's victory.

21.15. Propertius, *Elegiae* **2.10.19–20.** Propertius has vowed to abandon love poetry and focus instead on the military exploits of great Roman leaders. He will sing of Augustus's military triumphs. Meter: elegiac couplets.

Haec ego castra sequar; vātēs tua castra canendō
    magnus erō: servent hunc mihi fāta diem!

Notes: **vātēs, -is (-ium)**, m: seer, bard, poet; **canendō**: "by singing" (gerund); **servent**: "let (the fates) preserve."

Participles

1. **PARTICIPLES** are verbal adjectives. You have been translating them (presented as simple adjectives) since *NLP* 3. Like **verbs**, participles have tense (present, perfect, or future) and voice (active or passive). Like **adjectives**, a participle agrees with the noun it modifies in case, number, and gender.

2. There are only four types of participles in Latin: present active, perfect passive, future active, and future passive.

PART 1: PRESENT ACTIVE PARTICIPLES

3. The **PRESENT ACTIVE PARTICIPLE** describes what a particular noun is doing at the same time as the main action of the sentence. In English, it is best translated by adding "-ing" to the basic definition of the verb. Consider the following examples:

Livy, *ab Urbe Condita* 1.58.6: **Lucrētiam <u>sedentem</u> maestam in cubiculō inveniunt**. They find sorrowful Lucretia <u>sitting</u> in her room.

Augustus, *Res Gestae* 3.1: **Victorque omnibus veniam <u>petentibus</u> cīvibus pepercī**. And as conqueror, I spared all the citizens <u>seeking</u> pardon.

4. To form the nominative singular of the **PRESENT ACTIVE PARTICIPLE**, add **-ns** to the present stem. The vowel between the present stem and the participial ending changes depending upon the verb's conjugation. Study the table on the following page.

First Conjugation	am-a-ns (amantis)	loving
Second Conjugation	doc-e-ns (docentis)	teaching
Third Conjugation	mitt-e-ns (mittentis)	sending
Third Conjugation (-io)	cap-ie-ns (capientis)	seizing
Fourth Conjugation	aud-ie-ns (audientis)	hearing

5. **PRESENT ACTIVE PARTICIPLE** is a **third declension i-stem adjective** and follows the paradigm of third declension adjectives like *ingens (ingentis)* and *sapiens (sapientis)*. Study the following table:

DECLENSION OF PRESENT ACTIVE PARTICIPLE

Case	Masculine	Feminine	Neuter
Singular			
Nominative	amans	amans	amans
Genitive	amantis	amantis	amantis
Dative	amantī	amantī	amantī
Accusative	amantem	amantem	amans
Ablative	amantī/ amante	amantī/amante	amantī/amante
Plural			
Nominative	amantēs	amantēs	amantia
Genitive	amantium	amantium	amantium
Dative	amantibus	amantibus	amantibus
Accusative	amantēs	amantēs	amantia
Ablative	amantibus	amantibus	amantibus

6. **PRESENT PARTICIPLES OF DEPONENT VERBS** follow the same pattern as regular verbs. In other words, deponent verbs have present **active** participles with **active** meanings. Study the following table:

First Conjugation	cōn-a-ns (cōnantis)	trying
Second Conjugation	pollic-e-ns (pollicentis)	promising
Third Conjugation	loqu-e-ns (loquentis)	speaking
Third Conjugation (-io)	ingred-ie-ns (ingredientis)	entering
Fourth Conjugation	or-ie-ns (orientis)	rising

7. **PRESENT ACTIVE PARTICIPLES OF IRREGULAR VERBS** follow the same pattern as regular verbs. N.B. There is no present active participle for *esse* or *posse*. Study the following table:

volō, velle	vol-e-ns (vol**ent**is)	wanting
mālō, mālle	māl-e-ns (māl**ent**is)	preferring
nōlō, nolle	nōl-e-ns (nōl**ent**is)	not wanting
eō, īre	i-e-ns (i**ent**is)	going
ferō, ferre	fer-e-ns (fer**ent**is)	carrying
fīō, fierī	fī-e-ns (fi**ent**is)	becoming

PART 2: PERFECT PASSIVE PARTICIPLES

8. **PERFECT PASSIVE PARTICIPLE** describes what happened to a particular noun before the main action of the sentence. In English, it is best translated as "having been _____ed" (in some instances the "having been" can even be dropped). Consider the following examples:

Martial 1.33.1–2: **<u>Āmissum</u> nōn flet cum sōla est Gellia patrem; / sī quis adest, <u>iussae</u> prōsiliunt lacrimae.** When she is alone, Gellia does not weep for her <u>lost</u> father (literally: her father having been lost); if anyone is at hand, <u>summoned</u> tears (literally: tears having been summoned) leap forth.

Augustus, *Res Gestae* 1.1: **Annōs undēvīginti <u>nātus</u>, exercitum prīvātō consiliō et prīvātā impensā comparāvī, per quem rem pūblicam ā dominātiōne factiōnis <u>oppressam</u> in lībertātem vindicāvī.** At nineteen years old (literally: <u>having been born for nineteen years</u>), under my personal plan and at private expense, I raised an army through which I delivered into liberty the Republic <u>(having been) crushed</u> by the despotism of a faction.

9. The **PERFECT PASSIVE PARTICIPLE** is the **fourth principal part** of the verb. It takes the endings of first and second declension adjectives (i.e., **bonus, -a, -um**) that you learned in *NLP* 2. Study the table on the following page.

First Conjugation	amāt**us, -a, -um**	having been loved
Second Conjugation	doct**us, -a, -um**	having been taught
Third Conjugation	miss**us, -a, -um**	having been sent
Third Conjugation (-io)	capt**us, -a, -um**	having been seized
Fourth Conjugation	audīt**us, -a, -um**	having been heard

10. **PERFECT PARTICIPLES OF DEPONENT VERBS** are formed by dropping *sum* from the last principal part. Even though perfect participles of deponent verbs look identical to the perfect passive participles of regular verbs, they have **active** meanings. Study the following table:

First Conjugation	cōnāt**us, -a, -um**	having tried
Second Conjugation	pollicit**us, -a, -um**	having promised
Third Conjugation	locūt**us, -a, -um**	having spoken
Third Conjugation (-io)	ingress**us, -a, -um**	having entered
Fourth Conjugation	ort**us, -a, -um**	having risen

PART 3: FUTURE ACTIVE PARTICIPLES

11. The **FUTURE ACTIVE PARTICIPLE** describes what a particular noun will do after the main action of the sentence. In English, it is best translated as "about to _____." Consider the following examples:

    Vergil, *Aeneid* 4.308: **Nec morit<u>ū</u>ra tenet crūdēlī fūnere Dīdō?** Nor does Dido <u>about to die</u> by a cruel death detain (you)?

    Ovid, *Metamorphoses* 2.620: **Vīdit et <u>arsūrōs</u> suprēmīs ignibus artūs.** And he saw limbs <u>about to burn</u> in the last fires.

12. The **FUTURE ACTIVE PARTICIPLE** is formed by inserting **-ūr-** between the stem and the adjective ending of the **fourth principal part** of the verb. Like perfect passive participles, future active participles decline as first and second declension adjectives. Study the following table:

First Conjugation	amāt<u>**ūr**</u>**us, -a, -um**	about to love
Second Conjugation	doct<u>**ūr**</u>**us, -a, -um**	about to teach
Third Conjugation	miss<u>**ūr**</u>**us, -a, -um**	about to send
Third Conjugation (-io)	capt<u>**ūr**</u>**us, -a, -um**	about to seize
Fourth Conjugation	audīt<u>**ūr**</u>**us, -a, -um**	about to hear

13. **FUTURE ACTIVE PARTICIPLES OF DEPONENT VERBS** follow the same pattern as regular verbs. In other words, deponent verbs have future **active** participles with **active** meanings. Study the following table:

First Conjugation	cōnātūrus, -a, -um	about to try
Second Conjugation	pollicitūrus, -a, -um	about to promise
Third Conjugation	locūtūrus, -a, -um	about to speak
Third Conjugation (-io)	ingressūrus, -a, -um	about to enter
Fourth Conjugation	ortūrus, -a, -um	about to rise

PART 4: FUTURE PASSIVE PARTICIPLES

14. The **FUTURE PASSIVE PARTICIPLE** describes what will be done to a particular noun after the main action of the sentence. In English, it is best translated as "(about) to be _____ed." This participle is also known as the **GERUNDIVE** and will be presented in more detail in *NLP* 35. For now, consider the following examples:

Vitruvius, *de Architectura* 2.6.1: **Est etiam genus pulveris, quod efficit nātūrāliter rēs admīrandās.** It (Roman concrete) is also a type of dust, which naturally makes things (about) to be admired.

Caesar, *de Bello Gallico* 1.3.3: **Ad eās rēs conficiendās Orgetorix dēligitur.** Orgetorix is chosen for these things (about) to be completed (i.e., "for completing these things").

15. The **FUTURE PASSIVE PARTICIPLE** is formed by adding **-nd-** to the **present stem** of the verb, and then first and second declension adjective endings. The vowel between the present stem and the participial ending changes depending upon the verb's conjugation. Study the following table:

First Conjugation	am-a-**ndus**, -a, -um	about to be loved
Second Conjugation	doc-e-**ndus**, -a, -um	about to be taught
Third Conjugation	mitt-e-**ndus**, -a, -um	about to be sent
Third Conjugation (-io)	cap-ie-**ndus**, -a, -um	about to be seized
Fourth Conjugation	aud-ie-**ndus**, -a, -um	about to be heard

I. Required Vocabulary

NOUNS

arvum, -ī, n: region, country, field
pontus, -ī, m: sea

aequor, -oris, n: level surface, sea
auris, -is (-ium), f: ear
murmur, murmuris, n: murmur, roar, rumble
ratiō, -iōnis, f: account, reckoning, reasoning, method
voluptās, -ātis, f: pleasure, enjoyment

cursus, -ūs, m: course, running, race
vultus, -ūs, m: face, appearance

faciēs, -iēī, f: shape, form, appearance

ADJECTIVES

dūrus, -a, -um: hard, inflexible, harsh
īmus, -a, -um: lowest, deepest

mollis, -e: soft, supple
potens (-entis): powerful

VERBS

arō, -āre, -āvī, -ātus: plow
errō, -āre, -āvī, -ātus: wander, stray

misceō, -ēre, -uī, mixtus: mix, mingle

cēdō, -ere, cessī, cessus: proceed, yield
cernō, -ere, crēvī, crētus: discern, distinguish, see
cingō, -ere, cinxī, cinctus: gird, wreathe, crown
condō, -ere, -didī, -ditus: build, found; plunge, conceal, hide, store
currō, -ere, cucurrī, cursus: run, rush
disiiciō, -ere, -iēcī, -iectus: scatter, rout, destroy
tegō, -ere, texī, tectus: cover, hide

hortor, -ārī, hortātus sum: encourage, urge, exhort

patior, -ī, passus sum: suffer, endure

CONJUNCTIONS AND ADVERBS
frustrā: in vain
haud: by no means, not at all
ultrā (+ accusative): on the other side; beyond, farther (as an adverb)

II. Translate the following sentences from Latin to English or English to Latin.

1. Multum terrā marīque passī urbem novam condidimus.
2. Aenēas ad coniugem plūra locūtūram cucurrit.
3. Tēla ingentia tenens mīles hostem caedere voluit.
4. Nāvēs disiectās tōtō aequore vīderātis.
5. Fēminae in fīnibus nostrīs errantī lēgēs dedī.
6. Arvum arandum invenīre vōbīs necesse erat.
7. Exercitus in proeliō victūrus equōs potentēs hortātus est.
8. In prōvinciam intrantēs frātrēs sorōrēsque cernis.
9. Yielding to the crowd, the poets wrote about the pleasures of the soul.
10. Having suffered for so many years in the harsh war, we know the rewards of life.
11. I saw the mothers teaching the children.
12. In vain you (plural) were encouraging the freedmen and freedwomen, about to follow their friend.

Roman Gods and Mythology

For the Romans there were essentially two pantheons, the gods of myth and the gods of cult. Although the gods of myth ultimately derived from the anthropomorphized forces of nature, and despite rationalizing arguments from Cicero and Lucretius (who asserted that the gods exist yet have no interest in human affairs), the Romans, and the Greeks before them, created and enjoyed a rich mythological tradition in which the gods were just like human beings, only bigger, better, stronger, prettier, and more powerful. Populating a rich literature, the gods interacted directly with humans as lovers, parents, friends, and enemies.

These mythological tales helped explain the natural world: thunder is caused by Jupiter; earthquakes ensue when Neptune strikes the earth with his trident; seasons occur because Ceres goes into mourning when her daughter lives with her husband Pluto in the underworld; spiders weave because the great weaver Arachne defied Minerva and was transformed into a web-weaving creature. These stories also explain human institutions: women cannot vote because of the competition between Neptune and Minerva for the city of Athens. All the people were invited to cast votes, but, since there were more women than men in Athens and all the women cast their votes for Minerva, the city went to Minerva (Athena of the Greek pantheon). Neptune became so enraged that he threatened to destroy the city until the men agreed never to let women vote again.

Other myths recount historical events (e.g., the Trojan War is the legendary backdrop for Homer, Vergil, Ovid, and others) and local traditions (e.g., the cult of Hercules prevails in central Italy because there the hero vanquished Cacus, a fire-breathing cannibal). Cities traced their foundations to great heroes (invariably the sons of gods). Rome's founder Romulus was the son of Mars, and his mother was a descendant of Venus. Nonetheless, there was skepticism; Livy suggests that Rhea Silvia was raped by Mars, or "so she claimed" to hide her shame. Even in the historical period, divine descent proved a powerful means of enhancing a political career. Most famously, Julius Caesar, eulogizing his aunt in 68 BCE (Suetonius, *de Vita Iulii* 6), traced his lineage directly to Venus. Throughout his career, he promoted the cult, exploiting her image on coin issues from 47 BCE onward and dedicating a temple to Venus Genetrix in the *Forum Romanum* in 46 BCE.

In Latin, we find the richest single source of mythology in Ovid. As we learned in *NLP* 2, Ovid's corpus includes the *Heroides*, a collection of letters from mythological ladies to their heroic paramours (e.g., Dido to Aeneas, Medea to Jason, Penelope to Ulysses). The *Fasti* records the mythological origins of many festivals. But Ovid's masterpiece is the *Metamorphoses* which chronicles the history of the world from its creation to the apotheosis of Julius Caesar. Some 250 mythological tales are woven together by divine transformations (rocks into people, people into animals, plants, constellations, and gods) set ultimately against the backdrop of the Augustan cultural and political milieu.

Knowledge of mythology, finally, was a sign of literary erudition. It is the currency of poets to make casual references to mythological characters and events—and we find these offhand citations in Catullus, Horace, Tibullus, Propertius, and Martial, all lauding especially Apollo, the Muses, Mercury, Venus, and Bacchus, deities who inspired eloquence or conviviality. Silver Age poets, like Statius, particularly reveled in constructing opaque allusions to the most obscure mythological traditions.

SUGGESTIONS FOR FURTHER READING:

Bremmer, J. N. and N. M. Horsfall. *Roman Myth and Mythography.* University of London Institute of Classical Studies, 1987.

Camps, W. A. *An Introduction to Vergil's* Aeneid. Oxford, 1969.

Feldherr, Andrew. *Playing Gods: Ovid's* Metamorphoses *and the Politics of Fiction.* Princeton, 2010.

Wiseman, T. P. *The Myths of Rome.* Exeter, 2004.

PASSAGES

22.1. Ovid, *Metamorphoses* **1.607–11.** To hide her from his jealous wife, Jupiter turns his latest conquest, Io, into a beautiful white cow. Not fooled, Juno demands the cow as a gift and sends her henchman, the hundred-eyed Argos, to watch the hapless "cow-girl." In retaliation, Jupiter sends his son Mercury to slay Argos, whose one hundred eyes are placed in the tail feathers of Juno's favorite bird, the peacock. Io is eventually restored to human form, and her distant descendants will include the god Dionysus and the heroes Perseus and Hercules. Juno here laments her husband's infidelity and her own wounded honor. Meter: dactylic hexameter.

Quem postquam caelō nōn repperit, "Aut ego fallor
aut ego laedor" ait dēlapsaque ab aethere summō
constitit in terrīs nebulāsque recēdere iussit.
Coniugis adventum praesenserat, inque nitentem
Īnachidōs vultūs mūtāverat ille iuvencam.

Notes: **quem**: here, Jupiter; **repperiō, -ere, repperī, repertus**: find, discover (construe Juno as the subject); **laedō, -ere, laesī, laesus**: wound, injure, strike; **dēlābor, -ī, -lapsus**: glide down, sink; **aether, aetheris**, m: upper air, aether; **consistō, -ere, -stitī, -stitus**: stop, halt, stand still; **nebula, -ae**, f: vapor, fog, mist; **recēdō, -ere, -cessī, -cessus**: recede, retreat, ebb; **adventus, -ūs**, m: arrival; **praesentiō, -īre, -sensī, -sensus**: perceive in advance (construe Jupiter as the subject); **niteō, -ēre, -uī**: shine, glitter; **Ĭnachis, Ĭnachidŏs**, f: daughter of Inachus (*Ĭnachidŏs*: Greek genitive); **iuvenca, -ae**, f: heifer, cow.

22.2. Vergil, *Aeneid* **1.67–70.** Juno entreats Aeolus, king of the winds, to send a great storm against the Trojans. Meter: dactylic hexameter.

"Gens inimīca mihī Tyrrhēnum nāvigat aequor,
Īlium in Ītaliam portans victōsque Penātēs:
incute vim ventīs submersāsque obrue puppīs,
aut age dīversōs et disiice corpora pontō."

Notes: **inimīcus, -a, -um** (+ dative): hostile (to); **Tyrrhēnus, -a, -um**: Tyrrhenian, of Etruria (an area in northwestern Italy where the Etruscans dwelled); **nāvigō, -āre, -āvī, -ātus**: sail; **Īlium, -ī**, n: Troy; **Ītalia, -iae**, f: Italy; **portō, -āre, -āvī, -ātus**: carry; **incutiō, -ere, -cussī, -cussus**: strike; **submergō, -ere, -mersī, -mersus**: sink; **obruō, -ere, -uī, obrutus**: overwhelm, crush; **puppis, -is (-ium)**, f: stern, ship; **dīversus, -a, -um**: opposite, diverse (e.g., into separate directions).

22.3. Vergil, *Aeneid* **1.128–30.** Neptune, the god of the sea, discovers that Aeolus has overstepped his authority by attacking the Trojan fleet with a storm. Meter: dactylic hexameter.

Disiectam Aenēae tōtō videt aequore classem,
fluctibus oppressōs Trōās caelīque ruīnā,
nec latuēre dolī frātrem Iunōnis et īrae.

Notes: **Aenēās, -ae**, m: Aeneas (*Aenēae*: Greek genitive); **opprimō, -ere, -pressī, -pressus**: crush, overwhelm; **Trŏs, Trŏis**, m: Trojan (*Trōās*: Greek accusative plural); **ruīna, -ae**, f: downfall, collapse; **lateō, -ēre, latuī**: lie hidden, escape the notice of; **dolus, -ī**, m: deceit, trick.

22.4. Vergil, *Aeneid* **12.829–33.** Jupiter convinces Juno to stop her relentless pursuit of the Trojans. In return, he guarantees that the Trojans will relinquish their ancestral ways, adopting instead Italian customs. Meter: dactylic hexameter.

Ollī subrīdens hominum rērumque repertor:
"Es germāna Iovis Saturnīque altera prōlēs,
īrārum tantōs volvis sub pectore fluctūs.
Vērum age et inceptum frustrā summitte furōrem:
dō quod vīs, et mē victusque volēnsque remittō."

Notes: **ollī** = *illī*; **subrīdeō, -ēre, -rīsī, -rīsus**: smile; **repertor, -ōris**, m: inventor, discoverer, author, creator; **germāna, -ae**, f: true sister; **Saturnus, -ī**, m: Saturn, the mythical king of Latium during the golden age; **prōlēs, -is (-ium)**, f: offspring; **volvō, -ere, volvī, volūtus**: roll, wind, turn over; **vērum**: but; **summittō, -ere, -mīsī, -missus**: moderate, relieve; **furor, -ōris**, m: madness, rage, insanity; **remittō, -ere, -mīsī, -missus**: send back, relax.

22.5. Ovid, *Metamorphoses* 5.420–24. While Ceres' teenage daughter Proserpina was gathering flowers in a meadow, Pluto, the god of the dead, kidnapped her. Ceres, the goddess of grain, grieved the loss of her daughter, causing crops to fail and famished men to die. Here Ovid vividly describes the moment that Pluto's chariot descends to the underworld. Meter: dactylic hexameter.

Haud ultrā tenuit Saturnius īram
terribilēsque hortātus equōs in gurgitis īma
contortum validō sceptrum rēgāle lacertō
condidit; icta viam tellūs in Tartara fēcit
et prōnōs currūs mediō crātēre recēpit.

Notes: **Saturnius, -a, -um**: of Saturn (Pluto was a son of Saturn); **terribilis, -e**: frightful; **gurges, gurgitis**, m: whirlpool; **īma**: depths (accusative plural neuter); **contorqueō, -ēre, -torsī, -tortus**: twist, brandish; **validus, -a, -um**: strong; **sceptrum, -ī**, n: scepter; **rēgālis, -e**: royal, regal; **lacertus, -ī**, m: upper arm, shoulder; **iciō, -ere, īcī, ictus**: strike, hit; **tellūs, tellūris**, f: earth; **Tartara, -ōrum**, n (plural): the underworld, Tartarus; **prōnus, -a, -um**: headlong, rushing down; **crātēr, crātēris**, m: crater, abyss.

22.6. Ovid, *Metamorphoses* 6.32–33. An excellent weaver, Arachne arrogantly boasts that her own talent is greater than Minerva's, the goddess who oversees this craft. Disguised as an old woman, Minerva advises Arachne to apologize for her unforgivable hubris. Meter: dactylic hexameter.

"Cēde deae veniamque tuīs, temerāria, dictīs
supplice vōce rogā: veniam dabit illa rogantī."

Notes: **venia, -iae**, f: favor, indulgence, pardon; **temerārius, -a, -um**: thoughtless, rash, reckless; **dictum, -ī**, n: word; **supplex (supplicis)**: suppliant, begging.

22.7. Vergil, *Aeneid* 11.557–60. A tyrannical king of the Volsci in Italy, expelled by his people, Metabus escapes with his infant daughter Camilla. In order to save her, Metabus ties the baby to a spear and throws the weapon across the river. Here he entrusts the girl to Diana, goddess of the hunt. In return for her life, Camilla later becomes a devotee of Diana, a formidable warrior, and trusted ally of Aeneas' enemy Turnus. Meter: dactylic hexameter.

"Alma, tibi hanc, nemorum cultrix, Lātōnia virgō,
ipse pater famulam voveō; tua prīma per aurās
tēla tenens supplex hostem fugit. Accipe, testor,
dīva, tuam, quae nunc dubiīs committitur aurīs."

Notes: **almus, -a, -um**: nourishing, kind; **cultrix, cultricis**, f: cultivator, protector; **Lātōnius, -a, -um**: of Latona (mother of Apollo and Diana); **famula, -ae**, f: handmaid, female servant; **voveō, -ēre, vōvī, vōtus**: vow, pledge, offer; **aura, -ae**, f: air, wind, breeze; **supplex**: see *NLP* 22.6 (here, Camilla); **testor, -ārī**: call to witness, swear; **tuam**: in apposition with *Camillam*, the implied direct object of *accipe*; **dubius, -a, -um**: doubtful, wavering, uncertain; **committō, -ere, -mīsī, -missus**: entrust, forfeit.

22.8. Ovid, *Metamorphoses* 4.182–87. Married to Vulcan, Venus pursues an affair with Mars. Frustrated at his wife's infidelity, Vulcan sets an elaborate trap in their marriage bed to catch the lovers. Meter: dactylic hexameter.

Ut vēnēre torum coniunx et adulter in ūnum,
arte virī vinclīsque novā ratiōne parātīs,
in mediīs ambō dēprensī amplexibus haerent.
Lemnius extemplō valvās patefēcit eburnās
inmīsitque deōs; illī iacuēre ligātī
turpiter.

Notes: **ut**: when; **torus, -ī**, m: marriage couch; **adulter, adulterī**, m: adulterer; **vinclum, -ī**, n: chain; **dēprēhendō, -ere, -hensī, -hensus**: seize, catch; **amplexus, -ūs**, m: embrace; **haereō, -ēre, haesī, haesus**: cling, adhere to; **Lemnius, -a, -um**: of Lemnos, an island sacred to Vulcan, where he had one of his smithies; **extemplō**: immediately; **valvae, -ārum**, f (plural): folding doors; **patefaciō, -ere, -fēcī, -factus**: throw open, lay open; **eburnus, -a, -um**: made of ivory; **inmittō, -ere, -mīsī, -missus**: send in, allow; **ligō, -āre, -āvī, -ātus**: bind, tie; **turpiter**: shamefully.

22.9. Vergil, *Aeneid* **8.387–90.** Vergil here describes Vulcan's passionate reaction after his wife Venus asks him to forge new armor for her illegitimate son (Aeneas was Anchises' son, not Vulcan's). Meter: dactylic hexameter.

Dixerat, et niveīs hinc atque hinc dīva lacertīs
cunctantem amplexū mollī fovet. Ille repente
accēpit solitam flammam, nōtusque medullās
intrāvit calor et labefacta per ossa cucurrit.

Notes: **niveus, -a, -um**: snowy, white as snow; **lacertīs**: see *NLP* 22.5; **cunctor, -ārī, cunctātus**: delay, linger, hesitate; **amplexū**: see *NLP* 22.8; **foveō, -ēre, fōvī, fōtus**: keep warm, cherish, caress; **repente**: suddenly, unexpectedly; **solitus, -a, -um**: customary, usual; **medulla, -ae**, f: marrow, heart; **calor, -ōris**, m: warmth, heat, glow; **labefaciō, -ere, -fēcī, -factus**: loosen, shake, make unsteady; **os, ossis**, n: bone.

22.10. Ovid, *Metamorphoses* **1.525–26.** Daphne runs away from her divine suitor Apollo in mid-speech. Meter: dactylic hexameter.

Plūra locūtūrum timidō Pēnēia cursū
fūgit cumque ipsō verba inperfecta relīquit.

Notes: **timidus, -a, -um**: fearful, timid; **Pēnēia, Pēnēiae**, f: daughter of Peneus (Daphne); **inperfectus, -a, -um**: unfinished, incomplete.

22.11. Vergil, *Aeneid* **4.246–51.** Aeneas has tarried at Carthage with Queen Dido, neglecting his duty and the destiny of his people. Jupiter finally sends his son Mercury, the messenger god, to recall Aeneas to his mission. As Mercury flies to Carthage, he sees the Atlas Mountains in western Africa, long thought to be the Titan Atlas who supports the vault of the sky and here vividly described. Meter: dactylic hexameter.

Iamque volans apicem et latera ardua cernit
Atlantis dūrī caelum quī vertice fulcit,
Atlantis, cinctum adsiduē cui nūbibus atrīs
pīniferum caput et ventō pulsātur et imbrī,
nix umerōs infūsa tegit, tum flūmina mentō
praecipitant senis, et glaciē riget horrida barba.

Notes: **iamque**: already, and now; **volō, -āre, -āvī**: fly (over), speed; **apex, apicis**, m: peak, summit, head; **arduus, -a, -um**: lofty, steep, towering; **Atlās, Atlantis**, m: the

Titan Atlas, Mercury's grandfather; **vertex, verticis**, m: crown of the head; **fulciō, -īre, fulsī, fulsus**: prop up, support; **cinctum** (*est*); **adsiduē**: constantly; **nūbes, -is (-ium)**, f: cloud; **āter, atra, atrum**: black, dark; **pīnifer, -fera, -ferum**: pine-bearing; **pellō, -ere, pepulī, pulsus**: beat, strike; **nix, nivis (-ium)**, f: snow; **umerus, -ī**, m: shoulder; **infundō, -ere, -fūdī, -fūsus**: pour over; **mentum, -ī**, n: chin, beard; **praecipitō, -āre, -āvī, -ātus**: fall headlong (down), hurry; **senex, senis**, m: old man; **glaciēs, -iēī**, f: ice; **rigeō, -ēre, -uī**: be stiff (with); **horridus, -a, -um**: rough, shaggy; **barba, -ae**, f: beard.

22.12. Horace, *Carmina* **2.19.1–4.** Horace opens his Ode to Bacchus, the god of wine, music and ecstasy, with the claim that he has actually seen the god. Meter: Alcaic strophe.

> Bacchum in rēmōtīs carmina rūpibus
> vīdī docentem, crēdite, posterī,
>   Nymphāsque discentīs et aurīs
>   capripedum Satyrōrum acūtās.

Notes: **rēmōtus, -a, -um**: distant, remote; **rūpes, -is (-ium)**, f: rock, cliff, crag; **nympha, -ae**, f: nymph, maiden; **capripēs (-pedis)**: goat-footed; **satyrus, -ī**, m: Satyr, a half-human, half-equine demigod of the forest with a horse's tail and cloven hooves; **acūtus, -a, -um**: pointed, sharpened.

EXTRA PASSAGES: HEALING BOTANICALS

Harkening back to the agricultural origins of Roman religion, most gods are associated with various plants, and many of these botanicals have healing properties.

22.13. Pliny the Elder, *Naturalis Historia* **21.140.** The iris, the eponymous flower of Juno's messenger, the goddess of the rainbow, was prescribed for teething and coughing babies.

> Īris rūfa melior quam candida. Infantibus eam circumligārī salūtāre est, dentientibus praecipuē et tussientibus.

Notes: **īris, īridis**, f: iris; **rūfus, -a, -um**: red, ruddy; **candidus, -a, -um**: shining, bright, white; **infans (-antis)**: unspeaking (often referring to little children); **eam**: "with respect to it" (accusative of respect); **circumligō, -āre, -āvī, -ātus**: bind round with, wrap; **salūtāris, -e**: healthful; **dentiō, -īre**: cut teeth, teethe; **praecipuē**: especially; **tussiō, -īre**: cough.

22.14. Pliny the Elder, *Naturalis Historia* 22.55. The lotus, sacred to Isis (assimilated to the Roman goddess Ceres and Greek goddess Demeter) was a flower with many medicinal uses, particularly as a remedy for eye complaints.

Is enim inter herbās subnascentēs deōrum voluptātī lōton prīmam nōmināvit. Folia eius cum melle oculōrum cicātrīcēs, argema, nūbeculās discutiunt.

Notes: **is**: here, Homer; **herba, -ae**, f: plant; **subnascor, -ī, -nātus**: grow up, arise; **lōtos, -ī**, f: lotus (*lōton* = Greek accusative); **nōminō, -āre, -āvī, -ātus**: name, call, mention; **folium, -iī**, n: leaf; **mel, mellis**, n: honey, sweetness; **cicātrix, cicātrīcis**, f: scar, **argema, argematis**, n: white spot or ulcer in the eye; **nūbecula, -ae**, f: cloud, dark spot (in the eye); **discutiō, -ere, -cussī, -cussus**: dissolve, dissipate.

22.15. Pliny the Elder, *Naturalis Historia* 21.170. When Apollo's young Spartan lover, Hyacinthus, was accidentally killed by a stray discus, the god made the eponymous flower grow from the lad's blood. Pliny tells us here that the hyacinth was thought capable of postponing puberty.

Rādix est bulbācea, mangōnicīs venāliciīs pulchrē nōta, quae ē vīno dulcī inlita pūbertātem coercet et nōn patitur ērumpere.

Notes: **rādix, rādīcis**, f: root; **bulbāceus, -a, -um**: bulbous; **mangōnicus, -a, -um**: a salesman's; **venālicius, -iī**, m: slave dealer; **mangōnicīs venāliciīs**: Pliny is using the adjective as a substantive, and the noun as an adjective; **inlinō, -ere, -lēvī, -litus**: smear, anoint; **pūbertās, -ātis**, f: puberty, signs of puberty; **coerceō, -ēre, -cuī, -citus**: limit, restrain; **ērumpō, -ere, -rūpī, -ruptus**: break open, develop.

Ablatives Absolute

1. Ablatives absolute are phrases, separate or "absolute" from the grammar of the sentence, and typically consisting of a noun and a participle in the ablative case. The Latin participles used for this construction can be any of those learned in *NLP* 22 (i.e., present active, perfect passive, future active, or future passive). Consider the following examples:

Ovid, *Amores* 1.1.1–2: **Arma gravī numerō violentaque bella parābam / ēdere, māteriā conveniente modīs**. I was preparing to publish arms and violent wars in a serious meter, <u>the material matching the verses</u> (i.e., "while the material was matching the meter").

Aberdeen Bestiary 22r: **<u>Nīchomēde rēge interfectō</u>, equus eius inediā vītam expulit**. <u>The king Nicomedus having been killed</u> (i.e., "after the king Nicomedus had been killed"), his horse expelled life because of fasting.

Tacitus, *Annales* 12.25.2: **Sē quoque accingeret, <u>iuvene partem cūrārum capessītūrō</u>**. He also would prepare himself, <u>the young man about to undertake his part of the concerns</u> (i.e., "since the young man would undertake his part of the concerns").

Tacitus, *Annales* 1.26.2: **Cūr vēnisset, neque <u>augendīs mīlitum stīpendiīs</u> neque <u>adlevandīs labōribus</u>**? Why had he come, neither <u>the soldiers' pay to be increased</u> nor <u>their labor to be diminished</u> (i.e., "since the soldiers' pay was not to be increased, nor was their labor to be diminished")?

2. An ablative absolute does not always feature a participle. It can take the form of two nouns in the ablative case or a noun and adjective in the

ablative case, as long as the phrase remains "absolute" from the grammar of the sentence. Consider the following examples:

Martial 5.10.7: **Ennius est lectus <u>salvō</u> tibi, Rōma, <u>Marōne</u>.** Ennius was read by you, Rome, <u>Maro (Vergil) (being) alive</u> (i.e., "while Maro (Vergil) was living").

Tacitus, *Annales* 3.37.1: **<u>Auctōre principe</u> ac dēcrētō senātūs punītī (sunt).** <u>The emperor as the instigator</u> (i.e., "while the emperor was the instigator") and by a decree of the Senate, they were punished.

3. Ablatives absolute can replace many types of subordinate clauses. For example, they can indicate **when** the action of the sentence occurs (**temporal**). Consider the following examples:

Ovid, *Metamorphoses* 8.208: **<u>Mē duce</u> carpe viam!** Take the road, <u>me (being) leader</u> (i.e., "while I am leading").

Livy, *ab Urbe Condita* 45.9.3: **Perseus Q. Fulviō (et) <L.> Manliō consulibus regnum accēpit, ā senātū rex est appellātus M. Iūniō A. Manliō consulibus.** Perseus received the reign, <u>Q. Fulvius (and) L. Manlius as consuls</u> (i.e., "when Fulvius and Manlius were consuls"), he was named king by the senate, <u>M. Iunius and A. Manlius as consuls</u> (i.e., "when Iunius and Manlius were consuls").

4. Ablatives absolute can indicate **why** the action of the sentence occurs (**causal**). Consider the following examples:

Tacitus, *Annales* 1.2.1: **<u>Brūtō et Cassiō caesīs</u>, nulla iam pūblica arma.** <u>Brutus and Cassius having been killed</u> (i.e., "because they had been killed"), no longer were there public arms.

Caesar, *de Bello Gallico* 7.32.2: **Iam <u>prope hieme confectā</u> cum ipsō annī tempore ad gerendum bellum vocārētur et ad hostem proficiscī constituisset** . . . Now <u>winter almost completed</u> (i.e., "since winter had almost been completed), when, at that very time of year, he (Caesar) was summoned for the purpose of waging war and he had decided to set out against the enemy . . .

5. Ablatives absolute can stand in opposition to the action of the sentence (**concessive**). Consider the following examples:

Tacitus, *Annales* 2.80.2: **Consisterent in aciē, nōn pugnātūrīs mīlitibus**. They could stand in battle array, <u>the soldiers not about to fight</u> (i.e., "although the soldiers would not fight").

Tacitus, *Annales* 1.55.1: **Drūsō Caesare (et) C. Norbanō consulibus, dēcernitur Germānicō triumphus manente bellō**. When Drusus Caesar (and) Gaius Norbanus were consuls, a triumph is decreed for Germanicus, <u>the war continuing</u> (i.e., "although the war was still continuing").

6. Ablatives absolute can indicate a **condition** necessary for the action of the sentence (**conditional**). Consider the following examples:

Cato, *de Agricultura* 141: "**Cum dīvīs volentibus quodque bene ēveniat, mandō tibi . . .**" "When, the gods willing (i.e., "if the gods are willing"), this turns out well, I entrust to you. . . ."

Propertius, *Elegiae* 1.14.16: **Nulla mihī tristī praemia sint Venere!** May there be no rewards for me, <u>Venus (being) sad</u> (i.e., "if Venus is sad").

7. Ablatives absolute can indicate the **circumstances** under which the action of the sentence occurs (**circumstantial**).

Ovid, *Epistulae ex Ponto* 4.4.36–41: **Inde domum repetēs, tōtō comitante senātū**. Then you will return home, <u>all the Senate following</u> (i.e., "while all the Senate follows").

Caesar, *de Bello Gallico* 7.73.2: **Itaque truncīs arborum aut admodum firmīs rāmīs abscisīs atque hōrum dēlībrātīs ac praeacūtīs cacūminibus** perpetuae fossae quīnōs pedēs altae dūcēbantur. And so, <u>the trunks of the trees or the very strong branches having been cut down</u> (i.e., "after the trunks of the trees or the very strong branches had been cut down"), and <u>the tops of them stripped and sharpened</u> (i.e., "after the tops of them had been stripped and sharpened"), continuous ditches, five feet deep, were drawn out.

8. Relative pronouns often act as the "noun" of an ablative absolute and link something from earlier in the narrative to the participle in the absolute phrase. Consider the following examples:

Cicero, *Philippica* 1.3: **Quō recitātō, auctōritātem eius summō studiō secūtī sumus.** This (the senatorial decree) having been recited (i.e., "after this had been recited"), we followed its authority with the greatest eagerness.

Caesar, *de Bello Gallico* 3.14.7: **Quibus abscīsīs, antemnae necessāriō concidēbant.** These things (the rigging ropes) having been destroyed (i.e., "when these things had been destroyed"), the yardarms fell because of necessity.

I. Required Vocabulary

NOUNS

cūra, -ae, f: concern, care, trouble, distress
domina, -ae, f: mistress, lady friend
fenestra, -ae, f: window
turba, -ae, f: crowd

campus, -ī, m: plain, field
iugum, -ī, n: yoke, team, cross-bar, ridge
lēgātus, -ī, m: envoy, delegate
pretium, -iī, n: price, reward
somnus, -ī, m: sleep

consul, consulis, m: a high political office in Rome
ōs, oris, n: mouth, face
prex, precis, f: request, entreaty

impetus, -ūs, m: attack, assault, charge

ADJECTIVES

beātus, -a, -um: happy, fortunate
honestus, -a, -um: respectable, honorable, proper, virtuous
lātus, -a, -um: broad, wide
saevus, -a, -um: fierce, raging, violent

VERBS

celebrō, -āre, -āvī, -ātus: practice, repeat, celebrate, make known

immineō, -ēre: overhang, threaten
maneō, -ēre, mansī, mansus: remain, stay
prohibeō, -ēre, -uī, -itus: restrain, hinder

vertō, -ere, vertī, versus: turn, destroy

laetor, -ārī, laetus sum: rejoice, be glad

pereō, -īre, -iī, -ītus: waste, be lost, perish

CONJUNCTIONS AND ADVERBS
adeō: thus far, truly
procul: from a distance
quā: where, how
sīve . . . sīve: whether . . . or
usque: continuously, all the way

II. Translate the following sentences from Latin to English or English to Latin.

1. Caesar plūrēs legiōnēs ad Britanniam mīsit et, multīs oppidīs captīs, castra posuit.
2. Ō Cicerō, tē consule, Rōma erat beāta.
3. Cīvēs adeō laetābantur, exercitū Rōmānō in prōvinciā manente.
4. Lēgātīs prō imperātōre locūtūrīs, hostēs impetum relinquēbant.
5. Līberīs in silvīs errantibus, parentēs precibus grātiam rogāvērunt.
6. Equī ā campīs vertērunt, montibus imminentibus.
7. Rōmulō rēge, populus bellum saevum passus est.
8. Nullō prohibente, poētās doctōs celebrābāmus.
9. Many wounds having been received, the soldier was sent to the countryside.
10. Our children rejoicing, we built a temple.
11. The horses having been hindered by their yokes, the fields were not plowed.
12. The crowd encouraging the consul, the entreaties of the woman were heard.

The Roman Countryside:
Simplicity, Agriculture, and Tradition

Rome's very foundation legend plays into a long tradition that idealizes the countryside and country living as simple and country dwellers as divinely favored. Twin
boys, abandoned on a riverbank and raised by kindly shepherds, grew up to found
a mighty city that would rule the world by the authority of the gods. Romulus and
Remus remained shepherds, and, long after their deaths, Roman legend continued
to exalt farming. Most famously, Cincinnatus was in his fields at his plow when a
senatorial delegation recalled the retired statesman to service. Cicero described
farming as the most profitable and delightful occupation, and the one most becoming to a free man (*de Officiis* 1.151). How much land a family owned determined that
family's level of importance and influence. Land-owning citizens voted first in the
Comitia Centuriāta, and their votes carried the most weight. Only the landed were
permitted to fight in the army—until the Marian reforms of the early first century
BCE, when the promise of a land grant to retiring soldiers was a powerful recruiting
incentive (see *NLP* 7). Senatorial alliances were struck and broken in efforts to
secure these land grants. Pompey's boon for his participation in the so-called first
triumvirate was land for his veterans, by which he assured their continuing loyalty. Land was wealth, and wealth was power.

The ideal of the gentleman farmer derived from the archetype of ancient
Roman self-sufficiency. Agricultural handbooks penned by Cato, Columella, and
Varro were intended not just as practical guides to working the earth. They were
compendia of everything a *pater familias* might need to know in order to manage
a country estate: what to plant when, how to care for the needs of slaves, and what
remedies were prescribed for common medical ailments. Such handbooks were
the practical side of a rich literary tradition, beginning with Hesiod's *Works and
Days* (in Greek) and perfected by Vergil's *Georgics*, a versified and highly stylized
account of agricultural topics and tensions.

Life in the country was almost universally depicted as idealized and free from
the perils, overcrowding, and filth of the city. Horace's Country Mouse is eager to
return to his dull life after a visit to the "glamorous" city (*Sermones* 2.6.79–117).
Propertius (2.19) lauds the country for its lack of tempting traps, and Tibullus
idealizes the rustic vintage festival (2.1). Horace and Vergil cherished their

country villas. Pliny the Younger and Martial relished the slower pace of life in the country and the freedom from business afforded by life there.

SUGGESTIONS FOR FURTHER READING:

Dyson, Stephen L. *The Roman Countryside*. Duckworth, 2003.

Rosenmeyer, T. *The Green Cabinet: Theocritus and the European Pastoral Lyric*. University of California, 1969.

Thibodeau, Philip. *Playing the Farmer: Representations of Rural Life in Vergil's Georgics*. University of California, 2011.

PASSAGES

23.1. Vergil, *Eclogues* **1.77–78.** The *Eclogues* took their inspiration from the Greek *Idylls* of Theocritus whose eloquent shepherds sang to each other while the sheep blissfully grazed the countryside. However, unlike Theocritus, Vergil also politicized these poems, subtly reflecting the tensions of the late Republic: peace and civil war, tradition and modernity, duty and retreat from public life. Meter: dactylic hexameter.

> Nōn mē pascente, capellae,
> flōrentem cytisum et salicēs carpētis amārās.

Notes: **pascō, -ere, pāvī, pastus**: feed, provide food for the flocks; **capella, -ae**, f: she-goat; **flōreō, -ēre, -uī**: bloom, flower; **cytisus, -ī**, m/f: clover; **salix, salicis**, f: willow; **carpō, -ere, carpsī, carptus**: pluck; **amārus, -a, -um**: bitter.

23.2. Horace, *Carmina* **3.13.13–16.** Horace here sings the praises of the Bandusian spring on his country estate (see *NLP* 17.13). Meter: fourth Asclepiadean.

> Fīēs nōbilium tū quoque fontium,
> mē dīcente cavīs impositam īlicem
>   saxīs, unde loquācēs
>   lymphae dēsiliunt tuae.

Notes: construe *pars* as a subject complement with *fīēs*; **cavus, -a, -um**: hollow, sunken, deep; **impositam īlicem**: "that the holm-oak was placed" (indirect statement); **impōnō, -ere, -posuī, -positus**: set in, put in; **īlex, īlicis**, f: holm-oak; **loquax (loquācis)**: talkative, garrulous, loquacious; **lympha, -ae**, f: clear water; **dēsiliō, -īre, -siluī, -sultus**: leap down.

23.3. Vergil, *Eclogues* **4.11–14.** In this poem, Vergil transforms the idyllic landscape into an opportunity for political commentary as he artfully predicts a Golden Age in which the birth of a special child (most likely Octavian's—his first wife Scribonia was pregnant with Julia when this poem was published) ushers in an age of peace and prosperity. Meter: dactylic hexameter.

> Tēque, adeō decus hōc aevī, tē consule, inībit,
> Pollio, et incipient magnī prōcēdere mensēs;
> tē duce, sī qua manent sceleris vestīgia nostrī,
> inrita perpetuā solvent formīdine terrās.

Notes: notice the anaphora (or rhetorical repetition) of *tē* (the first *tē* emphasizes the second *tē* in the ablative absolute); **aevum, -ī,** n: generation, age; **ineō, -īre, -īvī** or **iī, -itus**: enter, begin; **Polliō, -iōnis,** m: Gaius Asinius Pollio, consul in 40 BCE, Roman statesman and litterateur, and Vergil's friend and patron; **prōcēdō, -ere, -cessī, -cessus**: proceed; **mensis, -is (-ium),** m: month; **qua** = *aliqua*; **inritus, -a, -um**: useless, ineffective; **perpetuus, -a, -um**: continuous, uninterrupted; **formīdō, formīdinis,** f: dread, terror.

23.4. Ovid, *Amores* **1.13.11–16.** Ovid here describes how wicked Aurora (Dawn) makes the lives of Romans, including farmers, difficult. Meter: elegiac couplets.

> Ante tuōs ortūs melius sua sīdera servat
>   nāvita nec mediā nescius errat aquā;
> tē surgit quamvīs lassus veniente viātor,
>   et mīlēs saevās aptat ad arma manūs.
> Prīma bidente vidēs onerātōs arva colentēs;
>   prīma vocās tardōs sub iuga panda bovēs.

Notes: **nāvita, -ae,** m: sailor; **nescius, -a, -um**: unaware, ignorant; **surgo, -ere, surrexī, surrectus**: rise; **lassus, -a, -um**: tired, weary; **viātor, -ōris,** m: traveler; **aptō, -āre, -āvī, -ātus**: fit, adjust, furnish; **bidens, -entis (-ium),** m: two-pronged hoe; **onerō, -āre, -āvī, -ātus**: load, burden; **tardus, -a, -um**: slow; **pandus, -a, -um**: spreading around in a curved arch; **bōs, bovis,** m/f: ox, cow.

23.5. Livy, *ab Urbe Condita* **1.4.9.** The countryside was a crucial element of Rome's foundation myths: Romulus and Remus, abandoned at birth, are suckled by a she-wolf and then raised by shepherds. As they grow up, they join with other young shepherds to hunt, conduct raids on robbers, and have fun.

Hinc rōbore corporibus animīsque sumptō iam nōn ferās tantum subsistere sed in latrōnēs praedā onustōs impetūs facere pastōribusque rapta dīvidere et cum hīs—crescente in diēs grege iuvenum—sēria ac iocōs celebrāre.

Notes: **rōbur, rōboris**, n: oak, flower, strength; **fera, -ae**, f: wild animal; **subsistō, -ere, substitī**: halt, cause to stop (historical infinitive: translate this and the other infinitives in the passage as third person plural present tense verbs); **latrō, -ōnis**, m: bandit, brigand; **praeda, -ae**, f: plunder, booty; **onustus, -a, -um**: laden, burdened; **pastor, -ōris**, m: shepherd; **dīvidō, -ere, -vīsī, -vīsus**: divide, separate; **grex, gregis**, m: flock, herd; **sēria, -iōrum**, n (plural): serious affairs; **iocus, -ī**, m: joke, jest, sport.

23.6. Livy, *ab Urbe Condita* **3.26.10.** Cincinnatus had served Rome with distinction as consul in 460 BCE, afterwards returning to his farm. In the face of attacks from hostile neighbors and losses suffered by the consular army, the Roman Senate elected Cincinnatus as dictator—a constitutional office of absolute authority that was filled only in times of emergency. As soon as the war was resolved, Cincinnatus resigned immediately and peacefully, exchanging the *fasces* of office for the plowshare. This story inspired Jean-Antoine Houdan's statue of George Washington who, to the amazement of the rest of the world, stepped down from the presidency after two terms. Here, the senatorial delegation approaches Cincinnatus at his plow.

Abstersō pulvere ac sūdōre vēlātus prōcessit, dictātōrem eum lēgātī grātulantēs consalūtant, in urbem vocant; quī terror sit in exercitū exponunt.

Notes: **abstergeō, -ēre, -stersī, -stersus**: wipe away; **pulvis, pulveris**, m: dust; **sūdor, -ōris**, m: sweat; **vēlō, -āre, -āvī, -ātus**: cover (with his toga); **prōcessit**: see *NLP* 23.2 **dictātor, -ōris**, m: dictator; **grātulor, -ārī, grātulātus sum**: congratulate; **consalūtō, -āre, -āvī, -ātus**: greet, hail, salute; **terror, -ōris**, m: fright, dread; **sit**: "there is" (present subjunctive); **expōnō, -ere, -posuī, -positus**: expose, explain.

23.7. Pliny the Elder, *Naturalis Historia* **18.19.** Agriculture as an honorable and dignified occupation long remained part of the fabric of the Roman self-identity. The fact that even the highest-born citizens (e.g., Cincinnatus) actually worked the fields with their own hands was considered one of the contributing factors to Rome's political and military success.

Ipsōrum tunc manibus imperātōrum colēbantur agrī, ut fās est crēdere—gaudente terrā vōmere laureātō et triumphālī arātōre— sīve illī eādem cūrā sēmina tractābant, quā bella, eādemque dīligentiā arva dispōnēbant, quā castra, sīve honestīs manibus omnia laetius prōveniunt, quoniam et cūriōsius fīunt.

Notes: **vōmer, -eris**, m: plowshare; **laureātus, -a, -um**: crowned with laurel; **triumphālis, -e**: triumphal, relating to a triumphal parade (see *NLP 7*); **arātor, -ōris**, m: plowman; **sēmen, sēminis**, n: seed, seedling; **tractō, -āre, -āvī, -ātus**: drag, haul, manage; **dīligentia, -iae**, f: carefulness, attentiveness, accuracy; **dispōnō, -ere, -posuī, -positus**: arrange, distribute; **prōveniō, -īre, -vēnī, -ventus**: come forth; **cūriōsus, -a, -um**: careful, attentive, diligent.

23.8. Propertius, *Elegiae* **2.19.1–4.** The Romans considered rural living to be naturally more upright because the country lacked the seductions of the city. Here, Propertius takes solace that his mistress Cynthia is safe from city-dwelling suitors. Meter: elegiac couplets.

Etsī mē invītō discēdis, Cynthia, Rōmā,
    laetor quod sine mē dēvia rūra colēs.
Nullus erit castīs iuvenis corruptor in agrīs,
    quī tē blanditiīs nōn sinat esse probam.

Notes: **etsī**: although, even if; **invītus, -a, -um**: unwilling; **discēdō, -ere, -cessī**: depart, go away; **dēvius, -a, -um**: pathless; **castus, -a, -um**: pure, chaste; **corruptor, -ōris**, m: seducer, corruptor; **blanditia, -iae**, f: flattery, charm; **sinat**: "(who) will not allow" (present subjunctive); **probus, -a, -um**: good, virtuous, honorable.

23.9. Martial 3.58.1–9. Martial praises the rustic charms of his friend Faustinus's country villa, tucked away in the resort area of Baiae on the Bay of Naples. Meter: limping iambics.

Bāiāna nostrī villa, Basse, Faustīnī
nōn ōtiōsīs ordināta myrtētīs
viduāque platanō tonsilīque buxētō
ingrāta lātī spatia dētinet campī,

sed rūre vērō barbarōque laetātur.
Hīc farta premitur angulō Cerēs omnī,
et multa fragrat testa senibus autumnīs;
hīc post Novembrēs, imminente iam brūmā,
serās putātor horridus refert ūvās.

Notes: The nominative adjectives *ordināta* and *ingrāta* modify *villa* in the first half of this passage; **Bāiānus, -a, -um**: of Baiae, a resort town on the Bay of Naples, famous for its thermo-mineral baths, often represented in literature as a "harbor of vice" (see Seneca the Younger, *Epistulae Morales* 55.6); **Bassus, -ī**, m: a contemporary poet frequently addressed by Martial; **Faustīnus, -ī**, m: a regular addressee in Martial, possibly Minucius Faustinus, suffect consul in 91 CE; **ōtiōsus, -a, -um**: at leisure; **ordinō, -āre, -āvī, -ātus**: set in order, arrange; **myrtētum, -ī**, n: grove of myrtle trees; **viduus, -a, -um**: destitute; **platanus, -ī**, f: plane tree; **tonsilis, -e**: shorn, clipped, cut; **buxētum, -ī**, n: a boxwood plantation; **ingrātus, -a, -um**: unpleasant; **dētineō, -ēre, -uī, -tentus**: occupy; **barbarus, -a, -um**: rough, uncultivated; **farciō, -īre, farsī, fartus**: stuff, gorge; **angulus, -ī**, m: corner, angle; **Cerēs, -eris**, f: the Roman goddess of agriculture, a metonym for "grain"; **fragrō, -āre, -āvī, -ātus**: emit a sweet smell, be redolent; **testa, -ae**, f: earthenware jar; **senex (senis)**: old, ancient, aged (wine); **autumnus, -a, -um**: autumnal (here used substantively as "autumnal wines"); **Novembris, -is**, m: November, the ninth month in the traditional Roman calendar; **brūma, -ae**, f: the shortest day of the year, winter solstice, cold, winter; **serus, -a, -um**: late (-harvest); **putātor, -ōris**, m: pruner; **horridus, -a, -um**: rough, shaggy, bristly; **ūva, -ae**, f: vine, grape.

23.10. Seneca the Younger, *Epistulae* 86.1. Seneca visits the country estate of Scipio Africanus, hero of the Second Punic War (see *NLP* 20), where the great man retired after withdrawing from politics and where he died.

In ipsā Scīpiōnis Africānī villā iacens haec tibi scrībō, adōrātīs mānibus eius et ārā, quam sepulchrum esse tantī virī suspicor.

Notes: **Scīpiō Africānus, Scīpiōnis Africānī**, m: a Roman man's name; **adōrō, -āre, -āvī, -ātus**: address, entreat, honor, worship; **āra, -ae**, f: altar; **sepulchrum, -ī**, n: tomb; **suspicor, -ārī, suspicātus sum**: surmise, suppose.

23.11. Pliny the Younger, *Epistulae* 9.36.2–3. Pliny describes the leisurely schedule of his days at his country estate at Tifernum Tiberinum, north of Rome.

Notārium vocō et, diē admissō, quae formāveram dictō. Abit rursusque rēvocātur rursusque dīmittitur. Ubi hōrā quartā vel quintā—neque enim certum dīmensumque tempus—ut diēs suāsit, in xystum mē vel cryptoporticum conferō, reliqua meditor et dictō.

Notes: **notārius, -iī**, m: secretary; **admittō, -ere, -mīsī, -missus**: admit, let in; **formō, -āre, -āvī, -ātus**: shape, arrange, regulate, plan; **dictō, -āre, -āvī, -ātus**: repeat, dictate, have (something) written down; **rēvocō, -āre, -āvī, -ātus**: call back, recall; **dīmittō, -ere, -mīsī, -missus**: send away; **hōra, -ae**, f: hour; **dīmētior, -īrī, dīmensus sum**: measure out; **suādeō, -ēre, suāsī, suāsus**: recommend, advise; **cryptoporticus, -ūs**, f: covered passage; **conferō, -ferre, -tulī, -lātus**: collect, bring together, bring (someone/thing) to (a particular place); **meditor, -ārī, meditātus sum**: think over, consider.

23.12. Martial 10.58.1–6. Martial contrasts the soothing allurements of the country with the unrelenting professional demands of life in the big city. Meter: elegiac couplets.

Anxuris aequoreī placidōs, Frontīne, recessūs
    et propius Bāiās lītoreamque domum,
et quod inhūmānae—Cancrō fervente—cicādae
    nōn nōvēre nemus, flūmineōsque lacūs
dum coluī, doctās tēcum celebrāre vacābat
    Pīeridās: nunc nōs maxima Rōma terit.

Notes: **Anxur, Anxuris**, n: a coastal town between Rome and Naples; **aequoreus, -a, -um**: watery, maritime, by-the-sea; **placidus, -a, -um**: quiet, gentle, calm; **Frontīnus, -ī**, m: probably Sextus Julius Frontinus, author of *de Aquaeductu urbis Romae*; **recessus, -ūs**, m: retreat, recess, secluded spot; **propius**: rather close; **Bāiae, Bāiārum**, f: (plural): Baiae (see *NLP* 23.9); **lītoreus, -a, -um**: coastal; **inhūmānus, -a, -um**: cruel, barbarous, uncivil; **Cancer, Cancrī**, m: crab, Cancer, the sign of the zodiac in which the sun appears at the summer solstice (i.e., a hot season); **ferveō, -ēre, ferbuī**: boil, seethe; **cicāda, -ae**, f: tree cricket; **flūmineus, -a, -um**: watery, of a river; **vacābat**: "there was leisure to" (impersonal); **Pīeris, Pīeridis**, f: the Muses (*Pīeridās*: Greek accusative); **terō, -ere, trīvī, trītus**; rub, wear away, wear oneself out.

EXTRA PASSAGES: URBAN PERILS

During the first centuries BCE and CE, Rome was a bustling international city with a cosmopolitan population of about one million people. The city was crowded, noisy, and dirty, and petty crime was a common complaint. The poor lived in tiny, dark apartments, often in multistory buildings with paper-thin walls, sharing cooking and bathroom facilities. Despite these hardships, life in the city offered opportunity, commerce, and culture, much as it does today.

23.13. Ovid, *Ars Amatoria* 1.139–40. The crowds at the Circus Maximus provide the perfect cover for flirtation and seduction. Meter: elegiac couplets.

> Proximus ā dominā, nullō prohibente, sedētō;
> > iunge tuum laterī quā potes usque latus.

Notes: **sedeō, -ēre, sēdī, sessus:** sit, settle; **iungō, -ere, iunxī, iunctus:** join.

23.14. Juvenal, *Saturae* 3.239–42. Juvenal complains about the city traffic and aggressive drivers. Meter: dactylic hexameter.

> Sī vocat officium, turbā cēdente, vehētur
> dīves et ingentī curret super ōra Liburnā
> atque obiter leget aut scrībet vel dormiet intus;
> namque facit somnum clausā lectīca fenestrā.

Notes: **vehō, -ere, vexī, vectus:** carry, convey; **ōs, ōris,** n: face; **Liburna, -ae,** f: a small galley used by the Roman navy for raids and patrols (Juvenal compares the rich man's vehicle to this naval ship); **obiter:** in passing; **intus:** within; **lectīca, -ae,** f: litter.

23.15. Pliny the Younger, *Epistulae* 10.33.1. Pliny describes a devastating fire that struck Nicomedia, one of the towns in Bithynia-Pontus, the province that he governed (110–13 CE).

> Cum dīversam partem prōvinciae circumīrem, Nīcomēdiae vastissimum incendium multās prīvātōrum domōs et duō pūblica opera, quamquam viā interiacente, Gerūsian et Īsēon absumpsit.

Notes: **dīversus, -a, -um:** remote; **circumīrem:** "when I toured" (imperfect subjunctive); **Nīcomēdia, -iae,** f: the capital of the Roman province Bithynia-Pontus (western Turkey) (locative); **vastus, -a, -um:** enormous; **incendium, -iī,** n: fire; **prīvātus, -ī,** m: private citizen; **quamquam:** although; **interiaceō, -ēre, -uī, -iacitus:** lie between; **Gerūsia, -iae,** f: the meeting house for a council of old men (*Gerūsian:* Greek accusative); **Īsēum, -ī,** n: temple of Isis (*Īsēon:* Greek accusative); **absumō, -ere, -sumpsī, -sumptus:** waste, consume.

LESSON 24

Indirect Statement

1. Verbs of saying, thinking, knowing, hearing, and feeling often introduce indirect statements (a construction also known as indirect discourse or *oratio obliqua*). In Latin, indirect statements are characterized by a subject in the accusative case and an infinitive verb. Consider the following examples:

Ovid, *Amores* 1.14.35: **Quid <u>male dispositōs</u> <u>quereris periisse capillōs?</u>** Why <u>do you complain</u> that your well arranged hair has perished badly?

Catullus 1.3–4: **Namque tū solēbās / <u>meās esse aliquid putāre</u> nugās.** For you were accustomed <u>to think</u> that my trifles were something.

2. There are six infinitives in Latin:

   present active (see *NLP* 1)
   present passive (see *NLP* 17)
   perfect active (see *NLP* 13)
   perfect passive (see *NLP* 18)
   future active (see below)
   future passive (see below)

Study the tables on the following pages (most of which should be review).

INFINITIVES OF REGULAR VERBS

Tense and Voice	1st Conj.	2nd Conj.	3rd Conj.	3rd Conj. (-io)	4th Conj.
Present Active	amāre: to love	docēre: to teach	mittere: to send	capere: to take	audīre: to hear
Present Passive	amārī: to be loved	docērī: to be taught	mittī: to be sent	capī: to be taken	audīrī: to be heard
Perfect Active	amāvisse: to have loved	docuisse: to have taught	mīsisse: to have sent	cēpisse: to have taken	audīvisse: to have heard
Perfect Passive	amātus, -a, -um esse: to have been loved	doctus, -a, -um esse: to have been taught	missus, -a, -um esse: to have been sent	captus, -a, -um esse: to have been taken	audītus, -a, -um esse: to have been heard
Future Active	amātūrus, -a, -um esse: to be about to love	doctūrus, -a, -um esse: to be about to teach	missūrus, -a, -um esse: to be about to send	captūrus, -a, -um esse: to be about to take	audītūrus, -a, -um esse: to be about to hear
Future Passive	amātum īrī: to be about to be loved	doctum īrī: to be about to be taught	missum īrī: to be about to be sent	captum īrī: to be about to be taken	audītum īrī: to be about to be heard

INFINITIVES OF DEPONENT VERBS

Tense and Voice	1st Conj.	2nd Conj.	3rd Conj.	3rd Conj. (-io)	4th Conj.
Present Deponent	cōnārī: to try	pollicērī: to promise	loquī: to speak	ingredī: to enter	orīrī: to rise
Perfect Deponent	cōnātus, -a, -um esse: to have tried	pollicitus, -a, -um esse: to have promised	locūtus, -a, -um esse: to have spoken	ingressus, -a, -um esse: to have entered	ortus, -a, -um esse: to have risen
Future Deponent	cōnātūrus, -a, -um esse: to be about to try	pollicitūrus, -a, -um esse: to be about to promise	locūtūrus, -a, -um esse: to be about to speak	ingressūrus, -a, -um esse: to be about to enter	ortūrus, -a, -um esse: to be about to rise

INFINITIVES OF IRREGULAR VERBS

Tense	sum	possum	volō	mālō	nōlō	eō	fiō
Present	esse: to be	posse: to be able	velle: to want	mālle: to prefer	nōlle: to be unwilling	īre: to go	fierī: to become
Perfect	fuisse: to have been	potuisse: to have been able	voluisse: to have wanted	māluisse: to have preferred	nōluisse: to have been unwilling	īvisse: to have gone	factus, -a, -um esse: to have become
Future	futūrus, -a, -um esse: to be about to be	——	——	——	——	itūrus, -a, -um esse: to be about to go	——

N.B. The future active infinitive of *sum* (*futūrus, -a, -um*) is sometimes rendered as **FORE**.

N.B. The first word of the future passive infinitive is not a participle, but a supine— a verbal noun that you will learn in *NLP* 36. It does not decline to agree with its subject (as do the participles of the perfect passive and future active infinitives), but retains its -*um* ending.

3. The infinitives of indirect statements are translated relative to the main verb of the sentence:

   • **PRESENT INFINITIVES** are translated as the **same time** as the main verb
   • **PERFECT INFINITIVES** are translated as occurring **before** the main verb
   • **FUTURE INFINITIVES** are translated as occurring **after** the main verb

Consider the following examples and note how the translation of the infinitive in indirect statement shifts as the tense of the main verb changes:

Catullus 12.4: **Hoc salsum esse putās**? <u>Do you think</u> that this <u>is</u> witty?
    The main verb, *putās*, is in the present tense, and the infinitive in indirect statement, *esse*, is also in the present tense. The indirect statement occurs at the same time as the main verb.

Caesar, *de Bello Gallico* 5.41.7: **Cicerō ad haec ūnum modo <u>respondit</u>: nōn <u>esse</u> consuētūdinem populī Rōmānī accipere ab hoste armātō condiciōnem.** To these things Cicero <u>responded</u> only one thing: that it <u>was</u> not a habit of the Roman people to accept a condition from an armed enemy.

> The main verb, *respondit*, is in the perfect tense, and the infinitive in indirect statement, *esse*, is in the present tense. The indirect statement occurs at the same time as the main verb.

Livy, *ab Urbe Condita* 1.1.6: **Aliī proeliō <u>victum (esse)</u> Latīnum pācem cum Aenēā, deinde affinitātem <u>iunxisse</u> <u>trādunt</u>.** Some <u>hand down</u> that Latinus <u>was conquered</u> in battle (and) that <u>he joined</u> a peace with Aeneas, then a family alliance.

> The main verb, *trādunt*, is in the present tense, and the infinitives in indirect statement, *victum (esse) iunxisse*, are in the perfect tense. The indirect statement occurs before the main verb.

Caesar, *de Bello Gallico* 1.5.1: **Ubi iam sē ad eam rem <u>parātōs esse</u> <u>arbitrātī sunt</u>, oppida sua omnia, numerō ad duodecim, vīcōs ad quadringentōs, reliqua prīvāta aedificia incendunt.** When they now <u>thought</u> that they <u>had been prepared</u> for this matter, they set fire to all their towns, twelve in number, (their) villages, four hundred (in number) (and) the remaining private buildings.

> The main verb, *arbitrātī sunt*, is in the perfect tense, and the infinitive in indirect statement, *parātōs esse*, is also in the perfect tense. The indirect statement occurs before the main verb.

Caesar, *de Bello Gallico* 1.3.6: **Sē suīs cōpiīs suōque exercitū illīs regna <u>conciliātūrum (esse)</u> <u>confirmat</u>.** He (Orgetorix) <u>confirms</u> that he <u>will acquire</u> the kingdoms for them with his own resources and with his own army.

> The main verb, *confirmat*, is in the present tense, and the infinitive in indirect statement, *conciliātūrum (esse)*, is in the future tense. The indirect statement occurs after the main verb.

Caesar, *de Bello Gallico* 4.9.1: **Lēgātī haec sē ad suōs <u>relātūrōs</u> <u>dīxērunt</u> et rē dēlīberātā post diem tertium ad Caesarem <u>reversūrōs</u>.** The envoys <u>said</u> that they <u>would report</u> these things to their people and that, with the matter discussed, they <u>would return</u> to Caesar after the third day.

The main verb, *dīxērunt*, is in the perfect tense, and the infinitives in indirect statement, *relātūrōs* (*esse*) and *reversūrōs* (*esse*), are in the future tense. The actions of the indirect statements occur after the main verb.

4. In indirect statements with PERFECT PASSIVE or FUTURE ACTIVE infinitives, *esse* is often omitted. Consider the following examples:

Pliny, *Naturalis Historia* 22.12: **Scrīpsit et Sulla dictātor ab exercitū sē quoque dōnātum apud Nōlam lēgātum bellō Marsicō.** The dictator Sulla even <u>wrote</u> that he, as legate during the Marsican War, also <u>had been granted</u> (a grass crown) by the army at Nola.

Understand *dōnātum* (*esse*).

Adamnanus, *de Vita Sancti Columbae* 1.1: **Tōtus populus prōmittit sē post reversiōnem dē bellō crēditūrum et baptismum susceptūrum.** The entire population <u>promises</u> that after their return from war they <u>will believe</u> and they <u>will receive</u> baptism.

Understand *crēditūrum* (*esse*) and *susceptūrum* (*esse*).

5. Indirect statements can also be introduced by participles, and they can even occur within ablatives absolute. Consider the following examples:

Horace, *Carmina* 3.7.9–11: **Atquī sollicitae nuntius hospitae,/ suspīrāre Chloen et miseram tuīs / dīcens ignibus ūrī . . .** And so the messenger of a worried hostess, <u>saying</u> that miserable Chloe <u>sighs</u> and <u>is burned</u> by your fires . . .

Suetonius, *Vita Caligulae* 51.2: **Dīcente quōdam nōn mediocrem fore consternātiōnem sīcunde hostis appareat . . .** With someone <u>declaring</u> that the confusion <u>would not be</u> moderate if the enemy would appear from anywhere . . .

I. Required Vocabulary

NOUNS

fātum, -ī, n: fate
medicus, -ī, m: doctor, physician
prōdigium, -iī, n: prodigy, portent

bōs, bovis, m / f: ox, bull, cow
caedēs, -is (-ium), f: killing, slaughter
fax, facis, f: torch
lapis, lapidis, m: stone
mulier, mulieris, f: woman
pēs, pedis, m: foot, foot soldier

ADJECTIVES

falsus, -a, -um: deceptive, false, fake

tristis, -e: sad, gloomy

VERBS

cūrō, -āre, -āvī, -ātus: care for, attend to
nuntiō, -āre, -āvī, -ātus: announce
turbō, -āre, -āvī, -ātus: disturb, throw into confusion

taceō, -ēre, -uī, -itus: be silent
terreō, -ēre, -uī: frighten, terrify

canō, -ere, cecinī, cantus: sing, prophesy
ēdō, -ere, -didī, -ditus: bring forth, explain, emit
gignō, -ere, genuī, genitus: bear, bring forth
pariō, -ere, peperī, partus: bring forth, bear, give birth (to)

offerō, -ferre, obtulī, oblātus: present, offer

morior, -ī, mortuus sum: die
nascor, -ī, nātus sum: be born, come into existence

fore = *futurus, -a, -um esse*

CONJUNCTIONS AND ADVERBS

crās: tomorrow
paulō, paulum: a little
semel: once
simul: at once, at the same time
subitō: suddenly

II. Translate the following sentences from
Latin to English or English to Latin.

1. Poēta sanctus canit vōs diū victūrōs esse.
2. Huic medicō nuntiātum est illōs mīlitēs vulnera multa accēpisse.
3. Tua māter scrībit amīcam suam crās moritūram esse.
4. Audīvimus caedem saevam terrēre equōs bovēsque.
5. Mulierēs in īram turbātae locūtae sunt sē cum legiōnibus impetum factūrās esse.
6. Intellexī sorōrem meam duo līberōs peperisse.
7. Cīvēs putāvērunt consulēs eō annō esse pessimōs.
8. Caesar invenit aliquōs lēgātōs bellum gerere nōn cupere.
9. Romulus and Remus announced that two prodigies were perceived in the sky.
10. You (singular) write that your legion is pitching camp.
11. Hispulla said that her spouse Corellius had died.
12. The army thinks that Caesar has presented the best plans.

Prodigies and Paradoxa

The Romans strongly believed that the gods sent signs, both solicited and im-promptu. Priests were trained to interpret signs from birds (augury) and entrails (*haruspicium*) in the context of Roman state business. Spontaneous signs, the marvelous and paradoxical, manifested in all manner of natural anomalies, giving cause for alarm and sometimes even fear. Such prodigies included unusual births (hermaphrodites, hawk-taloned piglets, two-headed fetuses), the strange behavior of animals (swarms of bees), atmospheric anomalies (earthquakes, comets, eclipses, showers of blood or stones, lightning strikes), and plagues. Almost in-variably such occurrences were thought to indicate divine displeasure.

Prodigies were commonly featured in Republican historiography (Livy, for ex-ample, reports and analyzes many *paradoxa*). Consuls received reports of prodi-gies, which in turn they relayed to the Senate to determine which *paradoxa* were authentic divine warnings. Written in Greek hexameters, the Sibylline books were consulted in regard to prodigies that were deemed urgent matters of public concern, usually with the aim to avert political calamity and expiate divine anger. The Sibylline books often prescribed religious observances or mandated new (Greek) cults. For example, the cult of Asclepius, the healer god, was imported to alleviate a plague in 293 BCE (Livy, *ab Urbe Condita* 10.17), and Cybele's strange Eastern rite and eunuch priests were brought to Rome to aid the failing war effort against Hannibal in 205 BCE (*ab Urbe Condita* 29.10–14). In 69 CE, portents and oracles presaged the rise of Vespasian (Tacitus, *Historia* 1.10.3), and Galba was condemned for disregarding meteorological signs (*Historia* 1.18.1).

The cultural milieu of the first century CE was imbued with *paradoxa* and fantasy. In vogue was the so-called Third Style of Pompeian wall painting, which spotlighted delicately (and unrealistically) wrought architectural features, as well as fantastical hybrid animals in Egyptianizing landscapes. Dwarfs were popular both in the arena and as mascots at court (Pliny the Elder tells us that Augustus's granddaughter Julia kept as a "pet" a dwarf whom she called Conopas, *Naturalis Historia* 7.75). Reflecting the intellectual tastes of his times, while omitting politically significant sites, the geographer Mela describes *paradoxa*, and the historian Tacitus employs *paradoxa* in his editorial arsenal. It was in this culture that Petronius composed his picaresque *Satyrica*, a novel of ostentatious and grotesque extravagance, and that Apuleius penned his *Metamorphoses*, a tale of a man turned into a donkey turned back into a man after conversion to the cult of Isis. The first century CE was a time of discovery, and, as Roman knowledge extended further afield, increasingly strange reports of bizarre peoples, plants, and animals came to Rome. Pliny the Elder summarizes Rome's curiosity in these observations: *nam mihi contuentī semper suasit rērum nātūra nihil incrēdibile existimāre dē eā* ("for the nature of things has always persuaded me, while I was observing it, to think nothing impossible about it": *Naturalis Historia* 11.6).

SUGGESTIONS FOR FURTHER READING:

Barton, Carlin A. *The Sorrows of the Ancient Romans: The Gladiator and the Monster.* Princeton, 1993.

Beagon, Mary. *Roman Nature: The Thought of Pliny the Elder.* Oxford, 1992.

Davies, J. P. *Rome's Religious History: Livy, Tacitus and Ammianus on their Gods.* Cambridge, 2004.

PASSAGES

24.1. Vergil, *Aeneid* **7.79–80.** When a swarm of bees suddenly appears in Latinus's palace, a prophet predicts that a foreign hero will approach the kingdom with an army. Immediately after this prediction, Lavinia's head bursts into flames and the following prediction is made. Meter: dactylic hexameter.

Namque fore inlustrem fāmā fātīsque canēbant
ipsam, sed populō magnum portendere bellum.

Notes: **inlustris, -e**: bright, distinguished, famous; **ipsam**: Lavinia; **portendō, -ere, -tendī, -tentus**: indicate, predict.

24.2. Livy, *ab Urbe Condita* **43.13.3.** Living in an era when such strange occurrences are no longer recorded, Livy tackles contemporary skepticism about the validity of portents and signs as genuine messages from the gods. Deferring to ancient wisdom, he defends his choice to include these unbelievable events. Here he launches into a lengthy list of portents for the year 169 BCE.

Anagniā duo prōdigia eō annō sunt nuntiāta, facem in caelō conspectam et bovem fēminam locūtam.

Notes: **Anagnia, -iae**, f: a small town near Rome; **conspectam** (*esse*); **conspiciō, -ere, -spexī, -spectus**: behold, perceive; (*tamquam*) **fēminam**; **locūtam** (*esse*).

24.3. Tacitus, *Annales* **6.28.4.** The phoenix was a legendary bird that periodically regenerated itself, was consumed by fire at death, and then was reborn anew from its own ashes. In 34 CE, a phoenix was presumably sighted in Egypt. Yet debate over the interval between appearances of the phoenix (500 or 1,461 years) led some to dispute the authenticity of the report.

Nōn nullī falsum hunc phoenīcem neque Arabum ē terrīs crēdidēre nihilque ūsurpāvisse ex hīs quae vetus memoria firmāvit.

Notes: **nōn nullī**: "some"; construe *fuisse* as the infinitive that governs the first indirect statement; **phoenix, phoenīcis**, m, phoenix; **Arabum** = *Arabōrum*; **Arabī, -ōrum**, m (plural): Arabs, people from Arabia; **ūsurpō, -āre, -āvī, -ātus**: employ, appropriate; **firmō, -āre, -āvī, -ātus**: strengthen, assert, maintain.

24.4. Suetonius, *Vita Caligulae* 57.1. Signs of Caligula's impending assassination.

Futūrae caedis multa prōdigia exstitērunt. Olympiae simulācrum Iovis, quod dissolvī transferrīque Rōmam placuerat, tantum cachinnum repente ēdidit, ut māchinīs labefactīs opificēs diffūgerint; supervēnitque īlicō quidam Cassius nōmine, iussum sē somniō affirmans immolāre taurum Iovī.

Notes: **exstō, -āre, -stitī**: appear, exist; **Olympia, -iae**, f: the site of Jupiter's famous temple and games in the northern Peloponnese (*Olympiae*: locative); **simulācrum, -ī**, n: image, likeness, statue; **Iuppiter, Iovis**, m: Jupiter; **dissolvō, -ere, -solvī, -solūtus**: loosen, destroy; **transferō, -ferre, -tulī, -lātus**: bring across; **cachinnus, -ī**, m: raucous laughter; **repente**: suddenly; **ut diffūgerint**: "that (the workers) scattered" (perfect subjunctive); **māchina, -ae**, f: machine, device, here "scaffolding"; **labefaciō, -ere, -fēcī, -factus**: shake, totter; **opifex, opificis**, m/f: worker; **superveniō, -īre, -vēnī, -ventus**: arrive; **īlicō**: in that very spot; **Cassius, -iī**, m: the name of an otherwise unknown Roman man; **iussum** (*esse*); **somnium, -iī**, n: dream; **affirmō, -āre, -āvī, -ātus**: declare, assert; **immolō, -āre, -āvī, -ātus**: sacrifice, **taurus, -ī**, m: bull.

24.5. Pliny the Elder, *Naturalis Historia* 7.35. Pliny here claims to have seen the preserved remains of a mythical composite creature, commonly known as a "Centaur."

Claudius Caesar scrībit hippocentaurum in Thessaliā nātum eōdem diē interisse; et nōs principātū eius adlātum illī ex Aegyptō in melle vīdimus.

Notes: **hippocentaurus, -ī**, m: centaur (part horse, part human); **Thessalia, -iae**, f: a remote region of northern Greece, a notorious hotbed of magic and witchcraft; **intereō, -īre, -īvī, -itūrus**: perish, die; **principātus, -ūs**, m: rule, reign; **eius**: Claudius; **adlātum** (*esse*); **adferō, -ferre, -tulī, -lātus**: carry, convey, "preserve"; **illī**: Claudius; **Aegyptus, -ī**, m: Egypt; **mel, mellis**, n: honey.

24.6. Pliny the Elder, *Naturalis Historia* 7.46. Breech births were considered unlucky or inauspicious, and those so born were frequently called Agrippa ("with difficulty"). Nero's own great-grandfather Agrippa was one of the few breech babies to have enjoyed a successful political career at Rome, according to Pliny. But his "success" was bittersweet. Agrippa's unusual birth presaged misfortune for the world through his descendants, including the self-indulgent, immature Nero who was, likewise, a breech baby.

Nerōnem quoque—paulō ante principem et tōtō principātū suō hostem generis hūmānī—pedibus genitum scrībit parens eius Agrippīna. Rītus nātūrae hominem capite gignī, mōs est pedibus efferrī.

Notes: **Nerō, -ōnis**, m: Nero; **principātū**: see *NLP* 24.5; **pēs, pedis**, m: here, "feet-first"; **genitum** (*esse*); **Agrippīna, -ae**, f: Nero's mother; **rītus, -ūs**, m: custom, practice; **efferō, -ferre, -tulī, -lātus**: bring out.

24.7. Pliny the Younger, *Epistulae* **7.27.2–3.** Serving on the staff of a quaestor in Africa, a young Curtius Rufus saw an apparition of a woman who foretold (accurately) his successful political career, including his governorship of Africa.

Inclīnātō diē spatiābātur in porticū; offertur eī mulieris figūra hūmāna grandior pulchriorque. Perterritō Āfricam sē futūrōrum praenuntiam dixit: itūrum enim Rōmam honōrēsque gestūrum, atque etiam cum summō imperiō in eandem prōvinciam reversūrum, ibique moritūrum. Facta sunt omnia.

Notes: **inclīnō, -āre, -āvī, -ātus**: bend, incline, sink (i.e., it was late afternoon); **spatior, -ārī**: walk, stroll; **porticus, -ūs**, f: colonnade, gallery; **eī**: Curtius Rufus; **figūra, -ae**, f: form, shape, figure; **perterreō, -ēre, -uī, -itus**: frighten, terrify; **Āfrica, -ae**, f: the province of Africa (the Mediterranean coast of Africa roughly between Algeria and Egypt); **Āfricam** (*esse*) **sē**; **praenuntia, -iae**, f: herald, harbinger; **itūrum** (*esse*); **gestūrum** (*esse*); **reversūrum** (*esse*); **revertō, -ere, vertī, versus**: return; **moritūrum** (*esse*).

24.8. Plautus, *Mostellaria* **489–90.** To cover for the transgressions of his love-stricken young master Philolaches, the slave Tranio insists that Theopropides' house is haunted and that, in his absence, his son was visited by a ghost.

Theopropides. Quis homo? An gnātus meus? **Tranio.** St, tacē, auscultā modo. Ait vēnisse illum in somnīs ad sē mortuom.

Notes: **an**: or; **gnātus, -ī**, m: son; **st**: hush!; **auscultō, -āre, -āvī, -ātus**: listen attentively; **ait**: "he (your son) said"; **mortuom** = *mortuum* from *mortuus, -a, -um*: dead.

24.9. Petronius, *Satyricon* 62. One of Trimalchio's guests, Niceros, recounts his encounter with a werewolf. On his way to visit his girlfriend, Niceros was walking with a soldier who wandered off into a cemetery, but tarried too long. Niceros went to investigate, finding the soldier stark naked on the road—just before the transformation—and his clothes turned to stone. Niceros ran in terror to his girlfriend's house, where he found the soldier, wounded but restored to human form.

Ut vērō domum vēnī, iacēbat mīles meus in lectō tanquam bovis, et collum illīus medicus cūrābat. Intellexī illum versipellem esse.

Notes: **ut**: when; **lectus, -ī**, m: couch, bed; **tanquam** = *tamquam*; (*in modo*) **bovis**; **collum, -ī**, n: neck; **versipellis, -is (-ium)**, m: shape-changer, werewolf.

24.10. Pliny the Elder, *Naturalis Historia* 8.6. Some elephants, apparently, could read and write in Greek.

Mūciānus III consul auctor est aliquem ex iīs et litterārum ductūs Graecārum didicisse solitumque perscrībere eius linguae verbīs: "Ipse ego haec scripsī et spolia Celtica dicāvī."

Notes: **Mūciānus, -ī**, m: Gaius Licinius Mucianus, author, statesman, and general who served under Corbulo in Armenia (see *NLP* 21) but, failing to mollify the Jewish revolt in 66 CE, was replaced by Vespasian; **III**: three times; **iīs** (*elephantīs*); **ductus, -ūs**, m: drawing, leading; **Graecus, -a, -um**: Greek; **solitum** (*esse*); **perscrībō, -ere, -scripsī, -scriptus**: write in full (i.e., without abbreviations); **spolium, -iī**, n: plunder, spoils; **Celticus, -a, -um**: Celtic; **dicō, -āre, -āvī, -ātus**: dedicate.

24.11. Pliny the Elder, *Naturalis Historia* 7.23. Among many strange things that happen in India, some newborn babies immediately turn gray.

Ctēsiās scrībit, et in quādam gente Indiae fēminās semel in vītā parere genitōsque confestim cānescere.

Notes: **Ctēsiās, -ae**, m; a famous Greek physician from Caria in Turkey, fifth century BCE; **India, -iae**, f: India; **confestim**: immediately, suddenly; **cānescō, -ere**: become white, become old.

24.12. Pliny the Elder, *Naturalis Historia* 7.36. Gender was a complex question in antiquity: mythology preserves tales of cross-dressing heroes (Achilles and Hercules); a female physician masqueraded as a man to win clients;

Nero sought a sex change operation for Sporus, one of his favorites; and Elagabalus (ruled 218–220 CE) sought the procedure for himself. Pliny here reports an historical account of a sex-change operation but omits the medical details.

Ex fēminīs mūtārī in marēs nōn est fābulōsum. Invēnimus in annālibus—P. Liciniō Crassō C. Cassiō Longīnō cons(ulibus)— Casīnī puerum factum ex virgine sub parentibus iussūque haruspicum dēportātum in insulam dēsertam.

Notes: **mūtārī**: impersonal passive; **mas, maris**, m: male; **fābulōsus, -a, -um**: fabled, storied; **annālēs, -ium**, m (plural): yearly records; **Publius Licinius Crassus, Publiī Liciniī Crassī**, m: consul in 171 BCE; **Caius Cassius Longīnus, Caiī Cassiī Longīnī**, m: consul in 171 BCE, recalled to Rome for deliberately disobeying senatorial orders in the Third Macedonian War, he was elected censor in 154 BCE; **Casīnum, -ī**, n: a town in the mountains of central Italy between Rome and Naples; **factum** (*esse*); **iussū**: by the command; **haruspex, -icis**, m: a priest who read the will of the gods by examining the entrails of sacrificial animals, according to ancient Etruscan practices; **dēportātum** (*esse*); **dēportō, -āre, -āvī, -ātus**: carry off, carry away; **dēsertus, -a, -um**: uninhabited.

EXTRA PASSAGES: HEALTH AND WELL-BEING

Prodigies and portents were remarkable for their rarity, but physical health and mental well-being were of universal concern (see also *NLP* 33 and the Extra Passages in *NLP* 22).

24.13. Vegetius, *de Re Militari* 3.2. From Hippocrates onward, the health benefits of exercise were recognized.

Sed reī mīlitāris perītī plus cotidiāna armōrum exercitia ad sānitātem mīlitum putāvērunt prōdesse quam medicōs.

Notes: **mīlitāris, -e**: of war, of a soldier, military; **perītus, -a, -um** (+ genitive): skillful (in), expert (in); **cotidiānus, -a, -um**: daily; **exercitium, -iī**, n: practice, exercise; **sānitās, -ātis**, f: health; **prōsum, prōdesse, -fuī, -futūrus**: be useful (to), benefit.

24.14. Cicero, *ad Familares* 14.8. Cicero writes to his wife who has fallen ill in 47 BCE.

Nam mihi et scriptum et nuntiātum est tē in febrim subitō incidisse.

Notes: **scriptum** (*esse*); **nuntiātum** (*esse*); **febris, -is (-ium)**, f: fever; **incidō, -ere, -cidī, -cāsus**: fall in / on.

24.15. Pliny the Younger, *Epistulae* 1.12.9–10. Pliny here laments the impending suicide of his friend Corellius Rufus, a senator who served with distinction as governor of Upper Germany, long suffering from gout.

Mīsit ad mē uxor eius Hispulla commūnem amīcum C. Geminium cum tristissimō nuntiō, destināsse Corellium morī, nec aut suīs aut fīliae precibus inflectī; sōlum superesse mē, ā quō rēvocārī posset ad vītam. Cucurrī.

Notes: **eius**: Corellius Rufus; **Hispulla, -ae**, f: Corellius's faithful wife; **commūnis, -e**: common; **Caius Geminius, Caiī Geminiī**, m: a mutual friend of Pliny and Corellius Rufus and the addressee of several of Pliny's letters; **nuntium, -iī**, n: message; **destinā(vi)sse**; **dēstinō, -āre, -āvī, -ātus**: intend (to), be determined (to); **inflectō, -ere, -flexī, -flexus**: bend, change; **supersum, -esse, fuī, -futūrus**: remain, survive; **rēvocō, -āre, -āvī, -ātus**: call back, recall, revive; **posset**: "might be able to" (imperfect subjunctive).

Correlatives

1. Correlatives indicate a complementary relationship between two words or two phrases in the same sentence. The most familiar of these correlatives are the coordinating conjunctions that you have seen since the early lessons of this book. Review the following passages (only the last one presents a new correlative):

Horace, *Carmina* 1.1.2 (*NLP* 4.5): **Ō <u>et</u> praesidium <u>et</u> dulce decus meum.** O (Maecenas), <u>both</u> my defense <u>and</u> my sweet glory.

Catullus 12.10–11 (*NLP* 4.3): **Quārē <u>aut</u> hendecasyllabōs trecentōs / exspectā, <u>aut</u> mihi linteum remitte!** Therefore <u>either</u> await 300 hendecasyllables <u>or</u> send me back my napkin!

Vergil, *Aeneid* 4.380: **<u>Neque</u> tē teneō <u>neque</u> dicta refellō.** I <u>neither</u> detain you <u>nor</u> refute (your) words.

Livy, *ab Urbe Condita* 9.10.1: **Mōvit patrēs conscriptōs <u>cum</u> causa <u>tum</u> auctor, <u>nec</u> cēterōs <u>sōlum</u> <u>sed</u> tribūnōs <u>etiam</u> plebēī.** <u>Not only</u> the speech <u>but also</u> the author moved the senators, and <u>not only</u> the rest (of them) <u>but also</u> the tribunes of the plebs.

2. We have also seen pronouns, especially the demonstratives, act as correlatives. Review the following examples:

Pliny the Younger, *Epistulae* 6.16.22 (*NLP* 9.13): **<u>Aliud</u> est enim epistulam, <u>aliud</u> historiam, <u>aliud</u> amīcō, <u>aliud</u> omnibus scrībere.** For it is <u>one thing</u> to write a letter, <u>another thing</u> (to write) history; it is <u>one thing</u> (to write) for a friend, <u>another thing</u> (to write) for everyone.

Ovid, *Metamorphoses* 1.428–29: **Et eōdem in corpore saepe/altera pars vīvit, rudis est pars altera tellus.** And in the same body <u>one</u> part often lives, the <u>other</u> part is earth with debris.

Ovid, *Fasti* 5.392: **Et causam adventūs hic rogat, ille docet.** And <u>the latter</u> (Chiron) asks the reason for his arrival, (and) <u>the former</u> (Hercules) replies.

3. Some of the more complex correlatives pair a demonstrative pronoun with comparative adjective, or a comparative adverb with a corresponding relative pronoun, comparative adjective or comparative adverb. Consider the following examples:

Caesar, *de Bello Gallico* 1.14.1: **Atque eō gravius ferre quō minus meritō populī Rōmānī accidissent.** And <u>the more</u> severely he endured (the situation), <u>the less</u> deservedly the Roman people had experienced it.

Caesar, *de Bello Gallico* 7.18.1: **Eō profectum quō nostrōs posterō diē pābulātum ventūrōs arbitrārētur.** Caesar set out <u>to that place</u> <u>where</u> he thought our men would come on the following day to forage.

4. Other more complex correlatives involve a main clause that features one of the following adjectives or adverbs:

tantus, -a, -um: so great, so much
tālis, -e: of such a kind
tam: so
tot: so many
totiens: so often

and a corresponding relative clause introduced by

quantus, -a, -um: how much
quālis, -e: what sort
quam: as
quot: how many
quotiens: how often

Remember that the adjectives decline to agree in case, number, and gender with the nouns they modify. Consider the following examples:

Caesar, *de Bello Gallico* 2.11.6: **Ita sine ullō perīculō <u>tantam</u> eōrum multitūdinem nostrī interfēcērunt <u>quantum</u> fuit diēī spatium.** Thus without any danger, our men killed <u>as great</u> a crowd of them <u>as</u> was the extent of the day.

Ovid, *Metamorphoses* 8.49–50: **Sī quae tē peperit, <u>tālis</u>, pulcherrimē rēgum, / <u>quālis</u> es, ipsa fuit.** If she who birthed you, most beautiful of kings, was herself <u>such a</u> (woman) <u>as</u> you are.

Tacitus, *Agricola* 32: **<u>Tam</u> dēserent illōs cēterī Germānī <u>quam</u> nūper Ūsīpī reliquērunt.** The other Germans will abandon them as <u>recently</u> as the Usipi left (them).

Cicero, *ad Brutum* 1.16: **Valdē cārē aestimās <u>tot</u> annōs <u>quot</u> ista aetās recipit.** You value very dearly <u>as many</u> years <u>as</u> that life of yours receives.

Cicero, *ad Atticum* 1.14.3: **<u>Quotiens</u> coniugem, <u>quotiens</u> domum, <u>quotiens</u> patriam vidēret, <u>totiens</u> sē beneficium meum vidēre.** <u>As often as</u> he saw his wife, <u>as often as</u> (he saw) his house, <u>as often as</u> (he saw) his country, <u>so often</u> did he see my kindness.

I. Required Vocabulary

NOUNS

sapientia, -iae, f: wisdom, discernment, prudence

beneficium, -iī, n: favor, kindness, service

vōtum, -ī, n: vow, solemn promise

fūnus, fūneris, n: funeral, burial, funeral rite

laus, laudis, f: praise

nūmen, nūminis, n: divine spirit

ops, opis, f: power, means

ōrātiō, -iōnis, f: speech

ADJECTIVES

exiguus, -a, -um: small, scanty

quantus, -a, -um: how much

mortālis, -e: mortal, transitory, human

VERBS

creō, -āre, -āvī, -ātus: create, make

existimō, -āre, -āvī, -ātus: value, esteem, judge, think

properō, -āre, -āvī, -ātus: hurry

dēcernō, -ere, -crēvī, -crētus: decide, settle, propose

dēficiō, -ere, -fēcī, -fectus: fail, run short

descisco, -ere, -scīvī, -scītus: desert, withdraw, revolt, break away

prōcēdō, -ere, -cessī, -cessus: proceed, advance

tollō, -ere, sustulī, sublātus: lift up

absum, -esse, āfuī, āfutūrus: be absent, be removed

ait: he said (aiunt: they said)

PREPOSITIONS

adversus (+ accusative): against

CONJUNCTIONS, ADVERBS, AND CORRELATIVE EXPRESSIONS

dēnique: finally, at last, further

satis or sat: enough, sufficiently

cum . . . tum: both . . . and; not only . . . but also

eō . . . quō: the more . . . the more; there . . . where

talis . . . qualis: such . . . as

tam . . . quam: as . . . as

tantus . . . quantus: so great . . . as

tantō . . . quantō: the more . . . the more

totiens . . . quotiens: so often . . . as

tot . . . quot: so much / as many . . . as

II. Translate the following sentences from Latin to English or English to Latin.

1. Ōrātiōnem tālem dat Cicerō quālem Catilīna numquam dēdit.

2. Post Lucrētiae mortem Brutus erat dux tantus quantus fuerat optimus rex.

3. Caesar tot in bellīs vincet quot in annō diēs sunt.

4. Dē nostrīs beneficiīs quotiens cōgitābis totiens dē sapientiā putābis.

5. Vōta tam multa erant quam in caelō astra erant.

6. Temporis tantum dēcrēvit quantum necesse erat.

7. Tālis māter Agrippīna quālem omnēs līberī timent.

8. In bonō exercitū eō māior laus quō in malō culpa est.

9. Caesar was as great a general as Cincinnatus had been.

10. We wrote to our brothers and sisters as often as our mothers and fathers had written to us.

11. Value me as most friendly to you and such a citizen as Rome ought to make.

12. We heard as many sweet songs as the poet was able to sing.

The Roman Republic

In 509 BCE, according to legend, in response to the outrages committed against Lucretia, the men of Rome rejected two and a half centuries of kingship in favor of a system of self-government where—in theory—the best men would rise to the highest offices and govern the state in the best possible way (see *NLP* 3). The resulting republican system of government was based on an informal, largely unwritten, and ever-evolving "constitution" of traditions as Rome herself expanded into Italy and beyond. Our best source, aside from the large corpus of jurisprudence, is the Greek historian Polybius (c. 200–118 BCE), whose *Histories* were written in Greek to explain to a Greek readership how and why Rome rose to prominence so quickly.

Polybius described the Roman republican system as featuring three branches of government: assemblies, Senate, and the consulship (6.11–18). He particularly admired how the branches incorporated contrasting philosophies and models of government to complement and balance each other, yielding the best possible practices. The assemblies resembled a democracy wherein all Roman (male) citizens came together to elect magistrates, enact laws, and declare war or peace. The Senate corresponded to an oligarchy, serving as an advisory body to the magistrates (on foreign and domestic policy, finances, religion, and legislation), ratifying popular deliberations, and acting as judges. The two annually elected consuls together mirrored a monarchy, and their fundamental responsibility was to oversee foreign policy.

Within this system were automatic checks and balances. The consuls needed the support of the assemblies for election to office in the first place. The Senate could refuse to ratify deliberations of the popular assemblies (including elections). The consuls required senatorial support for money to fund their actions while in office. The Senate could hold a consul accountable for his actions and bring him to trial after his term of office (so Caesar feared in 49 BCE, preferring to go to war rather than risk trial and end his political career; magistrates were immune from legal proceedings while they held certain higher offices, including the praetorship, consulship, and provincial governorship—but **only** while in office). The Senate was also responsible for assigning provincial governorships to the outgoing consuls— a rich opportunity to enhance personal glory and wealth. Finally, war was the unifying arc: the assemblies declared war, voted for the funds to underwrite warfare, and their members served as troops in the army; the Senate advised and criticized the course of a war and conclusion of peace treaties, and senators awarded or denied military triumphal parades to victorious consul-generals; the consuls were responsible for leading Roman troops in the field.

Only a small portion of the population could play this game—canvassing for votes was an expensive business, and family connections were critically important. Cicero was right to be proud of his status as a *novus homo*, the first man in his family to attain the consulship. There was a strict sequence of one-year-long public offices sought by aspiring statesmen. The first rung in this *cursus honōrum* was the office of the quaestor, a financial magistrate whose minimum age was thirty-one. Upon completion of the term, quaestors were automatically enrolled in the Senate, where they served for life unless removed by a censor. At age thirty-six, Roman statesmen were eligible to hold the office of aedile, responsible for maintaining public infrastructure (buildings, archives, streets, water supply, weights and measures, grain supply) and sponsoring games (a sure means of securing popular support, as Caesar proved by the extravagant games he hosted during his aedileship in 65 BCE—with Crassus's money). At age thirty-nine, a politician could seek election as praetor, whose fundamental responsibility included supervising the defense of the city and who had the right to govern a province afterwards. The consulship was open to men aged forty-two and older (Cicero was likewise right to be proud that he had risen through the ranks of the *cursus honōrum* at the youngest possible age).

This informal constitution also called for the appointment of occasional magistrates. Censors held office for eighteen months, once every five years. The censor reviewed the rolls of the Senate, disenrolling those men who either lacked moral probity or—more commonly—expressed political views contrary to the censor's (In 50 BCE, Appius Claudius Pulcher expunged the historian Sallust for "immorality." It is more likely that Sallust's expulsion resulted from a personal vendetta—he had expressed opposition to the censor Appius's friend Cicero; under Caesar's influence, Sallust was reinstated by a sympathetic censor in 49 BCE.) Dictators were appointed during times of emergency, to hold office for a term of six months or until the emergency was resolved, whichever came first (Cincinnatus and Sulla both stepped down from office into quiet retirement; Caesar's declaration of himself as "dictator for life" was extraordinary and shocking).

As Rome grew, constitutional convention adapted itself to the changing political climate. The fifth century BCE in particular was rife with transition as the patricians (descended from Romulus's original one hundred senators) and plebeians (the non-noble families) came into contention in the so-called Conflict of the Orders. In 494 BCE, the plebeians withdrew their military support and demanded a written code of law, resulting eventually in the Twelve Tables, which formalized the right to appeal and the right for personal liberty (see *NLP* 35). A series of political revisions ensued, including new magistracies and the expansion of the candidate pool to include plebeians. Soon the quaestorship and aedileship were opened to plebeians, and by 367 BCE one of the two annually elected consuls was required by law to be plebeian. The office of Tribune of the Plebs was a powerful one that could be held *only* by a politician from a plebeian family. Responsible for defending the lives and property of plebeians, these Tribunes had the authority to convene the Senate and summon the plebeians to assembly, as well as the power to veto laws, elections, and decrees of the senate (Cicero's exile was orchestrated by Tribunes of the Plebs, as was his recall: see *NLP* 9). Unlike other offices, the tribuneship could be held only once. Roman sensibilities allowed for a peculiar loophole: a Tribune of the Plebs had to be plebeian only according to the law, not necessarily by birth. Publius Clodius Pulcher, born to an ancient elite family (he was born a Claudius), had himself adopted into the plebeian branch of the family (Clodius) by a younger man, so he could stand for the tribuneship and seek revenge against his political enemy, Cicero.

SUGGESTIONS FOR FURTHER READING:

Beck, Hans, Antonio Duplá, Martin Jehne and Francisco Pina Polo. *Consuls and Res Publica: Holding High Office in the Roman Republic.* Cambridge, 2011.
Brennan, T. Corey. *The Praetorship in the Roman Republic.* Oxford, 2001.
Gwynn, David M. *The Roman Republic: A Very Short Introduction.* Oxford, 2012.
Lendon, J. E. *Empire of Honour: The Art of Government in the Roman World.* Oxford, 1997.
Lintott, Andrew. *The Constitution of the Roman Republic.* Oxford, 2003.

PASSAGES

25.1. Cicero, *ad Brutum* 1.1.2. In this letter, dated May, 43 BCE, Cicero attempts to reconcile his friend Brutus with the Tribune-elect, Lucius Clodius.

Clōdium tibi amīcissimum existimā cīvemque tālem quālis et prūdentissimus et fortūnā optimā esse dēbet.

Notes: **prūdens (-entis)**: skilled, discreet, wise.

25.2. Cicero, *pro Marcello* 19. Marcellus was one of the consuls of 49 BCE who legally stripped Caesar of his command, thereby sparking civil war. In 46 BCE, however, Caesar pardoned Marcellus, as he did so many of his enemies, which in turn inspired Cicero to thank the dictator for his magnanimity on behalf of fellow Republican Marcellus (and himself), as here, believing, perhaps, that Caesar intended to restore the Republic.

Dē nōbīs, quōs in Rēpūblica tēcum simul esse voluistī, quotiens cōgitābis, totiens dē maximīs tuīs beneficiīs, totiens dē incrēdibilī līberālitāte, totiens dē singulārī sapientiā tuā cōgitābis.

Notes: **incrēdibilis, -e**: extraordinary; **līberālitās, -ātis**, f: kindness, courtesy, generosity; **singulāris, -e**: single, individual, unique.

25.3. Cicero, *pro Sestio* 28. Here Cicero chastises Clodius Pulcher's ally, Lucius Calpurnius Piso Caesonius, who in 56 BCE brought a (likely trumped-up) charge of *vis* (violence to the state) against Cicero's ally Sestius, among the Tribunes who advocated the orator's recall (see *NLP* 9).

Advocat contiōnem, habet ōrātiōnem tālem consul quālem numquam Catilīna victor habuisset.

Notes: **advocō, -āre, -āvī, -ātus**: call, summon; **contiō, -iōnis**, f: assembly, public meeting; **Catilīna, -ae**, m: Catiline; **habuisset**: "(Catiline) would have delivered" (pluperfect subjunctive).

25.4. Cicero, *Philippica* 3.9. Here, Cicero compares Antony to Rome's last king, Tarquinius Superbus, whose atrocities sparked civil war, leading to the establishment of the Republic in 509 BCE. Antony's actions pose a far greater threat to Rome's survival.

Quid Tarquinius tāle, quālia innumerābilia et facit et fēcit Antōnius?

Notes: **quid** (*scelus fēcit*); **Tarquinius, -iī**, m: Tarquinius Superbus, an Etruscan king of Rome (ruled 535–509 BCE); **innumerābilia** (*scelera*); **innumerābilis, -e**: countless; **Antōnius, -iī**, m: Marc Antony, Caesar's lieutenant responsible for Cicero's execution in 43 BCE.

25.5. Cicero, *de Provinciis Consularibus* 26. Weighing in on the distribution of provincial governorships for the outgoing consuls (staunch Ciceronians), Cicero launches into a long digression concerning his own political enemies, including Caesar. Cicero here reminds the Senate of his own support for the *supplicātiō* awarded after Caesar's conquest of the Belgae the previous year (57 BCE).

Supplicātiōnem quindecim diērum dēcrēvī sententiā meā. Reī pūblicae satis erat tot diērum quot C. Mariō; dīs immortālibus nōn erat exigua eadem grātulātiō quae ex maximīs bellīs.

Notes: **supplicātiō, -iōnis**, f: solemn thanksgiving to the gods, decreed by the Senate after great victories—often a prelude to a triumphal parade, or to avert the anger of the gods in the face of public danger or prodigies. A *supplicātiō*'s length was proportional to the importance of the event to be commemorated, lasting as little as one day, or more commonly three to five, growing to twenty (for Caesar's subjugation of Vercingetorix), and even forty or fifty; **Caius Marius, Caiī Mariī**, m: Gaius Marius, the great army reformer who saw spectacular successes against Jugurtha in 104 BCE and the Germanic tribes in 104–101 BCE (see *NLP 7*), who likewise enjoyed lengthy *supplicātiōnēs* for these victories; **immortālis, -e**: deathless, everlasting, imperishable; **grātulātiō, -iōnis**, f: joy, festival of thanksgiving.

25.6. Ovid, *Fasti* 1.599–600. Political careers were launched and sustained by military victories, and successful generals often took the toponyms of conquered peoples as names of honor for themselves (e.g., Scipio Africanus) or their children (e.g., Germanicus, Britannicus). Ovid here may refer to Julius Caesar or, more likely, to Augustus, whose own career, though unusual, mostly adhered to Roman republican constitutional law. In 27 BCE, Augustus declared the Republic restored (*Res Gestae* 34.1). Meter: elegiac couplets.

> Sī petat ā victīs, tot sūmet nōmina Caesar
> quot numerō gentēs maximus orbis habet.

Notes: **petat**: "he should demand" (present subjunctive) (construe *nōmina* as the direct object).

25.7. Livy, *ab Urbe Condita* 6.18.6. In a rousing speech, Manlius stirs the people to unite against the Senate.

> Quot enim clientēs circā singulōs fuistis patrōnōs, tot nunc adversus ūnum hostem eritis.

Notes: **cliens, -entis**, m: client, dependent; **patrōnus, -ī**, m: protector, defender, patron.

25.8. Livy, *ab Urbe Condita* 30.28.7. At the close of the Second Punic War in 202 BCE, Livy remarks on Hannibal's successes in the field with reference to a powerful symbol of the Republic. Consisting of an axehead and bundle of birch rods, strapped together with red leather, the fasces signified the absolute but constitutional authority of praetors, consuls, dictators, and generals in republican Rome.

> Nōn esse hodiē tot fascēs magistrātibus populī Rōmānī quot captōs ex caede imperātōrum prae sē ferre posset Hannibal.

Notes: **esse**: "there are" (historical infinitive); **fascis, -is (-ium)**, m: bundle, fasces; **magistrātus, -ūs**, m: magistrate, state official; **prae** (+ ablative): before, in front; **posset**: "he (Hannibal) was able" (imperfect subjunctive).

25.9. Sallust, *Historiae* 1.67.17. Marcus Aemilius Lepidus (the grandfather of the triumvir) rose to prominence under Sulla; but opposing Sulla's constitution during his consulship (78 BCE) he moved, for example, to restore the prerogatives of the Tribunes of the Plebs which had been harshly curtailed under Sulla. As governor of Gallia Transalpina, promising recall for those exiled by Sulla, Lepidus gathered allies and fomented civil war. He was defeated by a senatorial army in pitched battle in the Campus Martius in 77 BCE. Here, Lucius Marcus Philippus persuades the Senate to take action against Lepidus.

Quantō mehercule avidius pācem petīeritis, tantō bellum ācrius erit, cum intelleget sē metū magis quam aequō et bonō sustentātum.

Notes: **mehercule**: by Hercules!; **avidus, -a, -um**: greedy, eager, passionate; **petī(v)eritis**; **sē**: Lepidus; **aequum, -ī**, n: fairness, equanimity; **sustentātum** (*esse*); **sustentō, -āre, -āvī, -ātus**: support, sustain.

25.10. Caesar, *de Bello Civili* 1.81.4. In 49 BCE at Ilerda in northern Spain, Caesar engages Pompey's lieutenant Lucius Afranius in a strategic game of cat and mouse. Here we see that, despite their best efforts, the Pompeians cannot pitch a camp that has adequate access to resources.

Sed quantum opere prōcesserant et castra prōtulerant, tantō aberant ab aquā longius.

Notes: **prōferō, -ferre, -tulī, -lātus**: bring forth, advance, enlarge, extend.

25.11. Caesar, *de Bello Civili* 3.78.2. In 48 BCE, Caesar was balancing practical obligations with strategic concerns: attending to his troops and preparing for imminent battle with Pompey.

Sed hīs rēbus tantum temporis tribuit, quantum erat properantī necesse.

Notes: **hīs rēbus**: i.e., to paying troops and attending to the wounded; **tribuō, -ere, -uī, -ūtus**: allot, assign.

25.12. Velleius Paterculus 2.2.2. Velleius Paterculus assesses the sterling character of Tiberius Gracchus, Tribune of the Plebs in 133 BCE, whose agrarian reforms aimed to transfer wealth to the poor, causing political turmoil.

Prōpositō sanctissimus, tantīs dēnique adornātus virtūtibus, quantās perfecta et nātūrā et industriā mortālis condiciō recipit, P. Muciō Scaevolā L. Calpurniō consulibus (abhinc annōs centum sexaginta duōs) dēscīvit ā bonīs, pollicitusque tōtī Ītāliae cīvitātem.

Notes: **prōpositum, -ī**, n: design, purpose, plan; **adornō, -āre, -āvī, -ātus**: endow (with), furnish; **perfectus, -a, -um**: excellent; **industria, -iae**, f: diligence; **condiciō, -iōnis**, f: circumstance; **Publius Mucius Scaevola, Publiī Muciī Scaevolae**, m: consul in 133 BCE, allowed Gracchus's second consecutive candidacy for the tribuneship since it seemed to be the will of the people; **Lūcius Calpurnius Pīso, Lūciī Calpurniī Pīsōnis**, m: historian, opponent of Gracchus, and plebeian consul for 133 BCE; **abhinc**: hereafter, ago; **bonīs**: the conservative party in the Senate (see *NLP* 32); **pollicitus** (*est*).

EXTRA PASSAGES: THE ROMAN FAMILY

The Roman family was essentially a microcosm of the Roman state, and the two institutions are often inextricable. The state protected the family (its citizens), and the family contributed to the state by producing citizens and facilitating its defense. One's obligations to the state were determined largely by family connections. But family members also had obligations to one another: to promote political careers and happy marriages. As the Romans expanded their boundaries, they found that this emphasis on family was shared by many neighboring cultures.

25.13. Cicero, *ad Familiares* 7.7.1. A large collection of affectionate and supportive correspondence between Cicero and his brother Quintus survives. Cicero often remembered family members in his letters to friends, as here, when he observes to his friend Trebatius Testa, currently (54 BCE) serving in Britain with Caesar, that Quintus, also among Caesar's *lēgātī* in Britain, has been the better correspondent.

Illud soleō mīrārī, nōn mē totiens accipere tuās litterās, quotiens ā Quintō mihi frātre adferantur.

Notes: **adferantur**: "(letters) are brought to (me)" (present subjunctive).

25.14. Caesar, *de Bello Gallico* 6.19.1. In Germany, as in Rome, marriages are often business partnerships.

Virī, quantās pecūniās ab uxōribus dōtis nōmine accēpērunt, tantās ex suīs bonīs aestimātiōne factā cum dōtibus communicant.

Notes: **dōs, dōtis**, f: dowry; **aestimātiō, -iōnis**, f: appraisal, valuation; **communicō, -āre, -āvī, -ātus**: share, divide.

25.15. Tacitus, *Agricola* 6.1–2. Agricola's marriage to Domitia Decidiana, from a wealthy family, was a happy one, in part because of their mutual respect.

Vixēruntque mīrā concordiā, per mūtuam cāritātem et in vicem sē antepōnendō, nisi quod in bonā uxōre tantō māior laus, quantō in malā plūs culpae est.

Notes: **mīrus, -a, -um**: wonderful, astonishing; **concordia, -iae**, f: harmony; **mūtuus, -a, -um**: reciprocal, equal; **cāritās, -ātis**, f: dearness, esteem, affection; **in vicem**: in turn; **antepōnendō**: "by setting (another) above" (gerund).

Present and Imperfect Subjunctives

1. Most of the verbs that you have learned since *NLP* 1 reflect the indicative mood, which presents the action of the sentence as a statement of fact. In this lesson, you will begin to learn the forms and basic uses of the subjunctive mood, which allows us to indicate the possibility or hope of an action. In English, we often communicate these ideas with the modal verbs "may," "might," "can," "could," "would," and "should." For now, we are going to focus on the "independent" uses of the present and imperfect subjunctives (i.e., when these forms function as the main verb of a sentence).

2. When the main verb of a Latin sentence appears in the present subjunctive, the force is commonly **HORTATORY** (for first person verbs) or **JUSSIVE** (for second and third person verbs), expressing a polite command. These hortatory and jussive subjunctives are negated by *nē* (not *nōn*). Consider the following examples:

   Catullus 34.3–4: **Diānam puerī integrī / puellaeque <u>canāmus</u>**. <u>Let us</u> vigorous boys and girls <u>sing</u> of Diana. (hortatory subjunctive)

   Catullus 5.1: **<u>Vīvāmus</u>, mea Lesbia, atque <u>amēmus</u>**. <u>Let us live</u>, my Lesbia, and <u>let us love</u>. (hortatory subjunctive)

   Caesar, *de Bello Civili* 1.9.5: **<u>Proficiscātur</u> Pompēius in suās prōvinciās**. <u>Let</u> Pompey <u>set out</u> into his provinces. (jussive subjunctive)

3. Main verbs in the present subjunctive sometimes have an **OPTATIVE** force, expressing a concession or desire. Often, but not always, these optative

subjunctives are introduced by the Latin interjection *utinam* ("would that
. . .") and negated by *nē*. Consider the following examples:

Horace, *Carmina* 2.6.5–6: **Tībur Argeō positum colōnō / <u>sit</u> meae sēdēs
<u>utinam</u> senectae**: <u>Would that</u> the Tibur, founded by a Greek settler, <u>be</u> the
seat of my old age!

CIL VI 30738: **Nē quid hīc <u>fīat</u> mal[ī]**! <u>May</u> nothing bad <u>happen</u> here!

4. Main verbs in the subjunctive can also have a **POTENTIAL** force, when
the action of the verb is deemed possible but not necessarily desired.
These potential subjunctives are negated by *nōn*, just like indicative verbs.
Consider the following examples:

CIL IV 10656: **Ursī mē <u>comēdant</u>**. Bears <u>may</u> (i.e., could) <u>eat</u> me.

Cicero, *Philippica* 14.18: **Ego enim malīs sententiīs vincī nōn possum, bonīs
forsitan <u>possim</u> et libenter**. For I cannot be defeated by evil sentiments, (but)
perhaps I <u>could</u>, and willingly, (be defeated) by good ones.

5. A main verb in the subjunctive is **DELIBERATIVE** when the speaker seeks
advice in the form of a question. These deliberative subjunctives are negated with *nōn*. Consider the following examples:

Cicero, *ad Atticum* 1.13: **Novī tibi quidnam <u>scrībam</u>?** What additional news
<u>should I write</u> to you?

Ovid, *Metamorphoses* 1.617–18: **Quid <u>faciat</u>? Crūdēle suōs addīcere amōrēs / nōn
dare suspectum est.** What <u>should he do</u>? It is cruel to sentence one's lovers, (but)
it is suspicious not to hand (them) over.

6. To form the **PRESENT ACTIVE SUBJUNCTIVE**, use the same personal endings for the active voice that you learned in *NLP* 1. Change the vowel signifier for each conjugation accordingly:

for the first conjugation, change **-a-** to **-e-**
for the second conjugation, change **-e-** to **-ea-**
for the third conjugation, change **-i-** to **-a-**
for the third conjugation (–io) and fourth conjugation, change **-i-** to **-ia-**

These shifts in vowel signifiers will add another challenge to your translation work. For example, it is easy to confuse the present active subjunctive forms of the first conjugation with the present active indicative forms of the second conjugation (both have the vowel signifier -e-). In other words, you must know to what conjugation a verb belongs so that you can accurately determine whether the verb is indicative or subjunctive. Study the following table:

PRESENT ACTIVE SUBJUNCTIVE

	1st Conj.	2nd Conj.	3rd Conj.	3rd Conj. (-io)	4th Conj.
Singular					
1st	am**em**	doce**am**	mitt**am**	capi**am**	audi**am**
2nd	am**ēs**	doce**ās**	mitt**ās**	capi**ās**	audi**ās**
3rd	am**et**	doce**at**	mitt**at**	capi**at**	audi**at**
Plural					
1st	am**ēmus**	doce**āmus**	mitt**āmus**	capi**āmus**	audi**āmus**
2nd	am**ētis**	doce**ātis**	mitt**ātis**	capi**ātis**	audi**ātis**
3rd	am**ent**	doce**ant**	mitt**ant**	capi**ant**	audi**ant**

7. To form the **PRESENT PASSIVE SUBJUNCTIVE**, use the same personal endings for the passive voice that you learned in *NLP* 17. Change the vowel signifiers according to the same system outlined above. Study the following table:

PRESENT PASSIVE SUBJUNCTIVE

	1st Conj.	2nd Conj.	3rd Conj.	3rd Conj. (-io)	4th Conj.
Singular					
1st	am**er**	doce**ar**	mitt**ar**	capi**ar**	audi**ar**
2nd	am**ēris** / am**ēre**	doce**āris** / doce**āre**	mitt**āris** / mitt**āre**	capi**āris** / capi**āre**	audi**āris** / audi**āre**
3rd	am**ētur**	doce**ātur**	mitt**ātur**	capi**ātur**	audi**ātur**
Plural					
1st	am**ēmur**	doce**āmur**	mitt**āmur**	capi**āmur**	audi**āmur**
2nd	am**ēminī**	doce**āminī**	mitt**āminī**	capi**āminī**	audi**āminī**
3rd	am**entur**	doce**antur**	mitt**antur**	capi**antur**	audi**antur**

8. To form the **PRESENT SUBJUNCTIVE OF DEPONENT VERBS**, use the same personal endings for the passive voice that you learned in *NLP* 17. Change the vowel signifiers according to the same system outlined in section 6 above. Study the following table:

PRESENT SUBJUNCTIVE OF DEPONENT VERBS

	1st Conj.	2nd Conj.	3rd Conj.	3rd Conj. (-io)	4th Conj.
Singular					
1st	cōner	pollicear	loquar	ingrediar	oriar
2nd	cōnēris / cōnēre	polliceāris / polliceāre	loquāris / loquāre	ingrediāris / ingrediāre	oriāris / oriāre
3rd	cōnētur	polliceātur	loquātur	ingrediātur	oriātur
Plural					
1st	cōnēmur	polliceāmur	loquāmur	ingrediāmur	oriāmur
2nd	cōnēminī	polliceāminī	loquāminī	ingrediāminī	oriāminī
3rd	cōnentur	polliceantur	loquantur	ingrediantur	oriantur

9. To form the **PRESENT ACTIVE SUBJUNCTIVE OF IRREGULAR VERBS**, use the same personal endings for the active voice that you learned in *NLP* 1. Notice how the stems remain constant, but these subjunctive stems must be memorized. Study the following table:

PRESENT SUBJUNCTIVE OF IRREGULAR VERBS

	sum	possum	volō	mālō	nōlō	eō	fīō
Singular							
1st	sim	possim	velim	mālim	nōlim	eam	fīam
2nd	sīs	possīs	velīs	mālīs	nōlīs	eās	fīās
3rd	sit	possit	velit	mālit	nōlit	eat	fīat
Plural							
1st	sīmus	possīmus	velīmus	mālīmus	nōlīmus	eāmus	fīāmus
2nd	sītis	possītis	velītis	mālītis	nōlītis	eātis	fīātis
3rd	sint	possint	velint	mālint	nōlint	eant	fīant

10. To form the **PRESENT SUBJUNCTIVE OF *FERŌ***, attach the same personal endings for the active and passive voice that you learned in *NLP* 1 and 17. *Ferō* uses the subjunctive vowel signifier of the third conjugation. Study the following table:

PRESENT SUBJUNCTIVE OF *FERŌ*

	Active	Passive
Singular		
1st	fera**m**	fera**r**
2nd	fer**ās**	ferā**ris** / ferā**re**
3rd	fera**t**	ferā**tur**
Plural		
1st	ferā**mus**	ferā**mur**
2nd	ferā**tis**	ferā**minī**
3rd	fera**nt**	fera**ntur**

11. Imperfect subjunctives can also be used as the main verbs of sentences to indicate that the action of the verb has happened "contrary to expectation." Consider the following examples:

Caesar, *de Bello Gallico* 1.40: **Quid tandem <u>verērentur</u>?** Finally, what <u>should they have feared</u>?

Vergil, *Aeneid* 1.575–76: **Atque utinam rex ipse Notō compulsus eōdem / <u>adforet</u> Aenēās!** And would that the king himself, Aeneas, driven by the same North Wind, <u>were present</u>!

12. To form the **IMPERFECT ACTIVE SUBJUNCTIVE**, attach the same personal endings for the active voice that you learned in *NLP* 1 to the present active infinitive (the second principal part). Study the table on the following page.

IMPERFECT ACTIVE SUBJUNCTIVE

	1st Conj.	2nd Conj.	3rd Conj.	3rd Conj. (-io)	4th Conj.
Singular					
1st	amārem	docērem	mitterem	caperem	audīrem
2nd	amārēs	docērēs	mitterēs	caperēs	audīrēs
3rd	amāret	docēret	mitteret	caperet	audīret
Plural					
1st	amārēmus	docērēmus	mitterēmus	caperēmus	audīrēmus
2nd	amārētis	docērētis	mitterētis	caperētis	audīrētis
3rd	amārent	docērent	mitterent	caperent	audīrent

13. To form the **IMPERFECT PASSIVE SUBJUNCTIVE,** attach the same personal endings for the passive voice that you learned in *NLP* 17 to the present active infinitive (the second principal part). Study the following table:

IMPERFECT PASSIVE SUBJUNCTIVE

	1st Conj.	2nd Conj.	3rd Conj.	3rd Conj. (-io)	4th Conj.
Singular					
1st	amārer	docērer	mitterer	caperer	audīrer
2nd	amārēris / amārēre	docērēris / docērēre	mitterēris / mitterēre	caperēris / caperēre	audīrēris / audīrēre
3rd	amārētur	docērētur	mitterētur	caperētur	audīrētur
Plural					
1st	amārēmur	docērēmur	mitterēmur	caperēmur	audīrēmur
2nd	amārēminī	docērēminī	mitterēminī	caperēminī	audīrēminī
3rd	amārentur	docērentur	mitterentur	caperentur	audīrentur

14. To form the **IMPERFECT SUBJUNCTIVE OF DEPONENT VERBS,** you must convert the deponent infinitive to a present active infinitive (even though no such form technically exists) and then attach the same personal endings for the passive voice that you learned in *NLP* 17. Study the table on the following page.

IMPERFECT SUBJUNCTIVE OF DEPONENT VERBS

	1st Conj.	2nd Conj.	3rd Conj.	3rd Conj. (-io)	4th Conj.
Singular					
1st	cōnārer	pollicērer	loquērer	ingrederer	orīrer
2nd	cōnārēris / cōnārēre	pollicērēris / pollicērēre	loquērēris / loquērēre	ingredērēris / ingredērēre	orīrēris / orīrēre
3rd	cōnārētur	pollicērētur	loquērētur	ingredērētur	orīrētur
Plural					
1st	cōnārēmur	pollicērēmur	loquērēmur	ingredērēmur	orīrēmur
2nd	cōnārēminī	pollicērēminī	loquērēminī	ingredērēminī	orīrēminī
3rd	cōnārentur	pollicērentur	loquērentur	ingredērentur	orīrentur

15. To form the **IMPERFECT SUBJUNCTIVE OF IRREGULAR VERBS**, attach the same personal endings for the active voice that you learned in *NLP* 1 to the present active infinitive (the second principal part). These verbs have no passive forms. Study the following table:

IMPERFECT SUBJUNCTIVE OF IRREGULAR VERBS

	Sum	Possum	Volō	Mālō	Nōlō	Eō	Fiō
Singular							
1st	essem	possem	vellem	māllem	nōllem	īrem	fierem
2nd	essēs	possēs	vellēs	māllēs	nōllēs	īrēs	fierēs
3rd	esset	posset	vellet	māllet	nōllet	īret	fieret
Plural							
1st	essēmus	possēmus	vellēmus	māllēmus	nōllēmus	īrēmus	fierēmus
2nd	essētis	possētis	vellētis	māllētis	nōllētis	īrētis	fierētis
3rd	essent	possent	vellent	māllent	nōllent	īrent	fierent

N.B. The imperfect subjunctive of *sum* and its compounds can also be formed from the alternate future active infinitive *fore* (see *NLP* 24):

Person	Singular	Plural
1st	**forem**	**forēmus**
2nd	**forēs**	**forētis**
3rd	**foret**	**forent**

16. To form the **IMPERFECT SUBJUNCTIVE OF *FERŌ***, attach the same personal endings for the active and passive voice that you learned in *NLP* 1 and 17 to the present active infinitive (the second principal part). Study the following table:

IMPERFECT SUBJUNCTIVE OF *FERŌ*

	Active	Passive
Singular		
1st	ferre**m**	ferre**r**
2nd	ferrē**s**	ferrē**ris**/ferrē**re**
3rd	ferre**t**	ferrē**tur**
Plural		
1st	ferrē**mus**	ferrē**mur**
2nd	ferrē**tis**	ferrē**minī**
3rd	ferre**nt**	ferre**ntur**

I. Required Vocabulary

NOUNS

anima, -ae, f: soul, spirit
coma, -ae, f: hair, foliage
iānua, -ae, f: door

ingenium, -iī, n: talent, ability, nature, character

aetās, -ātis, f: lifetime, generation, age
flōs, flōris, m: flower

ADJECTIVES

aeternus, -a, -um: eternal
castus, -a, -um: pure, chaste, innocent, virtuous
inimīcus, -a, -um (+ dative): hostile
secundus, -a, -um: favorable

difficilis, -e: difficult, obstinate
pauper (-eris): poor

VERBS

sonō, -āre, -āvī, -ātus: resound, make a sound

mereō, -ēre, -uī, -itus: deserve, earn, obtain

pateō, -ēre, -uī: lie open

corrumpō, -ere, -rūpī, -ruptus: destroy, weaken, mar, spoil

dēserō, -ere, -seruī, -sertus: desert, abandon, leave, forsake

aperiō, -īre, -uī, apertus: uncover, lay open, reveal

queror, querī, questus sum: complain

conferō, -ferre, -tulī, -lātus: bring together, collect, apply, devote

supersum, -esse, -fuī, -futūrus: remain, abound

CONJUNCTIONS AND ADVERBS

fortasse: perhaps

nē: lest, so that . . . not

nī: if not, unless

quamquam: although, however

umquam: ever

utinam: would that

velut: just as, just like

II. Translate the following sentences from Latin to English or English to Latin.

1. Mea amīca dīcat sē mē semper amātūram esse.
2. Vīvāmus diū, mī Cicerō, atque videāmus populī Rōmānī ingenium.
3. Quamquam sīdere pulchrior Lesbia est, Catullus amōrem illīus dēserat.
4. Nē sit coma tibi dolōrī.
5. Utinam loquerem nec tacērem, sed carmina mea erant pessima.
6. Dē flōribus in templīs vestrīs nōn querar.
7. Mortēs amīcōrum mē corrumperent!
8. Mūnera nē poscās! Sum tam pauper et nihil praemiī mihi est.
9. Would that the Roman army be victorious in the long war.
10. What should I do? I have destroyed my little book of songs.
11. Perhaps the difficult door may lie open for me alone.
12. Let the favorable signs of this generation remain.

Latin Love Poetry

Although inspired by the personal lyric verses of the archaic Greek poets—Archilochus, Alcaeus, Sappho—and the learned allusions of their Hellenistic successors, the Romans invented love poetry. In the waning years of the Republic, Gaius Valerius Catullus (84–c. 54 BCE), one of the leading Neoteric poets, chronicled his love affair with Lesbia, a married woman whom many believe to be Clodia, the sister of Publius Clodius Pulcher and wife of Quintus Caecilius Metellus Celer. Clodia is featured prominently as an object of derision and subject of scandal in Cicero's *pro Caelio.* Whether or not Lesbia was a real historical figure or a literary construct of his imagination, Catullus presented his relationship with her as emotionally fraught—a series of tumultuous breakups and reconciliations that tossed the poet from the heights of joy to the depths of depression.

Catullus's Lesbia served as the model for a host of other *femmes fatales* who populated the verses of Rome's leading poets. Catullus's contemporary Gaius Cornelius Gallus (c. 70–26 BCE) composed elegiac couplets, nine lines of which survive, to explore his love for Lycoris. The relationship between poet and mistress grew in complexity as Albius Tibullus (c. 55–19 BCE) and Sextus Propertius (c. 50–15 BCE) explored the endless possibilities that verse offered for chronicling the courtship of a beautiful, enticing, and difficult-to-please woman. Tibullus penned couplets for Delia, and Propertius for Cynthia. Latin love poems were not, however, strictly the domain of male poets. Six poems, chronicling her love affair with Cerinthus, survive from Sulpicia, the niece of the famous literary patron Marcus Valerius Messalla Corvinus (five additional poems speak about these two lovers, but are attributed to another poet, known as *auctor dē Sulpicia* or *amīcus Sulpiciae*). Toward the end of this era of innovative amatory verse, Ovid (43 BCE–17 CE) courted his literary mistress, Corinna, throughout the three books of his *Amores*. Casting himself as an "expert in love and romance," he also took the genre of Latin love elegy one step further with his *Ars Amatoria,* a guide to the art of seduction, and with his *Remedia Amoris,* an instructive poem on ending and recovering from a love affair.

Although each literary relationship is distinct, all of these poets present themselves as helpless in the face of great love. The lover is often compared to a soldier on a military campaign: both need endurance and strength for difficult journeys and arduous battles; both need a variety of weapons in their arsenals; and both need to fight off enemies and obstacles to achieve success. Often scorned by their mistresses, the poets pursue them diligently in the face of rejection. They find themselves begging for attention outside their mistress's closed door (a poem describing such a pitiful picture is called a *paraklausithyron*) or planning elaborate birthday celebrations for them (such birthday poems are known as *genethliaca*). Although their efforts, for the most part, prove ineffectual, these Roman poets earn our sympathy (or, perhaps, our pity) as they struggle to impress and win over their elusive lovers.

SUGGESTIONS FOR FURTHER READING:

Liveley, Genevieve and Patricia Salzman-Mitchell, eds. *Latin Elegy and Narratology.* Ohio State University, 2008.

Miller, Paul Allen. *Subjecting Verses: Latin Love Elegy and the Emergence of the Real.* Princeton, 2003.

Spentzou, Efrossini. *The Roman Poetry of Love: Elegy and Politics in a Time of Revolution.* Bristol Classical Press, 2013.

Thorsen, Thea S. *The Cambridge Companion to Latin Love Elegy.* Cambridge, 2013.

PASSAGES

26.1. Catullus 6.1–3. Catullus teases his friend Flavius about his less than stunningly beautiful girlfriend. Meter: hendecasyllabics.

> Flāvī, "dēliciās tuās" Catullō,
> nī sint illepidae atque inēlegantēs,
> vellēs dīcere nec tacēre possēs.

Notes: **Flāvius, -iī**, m: a Roman man's name, meaning "Blondie"; **dēliciae, -iārum**, f (plural): "pet," "darling"; **illepidus, -a, -um**: ungraceful, awkward; **inēlegans (-antis)**: clumsy; **nī ... inēlegantēs**: litotes, an assertion made by denying the opposite.

26.2. Catullus 11.21–24. Catullus compares his love for Lesbia to a flower crushed by the passing plow. Vergil adopts this imagery when he describes

the death of Euryalus, a young warrior in Aeneas' army (*Aeneid* 9.435–36).
Meter: Sapphic strophe.

Nec meum respectet, ut ante, amōrem,
quī illīus culpā cecidit velut prātī
ultimī flōs, praetereunte postquam
     tactus arātrō est.

Notes: **respectō, -āre, -āvī, -ātus**: look back at, wait expectantly for (construe Lesbia as the subject); **ut**: as; **illīus**: Lesbia; **prātum, -ī**, n: meadow; **praetereō, -īre, -īvī** or **iī, -itus**: go beyond, pass (*praetereunte*: present active participle); **arātrum, -ī**, n: plow.

26.3. Catullus 92. Despite the reciprocal verbal abuse (or perhaps because of it), Lesbia and Catullus cannot help but love each other. Meter: elegiac couplets.

Lesbia mī dīcit semper male nec tacet umquam
     dē mē: Lesbia mē dispeream nī amat.
Quō signō? Quia sunt totidem mea: dēprecor illam
     assiduē, vērum dispeream nisi amō.

Notes: **dispereō, -īre, -īvī** or **iī, -itus**: perish, waste away; **totidem**: as many, so many; **dēprecor, -ārī, dēprecātus sum**: entreat; **assiduē**: constantly.

26.4. Horace, *Carmina* 3.9.21–24. Horace dramatizes the quarrel and reconciliation of two lovers both of whom have strayed. Here, the woman admits her attraction for the "other" man, but hopes to win back her lover by the ultimate declaration of love. Meter: second Asclepiadean.

"Quamquam sīdere pulchrior
     ille est, tu levior cortice et improbō
īrācundior Hadriā,
tēcum vīvere amem, tēcum obeam libens."

Notes: **cortex, corticis**, m / f: bark, cork; **improbus, -a, -um**: inferior, perverse, impudent; **īrācundus, -a, -um**: irascible, passionate, quick to anger; **Hadria, -iae**, m: the notoriously stormy Adriatic Sea; **obeō, -īre, -īvī** or **iī, -itus**: die; **libens (-entis)**: willing.

26.5. Tibullus, *Elegiae* 1.2.7–10. In this *paraklausithyron*, Tibullus curses the door itself for its heartlessness and then begs that it be his ally in this refined game of love. Meter: elegiac couplets.

Iānua difficilis dominī, tē verberet imber,
    tē Iovis imperiō fulmina missa petant.
Iānua, iam pateās ūnī mihi, victa querēlīs,
    neu—furtim versō cardine aperta—sonēs.

Notes: **verberō, -āre, -āvī, -ātus**: beat, strike; **fulmen, fulminis**, n: thunderbolt; **querēla, -ae**, f: complaint, lament, grievance; **neu**: and not; **furtim**: secretly, stealthily; **cardō, cardinis**, m: hinge.

26.6. Tibullus 1.6.85–86. Although Delia has been unfaithful to both her husband and Tibullus, the poet calls for reconciliation all around. Meter: elegiac couplets.

Haec aliīs maledicta cadant; nōs, Dēlia, amōris
    exemplum cānā sīmus uterque comā.

Notes: **maledictum, -ī**, n: curse; **exemplum, -ī**, n: example; **cānus, -a, -um**: gray, white.

26.7. Propertius, *Elegiae* 1.4.27–28. Rebuking his friend Bassus for trying to tempt him with other women instead of encouraging fidelity, Propertius praises the lovely Cynthia, with a plea that she always remain constant in her love. Meter: elegiac couplets.

Maneat sīc semper, adōrō,
    nec quicquam ex illā quod querar inveniam!

Notes: **sīc**: i.e., faithful and in love with Propertius; **adōrō, -āre, -āvī, -ātus**: entreat, pray.

26.8. Propertius, *Elegiae* 1.11.27–30. While Cynthia vacations at Baiae (see *NLP* 23.12), Propertius, worrying that she might give into temptation, wishes that she would go anywhere else, as soon as possible. Meter: elegiac couplets.

Tū modo quam prīmum corruptās dēsere Bāiās:
    multīs ista dabunt lītora discidium,
lītora quae fuerunt castīs inimīca puellīs:
    ah pereant Bāiae, crīmen amōris, aquae!

Notes: **quam prīmum**: as soon as possible; **Bāius, -a, -um**: of Baiae; **discidium, -iī**, n: separation, quarrel; **ah**: an interjection expressing irony.

26.9. Propertius, *Elegiae* 1.19.25–26. Musing over the transitory nature of life, Propertius asks Cynthia to continue loving him even after death. Meter: elegiac couplets.

Quārē, dum licet, inter nōs laetēmur amantēs:
　　nōn satis est ullō tempore longus amor.

Notes: **quārē**: therefore.

26.10. Ovid, *Amores* 1.7.67–68. In a fit of anger, Ovid has raised his hand against Corinna, causing her to weep and her hair to become disheveled. He begs forgiveness. Meter: elegiac couplets.

Nēve meī sceleris tam tristia signa supersint,
　　pōne recompositās in statiōne comās!

Notes: **nēve**: or . . . not; **recompōnō, -ere, -posuī, -positus**: readjust, rearrange; **statiō, -iōnis**, f: order.

26.11. Ovid, *Amores* 1.10.57–60. Ovid elevates the poor lover whose abstract gifts (poetry, among other things) are more lasting than the material gifts from rich lovers. Meter: elegiac couplets.

Officium pauper numeret studiumque fidemque;
　　quod quis habet, dominae conferat omne suae.
Est quoque carminibus meritās celebrāre puellās
　　dōs mea; quam voluī, nōta fit arte meā.

Notes: **numerō, -āre, -āvī, -ātus**: count, consider; **quis** = *aliquis*; **dōs, dōtis**, f: dowry.

26.12. Ovid, *Amores* 3.2.55–58. While at the races, Ovid enjoins Venus to look favorably on his new love affair. Meter: elegiac couplets.

Nōs tibi, blanda Venus, puerīsque potentibus arcū
　　plaudimus; inceptīs adnue, dīva, meīs
dāque novae mentem dominae! Patiātur amārī!
　　Adnuit et mōtū signa secunda dedit.

Notes: **blandus, -a, -um**: pleasant, gentle, alluring; **puerīs**: "Cupids"; **plaudō, -ere, plausī, plausus** (+ dative): applaud; **inceptum, -ī**, n: beginning, attempt, enterprise; **adnuō, -ere, -nuī, -nūtus**: nod assent, be favorable; **dare mentem**: pay attention; **mōtus, -ūs**, m: motion.

EXTRA PASSAGES: POETS PRAISE POETS

It was the highest form of praise for one writer to commemorate another, and we find encomia to famous Roman poets in many Latin authors. Some poets took great pains to link their work to the rich legacy of verse that preceded them; others yearned for the lasting recognition and sense of immortality that Homer and Vergil had earned.

26.13. Horace, *Carmina* 1.3.1–8. Horace honors his friend Vergil, embarking for Greece, with a *propempticon* (a "send-off" ode). Here, he entreats the gods of the sea to be propitious. Meter: second Asclepiadean.

> Sīc tē dīva potens Cyprī,
> sīc frātrēs Helenae, lūcida sīdera,
>   ventōrumque regat pater
> obstrictīs aliīs praeter Iāpyga.
>   Nāvis, quae tibi crēditum
> dēbēs Vergilium, fīnibus Atticīs
>   reddās incolumem—precor—
> et servēs animae dīmidium meae.

Notes: **Cyprus, -ī**, f: the island of Cyprus, sacred to Venus; **frātrēs**: Castor and Pollux, patrons of sailors; **Helena, -ae**, f: Helen, the beautiful daughter of Leda and Jupiter whose affair with Paris sparked the Trojan War; **lūcidus, -a, -um**: clear, bright; **ventōrum pater**: Aeolus, king of the winds; **obstringō, -ere, -strinxī, -strictus**: bind, tie, restrain; **Iāpyx, Iāpygis**, m: the northwest wind, thus favorable for ships sailing to Greece (*Iāpȳga*: Greek accusative); **crēditus, -a, -um**: entrusted (to); **Vergilius, -iī**, m: Vergil; **Atticus, -a, -um**: Attic, Athenian; **incolumis, -e**: safe; **precor, -ārī, precātus sum**: beg; **dīmidius, -a, -um**: half.

26.14. Martial 8.56.1–6. Like many of his contemporaries, Martial recognized that the current trend in literature lacked the dignity of the bygone Golden Age under Augustus. Martial offers a clever tongue-in-cheek solution to remedy the paucity of truly great literature. Meter: elegiac couplets.

> Temporibus nostrīs aetās cum cēdat avōrum
> 　　crēverit et māior cum duce Rōma suō,
> ingenium sacrī mīrāris desse Marōnis
> 　　nec quemquam tantā bella sonāre tubā.
> Sint Maecēnātēs, nōn dērunt, Flacce, Marōnēs
> 　　Vergiliumque tibī vel tua rūra dabunt.

Notes: **avus, -ī,** m: grandfather, ancestor; **dēsum, -esse, -fuī**: be lacking; **Marō, -ōnis,** m: Vergil's cognomen. A Maro was among Bacchus's teachers, and Maronia in Thrace was famous for its wine; **tuba, -ae,** f: war trumpet; **Maecēnās, -ātis,** m: friend of Augustus and patron of both Horace and Vergil, Maecenas gifted Horace with his beloved Sabine farm, and his name has come to be associated with generous cultural benefactors; **Flaccus, -ī,** m: Horace's cognomen, meaning "floppy-eared."

26.15. Pliny the Younger, *Epistulae* 3.21.6. Eulogizing Martial, his friend (and ours!), Pliny quotes poem 10.19, where Martial pokes good-hearted fun at the bookish and nerdy Pliny. After asserting that he did not take the poem seriously, Pliny declares the friendly terms on which they parted and wonders if Martial's light verses will endure the test of time.

> Tametsī, quid hominī potest darī māius quam glōria et laus et
> aeternitās? At nōn erunt aeterna, quae scripsit; nōn erunt fortasse;
> ille tamen scripsit, tamquam essent futūra.

Notes: **tametsī**: notwithstanding; **aeternitās, -ātis,** f: eternity.

Perfect and Pluperfect Subjunctives and Cum Clauses

PART 1: PERFECT AND PLUPERFECT SUBJUNCTIVES

1. In *NLP* 26, you learned two of the four tenses of the subjunctive mood (present and imperfect). In this lesson, you will learn the forms of the other two tenses (perfect and pluperfect) and their use in independent clauses.

2. The perfect subjunctive can be used with *nē* to indicate a **NEGATIVE COMMAND.** Consider the following examples:

   Horace, *Saturae* 2.3.220: **Nē dixeris**. Don't say (it).

   Horace, *Carmina* 1.11.1–2: **Tū nē quaesīeris (scīre nefās) quem mihi, quem tibi / fīnem dī dederint**. Don't ask (it is impious to know) what end the gods have granted to me, what (end the gods have granted) to you.

3. To form the **PERFECT ACTIVE SUBJUNCTIVE**, add -eri- to the **perfect active stem** (from the third principal part) and then use the same personal endings for the active voice that you learned in *NLP* 1. N.B. The perfect active subjunctive endings are almost identical to those of the future perfect active indicative that you learned in *NLP* 13. The only difference is the first person singular (-**erō** for the future perfect active indicative, -**erim** for the perfect active subjunctive). Only context will help you determine

whether the verb is future perfect indicative or perfect active subjunctive. Study the following table:

PERFECT ACTIVE SUBJUNCTIVE

	1st Conj.	2nd Conj.	3rd Conj.	3rd Conj. (-io)	4th Conj.
Singular					
1st	amāv**erim**	docu**erim**	mīs**erim**	cēp**erim**	audīv**erim**
2nd	amāv**eris**	docu**eris**	mīs**eris**	cēp**eris**	audīv**eris**
3rd	amāv**erit**	docu**erit**	mīs**erit**	cēp**erit**	audīv**erit**
Plural					
1st	amāv**erimus**	docu**erimus**	mīs**erimus**	cēp**erimus**	audīv**erimus**
2nd	amāv**eritis**	docu**eritis**	mīs**eritis**	cēp**eritis**	audīv**eritis**
3rd	amāv**erint**	docu**erint**	mīs**erint**	cēp**erint**	audīv**erint**

4. To form the **PERFECT PASSIVE SUBJUNCTIVE**, use the perfect passive participle (i.e., the fourth principal part), declined to agree in case, number, and gender with the subject, completed by the **present subjunctive of *esse***. Note the similarity between the perfect passive indicative and the perfect passive subjunctive. The only change occurs in the form of *esse*: the present indicative of *esse* shifts to the **present subjunctive of *esse***. Study the following table:

PERFECT PASSIVE SUBJUNCTIVE

	1st Conj.	2nd Conj.	3rd Conj.	3rd Conj. (-io)	4th Conj.
Singular					
1st	amātus, -a, -um **sim**	doctus, -a, -um **sim**	missus, -a, -um **sim**	captus, -a, -um **sim**	audītus, -a, -um **sim**
2nd	amātus, -a, -um **sīs**	doctus, -a, -um **sīs**	missus, -a, -um **sīs**	captus, -a, -um **sīs**	audītus, -a, -um **sīs**
3rd	amātus, -a, -um **sit**	doctus, -a, -um **sit**	missus, -a, -um **sit**	captus, -a, -um **sit**	audītus, -a, -um **sit**
Plural					
1st	amātī, -ae, -a **sīmus**	doctī, -ae, -a **sīmus**	missī, -ae, -a **sīmus**	captī, -ae, -a **sīmus**	audītī, -ae, -a **sīmus**
2nd	amātī, -ae, -a **sītis**	doctī, -ae, -a **sītis**	missī, -ae, -a **sītis**	captī, -ae, -a **sītis**	audītī, -ae, -a **sītis**
3rd	amātī, -ae, -a **sint**	doctī, -ae, -a **sint**	missī, -ae, -a **sint**	captī, -ae, -a **sint**	audītī, -ae, -a **sint**

5. To form the **PERFECT DEPONENT SUBJUNCTIVE**, use the perfect deponent participle (i.e., the third principal part), declined to agree in case, number, and gender with the subject, completed by the **present subjunctive of *esse***. Note the similarity between the perfect deponent indicative and the perfect deponent subjunctive. As with regular verbs, the only change occurs in the second word of the verb form: the present indicative of *esse* shifts to the **present subjunctive of *esse***. N.B. The perfect deponent subjunctive is translated as active, despite its "passive-looking" form. Study the following table:

PERFECT DEPONENT SUBJUNCTIVE

	1st Conj.	2nd Conj.	3rd Conj.	3rd Conj. (-io)	4th Conj.
Singular					
1st	cōnātus, -a, -um sim	pollicitus, -a, -um sim	locūtus, -a, -um sim	ingressus, -a, -um sim	ortus, -a, -um sim
2nd	cōnātus, -a, -um sīs	pollicitus, -a, -um sīs	locūtus, -a, -um sīs	ingressus, -a, -um sīs	ortus, -a, -um sīs
3rd	cōnātus, -a, -um sit	pollicitus, -a, -um sit	locūtus, -a, -um sit	ingressus, -a, -um sit	ortus, -a, -um sit
Plural					
1st	cōnātī, -ae, -a sīmus	pollicitī, -ae, -a sīmus	locūtī, -ae, -a sīmus	ingressī, -ae, -a sīmus	ortī, -ae, -a sīmus
2nd	cōnātī, -ae, -a sītis	pollicitī, -ae, -a sītis	locūtī, -ae, -a sītis	ingressī, -ae, -a sītis	ortī, -ae, -a sītis
3rd	cōnātī, -ae, -a sint	pollicitī, -ae, -a sint	locūtī, -ae, -a sint	ingressī, -ae, -a sint	ortī, -ae, -a sint

6. Pluperfect subjunctives, just like imperfect subjunctives, can be used as main verbs to indicate that the action of the verb has happened "**CONTRARY TO FACT**." Consider the following examples:

Vergil, *Aeneid* 2.110: **Fēcissentque utinam!** And would that <u>they had done</u> (so)!

Vegetius, *de Re Militari* 1.1: **Quid enim adversus Gallōrum multitūdinem paucitās Rōmāna valuisset?** For why <u>would</u> Roman scarcity <u>have prevailed</u> against the crowd of Gauls?

7. To form the **PLUPERFECT ACTIVE SUBJUNCTIVE**, add the same personal endings for the active voice that you learned in *NLP* 1 to the **perfect active infinitive** (see *NLP* 13). (Remember that you added these same endings to the present active infinitive to form the imperfect active subjunctive.) Study the following table:

PLUPERFECT ACTIVE SUBJUNCTIVE

	1st Conj.	2nd Conj.	3rd Conj.	3rd Conj. (-io)	4th Conj.
Singular					
1st	amāvissem	docuissem	mīsissem	cēpissem	audīvissem
2nd	amāvissēs	docuissēs	mīsissēs	cēpissēs	audīvissēs
3rd	amāvisset	docuisset	mīsisset	cēpisset	audīvisset
Plural					
1st	amāvissēmus	docuissēmus	mīsissēmus	cēpissēmus	audīvissēmus
2nd	amāvissētis	docuissētis	mīsissētis	cēpissētis	audīvissētis
3rd	amāvissent	docuissent	mīsissent	cēpissent	audīvissent

8. To form the **PLUPERFECT PASSIVE SUBJUNCTIVE**, use the perfect passive participle, declined to agree in case, number, and gender with the subject, completed by the **imperfect subjunctive of** *esse*. Note the similarity between the pluperfect passive indicative and the pluperfect passive subjunctive. The only change occurs in the form of *esse*: the imperfect indicative of *esse* shifts to the imperfect subjunctive of *esse*. Study the following table:

PLUPERFECT PASSIVE SUBJUNCTIVE

	1st Conj.	2nd Conj.	3rd Conj.	3rd Conj. (-io)	4th Conj.
Singular					
1st	amātus, -a, -um essem	doctus, -a, -um essem	missus, -a, -um essem	captus, -a, -um essem	audītus, -a, -um essem
2nd	amātus, -a, -um essēs	doctus, -a, -um essēs	missus, -a, -um essēs	captus, -a, -um essēs	audītus, -a, -um essēs
3rd	amātus, -a, -um esset	doctus, -a, -um esset	missus, -a, -um esset	captus, -a, -um esset	audītus, -a, -um esset

(continued)

Plural					
1st	amātī, -ae, -a essēmus	doctī, -ae, -a essēmus	missī, -ae, -a essēmus	captī, -ae, -a essēmus	audītī, -ae, -a essēmus
2nd	amātī, -ae, -a essētis	doctī, -ae, -a essētis	missī, -ae, -a essētis	captī, -ae, -a essētis	audītī, -ae, -a essētis
3rd	amātī, -ae, -a essent	doctī, -ae, -a essent	missī, -ae, -a essent	captī, -ae, -a essent	audītī, -ae, -a essent

9. To form the **PLUPERFECT DEPONENT SUBJUNCTIVE**, use the perfect passive participle, declined to agree in case, number, and gender with the subject, completed by the **imperfect subjunctive of** *esse*. Note the similarity between the pluperfect passive indicative and the pluperfect passive subjunctive. As with regular verbs, the only change occurs in the form of *esse*: the imperfect indicative of *esse* shifts to the imperfect subjunctive of *esse*. N.B. The pluperfect deponent subjunctive is translated as active, despite its "passive-looking" form. Study the following table:

PLUPERFECT DEPONENT SUBJUNCTIVE

	1st Conj.	2nd Conj.	3rd Conj.	3rd Conj. (-io)	4th Conj.
Singular					
1st	cōnātus, -a, -um essem	pollicitus, -a, -um essem	locūtus, -a, -um essem	ingressus, -a, -um essem	ortus, -a, -um essem
2nd	cōnātus, -a, -um essēs	pollicitus, -a, -um essēs	locūtus, -a, -um essēs	ingressus, -a, -um essēs	ortus, -a, -um essēs
3rd	cōnātus, -a, -um esset	pollicitus, -a, -um esset	locūtus, -a, -um esset	ingressus, -a, -um esset	ortus, -a, -um esset
Plural					
1st	cōnātī, -ae, -a essēmus	pollicitī, -ae, -a essēmus	locūtī, -ae, -a essēmus	ingressī, -ae, -a essēmus	ortī, -ae, -a essēmus
2nd	cōnātī, -ae, -a essētis	pollicitī, -ae, -a essētis	locūtī, -ae, -a essētis	ingressī, -ae, -a essētis	ortī, -ae, -a essētis
3rd	cōnātī, -ae, -a essent	pollicitī, -ae, -a essent	locūtī, -ae, -a essent	ingressī, -ae, -a essent	ortī, -ae, -a essent

PART 2: CUM CLAUSES

10. As a conjunction, **cum** introduces several types of subordinate clauses that feature both indicative and subjunctive verbs. You have already learned the **CUM TEMPORAL CLAUSE** with indicative verbs, defining **when** an action occurs. Consider the following examples:

Martial 3.4.8: **Veniet, <u>cum citharoedus erit</u>**. He will come <u>when he will be a cithara player</u>.

Horace, *Carmina* 1.13.1–4: **<u>Cum tū</u>, Lȳdia, <u>Tēlephī</u> / cervīcem roseam, cērea Tēlephī / <u>laudās</u> bracchia**, vae, meum / fervens difficilī bīle tumet iecur. <u>When you</u>, Lydia, <u>praise</u> the rosy neck of Telephus (and) the smooth arms of Telephus, alas, my boiling liver swells with difficult wrath.

11. A cum temporal clause with an imperfect or pluperfect subjunctive, often called a **CUM CIRCUMSTANTIAL CLAUSE**, can express the circumstances under which the main action of the sentence occurs. Consider the following examples:

Caesar, *de Bello Gallico* 1.4.3: **<u>Cum cīvitās ob eam rem incitāta armīs iūs suum exsequī cōnārētur</u> multitūdinemque hominum ex agrīs magistrātūs <u>cogerent</u>, Orgetorix mortuus est**. <u>While the state, roused to arms on account of this affair, tried to pursue its own justice and (while) the magistrates forced a crowd of men from the fields</u>, Orgetorix died.

Martial 1.12.7–8: **Nam subitō conlapsa ruit, <u>cum mōle sub illā</u> / gestātus bīiugīs Rēgulus <u>esset</u> equīs**. For suddenly it fell, having collapsed <u>while Regulus had been carried</u> under that mass in his two-yoked chariot.

CIL VI 10096: **<u>Heic viridis aetās cum flōreret</u> artibus / crescente et aevō glōriam <u>conscenderet</u>, / properāvit hōra tristis fātālis mea / et dēnegāvit ultrā veitae spīritum**. <u>While this blooming age flourished with skills and attained glory with growing age</u>, my sad fatal hour hastened and finally refused the spirit of life.

12. Cum clauses can express why an action occurs (**CUM CAUSAL**), particularly if accompanied by *praesertim* (especially), *quippe* (naturally), or *utpote* (inasmuch as). **CUM CAUSAL** clauses almost always feature a subjunctive verb. Consider the following examples:

Cicero, *ad Atticum* 1.16.14: **Sed tamen nōn possum reprehendere consilium tuum, <u>praesertim cum egomet in prōvinciam nōn</u> <u>sim profectus</u>.** But nonetheless I am not able to reproach your counsel, <u>especially since I myself</u> <u>have</u> <u>not</u> <u>set out</u> into the province.

Pliny, *Naturalis Historia* 31.27: **Hanc putant nimiō frigōre esse noxiam, <u>utpote cum prōfluens ipsa</u> <u>lapidescat</u>.** They think that this (water) is harmful because of excessive cold, <u>since (*utpote cum*) flowing (as it flows) it</u> <u>becomes stony</u>.

13. Cum clauses can express concession (**CUM CONCESSIVE**), especially if accompanied by *tamen*. These clauses almost always feature a subjunctive verb. Consider the following examples:

Caesar, *de Bello Gallico* 3.22.4: **<u>Cum ad arma mīlitēs</u> <u>concurrissent</u> <u>vehementerque ibi</u> <u>pugnātum esset</u>, repulsus in oppidum tamen.** <u>Although the soldiers</u> <u>had rushed</u> to arms and there <u>had been</u> vigorous <u>fighting</u> <u>in that place</u>, nonetheless he (Adiatunnus) was driven back into the town.

Pliny the Younger, *Epistulae* 4.9.18: **<u>Caepiō cum</u> <u>putāret</u> <u>licēre</u> senātuī—sīcut licet—<u>et mītigāre lēgēs et intendere</u>, nōn sine ratiōne veniam dedit.** <u>Although Caepio</u> <u>thought</u> <u>it was permitted</u> <u>for the Senate to mitigate and increase laws</u>—just as it is permitted—not without reason did he offer leniency.

I. Required Vocabulary

NOUNS

    exemplum, -ī, n: example, sample
    ferrum, -ī, n: iron, sword
    forum, -ī, n: forum, open square, marketplace
    gladius, -iī, m: sword
    odium, -iī, n: hatred

clāmor, -ōris, m: cry, shout
dēlātor, -ōris, m: informer

PRONOUNS

quisquis, quaeque, quicquid or **quidquid**: whoever, whatever

ADJECTIVES

cunctus, -a, -um: entire, the whole (singular); all (plural)
dexter, dext(e)ra, dext(e)rum: skillful, right (hand)
plēnus, -a, -um (+ ablative): full
posterus, -a, -um: following, next

VERBS

dōnō, -āre, -āvī, -ātus: present, bestow, award, consecrate

doleō, -ēre, -uī, -itus: suffer pain, grieve

addō, -ere, -didī, -ditus: bring, add, join, place
compōnō, -ere, -posuī, -positus: bring together, collect, arrange, settle
prōdō, -ere, -didī, -ditus: put forth, proclaim, abandon, betray
repetō, -ere, -īvī/iī, -ītus: seek again, recall

ōdī, ōdisse (defective verb): hate, detest

CONJUNCTIONS

dōnec: until

II. Translate the following sentences from Latin to English or English to Latin.

1. Imperātorī tempus beātō erit cum exempla optima didicerit.
2. Pessima carmina urbibus in amoenīs nē prōdideritis.
3. Cum mīlitēs officia propter pietātem fēcissent, Rōmae tamen bellum longum gestum est.
4. Cum pācem sine armīs peterēmus, hostēs impetum nostram in patriam ingredientēs fēcēre.
5. Utinam dēlātōrēs tacēre potuissent!
6. Posterō diē, mulierēs cum nemus in antīquum ingressae essent, līberīs suīs dē vītā locūtae sunt.

7. Cum populī Rōmānī aeterna templa dōnent, dī operibus crescentibus praesidium offerre volent.

8. In dolōre metūque cucurrī, praesertim cum cīvēs domum venientēs magnō clamōre audīrem.

9. Don't think that I have died by the sword.

10. Although we had escaped the town, nevertheless we suffered and lived with the worst hatred.

11. Would that the informers had broken the gates and seen the crimes!

12. I hate the city and the forum, especially since I am so poor.

Virtus, Dignitas, et Pietas

Roman society was class-oriented, with rules governing to what extent people born into different classes interacted with one another, and especially how those within a class (particularly the senatorial class) treated one another. These rules softened as the state evolved, but the underlying prejudices lingered. Some Romans were free-born, while others were slave or freed (see *NLP* 12 and 15). Some Romans were born into patrician families, tracing their lineage back to Romulus's original one hundred Senators. Others were born into the noble class of equestrians, those families with sufficient wealth to maintain a horse (and thus forming the cavalry of the early Roman army, c. 400 BCE), but lacking the distinction of patrician ancestry. The plebeian class included the masses, who were excluded from holding priesthoods and serving in elected offices until reforms that ensued from the "Conflict of the Orders" (see *NLP* 25); these included political equality with patricians and the right of intermarriage. Finally, some occupations and social circumstances were considered so unbecoming to Roman dignity that further restrictions were applied. These *infāmēs* (disreputable people, who had either lost or never had *fāma*: a "good reputation") included entertainers, pimps, soldiers who had been dishonorably discharged, convicted criminals, and all *lībertī*. *Infāmēs* were barred from political and priestly appointments and were strictly denied the right of intermarriage with "respectable" Romans.

Despite virtual political and social equality, convention preserved distinctions between the classes. Wealth was always a determining factor, but it could never purchase respectability. There was, however, mobility, as plebeians could become patrician by adoption, or vice versa (most famously, Publius Clodius Pulcher: see *NLP* 25). The Roman Republic was dominated by powerful men who considered it their right to pursue personal glory as a means of enhancing this power and wealth. Under this sense of entitlement, ambitions were fueled or frustrated, and some leading politicians went to extremes to protect or restore their "good names" or avenge slights to personal honor. After two ignominious defeats for the consulship (including a loss in 63 BCE made more shameful because it was to a *novus homo*, Cicero: see *NLP* 25), frustrated ambition compelled Lucius Sergius Catilina to organize a widespread conspiracy against the government, resulting in Catiline's death in pitched battle outside Rome. Not long after, Clodius sought election as Tribune of the Plebs for many reasons, including to secure the exile of Cicero, who had given damaging evidence when Clodius was charged with trespassing into the very secret and sacred rites of the Bona Dea in 61 BCE (the jury was bribed, and Clodius was acquitted by a narrow margin; his *dignitās*, nonetheless, was wounded). Cicero never held another public office in Rome after his exile (aside from the governorship of Cilicia in 51 BCE when eligible men were in short supply), despite his assiduous efforts. Finally, Gaius Julius Caesar took extraordinary steps to preserve his *dignitās* and maintain his *imperium*, the constitutional prerogative of higher office that guaranteed the right to lead an army and immunity from lawsuits while in office (see also *NLP* 25). As consul in 59 BCE, Caesar illegally ignored his consular colleague Marcus Calpurnius Bibulus, and his enemies were eager to bring him to trial. In all likelihood Caesar would have been convicted and possibly exiled, bringing his political career to an end. Instead, Caesar chose civil war over losing face to the Senate.

Such glory was worthless without honor. And, to the Roman mind, this meant adhering stringently to the code of *pietās*, the keystone of the Roman ideal. *Pietās* entailed a devotion to duty: duty to one's family and ancestors, to the state, and to the gods who protected the state. Vergil showcased these ideals in his portrait of the hero *pius Aenēās* in the *Aeneid*. Caesar may have sincerely believed that he was the only man capable of governing Rome for the good by the 40s BCE; Cicero further maintained that his precautions saved the Republic from Catiline in 63 BCE. They were following in the footsteps of such legendary heroes as Porsenna, the Horatii triplets, and Horatius Cocles, who all had been willing to die for the state. In addition, those who chose suicide over life as a prisoner of war were lauded, as were those who preferred to end their lives before bringing shame on their families or before submitting to the unjust demands of an unjust ruler. Condemned were cowards, along with those who dishonored or neglected the gods of the state: thus, Turnus dishonored Mars by wearing Pallas' baldric into battle (*NLP* 27.1), and an entire generation dishonored the Roman state gods by neglecting the state cult and allowing temples to fall into neglect.

SUGGESTIONS FOR FURTHER READING:

Garrison, James. *Pietas from Vergil to Dryden*. Pennsylvania State University, 1992.
Konstan, David. *Friendship in the Classical World*. Cambridge, 1997.
McDonnell, Myles. *Roman Manliness:* Virtus *and the Roman Republic*. Cambridge, 2009.
Wray, David. *Catullus and the Poetics of Roman Manhood*. Cambridge, 2007.

PASSAGES

27.1. Vergil, *Aeneid* **10.503–505.** After slaying Pallas, the son of Evander whom Aeneas had sworn to protect, Turnus stripped the body of its beautifully wrought sword belt, which he then brazenly wore into battle. In the final duel of the *Aeneid*, Aeneas hesitates, contemplating mercy, until he catches sight of his young friend's baldric on Turnus's waist. Vergil uses both Aeneas and Turnus to explore the boundaries of *virtus*, *dignitās*, and *pietās*. Meter: dactylic hexameter.

Turnō tempus erit magnō cum optāverit emptum
intactum Pallanta, et cum spolia ista diemque
ōderit.

Notes: **Turnus, -ī**, m: Turnus, the prince of the Rutulians, against whom Aeneas fights when he reaches Italy; **magnō**: "at a great price" (ablative of price); **emō, -ere, ēmī, emptus**: buy, purchase; **intactus, -a, -um**: untouched; **Pallās, -antis**, m: son of Evander, Aeneas' Greek ally in Italy (*Pallanta*: Greek accusative); **spolium, -iī**, n: plunder, booty, arms stripped from an enemy.

27.2. Vergil, *Aeneid* **12.435–40.** As Aeneas prepares for his duel with Turnus, he has a father-son chat with Ascanius on the Roman virtues of military courage and bravery. Meter: dactylic hexameter.

> "Disce, puer, virtūtem ex mē vērumque labōrem,
> fortūnam ex aliīs. Nunc tē mea dextera bellō
> dēfensum dabit et magna inter praemia dūcet.
> Tū facitō, mox cum mātūra adolēverit aetās—
> sīs memor—et tē animō repetentem exempla tuōrum
> et pater Aenēās et avunculus excitet Hector."

Notes: **dēfensus, -a, -um:** defended; **mātūrus, -a, -um:** mature, ripe, grown up; **adolescō, -ere, -lēvī:** mature, grow up, become established; **memor (-oris):** mindful, thoughtful, prudent; **avunculus, -ī, m:** maternal uncle; **excitō, -āre, -āvī, -ātus:** rouse, inspire; **Hector, -ōris, m:** Priam's bravest son, brother of Ascanius's mother, Creusa.

27.3. Livy, *ab Urbe Condita* **1.25.1.** During the reign of Tullius Hostilius (ruled 674–642 BCE), when Rome was at war with Alba Longa, the two states agreed to settle their conflict in a single pitched battle between chosen champions. Each side boasted a set of brave triplets (the Roman Horatii and Alba Longan Curatii), who eagerly accepted. In the end, five of the champions lost their lives (the greatest and most honorable sacrifice a young Roman could make for his country), and Rome won the war. Here the six young men enter the arena of battle.

> Cum suī utrōsque adhortārentur deōs patriōs, patriam, ac parentēs, quidquid cīvium domī, quidquid in exercitū sit, illōrum tunc arma, illōrum intuērī manūs—ferōcēs et suōpte ingeniō et plēnī adhortantium vōcibus in medium inter duās aciēs prōcēdunt.

Notes: **suī** (*cīvēs*); **adhortor, -ārī, adhortātus sum** (+ accusative / infinitive): exhort, encourage; **patrius, -a, -um:** paternal; **intueor, -ērī, intuitus sum:** consider, regard, contemplate; **ferox (ferōcis):** courageous, warlike, brave, high-spirited; **-pte:** -self, own (an intensifying enclitic attached to personal, possessive, or reflexive pronouns).

27.4. Martial 1.21. In 508 BCE, the young Roman Republic was at war with the Etruscan king Lars Porsenna of nearby Clusium. As Porsenna's army besieged Rome, the Senate at Rome allowed Mucius Scaevola to infiltrate the Etruscan camp to execute the king. Scaevola killed a well-dressed man who seemed to be supervising the distribution of pay vouchers, assuming that this dandy must be the king. Scaevola killed the secretary by mistake. Martial here describes Scaevola's rash reaction to Porsenna's threats of death, and Porsenna's subsequent reaction to this strange but brave Roman (whose cognomen means "lefty," for the obvious reason—described in the first couplet). The king soon opened up negotiations with Rome, and the war was ended. Meter: elegiac couplets.

> Cum peteret rēgem dēcepta satellite dextra,
> > ingessit sacrīs sē peritūra focīs.
> Sed tam saeva pius mīrācula nōn tulit hostis
> > et raptum flammīs iussit abīre virum:
> ūrere quam potuit contemptō Mūcius igne,
> > hanc spectāre manum Porsena nōn potuit.
> Māior dēceptae fāma est et glōria dextrae:
> > sī nōn errāsset, fēcerat illa minus.

Notes: **dēcipiō, -ere, -cēpī, -ceptus**: deceive, cheat; **satelles, satellitis**, m/f: attendant, companion, guard; **ingerō, -ere, -gessī, -gestus**: throw in, press upon; **focus, -ī**, m: fireplace, hearth; **mīrāculum, -ī**, n: prodigy, miracle; **ūrō, -ere, ussī, ustus**: burn; **quam** (*dextram*); **dēcipiō, -ere, -cēpī, -ceptus**: catch, ensnare, elude; **errā(vi)sset**; **illa** (*dextra*).

27.5. Livy, *ab Urbe Condita* 3.27.1. Cincinnatus was twice called out of retirement to serve as dictator in times of emergency at Rome. Having just accepted the obligation in 458 BCE against the neighboring Aequi and

Sabines, his first act was to appoint a capable and talented man to the very important advisory and tactical post of the *Magister Equitum*.

Posterō diē dictātor cum ante lūcem in forum vēnisset, magistrum equitum dīcit L. Tarquitium, patriciae gentis, sed quī, cum stīpendia pedibus propter paupertātem fēcisset, bellō tamen prīmus longē Rōmānae iuventūtis habitus esset.

Notes: **dictātor, -ōris**, m: a constitutional officer, elected by the Senate, who served a term of six months or until the crisis was resolved, whichever came first; **magister equitum, magistrī equitum**, m: master of the horse, cavalry commander under a Roman dictator; **Lūcius Tarquitius, Lūciī Tarquitiī**, m: known only from this passage in Livy, the cognomen suggests Etruscan ancestry; **patricius, -a, -um**: patrician, of the Roman noble class; **stīpendium, -iī**, n: pay, wage; **pedibus**: dative of reference; **paupertās, -ātis**, f: poverty (i.e., Tarquinius was too poor to maintain a horse); **iuventus, -ūtis**, f: youth.

27.6. Lucan, *Pharsalia* **4.511–12.** Facing certain defeat from Pompey's superior forces, Caesar's fictional lieutenant Vulteius urges his men to mass suicide, a far more honorable death than capture in war. Meter: dactylic hexameter.

Nē nōs, cum calidō fodiēmus viscera ferrō,
dēspērāsse putent.

Notes: **calidus, -a, -um**: warm; **fodiō, -ere, fōdī, fōssus**: dig through, goad; **viscera, -um**, n (plural): internal organs, guts; **dēspērā(vi)sse**; **dēspērō, -āre, -āvī, -ātus**: be hopeless, despair, give up.

27.7. Tacitus, *Annales* **1.32.2.** In 14 CE, after the death of Augustus, the armies in Germany incited mutiny, proclaiming the grievances of long years of arduous service at very low pay. The soldiers have just attacked their centurions (the senior professional officers), the brunt of their long resentment, mauling many and killing some. One centurion, Septimius, managed to escape and here seeks refuge with Caecina, the legate (commander in the field), powerless to save the hapless Septimius from the angry mob.

Septimius cum perfūgisset ad tribūnal pedibusque Caecinae advolverētur, eō usque flagitātus est dōnec ad exitium derētur.

Notes: **Septimius, -iī**, m: one of Germanicus's centurions; **perfugiō, -ere, -fūgī, -fūgitūrus**: flee for refuge; **tribūnal, -ālis (-ium)**, n: tribunal, raised platform; **(Aulus) Caecina, (Aulī) Caecinae**, m: the Roman general in charge of troops on the Rhine during the campaign of retaliation after the Teutoberg forest disaster (wherein Quinctilius Varus managed to lose three entire legions and their standards). Caecina was awarded triumphal honors in 15 CE; **advolvō, -ere, -volvī, -volūtus**: roll towards, grovel; **eō usque**: up to the time; **flagitō, -āre, -āvī, -ātus**: demand urgently; **exitium, -iī**, n: destruction, ruin; **dēdō, -ere, dēdidī, dēditus**: give up, surrender.

27.8. Tacitus, *Annales* 1.40.3. In the heat of the mutiny of 14 CE Germanicus tried to send away his family for their own safety. Agrippina here proclaims her own distinguished character and ancestry.

> Diū cunctātus aspernantem uxōrem—cum sē dīvō Augustō ortam neque dēgenerem ad perīcula testārētur—postrēmō uterum eius et commūnem fīlium multō cum flētū complexus ut abīret perpulit.

Notes: **cunctor, -ārī, cunctātus sum**: linger, delay; **aspernor, -ārī, aspernātus sum**: scorn, despise, reject (i.e., the suggestion that she leave camp); **sē**: Agrippina; **ortam** (*esse*); **dēgener (-is)**: degenerate, ignoble, base, inferior; **testor, -ārī, testātus sum**: bear witness, give evidence, protest; **postrēmō**: finally, at last; **uterus, -ī**, m: womb (at the time, Agrippina was pregnant); **commūnis, -e**: common, shared (little Caligula); **flētus, -ūs**, m: weeping; **complector, -ī, complexus**: embrace; **ut abīret**: "that she go away" (indirect command); **perpellō, -ere, -pulī, -pulsus**: force, compel, prevail upon.

27.9. Martial 1.13. Implicated in a plot against Claudius, Caecina Paetus was ordered to commit suicide, but found himself too cowardly to do so. His courageous wife, Arria, snatching the dagger and plunging it into her own chest, condemns her husband's ignominy with her dying words. (Pliny the Younger's version, *Epistulae* 3.16, has Arria pleading with the emperor for her husband's life and condemning another aristocratic woman for surviving her husband's political suicide.) Meter: elegiac couplets.

> Casta suō gladium cum trāderet Arria Paetō,
> quem dē visceribus strinxerat ipsa suīs,
> "Sī qua fidēs, vulnus quod fēcī nōn dolet," inquit
> "sed tū quod faciēs, hoc mihi, Paete, dolet."

Notes: **visceribus**: see *NLP* 27.6; **stringō, -ere, strinxī, strictus**: pluck, draw; **qua** = *aliqua*.

27.10. Tacitus, *Annales* **11.21.1.** Curtius Rufus, our friend from *NLP* 24.7, was a distinguished politician and soldier whose ancestry was obscure.

Dē orīgine Curtiī Rūfī, quem gladiātōre genitum quīdam prōdidēre, neque falsa prompserim et vēra exequī pudet.

Notes: **orīgō, orīginis**: f: source, beginning, origin; **genitum** (*esse*); **prōmō, -ere, prompsī, promptus**: produce, bring forth, disclose, express; **ex(s)equor, -ī, exsecūtus sum**: pursue, persist in.

27.11. Tacitus, *Agricola* **42.3.** Although Agricola had expressed the desire to retire from politics, late in his career he was offered the governorship of Asia or Africa (either one, a plush assignment after perilous Britain). Agricola refused the appointment.

Quī parātus simulātiōne, in adrogantiam compositus, et audiit precēs excūsantis, et, cum adnuisset, agī sibi grātiās passus est, nec ērubuit beneficiī invidiā.

Notes: **quī**: Domitian; **simulātiō, -iōnis**, f: pretense; **adrogantia, -iae**, f: insolence, conceit, haughtiness; **excūsō, -āre, -āvī, -ātus**: excuse, exempt from blame, apologize (construe with an understood *Agricolae* who apologized for declining a provincial command); **adnuō, -ere, -uī, -ūtus**: nod assent, agree; **ērubescō, -ere, ērubuī**: blush; **invidia, -iae**, f: envy, ill will.

27.12. Pliny the Elder, *Naturalis Historia* **22.9.** Of the accolades awarded to Roman soldiers, the crown of grass (*corōna obsidiōnālis*: siege crown) was the most prestigious, conferred on a man who had ended a siege (Pliny cites only six recipients, Augustus being the last).

Dōnātus est eā L. Siccius Dentātus semel, cum cīvicās quattuor-decim meruisset dēpugnāssetque centiens vīciens, semper victor.

Notes: **eā**: *corōna obsidiōnālis*; **Lūcius Siccius Dentātus, Lūciī Siciī Dentātī**, m: c. 514–450 BCE, a highly decorated soldier, surviving 120 battles, receiving 45 "honorable" wounds, also awarded three *corōnae mūrālēs* (for being the first man over an enemy wall) and eight *corōnae aureae* (for general acts of gallantry), in addition to countless lesser accolades. His cognomen means "toothy"; **cīvicās**: the *corōna cīvica*, awarded to a man who had saved the life of a fellow Roman citizen; (**dēpugnā[vi]sset**) **dēpugnō, -āre, -āvī, -ātus**: fight hard; **centiens**: a hundred time; **vīciens**: twenty times.

EXTRA PASSAGES: INFORMERS

In times of political crisis, there will always be certain individuals willing to give evidence (authentic or fabricated) against honest men and women whose only "crime" is subscription to rival political philosophies. Acting to curry favor with those in power, to advance their own political careers, or to enhance personal fortunes, informers were widely condemned in Roman literature.

27.13. Tacitus, *Historiae* 1.2. According to Tacitus, the political climate in the waning years of the Julio-Claudian dynasty censured virtue and rewarded corruption. Nonetheless, there was abiding resentment of those who advanced by means of treachery and deceit.

> Nec minus praemia dēlātōrum invīsa quam scelera—cum aliī sacerdōtia et consulātūs ut spolia adeptī, procūrātiōnēs aliī et interiōrem potentiam, agerent verterent cuncta odiō et terrōre.

Notes: as often in Tacitus, forms of *esse* are omitted; **invīsus, -a, -um**: hated; **consulātus, -ūs**, m: consulship; **ut**: as, like; **spolia**: see *NLP* 27.1; **adipiscor, -ī, adeptus sum**: obtain; **procūrātiō, -iōnis**, f: a managerial or administrative post; **interior, -ius (-iōris)**: inner, "confidential"; **potentia, -iae**, f: power; **agerent** (*et*) **verterent**; **terror, -ōris**, m: fear, terror, dread.

27.14. Tacitus, *Annales* 3.37.1. In 21 CE, before the notorious spate of treason trials under Sejanus, Tiberius condemns two Romans for attempting to lay a fabricated charge of treason against a political rival. These three men are otherwise unknown.

> Et Considius Aequus et Caelius Cursor equitēs Rōmānī, quod fictīs māiestātis crīminibus Magium Caecilianum praetōrem petīvissent, auctōre principe ac dēcrētō senātūs pūnitī.

Notes: **Considius Aequus, Considiī Aequī**, m: a Roman *eques*; **Caelius Cursor, Caeliī Cursōris**, m: a Roman *eques*; **fictus, -a, -um**: feigned, false; **māiestās, -ātis**, f: dignity, majesty, treason; **dēcrētum, -ī**, n: resolution, decree; **pūnitī** (*sunt*); **pūniō, -īre, -īvī, -ītus**: punish.

27.15. Juvenal, *Saturae* 4.46–48. A fisherman has just caught a fish of such epic proportions that it is fit only for the emperor—to sell it on the market would surely be an act of treason. There ensues a crisis of state wherein the royal cabinet must decide how to prepare the fish. Here we learn that informers lurk everywhere. Meter: dactylic hexameter.

> Quis enim prōpōnere tālem
> aut emere audēret, cum plēna et lītora multō
> dēlātōre forent?

Notes: **prōpōnō, -ere, -posuī, -positus**: display; **tālem** (*piscem: piscis, -is*, m: fish); **emō, -ere, ēmī, emptus**: buy, purchase; **forent** = *futūrī essent.*

Purpose Clauses

1. A **PURPOSE CLAUSE**, introduced by **ut** for positive clauses and **nē** for negative clauses, explains the end or purpose of the main action. Consider the following examples:

Caesar, *de Bello Gallico* 7.70.2: **Labōrantibus nostrīs Caesar Germānōs summittit legiōnēsque prō castrīs constituit, <u>nē qua subitō irruptiō ab hostium peditātū fīat</u>**. Caesar sends the Germans as reinforcements to our men laboring and he establishes the legions in front of the camps <u>lest any incursion by the infantry of the enemy suddenly happen</u>.

Vegetius, *de Re Militari* 2.1: **Exercitus ex rē ipsā atque opere exercitiī nōmen accēpit, <u>ut eī numquam licēret oblīviscī</u> quod vocābātur**. The army received its name from the very circumstance and work of the training <u>so that it was never allowed for it to forget what it was called</u>.

2. The main clause may contain a correlative adverb such as *ideō* (for that reason), *idcircō* (on that account), *eō consiliō* (with this plan). Consider the following examples:

Cicero, *pro Caelio* 14.33: **<u>Ideō</u> viam mūnīvī, <u>ut eam tū aliēnīs virīs comitāta celebrārēs</u>?** Did I fortify the road <u>for this reason</u>, <u>so that you should frequent it escorted by strange men</u>?

Cicero, *ad Atticum* 2.14.2: **C. Arrius proximus est vīcīnus, immō ille quidem iam contubernālis, quī etiam sē <u>idcircō</u> Rōmam īre negat <u>ut hīc mēcum tōtōs diēs philosophētur</u>**. Caius Arrius is my next door neighbor, or rather indeed my tent-mate, who also refuses to go to Rome <u>on this account</u>, <u>so that he may philosophize here with me all day long</u>.

3. Relative clauses that feature subjunctive verbs can also convey purpose. Consider the following examples:

Catullus 7.9–12: **Tam tē bāsia multa bāsiāre / vēsānō satis et super Catullō est, / quae nec pernumerāre cūriōsī / possint nec malā fascināre linguā**. That you kiss so many kisses is enough and more than enough for mad Catullus, <u>so that meddlesome (old men) are not able to count them or bewitch them with an evil tongue.</u>

Sallust, *Bellum Iugurthinum* 46.2: **Igitur lēgātōs ad consulem cum suppliciīs mittit, quī tantummodo ipsī līberīsque vītam peterent, alia omnia dederent populō Rōmānō**. He therefore sends envoys to the consul with supplications, <u>who were to seek only life for himself and his children, and (who were) to offer all other things to the Roman people.</u>

4. Purpose clauses containing a comparative adjective or adverb are often introduced by *quō*. Consider the following examples:

Caesar, *de Bello Gallico* 2.25.2: **Reliquōs cohortātus mīlitēs signa inferre et manipulōs laxāre iussit, quō facilius gladiīs ūtī possent**. Having encouraged the remaining soldiers, he ordered them to bring in the standards and to open up the ranks, <u>so that they might be able to use their swords more easily.</u>

Tacitus, *Annales* 1.3.5: **Adscīrīque per adoptiōnem ā Tiberiō iussit, quamquam esset in domō Tiberiī fīlius iuvenis, sed quō plūribus mūnīmentīs insisteret**. And he (Augustus) ordered (Germanicus) to be admitted through adoption by Tiberius, although there was a young son in Tiberius's house, but <u>so that he (Augustus) could stand with more safeguards.</u>

5. Latin typically employs the following **SEQUENCE OF TENSES** for purpose clauses:

   (a) when the main verb is present or future tense, the subjunctive verb in the purpose clause is present tense (primary sequence)
   (b) when the main verb is one of the past tenses (imperfect, perfect, or pluperfect), the subjunctive verb in the purpose clause is imperfect tense (secondary sequence)

Consider the following examples:

Ovid, *Ars Amatoria* 1.157–58: **Respice praetereā, post vōs quīcumque sedēbit, / nē premat oppositō mollia terga genū**. Moreover, <u>look back</u> at whoever will sit behind you so that <u>he does not press</u> (your) soft back with an interposing knee. (primary sequence)

Caesar, *de Bello Civili* 1.26.1: **Ad opera Caesaris adpellēbat, ut ratēs perrumperet atque opera disturbāret**. He (Pompey) <u>drove</u> (his men) through Caesar's works so they might <u>break through</u> the rafts and <u>demolish</u> the works. (secondary sequence)

This table summarizes the sequence of tenses for purpose clauses:

SEQUENCE OF TENSES FOR PURPOSE CLAUSES

Primary Sequence		Secondary Sequence	
Main Verb	Subjunctive Verb	Main Verb	Subjunctive Verb
Present Future	Present	Imperfect Perfect Pluperfect	Imperfect

I. Required Vocabulary

NOUNS

dolus, -ī, m: deceit, trick
lupus, -ī, m: wolf
marītus, -ī, m: husband

cruor, -ōris, m: blood, gore
līmen, līminis, n: threshold, entrance, home

ADJECTIVES

praeclārus, -a, -um: bright, distinguished, excellent
sānus, -a, -um: sound, healthy, sane
vacuus, -a, -um: empty, idle

suāvis, -e: sweet, agreeable, pleasant

VERBS

comparō, -āre, -āvī, -ātus: provide, furnish, prepare
dubitō, -āre, -āvī, -ātus: waver, hesitate

accēdō, -ere, -cessī, -cessus: approach
ēripiō, -ere, -uī, -reptus: snatch, tear away
fingō, -ere, finxī, fictus: shape, invent
impōnō, -ere, -posuī, -positus: place upon, impose
intendō, -ere, -tendī, -tentus: aim, stretch, strain, exert
surgō, -ere, surrexī, surrectus: rise

conveniō, -īre, -vēnī, -ventus: come together, meet with

CONJUNCTIONS AND ADVERBS

cūr: why
prōtinus: immediately
scīlicet: evidently, certainly, of course
ubique: everywhere
ut / utī: as, like, how (with indicative verbs); so that (with subjunctive verbs)
-ve: or

II. Translate the following sentences from Latin to English or English to Latin.

1. Marītus dolōs comparat nē uxor lēgēs sibi impōnat.
2. Convenimus eō consiliō ut diū hīc habitēmus et dīvitēs sīmus.
3. Ō parentēs, ēripite līberōs vestrōs nē cruōrem videant et dē malō discant.
4. Mīlitēs oppidum tenēbant ut exercitus Rōmānus in bellō vincere cōnārētur.
5. Prōtinus accessī ut mūnus populō in nōmine meō darem.
6. Ō Catulle, opus tuum surgat in dulcibus modīs ut carminibus plūs gaudeāmus.
7. Dēlātōrēs dubitāvērunt ut consilium melius caperent.
8. Cīvis templa optima petīvit nē dī sibi nocērent.
9. Although we are escaping the city, nevertheless we want to meet with Caesar in order to make an end of the war.

10. Let the army seize the hill so that it may be able to pitch camp.

11. If only the mothers had not seen their children. They approached in order to protect them.

12. Don't (plural) follow the crowd in order that I still trust you.

Magic and the Occult

Magic consists of attempts to manipulate the natural world or human mind for good or ill, and its practitioners in Rome were both professionals and amateurs. Our word "magic" ultimately derives from a Persian guild of dream interpreters and royal advisors, but the Greek term *magus* soon became associated with the practices of nefarious sorcerers. The concept, however, was complex. Magic overlaps with religion and medicine, it anticipates alchemy and chemistry, and it straddles the natural and the paranormal. Fundamentally, magic is a science based on "secret" knowledge.

Mythology is replete with examples of magic. Gods change their shape at will. Jupiter is a bull, a swan, a shower of golden rain. Ceres becomes a mare to escape the advances of Neptune, god of horses, who in turn assumes the form of a stallion for the chase. Gods readily transform people into animals (dolphins, bears, spiders, birds) or plants—the fate of many of Apollo's ill-fortuned lovers: Daphne becomes the laurel; Cyparissus, the mournful cypress tree; Clytie, the sunflower. And animals are transformed into people: the Myrmidons who follow Achilles were once ants.

Mythology also preserves the tradition of two powerful witches: Circe and her niece Medea. An expert pharmacologist, Circe uses her knowledge of drugs to transform her enemies into animals, most famously changing Odysseus's crew into pigs. Her magic is useless against Odysseus, to whom the gods had given *moly*, a powerful antidote. Circe also advises Odysseus on summoning and controlling the dead. Like her aunt, Medea is an expert in drugs, which she uses for healing wounds and restoring youth. Her salves protect Jason from fire-breathing bulls, and her chants lull to sleep the serpent that guarded the golden fleece. The elegant Circe and Medea contrast sharply with the hag-witches that populate Roman literature, including Horace's Canidia (*NLP* 28.6-7), Propertius's Acanthis

(*NLP* 28.8), Lucan's Erichtho (*Pharsalia* 6.414–830), and Apuleius's Meroë (*Metamorphoses* 1.5–19).

Words and incantations also prove magically powerful. Cato the Elder recorded a treatment that involved brandishing a knife and two pieces of reed over a fractured bone while the healer chanted the nonsensical *motas vaeta daries dardares astataries dissunapiter* (*de Agricultura* 160). Other magical phrases were thought to increase the efficacy of erotic seduction, and their repetition supposedly heightened or intensified the chances for the desired outcome. Particularly powerful implements of retribution were curse tablets, usually inscribed on thin sheets of lead which were then folded, rolled, or nailed and finally deposited near conduits to the underworld—battle sites, fresh graves, hot springs—in the hopes that chthonic (underworld) gods would fulfill the curse. Binding-curse tablets ranged from simple lists of names to elaborate compositions invoking foreign gods, or featuring words either jumbled or arrayed into a magical pattern. Many curses concerned rivals in sport or love, erotic separation or attraction, and justice, featuring prayers for the restoration of stolen property and punishment of the thief.

Physical objects also had magical properties. To protect the wearer from ailment, lawsuit, or black magic, amulets were ubiquitous—rings, bracelets, pendants, or even pieces of thread that could encircle a body part. Magical texts inscribed on thin sheets of silver or gold were rolled into copper tubes to be worn protectively around the neck. Pliny reports a method of contraception that involved a bracelet containing a spider (*Naturalis Historia* 29.85). He also notes (without endorsement) that the Magi claimed that touching the corresponding tooth of a hyena could cure a toothache (*Naturalis Historia* 29.95, an example of "sympathetic" magic, based on imitation or correspondence). To restore the straying affections of Delphis, Simaetha employed a magic wheel, melted a wax "voodoo" doll, and sprinkled drugs on Delphis' doorstep (Theocritus, *Idyll* 2). In fact, voodoo dolls were common, made from a variety of materials and frequently accompanied by curse tablets. These dolls were often mutilated and then enclosed in miniature coffins. Similarly, a clay dog, fitted with the eyes of a live bat and deposited at a crossroad, was prescribed to cause sleeplessness in a potential lover (*PGM* IV.1943–66). Since bats are nocturnal, it was believed that their eyes would stay open all night long, causing a corresponding (sympathetic) nocturnal wakefulness in the victim. The difficulty of obtaining the bat's eyes likely also increased the spell's potency.

Many spells make reference to Hecate, the goddess associated with the moon, magic, sorcery, dogs, and the underworld. Hecate was often depicted in triplicate form holding torches, keys, or other magical implements. Her statue was also often erected at the dangerous junction of roadways (Oedipus, for example, killed his father at a crossroad). The moon itself was a powerful magical symbol, and common in literary magic is the act of "drawing down the moon" by witches (usually from Thessaly) in honor of Hecate, usually with erotic intent. Growing pale or blood-red during the process, the moon supposedly deposited foam on the earth, which was then collected for use in love potions. This power came at a high price. Thessalian women who succeeded in drawing down the moon lost either their children or an eye. The raucous noise of clashing bronze cymbals could, however, thwart attempts to "draw down the moon." This tradition may relate to lunar eclipses (when the moon does in fact turn blood-red), which were themselves the source of superstition and fear.

Magic, in its many forms, is widely attested and often condemned. Pliny the Elder considered the Magi foolish, misinformed, and deceptive. The best single critical source from anitiquity is Apuleius's *Apologia*, wherein he defends himself against a charge of magic while fully discussing many aspects and practices of magic in the first to second centuries CE.

SUGGESTIONS FOR FURTHER READING:

Faraone, C. A. *Ancient Greek Love Magic*. Harvard, 1999.

Faraone, C. A. and Dirk Obbink, eds. *Magika Hiera: Ancient Greek Magic and Religion*. Oxford, 1991.

Gager, John G. *Curse Tablets and Binding Spells from the Ancient World*. Oxford, 1992.

Lloyd, G. E. R. *Magic, Reason, and Experience: Studies in the Origins and Development of Greek Science*. Cambridge, 1979.

Luck, G. *Arcana Mundi: Magic and the Occult in the Greek and Roman Worlds*. 2nd ed. Johns Hopkins, 2006.

Ogden, Daniel. *Magic, Witchcraft and Ghosts in the Greek and Roman Worlds: A Sourcebook*. 2nd ed. Oxford, 2009.

PASSAGES

28.1. Ovid, *Fasti* 4.907–909. Observed on April 25, the Robigalia was a ritual of agricultural magic to ward off mildew from the crops. To Ovid's query (here) the priest explains that a dog (an unusual sacrifice) is offered as a sympathetic token against Canis Minor, whose early rising will cause the crops to ripen too quickly. Meter: elegiac couplets.

Flāmen in antīquae lūcum Rōbīginis ībat,
        exta canis flammīs, exta datūrus ovis.
Prōtinus accessī, rītūs nē nescius essem.

Notes: **flāmen, flāminis**, m: priest; **lūcus, -ī**, m: sacred grove; **rōbīgō, rōbīginis**, f: rust, mildew (here, personified as the goddess who protects the crops from mildew); **exta, -ōrum**, n (plural): entrails of a sacrificial animal; **ovis, -is (-ium)**, f: sheep; **rītus, -ūs**, m: ceremony, custom; **nescius, -a, -um**: ignorant.

28.2. Apuleius, *Apologia* 63. Accused of using magic to gain the favor (and fortune) of a wealthy widow, Apuleius dismisses each charge in turn. He denies having used a voodoo doll, an emaciated, disemboweled figure "resembling an evil ghost" and "a clear sign of magic." Here he suggests why his accusers did not require him to produce the dreadful object.

Quod sī compertum habēbātis tam envidens signum magiae, cūr mihi ut exhibērem nōn dēnuntiāstis? An ut possētis in rem absentem līberē mentīrī?

Notes: **quod** = *aliquod*; **compertus, -a, -um**: proven, verified; **envidens** = *invidens*; **invideō, -ēre, -vīdī, -vīsus**: grudge, envy, be a source of ill will; **magia, -iae**, f: magic, sorcery; **ut exhibērem**: "that I produce" ("to produce": indirect command); **dēnuntiā(vi)stis; dēnuntiō, -āre, -āvī, -ātus**: declare, order; **absens (-entis)**: absent (*in absentem rem*: "against an absent object"); **mentior, -īrī, mentītus sum**: lie, cheat, pretend.

28.3. Ovid, *Fasti* 1.141–42. Hecate's power is enhanced by her (statue's) ability to look in three directions at once. Meter: elegiac couplets.

Ōra vidēs Hecatēs in trēs vertentia partēs,
        servet ut in ternās compita secta viās.

Notes: **Hecate, -ēs**, f: Hecate; **ternī, -ae, -a** (plural): three each; **compitum, -ī**, n: crossroads; **secō, -āre, -uī, sectus**: cut, divide.

28.4. Ovid, *Metamorphoses* 7.297–99. After Jason returned to Iolchus with the golden fleece, his uncle Pelias still refused to cede the throne. Medea's solution is diabolical and absolute. She conspires to have the daughters themselves kill their wicked father. Here she tries to win their trust. Meter: dactylic hexameter.

> Nēve dolī cessent, odium cum coniuge falsum
> Phāsias adsimulat Peliaeque ad līmina supplex
> confugit.

Notes: **nēve:** so that . . . not; **cessō, -āre, -āvī, -ātus:** stop; **Phāsias, Phāsiadis,** m/f: someone from Colchis (Medea's father was Aeëtes, king of Colchis on the Black Sea); **adsimulō, -āre, -āvī, -ātus:** pretend; **Peliās, -ae,** m: Pelias, the king of Iolchus in Thessaly who sent Jason on the quest for the golden fleece; **supplex (supplicis):** kneeling, entreating, as a suppliant; **confugiō, -ere, -fūgī, -fugitus:** flee, take refuge.

28.5. Ovid, *Metamorphoses* 7.332–35. Seducing the daughters of Pelias with an aged ram that has supposedly been restored to youth, Medea promises to do the same for the king, but withholds the efficacious drugs. Here Medea enjoins the daughters to commit the unspeakable act. Meter: dactylic hexameter.

> "Quid nunc dubitātis, inertēs?
> Stringite" ait "gladiōs veteremque haurīte cruōrem,
> ut rēpleam vacuās iuvenālī sanguine vēnās!
> In manibus vestrīs vīta est aetāsque parentis."

Notes: **quid:** why; **iners (-ertis):** idle, sluggish; **stringō, -ere, strinxī, strictus:** draw tight, draw; **hauriō, -īre, hausī, haustus:** drain, spill, shed; **rēpleō, -ēre, -ēvī, -ētus:** replenish; **iuvenālis, -e:** youthful; **vēna, -ae,** f: vein, blood vessel (the ancients distinguished between arteries and veins but believed that only veins transported blood, while arteries were full of air).

28.6. Horace, *Sermones* 1.8.28–29. In this satire, a garden statue plays witness to acts of black magic and necromancy orchestrated by the notorious witch Canidia and her band. Meter: dactylic hexameter.

> Cruor in fossam confūsus, ut inde
> Mānīs ēlicerent animās responsa datūrās.

Notes: **fossa, -ae,** f: ditch, trench; **confūsus (*est*); confundō, -ere, -fūdī, -fūsus:** pour together, mix, mingle; **ēliciō, -ere, -uī, -itus:** entice, lure out (it is the witches who lure); **animās:** construe in apposition with *Mānīs*; **responsa:** substantive participle.

28.7. Horace, *Epodes* 17.27–29. In this epode, Horace supplicates Canidia, who soundly scorns his petition. Here he recants his former denial of her powers (see also *Epode* 5). Meter: iambic trimeter.

> Ergō negātum vincor ut crēdam miser:
> Sābella pectus increpāre carmina
> caputque Marsā dissilīre nēniā.

Notes: (*quod*) **negātum** (*esse*) (indirect statement depending on *crēdam*); **Sābellus, -a, -um**: Sabine. An old Sabine woman had uttered a protective folk-magical charm over Horace in his youth (*Sermones* 1.9.29–30); **increpō, -āre, -āvī, -ātus**: rustle, rebuke; **Marsus, -a, -um**: Marsian (the Marsi were an ancient Italic peoples renowned for curing serpent bites); **dissiliō, -īre, -uī**: burst, split; **nēnia, -iae**, f: funeral song, dirge, incantation.

28.8. Propertius, *Elegiae* 4.5.13–16. Propertius curses Acanthis, a dead bawd-witch (an unscrupulous "matchmaker") whose spells impelled his girlfriend to extort gifts from the poet while also taking on competing lovers. Propertius here describes some of Acanthis' magical tricks (including lycanthropy). Meter: elegiac couplets.

> Audax cantātae lēgēs impōnere lūnae
>   et sua nocturnō fallere terga lupō;
> posset ut intentōs astū caecāre marītōs,
>   cornīcum immeritās ēruit ungue genās.

Notes: **audax** (*est*); **cantātae**: "bewitched"; **nocturnus, -a, -um**: nocturnal; **tergum, -ī**, n: back; **intentōs**: e.g., to spy on their wives; **intentus, -a, -um**: eager, attentive; **astus, -ūs**, m: cunning, guile; **caecō, -āre, -āvī, -ātus**: blind; **cornis, cornīcis**, f: crow (construe with *ungue*); **immeritus, -a, -um**: guiltless, undeserving, innocent; **ēruō, -ere, -uī, -utus**: tear, dig, pluck out; **unguis, -is (-ium)**, m: nail, claw, talon; **gena, -ae**, f: cheek.

28.9. Apuleius, *Metamorphoses* 1.8. The merchant Aristomenes recounts a chilling tale of a Thessalian witch masquerading as an innkeeper and playing havoc with competitors and unfaithful lovers. Here we see how casually she makes men fall in love with her.

> Nam ut sē ament efflictim nōn modo incolae vērum etiam Indī vel Aethiopēs utrīque vel ipsī Anticthonēs, folia sunt artis et nūgae merae.

Notes: **efflictim**: passionately, desperately, to distraction; **incola, -ae**, m/f: inhabitant, resident; **Indī, -ōrum**, m (plural): inhabitants of the Indian subcontinent; **Aethiops, Aethiopis**, m: an Ethiopian, dwelling in the exotic land beloved by the sun god; **utrīque**: the ancients believed that there were two Ethiopias, one in the east, the other in the west; **Anticthonēs, -um**, m (plural): the inhabitants of the Antipodes in the southern regions; **folium, -iī**, n; trifle; **nūgae, -ārum**, f (plural): jests, frivolities; **merus, -a, -um**: pure, unmixed.

28.10. **Pliny the Younger,** *Epistulae* **7.27.7.** When the Stoic philosopher Athenodorus came to Athens, he took a house with suspiciously low rent because of its resident ghost. Quite eager to ascertain for himself whether ghosts really do exist, Athenodorus here prepares to work through the night, when ghosts are active. In the end, Athenodorus met his ghost and solved a murder mystery.

Ipse ad scrībendum animum, oculōs, manum intendit, nē vacua mens audīta simulācra et inānēs sibi metūs fingeret.

Notes: **ipse**: Athenodorus; **ad scrībendum**: "to writing" (gerund); **simulācrum, -ī**, n: image, likeness; **inānis, -e**: empty, void.

28.11. *CIL* **VI 19747:** Rome. A young child snatched by a witch issues a warning from the grave.

Iūcundus, (servus) Līviae Drūsī Caesaris, f(īlius) Gryphī et Vītālis, in quartum surgens comprensus dēprimor annum cum possem mātrī dulcis et esse patrī. Ēripuit mē saga(e) manus, crūdēlis ubique, cum manet in terrīs et noc(u)it arte suā. Vōs vestrōs nātōs concustōdīte, parentēs, nī dolor in totō pectore fixsus e[s]t!

Notes: **Iūcundus, -ī**, m: presumably the child's name, meaning "sweet, pleasant, delightful"; **Līviae** (*uxōris*) **Drūsī**; **Līvia, -iae**, f: Tiberius's niece, married to her cousin Drusus, whom she supposedly poisoned in 23 CE to help advance her lover Sejanus (see *NLP* 27); **Drūsus Caesar, Drūsī Caesaris**, m: Tiberius's son; **Gryphus, -ī**, m: a Greek man's name, related to the mythical gryphon; **Vītālis, -is**, f: a woman's name meaning "full of life"; **compre(he)ndō, -ere, -(he)ndī, -(he)nsus**: take, seize; **dēprimō, -ere, -pressī, -pressus**: press, sink, plant (in the ground); **saga, -ae**, f: witch; **crūdēlis, -e**: cruel, heartless; **concustōdiō, -īre, -īvī, -ītus**: keep a very close watch; **nī** = *nē*; **fixsus** = *fixus*; **fīgō, -ere, fixī, fixus**: attach, affix; *est* is a slip for *sit* and may reflect vernacular usage, just as grammatical errors are common in spoken English.

28.12. *Tabulae Sulis* **62.** A bath-goer's cloak has been stolen, and the victim seeks its return.

Dō[nāvī] [S]ūlis ut hoc ante diēs novem—[sī lī]ber sī ser(v)us sī [lī] bera sī serva [sī] pu <er> sī puell[a—i]n rostr[ō] s[uō] dēfera[t] caballārem. S[ī ser(v)us sī līber sī] serva sī lībera sī puer [sī puella] in suō rostrō dēfer[at].

Notes: **dōnāvī**: supply *vōtum* as the direct object; **Sūlis, -is**, f (attested only in the genitive and dative singular): Sulis Minerva, the Celtic goddess who presides over the hot springs at Bath, England, the recipient of over 130 curse tablets. The ancients believed that hot springs were entrances to the underworld, and that depositing curses in such places enhanced their efficacy (*Sulis*: here, the genitive is confused with the grammatically correct dative); **sī . . . sī . . . sī**: whether . . . or . . . or; **rostrum, -ī**, n: beak, bow of a ship; **caballāris, -e**: related to a horse (i.e., a horse blanket); **dēferat**: construe *fūr, fūris*, m/f: thief as the subject.

EXTRA PASSAGES: APULEIUS'S *METAMORPHOSES*

One of the most beloved episodes in Apuleius's *Metamorphoses* (a novel permeated by the occult) is the endearing tale of Cupid and Psyche. Psyche was so beautiful that her countrymen worshipped her above Venus. Soon Venus's son Cupid fell in love with the pretty girl, and he whisked her away, providing her with an affectionate and luxurious home, so long as she never asked to look on his true face and learn his real identity. Goaded by her faithless sisters, Psyche eventually sneaked a look in the middle of the night, unwittingly wounding her immortal paramour. A jealous and wrathful Venus then set a series of impossible tasks for Psyche's retribution, including a visit to the underworld. Recovered from his wounds, and finding Psyche sleeping deeply, Cupid removed the sleep from her face. The pair lived happily ever after. Psyche's name is Greek for both "butterfly" and "soul," and the tale is regarded as an allegory for the soul's immortality. It is a favorite of artists, sculpted by Canova, and retold by C. S. Lewis ('*Til We Have Faces*).

28.13. Apuleius, *Metamorphoses* 5.11. Here Cupid advises Psyche to be wary of her treacherous sisters.

"Perfidae lupulae magnīs cōnātibus nefāriās insidiās tibi comparant, quārum summa est, ut tē suādeant meōs explōrāre vultūs."

Notes: **perfidus, -a, -um**: faithless, treacherous; **lupula, -ae**, f: little wolf, prostitute, whore; **cōnātus, -ūs**, m: exertion, attempt; **nefārius, -a, -um**: wicked, abominable; **insidia, -iārum**, f (plural): ambush, snare, trap; **suādeō, -ēre, suāsī, suāsus** (+ dative): recommend, advise, persuade; **explōrō, -āre, -āvī, -ātus**: search, investigate, explore.

28.14. Apuleius, *Metamorphoses* 5.24. Driven by her sisters to murder her husband, Psyche has finally caught sight of the sleeping Cupid's true face. She saw not a beast, as she had expected, but a beautiful young man. In her shock, she accidentally wounded him. When he awakes, discovering the betrayal (she has broken the only restriction) and the wound, he rebukes her with a startling revelation, delivered with stunning irony.

"Praeclārus ille sagittārius ipse mē tēlō meō percussī tēque coniugem meam fēcī, ut bestia scīlicet tibi vidērer et ferrō caput excīderēs meum, quod istōs amātōrēs tuōs oculōs gerit."

Notes: **sagittārius, -iī**, m: archer, bowman; **percutiō, -ere, -cussī, -cussus**: strike hard, pierce; **bestia, -iae**, f: wild beast; **excīdō, -ere, -cīdī, -cīsus**: cut; **amātor, -ōris**, m: lover (*amātōrēs*: in apposition with *oculōs*).

28.15. Apuleius, *Metamorphoses* 6.11. While Venus punishes Psyche, Cupid is kept under close guard.

Interim Cupīdō—sōlus interiōris domūs ūnicī cubiculī custōdiā clausus—coercēbātur acriter, partim nē petulantī luxuriē vulnus gravāret, partim nē cum suā cupītā convenīret.

Notes: **Cupīdō, Cupīdinis**, m: Venus's arrow-wielding son; **interior, -ius**: inner, middle; **ūnicus, -a, -um**: one, single; **cubiculum, -ī**, n: bedroom; **custōdia, -iae**, f: guard, custody, care; **coerceō, -ēre, -cuī, -citus**: enclose, shut in, restrain; **partim**: partly; **petulans (-antis)**: petulant, impudent, lascivious; **luxuriēs, -ēī**, f: excess, extravagance; **gravō, -āre, -āvī, -ātus**: aggravate, oppress, trouble; **cupīta**: substantive.

Result Clauses

A **RESULT CLAUSE** or **CONSECUTIVE CLAUSE**, introduced by **ut** for positive clauses and **ut ... nōn** for negative clauses, shows the effect or outcome of the main action of the sentence. These result clauses are frequently introduced by *adeō, ita, tālis, tam, tantus, sīc, usque eō, valdē,* in the main clause. Consider the following examples:

Martial 7.7.8–10: **Adeōque mentēs omnium tenēs ūnus / ut ipsa magnī turba nesciat Circī / utrumque currat Passerīnus an Tigris**. And you alone hold the minds of all <u>to such an extent</u> that the very crowd of the Great Circus does not know whether Passerinus or the Tigris River is running.

Vegetius, *de Re Militari* 1.18: **Tantaque cūra erat, ut nōn sōlum ā dextrīs sed etiam ā sinistrīs partibus et insilīre et dēsilīre condiscerent**. And there was <u>such great</u> care (in training) <u>that they (the soldiers) learned both to mount and to dismount (horses) not only from the right but even from the left sides.</u>

Cicero, *in Verrem* 1.1.8: **Usque eō senātōria iūdicia perdita profligātaque esse arbitrātur, ut hoc palam dictitet** ... He thinks that senatorial decisions are <u>so</u> corrupt and dissolute <u>that he openly asserts this</u> ...

1. Result clauses can also be negated by *ut ... nec, ut ... neque, ut ... nēmō, ut ... nullus, ut ... nihil*. Consider the following examples:

Aberdeen Bestiary 15r: **Mārēs in sompnum ita concīdunt ut nec vulneribus excitārī queant**. Male (bears) fall into so deep a sleep <u>that</u> they are <u>not</u> able to be aroused by wounds.

Cicero, *ad Atticum* 3.11.2: **Quem ita adfectum meā aerumnā esse arbitror ut tē ipsum consōlārī nēmō possit**. (You) whom I believe to be so affected by my hardship <u>that no one</u> is able to console you yourself.

Cicero, *ad Atticum* 3.8.3: **Atque ita perturbātō sum animō dē Quintē ut nihil queam statuere**. And indeed I am with so disturbed a mind ("such anxiety") about (my brother) Quintus <u>that</u> I am able to decide <u>nothing</u>.

2. Result clauses can also function substantively as the direct objects of verbs like *faciō* and its compounds (e.g., *afficiō, conficiō, efficiō*), or as the subjects of impersonal verbs like *fit, accidit, contingit*, and *necesse est*. Consider the following examples of **NOUN RESULT CLAUSES**:

Martial 5.28.1–2: **Ut bene loquātur sentiatque Māmercus, / efficere nullīs, Aule, mōribus possīs**. By none of your habits, Aulus, would you able <u>to bring it about</u> <u>that Mamercus speaks and thinks well</u>. (The result clause is the object of *efficere*.)

Frontinus, *de Aquaeductu Urbis Romae* 2.75: **Unde fit ut ductūs pūblicī hominibus prīvātīs vel ad hortōrum ūsūs itinera suspendant**. Whence <u>it</u> <u>happens</u> <u>that the paths of the public aqueduct are suspended for private citizens or for the uses of gardens</u>. (The result clause is the subject of *fit*.)

Aberdeen Bestiary 7r: **Et sī contigerit ut querātur ā vēnātōribus, venit ad eum odor vēnātōrum**. And if <u>it will have happened</u> <u>that it (a lion) is sought by hunters</u>, the scent of the hunters comes to him. (The result clause is the subject of *contigerit*.)

3. All of these result clauses typically employ the same **SEQUENCE OF TENSES** that you learned for purpose clauses in *NLP* 28:

(a) when the main verb is present or future tense, the subjunctive verb in the result clause is present tense (primary sequence)

(b) when the main verb is one of the past tenses (imperfect, perfect, or pluperfect), the subjunctive verb in the result clause is imperfect tense (secondary sequence)

Consider the following examples:

Aberdeen Bestiary 23v: **Nam tantō acūtē <u>cernit</u>, ut fulgōre lūminis noctis tenebrās <u>superet</u>**. For (the mouse) <u>sees</u> so sharply that it <u>overcomes</u> the darkness of the night by means of the brightness of its eye. (primary sequence)

Caesar, *de Bello Gallico* 1.38.4: **Nātūra locī sīc <u>mūniēbātur</u> ut magnam ad dūcendum bellum <u>daret</u> facultātem**. The nature of the place <u>was so well fortified</u> that it <u>gave</u> great opportunity for waging war. (secondary sequence)

I. Required Vocabulary

NOUNS

> **Britannia, -iae**, f: Britain
> **hōra, -ae**, f: hour
> **victōria, -iae**, f: victory

> **agmen, agminis**, n: stream, band, column, army in marching order
> **comes, comitis**, m/f: companion, associate
> **conditiō (condiciō), -iōnis**, f: stipulation, provision, state, condition
> **cor, cordis**, n: heart
> **necessitās, -ātis**, f: necessity, need, poverty, difficult situation
> **sacerdōs, sacerdōtis**, m/f: priest(ess), bishop
> **testis, -is (-ium)**, m/f: witness

ADJECTIVES

> **clārus, -a, -um**: bright, clear, loud, distinct, distinguished
> **inferus, -a, -um**: low, southern
> **īrātus, -a, -um**: angry

VERBS

> **damnō, -āre, -āvī, -ātus**: condemn, discredit
> **stō, stāre, stetī, status**: stand

> **afficiō, -ere, -fēcī, -fectus**: influence, affect
> **fluō, -ere, fluxī, fluxus**: flow
> **quaerō, -ere, quaesīvī, quaesītus**: look for, seek
> **trahō, -ere, traxī, tractus**: draw, drag, derive, prolong

CONJUNCTIONS AND ADVERBS

eō: there
licet: although, granted that
p(a)ene: nearly, almost
quippe: certainly, to be sure

II. Translate the following sentences from Latin to English or English to Latin.

1. Sacerdōtēs voluptāte adeō afficiuntur ut grātiās dīs agere oblīviscantur.

2. Carmina sīc clarē canentur ut mulierēs puellaeque ea in proximā urbe audiant.

3. Agmen in proeliō tam forte fuit ut omnēs hostēs vinceret.

4. Gentēs orbis terrārum tālibus tempestātibus movēbantur ut agrōs colere nōn possent.

5. Tantus cordis meī dolor erat ut neque victōriam neque pācem quaererem.

6. Equī celeriter ita currunt ut populī Rōmānī nōn cognoscant utrum mortālēs an dīvī sint.

7. Cicerō in Antōnium odium tāle habuit ut quattuordecim ōrātiōnēs ā sē dīcerentur.

8. Extrēmā in Britanniae parte lux lūnae tanta vidēbātur ut sōlem orīrī putārēmus.

9. It was fitting that the king was so just that he was not influenced by his companions.

10. So great was the victory in Britain that all the citizens rejoiced.

11. It happened that all the witnesses and informers were absent.

12. I am so angry that I cannot listen to the priestesses.

Medieval and Renaissance Anglo-Latin Writers

As the Roman Empire grew, Latin became the standard language of business, politics, and education in the western Mediterranean. Many prominent writers came not from Rome or even Italy, as we saw in the extra passages of *NLP* 20, which featured writers from North Africa. As the Roman Empire faded, giving way to the new kingdoms established by Germanic invaders in the fifth century CE, Latin endured as the international language of the Christian church and then of science and diplomacy well into the eighteenth century.

From the Middle Ages to the Renaissance, the British Isles enjoyed a rich tradition of Anglo-Latin literature. Although spoken Latin was quickly replaced by English and Gaelic when the Roman army withdrew in the early fifth century CE, Latin endured in the British churches as well as on the mainland. For the most part, Anglo-Latin remained grammatically and syntactically "pure," and many scholars have described the Latin of the British Isles as archaic and conservative. Nonetheless, British writers employed vernacular words and forms, and their Latin is lively and engaging, reflecting a myriad of styles and approaches from the simple and straightforward to the complex and opaque.

The Church was the focus of intellectual activity in the Middle Ages, and the Celto-Anglo church was vibrant. One of the most stunning illuminated manuscripts is the *Book of Kells,* an ornately decorated copy of the Gospels and a masterpiece of liturgical calligraphy produced by Irish monks around 800 CE. British clerics also produced significant original works that contributed greatly to the intellectual climate in Britain and abroad. Among important hagiographies (lives of saints), are Adamnanus's *de Vita Sancti Columbae,* which celebrates Columba (521–597 CE), the Irish monk who spread Christianity into Scotland. Adamnanus (627/8–704 CE) provides insight into the early Church and its conflicts with the Picts. Equally famous was Alcuin of York (735–804 CE), who was described by Charlemagne's biographer Einhard as "the most learned man anywhere" (*virum undecumque doctissimum*: 25). Alcuin's works included poetry and treatises on theology, Christian dogma, and grammar and rhetoric. Invited to court by Charlemagne, Alcuin became a leading teacher on the Continent, helping to shape the Carolingian Renaissance. Finally, Anselm of Canterbury (1033–1109 CE) rose to become archbishop of Canterbury, but his liturgical conflicts with King William II forced him into self-exile: Anselm advocated a universal self-governing church; William preferred to maintain royal authority over the church in England. Anselm's *Proslogion* (1077–1078) provides an ontological proof of the existence of God. He also left a large corpus of personal correspondence recording his own thoughts and deeds, his conflicts with the crown, and his exile.

Also rich is the long tradition of historical chroniclers. The *De Excidio et Conquestu Britanniae* of Gildas (c. 500–570 CE) recounts the post-Roman history of the island. Gildas' complex and opaque literary style earned him the epithet "*Sapiens*." The *Historia Ecclesiastica Gentis Anglorum* of the Venerable Bede (672/3–735 CE) recounts the history of the island from the Roman invasion to his own day, following a traditional annalistic approach. Although Bede took liturgical writers as his models, his style owes much to classical paradigms, including Julius Caesar, whose geographical excurses inspired Bede's topographical accounts and whose complex but unpretentious style Bede seems to imitate. Last, the influential *Historia Brittonum* (c. 830 CE), which helped to shape the legend of Arthur, has been ascribed to the pen of the ninth-century Welsh monk Nennius. *Historia Regni Henrici Septimi Regis Angliae* of Sir Francis Bacon (1561–1626 CE) focuses on the reign of one king, Henry VII, who usurped power in 1485 and established the house of Tudor.

Philosophy also flourished in Anglo-Latin literature. The *Utopia* of Sir Thomas More (1478–1535 CE) envisions the religious, political, and social mores of a fictional island utopia. Bacon's *Nova Atlantis* looks to an aspirational future era of discovery and learning, anticipating the modern research university at its very best. Bacon's novel, appearing first in Latin (1624 CE), was also published in English translation (1627 CE). Thomas Hobbes (1588–1679 CE) wrote broadly in both Latin and English on history, literature (including a discourse on Tacitus), physics, and political science, where he advocated for the absolute authority of the sovereign but also believed in the natural equality of all human beings and in the notion that legitimate political power must be representative. John Milton (1608–1674 CE), who was most famous for his English-language *Paradise Lost* and who believed strongly in self-determination, composed Latin poems. As an English civil servant he also conducted foreign correspondence in Latin. His *Defensio pro Populo Anglicano,* commissioned by Cromwell's Parliament, was a polemical defense of the parliamentary (non-regal) government. Milton's clean style and wide learning were broadly admired.

Finally, British natural scientists writing in Latin were especially influential. In *NLP* 19, we delighted in the charming descriptions of animals in the Aberdeen Bestiary. Bacon's *Novum Organum Scientiarum* (*New Methods of Science*) outlines a system of logic utilizing the process of reduction and inductive reasoning that was essential in the development of the modern scientific method. Sir Isaac Newton (1642–1727 CE) whose advances in mathematics and physics revolutionized the scientific world, also stands at a point of literary transition. His influential first work, *Philosophiae Naturalis Principia Mathematica,* was composed in Latin, but his last, *Opticks* (1704 CE), was in English, reflecting changing sensibilities as Protestantism took hold in western Europe and with it a transition to the academic use of national languages.

SUGGESTIONS FOR FURTHER READING:

Echard, Siân and Gernot R. Wieland, eds. *Anglo-Latin and Its Heritage: Essays in Honour of A. G. Rigg on his 64th Birthday.* Publications of the Journal of Medieval Latin 4. Brepols, 2001.

Lapidge, Michael. *Anglo-Latin Literature, 900–1066.* Hambledon, 1993.

Lapidge, Michael. *Anglo-Latin Literature, 600–899.* Hambledon, 1996.

Rigg, A. G. *A History of Anglo-Latin Literature, 1066–1422.* Cambridge, 1992.

PASSAGES

29.1. Adamnanus, *de Vita Sancti Columbae* **1.29.** When Columba sings, he is heard for miles!

Sed tamen eādem hōrā quī ultrā mille passuum longinquitātem stābant, sīc clārē eandem audiēbant vōcem, ut illōs—quōs canēbat—versiculōs etiam per singulās possent distinguere syllabās.

Notes: **longinquitās, -ātis,** f: length, distance; **versiculus, -ī,** m: little line of verse; **distinguō, -ere, -stinxī, -stinctus:** separate distinguish, "make out"; **syllaba, -ae,** f: syllable.

29.2. Adamnanus, *de Vita Sancti Columbae* **1.29.** The spirit of Columba has the ability to refresh and gladden travel-worn monks, as we learn from one of the brothers of his order.

"Sed et quandam in corde insuētam et incomparābilem infūsam laetificātiōnem, quae mē subitō mīrābiliter consōlātur, et in tantum laetificat ut nullīus maerōris, nullīus lābōris, meminisse possim."

Notes: supply *sentiō* as the main verb governing the passage; **insuētus, -a, -um**: un-accustomed, unusual; **incomparābilis, -e**: incomparable; **infūsam** (*esse*); **infundō, -ere, -fūdī, -fūsus**: pour in / over; **laetificātiō, -iōnis**, f: happiness; **mīrābiliter**: won-derfully; **consōlor, -ārī, consōlātus sum**: comfort, encourage; **in tantum**: "to such a degree"; **laetificō, -āre, -āvī, -ātus**: cheer, gladden, delight; **maeror, -ōris**, m: sorrow, sadness, grief.

29.3. Alcuin, *Disputatio de Rhetorica et Virtutibus Sapientissimi Regis Karli et Albini Magistri* **15.** In his discussion of transgressions and their punish-ments, Alcuin muses over whether leeway should be allowed in extenuat-ing circumstances. For example, according to Spartan law, an official charged with providing victims for a state sacrifice must be put to death should he not fulfill his duty. Alcuin's Spartan official faces the extenuat-ing obstacle of a swelling river, even marching the collected victims along the riverbank to prove his good faith. Does the official deserve capital pun-ishment for having failed in his duties despite his efforts and good intentions?

In urbem ex agrō coepit agere, cum subitō magnīs commōtus tempestātibus fluvius Eurōtās. Is, quī praeter Lacedaemoniam fluit, ita magnus et vehemens factus est, ut eō trādūcī victimae nullō modō possent.

Notes: supply "Spartan official" as the subject of *coepit*; **commōtus** (*est*); **commoveō, -ēre, -mōvī, -mōtus**: move, shake, disturb; **fluvius, -iī**, m: stream, river; **Eurōtās, -ātis**, m: the principal river in the southern Peloponnese; **Lacedaemonia, -iae**, f: Laco-nia in the Peloponnese, whose capital was Sparta; **vehemens (-entis)**: violent, furious; **trādūcō, -ere, -duxī, -ductus**: lead across; **victima, -ae**, f: animal offered in sacrifice to a god.

29.4. Bede, *Historiam Ecclesiasticum Gentis Anglorum* **1.13.** In 423 CE, the cen-tral administration of the Roman Empire (the "Republic") is unable to respond to British appeals for aid because of the more immediate threat of marauding bands from the Central Asian steppes.

Attila tamen ipse adeō intolerābilis reī pūblicae remansit hostis, ut tōtam pene Eurōpam, excisīs invāsīsque cīvitātibus atque castellīs, conrōderet.

Notes: **Attila, -ae**, m: leader of the Huns, 434–453 CE; **intolerābilis, -e**: unbearable, intolerable; **remaneō, -ēre, -mansī**: remain, continue; **Eurōpa, -ae**, f: the continent of Europe, named for Cadmus's daughter, who was abducted by Jupiter and abandoned by him on Crete. Her sons with Jupiter include Minos and Sarpedon; **excīdō, -ere, -cīdī, -cīsus**: cut out, destroy, demolish; **invādō, -ere, -vāsī, -vāsus**: enter, attack, assault; **castellum, -ī**, n: fortress, castle; **conrōdō, -ere, -rōsī, -rōsus**: gnaw to pieces, chew up.

29.5. Bede, *Historiam Ecclesiasticum Gentis Anglorum* **2.5.** In 616 CE the great Christian king Ethelbert died. His successor, his wicked son Eadbald, as we learn here, rejected his father's faith, restored idolatry, and committed many outrages against decency.

Sīquidem nōn sōlum fidem Christī recipere nōluerat, sed et fornicātiōne pollutus est tālī—quālem nec inter gentēs audītam apostolus testātur—ita ut uxōrem patris habēret.

Notes: **sīquidem**: accordingly, in fact, indeed; **Christus, -ī**, m: the anointed prophet of the Christian faith; **fornicātiō, -iōnis**, f: sex between unmarried partners, fornication; **polluō, -ere, -uī, -ūtus**: defile, pollute; **apostolus, -ī**, m: apostle, missionary (Augustine of Canterbury, responsible for Ethelbert's conversion); **audītam** (*esse*); **testor, -ārī, testātus sum**: attest, bear witness (+ indirect statement).

29.6. Bede, *Historiam Ecclesiasticum Gentis Anglorum* **4.23.** St. Hilda (614–680 CE), niece of Edwin king of Northumbria and founder of the abbey at Streaneshalch (Whitby), was a woman of remarkable energy and wisdom.

Tantae autem erat ipsa prūdentiae, ut nōn sōlum mediocrēs quīque in necessitātibus suīs, sed etiam rēgēs ac principēs nōnnumquam ab eā consilium quaererent, et invenīrent.

Notes: **prūdentia, -iae**, f: discretion, sagacity; **mediocris, -e**: moderate, ordinary (substantive); (*ali*)*quīque*; **nōnnumquam**: sometimes.

29.7. Nennius (?), *Historia Brittonum* **39.** The warlord Vortigern, who seized power in the fifth century CE, married his own daughter, by whom he had a son. St. Germanus of Auxerre in Gaul (378–448 CE), visiting Britain around 430 CE to deal with heresies, asked that Vortigern's incestuous child be presented, and then the holy man offered to take the boy on as his disciple and "son." Here Vortigern, both embarrassed and offended, is excommunicated.

Sed surrexit et īrātus est valdē, ut ā faciē Sanctī Germānī fugeret, et maledictus est et damnātus ā Sanctō Germānō et omnī Brittōnum conciliō.

Notes: **īrascor, -ī, īrātus sum**: be angry; **valdē**: very much, exceedingly; **maledīcō, -ere, -dixī, -dictus**: abuse, curse; **Brittō, -ōnis**, m: Briton; **concilium, -iī**, n: assembly, council.

29.8. Sir Francis Bacon, *Historia Regni Henrici Septimi Regis Angliae* **2.2.** In 1487, Elizabeth Woodville (1437–1492), queen consort of Edward IV, had helped secure the ascension of her son-in-law Henry VII in 1485, thus ending the War of the Roses. Bacon strongly suggests that her implicit (and alleged) involvement in a rebellion of 1486, despite her earlier support, induced Henry to cloister the queen dowager at the abbey at Bermondsey, where she lived regally with a generous pension.

Rex ita afficiēbātur ut rēgīnam illam repente in monastēriō dē Bermondsey conclūserit, omnēsque fortūnās eius et reditūs fiscō applicārit.

Notes: **rēgīna, -ae**, f: queen (Elizabeth Woodville); **repente**: suddenly; **monastērium, -iī**, n: monastery; **Bermondsey** (indeclinable): a monastery established before 715 CE; **conclūdō, -ere, -clūsī, -clūsus**: enclose, confine; **reditus, -ūs**, m: income, revenue; **fiscus, -ī**, m: state treasury, privy purse; **applicā(ve)rit; applicō, -āre, -āvī, -ātus**: apply, devote.

29.9. Sir Francis Bacon, *Historia Regni Henrici Septimi Regis Angliae* **2.11.** King Henry sent John, earl of Oxford, to intercept John de la Pole, Earl of Lincoln, who had endorsed Lambert Simnel, the ten-year-old pretender to the throne who was crowned "Edward VI" in Dublin in 1487. The young pretender was later pardoned and employed in the royal kitchens. Bacon implies here that Henry first pursued a diplomatic resolution. The Tower of London was historically a regal residence, famously used as a prison for Mary, queen of Scots and other disenfranchised royals.

At licet rex aurem eī benignam reservāret, erat tamen conditiō temporis tam perīculōsa ut statim mīserit comitem Oxoniae.

Notes: **benignus, -a, -um**: kind, friendly; **reservō, -āre, -āvī, -ātus**: reserve, keep; **perīculōsus, -a, -um**: dangerous; **Oxonia, -iae**, f: Oxford (i.e., the earl of Oxford); **obviam**: towards, to meet; **turris, -is (-ium)**, f: tower; **Londīnensis, -e**: of London; **perdūcō, -ere, -duxī, -ductus**: lead through, bring along.

29.10. Sir Francis Bacon, *Historia Regni Henrici Septimi Regis Angliae* 2.14. In June of 1487, the earl of Lincoln led his army to central England, where Henry's forces were already mustered, in preparation for the Battle of Stoke Field, a tiny village near Newark where the earl was soundly defeated.

Properē exercitum duxit ita ut inter castra hostium et oppidum Newarcī sē medium sisteret, nōlens eōrum exercitum illīus oppidī commoditāte gaudēre.

Notes: **properē**: quickly; **Newarcus, -ī**, m: Newark; **sistō, -ere, stitī, status**: stand, stop; **nōlens** + accusative / infinitive; **eōrum**: the king (plural, out of respect); **illīus**: the earl of Lincoln; **commoditās, -ātis**, f: symmetry, convenience, advantage.

29.11. Sir Thomas More, *Utopia* 1 (p. 78, Logan). More recounts a merry dialogue between a joker and a group of clerics. The joker has just suggested that all the poor be sent to Benedictine monasteries where the men should become lay brothers and the women nuns. None of the clerics are amused by this flippancy, except for one.

Cēterum theologus, quīdam frāter, hōc dictō in sacerdōtēs ac monachōs adeō est exhilarātus, ut iam ipse quoque coeperit lūdere.

Notes: **theologus, -ī**, m: theologian; **dictum, -ī**, n: word, witticism; **in**: "in the midst of"; **monachus, -ī**, m: monk; **exhilarō, -āre, -āvī, -ātus**: cheer up; **lūdō, -ere, lūsī, lūsus**: play, sport, tease.

29.12. Sir Thomas More, *Utopia* 1 (p. 100, Logan). In Utopia there is no need of ambition or greed.

Tam commodē rēs administrantur, ut et virtūtī pretium sit.
Notes: **commodē**: properly; **administrō, -āre, -āvī, -ātus**: manage.

EXTRA PASSAGES: ROMAN BRITAIN

Britain was an exotic place to the Romans, where even the weather, like its bellicose inhabitants, behaved strangely. Britain was the "outpost of the Empire," the last territory to come under Roman hegemony and never fully Romanized.

29.13. Caesar, *de Bello Gallico* 4.28.2. As a contingent of ships conveying cavalry reinforcements for Caesar's invasion of Britain in 55 BCE draws near the island, a combination of violent storm and high tides forces them off course.

Quae cum adpropinquārent Britanniae et ex castrīs vidērentur, tanta tempestās subitō coorta est ut nulla eārum cursum tenēre posset, sed aliae eōdem unde erant profectae referrentur, aliae ad inferiōrem partem insulae, quae est propius sōlis occāsum, magnō suō cum perīculō dēicerentur.
Notes: **quae** (*nāvēs*); **adpropinquō, -āre, -āvī, -ātus**: approach; **coorior, -īrī, coortus sum**: arise, appear, break out; **nulla** (*nāvis*); **eōdem** (*locō*); **occāsus, -ūs**, m: setting, west; **dēiciō, -ere, -iēcī, -iectus**: throw, cast, hurl, throw off course.

29.14. Tacitus, *Agricola* 12.3. Among the remarkable features of Britain is its higher latitude, affecting the length of days.

Nox clāra et extrēmā Britanniae parte brevis, ut fīnem atque initium lūcis exiguō discrīmine internoscās.
Notes: **discrīmen, discrīminis**, n: interval; **internoscō, -ere, -nōvī, -nōtus**: distinguish between; Tacitus here omits the adverb that triggers the result clause.

29.15. Tacitus, *Annales* **14.34.2.** The entire nation of the Iceni comes out to witness the final battle between Boudicca and the Romans in 61 CE. Boudicca was defeated, her army crushed, and even the women and pack animals were slaughtered. Today Boudicca and her two daughters are commemorated in an elegant statue next to Westminster Bridge and the Houses of Parliament in London.

At Britannōrum cōpiae passim per catervās et turmās exultābant—
quanta nōn aliās multitūdō, et animō adeō ferōcī, ut coniugēs
quoque testēs victōriae sēcum traherent plaustrīsque impōnerent,
quae super extrēmum ambitum campī pōsuerant.

Notes: **passim:** everywhere; **caterva, -ae,** f: crowd, troop; **turma, -ae,** f: cavalry band, troop, throng; **exultō, -āre, -āvī, -ātus:** rejoice, prance about; **nōn aliās:** for no other reason, in no other way; **ferox (-ōcis):** courageous, warlike, brave; **plaustrum, -ī,** n: wagon, cart; **ambitus, -ūs,** m: circuit, edge.

Indirect Commands

1. An **INDIRECT COMMAND**, introduced by **ut** for positive clauses and **nē** for negative clauses, often follows verbs of commanding, urging, and begging. Indirect commands convey encouragement, orders, or warnings. They are considered substantive clauses of purpose (sometimes known as jussive noun clauses) and function as the subject or direct object of the "commanding" verbs that govern them. Consider the following examples:

Plautus, *Mercator* 426–27: **Senex est quidam, quī illam <u>mandāvit</u> mihi / <u>ut</u> <u>emerem</u>**. There is a certain old man who <u>commanded</u> me <u>to buy her</u>.
    The underlined clause is the direct object of *mandāvit*.

Ovid, *Metamorphoses* 2.564–65: **Mea poena volucrēs / <u>admonuisse</u> potest, <u>nē</u> vōce perīcula quaerant**. My punishment is able <u>to have warned</u> (other) birds <u>not to seek troubles with a chirp</u>.
    The underlined clause is the direct object of *admonuisse*.

Frontinus, *de Aquaeductu Urbis Romae* 2.104: **Ā senātū <u>est imperātum</u> ut inspicerent aquās pūblicās inīrentque numerum salientium pūblicōrum**. It <u>has been commanded</u> by the Senate <u>that they inspect the public waterworks and calculate the number of public fountains</u>.
    The underlined clause is the subject of *imperātum est*.

2. The following verbs typically introduce indirect commands:

    cohortor, -ārī, -ātus: encourage, incite
    hortor, -ārī, -ātus: encourage, urge
    imperō, -āre, -āvī, -ātus (+ dative): order

moneō, -ēre, -uī, -itus: warn
orō, -āre, -āvī, -ātus: speak, beg
persuādeō, -ēre, -suāsī, -suāsus (+ dative): convince, prevail upon
postulō, -āre, -āvī, -ātus: demand
prōnuntiō, -āre, -āvī, -ātus: declare
rogō, -āre, -āvī, -ātus: speak, beg
suādeō, -ēre, suāsī, suāsus (+ dative): advise, persuade, urge

N.B. Some Latin verbs, such as *iubeō* ("I order") and *vetō* ("I forbid"), take an infinitive rather than an indirect command, as in these examples:

Cicero, *ad Familiares* 7.2.3: **Quam ob rem valdē <u>iubeō</u> <u>gaudēre</u> tē**. For this reason <u>I order</u> you <u>to rejoice</u> very much.

Vergil, *Aeneid* 12.806: **Ulterius <u>temptāre</u> <u>vetō</u>**. I <u>forbid</u> (you) <u>to try</u> more.

3. In poetry, the conjunction *ut* is occasionally omitted from the indirect command. Consider the following examples:

Martial 5.49.12: **<u>Vītēs</u> <u>censeō</u> porticum Philippī**. <u>I advise</u> <u>you to avoid</u> Philippus's colonnade.

Horace, *Carmina* 1.2.30: **Tandem <u>veniās</u> <u>precāmur</u>**. Finally, we <u>beg</u> that you come.

4. Indirect commands typically employ the same **SEQUENCE OF TENSES** that you learned for purpose clauses in *NLP* 28 and result clauses in *NLP* 29:

   (a) when the main verb is present or future tense, the subjunctive verb in the indirect command is present tense (primary sequence)
   (b) when the main verb is one of the past tenses (imperfect, perfect, or pluperfect), the subjunctive verb in indirect command is imperfect tense (secondary sequence)

Consider the following examples:

Plautus, *Bacchides* 702: **Enim nīl nisi ut <u>amētis</u> <u>imperō</u>**. For I <u>command</u> nothing except that <u>you love (me)</u>. (primary sequence)

Caesar, *de Bello Gallico* 3.26.1: **Crassus equitum praefectōs <u>cohortātus</u>, ut magnīs praemiīs pollicitātiōnibusque suōs <u>excitārent</u>, quid fierī vellet ostendit.** Crassus, <u>having urged</u> the cavalry prefects <u>to rouse</u> their own men with great rewards and promises, showed them what he wanted to happen. (secondary sequence)

I. Required Vocabulary

NOUNS

poena, -ae, f: punishment, penalty (**poenam dare**: to pay the penalty)

socius, -iī, m: ally, follower
tribūnus, -ī, m: tribune, representative

coniūrātiō, -iōnis, f: conspiracy
ordō, ordinis, m: series, row, rank

ADJECTIVES

perpetuus, -a, -um: continuous, uninterrupted

commūnis, -e: shared, universal, general

VERBS

occupō, -āre, -āvī, -ātus: take possession, seize
orō, -āre, -āvī, -ātus: speak, beg
postulō, -āre, -āvī, -ātus: demand
prōnuntiō, -āre, -āvī, -ātus: declare

persuādeō, -ēre, -suāsī, -suāsus (+ dative): convince, prevail upon
suādeō, -ēre, suāsī, suāsus (+ dative): advise, persuade, urge

cōgō, -ere, coēgī, coactus: compel, force
dīmittō, -ere, -mīsī, -missus: send away, lose
discēdō, -ere, -cessī: depart, go away
impellō, -ere, -pulī, -pulsus: incite, impel
parcō, -ere, pepercī (+ dative): spare, refrain from injuring
pendō, -ere, pependī, pensus: pay, weigh out

cohortor, -ārī, cohortātus sum: encourage, incite

adeō, -īre, -iī, -itus: approach
exeō, -īre, -īvī or -iī, -itus: go out
transeō, -īre, -īvī or -iī, -itus: cross

PREPOSITIONS
    prope (+ accusative): near (can also function as an adverb)

CONJUNCTIONS AND ADVERBS
    priusquam: before
    ūnā: together (with)

II. Translate the following sentences from Latin to English or English to Latin.

1. Sociīs persuāsit ut dē castrīs suīs cum omnibus populīs discēderent.
2. Propter coniūrātiōnem cīvēs ōrāvērunt nē līberōs omnēs condemnārēmus.
3. Hōs cohortārī nōn poteram ut flūmen transīrent atque Rōmam adīrent.
4. Caesar mīlitibus imperat ut oppida occupent sed nē hostēs caedant.
5. Cicerō senātum hortātus est nē Catilīnae parceret.
6. Posterō diē imperātor pervēnit postulāvitque nē tribūnī līberōs suōs in perīcula dīmitterent.
7. Petimus ut antiquam virtūtem quam diūtissimē teneās.
8. Mīlitibus morantibus tribūnus prōnuntiat ut quisque eōrum castra pōnat.
9. The general encouraged the ranks to cross the fields and approach the city.
10. The allies persuade Caesar to spare them.
11. The mothers begged the king not to compel their children to pay the penalty.
12. The consul orders the Roman citizens to seek glory and honor.

Caesar's De Bello Gallico

It was typical for a consul at Rome to assume the governorship of a province after his term of office. By 59 BCE, Julius Caesar was deeply in debt after two costly political offices: the aedileship of 65 BCE, when he hosted lavish athletic games, and his consulship. Thus Caesar lobbied for provinces that would provide opportunities for foreign wars, whereby he could plunder and then repay his creditors.

In 58 BCE, Caesar assumed a five-year term as governor of Illyricum (northwest of Greece), Cisalpine Gaul, and Transalpine Gaul, with four legions under his command. In addition to acquiring wealth, Caesar was also motivated by the desire for personal glory and avenging an old injury: the Gallic invasion and sack of Rome in 390 BCE (*de Bello Gallico* 1.30). At Luca in 56 BCE Caesar's appointment was extended for another term, and he served as governor for an unprecedented eight years (the typical term for a provincial governor was a single three- or five-year term).

While in winter quarters, Caesar composed the *Commentarii*, which he then sent to Rome, in part as a record of his achievements, and in part as a means of preserving popular support back in Rome. In addition to the *Commentarii de Bello Gallico* and *Commentarii de Bello Civili*, Caesar also penned a now lost two-volume *de Analogia* (on eliminating grammatical irregularities) dedicated to Cicero, and an *Anti-Cato* in reaction to Cicero's *Cato*, an encomium to the hyper-republican, pro-senatorial, anti-Caesarian Cato, who died in battle at Utica in 46 BCE. Scholars agree on the excellence of Caesar's lucid, unadorned style (in contrast to the complex periods of Cicero), but are divided on Caesar's literary intent. Some take Caesar at his word, as producing an honest account of events in Gaul. Others see Caesar as a calculating tyrant whose *Commentarii* are a shameless propagandistic manipulation of events for political advancement. The truth probably lies somewhere in the middle. Caesar naturally attempted to present himself in the best light, and he should not be judged by the modern ideal of "historical impartiality," a concept that was interpreted quite differently in antiquity. Nonetheless, verbal technique was politically significant, and it is likely that Caesar's unequivocal style was intended to convey a political message, linking him with the "popular" political party at Rome (see *NLP* 32).

Famously written in the third person, the *Commentarii de Bello Gallico* is arranged in eight books, each covering one year of Caesar's governorship. The work opens with a quick survey of the Gallic provinces and their peoples before launching into the initial campaigns: Caesar's victories against the Helvetian prince Orgetorix, who rallied his people to emigrate and unite against Rome, and against the Germanic warlord Ariovistus, who threatened the Arverni and Sequani, Roman allies in Gaul. In 57 BCE (Book 2), Caesar turns his attentions to the Belgae, who rallied to stave off the expansion of Roman military power in Gaul, culminating in a bloody Roman victory. In 56 BCE (Book 3), Caesar subdues the seafaring Veneti, whose breach of diplomacy—the capture and imprisonment of Roman envoys—was unforgivable. In 55 BCE (Book 4), Caesar comes again into conflict with the Germanic Suebi, who, after crossing into Gaul, treacherously attacked Roman troops during peace negotiations. At this point Caesar alarmed the Germans by building a bridge over the Rhine and crossing into their territory. Caesar campaigned in Britain in 55 BCE (Book 4), surviving several skirmishes and eventually routing the Britons before returning to the Continent to his winter quarters. Returning to Britain in 54 BCE (Book 5), and bringing Gallic hostages with him to prevent insurrection in Gaul, Caesar initially faced an army of united British tribes. In time, these powerful tribes sought alliances with Rome, and Caesar returned to Gaul in victory. That winter, however, Gallic troops led by the Eburonian Ambiorix attacked two camps of Roman soldiers. Book 6 focuses on Caesar's efforts to avenge those soldiers slain by Ambiorix, and describes the devastation of Ambiorix's allies. Caesar again crossed into Germany, hoping that a show of Roman power would discourage the Germans from aiding Ambiorix. Caesar's account pauses for ethnographies of the Gauls and Germans, including a digression on the strange animals of the Hercynian forest in Germany. In 52 BCE (Book 7), Caesar faced Vercingetorix, a nobleman of the Averni, who rallied the Gallic tribes into a united force in order to oust their Roman invaders. Caesar's account culminates with the demoralizing Roman defeat at Gergovia and the description of Caesar's stunning and complex siegeworks at Alesia, where Vercingetorix finally surrendered. In 51 BCE (Book 8, almost certainly composed by his lieutenant Aulus Hirtius), Caesar dealt with a number of further revolts—quelled swiftly and mercilessly—before ending his term and turning his attentions to the war being fomented by his political enemies in the city.

De Bello Gallico is an extraordinary work. Caesar focuses on the terrain, the movements of his enemies, his own changing strategy, his unabating concern for the well-being of his men, and his staunch defense of Rome's allies. Hardly modest or reticent, Caesar preserves the full experience of the army on campaign, from supply lines to forced marches, raids, sieges, and combat, withholding neither the enemy's brutality nor his own. Assuming a readership familiar with technical military details, Caesar provides unique insight into the psyche of a general on campaign and a record of the achievements of a brilliant strategist, who was greatly admired by the militarily adept Napoléon Bonaparte and whose methods continue to be studied. The French populist emperor Napoléon III, who funded excavations of Caesarian battle sites and reputedly traveled with a copy of *de Bello Gallico*, wrote *A History of Julius Caesar*, comparing the Roman dictator to himself and his famous uncle, Napoléon Bonaparte.

Caesar's *de Bello Gallico* remains a mainstay of Latin language education because of the clarity of its language and rhetorical interest. The work also inspired Vincent d'Indy's *De Bello Gallico*, an opera recounting the French struggle against the Germans in World War I, as well as René Goscinny's comic book series *Asterix and Obelix*, whose eponymous heroes inhabit the unconquered "fourth part" of Gaul.

SUGGESTIONS FOR FURTHER READING:

Canfora, Luciano. *Julius Caesar: The People's Dictator.* University of Edinburgh, 2006.

Fuller, J. F. C. *Julius Caesar: Man, Soldier, and Tyrant.* Rutgers University, 1965.

Jimenez, Ramon. *Caesar Against the Celts.* Sarpedon, 1996.

Meier, Christian. *Caesar: A Biography.* Translated by David McLintock. HarperCollins, 1982.

Weinstock, Stefan. *Divus Julius.* Oxford, 1971.

PASSAGES

30.1. Caesar, *de Bello Gallico* **1.2.1.** By 61 BCE, Orgetorix, a wealthy Helvetian aristocrat, instigated a Helvetian migration into southwestern Gaul, eventually provoking conflict with Caesar.

Is, M. Messālā et M. Pūpiō Pīsōne consulibus, regnī cupiditāte inductus coniūrātiōnem nōbilitātis fēcit et cīvitātī persuāsit ut dē fīnibus suīs cum omnibus cōpiīs exīrent.

Notes: **is**: Orgetorix; **Marcus Messāla, Marcī Messālae**, m: a talented orator who served as praetor during Cicero's consulship in 63 BCE; **Marcus Pūpius Pīsō, Marcī Pūpiī Pīsōnis**, m: a Roman statesman who served under Sulla during the civil wars of the 80s BCE (see *NLP* 32), and then under Pompey against Mithridates; **cupiditās, -ātis**, f: desire, ambition; **indūcō, -ere, -duxī, -ductus**: lead in, bring in; **nōbilitās, -ātis**, f: renown, glory.

30.2. Caesar, *de Bello Gallico* **1.3.5.** In preparation for the Gallic migration, Orgetorix advises his allies.

Is sibi lēgātiōnem ad cīvitātēs suscēpit. In eō itinere persuādet Casticō, Catamantāloedis fīliō, Sēquanō—cuius pater regnum in Sēquanīs multōs annōs obtinuerat et ā senātū populī Rōmānī amīcus appellātus erat—ut regnum in cīvitāte suā occupāret, quod pater ante habuerat. Itemque Dumnorīgī Aeduō, frātrī Dīviciācī, quī eō tempore prīncipātum in cīvitāte obtinēbat ac maximē plēbī acceptus erat, ut idem cōnārētur persuādet. Eīque fīliam suam in mātrimōnium dat.

Notes: **is**: Orgetorix; **lēgātiō, -iōnis**, f: embassy; **Casticus, -ī**, m: a Sequani nobleman; **Catamantaloedes, -is**, m: a nobleman of the Sequani; **Sēquanus, -ī**, m: a member of a Celtic tribe dwelling west of the Helvetians; **obtineō, -ēre, -uī, -tentus**: hold, obtain, gain; **Dumnorix, -īgis**, m: an Aeduan nobleman; **Aeduī, -ōrum**, m (plural): a Celtic tribe of central Gaul; **Dīviciācus, -ī**, m: an Aeduan nobleman who served as a Druidic priest, whose name may mean "avenger." The Aedui appointed Diviciacus as their spokesman during negotiations with Caesar after Dumnorix's defeat; **prīncipātus, -ūs**, m: principate, rule; **mātrimōnium, -iī**, n: marriage.

30.3. Caesar, *de Bello Gallico* **1.5.4.** After Orgetorix's trial and death, the Helvetians are determined to follow through with their plan to emigrate, and they approach other neighboring tribes to join them.

Persuādent Rauricīs et Tulingīs et Latobrīgīs fīnitimīs ūtī, eōdem ūsī consiliō—oppidīs suīs vīcīsque exustīs—ūnā cum iīs proficiscantur. Boiōsque—quī trans Rhēnum incoluerant et in agrum Nōricum transierant Nōrēiamque oppugnābant—receptōs ad sē sociōs sibi adsciscunt.

Notes: **Rauricī, -ōrum**, m (plural): a Celtic tribe dwelling west of the Helvetians; **Tulingī, -ōrum**, m (plural): a Celtic tribe dwelling north of the Helvetians; **Latobrīgī, -ōrum**, m (plural): a Celtic tribe dwelling north of the Helvetians; **fīnitimus, -a, -um**: bordering, adjacent; **vīcus, -ī**, m: village, district; **exūrō, -ere, -ussī, -ustus**: burn up, destroy; **Boiī, -ōrum**, m (plural): a scattered Celtic tribe that settled in northern Italy, central Gaul, and central Germany; **Rhēnus, -ī**, m: the Rhine River; **incolō, -ere, -uī**: live, dwell, inhabit; **Nōricus, -a, -um**: Noric (the territory of Noricum was located between the Alps and the Danube); **Nōrēia, -ae**, f: a town in Noricum; **oppugnō, -āre, -āvī, -ātus**: attack; **adsciscō, -ere, -scīvī, -scītus**: receive, admit, approve.

30.4. Caesar, *de Bello Gallico* **4.27.4.** In 55 BCE, the Britons, who have just been defeated by the Romans in battle, sue for peace.

In petendā pāce eius reī culpam in multitūdinem contulērunt, et propter imprūdentiam ut ignoscerētur petīvērunt.

Notes: **in petendā pāce**: "in seeking peace" (gerundive); **imprūdentia, -iae**, f: ignorance; **ignoscō, -ere, ignōvī, ignōtus** (+ dative): forgive, overlook (construe with *culpa*).

30.5. Caesar, *de Bello Gallico* **5.34.3.** Ambiorix's strategy to counter Roman battlefield skill and bravery.

Quā rē animadversā Ambiorix prōnuntiārī iubet, ut procul tēla coniciant neu propius accēdant et, quam in partem Rōmānī impetum fēcerint, cēdant.

Notes: **animadvertō, -ere, -vertī, -versus**: notice, observe; **coniciō, -ere, -iēcī, -iectus**: throw, hurl; **neu**: and not; **propius**: closer.

30.6. Caesar, *de Bello Gallico* **5.36.1.** Caesar's lieutenant Sabinus requests a parlay with Ambiorix, in whose goodwill he continues to trust.

Hīs rēbus permōtus Quintus Titūrius, cum procul Ambiorīgem suōs cohortantem conspexisset, interpretem suum Gnaeum Pompēium ad eum mittit rogātum ut sibi mīlitibusque parcat.

Notes: **hīs rēbus**: i.e., Roman military setbacks; **permoveō, -ēre, -mōvī, -mōtus**: stir up, excite, agitate, disturb; **Quintus Titūrius Sabīnus, Quintī Titūriī Sabīnī**, m: Caesar's lieutenant; **Ambiorix, -īgis**, m; **conspiciō, -ere, -spexī, -spectus**: catch sight of, perceive; **interpres, interpretis**, m/f: mediator, messenger; **Gnaeus Pompēius, Gnaeī Pompēiī**, m: a Gallic ally who had taken the name of his Roman patron; **eum**: Ambiorix; **rogātum**: "to ask" (supine: see *NLP* 36).

30.7. Caesar, *de Bello Gallico* **5.36.3.** Sabinus here urges his fellow lieutenant Cotta to meet with Ambiorix.

Ille cum Cottā sauciō commūnicat, sī videātur, pugnā ut excēdant et cum Ambiorīge ūnā colloquantur.

Notes: **Cotta, -ae**, m: Caesar's lieutenant who served with distinction in Britain and Gaul; **saucius, -a, -um**: wounded; **commūnicō, -āre, -āvī, -ātus**: confer (with); **videātur**: "it seems best"; **exēdō, -ere, -cessī, -cessus**: leave; **colloquor, -loquī, collocūtus sum**: negotiate (with).

30.8. Caesar, *de Bello Gallico* **5.37.1.** Ambiorix agrees to meet with Sabinus, who comes with an armed guard. In the end, Ambiorix executes the naïve Sabinus.

Sabīnus quōs in praesentia tribūnōs mīlitum circum sē habēbat et prīmōrum ordinum centuriōnēs sē sequī iubet; et—cum propius Ambiorīgem accessisset—iussus arma abicere, imperātum facit suīsque ut idem faciant imperat.

Notes: **in praesentia**: "for the present"; **circum** (+ accusative): around; **prīmus ordō, prīmī ordinis**, m: a centurion of the first cohort (these officers outranked the other legionary centurions); **centuriō, -iōnis**, m: centurion, commander of 100 men; **propius**: see *NLP* 30.5; **imperātum, -ī**, n: command, order; **abiciō, -ere, -iēcī, -iectus**: throw down.

30.9. Caesar, *de Bello Gallico* **5.38.2.** After Sabinus's execution, and Cotta's death in battle, Ambiorix rallies other anti-Roman tribes.

Rē dēmonstrātā, Aduatucīsque concitātīs, posterō diē in Nerviōs pervēnit hortāturque, nē suī in perpetuum līberandī atque ulciscendī Rōmānōs prō eīs—quās accēperint—iniūriīs occāsiōnem dīmittant.

Notes: **dēmonstrō, -āre, -āvī, -ātus**: explain, describe clearly; **Aduatucī, -ōrum**, m (plural): a Germanic tribe dwelling in eastern Gallia Beligica; **concitō, -āre, -āvī, -ātus**: stir up, incite; **Nerviī, -iōrum**, m (plural): a powerful Belgic tribe dwelling in northern Gaul; **in perpetuum**: forever; **līberandī atque ulciscendī**: "of freeing (themselves from) and taking vengeance (against)" (gerundives, construe with *occāsiōnem*); **occāsiō, -iōnis**, f: opportunity.

30.10. Caesar, *de Bello Gallico* 5.48.2. Having just learned of Sabinus's death and the dangers faced by his lieutenants throughout Gaul, Caesar succeeds in sending a dispatch (written in Greek) to Cicero's brother Quintus, who distinguished himself during the Nervi siege.

Tum cuidam ex equitibus Gallīs magnīs praemiīs persuādet utī ad Cicerōnem epistolam dēferat.

Notes: **Gallus, -a, -um**: Gallic; **epistolam** = *epistulam*.

30.11. Caesar, *de Bello Gallico* 6.9.7. In 53 BCE, hoping to lure out Ambiorix, Caesar campaigned against the Germans across the Rhine. Here, fearing that Roman retribution might be universal, the Ubii (a Germanic tribe) remind Caesar of their loyalty, and they seek his protection.

Petunt atque ōrant ut sibi parcat, nē commūnī odiō Germānōrum innocentēs prō nocentibus poenās pendant.

Notes: **Germānus, -a, -um**: of Germany, of a German; **innocens (-entis)**: innocent, blameless; **nocens (-entis)**: guilty.

30.12. Caesar, *de Bello Gallico* 7.71.1–2. In 52 BCE, the Gallic leader Vercingetorix raises troops to fight against Caesar.

Vercingetorix, priusquam mūnītiōnēs ab Rōmānīs perficiantur, consilium capit omnem ab sē equitātum noctū dīmittere. Discēdentibus mandat ut suam quisque eōrum cīvitātem adeat omnēsque—quī per aetātem arma ferre possint—ad bellum cogant.

Notes: **mūnītiō, -iōnis**, f: fortification; **perficiō, -ere, -fēcī, -fectus**: complete, accomplish; **consilium capere**: to form a plan; **equitātus, -ūs**, m: cavalry; **noctū**: at night; **mandō, -āre, -āvī, -ātus**: commit, entrust, order; **per aetātem**: "by reason of age."

EXTRA PASSAGES: MARCUS LICINIUS CRASSUS

Marcus Licinius Crassus began his influential political career as one of Sulla's lieutenants during the civil war of the 80s BCE (between Sulla and Marius: see *NLP* 32), after which he amassed a large fortune through real-estate speculation. Together with Pompey, after routing the slave revolt led by Spartacus, he demanded the consulship for 70 BCE. Crassus quickly recognized Julius Caesar's potential and became his financial benefactor, underwriting the games of Caesar's aedileship, which helped to guarantee the rising politician's popularity. By 59 BCE, Caesar, Crassus, and Pompey entered into a powerful but unofficial partnership (the so-called first triumvirate), agreeing to protect one another's political interests—thus securing the governorship of Gaul for Caesar, a land grant to settle veterans who had served under Pompey, and lucrative tax contracts for Crassus. This agreement was renewed in 56 BCE. After his second co-consulship with Pompey in 55 BCE, Crassus obtained the governorship of Syria, from which he launched a campaign into Parthia, seeking military glory in his own right. Lacking Caesar's charisma and military genius, Crassus found himself unequal to the task of leading infantry troops against swift, highly skilled mounted archers. Crassus died in battle at Carrhae in Turkey, and—to his great shame—his battle standards were taken by the Parthians. (They were eventually returned to Rome in 20 BCE.)

30.13. Cicero, *ad Quintum Fratrem* 2.8.2. In 55 BCE, Cicero wished the Senate to pass some unspecified legislation on buildings and inscriptions (*operibus atque inscriptionibus*). Pompey seemed favorable but recommended discussing the matter with his co-consul, Crassus.

Cum Crassō sē dixit loquī velle mihique, ut idem facerem, suāsit.

Notes: **sē**: Pompey.

30.14. Sallust, *Bellum Catilinae* 48.4. At a meeting of the Senate on December 4, 63 BCE, Lucius Tarquinius, who had been arrested while setting out to join Catiline, unsuccessfully attempted to implicate Crassus in the Catilinarian conspiracy.

Praetereā sē missum ā M. Crasso, quī Catilīnae nuntiāret, nē eum Lentulus et Cethēgus aliīque ex coniūrātiōne dēprehensī terrērent eōque magis, properāret ad urbem accēdere, quō et cēterōrum animōs reficeret et illī facilius ē perīculō ēriperentur.

Notes: construe the passage with an understood *dixit*; **praetereā**: besides, moreover; **sē**: Lucius Tarquinius; **missum** (*esse*); **Catilīna, -ae**, m: the orchestrator of the plot; **eum**: Catiline; **Lentulus, -ī**, m: Catiline's ally Publius Cornelius Lentulus, the praetor who attempted to bribe the Allobroges (a Gallic tribe) to support Catiline's cause; **Cethēgus, -ī**, m: Catiline's ally Caius Cornelius Cethegus, one of the five leaders of the conspiracy; **dēprehendō, -ere, -hendī, -hensus**: seize, catch, observe; **eōque magis**: all the more; **quō**: where; **reficiō, -ere, -fēcī, -fectus**: restore, repair.

30.15. Suetonius, *Vita Iuliae* 24.1. In the spring of 56 BCE, Caesar summoned Pompey and Crassus to Luca to refresh their agreement and protect his own interests in Rome.

Crassum Pompēiumque in urbem prōvinciae suae Lūcam extractōs conpulit, ut dētrūdendī Domitiī causā consulātum alterum peterent.

Notes: **Lūca, -ae**, f: a town in Cisalpine Gaul; **extrahō, -ere, -traxī, -tractus**: draw out; **conpellō, -ere, -pulī, -pulsus**: force, compell; **dētrūdendī Domitiī causā**: "for the sake of dislodging Domitius" (gerundive). Lucius Domitius Ahenobarbus was among Caesar's most outspoken opponents; **consulātus, -ūs**, m: consulship.

Indirect Questions

1. **INDIRECT QUESTIONS** follow verbs of asking, doubting, or knowing, and they convey a query. Indirect questions are often introduced by **INTERROGATIVE CONJUNCTIONS**, including, but not limited to, the following:

cūr: why
quam: how
quārē: why
quō: where, to what place
ubi: when, where
unde: from where
utī: how
utrum . . . an: whether . . . or

Consider the following examples:

Cicero, *ad Atticum* 12.41.1: **Utrum sim factūrus eō ipsō diē <u>sciēs</u>**. <u>You will know</u> whether I would do (it) on that very day.

Horace, *Carmina* 1.8.1–3: **Lȳdia, <u>dīc</u>, per omnīs / tē deōs, ōrō, Sybarin cūr properēs amandō / perdere**. Lydia, <u>speak</u>, by all the gods, I beg you, <u>why do you hurry to destroy Sybaris by loving (him)?</u>

Cicero, *ad Atticum* 2.1.6: **Hoc facere illum mihi quam prōsit <u>nesciō</u>**. <u>I do not know</u> how it benefits me to make him this (i.e., a better citizen).

2. Indirect questions can also be introduced by **INTERROGATIVE PRONOUNS AND ADJECTIVES** (see *NLP* 16). (N.B. Interrogative pronouns and

adjectives closely resemble relative pronouns and adjectives. Other clues will help you to determine the exact construction. Focus on the **verb** that triggers the clause.) Consider the following examples:

Martial 5.33.1–2: **Quī sit / nesciō**. <u>I do not know</u> who he is.

Martial 5.5.61–2: **Cui trādās, Lupe, fīlium magistrō / quaeris** sollicitus diu **rogāsque**. Anxious for a long time, Lupus, <u>you seek and you ask</u> to which teacher you should hand over your son.

3. The following verbs often trigger indirect questions:

    memorō, -āre, -āvī, -ātus: mention, bring up
    mīror, -ārī, mīrātus sum: wonder
    nesciō, -īre, -īvī, -ītus: not know
    orō, -āre, -āvī, -ātus: ask, beg
    petō, -ere, -īvī / -iī, -ītus: seek, demand, ask, beg
    quaerō, -ere, quaesīvī, quaesītus: look for, seek
    requīrō, -ere, -quīsīvī, -quisītus: seek again, search for
    rogō, -āre, -āvī, -ātus: ask
    sciō, -īre, -īvī, -ītus: know
    videō, -ēre, vīdī, vīsus: see, look at, watch

N.B. Many of these verbs can also trigger either indirect statements or indirect commands. Again, you need to use other clues to determine the syntax. Focus on whether the sentence contains accusative / infinitive constructions, or interrogative conjunctions and subjunctive verbs.

4. Less frequently, indirect questions can be triggered by nouns, adjectives, or participles of asking, doubting, or knowing. Some of these expressions include, but are not limited to, the following:

    conscius sum: I am aware
    dubium est: there is a doubt, it is doubtful
    inscius sum: I am unaware
    quaesitum est: there is a question

Consider the following examples:

Ovid, *Metamorphoses* 11.716–17: **Prīmōque, quid illud / esset, erat dubium**. And at first there was <u>doubt</u> <u>as to what that was</u>.

Cicero, *ad Familiares* 13.8.1: **Quum et mihi conscius essem, quantī tē facerem, et tuam ergā mē benevolentiam expertus essem, non dubitāvī ā tē petere**... And since I was <u>aware</u> <u>of how much I made of you and how much I put to the test your kindness toward me</u>, I did not hesitate to seek from you ...

Cicero, *pro Milone* 26: **Quin etiam M. Favoniō, fortissimō virō, quaerentī ex eō quā spē fureret Milōne vīvō, respondit** . . . But he even responded to Marcus Favonius, a very brave man, <u>asking</u> him <u>in what hope he was raging</u> while Milo was still alive . . .

5. For indirect questions, Latin employs a slightly different SEQUENCE OF TENSES than the one you learned for purpose clauses, result clauses, and indirect commands.

    (a) when the main verb is present or future tense, the subjunctive verb in the indirect question is present or perfect tense (primary sequence)
    (b) when the main verb is one of the past tenses (imperfect, perfect, or pluperfect), the subjunctive verb in the indirect question is imperfect or pluperfect tense (secondary sequence)

Consider the following examples:

Martial 5.36: **Laudātus nostrō quīdam, Faustīne, libellō / dissimulat, quasi nīl debeat**. A certain man praised in our little book, Faustinus, <u>pretends</u> as if <u>he owes</u> nothing.
   Primary sequence with a present tense verb in the main clause and present tense subjunctive verb in the indirect question.

Pliny the Elder, *Naturalis Historia* 8.132: **Quōnam modō intellexerint mīror**. I <u>wonder</u> how <u>they knew</u>.
   Primary sequence with a present tense verb in the main clause and perfect tense subjunctive verb in the indirect question.

Cicero, *ad Atticum* 3.8.2: **Ille incertus ubi ego <u>essem</u> fortasse alium cursum petīvit**. Uncertain where I <u>was</u>, perhaps <u>he sought</u> another course.

    Secondary sequence with a perfect tense verb in the main clause and imperfect tense subjunctive verb in the indirect question. N.B. Although the indirect question depends on the adjective *incertus*, the tense of the subjunctive verb of the indirect question is determined by its relationship to the main verb.

Martial 1.23.3: **<u>Mīrābar</u> quārē numquam mē, Cotta, <u>vocāssēs</u>**. I was <u>wondering</u>, Cotta, why you had never <u>called</u> me.

    Secondary sequence with an imperfect tense verb in the main clause and pluperfect tense subjunctive verb in the indirect question.

This table summarizes the sequence of tenses for indirect questions:

SEQUENCE OF TENSES FOR INDIRECT QUESTIONS

Primary		Secondary	
Main Verb	Subjunctive Verb	Main Verb	Subjunctive Verb
Present Future	Present (current action) Perfect (past action)	Imperfect Perfect Pluperfect	Imperfect (current action) Pluperfect (past action)

I. Required Vocabulary

NOUNS

    mensa, -ae, f: table, course, meal
    rēgīna, -ae, f: queen

    famēs, -is (-ium), f: hunger
    iuventus, -ūtis, f: youth, the prime of life

    cāsus, -ūs, m: misfortune, fall
    sensus, -ūs, m: feeling, sense, understanding

    spēs, spēī, f: hope

ADJECTIVES

aeger, aegra, aegrum: sick, weary
dubius, -a, -um: doubtful, uncertain, wavering
rārus, -a, -um: scattered
rēgius, -a, -um: royal
varius, -a, -um: varied, different

insignis, -e: notable, remarkable
lēvis, -e: smooth, delicate

VERBS

memorō, -āre, -āvī, -ātus: remind, relate

lateō, -ēre, -uī: lie hidden

alō, -ere, -uī, alitus: nourish
effundō, -ere, -fūdī, -fūsus: pour out, squander, waste
laedō, -ere, laesī, laesus: hurt, wound, injure
requīrō, -ere, -quīsīvī, -quisītus: seek again, search for
respiciō, -ere, -spexī, -spectus: look back
tendō, -ere, tetendī, tentus: hasten, direct

PREPOSITIONS

circum (+ accusative): around

CONJUNCTIONS AND ADVERBS

forsitan: perhaps
quārē: why
quō: where, to what place
quō modō or **quōmodō**: how
seu: whether, or if

II. Translate the following sentences from Latin to English or English to Latin.

1. Ō Mūsa, nōbīs memorā cūr dolens rēgīna deum insignem pietāte virum laeserit.
2. Interim vidēbātis utī hostēs circum moenia pugnantēs fugerent.

3. Longō sermōne requīsīvimus, inter spemque metumque dubiī, seu amīcī nostrī vīverent sīve morerentur.

4. Sociī quae Rōmānōrum populōrum fuerint fāta petunt.

5. Sacerdōtēs spectāre tetendēre quantōs casūs dī ferrent.

6. Deinde quaerēmus quō modō imperātor fortis labōrem dūcat.

7. Ō rēgīna, iubēs nōs dīcere dolōrem malum: utī Trōiānae dīvitiae āmissae sint.

8. Videāmus utrum regnum in regiōnēs clārissimās an dūrissmās pateat.

9. You (plural) ask where the legions are pitching camp.

10. The citizens recalled how Caesar killed the enemy in battle.

11. The informer demanded why the citizens had lost so much money and property (goods).

12. We wonder whether the soldiers have endured or died in the war.

Publius Vergilius Maro (70–19 BCE)

Publius Vergilius Maro was born on 15 October 70 BCE on the family estate in the little village of Andes near Mantua. Broadly educated, Vergil studied rhetoric in Milan and Rome, and he joined the Epicurean school at Naples. His family lands were confiscated during the veteran resettlement program of 42–40 BCE, but later restored.

In 37 BCE Vergil published his *Eclogues*, ten pastoral pieces inspired by the Greek poet Theocritus (third century BCE). He altered the idyllic landscape of his Hellenistic predecessor by interjecting into the pastoral world elements of danger and political intrigue—the very things that were permeating Roman society in the waning years of the Republic. Vergil's shepherds were not mere tenders of sheep, enveloped by romantic visions of beautiful nymphs, but fierce commentators on Roman society.

Soon after the publication of the *Eclogues*, Vergil came to the attention of Maecenas, Octavian's trusted advisor and an important patron of the arts at Rome. By 29 BCE the poet completed his *Georgics*, a versified agricultural account in four books, in the tradition of Hesiod's *Works and Days*. Embedded in these discussions of Roman farming lie the seeds of Vergil's epic spirit. The *Georgics* end with an *epyllion*, or "little epic," which relates the story of the famous musician Orpheus and his beloved wife, Eurydice, who dies from a poisonous snakebite. Orpheus journeys to the underworld to plead for the restoration of his wife. His lyre playing so moves Proserpina that she grants Eurydice's return—provided that Orpheus not look upon his wife until they are both in the light of the upper world. They are almost home when Orpheus gives in to temptation and steals a glance at Eurydice, who in turn vanishes into thin air.

Vergil spent the remainder of his life on the *Aeneid*, a Roman national epic celebrating her legendary founder, Aeneas, perhaps the greatest poem in Latin and Rome's answer to Homer's *Iliad* and *Odyssey*. Vergil crafts a remarkable hero in Aeneas, a survivor of Troy who, while embodying the Roman ideals of *pietas*—devotion to family, state, and gods—also struggles with the burdens of such commitment. Despite his reluctance to assume the momentous duty of leading his Trojan survivors to Italy and establishing the community that will eventually become Rome, Aeneas triumphs.

Returning from Greece, Vergil died of illness at Brundisium on 21 September 19 BCE before completing his masterpiece. According to legend, dissatisfied with his work, Vergil left instructions for the manuscript to be burned if he died before finishing it!

SUGGESTIONS FOR FURTHER READING:

Desmond, Marilynn. *Reading Dido: Gender Textuality and the Medieval* Aeneid. University of Minnesota, 1994.

Farrell, Joseph and Michael C. J. Putnam. *A Companion to Vergil's* Aeneid *and Its Tradition*. Wiley, 2014.

Johnson, W. R. *Darkness Visible: A Study of Vergil's* Aeneid. University of California, 1979.

Panoussi, Vassiliki. *Greek Tragedy in Vergil's* Aeneid. Cambridge, 2014.

Volk, Katharina. *Vergil's* Eclogues. Oxford Readings in Classical Studies. Oxford, 2008.

Volk, Katharina. *Vergil's* Georgics. Oxford Readings in Classical Studies. Oxford, 2008.

Wiltshire, S. F. *Public and Private in Vergil's* Aeneid. University of Massachusetts, 1989.

PASSAGES

31.1. Vergil, *Aeneid* 1.8–11. In the opening lines, Vergil sets out both the plot and overarching themes of his great masterpiece. Here we learn that Aeneas' suffering is caused by the enmity of Juno, who had supported the Greek side in the Trojan War. Meter: dactylic hexameter.

Mūsa, mihī causās memorā, quō nūmine laesō,
quidve dolens, rēgīna deum tot volvere cāsūs
insignem pietāte virum, tot adīre labōrēs
impulerit. Tantaene animīs caelestibus īrae?

Notes: **volvō, -ere, volvī, volūtus**: roll, revolve, consider, endure; **de(ōr)um; caelestis, -e**: heavenly.

31.2. Vergil, *Aeneid* 1.216–19. Aeneas and his men have been driven to the shores of Carthage by a storm at sea. After enjoying a banquet of roasted venison, the men speculate about their missing colleagues. Meter: dactylic hexameter.

Postquam exempta famēs epulīs mensaeque remōtae,
āmissōs longō sociōs sermōne requīrunt,
spemque metumque inter dubiī, seu vīvere crēdant,
sīve extrēma patī nec iam exaudīre vocātōs.

Notes: **exempta** (*est*); **eximō, -ere, -ēmī, -emptus**: remove; **epulae, -ārum**, f (plural): banquet, feast; **remōtae** (*sunt*); **removeō, -ēre, -mōvī, -mōtus**: move back, withdraw; **inter**: here, the preposition follows its two objects for the sake of the meter; **extrēmum, -ī**, n: end (here, "death"); **exaudiō, -īre, -īvī, -ītus**: hear plainly.

31.3. Vergil, *Aeneid* 1.466–68. As Aeneas tours Dido's burgeoning city, he sees many sights, including a mural that depicts highlights of the Trojan War. Meter: dactylic hexameter.

Namque vidēbat, utī bellantēs Pergama circum
hāc fugerent Grāiī, premeret Trōiāna iuventus,
hāc Phryges, instāret currū cristātus Achīllēs.

Notes: **bellō, -āre, -āvī, -ātus**: wage war; **Pergama, -ōrum**, n (plural): the citadel of Troy; **hāc . . . hāc**: "in this scene . . . in that scene"; **Grāiī, -ōrum**, m (plural): Greeks; **Phryges, -um**: Trojans; **Phrygēs** (*fugerent*); **instō, -āre, institī**: press upon, pursue, harass, solicit; **cristātus, -a, -um**: tufted, plumed, crested; **Achīllēs, -is**, m: the Greek hero who dragged the corpse of Troy's champion, Hector, around the walls of Troy.

31.4. Vergil, *Aeneid* 1.718–20. Venus has sent her son Cupid, disguised as Aeneas' young child Ascanius, to make Dido fall in love with the Trojan warrior. Here Cupid-Ascanius works his mischief as he sits on the queen's lap. Meter: dactylic hexameter.

Haec oculīs, haec pectore tōtō
haeret et interdum gremiō fovet, inscia Dīdō,
insīdat quantus miserae deus.

Notes: **haec**: Dido; **haereō, -ēre, haesī, haesus**: cling, adhere to; **interdum**: sometimes; **gremium, -iī**, n: lap, bosom; **foveō, -ēre, fōvī, fōtus**: keep warm, cherish, caress; **inscius, -a, -um**: ignorant (of), not knowing; **Dīdō, -ūs**, f: the founder of Carthage; **insīdō, -ere, -sēdī, -sessus** (+ dative): settle (on), take possession.

31.5. Vergil, *Aeneid* 2.3–6. Dido has asked Aeneas to describe the last night of the Trojan War and his own escape from the war-torn city. Aeneas complies with her painful request. Meter: dactylic hexameter.

"Infandum, rēgīna, iubēs renovāre dolōrem,
Trōiānās ut opēs et lāmentābile regnum
ēruerint Danaī, quaeque ipse miserrima vīdī
et quōrum pars magna fuī."

Notes: **infandus, -a, -um**: unutterable, abominable; **renovō, -āre, -āvī, -ātus**: restore, renew; **lāmentābilis, -e**: doleful, lamentable; **ēruō, -ere, -ruī, -rutus**: overthrow, destroy; **Danaī, -ōrum**, m (plural): Greeks.

31.6. Vergil, *Aeneid* **2.506.** Priam, the king of Troy, was killed at an altar by Pyrrhus, the son of Achilles. Meter: dactylic hexameter.

Forsitan et Priamī fuerint quae fāta requīrās.

Notes: **Priamus, -ī,** m: the aged king of Troy.

31.7. Vergil, *Aeneid* **2.564–66.** After leaving Priam's palace, Aeneas finds himself alone in the city, speculating about the fate of his comrades. Meter: dactylic hexameter.

Respiciō et, quae sit mē circum cōpia, lustrō.
Dēseruēre omnēs dēfessī, et corpora saltū
ad terram mīsēre aut ignibus aegra dedēre.

Notes: **lustrō, -āre, -āvī, -ātus:** survey, look around; **dēfessus, -a, -um:** weary, exhausted; **saltus, -ūs,** m: leap, jump.

31.8. Vergil, *Aeneid* **2.736–40.** After escaping the burning city with his family, Aeneas discovers that his wife Creusa has fallen behind. Here, he returns to the now deserted city to look for her. In this passage, Vergil substitutes indicative verbs for the subjunctive verbs in the indirect question to make the probability of Creusa's misfortune all the more vivid. Meter: dactylic hexameter.

Namque āvia cursū
dum sequor et nōtā excēdō regiōne viārum,
heu miserō coniunx fātōne ērepta Creūsa
substitit, errāvitne viā seu lapsa resēdit,
incertum. Nec post oculīs est reddita nostrīs.

Notes: **āvium, -ī,** n: wilderness, remote region; **excēdō, -ere, -cessī, -cessus:** go out, withdraw; **heu:** alas; **subsistō, -ere, substitī:** stand still, remain standing; **labor, -ī, lapsus sum:** fall, glide, perish; **resīdō, -ere, -sēdī:** sit down; **incertus, -a, -um:** uncertain, doubtful; **incertum** (*erat*).

31.9. Vergil, *Aeneid* **5.4–7.** As Aeneas sails from Carthage, he sees the flames of Dido's funeral pyre. Meter: dactylic hexameter.

Quae tantum accenderit ignem
causa latet; dūrī magnō sed amōre dolōrēs
pollūtō nōtumque furens quid fēmina possit
triste per augurium Teucrōrum pectora ducunt.

Notes: **accendō, -ere, -ī, accensus:** ignite, set on fire; **polluō, -ere, -uī, -ūtus:** defile; **furō, -ere:** rage, be mad; **nōtum, -ī, n:** knowledge, knowing; **possit** (*facere*); **augurium, -iī, n:** augury, the observation and interpretation of omens, prophecy; **Teucrus, -a, -um:** Trojan.

31.10. Vergil, *Aeneid* **6.197–98.** After long searching in vain for a golden bough, the token that will grant a living person entrance to the underworld, Aeneas sees a sign—two doves sent by his mother—whose flight path he now follows. Meter: dactylic hexameter.

Vestīgia pressit
observans quae signa ferant, quō tendere pergant.

Notes: **observō, -āre, -āvī, -ātus:** watch, attend to.

31.11. Vergil, *Aeneid* **7.812–17.** Here we meet the great *bellatrix* Camilla, the formidable ally of Aeneas' enemy Turnus, and a desirable bride. Meter: dactylic hexameter.

Illam omnis tectīs agrīsque effūsa iuventus
turbaque mīrātur mātrum et prōspectat euntem,
attonitīs inhians animīs ut rēgius ostrō
vēlet honos lēvīs umerōs, ut fībula crīnem
aurō internectat, Lyciam ut gerat ipsa pharetram
et pastōrālem praefīxā cuspide myrtum.

Notes: **illam:** Camilla; **prōspiciō, -ere, -spexī, -spectus:** see, look out, take care; **attonitus, -a, -um:** thunderstruck, terrified; **inhiō, -āre:** stand agape, desire, covet; **ostrum, -ī, n:** purple dye; **vēlō, -āre, -āvī, -ātus:** cover, wrap, hide; **honos** = *honor*; **umerus, -ī, m:** shoulder; **fībula, -ae,** f: buckle, clasp; **crīnis, -is (-ium),** m: hair; **internectō, -ere:** bind; **Lycius, -a, -um:** Lycian, from western Turkey, an exotic eastern land; **pharetra, -ae,** f: quiver; **pastōrālis, -e:** of a shepherd, pastoral; **praefīgō, -ere, -fixī, -fixus:** fasten, pierce; **cuspis, cuspidis,** f: point (of a spear); **myrtus, -ī,** f: myrtle tree, staff of myrtle wood.

31.12. Vergil, *Aeneid* 12.914–18. In the final duel between Turnus and Aeneas, the once swaggering and brash Turnus begins to waver, fearing death and despairing that there is no escape. Meter: dactylic hexameter.

> Tum pectore sensūs
> vertuntur variī. Rutulōs aspectat et urbem,
> cunctāturque metū lētumque instāre tremescit.
> Nec quō sē ēripiat, nec quā vī tendat in hostem,
> nec currūs usquam videt aurīgamve sorōrem.

Notes: **Rutulus, -ī**, m: a Rutulian, a follower of Turnus; **aspectō, -āre**: look at, observe; **cunctor, -ārī, cunctātus sum**: delay, hesitate; **lētum, -ī**, n: death; **instō, -āre, institī**: press upon, pursue, harass, solicit; **tremescō, -ere**: tremble, quake (+ infinitive); **usquam**: ever; **aurīga, -ae**, m: charioteer; **sorōrem**: Turnus's sister Juturna had whisked him out of battle as Aeneas was seeking to engage him in combat: *Aeneid* 12.468–80.

EXTRA PASSAGES: TITUS LUCRETIUS CARUS

Among Vergil's literary models was Titus Lucretius Carus (99–55 BCE), an Epicurean philosopher who used the medium of poetry to make the difficult lessons of philosophy more palatable to the educated reader. Lucretius describes this maverick approach as "honeying the cup" (philosophy was usually composed in prose, which was considered less aesthetically pleasing). In the six books of his *de Rerum Natura*, Lucretius explains this philosophical system, devised by the eponymous founder of the system, Epicurus (341–240 BCE). Epicurus had adapted the atomic theory of Democritus (fifth century BCE) into a fully integrated system of physics and ethics. All material objects are comprised of atoms (literally, "uncuttable" objects) and void. These atoms come together into various configuration to form all sensible objects, including inanimate objects, animals, people, and even souls. When a person dies, the atoms of both body and soul dissipate to form new bodies and new souls. Therefore, there is no reason to fear death. Nor is there cause for superstition or fear of natural phenomena (thunder, illness), which can all be explained quite sensibly by the simple tenets of Epicurean physics. The goal of the Epicurean disciple is a life free from anxiety, obtained by seeking tranquillity (*ataraxia*) through an understanding of the natural world. Because the Epicureans also believed that abstention from public life contributed to this tranquillity, the philosophy found little favor among the *pietas*-driven Romans, who much preferred Stoicism, a system that expounded much the same ethics (integrated with Stoic physics) while also advocating that well-born citizens fulfill obligations to the state.

31.13. Lucretius, *de Rerum Natura* 1.55–57. Lucretius emphasizes that the universe works according to strict scientific principles and the gods have no interest in human affairs. Meter: dactylic hexameter.

> Disserere incipiam et rērum prīmordia pandam,
> unde omnīs nātūra creet rēs, auctet alatque,
> quōve eadem rursum nātūra perempta resolvat.

Notes: **disserō, -ere, -ruī, -sertus**: explain; **prīmordium, -iī,** n: origin, beginnings; **pandō, -ere, -ī, pandus** or **passus**: unfold, reveal; **auctō, -āre, -āvī, -ātus**: increase; **quō** (*modō*); **perimō, -ere, -ēmī, -emptus**: destroy, kill, prevent; **resolvō, -ere, -solvī, -solūtus**: weaken.

31.14. Lucretius, *de Rerum Natura* 1.645–46. Here Lucretius debunks Heraclitus's theory that fire is the basic material of the universe. Meter: dactylic hexameter.

> Nam cūr tam variae rēs possent esse, requīrō,
> ex ūnō sī sunt ignī pūrōque creātae?

Notes: **pūrus, -a, -um**: clean, pure.

31.15. Lucretius, *de Rerum Natura* 4.269–70. The Epicurean theory of optics. Meter: dactylic hexameter.

> Nunc age. Cūr ultrā speculum videātur imāgo
> percipe: nam certē penitus remmōta vidētur.

Notes: **speculum, -ī,** n: mirror; **percipiō, -ere, -cēpī, -ceptus**: learn; **penitus**: deep within, thoroughly; **rem(m)oveō, -ēre, -mōvī, -mōtus**: remove, withdraw.

Fear Clauses

1. **FEAR CLAUSES** also feature subjunctive verbs. They are introduced by **NĒ** for positive clauses (to emphasize what the speaker fears **will** happen, but hopes **will not** happen) and **NĒ NŌN** or **UT** for negative clauses (to emphasize what the speaker fears **will not** happen but hopes **will**). Consider the following examples:

Cicero, *ad Atticum* 9.7.3: **Sed <u>vereor</u> <u>nē Pompēiō quid oneris impōnam</u>**. But <u>I fear</u> <u>that I would put something of a burden on Pompey</u> (i.e., Cicero hopes **not** to burden Pompey, but fears that he does).

Ovid, *Metamorphoses* 10.56: **Hic, <u>nē dēficeret</u>, <u>metuens</u> . . .** This man (Orpheus), <u>fearing</u> <u>that she (Eurydice) would die</u> . . . (i.e., he hopes that she has **not** died, but fears that she has).

Cicero, *ad Familiarēs* 14.2.3: **<u>Timeō</u> <u>ut sustineās</u>**. <u>I fear</u> <u>that you are not persevering</u> (i.e., Cicero hopes that his wife and daughter **will** persevere, but fears that they are not).

Cicero, *in Catilinam* 4.14: **Quī <u>verērī</u> videntur, <u>ut habeam satis praesidiī</u> . . .** Those who seem <u>to fear</u> <u>that I may not have enough protection</u> . . . (i.e., they seem to hope that I **will** have enough protection, but fear that I do not).

2. The following verbs often trigger fear clauses (you should consider this list additional required vocabulary):

metuō, -ere, uī, -ūtus: be afraid, fear
paveō, -ēre, pāvī: be scared (of), be terrified (at)
timeō, -ēre, -uī: be afraid, fear
vereor, -ērī, veritus sum: revere, respect, fear, dread

3. **NOUNS OF FEARING** (*metus, terror, timor, pavor*, etc.) can also introduce fear clauses. Consider the following examples:

Sallust, *Historiae* 4.50: **Ingens <u>terror</u> erat, <u>nē ex latere nova mūnīmenta madōre īnfirmārentur</u>**. There was great <u>terror</u> <u>that the new fortifications (made) of brick were being weakened by moisture</u>.

Celsus, *de Materia Medica* 2.7.2: **<u>Nē in malum habitum corpus eius recīdat</u>, metus est**. There is a <u>fear</u> <u>that his body will relapse into its bad habit</u>.

4. For fear clauses, Latin employs the same **SEQUENCE OF TENSES** that you learned in *NLP* 31 for indirect questions:

   (a) when the main verb is present or future tense, the subjunctive verb in the fear clause is present tense or perfect tense (primary sequence)
   (b) when the main verb is one of the past tenses (imperfect, perfect, or pluperfect), the subjunctive verb in the fear clause is imperfect or pluperfect tense (secondary sequence)

Consider the following examples:

Celsus, *de Materia Medica* 7.26.30: **Sī <u>timēmus</u> nē quid intus <u>sit</u>** . . . If we <u>fear</u> that there <u>is</u> something inside . . .
   Primary sequence with a present tense verb triggering the fear clause and a present tense subjunctive verb in the fear clause.

Cicero, *ad Atticum* 14.17: **Quō quidem <u>metuō</u> nē magnō reī publicae malō <u>vēnerit</u>**. Indeed I <u>fear</u> that <u>he has come</u> for the purpose of great evil to the state.
   Primary sequence with a present tense verb in the main clause and a perfect tense subjunctive verb in the fear clause.

Caesar, *de Bello Gallico* 1.39.6: **Ut satis commodē supportārī <u>posset</u>, <u>timēre</u> <u>dīcēbant</u>**. <u>They were saying</u> <u>that they feared</u> that <u>it could not be conveyed</u> adequately enough.
   Secondary sequence with an imperfect tense verb in the main clause and an imperfect tense subjunctive verb in the fear clause.

Cicero, *ad Familiares* 9.16.1: **Tē ad scrībendum <u>incitāvit verentem</u> nē Silius suō nuntiō aliquid mihi sollicitūdinis <u>attulisset</u>.** He urged you to write, (you) <u>fearing</u> that Silius <u>had caused</u> me some anxiety with his announcement.

Secondary sequence with a perfect tense verb in the main clause and a pluperfect tense subjunctive verb in the fear clause.

I. Required Vocabulary

NOUNS

frūmentum, -ī, n: grain

mundus, -ī, m: universe, world

mūrus, -ī, m: wall

vallum, -ī, n: wall, entrenchment

cohors, -ortis (-ium), f: troop, company, cohort

os, ossis, n: bone

pecus, pecoris, n: flock

tellūs, tellūris, f: earth

terror, -ōris, m: dread, terror

timor, -ōris, m: fear, dread

equitātus, -ūs, m: cavalry

nefās (indeclinable): a violation of divine law, an impious act

ADJECTIVES

nocturnus, -a, -um: by night, nocturnal

vagus, -a, -um: wandering, roving

VERBS

constō, -stāre, -stitī, -stātus: agree, stand together, stand firm

ex(s)pectō, -āre, -āvī, -ātus: await, dread

praestō, -āre, -stitī, -stitus: offer, excel

vetō, -āre, vetuī, vetitus: forbid

moneō, -ēre, -uī: advise, warn

conficiō, -ere, -fēcī, -fectus: complete, carry out
conligō (colligō), -ere, -lēgī, -lectus: gather together, collect, infer
instituō, -ere, -stituī, -stitūtus: position, place, establish, decide
interficiō, -ere, -fēcī, -fectus: destroy, kill
ostendō, -ere, -tendī, -tensus: show, display
pellō, -ere, pepulī, pulsus: strike, drive away, dislodge
statuō, -ere, -uī, -ūtus: establish, settle, decide

circumveniō, -īre, -vēnī, -ventus: surround, encircle

fateor, -ērī, fassus sum: confess, acknowledge
vereor, -ērī, veritus sum: revere, respect, fear, dread

II. Translate the following sentences from Latin to English or English to Latin.

1. Gentēs timuērunt ut redīret aetās nova.
2. Verēmur nē quid malī tē capiat et ut portās murōsque servēs.
3. Metuō nē omne hoc pecus ad illud vallum pellātur.
4. Carmina pessima cantūrī metuunt ut suīs cum vōcibus nōbīs persuādeant.
5. Hostibus paene victīs, magnum in timōrem dux pervēnit, nē equitātus circumvenīrētur.
6. Exercitus, verens nē moenia nostra corrupta sint, aciem fortissimē pellere potest.
7. Imperātor cohortī prīmae timentī nē omnia dēficerent imperāvit ut ad hostēs impetum faceret.
8. Ut pecus agrīs in dūrissimīs errans satis frūmentī inveniat, metus est.
9. It is impious to fear that the Romans may not prevail in the battles.
10. We feared that the horses could not cross the river.
11. Let me confess that the soldiers are afraid that there is not enough money.
12. O friends, surround the walls and don't be afraid that you may be driven away by the harshest weapons.

Roman Civil Wars: The Political
Landscape of the First Century BCE

By the late second century BCE, the political climate began to change at Rome once again as factions in the Senate vied for power. These factions were hardly "political parties" in the modern sense. Members of each "party" were interested in the same goal—obtaining power, wealth, and reputation. They differed only in how they achieved and used their authority. The *Optimātēs* (whose members were called the "*Bonī*") worked through the Senate to retain senatorial prestige, maintain the rights of wealthy property owners, and protect the status quo. The *Populārēs*, instead, attempted to gain power through controlling the people and the popular assemblies. They promoted land distribution to the poor, debt cancellation, and subsidized (or free) grain.

In the second century BCE, only property owners were eligible for military service (see *NLP* 7), but constant foreign warfare kept men away from the fields during the growing season, eventually forcing families into bankruptcy. Thus, farmers moved to the city, creating a social crisis—a large, debt-ridden, unemployed urban population. Consequently, the number of men eligible for military service dwindled. To alleviate the growing crisis, Tiberius Gracchus, as Tribune of the Plebs (133 BCE), proposed agrarian reform: limiting the amount of land that a private citizen could own, and redistributing public lands to disenfranchised veterans. These reforms met with violent opposition from conservative (i.e., land-holding) senators and wealthy businessmen who managed the large plantations (*latifundia*) with slave labor and at great profit. The conflict eventually came to arms, resulting in Tiberius's brutal murder. Tiberius's younger brother Gaius, also as Tribune of the Plebs (123–122 BCE), sought far-reaching constitutional and judicial reform, intended either to protect the poorer classes or to weaken the enemies of his dead brother. In 121 BCE Gaius was executed by a pro-senatorial mob, as Tiberius had been.

Gaius Marius also sought power by currying favor with the people, and his military reforms utterly transformed the political landscape at Rome. An ambitious *novus homo* (the first in his family to hold the consulship), Marius served an unprecedented seven terms as consul (107, 104–100, 86 BCE, despite the Roman legal mandate of a ten-year hiatus between consulships). The candidacy for his second consulship was particularly unusual: he campaigned not in the city, as tradition and law dictated, but *in absentia*, from the field in Numidia. By his successes against both Jugurtha in Numidia (112–106 BCE) and the Cimbri and Teutones in Germany (113–101 BCE), where senatorial armies before him had failed, Marius attained great prestige and the support of the plebs and *equites* at Rome, but the condemnation of the Senate, who feared his ambition. Plutarch (*Life of Marius*) even called him the "third founder of Rome" for his successes against the fierce northern tribes. Marius's seminal reform was opening up military service to the landless.

Marius's former quaestor, the conservative Lucius Cornelius Sulla Felix, earned the favor of the equally conservative Senate and command of senatorial armies sent to quell uprisings in Italy during the Social Wars (91–88 BCE), when allied Italians were petitioning for full benefits of Roman citizenship to temper the onerous obligations of taxes and military service; the Senate then feared to give a command on Italian soil to the dangerously ambitious Marius. Sulla's successful service led to his first consulship in 88 BCE, a command against Mithridates VI of Pontus, who had rebelled against Roman authority, massacring Roman citizens in the East. It led as well to conflict with his former general Marius, who also had tried to secure a command against Mithridates. Sulla succeeded in vanquishing his former commander-in-chief, and, as dictator, in pushing though constitutional reforms that severely curtailed the powers of the Tribunes of the Plebs and the popular assemblies who had enabled Marius's unprecedented career in the first place.

Marius and Sulla both enjoyed their successes in large part because of the loyalty of their soldiers, who shared in the spoils of war and received grants of land upon retirement. This principle would shape the political landscape of the mid-first century BCE, and change forever the psychology of the Roman soldier, who now gave his allegiance to his general, not to the state. Sulla's lieutenant Gnaeus Pompeius Magnus achieved glory in vanquishing the Marians who had fled to Spain. Pompey succeeded in securing the allegiance of his veterans, who would serve as a loyal power base throughout his career. After the failure of senatorial armies against Spartacus in 73–72 BCE (see *NLP* 15), Pompey joined forces with another Sullan lieutenant, Marcus Licinius Crassus, to quell that rebellion, earning the leverage to demand the consulship (despite the fact that Pompey was too young by two years) and lucrative post-consular assignments. Pompey further increased his own power base (his "private army") when he vanquished Cilician pirates raiding the eastern coast of Italy and when he reorganized the eastern territories (including Judea) into a continuous belt of Roman provinces and client kingships, protected by and loyal to Pompey. Pompey's motivation for joining in the three-way alliance with Julius Caesar and Crassus was to secure land grants for his veterans (see *NLP* 30 Extra Passages).

Caesar was a charismatic and generous leader, popular with both the people and his men. Caesar consistently aimed to secure power through the popular assemblies. As tensions began to rise between Caesar and Pompey, Pompey curried favor with the Senate. In 52 BCE, when Rome was in turmoil after the murder of the former Tribune of the Plebs Publius Clodius Pulcher (see *NLP* 9), the Senate had asked Pompey to restore order in the city, and they declared him *Princeps Senātus* (giving him the right to speak first in the Senate).

After eight years of successful campaigning in the Gallic provinces, Caesar had amassed a dedicated power base that followed him into civil war against his former ally Pompey. As his governorship was coming to an end, Caesar desired to stand for the consulship *in absentiā*, hoping to avoid a lapse in his *imperium*. Had Caesar disbanded his army (thus relinquishing *imperium*) and returned to Rome to run for office, his enemies would have tried him in court for the irregularities of his first consulship, thus effectively ending his political career (a magistrate with *imperium* is protected from legal proceedings only while he holds *imperium*). Caesar attempted to compromise with the Senate, offering to disband part, but not all, of his army. The Senate rejected the compromise. The senatorial rejection was duly vetoed by the Tribunes of the Plebs (see *NLP* 25), including Marc Antony, who were protecting Caesar's interests in Rome and who were consequently driven out of the city. They fled to Caesar's camp on the Rubicon just north of Italy, giving the general a constitutional excuse to march on the city. He could claim that he was defending the rights and prerogatives of the people's chosen representatives.

In 49 BCE, civil war began anew between Caesar (defending the rights of the people) and Pompey (defending the authority of the Senate), culminating in Caesar's victory at Pharsalus on August 9, 48 BCE, and his avenging of Pompey, who was murdered in Egypt after Pharsalus. Caesar himself recounts the war in his *Commentarii de Bello Civili*. Declared "Dictator for life" and perpetual Consul, Caesar attempted to reconcile warring factions, but with little success. He spared his enemies, eschewed proscriptions, and granted a general amnesty. The Senate, alarmed at Caesar's accrual of power and honors, plotted his assassination on March 15, 44 BCE. The senatorial assassination launched Rome into yet another series of civil wars, as Caesar's lieutenants Marc Antony and Marcus Aemilius Lepidus joined forces with Caesar's heir, Gaius Octavian, to avenge the dictator's murder. Then Antony, aided by Caesar's lover Cleopatra (the queen of Egypt), and Octavian vied against each other. In the end, Octavian was victorious at the battle of Actium (September 2, 31 BCE), and Rome was irrevocably changed from republic to monarchy.

SUGGESTIONS FOR FURTHER READING:

Gruen, Erich. *The Last Generation of the Roman Republic.* University of California, 1974.

Jimenez, Ramon. *Caesar Against Rome: The Great Roman Civil War.* Da Capo, 2000.

Meier, Christian. *Caesar: A Biography.* Translated by David McLintock. Basic Books, 1982.

Syme, Ronald. *The Roman Revolution.* Oxford, 1968.

Taylor, Lily Ross. *Party Politics in the Age of Caesar.* University of California, 1949.

PASSAGES

32.1. Horace, *Carmina* 1.2.5–8. The Romans believed that civil war was divine punishment for neglecting the gods who protected Rome. Horace here compares the current state of affairs at Rome with an episode from mythology. In ages past, the people had refused to worship the gods, incurring the wrath of Jupiter, who in turn punished them with a devastating flood. Deucalion and his wife Pyrrha alone were spared for their singular devotion, and together they recreated the human race (the tale is vividly recounted by Ovid, *Metamorphoses* 1.253–312). Meter: Sapphic strophe.

Terruit gentīs, grave nē redīret
saeculum Pyrrhae nova monstra questae,
omne cum Prōtēus pecus ēgit altōs
    vīsere montīs.

Notes: **terruit**: "He (*Iuppiter*) made (them) fear that"; **saeculum, -ī**, n: age, generation; **Pyrrha, -ae**, f: the daughter of Pandora, the only woman to survive the flood sent by

Jupiter in his efforts to eradicate evil in the world; **monstrum, -ī**, n: sign, portent; **questae** + direct object; **Prōteus, -ī**, m: a god of the sea (the *-eu-* in *Prōteus* is a diphthong); **pecus**: i.e., marine animals; **vīsō, -ere, vīsī, vīsus**: come to see (infinitive of purpose).

32.2. Sallust, *Historiae* 1.48.20. In this address to the Roman people (against the dictator Sulla), Marcus Aemilius Lepidus advocates for returning land and personal property, and he calls for the people to resist Sulla's tyranny. Here Lepidus assures the people that Sulla is not as strong as they might suspect.

> Vereor nē—alīus alium principem expectantēs—ante capiāminī, nōn opibus eius, quae fūtilēs et corruptae sunt, sed vostrā sōcordiā.

Notes: **expectantēs**: in the plural to emphasize the distributive nature of the action (each of you, one by one, are collectively . . .); **fūtilis, -e**: worthless; **vostrā** = *vestrā*; **sōcordia, -iae**, f: folly, weakness, indolence, inactivity.

32.3. Cicero, *ad Atticum* 8.9.4. In this letter dated February 25, 49 BCE, Cicero recounts his conversation with Caesar's lieutenant Lucius Cornelius Balbus, whose eponymous uncle was a close personal friend of both Pompey and Caesar. Uncle and nephew alike seemed to believe (or hope) that Caesar desired reconciliation with his former friend.

> Īdem aiēbat nihil malle Caesarem quam ut Pompēium adsequeretur (id crēdō) et redīret in grātiam (id nōn crēdō). Et metuō nē omnis haec clēmentia ad ūnam illam crūdēlitātem conligātur. Balbus quidem Māior ad mē scrībit nihil malle Caesarem quam—prīncipe Pompēiō—sine metū vīvere. Tū, putō, haec crēdis.

Notes: **īdem**: the younger Balbus; **adsequor, -sequī, adsecūtus sum**: pursue, overtake; **clēmentia, -iae**, f: mildness, mercy; **crūdēlitās, -ātis**, f: cruelty, inhumanity.

32.4. Lucan, *Pharsalia* 7.95–96. Pompey—preferring to avoid the deaths of more Roman citizens—still hopes for victory through strategy, but his men are eager for the glory of battle. Meter: dactylic hexameter.

> "Cīvīlia bella
> gestūrī metuunt nē nōn cum sanguine vincant."

Notes: **cīvīlis, -e**: civil, civic.

32.5. Caesar, *de Bello Civili* **1.21.2.** In 49 BCE, as Caesar prepares a night attack on Corfinium, a Pompeian stronghold east of Rome, he worries that the cover of darkness might encourage unauthorized looting.

Tamen veritus nē mīlitum introitū et nocturnī temporis licentiā oppidum dīriperētur, eōs, quī vēnerant, collaudat atque in oppidum dīmittit; portās mūrōsque adservārī iubet.

Notes: **introitus, -ūs**, m: entrance, invasion; **licentia, -iae**, f: freedom, liberty; **dīripiō, -ere, -ripuī, -reptus**: plunder, pillage; **collaudō, -āre, -āvī, -ātus**: praise; **adservō, -āre, -āvī, -ātus**: preserve, guard.

32.6. Caesar, *de Bello Civili* **1.25.4.** Caesar decides to blockade the strategic port at Brundisium, in Italy's heel, to prevent his enemy from gaining control of the entire Adriatic Sea.

Veritusque nē ille Itāliam dīmittendam nōn existimāret, exitūs administrātiōnēsque Brundisīnī portūs impedīre īnstituit.

Notes: **veritus**: construe with Caesar as subject; **ille**: Pompey; **Itāliam dīmittendam**: "that Italy should be given over" (future passive periphrastic in indirect statement); **exitus, -ūs**, m: exit, egress; **administrātiō, -iōnis**, f: management, operation; **Brundisīnus, -a, -um**: of Brundisium; **portus, -ūs**, m: port; **impediō, -īre, -īvī, -ītus**: hinder, obstruct, block.

32.7. Caesar, *de Bello Civili* **1.61.2.** After Caesar succeeds in securing supplies and allegiance from the inhabitants of the Ebro valley in northern Spain, Pompey's lieutenants Lucius Afranius and Marcus Petreius begin to worry about their supply lines, while Pompeian morale disintegrates.

Hīs paene effectīs, magnum in timōrem Afrānius Petrēiusque perveniunt, nē omnīnō frūmentō pābulōque interclūderentur, quod multum Caesar equitātū valēbat.

Notes: **hīs**: i.e., Caesar's efforts to create a ford through a river, allowing him to cut the Pompeians from their supply lines; **omnīnō**: altogether, entirely; **pābulum, -ī**, n: fodder, forage; **interclūdō, -ere, -clūsī, -clūsus**: shut off (from), hinder (from).

32.8. Caesar, *de Bello Civili* 3.63.2. Near Dyrrachium, Pompey's troops stand between Caesar and the Adriatic. Hoping to avoid a multi-front battle, Caesar builds fortifications to enhance his strategic advantage.

Hoc enim superiōribus diēbus timens Caesar, nē nāvibus nostrī circumvenīrentur, duplicem eō locō fēcerat vallum, ut—sī ancipitī proeliō dīmicārētur—posset resistī.

Notes: **superus, -a, -um**: "preceding"; **duplex (duplicis)**: double; **anceps (ancipitis)**: double, twofold; **dīmicārētur**: impersonal passive; **dīmicō, -āre, -āvī**: brandish (a weapon), fight; **resistī**: impersonal passive; **resistō, -ere, restitī**: resist, oppose, withstand.

32.9. Caesar, *de Bello Civili* 3.89.4–5. Caesar's strategy for the battle of Pharsalus, August 9, 48 BCE, where he finally and definitively defeated Pompey.

Timens nē ā multitūdine equitum dextrum cornū circumvenīrētur, celeriter ex tertiā aciē singulās cohortēs dētraxit atque ex hīs quartam instituit equitātuīque opposuit; et quid fierī vellet ostendit; monuitque eius diēī victōriam in eārum cohortium virtūte constāre.

Notes: **dētrahō, -ere, -traxī, -tractus**: withdraw (something in the accusative case) from (someone in the dative case); **quartam** (*cohortem*); **oppōnō, -ere, -posuī, -positus**: place opposite; **monuit** + indirect statement; **constō, -āre, constitī, constātus**: depend on.

32.10. Cicero, *Philippica* 1.33. In the final rhetorical flourish of this powerful speech, Cicero impugns Marc Antony for preferring absolute power at any cost.

Illud magis vereor nē—ignōrans vērum iter glōriae—glōriōsum putēs plūs tē ūnum posse quam omnēs et metuī ā cīvibus tuīs quam dīligī mālīs.

Notes: this is a complex passage: **vereor nē** governs two verbs in the fear clause, each of which in turn governs accusative / infinitive constructions; **ignōrō, -āre, -āvī, -ātus**: be ignorant, not know; **glōriōsus, -a, -um**: glorious; **posse**: "be powerful."

32.11. Cicero, *Philippica* 2.32. In this rousing defense of Brutus and Caesar's other senatorial executioners, Cicero admits to having known of the plot, as a point of personal honor.

Etenim vereor nē aut cēlātum mē illīs ipsīs nōn honestum aut invītātum refugisse mihi sit turpissimum.

Notes: **etenim**: as a matter of fact; **cēlātum** (*esse*); **cēlō, -āre, -āvī, -ātus**: hide, keep in ignorance; **illīs ipsīs**: i.e., the plans to assassinate Caesar; **invītō, -āre, -āvī, -ātus**: summon, invite; **refugiō, -fugere, -fūgī**: flee back, shirk, avoid; **turpissimum sit** + two accusative / infinitive constructions.

32.12. Cicero, *Philippica* 2.86. Here, Cicero refers to the notorious Lupercal games of February, 44 BCE, when Marc Antony offered a royal (kingly) diadem to Caesar, who refused it partly, perhaps, because the title *rex* had acquired tyrannical associations after the expulsion of Tarquinius Superbus, Rome's last king.

Vereor nē imminuam summōrum virōrum glōriam. Dīcam tamen dolōre commōtus. Quid indignius quam vīvere eum, quī inposuerit diadēma, cum omnēs fateantur iūre interfectum esse?

Notes: **imminuō, -ere, -minuī, -minūtus**: diminish; **commoveō, -ēre, -mōvī, -mōtus**: shake, disturb; **indignus, -a, -um**: unworthy, shameful, disgraceful; **inposuerit** = *imposuerit* (referring to Antony's act of offering a crown to Caesar at the Lupercal games of 44 BCE); **diadēma, diadēmātis**, n: crown; **iūre**: rightly.

EXTRA PASSAGES: MARCUS ANNEAEUS LUCANUS

Born in Corduba, Spain, Marcus Anneaeus Lucanus (39–65 CE) was the grandson of Seneca the Elder and nephew of Seneca the Younger. Although once on friendly terms with Nero, Lucan participated in the Pisonian conspiracy against Nero's regime in 65 CE. A vast body of work was attributed to Lucan, including a *Medea*, *Laudes Neronis*, and *de Incendio Urbis*, but only the *Pharsalia* survives, a ten-book epic account of the civil war between Caesar and Pompey. After his death, Lucan was especially renowned for his youthfulness (he was twenty-six at the time of his death) and the speed at which he composed.

32.13. Lucan, *Pharsalia* 5.368–70. By sheer force of personality, Caesar quells a mutiny among his troops. Meter: dactylic hexameter.

> Ipse pavet nē tēla sibī dextraeque negentur
> ad scelus hoc Caesar. Vīcit patientia saevī
> spem ducis, et iugulōs nōn tantum praestitit ensīs.

Notes: **paveō, -ēre, pāvī**: quake with fear; **scelus**: i.e., civil war; **patientia, -iae**, f: endurance, submission; (*sed etiam*) **iugulōs; iugulum, -ī**, n: throat; **ensis, -is (-ium)**, m: sword.

32.14. Lucan, *Pharsalia* 6.579–86. Pompey's worthless son Sextus has invoked the atrocious witch Erichtho to foretell the war's outcome. Here she gleefully describes the impending slaughter. Meter: dactylic hexameter.

> Namque timens nē Mars alium vagus īret in orbem
> Ēmathis et tellūs tam multā caede carēret,
> pollūtōs cantū dīrīsque venēfica sūcīs
> conspersōs vetuit transmittere bella Philippōs:
> tōt mortēs habitūra suās ūsūraque mundī
> sanguine, caesōrum truncāre cadāvera rēgum
> spērat et Hesperiae cinerēs āvertere gentis
> ossaque nōbilium tantōsque adquīrere mānēs.

Notes: **Ēmathis (Ēmathidis)**: Macedonian (just north of Greece, Macedon, where the fighting now occurs); **careō, -ēre, -uī, -itūrus** (+ ablative): lack, be without; **polluō, -ere, -uī, -ūtus**: befoul, defile; **cantus, -ūs**, m: prophecy, incantation; **dīrus, -a, -um**: fearful, horrible, dire; **venēfica, -ae**, f: one who makes poison, a poisoner, witch (here, Emathis); **sūcus, -ī**, m: juice, sap; **conspergō, -ere, -spersī, -spersus**: sprinkle; **vetuit**: construe Erichtho as the subject (+ accusative/infinitive); **transmittō, -ere, -mīsī, -missus**: convey across, shift; **Philippī, -ōrum**, m: a city on the eastern coast of Macedonia where Octavian and Antony defeated Caesar's assassins in 42 BCE; **suās**: "as her own"; **truncō, -āre, -āvī, -ātus**: maim, mutilate; **cadāver, -eris**, n: dead body, carcass; **spērō, -āre, -āvī, -ātus** (+ complementary infinitive): hope; **Hesperius, -a, -um**: western; **cinis, cineris**, m: ash; **āvertō, -ere, -vertī, -versus**: turn away, steal; **adquīrō, -ere, -quīsīvī, -quīsītus**: acquire.

32.15. Lucan, *Pharsalia* 8.592–95. After fleeing Pharsalia, Pompey seeks asylum in Alexandria where he will be assassinated on orders from Ptolemy XIII in a misguided attempt to curry favor with Caesar. Pompey's troops are naturally anxious for their General's safety. Meter: dactylic hexameter.

Stētit anxia classis

ad ducis ēventum, metuens nōn arma nefāsque
sed nē summissīs precibus Pompēius adōret
sceptra suā dōnāta manū.

Notes: **stētit**: "lay at anchor"; **anxius, -a, -um**: uneasy, anxious; **ēventus, -ūs**, m: outcome, fate, chance; **summittō, -ere, -mīsī, -missus**: abase oneself, submit; **adōrō, -āre, -āvī, -ātus**: address, entreat, "grovel (at)"; **sceptrum, -ī**, n: scepter, royal authority (Pompey had been instrumental in extending Roman hegemony in the eastern Mediterranean).

LESSON 33

Relative Clauses
with the Subjunctive

1. In *NLP* 16, you learned to identify and translate **RELATIVE CLAUSES OF DESCRIPTION** which feature indicative verbs and provide further **factual** information about their antecedents. In this lesson, you will learn how the function of the relative clause changes when the verb shifts from indicative to subjunctive.

2. Relative clauses with subjunctive verbs often express generalizing characteristics (not factual information) about a particular noun. These clauses are described as **RELATIVE CLAUSES OF CHARACTERISTIC.** The antecedent is often indefinite, not specifying a particular person or thing, but rather a class or group (e.g., *sunt quī*: "there are some who"; *homo quī*: "a man who"; *multī quī*: "many who"; *nēmō quī*: "no one who"; *nōn nullī quī*: "some who"; *quī*: "a certain one who"; *quis quī*: "who [is there] who"). Consider the following examples:

Cicero, *ad Brutum* 1.14.2: **Erit cīvis nēmō quem quidem cīvem appellārī fās sit, quī sē nōn in tua castra <u>conferat</u>**. There will be no citizen whom indeed <u>it would be</u> right to be called a citizen, who <u>would</u> not <u>convey</u> himself into your camp.

Pliny the Younger, *Epistulae* 3.21.1–2: **Erat homo ingeniōsus acūtus ācer, et quī plūrimum in scrībendō et salis <u>habēret</u>**. He was a talented, intelligent, sharp person, and the sort who also <u>would have</u> much (of) wit in writing.

3. A relative clause with a subjunctive verb can also express **CAUSE** or **CONCESSION**. These clauses are often introduced by *ut*, *utpote*, or *quippe*. Consider the following examples:

Sallust, *Bellum Catilinae* 57.4: **Neque tamen Antōnius procul aberat, utpote quī magnō exercitū locīs aequiōribus expedītōs in fugā <u>sequerētur</u>**. And nonetheless Antonius was not far distant, insofar as he <u>followed</u> in flight the lightly armed soldiers with a large army on rather level terrain.

Cicero, *ad Familiares* 1.9.9: **Ibi multa dē meā sententiā questus est Caesar, quippe quī etiam Ravennae Crassum ante <u>vīdisset</u> ab eōque in mē <u>esset incēnsus</u>**. There Caesar, who of course <u>had</u> even already <u>seen</u> Crassus at Ravenna and <u>had been inflamed</u> against me by him, grumbled much about my opinion (i.e., because Crassus turned Caesar against Cicero).

Cicero, *ad Atticum* 2.24.4: **Ea nōs, utpote quī nihil contemnere <u>solērēmus</u>, nōn contemnābāmus sed nōn pertimescēbāmus**. Insofar as we <u>were accustomed</u> to despise nothing, we did not despise those things, but we did not fear them.

4. As you learned in *NLP* 28, relative clauses with subjunctive verbs can also express **PURPOSE**. Consider the following examples:

Caesar, *de Bello Gallico* 1.24.1: **Cōpiās suās Caesar in proximum collem subdūxit equitātumque, quī <u>sustinēret</u> hostium impetum, mīsit**. Caesar led his own troops to the closest hill and sent the cavalry who <u>were to check</u> the attack of the enemy (i.e., in order to check the attack of the enemy).

Caesar, *de Bello Gallico* 7.61.5: **Parvā manū Metiōsēdum versus missā, quae tantum <u>prōgrediātur</u> quantum nāvēs prōcessissent, reliquās cōpiās contrā Labiēnum duxērunt**. With a small band sent toward Metiosedum, which <u>was to advance</u> (i.e., in order to advance) as far as the ships had proceeded, they (the Aedui) led the remaining troops against Labienus.

5. For relative clauses with subjunctive verbs, Latin employs the same **SEQUENCE OF TENSES** that you learned in *NLP* 31 for indirect questions and in *NLP* 32 for fear clauses:

(a) when the main verb is present or future tense, the subjunctive verb
    in the relative clause is present or perfect tense (primary sequence)
(b) when the main verb is one of the past tenses (imperfect, perfect, or
    pluperfect), the subjunctive verb in the relative clause is imperfect or
    pluperfect tense (secondary sequence)

Consider the following examples:

Seneca the Younger, *ad Helviam* 6.6: **<u>Inveniō</u> quī <u>dīcant</u> inesse nātūrālem quandam inrītātiōnem animīs commūtandī sēdēs et transferendī domicilia.** <u>I find</u> there are those who <u>say</u> that there is a certain innate excitement for the minds of changing bases and transferring homes.

   Primary sequence with a present tense verb in the main clause and a present tense subjunctive verb in the relative clause.

Seneca the Younger, *Epistulae* 5.3: **Nōn <u>habeāmus</u> argentum in quod solidī aurī caelātūra <u>dēscenderit</u>, sed nōn putēmus frūgālitātis indicium aurō argentōque caruisse.** Let us not <u>have</u> silver into which an engraving of solid gold <u>stooped</u>, but let us not think that to have lacked silver and gold is proof of frugality.

   Primary sequence with a present tense verb in the main clause and a perfect tense subjunctive verb in the relative clause.

Seneca the Younger, *de Clementia* 1.1: **Egone ex omnibus mortālibus <u>placuī</u> <u>electusque sum</u>, quī in terrīs deōrum vice <u>fungerer</u>?** Have I of all mortals found favor and <u>been chosen</u> as the one who <u>performed</u> the part of the gods on earth?

   Secondary sequence with a perfect tense verbs in the main clause and an imperfect tense subjunctive verb in the relative clause.

Caesar, *de Bello Gallico* 7.27.2: **Eīs quī prīmī mūrum <u>ascendissent</u> praemia <u>prōposuit</u> mīlitibusque signum dedit.** He (Caesar) <u>proposed</u> rewards to those who <u>had climbed</u> the wall first, and he gave the signal to the soldiers.

   Secondary sequence with a perfect tense verb in the main clause and a pluperfect tense subjunctive verb in the relative clause.

I. Required Vocabulary

NOUNS

medicīna, -ae, f: treatment, remedy
mora, -ae, f: delay, hindrance
tenebrae, -ārum, f (plural): darkness, gloom

cibus, -ī, m: food
medicāmentum, -ī, n: drug, remedy
morbus, -ī, m: sickness, disease, illness
tergum, -ī, n: back
venēnum, -ī, n: poison

cinis, cineris, m/f: ash
exercitātiō, -iōnis, f: exercise, practice
febris, -is (-ium), m: fever
lībidō, lībidinis, f: desire, lust, passion
pondus, ponderis, n: weight
valētūdō, valētūdinis, f: health, soundness

PRONOUNS

quīcumque, quaecumque, quodcumque: whoever, whatever

ADJECTIVES

aliēnus, -a, -um: of another, strange, foreign
praecipuus, -a, -um: particular, special
singulī, -ae, -a (plural): each, one by one, one each

ūtilis, -e: useful, advantageous, helpful

VERBS

careō, -ēre, -uī (+ ablative): lack, be without

nesciō, -īre, -īvī, -ītus: not know, be unfamiliar, be ignorant of

īrascor, -ī, īrātus sum: be angry

ADVERBS

nōndum: not yet

II. Translate the following sentences from Latin to English or English to Latin.

1. Mentem vacuam nōlī habēre, quae vītam brevissimam esse nōn intellegat.
2. Sunt exercitātiōnēs et facilēs et brevēs, quibus mīlitēs corpora fortia facere possint.
3. Namque medicī medicāmenta dīlexēre quae valētūdinem efficerent.
4. Lībertīs ipsīs aliquid dabitur, quō fiant saniōrēs.
5. Nam quī decoris magnī dignissimī essent, lībidine praecipuō caruērunt.
6. Venēna tamen quaedam sunt, quibus febrem vincere possīmus.
7. Mātrēs līberīs suīs satis cibī dant, quī simul et corpus et animam alat.
8. Caesar cōpiās nōndum collēgit, quae in proeliō ante vīcissent.
9. The informers, who were not men of great virtue, persuaded the citizens to abandon the Republic.
10. Caesar wished to find allies, with whom he could wage war.
11. I lack friends who would go with me into the gloom.
12. We do not yet know when we can set out across the river with a cavalry, which can make an easy attack against a foreign enemy.

Health and Healing

Health is a universal concern, and the Romans were as interested in maintaining good health as in treating disease. Despite living well into his seventies, Augustus was sickly as a young man, and Seneca the Younger discusses his own weak constitution at length. Many upper-class Romans suffered from gout, a disease caused by an indulgent lifestyle. Wounds, from battle or the arena, were also common, as were broken bones, fevers, eye complaints, earaches, headaches, acne, and cancerous growths.

The first recourse for an ill Roman was the pervasive tradition of "home remedies," compiled for easy reference in a number of handbooks, including Cato the Elder's *de Agri Cultura*, Pliny the Elder's *Naturalis Historiae*, and Celsus's *de Medicina* (the medical books of a once much larger encyclopedia similar in scope to Pliny's). The Romans were proud of their culture of self-sufficiency (most homeowners grew medicinal herbs in their gardens), and the *pater familias* was responsible for all aspects of the health and well-being of his family members and slaves. Pliny and Celsus preserve many recipes for salves, pills, and syrups believed effective against an array of common complaints. Ingredients range from the mundane (wine, honey, oil) to the exotic and expensive. Saffron and myrrh, for example, were among the components for a cough drop (Celsus, *de Medicina* 5.25.10). Laurel root bark was prescribed for kidney stones and as an abortifacient. Galen advised avoiding stress to treat epilepsy.

When home remedies failed, the ill might seek treatment from the gods. Most Roman gods, including Juno, Diana, Apollo, Hercules, and the Dioscouri, were thought to have healing powers. Prayers, votive offerings, and amulets were commonly used to treat, ward off, or even inflict disease. In Britain, many of the curse tablets dedicated to Sulis Minerva at Aquae Sulis (Bath) recommend horrible disease as punishment for wrongdoing. The healing sanctuary, where a patient might sleep in the temple to seek a cure, was a Greek phenomenon. Wealthy Romans, however, also traveled far afield to take cures at Epidaurus or other sanctuaries, where physicians, priests, and dream interpreters worked together to heal those seeking cures—medicine in the ancient world was, in effect, a mix of science, religion, magic, and superstition. On the model of Greek healing sanctuaries is the temple complex of the Romano-Celtic god Mars Nodens at Lydney Park in southern Britain. The precinct included a temple to Mars Nodens, baths, incubation (sleeping-cure) chambers, and a hotel for the patient's family and friends. At Lydney Park, there survive many votives (thank offerings for successful cures), including bracelets and pins, coins, a bronze arm, and nine statuettes of dogs, sacred to Celtic healers and analogous to Asclepius's snake.

To become a physician in the ancient world, one did little more than hang out a shingle. Some physicians, usually Greeks, may have studied at the great healing sanctuaries of Asclepius at Cos or Epidaurus in Greece (as Galen did [129–204 CE]), but there was no oversight, no required training, and no process of certification. Nonetheless, there was a science behind the practice of medicine. Hippocrates (fifth century BCE) believed that health was maintained when the four humors (blood, yellow bile, black bile, and phlegm) were in balance. And this balance could be restored by various treatments, including diet or exercise.

For example, someone with a fever was thought to have too much "blood" (whose properties are hot and wet), and so a diet of dry, cooling foods was prescribed to restore the balance from hot and wet to neutral. Feverish patients were also treated by bloodletting with leeches—literally reducing the amount of blood in the body—and by sweating to siphon off hot moisture. Cupping was a popular practice which aimed to draw poisonous substances from the body. Pressed onto the skin was a cup containing a burning cloth that consumed the oxygen in the cup and produced a partial vacuum. The cup was suctioned onto the body, and "vicious humors" were thus removed. The physician Asclepiades (first century BCE) believed that disease was caused by microscopic corpuscles which blocked pores, and that health was restored when pores were unblocked. Asclepiades was popular at Rome for prescribing mild remedies: gentle exercise, wine, baths, and massage. Agatharchus, reputedly the first Greek physician to come to Rome, was in fact sponsored by the Roman Senate in 219 BCE, but he quickly earned the nickname *carnifex* ("butcher") because of his over-fondness for treating patients with surgery and cautery.

Most Romans had a great mistrust of Greek physicians who were deemed unreliable, unprofessional, and inept. Cato the Elder, in fact, forbade his son to have anything to do with Greek physicians because they had sworn, so Cato claimed, to kill all foreigners with their medicine (Pliny, *Naturalis Historiae* 29.14). Martial also enjoyed poking fun at Greek physicians (see especially 1.47, 5.9). Despite this general mistrust of the medical profession, personal physicians were often attached to wealthy families (Galen served as physician to the emperor Marcus Aurelius, who ruled 161–180 CE), and physicians were consulted in times of need. There were some specialties, including ophthalmology, umbilical-cord cutting, and bonesetting, but most physicians were general practitioners. Among specialists, surgeons took pride of place. Surgery was performed for childbirth and abortion, kidney stones (mentioned in the Hippocratic oath), cataracts, dental capping, and tumor (*fistulae*) removal. The sedative and pain-relieving properties of alcohol, opium, hemp, mandrake, and henbane were known, but anesthesia was not widely used. The surgeon had to be strong, dexterous, accurate, and fast. The art of surgery was advanced by physicians attached to the Roman army, and military hospitals were widespread (e.g., at Houseteads on Hadrian's Wall in Britain). Surgical tools were often finely wrought and specialized, and there survive surgical kits with probes, hooks, forceps, needles, scalpels, catheters, bone chisels, and vaginal specula. All of this speaks to a sophisticated and multifaceted approach to healthcare.

SUGGESTIONS FOR FURTHER READING:

Baker, Patricia A. *The Archaeology of Medicine in the Greco-Roman World.* Cambridge, 2013.

Edelstein, Ludwig. *Ancient Medicine.* Johns Hopkins, 1967.

King, Helen. *Greek and Roman Medicine.* Bristol Classical Press, 2001.

Mattern, Susan. *The Prince of Medicine: Galen in the Roman Empire.* Oxford, 2013.

Nutton, Vivian. *Ancient Medicine.* 2nd ed. London, 2012.

Scarborough, John. *Roman Medicine.* Cornell, 1969.

PASSAGES

33.1. Juvenal, *Saturae* **10.356–60.** The most valuable gifts from the gods are good health, virtue, and a simple life. Meter: dactylic hexameter.

> Ōrandum est ut sit mens sāna in corpore sānō.
> Fortem posce animum mortis terrōre carentem,
> quī spatium vītae extrēmum inter mūnera pōnat
> nātūrae, quī ferre queat quōscumque labōrēs.
> Nesciat īrascī, cupiat nihil.

Notes: **ōrandum est**: "it must be prayed (that)" (future passive periphrastic); **queō, quīre, quīvī**: be able to.

33.2. Seneca the Younger, *Epistulae* **15.4.** Seneca does not deem exercise appropriate for learned men and disdains those who are addicted to it. But he recognizes the importance of exercise (*mens sāna in corpore sānō*) and here suggests some efficient ones.

> Sunt exercitātiōnēs et facilēs et brevēs, quae corpus et sine morā
> lassent et temporī parcant, cuius praecipua ratiō habenda est:

cursus et cum aliquō pondere manūs mōtae et saltūs vel ille, quī in altum lēvat, vel ille, quī in longum mittit.

Notes: **lassō, -āre, -āvī, -ātus**: tire, wear out; **habenda est**: "must be kept" (future passive periphrastic); **aliquō . . . mōtae**: i.e., weight-lifting; **saltus, -ūs**, m: leap, jump; **lēvō, -āre, -āvī, -ātus**: lift; **in longum**: i.e., a long jump.

33.3. **Celsus,** *de Materia Medica* **1.2.7.** Moderate exercise is best.

Exercitātiōnis autem plērumque fīnis esse dēbet sūdor aut certē lassitūdō, quae citrā fatigātiōnem sit.

Notes: **sūdor, -ōris**, m: sweat; **lassitūdō, lassitūdinis**, f: weariness, fatigue; **citrā** (+ accusative): on this side, within, short of; **fatigātiō, -iōnis**, f: exhaustion.

33.4. **Pliny the Elder,** *Naturalis Historia* **29.15.** Cato attributes his own longevity to homegrown Roman medicines and treatments.

Subicit enim quā medicīnā sē et coniugem usque ad longam senectam perduxerit.

Notes: **subiciō, -ere, -iēcī, -iectus**: lay before, expose, explain (construe Cato as the subject); **senecta, -ae**, f: old age; **perdūcō, -ere, -duxī, -ductus**: prolong.

33.5. **Ovid,** *Remedia Amoris* **150.** The poets often describe love as an illness, and Ovid here suggests one of many cures: keep busy! Meter: elegiac couplets (pentameter line).

Dā vacuae mentī, quō teneātur, opus.

33.6. **Cicero,** *ad Familiares* **16.4.2.** Some physicians may require incentives to do their best work.

Medicō ipsī putō aliquid dandum esse, quō sit studiōsior.

Notes: **dandum esse**: "ought to be given" (future passive periphrastic); **studiōsus, -a, -um**: eager, devoted.

33.7. Tacitus, *Annales* 6.46.5. Despite failing health, Tiberius continued to indulge himself in every excess and to disdain physicians.

Sed, gravescente valētūdine, nihil ē lībidinibus omittēbat, in patientiā firmitūdinem simulans solitusque ēlūdere medicōrum artēs atque eōs quī post trīcēsimum aetātis annum ad internoscenda corporī suō ūtilia vel noxia aliēnī consiliī indigērent.

Notes: **gravescō, -āre**: grow oppressive, decline; **omittō, -ere, -mīsī, -missus**: lay aside, neglect, let off; **patientia, -iae**, f: forbearance, hardship; **firmitūdō, -inis**, f: strength; **simulō, -āre, -āvī, -ātus**: pretend; **ēlūdō, -ere, -lūsī, -lūsus**: escape, baffle; **ad internoscenda**: "for distinguishing between things (*ūtilia vel noxia*)" (gerundive); **indigeō, -ēre, -uī** (+ genitive): need, require, lack.

33.8. Pliny the Elder, *Naturalis Historia* 29.62. How to prepare bugs for treating sore ears.

Eōs, quī agrestēs sint et in malvā nascantur, cremātōs, cinere permixtō rosāceō, infundunt auribus.

Notes: **eōs**: bugs; **agrestis, -e**: rustic, wild; **malva, -ae**, f: mallow plant; **cremō, -āre, -āvī, -ātus**: burn; **permisceō, -ēre, -uī, -mixtus**: mix completely; **rosāceus, -a, -um**: made with rose (oil); **infundō, -ere, -fūdī, -fūsus**: pour in (construe *medicī* as the subject).

33.9. Celsus, *de Materia Medica* 2.5.1. The attentive physician can determine how long an illness might last.

Prōtinus tamen signa quaedam sunt, ex quibus colligere possīmus morbum—etsi nōn interēmit—longius tamen tempus habitūrum.

Notes: **etsi**: even if; **interimō, -ere, -ēmī, -emptus**: kill, destroy; **habitūrum** (*esse*).

33.10. Celsus, *de Materia Medica* 2.12.1c. In antiquity there was a fully developed philosophy of nutrition, and medical conditions were often treated by diet.

At ubi febrēs sunt, satius est eius reī causā cibōs pōtiōnēsque adsūmere, quī simul et alant et ventrem molliant.

Notes: **satius**: comparative of *satis*; **eius reī causā**: i.e., the fever; **pōtiō, -iōnis**, f: drink; **adsūmō, -ere, -sumpsī, -sumptus**: take up, consume; **venter, ventris**, m: belly; **molliō, -īre, -īvī, -ītus**: soften, soothe.

33.11. Celsus, *de Materia Medica* 5.20.6. A multi-ingredient recipe to expel bladder stones.

Expellere autem ex vēsīcā cum ūrīnā calculum vidētur haec compositiō: casiae, crocī, murrae, costī, nardī, cinnamōmī, dulcis rādīcis, balsamī, hyperīcī pārēs portiōnēs conteruntur. Deinde vīnum lēnē instillātur, et pastillī fiunt, quī singulī habeant sextans dēnāriī, hīque singulī cōtīdiē māne ieiūnō dantur.

Notes: **expellō, -ere, -pepulī, -pulsus**: drive out, expel; **vēsīca, -ae**, f: bladder; **ūrīna, -ae**, f: urine; **calculus, -ī**, m: stone; **compositiō, -iōnis**, f: mixture; **casia, -iae**, f: a fragrant tree whose aromatic bark is similar to cinnamon; **crocus, -ī**, m: crocus, saffron; **murra, -ae**, f: myrrh, the aromatic resin of a thorny tree; **costum, -ī**, n: an aromatic eastern plant whose root was a common medicinal ingredient; **nardus, -ī**, m: spikenard, a flowering plant of the valerian family; **cinnamōmum, -ī**, n: cinnamon; **rādex, rādīcis**, f: root, radish; **balsamum, -ī**, n: the fragrant gum of the balsam tree; **hyperīcon, -ī**, n: hypericum, a variety of St. John's wort; a small perennial with yellow flowers; **portiō, -iōnis**, f: portion, share; **conterō, -ere, -trīvī, -trītus**: crumble, wipe away, use up; **lēnē**: gently; **instillō, -āre, -āvī, -ātus**: pour in drop by drop; **pastillus, -ī**, m: lozenge; **sextans dēnāriī**: about 2/3 of a gram; **cōtīdiē**: daily; **māne**: in the morning; **ieiūnus, -a, -um**: fasting (substantive).

33.12. Celsus, *de Materia Medica* 5.27.3b. The Psylli, from North Africa, were reputedly able to use their bodies as an antidote to the bites of venomous creatures.

Homo adhibendus est, quī id vulnus exsūgat. Neque, Hercules, scientiam praecipuam habent iī, quī Psyllī nōminantur, sed audāciam ūsū ipsō confirmātam. Nam venēnum serpentis, ut quaedam etiam vēnātōria venēna, quibus Gallī praecipuē ūtuntur, nōn gustū, sed in vulnere nocent.

Notes: **adhibendus est**: "(a person) must be summoned" (future passive periphrastic); **exsūgō, -ere, -sūxī, -suctus**: suck out; **Hercules** = *mehercle*: by Hercules!; **scientia, -iae**, f: knowledge, understanding; **nōminō, -āre, -āvī, -ātus**: call, name; **audācia, -iae**, f: boldness, courage; **confirmō, -āre, -āvī, -ātus**: prove, strengthen; **serpens, -entis**, f: snake; **vēnātōrius, -a, -um**: of a hunter; **Gallī, -ōrum**, m (plural): the Gauls; **gustus, -ūs**, m: tasting; **nocent**: agrees in number with *quaedam venēna* rather than (more properly) *venēnum*.

EXTRA PASSAGES: SENECA THE YOUNGER

The son of the rhetorician Seneca the Elder, Lucius Annaeus Seneca (4–65 CE) was a man of many interests. Seneca the Younger wrote broadly on philosophy, morality, health, and the natural world, and he even composed tragedies. Born in Corduba, Spain, as a young boy he came to Rome, where he studied Stoic philosophy and rhetoric. Often in poor health, and frequently at odds with the imperial family, he was spared by Caligula (who thought Seneca would soon die) in 38 CE and was then exiled by Claudius in 41 CE. He was recalled to Rome in 49 CE by Agrippina to tutor her son Nero, whom the philosopher advised during the early years of Nero's principate, but his influence waned as Nero gained confidence. After Agrippina's death in 59 CE, Seneca cowardly endorsed Nero's accusations against his mother and then withdrew from public life, devoting himself to study and writing. Implicated in the Pisonian conspiracy, an aristocratic attempt against Nero in 65 CE, Seneca was ordered to commit suicide, along with many others, including his own nephew, the poet Lucan, whom we met in the Extra Passages of *NLP* 32.

33.13. Seneca the Younger, *Thyestes* 970–72. Atreus usurped the kingdom of Mycenae from his brother Thyestes, and Thyestes retaliated by seducing Atreus's wife. While his brother languished in exile, Atreus plotted a horrendous counter-retaliation. Pretending reconciliation, Atreus had Thyestes' sons prepared in a stew, on which the unknowing father feasted. Immediately after the gruesome banquet, Atreus here persists in his charade just before revealing the macabre truth. (N.B. Martial mocks this grim tale at *NLP* 11.11.) Meter: iambic trimeter.

> Fēstum diem, germāne, cōnsensū pārī
> celebrēmus; hic est, sceptra quī firmet mea
> solidamque pācis alliget certae fīdem.

Notes: **fēstus, -a, -um**: solemn, merry; **germānus, -ī**, m: brother; **cōnsensus, -ūs**, m: unanimity, concord; **hic** (*diēs*); **sceptrum, -ī**, n: scepter, kingship; **firmō, -āre, -āvī, -ātus**: strengthen, establish; **solidus, -a, -um**: firm, complete, unwavering, lasting; **alligō, -āre, -āvī, -ātus**: bind, entangle, bind by obligation.

33.14. Seneca the Younger, *Apocolocyntosis* **12.2.** The mood on the streets of Rome during Claudius's funeral.

Omnēs laetī, hilarēs: populus Rōmānus ambulābat tanquam līber, Agathō et paucī causidicī plorābant, sed plānē ex animō. Iūriscōnsultī ē tenebrīs prōcēdēbant, pallidī, gracilēs, vix animam habentēs, tanquam quī tum maximē revīvīscerent.

Notes: **hilaris, -e**: cheerful, lighthearted; **ambulō, -āre, -āvī, -ātus**: walk; **tanquam** = *tamquam*; **Agathō, -ōnis**, m: a Greek man's name; **causidicus, -ī**, m: lawyer, advocate; **plorō, -āre, -āvī, -ātus**: wail, weep; **iūriscōnsultus, -ī**, m: lawyer; **pallidus, -a, -um**: pale; **gracilis, -e**: thin, poor; **revīvīscō, -ere, -vīvixī, -vīvictus**: come to life again.

33.15. Seneca the Younger, *de Tranquilitate Animi* **11.9.** Wealth is transitory.

Quae sunt dīvitiae quās nōn egestās et famēs et mendīcitās ā tergō sequātur?

Notes: **egestās, -ātis**, f: extreme poverty; **mendīcitās, -ātis**, f: beggary.

Conditionals

1. **CONDITIONALS** are sentences that contain an "if" clause (**protasis**) and a conclusion (**apodosis**). Most conditional sentences are characterized as "**SIMPLE**"—the verbs in both halves of the sentence appear in the present, imperfect, perfect, or pluperfect indicative tenses. Consider the following examples:

   Pliny the Younger, *Epistulae* 1.13.4: **Sī <u>venit</u>, <u>queritur</u> sē diem—quia nōn perdidit—perdidisse**. If he <u>comes</u>, he <u>complains</u> that he has wasted the day—because he has not wasted it.
   > Present indicative verb in the protasis and present indicative verb in the apodosis.

   Pliny the Younger, *Epistulae* 1.10.1: **Sī quandō urbs nostra līberālibus studiīs <u>flōruit</u>, nunc maximē <u>flōret</u>**. If our city <u>has</u> ever <u>flourished</u> with the liberal arts, now especially it <u>flourishes</u>.
   > Perfect indicative verb in the protasis and present indicative verb in the apodosis.

   Tacitus, *Annales* 1.44.2: **Sī nocentem <u>adclāmāverant</u>, praeceps datus <u>trucidābātur</u>**. If they had <u>shouted</u> "guilty," he, given headlong, <u>was massacred</u>.
   > Pluperfect indicative verb in the protasis and imperfect indicative verb in the apodosis.

2. There are a number of special conditional sentences. When the verb in the protasis appears in the future or future perfect indicative and the verb in the

apodosis appears in the future indicative, the sentence is characterized as a **FUTURE MORE VIVID CONDITIONAL**. Consider the following examples:

Vitruvius, *de Architectura* 5.3.1: **Itaque sī cūriōsius ēligētur locus theātrō, vītābuntur vitia.** And thus if the place for the theater <u>will be chosen</u> very carefully, vices <u>will be avoided</u>.

    Future indicative verb in the protasis and future indicative verb in the apodosis.

Vitruvius, *de Architectura* 8.3.18: **Ovum in acētō sī diūtius positum fuerit, cortex eius mollescet et dissolvētur.** If an egg <u>will have been placed</u> in vinegar for a rather long time, its shell <u>will soften</u> and <u>be dissolved</u>.

    Future perfect indicative verb in the protasis and future indicative verb in the apodosis.

CIL VI 3105: **Quod sī forte tuus nōn mē vītāverit axis, excutiēre rotīs . . .** But if by chance your wagon <u>will</u> not <u>have avoided</u> me, you <u>will be shaken</u> off the wheels. . . .

    Future perfect indicative verb in the protasis and future indicative verb in the apodosis.

3. When the verbs in both halves of the conditional appear in the present subjunctive, the sentence is characterized as a **FUTURE LESS VIVID CONDITIONAL** (also called a "should-would" conditional). Consider the following examples:

Ovid, *Metamorphoses* 1.647–48: **Sī modo verba sequantur, / ōret opem nōmenque suum cāsūsque loquātur.** If only the words <u>should follow</u>, she (Io) <u>would beg</u> for help and <u>speak</u> her own name and misfortunes.

    Present subjunctive verbs in both the protasis and apodosis.

Horace, *Carmina* 3.3.65–67: **Ter sī resurgat mūrus aeneus, / auctōre Phoebō, ter pereat meīs / excīsus Argīvīs . . .** If the bronze wall <u>should rise</u> three times, Phoebus being the instigator, three times it <u>would perish</u>, destroyed by my Argives . . .

    Present subjunctive verbs in both the protasis and apodosis.

4. When the verbs in both halves of the conditional appear in the imperfect or pluperfect subjunctive, the sentence is characterized as a **CONTRARY TO FACT CONDITIONAL.** These sentences explore what would have happened if something else had occurred. The **imperfect subjunctive** in both halves of the conditional indicates a **PRESENT CONTRARY TO FACT CONDITIONAL**; the **pluperfect subjunctive** in both halves of the conditional indicates a **PAST CONTRARY TO FACT CONDITIONAL**. Often, however, as the third and fourth examples below indicate, Latin authors employ various combinations of the imperfect and pluperfect subjunctives as the context demands.

Ovid, *Metamorphoses* 1.361–62: **Sī tē quoque pontus habēret,/tē sequērer, coniunx, et mē quoque pontus habēret.** If the sea also <u>were to hold</u> you, I <u>would have followed you</u>, wife, and the sea <u>would</u> also <u>have held</u> me.
     Imperfect subjunctive verbs in both the protasis and apodosis.

Ovid, *Metamorphoses* 3.627–28: **Excussum mīsisset in aequora, sī nōn/haesissem, quamvīs āmens, in fūne retentus.** He <u>would have sent</u> (me) cast forth into the water, if I, although frantic, <u>had</u> not <u>clung</u> having held fast on the rope.
     Pluperfect subjunctive verbs in both the protasis and apodosis.

Tacitus, *Agricola* 2: **Memoriam quoque ipsam cum vōce perdidissēmus, sī tam in nostrā potestāte esset obliviscī quam tacēre.** We <u>would have destroyed</u> the memory itself too along with the voice, if it <u>were</u> so much in our power to forget as to be silent.
     Imperfect subjunctive verb in the protasis and pluperfect subjunctive verb in the apodosis.

Augustus, *Res Gestae* 20: **Sī vīvus nōn perfēcissem, perficī ab hērēdibus meīs iussī.** If I <u>had not completed</u> (it) while living, I <u>ordered</u> (it) to be completed by my heirs.
     Pluperfect subjunctive verb in the protasis and perfect indicative verb in the apodosis.

5. The following table summarizes the common varieties of conditional clauses:

Type of Conditional	Verb Tense/Mood in Protasis ("if" Clause)	Verb Tense/Mood in Apodosis ("then" Clause)
Simple	Indicative (any tense)	Indicative (any tense)
Future More Vivid	Future or Future Perfect Indicative	Future or Future Perfect Indicative
Future Less Vivid (should/would)	Present Subjunctive	Present Subjunctive
Contrary to Fact	Imperfect or Pluperfect Subjunctive	Imperfect or Pluperfect Subjunctive

I. Required Vocabulary

NOUNS

aevum, -ī, n: lifetime, age

arbor, -oris, f: tree, "mast" (of a ship)
cupīdō, cupīdinis, f: desire
hospes, hospitis, m: guest, host, stranger
senex, senis, m: old man

ADJECTIVES

niger, nigra, nigrum: black, dark-colored
tardus, -a, -um: slow, sluggish, dull

fēlix (fēlicis): fertile, favorable, lucky

VERBS

probō, -āre, -āvī, -ātus: prove, approve

concipiō, -ere, -cēpī, -ceptus: absorb, receive, grasp
ēligō, -ere, -lēgī, -lectus: choose, select
perdō, -ere, -didī, -ditus: destroy, ruin

insum, -esse, -fuī: be in
praesum, -esse, -fuī (+ dative): be in charge
transferō, -ferre, -tulī, -lātus: transfer, carry over

PREPOSITIONS

contrā (+ accusative): against, opposite (adverb and preposition)

CONJUNCTIONS AND ADVERBS

aliter: otherwise

II. Translate the following sentences from Latin to English or English to Latin.

1. Sī tē nōn cognōvissēmus, mīlitibus tuīs nōn crēdidissēmus.
2. Sī exercitus in terrā marīque vīcerit, patria nostra optima atque maxima erit.
3. Sī cīvēs rēgem pessimum sequī velint, imperium certē eī transferant.
4. Sī templum perderem, dī poenam dūrissimam ēligerent.
5. Sī eōs in urbe hāc habitāre patimur, magnae virtūtis sumus.
6. Nōn metuam morī, sī fāta mihi pepercerint.
7. Sī tam fēlīx nōn essēs, māior mortis metus quam vītae tibi esset.
8. Sī ego moriār, tū līberōs meōs amēs.
9. If the troops will have been conveyed to the city, they will pitch camp.
10. If ever you (plural) had wanted to speak on behalf of peace, you would have approved Caesar's plan.
11. If you (singular) were not condemning your brother of the crime, he would be a happy old man.
12. If the general should do otherwise, we would drive him out of the town immediately.

Romans and the "Other": "Race" in the Ancient World

Ancient Mediterranean civilizations had a strong sense of the "Other," of people who were "not Roman" or "not Greek," but they lacked our modern concept of "race." Climate, instead, determined physical and intellectual characteristics, and "ethnic" characteristics reflected the physical environment. Herodotus reports that "soft men come from soft places" (9.122.3). The author of the Hippocratic *Airs, Waters, Places* (c. 400 BCE) describes the northern Scythians as chilled, watery, and almost barren, like their wintry land (*AWP* 19), in contrast with the gentler peoples from warmer, milder regions where "manly courage could not be produced . . . for there pleasure necessarily reigns" (*AWP* 12). Vitruvius (6.1.4) bluntly declares that those dwelling in hot locales "fear to resist the sword" because of the thinness of their blood, yet the inhabitants of rugged, cold environs "stand against the sword without fear" because of their abundance of blood. For this reason, Vegetius (*de Re Militari* 1.2) asserts that the best military recruits come from temperate zones: although men from warmer areas may have more intelligence, their paucity of blood renders them cowardly; although men from colder climates may have more blood and consequently more courage, their lower intelligence compromises camp discipline. Men from temperate regions have sufficient intelligence so as not to imperil camp discipline, and sufficient blood so as not to fear being wounded. Medial climates were valued for engendering everything from good health (as with the Egyptians, whose climate lacks seasonal variation) to political preeminence (Pliny the Elder, *Naturalis Historia* 3.41 [*NLP* 10.11], among others, ascribes Roman ascendancy to Italy's pleasantly temperate climate).

Writers explore the Other to legitimize or criticize contemporary culture. For the Athenians, Centaurs and Amazons represent an inversion of acceptable social norms. Unlike proper Greek ladies, Amazon women reject marriage and deny their male children, delighting instead in war. The Amazons inhabit liminal areas, and their very existence threatens a well-regulated, male-ordered society. Like the Amazons, the mountain-dwelling composite Centaurs (half man, half horse) are bellicose, uncivilized, and unable to hold their liquor. Vanquishing such liminal peoples was among the standard labors of great heroes, including Hercules and Theseus, and both Amazons and Centaurs are metaphors for foreign foes.

In representing the Other, two contradictory trends prevail. On the one hand, liminal peoples are viewed as backward, savage, and barbaric (e.g., the Amazons and Centaurs), inferior to the culturally and technologically advanced Greeks and Romans. On the other hand, peoples at the "edges of the Earth" are often deemed morally superior, living a pure, simple life long abandoned by the corrupt center. These Other peoples are always, however, described in reference to contemporary society and institutions. When Aeneas surveys Dido's burgeoning Carthage, he remarks on how the Carthaginians pursue Roman conventions (Senate, laws, magistrates: Vergil, *Aeneid* 1.426–29). For Herodotus, the Egyptians are mirror opposites of the Greeks (women, for example, go to market, while the men weave: 2.35).

In Caesar (*de Bello Gallico* 6.11–28), the Gauls are pale, long-haired, trouser-wearing militants who count by nights rather than days. They believe in the transmigration of souls, and that they are descended from the god of the Underworld. Thus, not fearing death, the Gauls are intrepid in battle. For Tacitus (*Germania*), the Germans also serve as mythologized, distorting mirrors for Roman society. Eschewing urban infrastructure, jealously guarding chastity and fidelity (e.g., the Germans do not allow their widows to remarry), and staunchly rejecting the practice of exposing infants, the Germans represent an idealized view of primeval Roman purity—the "noble savage."

Further afield, even stranger peoples are imagined, straddling the idyllic and the monstrous. Like the Germans, the semi-nomadic Scythians on the Black Sea foreswear agriculture (the Germans do grow grain, but only for making beer, of which they are over-fond, as the Romans believe), and they keep wives in common. Like the Gauls, the Scythians practice human sacrifice. In Herodotus, the Scythians brutally scalp their enemies and drink their blood (4.64.1). In Homer, however, the Scythians are gentle, hospitable, and pious "milk-drinkers" (i.e., they do not drink wine, an essential aspect of Greek hospitality). In fact, Homer's Scythians are the most righteous of men (*Iliad* 8.16).

As early as Hesiod (eighth century BCE), we hear of swan-fighting Pygmies and people who live underground in Africa (*Catalogue of Women*). Especially resonant is the tradition of the "wonders of the East" that recounts tales of increasingly strange and weird hominids. In India, the Dog-Heads, despite their "doggyness," enjoy long life, purity, and justice, the hallmarks of the golden race. Among many other wonders, Pliny the Elder immortalizes Big-Heads, Shadow Feet, men whose ears are so large that they sleep in them, those whose feet are set backward, Illyrians who can kill with the glance of an eye, the one-eyed *Monocoli*, and the swift single-legged folk. Tacitus refers fleetingly to the hybrid Hellusii and Oxiones—with the faces of men and bodies of beasts—beyond the tribe of the Suebi in Germany, deeming such bizarre rumors "unknown" (*incompertum*) and therefore unverifiable (*Germania* 46.4).

The ancients believed that the edge of the world was reserved for those favored by the gods. The mythical Hyperboreans, dwelling "beyond Boreas," were celebrated as a carefree race living in a perfect climate. The Hyperboreans incidentally shared many features with the equally distant and mythologized, but very historical, Chinese (see *NLP* 10.10). There is one exception to the rule of liminality. Celebrated for its antiquity, mountainous and inaccessible Arcadia was regarded as a pastoral paradise, protected by its natural features, where its inhabitants still ate the food of the Golden Age (acorns) and practiced impeccable justice and hospitality. The Arcadians, however, seemed to straddle humanity and bestiality, and they were punished with lycanthropy whenever they transgressed acceptable social *mores* by committing human sacrifice and cannibalism.

SUGGESTIONS FOR FURTHER READING:

Almagor, E. and J. Skinner, eds. *Ancient Ethnography: New Approaches.* Bloomsbury Academic, 2013.

Beagon, Mary. *The Elder Pliny on the Human Animal:* Natural History *Book 7.* Oxford, 2005.

Campbell, G. L. *Strange Creatures: Anthropology in Antiquity.* Duckworth, 2006.

Ferguson, J. *Utopias of the Classical World.* Thames and Hudson, 1975.

Hartog, F. *The Mirror of Herodotus: The Representation of the Other in the Writing of History.* University of California, 1988.

Woolf, G. *Tales of the Barbarians: Ethnography and Empire in the Roman West.* Wiley-Blackwell, 2011.

PASSAGES

34.1. Vitruvius, *de Architectura* 6.1.9. The affects of climate on intelligence.

Ita nōn est mīrandum, sī acūtiōrēs efficit calidus āēr hominum mentēs, refrīgerātus autem contrā tardiōrēs.

Notes: **est mīrandum**: "we must (not) be amazed" (future passive periphrastic); **acūtus, -a, -um**: sharp, acute, quick-witted; **calidus, -a, -um**: warm, hot; **refrīgerō, -āre, -āvī, -ātus**: cool.

34.2. Pliny the Elder, *Naturalis Historia* **4.89.** In his geographical survey, Pliny has come to the extreme north, where he discusses the legendary, theoretical, and idealized race of the Hyperboreans. See *NLP* 10.9.

Pōne eōs montēs ultrāque Aquilōnem gens fēlix, sī crēdimus, quōs Hyperboreōs appellāvēre, annōsō dēgit aevō, fābulōsīs celebrāta mīrāculīs.

Notes: **pōne**: behind; **eōs montēs**: i.e., the Ripaean mountains of the far north; **Aquilō, -ōnis**, m: north wind; **annōsus, -a, -um**: full of years, long-lived; **dēgō, -ere, dēgī**: spend time, live; **fābulōsus, -a, -um**: fabled, renowned; **mīrāculum, -ī**, n: wonder, prodigy.

34.3. Tacitus, *Germania* **7.1.** In Germany, kings must earn the respect of their people.

Ducēs exemplō potius quam imperiō, sī promptī, sī conspicuī, sī ante aciem agant, admīrātiōne praesunt.

Notes: **potius quam**: rather than; **promptī** (*sunt*); **promptus, -a, -um**: ready, at hand; **conspicuī** (*sunt*); **conspicuus, -a, -um**: remarkable, visible, striking; **admīrātiō, -iōnis**, f: admiration, veneration.

34.4. Tacitus, *Germania* **17.1.** German clothing lacks the frills that one sees in Rome.

Tegumen omnibus sagum fībulā aut, sī dēsit, spīnā consertum.

Notes: **tegumen, teguminis**, n: covering; **sagum, -ī**, n: cloak made from coarse wool; **fībula, -ae**, f: clasp, brooch; **dēsum, -esse, -fuī**: be lacking; **spīna, -ae**, f: thorn; **conserō, -ere, -uī, -sertus**: fasten; construe the apodosis with *est*.

34.5. Tacitus, *Historiae* **5.13.** During his survey of the Jewish War that culminated in 70 CE, Tacitus explores the history and culture of the Jewish people, whom the Romans considered intractable.

Obstinātiō virīs fēminīsque pār; ac sī transferre sēdīs cōgerentur, māior vītae metus quam mortis.

Notes: **obstinātiō, -iōnis**, f: stubbornness; construe the apodosis with *esset*.

34.6. Pliny the Elder, *Naturalis Historia* 7.21. India is a remarkable land filled with strange peoples: dog-headed men, neckless folk with eyes in their shoulders, some with their feet turned backward, some with eight toes on each foot, others with feet large enough to provide shade in the heat of the summer. These bizarre physical features are reflected in an equally exotic landscape.

Arbōrēs quīdem tantae prōcēritātis trāduntur, ut sagittīs superiācī nequeant—et facit ūbertas solī, temperiēs caelī, aquārum abundantia, sī libeat crēdere, ut sub ūnā fīcō turmae condantur equitum.

Notes: **prōcēritās, -ātis**, f: height; **sagitta, -ae**, f: arrow; **superiāciō, -ere, -iēcī, -iactus**: shoot over the top of, overshoot; **nequeō, -īre, -īvī** or **-iī, -itus**: be unable; **ūbertas, -ātis**, f: fruitfulness, fertility, abundance; **abundantia, -iae**, f: richness, plenty; **fīcus, -ī**, f: fig tree; **turma, -ae**, f: troop, squadron.

34.7. Pliny the Elder, *Naturalis Historia* 6.89. Taprobane (perhaps modern Sri Lanka) was a mysterious place renowned for its wealth, honest people (they lacked courts and lawsuits), level economy (inflation was unknown), and aggressively democratic method of choosing kings.

Ēligī rēgem ā populō senectā clēmentiāque, līberōs nōn habentem, et, sī posteā gignat, abdicārī, nē fīat hērēditārium regnum.

Notes: this passage concludes a lengthy series of indirect statements; construe with *dīcunt*; **senecta, -ae**, f: old age; **clēmentia, -iae**, f: mercy, mildness; **abdicō, -āre, -āvī, -ātus**: renounce, reject, abdicate; **hērēditārius, -a, -um**: hereditary.

34.8. Pliny the Elder, *Naturalis Historia* **7.15.** Like the Psylli of North Africa (see *NLP* 33.12), the Marsi of Italy have remarkable powers against the venom of poisonous animals.

Simile et in Italiā Marsōrum genus dūrat, quōs ā Circae fīliō ortōs ferunt et ideō inesse iīs vim nātūrālem eam. Et tamen omnibus hominibus contrā serpentēs inest venēnum: ferunt ictās salīvā— ut ferventis aquae contactū—fugere, quod sī in faucēs penetrāverit, etiam morī.

Notes: **simile**: i.e., to the Psylli; **dūrō, -āre, -āvī, -ātus**: endure, be hardy; **Circē, -ae**, f: a famous mythological witch with great magical powers (see *NLP* 28); note the two indirect statements depending on the first *ferunt*; **nātūrālis, -e**: natural; **serpens, -entis (-ium)**, f: snake; **īciō, -ere, īcī, ictus**: strike, smite, hit; **ictās** (*serpentēs*); **salīva, -ae**, f: spittle, saliva; **ferveō, -ēre, ferbuī**: boil, seethe; **contactus, -ūs**, m: contact, touch; **faucēs, faucium**, f (plural) throat; **penetrō, -āre, -āvī, -ātus**: pass through, penetrate (construe *salīva* as the subject).

34.9. Martial 6.39.18–21. Martial mocks Cinna, whose wife has clearly been unfaithful. Meter: limping iambics (scazons).

Duae sorōrēs, illa nigra et haec rūfa,
Crotī choraulae vīlicīque sunt Carpī.
Iam Niobidārum grex tibī foret plēnus
sī spado Corēsus Dindymusque nōn esset.

Notes: **illa nigra**: this child's father may have been North African; **rūfus, -a, -um**: red, ruddy (this child's father may have been British or German); **Crotus, -ī**, m: a man's name from a Greek word meaning "rattle, finger-snapping, applause"; **choraulēs, -ae**, m: flute-player; **vīlicus, -ī**, m: steward, overseer; **sunt** (*fīliae*); **Carpus, -ī**, m: a man's name from a Greek word meaning "agricultural produce"; **Niobidēs, -ae**, m: child of Niobe, a mythological mother of fourteen children who boasted that she was a better mother than the gods. All of her children were slain as punishment for her hubris; **grex, gregis**, m/f: flock, herd, crowd, company; **tibi**: Cinna; **foret** = *futūrus esset*; **spadō, -ōnis**, m: eunuch; **Corēsus, -ī**, m: a man's name from a Greek word meaning "satisfy one's desires"; **Dindymus, -ī**, m: a man's name from the mountain in eastern Phrygia sacred to Cybele, who was worshipped by eunuch priests.

34.10. Horace, *Carmina* 3.9.9–16. This Ode captures an unusual dialogue between two ex-lovers who, in the end, are reconciled. Here they each praise their new paramours, from exotic corners of the Mediterranean world. Meter: second Asclepiadean.

> "Mē nunc Thressa Chloē regit,
> dulcīs docta modōs et citharae sciens,
>   prō quā nōn metuam morī,
> sī parcent animae fāta superstitī."

> "Mē torret face mūtuā
> Thūrīnī Calaïs fīlius Ornytī,
>   prō quō bis patiar morī,
> sī parcent puerō fāta superstitī."

Notes: **Thressus, -a, -um**: Thracian (semi-nomadic peoples who inhabited central Europe to the Black Sea, presented as warlike and polygamistic); **Chloē, -ēs**, f: a woman's name from a Greek word meaning "a plant's green shoot" (she was young); **modōs**: accusative of respect (with respect to . . .); **cithara, -ae**, f: cithara, a musical stringed instrument; **superstes (superstitis)**: surviving, outliving; **torreō, -ēre, -uī, tostus**: burn, enflame; **mūtuus, -a, -um**: mutual, reciprocal; **Thūrīnus, -a, -um**: from Thurii, a culturally Greek coastal city on Italy's instep; **Calaïs, -is**, m: the name of a young man, after the swift son of the north wind who joined the crew of the *Argo* in search of the golden fleece; **Ornytus, -ī**, m: a man's name, possibly referring to a son of Sisyphus, the mythological king who cheated death.

34.11. Catullus 84.1–2. Pronunciation is (and was) a clue to interpreting social status and ethnography. Catullus here satirizes the country bumpkin Arrius, who attempts to appear up-to-date with the latest fashions in pronunciation (i.e., emphasizing the "h" in *pulcher*). Arrius, however, overdoes it, getting many of the words wrong. Meter: elegiac couplets.

> "Chommoda" dīcēbat, sī quandō "commoda" vellet
>   dīcere, et "insidiās" Arrius "hinsidiās."

Notes: **chommoda** = *commoda*; **commodus, -a, -um**: opportune, timely; **hinsidiās** = *insidiās*; **insidiae, -ārum**, f (plural): ambush, plot.

34.12. Ovid, *Metamorphoses* 7.17–22. Medea, the exotic princess from the Black Sea, daughter of the king who possessed the golden fleece, was a foreigner, used by Juno and Venus as a pawn to help Jason retrieve the notorious fleece. Here, the young Medea, forced by the gods to fall in love with Jason, tries desperately to fight these feelings, which she knows to be foolish and dangerous. Meter: dactylic hexameter.

"Excute virgineō conceptās pectore flammās,
sī potes, infēlix! Sī possem, sānior essem!
Sed trahit invītam nova vīs, aliudque cupīdō,
mens aliud suādet: videō meliōra probōque,
dēteriōra sequor. Quid in hospite, rēgia virgō,
ūreris et thalamōs aliēnī concipis orbis?"

Notes: **excutiō, -ere, -cussī, -cussus**: shake off (from); **virgineus, -a, -um**: maidenly; **infelix (infelicis)**: unfortunate, unhappy, unlucky; **invītus, -a, -um**: unwilling; **dēterior, -ius**: unfavorable, weak (no positive degree); **ūrō, -ere, ussī, ustus**: burn; **thalamus, -ī, m**: marriage bed.

EXTRA PASSAGES: FOREIGN LEADERS

Ethnographies traditionally included lengthy discussions about foreign systems of government. Here we explore some non-Italian rulers who held power either abroad or at Rome.

34.13. Caesar, *de Bello Gallico* 6.11.4. In Gaul, leaders must continually prove their worth and protect their people, or they will lose power.

Suōs enim quisque opprimī et circumvenīrī nōn patitur, neque, aliter sī faciat, ullam inter suōs habet auctōritātem.

Notes: **opprimō, -ere, -pressī, -pressus**: overwhelm, crush.

34.14. Scriptores *Historiae Augustae: Vita Septimii Severi* **23.3.** Born in northern Africa to a mixed-race family (his father was Carthaginian, his mother was Roman), Septimius Severus pursued a political career at Rome, became embroiled in the civil wars of 191–193 CE, and finally usurped the throne in 193 CE. Severus was fluent in Punic, Greek, and Latin, which he spoke with a slight accent, and he was always embarrassed by his sisters' thick accents. Here we read Septimius's alleged last words.

"Turbātam Rem pūblicam ubique accēpī, pācātam etiam Brittannīs relinquō, senex ac pedibus aeger firmum imperium Antōnīnīs meīs relinquens, sī bonī erunt, imbēcillum, sī malī."

Notes: **pācō, -āre, -āvī, -ātus**: pacify; **Brittannīs**: dying at York, Severus campaigned in Britain during 208–211; **pedibus**: Severus may have suffered from gout; **firmus, -a, -um**: strong; **Antōnīnius, -iī**, m: Antonine (after assuming power, Severus secured for himself a posthumous adoption from Marcus Aurelius [Marcus Aurelius Antoninus Augustus, ruled 161–180 CE] to lend authority to his shaky political position; here he refers to his two sons, Geta and Caracalla); **imbēcillus, -a, -um**: weak, feeble (the sons, of course, were worthless: Caracalla murdered his brother and was himself assassinated in Turkey by one of his personal bodyguards in 217 CE).

34.15. Scriptores *Historiae Augustae Tyranni Triginta* **15.1.** From 253 to 268 CE, during the reign of Gallienus, thirty-two men claimed the principate or aspired to it. Odenatus never actually became emperor of Rome, but he was instrumental in protecting Roman interests in the East, if we are to believe this biographer.

Nisi Odenātus, princeps Palmȳrēnōrum, captō Valeriānō, fessīs Rōmānae Reīpūblicae vīribus sumpsisset imperium, in oriente perditae rēs essent.

Notes: **Palmȳrēnus, -a, -um**: of Palmyra, a city in Syria; **Valeriānus, -ī**, m: ruled 253–259 CE, famously taken prisoner by King Shapur I of Persia, who tortured his captive to death; **oriens (-entis)** m: the East.

Gerunds and Gerundives

1. Infinitives are neuter singular verbal nouns that can appear in the nominative case (e.g., as the subject of an impersonal verb: see *NLP* 20) or accusative case (as a complementary infinitive). **GERUNDS** are another type of verbal noun. In English, they end in "-ing" (e.g., "I love <u>swimming</u>"). In Latin, they can occur in the genitive, dative, accusative, and ablative cases, and can fulfill all the usual syntactic functions. Consider the following examples:

Vitruvius, *de Architectura* 5.3.2: **Āēr, conclūsus curvātūrā neque habens potestātem <u>vagandī</u>, <u>versandō</u> confervescit**. Air, restricted in an arched ceiling and not having the power <u>of circulating</u>, grows hot <u>by moving about</u>.
    Vagandī is a gerund in the genitive case. *Versandō* is a gerund in the ablative case.

Ovid, *Metamorphoses* 15.375–77: **Sēmina līmus habet viridēs generantia rānās, / et generat truncās pedibus, mox apta <u>natandō</u> / crūra dat**. Mud holds seeds producing green frogs, and it produces (frogs) deprived of feet, (but) soon it gives legs suitable <u>for swimming</u>.
    Natandō is a gerund in the dative case.

Vitruvius, *de Architectura* 2.1.6: **Cum autem cotīdiē <u>faciendō</u> tritiōrēs manūs ad <u>aedificandum</u> perfēcissent**.... When moreover <u>by working</u> daily they had made their hands more callused <u>for building</u>....
    Aedificandum is a gerund in the accusative case and *faciendō* is a gerund in the ablative case.

Martial 5.76.3–4: **Tū quoque cāvistī <u>cenandō</u> tam male semper/ne possēs umquam, Cinna, perīre fame.** <u>By</u> always <u>dining</u> so badly, Cinna, you also have taken precautions that you could never die from hunger.

    Cēnandō is a gerund in the ablative case.

2. In Latin, **GERUNDS** are formed from the present stem of the verb and are characterized by the -**nd**- that precedes the second declension neuter ending. The gerund does not exist in the nominative singular, and it has no plural forms. Study the following table:

Case	1st Conj.	2nd Conj.	3rd Conj.	3rd Conj. (-io)	4th Conj.
Nominative	–	–	–	–	–
Genitive	ama**ndī**	doce**ndī**	mitte**ndī**	capie**ndī**	audie**ndī**
Dative	ama**ndō**	doce**ndō**	mitte**ndō**	capie**ndō**	audie**ndō**
Accusative	ama**ndum**	doce**ndum**	mitte**ndum**	capie**ndum**	audie**ndum**
Ablative	ama**ndō**	doce**ndō**	mitte**ndō**	capie**ndō**	audie**ndō**

3. **GERUNDIVES**, otherwise known as future passive participles, are verbal adjectives. Consider the following examples:

Ovid, *Metamorphoses* 1.74: **Cessērunt nitidīs <u>habitandae</u> piscibus <u>undae</u>.** <u>Waves</u> <u>to be inhabited</u> by shining fish withdrew.

    The gerundive *habitandae* modifies the noun *undae*.

Juvenal, *Saturae* 1.95–96: **Nunc <u>sportula</u> prīmō / līmine parva sedet turbae rapienda togātae.** Now a little <u>basket</u>, <u>to be seized</u> by a togate crowd, sits on the first threshold.

    The gerundive *rapienda* modifies the noun *sportula*.

4. You first learned the paradigm for gerundives in *NLP* 22. These future passive participles are formed by adding -**nd**- to the present stem of the

verb, and then first and second declension adjective endings. The following table contains no new forms:

First Conjugation	ama**ndus**, -a, -um	(about) to be loved
Second Conjugation	doce**ndus**, -a, -um	(about) to be taught
Third Conjugation	mitte**ndus**, -a, -um	(about) to be sent
Third Conjugation (-io)	capie**ndus**, -a, -um	(about) to be seized
Fourth Conjugation	audie**ndus**, -a, -um	(about) to be heard

5. Gerunds can technically take direct objects, but Latin prefers to use a gerundive, or future passive participle, in agreement with a noun. Consider the following examples:

Vitruvius, *de Architectura* 10.13.1: **Carthāginiēnsēs ad G͟ā͟d͟ī͟s o͟p͟p͟u͟g͟n͟a͟n͟d͟ā͟s castra posuērunt**. The Carthaginians pitched camp for the purpose of a͟t͟t͟a͟c͟k͟-i͟n͟g͟ ͟G͟a͟d͟e͟s (literally "for Gades to be attacked").

Vegetius, *de Re Militari* 3.23: **Sed genus animālium, h͟a͟r͟ē͟n͟ī͟s et t͟o͟l͟e͟r͟a͟n͟d͟a͟e s͟i͟t͟ī aptum, confūsās etiam in pulvere ventō viās absque errōre dīrigere memorātur**. But (this) type of animal (the camel), suited to e͟n͟d͟u͟r͟i͟n͟g͟ ͟s͟a͟n͟d͟s a͟n͟d͟ ͟t͟h͟i͟r͟s͟t (literally "for sands and thirst to be endured"), recalls how to keep straight from error on roads even obscured in the dust by wind.

6. The gerund or gerundive can be used with the preposition *ad* or postpositions *causā* or *grātiā* to express purpose. Consider the following examples:

Caesar, *de Bello Gallico* 1.3.1: **Constituērunt ea quae a͟d͟ ͟p͟r͟o͟f͟i͟c͟i͟s͟c͟e͟n͟d͟u͟m pertinērent comparāre**. They decided to prepare those things which pertain t͟o͟ ͟s͟e͟t͟t͟i͟n͟g͟ ͟o͟u͟t.

Caesar, *de Bello Gallico* 1.3.3: **A͟d͟ ͟e͟ā͟s͟ ͟r͟ē͟s͟ ͟c͟o͟n͟f͟i͟c͟i͟e͟n͟d͟ā͟s Orgetorix dēligitur**. Orgetorix is chosen f͟o͟r͟ ͟c͟o͟m͟p͟l͟e͟t͟i͟n͟g͟ ͟t͟h͟e͟s͟e͟ ͟t͟h͟i͟n͟g͟s.

Caesar, *de Bello Gallico* 1.47.5: **Quid ad sē venīrent? An s͟p͟e͟c͟u͟l͟a͟n͟d͟ī͟ ͟c͟a͟u͟s͟ā?** Why did they come to him? F͟o͟r͟ ͟t͟h͟e͟ ͟p͟u͟r͟p͟o͟s͟e͟ ͟o͟f͟ ͟s͟p͟y͟i͟n͟g?

Cicero, *Philippica* 14.4: **Eiusdem D. Brūtī conservandī grātiā, consul sortītū ad bellum profectus A. Hirtius.** <u>For the sake of protecting this same Didius Brutus</u>, the consul Aulus Hirtius set out to war by lot.

I. Required Vocabulary

NOUNS

māteria, -iae, f: subject matter

iūdicium, -iī, n: trial, legal investigation, decision
lībertīnus, -ī, m: freedman
monumentum, -ī, n: memorial, monument

arx, arcis (-ium), f: citadel, fortress
hērēs, hērēdis, m: heir
iūs, iūris, n: right, law

ADJECTIVES

nūdus, -a, -um: plain, mere

VERBS

interrogō, -āre, -āvī, -ātus: examine, question

studeō, -ēre, -uī (+ dative): strive for, be devoted to, study

addūcō, -ere, -duxī, -ductus: bring, lead
committō, -ere, -mīsī, -missus: join, entrust to, bring together in a contest
concēdō, -ere, -cessī, -cessus: yield, grant
consulō, -ere, -uī, -sultus: consult
prōpōnō, -ere, -posuī, -positus: expose, display
rescrībō, -ere, -scrīpsī, -scriptus: write back, answer a petition
vehō, -ere, vexī, vectus: convey, carry

confiteor, -ērī, confessus sum: confess, reveal, acknowledge

auferō, -ferre, abstulī, ablātus: carry away, take away, remove
referō, -ferre, -tulī, -lātus: bring back, return, report
subeō, -īre, -īvī or **-iī, -itus**: approach, undergo, endure

II. Translate the following sentences from Latin to English or English to Latin.

1. Lībertīnus genere dīcendī optimō līberōs docēre cōnātus est.
2. Iūdicium erat ad hominēs malōs ab urbe auferendōs.
3. Cūr Iūliam amandō perdere vīs?
4. Caesar XXX legiōnēs arcis servandae grātiā mīsit.
5. Ego carminibus scrībendīs studeō et mē poētam clārissimum futūrum esse spērō.
6. Imperātor LXXV nāvēs ad vincendōs hostēs addūcī iussit.
7. Monumentum statuendum vidēbitis.
8. Nōs templī aedificandī causā in oppidum venīre confitēbāmur.
9. I desire to return to Rome in order to die.
10. My friend used to write many letters for the sake of encouraging his parents.
11. The soldiers set out to the provinces for the sake of waging war.
12. We will try to find material worthy of singing songs.

The Roman Legal System

At *Aeneid* 6.851–53, Anchises tells his son that the role of the Roman Empire will be to impose peace and order on the world:

> *Tū regere imperiō populōs, Rōmāne, mementō*
> *(hae tibi erunt artēs), pācīque impōnere mōrem,*
> *parcere subiectīs et dēbellāre superbōs.*

> You, Roman, remember to rule the people with imperial power
> (these will be skills for you), and to impose a way for peace,
> to spare the subjugated and to conquer the proud.

This "peace and order" (*imperiō, pācīque mōrem*) is established in a very real way through the institution of Roman law, which remains among the most enduring facets of Rome's legacy. Rhetoric, the art of speaking properly and developing persuasive arguments, was the cornerstone of Roman upper-class education, and most

Roman aristocrats, especially those with political ambitions, had some practical experience with the law courts. We also note that Cicero's speeches are legal documents, delivered as defenses or prosecutions to the Senate in its role as a judiciary body.

Roman history is replete with class conflict, and from this conflict, by 449 BCE, came the *Leges Duodecim Tabularum* (the "Twelve Tables": see *NLP* 25). Livy tells us that embassies were sent to Athens to study Solon's great democratic constitution, and that the Tables were established in a spirit of open debate (*ab Urbe Condita* 3.31). The final product was cut onto twelve ivory or bronze tablets, displayed in the Roman Forum where all citizens could consult them. The original tablets were destroyed during the Gallic siege of Rome in 390 BCE and survive only in short extracts from later writers. Our surviving fragments point to an unsystematic collection of rights and procedures regarding all the usual legal concerns: summoning someone to court, theft and petty crime, loans, paternal rights, marriage, guardianship, property rights, and state religion. The Twelve Tables provided the foundation of the incipient Roman legal system, ending the patrician monopoly on the justice system and formalizing the right of appeal for all citizens, regardless of class or income.

Over the years, the Twelve Tables became obsolete as laws were modernized and replaced with edicts from the urban praetors responsible for overseeing trials between Roman citizens. Private grievances were brought to the attention of a praetor, who then assigned a third-party *iūdex* (judge) to listen to both sides of the case (the "trial by a jury of peers" was introduced in England by the thirteenth century: *Magna Carta* article 39). The *iūdex*, who was not a "professional" lawyer in the modern sense and whose knowledge of law likely lacked any sophistication or depth, then issued a binding and unappealable verdict. As with many other aspects of Roman life (e.g., medicine: see *NLP* 33), the practice of law reflected the Roman ideal of self-sufficiency. Political crime (extortion), in contrast, fell to the purview of dedicated criminal courts with large panels of senatorial *iūdicēs*. Private law began to arise as a separate profession in the third and second centuries BCE, when politically ambitious and legally savvy Romans (*patrōnī*) began to offer legal advice to their *clientēs* in exchange for future electoral support. Cicero describes these *iūrisconsultī* (jurisconsults, amateur lawyers) disbursing legal advice in the Forum or in their homes (*de Oratore* 3.33), and one of

Trimalchio's dinner guests has purchased a set of law books for his clever son in the hope that the lad will acquire some law for "home use" (*ad domusiōnem*: Petronius, *Satyrica* 46).

Nonetheless, by the late Republic, some jurists began analyzing court rulings and isolating the underlying legal principles. This gave rise, eventually, to a genre of technical legal literature, represented by hundreds of juristic treatises penned from 30 BCE to 235 CE. These texts explore many aspects of private and state law, including provincial administration, the military, tax, and criminal law. The ninety-book *Digesta* of Lucius Salvius Iulianus, a prominent jurist of the early second century CE, whose creative approach and analogical reasoning is much admired, systematically expounds laws derived from the edicts of the praetors.

One of the most prominent writers on Roman law was Gaius (his full name is unknown to us), who practiced and taught law at Rome and Beirut in the second century CE. In the *Institutiones*, a collection of his elementary law lectures, Gaius employs the Socratic method, wherein he poses a legal query but leaves it unanswered. "Gaius noster," as Justinian affectionately calls him, was responsible for developing a new type of analytic legal literature, a natural focus for a Roman citizen working in the provinces. The *Institutiones* are the best known of Gaius's many legal treatises.

Other prominent jurisprudential writers—all as prolific as Gaius—include Aemilius Papinianus, long regarded as among the best Roman lawyers, on the staff of emperor Septimius Severus (ruled 193–211 CE) and who, like his emperor, may have hailed from North Africa. In his *Quaestiones* (in thirty-seven books), he explored the ethical basis of laws. Papinianus's contemporary Iulius Paulus was a celebrated imperial lawyer whose *Quaestiones* (in twenty-six books) and *Responsa* (in twenty-three books) were based on his extensive private practice as a legal consultant. Domitius Ulpianus, from Tyre in Lebanon, was another renowned Severan lawyer. Ulpian composed more than two hundred books in response to the *Constitūtio Antontiniāna*, decreed by Septimius Severus's older son Caracalla, who extended Roman citizenship to all free inhabitants of empire in 212 CE. Explaining Roman law to a new and diverse body of Roman citizens, Ulpian emphasized the universal character of Roman law and how it was based rationally in natural law.

Roman emperors had the authority to intervene in suits and trials, and citizens often appealed to the emperor with petitions on points of Roman law, both significant and trivial. Claudius (ruled 41–54 CE), a particularly active imperial *iūrisconsultus*, was thus mocked by Seneca the Younger (*Apocolocyntosis* 12). Pliny the Younger preserves Trajan's rescripts to his own administrative queries as governor of Bithynia-Pontus in 112 CE. By Trajan's reign (98–117 CE), the imperial rescript attained legal authority. Under Diocletian (ruled 284–305 CE), two legal collections of imperial rescripts were produced: the *Codex Gregorianus* by the obscure Gregorius in 291 CE, and the *Codex Hermogenianus* by the eponymous master of petitions in 295 CE. Theodosian II (ruled 408–450 CE) sponsored a new, more practical legal codification, in sixteen books, including general laws (edited for concision and clarity), but excluding rescripts. The *Codex Theodosianus* was superseded in 529 CE by the *Codex Iustinianus*, a collection of 5,000 laws. Justinian's *Codex* was supplemented by the *Institutiones*, an elementary textbook in four books, and the *Digesta*, a compendium in fifty books intended for advanced students. Justinian's comprehensive new collection included material from existing codices and recognized the authority of five legal writers in particular—Gaius, Papinianus, Paulus, Ulpian, and Ulpian's student Herennius Modestinus. Justinian aimed for a true codification of Roman law, excising redundant laws and resolving conflicting ones. The *Codex Iustinianus* was part of Justinian's effort to restore law and order (in part by reducing the number of lawsuits) and to extend the Empire, emphasizing the symbiosis of legal and military achievement.

Through Justinian's efforts, the Roman legal code survived. It provided the bedrock of civil law in western Europe well into the eighteenth century, supplanted in 1804 in France, for example, by the Napoleonic Code—a comprehensive, rational restructuring of French law, written in vernacular language, and rigorously excluding religious content. The categories of the Napoleonic Code, nonetheless, were drawn from Justinian's *Codex* rather than from contemporary French law. Although the Roman legal system continues to have an influence on British (and American) common law, the British *Magna Carta* of 1215 CE represents a break with Roman legal (and religious) tradition. The *Magna Carta* curtailed the powers of the king, established a notion of personal liberty, and, in its very first clause, called for the separation of church and state, a concept that would have been anathema in ancient Rome.

SUGGESTIONS FOR FURTHER READING:

Crook, John A. *Law and Life of Rome.* Cornell, 1967.
Harries, Jill. *Law and Crime in the Roman World.* Cambridge, 2007.
Johnston, David. *Roman Law in Context.* Cambridge, 1999.
Nicholas, Barry. *An Introduction to Roman Law.* Oxford, 1976.
Stein, Peter. *Roman Law in European History.* Cambridge, 1999.

PASSAGES

35.1. Justinian, *Digesta* **1.5.27.** Ex-slaves can never attain the legal status of free-born citizens.

Eum, quī sē lībertīnum esse fatētur, nec adoptandō patrōnus ingenuum facere potuit.

Notes: **adoptō, -āre, -āvī, -ātus:** choose, adopt; **patrōnus, -ī,** m: protector, defender, advocate, patron; **ingenuus, -a, -um:** native, natural, free-born.

35.2. Justinian, *Digesta* **1.7.40.2.** Eunuchs are permitted the legal right to draw up wills and name heirs, despite the Roman abhorrence of bodily deformity.

Spadō adrogandō suum hērēdem sibi adsciscere potest nec eī corporāle vitium impedimentō est.

Notes: **spadō, -ōnis,** m: eunuch; **adrogō, -āre, -āvī, -ātus:** claim, adjudge; **adsciscō, -ere, -scīvī, -scītus:** admit, adopt; **corporālis, -e:** corporeal, bodily; **impedimentum, -ī,** n: hindrance.

35.3. Justinian, *Digesta* **1.8.4** *praefatio* **1.** Fishing is allowed provided that …

Nēmō igitur ad lītus maris accēdere prohibētur piscandī causā, dum tamen ullīus et aedificiīs et monumentīs abstineātur.

Notes: **piscor, -ārī:** fish; **aedificium, -iī,** n: building; **abstineō, -ēre, -tinuī, -tentus:** hold back, keep away from.

35.4. Justinian, *Digesta* 2.1.3. The complex prerogative of *imperium* (see *NLP* 18).

Imperium aut merum aut mixtum est. Merum est imperium habēre gladiī potestātem ad animadvertendum facīnorōsōs hominēs, quod etiam "potestās" appellātur.

Notes: **merus, -a, -um**: pure, unmixed; **animadvertō, -ere, -vertī, -versus**: notice, punish; **facīnorōsus, -a, -um**: criminal, wicked, "full of crime."

35.5. Justinian, *Institutiones* 1.2.5. Although merely a decree of the Senate, the *senatūs consultum* came to have the force of law. Justinian here explains its the origins.

Senātūs consultum est quod senātus iubet atque constituit. Nam cum auctus est populus Rōmānus in eum modum ut difficile sit in ūnum eum convocārī lēgis sanciendae causā, aequum vīsum est senātum vice populī consulī.

Notes: **consultum, -ī**, n: resolution, decree; **augeō, -ēre, auxī, auctus**: enlarge, increase; **eum**: *populum Rōmānum*; **ūnum**: i.e., one deliberative body; **convocō, -āre, -āvī, -ātus**: assemble; **sanciō, -ere, sanxī, sanctus**: ratify, decree; **vice** (+ genitive): in place of.

35.6. Justinian, *Digesta* 27.10.1 *praefatio*. The state appoints guardians to oversee the finances of spendthrifts and lunatics.

Lēge Duodecim Tabulārum prōdigō interdīcitur bonōrum suōrum administrātiō, quod mōribus quidem ab initiō introductum est. Sed solent hodiē praetōrēs vel praesidēs—sī tālem hominem invēnerint, quī neque tempus neque fīnem expensārum habet, sed bona sua dīlacerandō et dissipandō profūdit—cūrātōrem eī dare exemplō furiōsī. Et tamdiū erunt ambō in cūrātiōne, quamdiū vel furiōsus sānitātem vel ille sānōs mōrēs recēperit.

Notes: **tabula, -ae**, f: tablet, panel; **prōdigus, -a, -um**: wasteful, lavish, prodigal; **interdīcō, -ere, -dixī, -dictus**: forbid, prohibit; **administrātiō, -iōnis**, f: management, care of affairs; **quod**: a thing which; **introdūcō, -ere, -duxī, -ductus**: lead in, introduce, guide; **praeses, praesidis**, m: guardian; **expensa, -ae**, f: expenditure; **dīlacerō, -āre, -āvī, -ātus**: tear to pieces, wound, jeopardize; **dissipō, -āre, -āvī, -ātus**: squander, waste; **profundō, -ere, -fūdī, -fūsus**: pour out, squander, waste; **cūrātor, -ōris**, m: manager, guardian; **furiōsus, -a, -um**: furious, mad, wild, lunatic (substantive); **tamdiū**: so long as; **cūrātiō, -iōnis**, f: administration, management; **quamdiū**: as long as, until; **sānitās, -ātis**, f: health, soundness of mind.

35.7. Justinian, *Digesta* **11.7.2.6.** On monuments.

Monumentum est, quod memoriae servandae grātiā existat.

Notes: **existō, -ere, -stitī, -stitus**: appear, come forth, arise.

35.8. Justinian, *Digesta* **14.2.3.** The financial responsibilities of travelers on passenger-carrying vessels.

Cum arbor aut aliud nāvis instrūmentum removendī commūnis perīculī causā dēiectum est, contribūtiō dēbētur.

Notes: **instrūmentum, -ī**, n: equipment; **removeō, -ēre, -mōvī, -mōtus**: withdraw, remove; **dēiciō, -ere, -iēcī, -iectus**: cast down, fell; **contribūtiō, -iōnis**, f: contribution, subsidy.

35.9. Justinian, *Digesta* **14.2.10** *praefatio.* The slave owner's liability if a slave dies in transit on a cargo ship.

Sī vehenda mancipia conduxistī, prō eō mancipiō, quod in nāve mortuum est, vectūra tibi nōn dēbētur.

Notes: **mancipium, -iī**, n: a slave acquired by the contract of a sale; **quod**: "with respect to that slave who"; **condūcō, -ere, -duxī, -ductus**: contract (a ship) for, hire; **vectūra, -ae**, f: fare, transport fee; **tibi**: the slave owner.

35.10. Justinian, *Digesta* **23.1.4** *praefatio* **1.4.1.** Roman law recognized many types of marriage ceremonies as binding—even marriages of mere consent. Neither bride nor groom had to be physically present at the wedding!

Sufficit nūdus consensus ad constituenda sponsālia. Dēnique constat et absentī absentem dēspondērī posse, et hoc cottīdiē fierī.

Notes: **sufficiō, -ere, -fēcī, -fectus**: be adequate; **consensus, -ūs**, m: agreement; **sponsālia, -ium**, n (plural): betrothal; **constat**: introduces two indirect statements; **absens (-entis)**: absent, missing (substantive); **dēspondeō, -ēre, -spondī, -sponsus**: pledge, promise, betroth, marry; **cottīdiē**: daily.

35.11. Justinian, *Digesta* 23.1.12.1. Despite the strict code of tradition and law that governed the behavior of women, a daughter could, in fact, though rarely, refuse her father's choice of groom.

Tunc autem sōlum dissentiendī ā patre licentia fīliae concēditur, sī indignum mōribus vel turpem sponsum eī pater ēligat.

Notes: **dissentiō, -īre, -sensī, -sensus**: oppose, disagree; **licentia, -iae**, f: freedom; **indignus, -a, -um**: unworthy, disgraceful, shameful; **sponsus, -ī**, m: groom.

35.12. Justinian, *Digesta* 24.2.2.2. The legal formula for ending an engagement.

In sponsālibus quoque discutiendīs placuit renuntiātiōnem intervenīre oportere: in quā rē haec verba probāta sunt: "condiciōne tuā nōn ūtor."

Notes: **sponsālia, -ium**, n (plural): betrothal, engagement; **discutiō, -ere, -cussī, -cussus**: shatter, break; **renuntiātiō, -iōnis**, f: public announcement; **interveniō, -īre, -vēnī, -ventus**: occur; **condiciō, -iōnis**, f: agreement, contract, condition, marriage.

EXTRA PASSAGES: ROMAN EDUCATION

Although Roman law protected the rights of the individual, it did not mandate education. Education was instead informal and *ad hoc*, overseen by the *paterfamilias* and emphasizing Roman morality. In wealthier households, a Greek slave was often retained to teach the children (e.g., Livius Andronicus, see *NLP* 12). But Cato the Elder, preferring not to entrust his son's upbringing to a foreigner, oversaw the boy's education directly. Schools were not institutionalized, and the school house, as such, was not universal. Martial (12.57.5) complains about noisy classes that start at dawn on the sidewalks—where no rent would be due. Individuals like Pliny the Younger, however, might endow a school or a teacher in a small town. Most children learned reading, writing, and arithmetic, but education usually stopped with vocational training. Some children continued with the *Grammaticus* curriculum, wherein boys (and some girls) would learn language and literature. As preparation for a career in law, wealthier boys would pursue the *Rhetor* curriculum under famous teachers at Rome or abroad (Cicero's prodigal son studied at Athens). We are fortunate to have Quintilian's (35–90s CE) twelve-book

Institutio Oratoria, which describes rhetorical training in detail, for the infant all the way up to the public servant.

35.13. **Quintilian,** *Institutio Oratoria* **1.1.26.** Even Roman babies played with toy blocks.

> Nōn exclūdō autem id quod est nōtum irrītandae ad discendum infantiae grātiā: eburneās etiam litterārum formās in lūsum offerre.

Notes: **exclūdō, -ere, -clūsī, -clūsus**: reject, rule out; **irrītō, -āre, -āvī, -ātus**: stir up, excite; **infantia, -iae,** f: infancy; **eburneus, -a, -um**: ivory; **lūsus, -ūs,** m: play.

35.14. **Pliny the Younger,** *Epistulae* **4.13.3.** Many small towns lacked the resources for their own schools, and children often had to travel miles for their education. Pliny tells his friend Tacitus that he has decided to endow a school in his hometown, Comum.

> Proximē cum in patriā meā fuī, vēnit ad mē salūtandum mūnicipis meī fīlius praetextātus. Huic ego "Studēs?" inquam. Respondit: "Etiam." "Ubi?" "Mediolānī." "Cūr nōn hīc?" Et pater eius—erat enim ūnā atque etiam ipse adduxerat puerum—"Quia nullōs hīc praeceptōrēs habēmus."

Notes: **proximē**: most recently; **salūtō, -āre, -āvī, -ātus**: greet; **mūniceps, mūnicipis,** m/f: fellow citizen; **praetextātus, -a, -um**: referring to the magisterial purple-bordered *toga praetexta* worn by Roman boys before they reached adulthood; **inquam**: "I said"; **Mediolānī**: at Milan; **hīc**: Comum; **ūnā**: together, along with; **praeceptor, -ōris,** m: teacher.

35.15. **Suetonius,** *de Grammaticis* **17.** The pedagogical tricks of a famous teacher.

> M. Verrius Flaccus lībertīnus docendī genere maximē clāruit. Namque ad exercitanda discentium ingenia aequālēs inter sē committere solēbat, prōpositā nōn sōlum māteriā quam scrīberent sed et praemiō quod victor auferret.

Notes: **clāreō, -ēre, -uī**: be distinguished, be illustrious, be famous; **exercitō, -āre, -āvī, -ātus**: train hard; **aequālis, -e**: equal, of the same skill level.

LESSON 36

Future Passive Periphrastics, Supines, and Other Subjunctive Clauses

1. The **FUTURE PASSIVE PERIPHRASTIC**, comprised of the gerundive (see *NLP* 35) and the verb "to be," is used to express necessity. Consider the following examples:

   Vitruvius, *de Architectura* 5.9.1: **Post scaenam porticūs <u>sunt constituendae</u>.** Behind the stage building, colonnades <u>must be established</u>.

   Ovid, *Fasti* 1.72: **Nunc <u>dīcenda</u> bonā <u>sunt</u> bona verba diē.** Now good words <u>must be spoken</u> on a good day.

   Caesar, *de Bello Gallico* 5.28.1: **Quod cīvitātem ignōbilem atque humilem Eburōnum suā sponte populō Rōmānō bellum facere ausam vix <u>erat</u> <u>crēdendum</u>.** <u>It was</u> hardly <u>believable</u> (literally: to be believed) that the obscure and lowly state of the Eburni dared to make war on the Roman people of their own free will.

2. The future passive periphrastic appears in many types of subordinate clauses, including indirect statements.

   Caesar, *de Bello Gallico* 7.73.2: **Quārē ad haec rursus opera <u>addendum (esse)</u> Caesar putāvit.** Wherefore Caesar thought that in turn there <u>ought to be an addition</u> to these works.
   Addendum (esse) is a future passive periphrastic in indirect statement.

Caesar, *de Bello Gallico* 1.7.3: **Concēdendum (esse) nōn putābat.** He did not think that (their request) <u>should be granted</u>.

Concedendum (esse) is a future passive periphrastic in indirect statement.

Justinian, *Digesta* 2.4.13: **Generāliter eās personās, quibus reverentia praestanda est, sine iussū praetōris in iūs vocāre nōn possumus.** Generally without an order of the praetor we are not able to summon to court those people to whom respect <u>must be owed</u>.

Praestanda est is a future passive periphrastic in a relative clause.

3. In Latin, most passive verbs and passive verb constructions are completed by an ablative of personal agent or an ablative of means. The future passive periphrastic, however, takes a **DATIVE OF AGENT**. Consider the following examples:

Catullus 61.46–47: **Quis deus magis est <u>amātīs</u> petendus <u>amantibus</u>?** What god ought to be sought more <u>by beloved lovers</u>?

Ovid, *Ars Amatoria* 1.386: **Nōn <u>tibi</u> ab ancillā est incipienda venus.** A love affair must not be begun <u>by you</u> from her maid.

Ovid, *Ars Amatoria* 1.44: **Quaerenda est <u>oculīs</u> apta puella <u>tuīs</u>.** A suitable girl must be sought <u>by your eyes</u>.

4. The **SUPINE** is another verbal noun formed from the fourth principal part of the Latin verb. Supines are declined like fourth declension nouns and occur only in the accusative and ablative singular. Study the following table:

Case	1st Conj.	2nd Conj.	3rd Conj.	3rd Conj. (-io)	4th Conj.
Accusative	amā**tum**	doc**tum**	mis**sum**	cap**tum**	audī**tum**
Ablative	amā**tū**	doc**tū**	mis**sū**	cap**tū**	audī**tū**

5. Supines in the accusative case are used to express purpose, especially after *īre* and other verbs of "coming and going." Consider the following examples:

Catullus 10.1–2: **Varus mē meus ad suōs amōrēs/<u>vīsum</u> duxerat ē forō otiōsum.** My Varus had led me, at leisure, from the Forum <u>to see</u> his love (i.e., "for the purpose of seeing his love").

Ovid, *Ars Amatoria* 1.99: **<u>Spectātum</u> veniunt; veniunt spectentur ut ipsae.** They (the women) come <u>to watch</u> (i.e., "for the purpose of watching"); they come in order that they themselves be watched.

6. Supines in the ablative case often function as ablatives of specification after certain Latin adjectives. Consider the following examples:

Pliny the Elder, *Naturalis Historia* 3.151: **Insulae in Ausoniō marī praeter iam dictās <u>memorātū</u> dignae nullae.** (There are) no islands in the Ausonian sea worthy <u>to mention</u>, except those already noted.

Pliny the Elder, *Naturalis Historia* 8.142: **Multa sunt <u>cognitū</u> digna, fidēlissimumque ante omnia hominī canis atque equus.** There are many (animals) worthy <u>to know</u>, and above all the most faithful to humankind (are) the dog and the horse.

7. You have already learned the most common uses of Latin subjunctive verbs. Less frequently, Latin employs the **SUBJUNCTIVE** in clauses introduced by the following:

dum: until
dummodo: provided that
priusquam: before
quandō: when
and other conjunctions

These additional subjunctive clauses follow the same sequence of tenses that you have already learned in *NLP* 28–33. Consider the following examples:

Caesar, *de Bello Gallico* 4.13.2: **Expectāre vērō <u>dum hostium cōpiae augērentur, equitātus reverterētur</u> summae dēmentiae esse iūdicābat.** Indeed he (Caesar) deemed it to be (of) the highest foolishness to wait <u>until the enemy troops were increased (and) the cavalry returned</u>.

Ovid, *Metamorphoses* 9.30: **<u>Dummodo pugnandō superem</u>, tū vince loquendō.** <u>Provided I conquer by fighting</u>, conquer (me) by speaking.

Caesar, *de Bello Gallico* 6.4.1: **<u>Priusquam id efficī posset</u>, adesse Rōmānōs nuntiātur.** <u>Before this was able to be done</u>, it is announced that the Romans are approaching.

Cicero, *ad Familiares* 7.23.4: **<u>Quandō tē exspectem</u>, faciēs mē, sī tibi vidētur, certiōrem.** You will make me more certain, if it seems best to you, <u>when I should expect you</u>.

I. Required Vocabulary

NOUNS

collum, -ī, n: neck
rāmus, -ī, m: branch, bough

genitor, -ōris, m: father
lūmen, lūminis, n: light, eye
religiō, -iōnis, f: obligation, scruples, observance of a religious ceremony
sors, sortis, f: lot, chance, oracular response
tūs, tūris, n: incense, frankincense
vestis, -is (-ium), f: garment, covering

ADJECTIVES

aptus, -a, -um (+ dative): fitting (for)
ēgregius, -a, -um: distinguished, extraordinary
ferus, -a, -um: savage, wild
ingrātus, -a, -um: unpleasant, thankless
pūrus, -a, -um: upright, faultless
ultimus, -a, -um: farthest, most distant, highest, greatest

mīrābilis, -e: extraordinary, unusual

VERBS

immolō, -āre, -āvī, -ātus: sacrifice

labōrō, -āre, -āvī, -ātus: work

superō, -āre, -āvī, -ātus: overcome, conquer

censeō, -ēre, -uī, censūs: advise, resolve, think, express an opinion

removeō, -ēre, -mōvī, -mōtus: move back, withdraw, be distant

arcessō, -ere, -īvī, -ītus: send for, summon

ēdūcō, -ere, -duxī, -ductus: lead out, march out

arbitror, -ārī, arbitrātus sum: think, perceive, judge

CONJUNCTIONS

dummodo: provided that

II. Translate the following sentences from Latin to English or English to Latin.

1. Haec omnia pūrē et castē nōbīs agenda sunt.
2. Genitōrem deōrum mihi vocandum esse arbitrātus sum.
3. Māter Magna optimā cum voluptāte accipienda est.
4. Lībertus ēgregius templum Iovis vīsum līberōs ex urbe duxerat.
5. Animālia fera gladiātōribus superanda erant.
6. Rōmānī sacerdōtēs, priusquam imperātor ad proelium proficiscerētur, immolāvērunt.
7. Quaerendum est etiam cūr hīc diū habitāverimus.
8. Carmina audītū digna poētīs doctīs scrībenda sunt.
9. The Republic must not be taken by the enemy.
10. We summoned the senators to watch the show.
11. I will lie on a covering fit for a god. Wonderful to say!
12. I think the branches ought to be moved back.

Roman Religion

Roman state religion differs greatly from the predominant faiths practiced in the West today. The Romans had no creed, no doctrine, and no liturgy. Roman religion was tolerant and nonsectarian (there is simply nothing to contradict). Belief was irrelevant. Action, instead, was the keystone. For the Romans, the purpose of religion was success, particularly the success of the state, not the moral transgressions of individuals. Roman religion aimed to maintain peace with the gods (*pax deōrum*) to secure success. *Pax deōrum* was preserved through the careful recitation and correct formulation of proper rituals duly performed in right and proper order at the specified times (*cultus deōrum*). In this way, one could avoid offending the gods.

Because of the deep symbiosis of state and religion, the concept of "separation of church and state" would have made no sense to the Romans. Citizens cultivated the gods, who in turn protected the state. There was, furthermore, a strong sense that neglect of state cult was responsible for the civil wars of the first century BCE: Rome suffered from divinely sent calamities because temples had fallen into disrepair and festivals had been neglected (Horace, *Carmina* 3.6). The Roman pantheon was extensive, but several gods were particularly important: the Capitoline Triad (Jupiter, Juno, and Minerva); Mars, the father of Romulus; Venus, the divine ancestress of the Julian house; Vesta, whose priestesses were prominent and powerful; and Janus, whose temple housed the armory.

State religion was overseen by elected politicians, including praetors and consuls, whose grant of *imperium* included the right to perform augury, that is, to look for signs from the gods as revealed through birds—numbers, pitch, flight patterns, or height. Augury was just one of several types of divination performed before any important business could proceed (public or private: marriage rites, meetings of the Senate, elections, battles). Widely practiced was the Etruscan tradition of *haruspicium*, whereby the livers of sacrificial animals were examined by trained professional priests. Divine signs, procured by augury or *haruspicium*, revealed *only* whether the proposed course of action was *fās*, that is, if the action was in accord with divine will, if the gods *favored* it on the day that the divination was performed (i.e., is it proper to vote or to fight?). Divination could *not* predict whether an act would succeed. If the event was postponed to another day, signs were sought and interpreted anew. Furthermore, actions could not proceed while an augur was looking for signs. This prerogative was abused in 59 BCE, when Caesar's consular colleague Marcus Bibulus constantly searched for and found such signs in his efforts to obstruct Caesar's agenda.

Divination was also performed by consulting the Sibylline books, which Lucius Tarquinius Superbus (ruled 535–509 BCE), Rome's last king, had purchased from Apollo's priestess, the Sibyl of Cumae. A collection of Greek hexameters, they were considered to be oracular proclamations from Apollo, who was consulted during times of political or social crisis, and who usually prescribed the importation of Greek cults: for example, Asclepius to avert a plague in 293 BCE, and the Magna Mater in 205 BCE, as a means of distracting an anxious populace during the Second Punic War.

Roman religion was coordinated by the *Pontifex Maximus*, elected for life from the rolls of the Senate, until Augustus assumed the position as an imperial prerogative. Several other priesthoods were maintained, including fifteen *flāminēs*, elected from the patricians, and whose special hats were eventually adopted by the cardinals of the Roman Catholic Church. Although the ancient Romans took no issue with priests holding political office (Julius Caesar was elected *Pontifex Maximus* in 63 BCE), a number of unusual restrictions essentially barred the *Flāmen Diālis* (high priest of Jupiter) from pursuing a political career. The *Flāmen Diālis* could not swear an oath, ride a horse, eat beans, touch a goat, have his hair cut by a slave or ex-slave, or sleep away from his own bed for three consecutive nights.

Aristocratic women also had powerful priestly opportunities. With a complement of six women from prominent families, and serving a term of thirty years, Vestal Virgins tended the sacred hearth of Rome and prepared the water and meal for sacred rites. Chosen between the ages of six and ten, the novitiate Vestal had to be free from physical defect, and she had to be the daughter of freeborn Roman citizens who were both still living (in other words, the girl had to be free from *miasma*, that is, unpolluted by the death of a close relative). Punishment for breaking the eponymous vow of chastity was burial alive, and Livy recounts several examples of Vestals who were charged with "unchastity," including Postumia, who in 420 BCE was told to stop dressing so fashionably (*ab Urbe Condita* 4.44), and Minucia, condemned in 337 BCE and buried alive near the Colline Gate (*ab Urbe Condita* 8.15). After her term expired, a retired Vestal could marry or retain social and economic autonomy.

The Vestals remained busy through the year keeping up with a vigorous calendar of religious observances. *Fēriae*, "festival days," occurred every several days. Much like modern weekends, *fēriae* gave Romans regular breaks from business obligations, including lawsuits. Ovid composed the *Fasti*, a festival calendar in elegiac couplets, which, sadly, survives only for the first half of the calendar year, January to June. In the *Fasti*, Ovid recounts the origins and rituals of both public and private festivals. During the pensive *Parentālia* (13–21 February) deceased ancestors were honored with an annual meal. At the raucous *Lupercālia* (February 15), goatskin-clad men raced down the Palatine Hill, whipping matrons who wished to become pregnant (an act of sympathetic magic and a precursor to the tossing of Mardi Gras beads). During the *Anna Perenna* (on the Ides of March), especially popular with the lower classes, Romans gathered on the banks of the Tiber, sharing picnics and drinking as many glasses of wine as years they wished yet to live (no wonder the senators chose this day for Caesar's assassination!). The *Parīlia* (21 April), Rome's birthday, was a day of public rejoicing and purification, when the city was greened, blood sacrifices were disallowed, and bonfires were lit. On 3 August; during the *Supplicia Canum* ("Punishment of the Dogs"), Juno's sacred geese were celebrated for raising the alarm against the invading Gauls in 390 BCE, and dogs, who had slept through that attack, were sacrificed. The *Lūdī Rōmānī*, annual games in honor of Jupiter Optimus Maximus, were held from September 4–9, featuring a parade and athletic competitions, which Vergil traced back to Ascanius's Trojan games in *Aeneid* Book 5. Both March (when the campaign season opened) and October (the close of the season) featured military festivals to purify the war trumpets before battle and the troops after contact with bloodshed. During the war-festival months the *Saliī*, an ancient priesthood of Mars, danced in the streets with their archaic *ancīla* (shields) and performed the nearly indecipherable and very ancient *Carmen Saliāre*. In early December, men were rigorously excluded from the *Bona Dea* festival, when Roman matrons sacrificed piglets to secure the fertility of crops and people (a huge scandal erupted when Clodius Pulcher infiltrated the *Bona Dea* of 62 BCE; see *NLP* 9). And finally, the winter solstice was celebrated in mid-December with the *Saturnālia*, when gifts were exchanged, slaves and masters reversed their roles, and the Master of the Revels saw to it that the party-goers acted as wildly as possible (or else he was replaced by a more attentive Master of the Revels).

Roman religion was polytheistic, and Romans took care to avoid offending local deities. Cato the Elder recommends propitiating woodland spirits with prayers and blood sacrifices before thinning a grove of trees (*de Agricultura* 139). Even foreign gods were welcomed into the pantheon. Macrobius preserves an ancient prayer urging the gods of Carthage to abandon their people and desert their temples. The gods of Carthage were invited to come instead to aid the Romans (*Saturnalia* 3.9.7, one of our extended Latin prose selections). State religion was impersonal and legalistic, and worshippers often found a more spiritual and personal religious experience with Eastern gods. The exotic cults of Isis, Mithras, and Cybele were viewed with anxiety, at times discouraged, but eventually mainstreamed. Like Roman state cult, these rites (and others) were polytheistic. Although the Jews were monotheistic, they did not deny the existence of non-Jewish gods. Jews alone worshipped the Jewish god, and they allowed non-Jews their own practices. Respecting the Jews for their antiquity (their culture predated the Trojan War), Rome deemed their peculiar religious beliefs acceptable because of the ideal of *mōs māiōrum*. The Jews were simply observing the very ancient customs of their ancestors. Christianity alone was rejected, regarded as high treason. Christians, who traced their beginnings to the reigns of Augustus and Tiberius, could hardly claim they were observing *mōs māiōrum*. Christians, furthermore, staunchly believed that only the Christian god existed. By denying the existence of the Roman pantheon, they thus jeopardized the *pax deōrum* and the very existence of the Roman state.

SUGGESTIONS FOR FURTHER READING:

Beard, Mary, John North, and Simon Price. *Religions of Rome*. 2 vols. Cambridge, 1998.
Ogilvie, R. M. *The Romans and Their Gods in the Age of Augustus*. Pimlico, 1969.
Rives, James B. *Religion in the Roman Empire*. Blackwell, 2006.
Scullard, H. H. *Festivals and Ceremonies of the Roman Republic*. London, 1981.
Warrior, Valerie M. *Roman Religion: A Sourcebook*. Focus, 2002.

PASSAGES

36.1. Augustine, *de Civitate Dei* 4.8. Here Augustine mocks the highly specialized and excessively large pantheon of the Romans.

Nec agrōrum mūnus ūnī alicuī deō committendum arbitrātī sunt, sed rūra deae Rūsīnae, iuga montium deō Iugātīnō; collibus deam Collatīnam, vallibus Vallōniam praefēcērunt.

Notes: **Rūsīna, -ae**, f: a goddess of the fields; **Iugātīnus, -ī**, m: a god of mountain ridges; **Collatīna, -ae**, f: a goddess of hills; **valles, -is (-ium)**, f: vale, valley; **Vallōnia, -iae**, f: a goddess of valleys; **praeficiō, -ere, -fēcī, -fectus**: set over, appoint as superintendent.

36.2. Ovid, *Fasti* 3.85–86. Mars, to whom the month of March is consecrated, is among the most powerful and important of the Roman gods. Meter: elegiac couplets.

Mars Latiō venerandus erat, quia praesidet armīs;
　　arma ferae gentī remque decusque dabant.

Notes: **Latium, -iī**, n: Latium, the district around Rome; **veneror, -ārī, venerātus sum**: revere, respect, worship; **praesideō, -ēre, -sēdī, -sessus**: watch over, protect, guard; **rem** (*pūblicam*).

36.3. Cicero, *de Divinatione* 1.29. Among the solemn duties of some Roman elected officials was the interpretation of signs from birds (augury). Some augurs, however, falsified or disregarded augury altogether—for political gain or spite. As consul in 59 BCE, Caesar ignored Bibulus's augury, and it was widely held that Crassus might have averted disaster and death at Carrhae had he not ignored the signs. Here Cicero defends Appius Claudius Pulcher who, as censor in 50 BCE, expelled Gaius Ateius Capito from the Senate for falsifying augury during his term as tribune in 55 BCE.

In quō Appius, collēga tuus, bonus augur, ut ex tē audīre soleō, nōn satis scienter virum bonum et cīvem ēgregium censor C. Ateium notāvit, quod ēmentītum auspicia subscrīberet.

Notes: **quō**: i.e., the charge of falsifying auspices; **collēga, -ae**, m: colleague; **augur, -uris**, m / f: augur, interpreter of divine signs from the birds; **scienter**: skillfully; **censor,**

-ōris, m: censor (see *NLP* 25); **notō, -āre, -āvī, -ātus**: mark, censure, charge; **quod**: with respect to the fact that; **ēmentior, -īrī, ēmentītus sum**: falsify; **auspicium, -iī**, n: divination (by observing birds); **subscrībō, -ere, -scrīpsī, -scrīptus**: record, endorse, charge.

36.4. Livy, *ab Urbe Condita* **8.9.1–2.** The Romans believed that the gods, when properly worshipped, would protect the state.

Rōmānī consulēs, priusquam ēdūcerent in aciem, immolāvērunt.

36.5. Livy, *ab Urbe Condita* **1.32.12.** The formulaic language by which each senator in turn ratified a declaration of war emphasized the divine favor of Roman justice.

"Dīc" inquit eī quem prīmum sententiam rogābat, "quid cēnsēs?" Tum ille: "Pūrō piōque duellō quaerendās cēnseō, itaque cōnsentiō cōnscīscōque." Inde ordine aliī rogābantur; quandōque pars māior eōrum quī aderant in eandem sententiam ībat, bellum erat cōnsēnsum.

Notes: **duellō** = *bellō*; (*rēs*) **quaerendās** (*esse*); **cōnsentiō, -īre, -sēnsī, -sēnsus**: agree; **cōnscīscō, -ere, -scīvī, -scītus**: decree.

36.6. Suetonius, *de Vita Tiberii* **2.2.** The Romans sought divine messages from many sources, including the sacred chickens whose appetite revealed divine favor or disfavor. Publius Claudius Pulcher would regret his skepticism after a naval engagement in 249 BCE during the First Punic War.

Claudius Pulcher apud Siciliam—nōn pāscentibus in auspicandō pullīs ac per contemptum religiōnis marī dēmersīs, quasi ut bīberent quandō ēsse nollent—proelium nāvāle iniit; superātusque.

Notes: **Sicilia, -iae**, f: Sicily; **pāscō, -ere, pāvī, pāstus**: feed, pasture; **auspicō, -āre, -āvī, -ātus**: take auspices; **pullus, -ī**, m: young animal, chicken, sacred chicken; **contemptus, -ūs**, m: disdain; **dēmergō, -ere, -mersī, -mersus**: plunge, sink, drown; **bibō, -ere, bibī**: drink; **ēdō, ēsse, ēdidī, ēditus**: eat; **ineō, -īre, -īvī** or **-iī, -itus**: enter, engage; **superātus** (*est*).

36.7. Cato the Elder, *de Agri Cultura* **134.** A litany of sacrifices performed just before the harvest.

Priusquam messim faciēs, porcam praecīdāneam hōc modō fierī oportet. Cererī porca praecīdānea porcō fēminā, priusquam hāsce frūgēs condās: fār, trīticum, hordeum, fabam, sēmen rāpīcium. Tūre, vīnō, Iānō, Iovī, Iunōnī praefātō, priusquam porcum fēminam immolābis.

Notes: **messis, -is (-ium)**, f: harvest; **porca, -ae**, f: sow; **praecīdānea, -ae**, f: preliminary sacrifice; **Cerēs, Cereris**, f: the Roman goddess of agriculture; **porcus fēmina, porcī fēminae**, f: sow; **-ce**: an emphatic enclitic (like *-que*) attached to demonstrative pronouns; **fār, farris**, n: spelt; **trīticum, -ī**, n: wheat; **hordeum, -ī**, n: barley; **faba, -ae**, f: bean; **sēmen, sēminis**, n: seed; **rāpīcius, -a, -um**: belonging to rapes or turnips; **tūre, vīnō** and **Iānō, Iovī, Iunōnī**: asyndeton; **Iānus, -ī**, m: the two-faced god who simultaneosly looks in both directions; **praefor, -ārī, praefātus sum**: say a prayer beforehand; **praefātō**: construe with an understood *tē*.

36.8. Ovid, *Fasti* **3.31–34.** After being raped by Mars in her sleep, Rhea Silvia recalls a strange metaphorical dream about the children she now carries—Romulus and Remus—represented in the dream by palm trees. The ancients believed that the gods sent messages, prophecies, and warnings through dreams. Meter: elegiac couplets.

Inde duae pariter, vīsū mīrābile, palmae
    surgunt: ex illīs altera māior erat,
et gravibus rāmīs tōtum prōtexerat orbem,
    contigeratque suā sīdera summa comā.

Notes: **pariter**: equally, together; **prōtegō, -ere, -texī, -tectus**: cover, protect.

36.9. Ovid, *Fasti* **3.575–76.** Many Roman festivals were rooted in the city's legendary past, including the popular *Anna Perenna*, celebrated on the Ides of March in honor of Dido's sister Anna. After Dido's suicide, Anna was driven out of Carthage to wander for three years before finding refuge in Italy (see *NLP* 20.9). Meter: elegiac couplets.

Signa recensuerat bis sōl sua, tertius ībat
    annus, et exiliō terra paranda nova est.

Notes: **signa**: the constellations of the zodiac; **recenseō, -ēre, -censuī, -census**: review, pass through; **ex(s)ilium, -iī**, n: exile.

36.10. Ovid, *Fasti* 4.133–38. Fortuna Virilis had the power to conceal female blemishes from male lovers. Worshippers propitiated the goddess (and her cult statue) with a bath on her feast day, April 1. Meter: elegiac couplets.

> Rīte deam colitis, Latiae mātrēsque nurūsque
> > et vōs, quīs vittae longaque vestis abest.
> Aurea marmoreō redimīcula dēmite collō,
> > dēmite dīvitiās: tōta lavanda dea est.
> Aurea siccātō redimīcula reddite collō:
> > nunc aliī flōrēs, nunc nova danda rosa est.

Notes: **rīte**: properly, duly; **Latius, -a, -um**: Latin; **nurus, -ūs**, f: young married woman; **quīs** = *quibus*; **vitta, -ae**, f: ribbon, fillet (worn by priests and sacrificial victims); **marmoreus, -a, -um**: of marble; **redimīculum, -ī**, n: fillet, fetter, chaplet; **dēmō, -ere, dempsī, demptus**: take away, subtract; **lavō, -āre, lāvī, lautus**: bathe; **siccō, -āre, -āvī, -ātus**: dry; **rosa, -ae**, f: rose.

36.11. Ovid, *Fasti* 4.412–16. In April, Rome celebrated the bounty of Ceres with games that were opened with a sacrifice of piglets, described here. Ceres was an approachable goddess who protected the lower classes and, as such, preferred this cheap, humble offering in contrast to the costlier bovines that Jupiter and Juno received. Oxen also played an important role in Roman agriculture, thus promoting Ceres' cult. Meter: elegiac couplets.

> Parva bonae Cererī, sint modo casta, placent.
> > Ā bove succinctī cultrōs removēte ministrī:
> bōs aret; ignāvam sacrificāte suem.
> > Apta iugō cervix nōn est ferienda secūrī:
> vīvat et in dūrā saepe labōret humō.

Notes: **modo** = *dummodo*; **succingō, -ere, -cinxī, -cinctus**: gird, tuck clothes in the girdle; **culter, cultrī**, m: knife; **minister, -strī**, m: attendant; **arō, -āre**: plough; **ignāvus, -a, -um**: idle, slothful, cowardly; **sacrifico, -āre, -āvī, -ātus**: offer sacrifice; **sūs, suis**, m/f: pig, hog; **cervix, cervīcis**, f: nape of the neck; **feriō, -īre**: strike; **secūris, -is (-ium)**, f: axe; **humus, -ī**, f: ground.

36.12. Ovid, *Fasti* **1.713–20.** The Romans believed that deities controlled every aspect of human life, and that whatever grants favor to humanity should be considered divine. From the late third century BCE there arose a cult of deified abstractions, including *Concordia, Disciplīna, Fortūna, Honos, Pietās, Victōria,* and *Virtus.* These abstractions were thought to bolster the success of the Empire, and they were used widely in imperial propaganda (e.g., coin issues and public art). Among the most widely exploited was *Pax,* celebrated on Augustus's exquisite *Ara Pācis* in Rome and whose gifts Ovid here extols. Meter: elegiac couplets.

> Dum dēsint hostēs, dēsit quoque causa triumphī:
> > tū ducibus bellō glōria māior eris.
> Sōla gerat mīles, quibus arma coerceat, arma;
> > cantēturque ferā nil nisi pompa tubā.
> Horreat Aeneadās et prīmus et ultimus orbis:
> > sīqua parum Rōmam terra timēbat, amet.
> Tūra, sacerdōtēs, pācālibus addite flammīs,
> > albaque perfūsā victima frōnte cadat.

Notes: **dēsum, -esse, -fuī**: be lacking; **triumphus, -ī,** m: triumphal procession; **coerceō, -ēre, -cuī, -citus**: enclose, limit, check; **pompa, -ae,** f: ceremonial procession; **tuba, -ae,** f: war trumpet; **horreō, -ēre, -uī**: shudder at, quake; **Aeneadēs, -ae,** m: de-scendant of Aeneas; **et prīmus et ultimus**: i.e., the lands closest to Rome and those farthest away; **sīquis, sīquae** or **sīqua, sīquid**: if anyone / thing; **pācālis, -e**: of peace; **alba**: sacrificial victims had to be white, unmarked, and physically flawless; **perfundō, -ere, -fūdī, -fūsus**: pour over (with incense); **victima, -ae,** f: sacrificial offering.

EXTRA PASSAGES: THE CULT OF CYBELE

Among the many foreign rites observed at Rome was the cult of Cybele (also known as the *Magna Mater*), imported to Rome from Phrygia (Turkey) in 205 BCE to aid the failing war effort against Hannibal (Livy, *ab Urbe Condita* 29.10–14). A multivalent goddess of fertility, mountains, disease, oracles, civic and martial protection, Cybele retained her exotic cult accoutrements: mystery rites, eunuch priests, and worshippers driven to ecstasy by wine and wild drum music. In April, the *Megalesia* honored Cybele with stage plays, chariot races, and a procession of her cult image accompanied by priests and initiates.

An elaborate Greek myth was constructed around the goddess. Cybele fell in love with the beautiful shepherd Attis whose philandering she could not endure. In turn, driven insane by Cybele's nagging and pouting, Attis castrated himself, providing the mythic paradigm for the eunuch priests. In art, Cybele is represented with a mural crown (to show her protective aspects), cornucopiae, and the brace of lions (Atalanta and Hippomenes) who draw her chariot, magnificently portrayed in the stunning Fountain of Cybele in Madrid (crafted by José Hermosilla and Ventura Rodríguez in the eighteenth century).

36.13. Ovid, *Fasti* 4.259–64. During times of crisis, the Romans consulted the Sibylline books (see *NLP* 24). Here Ovid recounts the Sibylline oracle that prescribed the importation of Cybele's cult. Meter: elegiac couplets.

> "Māter abest: mātrem iubeō, Rōmāne, requīrēs.
>   Cum veniet, castā est accipienda manū."
> Obscūrae sortis patrēs ambāgibus errant,
>   Quaeve parens absit, quōve petenda locō.
> Consulitur Paeān, "dīvum" que "arcessite Mātrem,"
>   inquit "in Īdaeō est invenienda iugō."

Notes: **iubeō** (*ut*); **obscūrus, -a, -um**: dark, secret; **ambāgēs, -is (-ium)**, f: winding path; **petenda** (*sit*); **Paeān, Paeānis**, m: the healer, an epithet of Apollo, the god of oracles; **Īdaeus, -a, -um**: related to Mt. Ida in the Troad.

36.14. Lucretius, *de Rerum Natura* 2.614–17. Cybele's retinue of eunuch priests. Meter: dactylic hexameter.

> Gallōs attribuunt, quia—nūmen quī violārint
> Mātris et ingrātī genitōribus inventī sint—
> significāre volunt indignōs esse putandōs,
> vīvam prōgeniem quī in ōrās lūminis ēdant.

Notes: **gallus, -ī**, m: a eunuch priest of Cybele; **attribuō, -ere, -buī, -būtus**: assign, appoint (construe "the Greeks" as the subject); **nūmen . . . sint**: construe as the subject of *esse putandōs*; **violā(ver)int; violō, -āre, -āvī, -ātus**: outrage, injure, violate; **significō, -āre, -āvī, -ātus**: indicate, show; **indignus, -a, -um**: unworthy; **vīvam . . . ēdant**: relative clause of purpose (construe with the subject of *esse putandōs*); **vīvus, -a, -um**: alive, living; **prōgeniēs, -iēī**, f: lineage, race; **ōra, -ae**, f: shore.

36.15. Catullus 63.58–64. Attis laments all that he has given up to join the cult of Cybele. Meter: galliambics.

Egone ā meā remōta haec ferar in nemora domō?
Patriā, bonīs, amīcīs, genitōribus aberō?
Aberō forō, palaestrā, stadiō et gymnasiīs?
Miser ā miser, querendum est etiam atque etiam, anime
quod enim genus figūrast, ego nōn quod obierim?
Ego mulier, ego adulescens, ego ephēbus, ego puer,
ego gymnasī fuī flōs, ego eram decus oleī.

Notes: **patriā . . . genitōribus**: asyndeton to heighten the crispness of the passage (see *NLP* 36.7); **palaestra, -ae**, f: wrestling arena, gymnasium; **stadium, -iī**, n: running track; **gymnasium, -iī**, n: sports center; **ā**: ah! (interjection of distress); **anime**: note the case; **figūrast** = *figūra est*; **figūra, -ae**, f: shape, form, image; **obierim**: deliberative subjunctive; **obeō, -īre, -īvī** or **-iī, -itus**: take on; **adulescens, -entis (-ium)**, m/f: youth, young person; **ephēbus, -ī**, m: youth, adolescent, a boy at puberty (according to Athenian law, an ephebe was between 18 and 20 years); **oleum, -ī**, n: oil, olive oil (Greek athletes rubbed themselves with oil to warm up their muscles and protect the skin from dehydration during competition).

Extended Latin Prose Passages

1. **Macrobius,** *Saturnalia* **3.9.7–8.** The *Saturnalia* is a compendium of ancient Roman religion, and here Macrobius (fifth century CE) recounts an ancient prayer formula intended to persuade the gods of the besieged city Carthage to transfer their allegiance to Rome.

Est autem carmen huiusmodī quō dī ēvocantur, cum oppugnātiōne cīvitās cingitur:

> Sī deus sī dea est cui populus cīvitāsque Carthāginiensis est in tūtēlā, tēque maximē, ille quī urbis huius populīque tūtēlam recēpistī, precor venerorque veniamque ā vōbīs petō ut vōs populum cīvitātemque Carthāginiensem dēserātis, loca templa sacra urbemque eōrum relinquātis absque hīs abeātis, eīque populō cīvitātī metum formīdinem oblīviōnem īniciātis, prōditīque Rōmam ad mē meōsque veniātis. Nostraque vōbīs loca templa sacra urbs acceptior probātiorque sit, mihique populōque Rōmānō mīlitibusque meīs praepositī sītīs ut sciāmus intelligāmusque. Sī ita fēceritis, voveō vōbīs templa lūdōsque factūrum.

Notes: **huiusmodī** = *huius modī*; **ēvocō, -āre, -āvī, -ātus:** call out; **oppugnātiō, -iōnis,** f: assault; **Carthāginiensis, -e:** Carthaginian; **tūtēla, -ae,** f: protection; **precor, -ārī, precātus sum:** ask, beg, beseech; **veneror, -ārī, venerātus sum:** beseech with awe; **venia, -iae,** f: indulgence, favor, grace; **dēserō, -ere, -seruī, -sertus:** abandon, forsake; **abs** = *ab*; **metum . . . oblīviōnem:** asyndeton (Macrobius has omitted the conjunction *et* to heighten the crispness of the prayer); **formīdō, formīdinis,** f: dread, terror; **oblīviō, -iōnis,** f: forgetfulness, oblivion; **īniciō, -ere, -iēcī, -iectus:** cast, infuse; **acceptus, -a, -um:** welcome, received; **nostraque . . . urbs:** another asyndeton; **probātus, -a, -um:** approved; **praepōnō, -ere, -posuī, -positus:** put before, prefer; **intelligāmus** = *intellēgāmus*; **voveō, -ēre, vōvī, vōtus:** vow, promise; **lūdus, -ī,** m: public games, spectacles.

2. Augustus, *Res Gestae* 25. Here Augustus recounts his military successes during the Civil Wars of the 40s and 30s BCE. To legitimize his position as *prīmus inter parēs* ("first among equals") at Rome, he emphasizes in particular that his campaigns enjoyed both popular and senatorial support.

[25.1] Mare pācāvī ā praedōnibus. Eō bellō servōrum, quī fūgerant ā dominīs suīs et arma contra rem pūblicam cēperant, triginta ferē millia capta dominīs ad supplicium sumendum trādidī.

[25.2] Iūrāvit in mea verba tōta Italia sponte suā, et mē bellī quō vīcī ad Actium ducem dēpoposcit; iūrāvērunt in eadem verba prōvinciae Galliae, Hispaniae, Āfrica, Sicilia, Sardinia.

[25.3] Quī sub signīs meīs tum mīlitāverint fuērunt senātōrēs plūrēs quam DCC, in iīs quī vel anteā vel posteā consulēs factī sunt ad eum diem quō scripta sunt haec LXXXIII, sacerdōtēs circiter CLXX.

Notes: Augustus's campaigns against Marc Antony culminated in Augustus's decisive victory at Actium, a small town on the western coast of Greece.

25.1: **pācō, -āre, -āvī, -ātus**: pacify, soothe; **praedō, -ōnis**, m: robber, pirate. Augustus here refers to the Sicilian uprising (44–36 BCE) led by Sextus Pompeius, son of Caesar's onetime ally Pompey; **captus, -a, -um**: captive (here, used substantively); **supplicium, -iī**, n: punishment, penalty.

25.2: **iūrō, -āre, -āvī, -ātus**: swear allegiance (to); **sponte suā**: "by its own will"; **Actium, -iī**, n: the small town in western Greece where Augustus's navy vanquished Marc Antony's, thus bringing an end to civil war at Rome. Actium became a powerful symbol in the *pax Augusta*; **dēposcō, -ere, -poposcī**: demand, request.

25.3: **mīlitō, -āre, -āvī, -ātus**: serve as a soldier; **senātor, -ōris**, m: senator; **anteā**: before, previously.

3. *Aberdeen Bestiary* 15r. Our anonymous author here describes the remarkable life cycle of bears (whom the ancients believed were born formless—hence giving rise to the etymology of *ursus*), their generation, and their ability to heal themselves of illnesses.

Dē ursō: Ursus fertur dictus quod ōre suō formet fētus, quasi "orsus." Nam aiunt eōs informēs generāre partūs et carnem quandam nascī quod māter lambendō in membra compōnit. Sed hoc inmātūritās facit partūs. Dēnique tricesimō diē generat, unde ēvenit ut precipitāta fēcunditās informis procreātur. Ursōrum caput invalidum, vīs maxima in brāchiīs et lumbīs, unde interdum erectī insistunt.

Etiam medendī industriam nōn pretermittunt. Sīquidem gravī affectī corde et sauciātī vulneribus medērī sibi sciunt. Herbē—cui nōmen est "flomus," ut Grēcī appellant—ulcera subicientēs sua, ut sōlō cūrentur ā tactū. Ursu erger formīcās dēvorat. Numidī ursī cēterīs prestant dumtaxat villīs profundiōribus.

Notes: **ursus, -ī,** m: bear; **formō, -āre, -āvī, -ātus:** shape, fashion; **fētus, -ūs,** m: offspring, cub; **ordior, -īrī, orsus sum:** begin; **informis, -e:** shapeless; **generō, -āre, -āvī, -ātus:** produce, beget; **partus, -ūs,** m: offspring, cub; **carō, carnis,** f: flesh; **quod** = *quam carnem*; **lambō, -ere, lambī:** lick; **membrum, -ī,** n: limb; **inmātūritās, -ātis,** f: immaturity (the cubs are born premature); **ēveniō, -īre, -vēnī, -ventus:** turn out, result, happen; **precipitō, -āre, -āvī, -ātus:** fall headlong, "drop"; **fēcunditās, -ātis,** f: fruitfulness (e.g., the cub); **procreō, -āre, -āvī, -ātus:** produce, beget; **invalidus, -a, -um:** weak; **brā(c)chium, -iī,** n: arm, forearm; **lumbus, -ī,** m: loin; **interdum:** occasionally; **ērigō, -ere, -rexī, -rectus:** lift up; **insistō, -ere, -stitī:** stand.

medeor, -ērī: heal, cure; **industria, -iae,** f: diligence, vigor; **pr(a)etermittō, -ere, -mīsī, -missus:** neglect, omit; **sīquidem:** consequently; **corde:** the Aberdeen manuscript gives *caede* as a variant reading; **sauciō, -āre, -āvī, -ātus:** wound, hurt; **herba, -ae,** f: stalk, blade, green plant; **herbē** = *herbae*; **flomus:** from Greek *phlomis, phlomidos,* f: a shrubby plant common in the Mediterranean and whose members include Jerusalem sage and the lampwick plant; **Grēcī** = *Graecī*; **ulcus, ulceris,** n: sore, ulcer; **subiciō, -ere, -iēcī, -iectus:** place under, expose; **tactus, -ūs,** m: touch; **Ursu** = *ursus*; **erger** = *aeger*; **formīca, -ae,** f: ant; **dēvorō, -āre, -āvī, -ātus:** swallow, gulp down; **Numid(ic)us, -a, -um:** Numidian, North African (the Numidian or Libyan bear was popular in the Roman arena and is likely identifiable with the now extinct Atlas bear); **prestant** = *praestant*; **dumtaxat:** precisely, only, merely; **villus, -ī,** m: shaggy hair; **profundus, -a, -um:** deep, dense.

4. Livy, *ab Urbe Condita* 21.37.1–4. Hannibal's troops meet with extreme difficulty as they attempt to cross the Alps along with their mules and elephants. Livy here describes the effort and ingenuity with which they made the final descent.

[37.1] Tandem nēquīquam iūmentīs atque hominibus fatīgātīs castra in iugō posita, aegerrimē ad id ipsum locō purgātō; tantum nivis fodiendum atque ēgerendum fuit.

[37.2] Inde ad rūpem mūniendam per quam ūnam via esse poterat, mīlitēs ductī, cum caedendum esset saxum, arboribus circā immānibus dēiectīs dētruncātīsque struem ingentem lignōrum faciunt eamque, cum et vīs ventī apta faciendō ignī coorta esset, succendunt ardentiaque saxa infūsō acētō putrefaciunt.

[37.3] Ita torridam incendiō rūpem ferrō pandunt molliuntque anfractibus modicīs clīvōs ut nōn iūmenta sōlum sed elephantī etiam dēdūcī possent.

[37.4] Quadrīduum circā rūpem consumptum, iūmentīs prope fāme absumptīs; nūda enim ferē cacūmina sunt et, sī quid est pābulī, obruunt nivēs.

Notes: 37.1. **nēquīquam**: in vain; **iūmentum, -ī,** n: beast of burden, mule; **fatīgātus, -a, -um**: weary, tired; **aegerrimē**: in the most exhaustive way; **ipsum** = *iugum*; **purgō, -āre, -āvī, -ātus**: clean, clear away; **nix, nivis (-ium),** f: snow; **fodiō, -ere, fōdī, fossus**: dig out; **ēgerō, -ere, -gessī, -gestus**: take away, remove.

37.2. **rūpēs, -is (-ium),** f: cliff; **mūniō, -īre, -īvī, -ītus**: fortify, strengthen, defend; **immānis, -e**: huge, enormous; **dēiciō, -ere, -iēcī, -iectus**: throw down, fling down; **dētruncō, -āre, -āvī, -ātus**: cut off, lop off; **struēs, -is (-ium),** f: pile, heap; **lignum, -ī,** n: wood; **coorior, -īrī, coortus sum**: rise, originate; **eam** = *struem*; **succendō, -ere, -cendī, -census**: set on fire; **ardeō, -ēre, arsī**: burn, glow; **infundo, -ere, -fūdī, -fūsus**: pour in, pour upon: **acētum, -ī,** n: vinegar; **putrefaciō, -ere, -fēcī, -factus**: rot, cause to crumble.

37.3. **torridus, -a, -um**: dried, scorched; **incendium, -ī,** n: fire, heat; **pandō, -ere, pandī, pansus**: open up, unfold, make accessible; **anfractus, -ūs,** m: curve; **modicus, -a, -um**: moderate, small; **clīvus, -ī,** m: hill; **elephantus, -ī,** m: elephant; **dēdūcō, -ere, -duxī, -ductus**: lead out.

37.4. **quadrīduum, -ī,** n: period of four days; **consūmō, -ere, -sumpsī, -sumptus**: use up, exhaust; **absūmō, -ere, -sumpsī, -sumptus**: claim; **cacūmen, cacūminis,** n: point, peak; **pābulum, -ī,** n: feed, fodder; **obruō, -ere, obruī, obrutus**: cover up, bury.

5. Sallust, *Bellum Jugurthinum* 5.7–6.1. The early life and education of Jugurtha, who would prove a bitter and stubborn enemy to Rome (see *NLP* 20.10).

[5.7] Is Adherbālem et Hiempsālem ex sēsē genuit, Iugurthamque fīlium Mastanabālis frātris, quem Masinissa, quod ortus ex concubīnā erat, prīvātum dērelīquerat, eōdem cultū—quō līberōs suōs—domī habuit.

[6.1] Quī ubi prīmum adolēvit, pollens vīribus, decōrā faciē, sed multō maximē ingeniō validus, nōn sē luxū neque inertiae corrumpendum dedit, sed, utī mōs gentis illīus est, equitāre, iaculārī; cursū cum aequālibus certāre et, cum omnīs glōriā anteīret, omnibus tamen cārus esse; ad hoc plēraque tempora in vēnandō agere, leōnem atque aliās ferās prīmus aut in prīmīs ferīre: plūrimum facere, [et] minimum ipse dē sē loquī.

Notes: 5.7: **is**: Micipsa, ruled Numidia 148–118 BCE; **Adherbāl, -ālis**, m: Micipsa's legitimate son; **Hiempsāl, -ālis**, m: the younger son of Micipsa, murdered by Jugurtha in 112 BCE; **Iugurtha, -ae**, m: the son of Micipsa's illegitimate half-brother; **Mastanabāl, -ālis**, m: Micipsa's illegitimate half-brother; **Masinissa, -ae**, m: the grandfather of Jugurtha, Adherbal, and Hiempsal; **ortus erat**: construe Jugurtha as the subject; **concubīna, -ae**, f: concubine; **prīvātus, -a, -um**: as a private citizen (not royal); **dērelinquō, -ere, -ī, -relictus**: forsake, abandon; **cultus, -ūs**, m: cultivation, training, education.

6.1: **quī**: Jugurtha; **adolēscō, -ere, -ēvī**: grow up; **pollens (-entis)**: strong; **decōrus, -a, -um**: beautiful, graceful; **validus, -a, -um**: strong, powerful; **luxus, -ūs**, m: excess, extravagance; **inertia, -iae**, f: slothfulness, lack of skill; **equitō, -āre, -āvī, -ātus**: ride a horse; **iaculor, -ārī, iaculātus sum**: throw a javelin; **aequālis, -e**: equal (in skill); **certō, -āre, -āvī, -ātus**: contend, struggle (*certāre*: historical infinitive, as are the remaining infinitives in this passage); **anteeō, -īre, -īvī or -iī, -itus**: go before, excel; **plērusque, -aque, -umque**: very many, a large part; **tempus agere**: "to spend time"; **vēnor, -ārī, vēnātus sum**: hunt; **leō, leōnis**, m: lion; **feriō, -īre, -īvī, -ītus**: strike, beat, hunt.

6. Tacitus, *Annales* 14.5.1–3. Nero grew tired of his mother Agrippina's meddling and made several attempts on her life, including botched poisonings and an elaborately staged boating "accident," as described here. In the end, Nero sends thugs who crudely execute her.

[14.5.1] Noctem sīderibus inlustrem et placidō marī quiētam quasi convincendum ad scelus dī praebuēre. Nec multum erat prōgressa nāvis, duobus ē numerō familiārium Agrippīnam comitantibus. Ex quīs Crepereius Gallus haud procul gubernāculīs adstābat. Ācerrōnia super pedēs cubitantis reclīnis paenitentiam fīliī et recuperātam mātris grātiam per gaudium memorābat. Cum—dātō signō—ruere tectum locī multō plumbō grave, pressusque Crepereius et statim exanimātus est.

[14.5.2] Agrippīna et Ācerrōnia ēminentibus lectī pariētibus ac forte validiōribus, quam ut onerī cēderent, prōtectae sunt. Nec dissolūtiō nāvigiī sequēbātur, turbātīs omnibus et quod plērīque ignārī etiam consciōs impediēbant. Visum dehinc rēmigibus ūnum in latus inclīnāre atque ita nāvem submergere; sed neque ipsīs promptus in rem subitam consensus, et aliī contrā nitentēs dedēre facultātem lēniōris in mare iactūs.

[14.5.3] Vērum Ācerrōnia (imprūdentiā dum sē Agrippīnam esse utque subvenīrētur mātrī principis clāmitat) contīs et rēmīs et quae fors obtulerat nāvālibus tēlīs conficitur. Agrippīna, silens eōque minus agnīta (ūnum tamen vulnus umerō excēpit), nandō deinde occursū lēnunculōrum Lucrīnum in lacum vecta villae suae infertur.

Notes: 14.5.1: **inlustris, -e**: clear, bright; **placidus, -a, -um**: gentle, still; **quiētus, -a, -um**: at peace, undisturbed, calm; **convincō, -ere, -vīcī, -victus**: demonstrate; **praebeō, -ēre, -uī, -itus**: provide, offer; **prōgredior, -gredī, prōgressus sum**: advance, go forth; **comitor, -ārī, comitātus sum**: attend, follow; **familiārium** (substantive); **quīs** = *quibus*; **Crepereius Gallus, Crepereiī Gallī**, m: Agrippina's servant, very likely a slave from Gaul, not attested in other accounts of her murder; **gubernāculum, -ī**, n: rudder, helm; **adstō, -stāre, -stitī**: stand by; **Ācerrōnia, -ae**, f: Acerronia Pollia, Agrippina's "bitter" friend, who was likely the daughter of Cnaueus Acerronius Proculus, Consul 36 CE; **cubitō, -āre, -āvī, -ātus**: sleep; **reclīnis, -e**: leaning back; **cubitantis** (*Agrippīnae*); **paenitentia, -iae**, f: regret, remorse; **recuperō, -āre, -āvī, -ātus**: recover; **gaudium, -iī**, n: joy; **ruō, -ere, ruī, rutus**: rush, hasten, fall (*ruere*: historical infinitive); **plumbum, -ī**, n: lead (presumably, Nero's agents covered the cabin roof with blocks of heavy lead to incite a leak; **exanimō, -āre, -āvī, -ātus**: kill.

14.5.2: **ēmineō, -ēre, -uī**: project, stand out; **pariēs, parietis**, m: wall; **forte**: by chance; **validus, -a, -um**: strong, powerful; **quam**: "so much"; **onus, oneris**, n: load, weight; **prōtegō, -ere, -texī, -tectus**: cover, protect; **dissolūtiō, -iōnis**, f: destruction, death; **nāvigium, -iī**, n: ship; **plērusque, plēraque, plērumque**: very many, a large part; **ignārus, -a, -um**: unaware, "out of the loop"; **conscius, -iī**, m/f: accomplice, accessory; **impediō, -īre, -īvī, -ītus**: hinder, obstruct; **visum** (*est*): "it seemed best"; **dehinc**: hence; **rēmex, rēmigis**, m: rower (the rowers, presumably, were complicit in the plot); **inclīnō, -āre, -āvī, -ātus**: bend, fall back; **submergō, -ere, -mersī, -mersus**: plunge under, sink; **ipsīs**: the rowers; **promptus, -a, -um**: eager, ready; **subitus, -a, -um**: sudden, unexpected; **consensus, -ūs**, m: agreement; **nītor, -ī, nixus sum**: support, lean strive, struggle; **facultās, -ātis**, f: opportunity, resource; **lēnis, -e**: gentle, smooth, easy; **iactus, -ūs**, m: throw, cast.

14.5.3: **vērum**: but; **imprūdentia, -iae**, f: ignorance, imprudence; **subveniō, -īre, -vēnī, -ventus**: rescue (impersonal passive); **clāmitō, -āre, -āvī, -ātus**: keep shouting; **contus, -ī**, m: lance, pike; **rēmus, -ī**, m: oar; **fors, fortis**, f: chance, luck; **silens (-entis)**: silent, still; **eō**: "all the", intensifying the comparativeness of *minus*; **agnoscō, -ere, -nōvī, -nītus**: recognize, know; **umerus, -ī**, m: shoulder; **excipiō, -ere, -cēpī, -ceptus**: receive; **nō, nāre, nāvī**: swim; **occursus, -ūs**, m: meeting; **lēnunculus, -ī**, m: small skiff, small boat; **Lucrīnus, -ī**, m: a lake near Baiae and renowned pleasure resort where many wealthy Romans, including Cicero, owned vacation villas; **inferō, -ferre, -tulī, -lātus**: bring in.

Extended Latin Poetry Passages

1. Horace, *Carmina* **1.9.** In this description of the change of seasons, from winter to spring, Horace urges his readers to enjoy life and the pleasures of the warmer weather, including dances and illicit love. Meter: Alcaic strophe.

Vidēs ut altā stet nive candidum
Sōracte nec iam sustineant onus
    silvae labōrantēs gelūque
      flūmina constiterint acūtō?

Dissolve frīgus ligna super focō   5
largē repōnens atque benignius
    dēprōme quadrīmum Sabīnā,
      ō Thaliarche, merum diōtā.

Permitte dīvīs cētera, quī simul
strāvēre ventōs aequore fervidō   10
    deproeliantīs, nec cupressī
      nec veterēs agitantur ornī.

Quid sit futūrum crās, fuge quaerere, et
quem fors diērum cumque dabit, lucrō
    adpōne nec dulcīs amōrēs   15
      sperne, puer, neque tū chorēās,

dōnec virentī cānitiēs abest
mōrōsa. Nunc et Campus et āreae
    lēnēsque sub noctem susurrī
    compositā repetantur hōrā,   20

nunc et latentis prōditor intumō
grātus puellae rīsus ab angulō
    pignusque dēreptum lacertīs
    aut digitō male pertinācī.

Notes: 1–8: **nix, nivis (-ium)**, f: snow; **candidus, -a, -um**: bright, gleaming; **Sōracte, -is**, n: a mountain northeast of Rome; **onus, oneris**, n: burden, load; **gelū, -ūs**, n: chill, frost; **acūtus, -a, -um**: sharp, piercing; **dissolvō, -ere, -solvī, -solūtus**: dissolve, melt; **frīgus, frīgoris**, n: cold, chill, frost; **lignum, -ī**, n: wood; **focus, -ī**, m: hearth, fireplace; **largē**: generously; **repōnō, -ere, -posuī, -positus**: put back, restore, replace; **benignus, -a, -um**: kind-hearted, favorable; **dēprōmō, -ere, -promsī, -promptus**: take down; **quadrīmus, -a, -um**: four-year-old; **Sabīnus, -a, -um**: Sabine; **Thaliarchus, -ī**, m: Greek for "master of the revels/banquet"; **merum, -ī**, n: undiluted wine; **diōta, -ae**, f: two-handled jar.

9–16: **permittō, -ere, -mīsī, -missus**: let go, surrender, concede; **sternō, -ere, strāvī, strātus**: calm down; **fervidus, -a, -um**: seething, violent; **dēproelior, -ārī**: battle fiercely; **cupressus, -ī**, f: cypress tree; **agitō, -āre, -āvī, -ātus**: set in motion, shake; **ornus, -ī**, f: ash tree; **fuge** (+ infinitive): "do not" . . . ; **quem . . . cumque**: whatever (tmesis, wherein two parts of a compound word are separated); **fors, fortis**, f: chance, luck; **lucrum, -ī**, n: profit, wealth; **adpōnō, -ere, -posuī, -positus**: assign, appoint; **spernō, -ere, spēvī, sprētus**: scorn, reject; **chorēa, -ae**, f: dance.

17–24: **vireō, -ēre, -uī**: be green, flourish; **cānitiēs, -ēī**, f: grayness, old age; **mōrōsus, -a, -um**: morose, fastidious; **Campus, -ī**, m: Campus Martius, a plain outside the earliest walls of the city where citizens convened for battle training and elections. By Nero's day, the site was fully built up with many famous landmarks, including the Pantheon, Augustus's *Ara Pacis* and the mausoleum of Augustus, the baths of Agrippa, and even apartment blocks; **ārea, -ae**, f: open space, park; **lēnis, -e**: gentle, soft; **susurrus, -ī**, m: whisper; **prōditor, -ōris**, m: betrayer, traitor; **intumus, -a, -um** = *intimus, -a, -um*: innermost, deepest; **rīsus, -ūs**, m: laughter; **angulus, -ī**, m: corner, nook; **pignus, pigneris**, n: pledge, assurance; **dēripiō, -ere, -ripuī, -reptus**: snatch away; **lacertus, -ī**, m: upper arm; **digitus, -ī**, m: finger; **pertinax (-ācis)**: tenacious, stubborn.

2. **Vergil**, *Aeneid* **4.198–218.** Iarbas, king of the Mauretani and a son of Jupiter, was among Dido's rejected suitors. When he hears the rumor of the "marriage" of Dido and Aeneas, Iarbas becomes enraged and calls into question Jupiter's power: Why would he allow his son to be treated so shamefully by

a foreign woman? As a suppliant with his palms upraised, Iarbas addresses Jupiter with this entreaty cast as a traditional prayer. Meter: dactylic hexameter.

Hic Hammōne satus raptā Garamantide nymphā
templa Iovī centum lātīs immānia regnīs,
centum ārās posuit vigilemque sacrāverat ignem,   200
excubiās dīvum aeternās, pecudumque cruōre
pingue solum et variīs flōrentia līmina sertīs.
Isque āmens animī et rūmōre accensus amārō
dīcitur ante ārās media inter nūmina dīvum
multa Iovem manibus supplex ōrāsse supīnīs: 205

"Iuppiter omnipotens, cui nunc Maurūsia pictīs
gens epulāta torīs Lēnaeum lībat honōrem,
aspicis haec? An tē, genitor, cum fulmina torquēs,
nēquīquam horrēmus, caecīque in nūbibus ignēs
terrificant animōs et inānia murmura miscent?   205

Fēmina, quae nostrīs errans in fīnibus urbem
exiguam pretiō posuit, cui lītus arandum
cuique locī lēgēs dedimus, cōnūbia nostra
reppulit ac dominum Aenēān in regna recēpit.
Et nunc ille Paris cum sēmivirō comitātū,   210
Maeoniā mentum mitrā crīnemque madentem
subnexus, raptō potitur: nōs mūnera templīs
quippe tuīs ferimus fāmamque fovēmus inānem."

Notes: 198–205: **hic**: Iarbas; **Hammōn, -ōnis**, m: Ammon, a North African god of oracles equated with Jupiter; **satus, -a, -um**: born (from), sprung (from); **Garamantis (-idis)**: of the Garamantes, a North African tribe who traced their lineage to the nymph Garamantis and Jupiter Ammon; **nympha, -ae**, f: nymph; **immānis, -e**: enormous, monstrous; **vigil (vigilis)**: wakeful; **sacrō, -āre, -āvī, -ātus**: consecrate, dedicate to a god; **excubiae, -iārum**, f (plural): watchfires; **dīv(ōr)um**; **pecus, pecudis**, n: cow, sheep; **pinguis, -e**: fat, rich, fertile; **flōreō, -ēre, -uī**: flower, bloom; **sertum, -ī**, n: garland; **is**: Iarbas; **āmens (-entis)**: mad, insane, senseless; **rūmor, -ōris**, m: report, rumor; **accendō, -ēre, -cendī, -census**: ignite, set on fire; **amārus, -a, -um**: bitter, pungent, acrimonious; **supplex (supplicis)**: suppliant;

ōrā(vi)sse (syncopated perfect infinitive); **supīnius, -a, -um**: spread out with the palms upwards.

206–210: **omnipotens (-entis)**: almighty, all-powerful; **Maurūsius, -a, -um**: Moorish; **pingō, -ere, pinxī, pictus**: paint, embroider; **epulātus, -a, -um**: having feasted, having banqueted; **torus, -ī, m**: banqueting couch; **Lēnaeus, -a, -um**: Bacchic, Dionysian; **lībō, -āre, -āvī, -ātus**: pour, offer (worshippers honored the gods with a libation of wine at the beginning of a banquet); **aspiciō, -ere, -spexī, -spectus**: gaze on, contemplate; **genitor, -ōris, m**: father, begetter; **fulmen, fulminis, n**: thunderbolt; **torqueō, -ēre, torsī, tortus**: twist, hurl; **nēquīquam**: in vain; **horreō, -ēre, -uī**: shudder at, quake; **caecus, -a, -um**: blind, hidden, dark; **nūbēs, -is (-ium), f**: cloud, mist, fog; **terrificō, -āre, -āvī, -ātus**: frighten, terrify; **inānis, -e**: empty, useless.

211–218: **cōnūbium, -iī, n**: marriage, wedlock, proposal; **repellō, -ere, reppulī, repulsus**: reject; **Aenēas, -ae, m**: Aeneas (*Aenēān*: Greek accusative); **Paris, Paridis, m**: Paris, the Trojan prince whose abduction of Helen caused the Trojan War; **sēmivirus, -a, -um**: half-man, effeminate; **comitātus, -ūs, m**: retinue, entourage; **Maeonius, -a, -um**: Lydian (western Turkey); **mentum, -ī, n**: chin; **mitra, -ae, f**: oriental headress, turban; **crīnis, -is (-ium), m**: hair; **madeō, -ēre, -uī**: be moist; **subnectō, -ere, -nectuī, -nexus**: bind under, fasten up (+ accusative of respect); **raptō** (*regnō*); **potior, -īrī, potitus sum** (+ ablative): acquire, gain possession of; **foveō, -ēre, fōvī, fōtus**: keep warm, caress, cherish.

3. Catullus 64.171–88. Catullus paved the way for Roman poets to explore Greco-Roman mythology and its hero culture in epic verse. In this *epyllion*, or "little epic," Catullus creates a poignant portrait of Ariadne and her grief at Theseus's decision to betray their pact (she had saved him from the Minotaur's labyrinth, and he, in turn, agreed to marry her) and abandon her on a deserted island. Meter: dactylic hexameter.

> Iuppiter omnipotens, utinam nē tempore prīmō
> Gnōsia Cēcropiae tetigissent lītora puppēs,
> indomitō nec dīra ferens stīpendia taurō
> perfidus in Crētam religāsset nāvita fūnem,
> nec malus hic cēlans dulcī crūdēlia formā   175
> consilia in nostrīs requiēsset sēdibus hospes!
> Nam quō mē referam? Quālī spē perdita nītor?
> Idaeōsne petam montēs? At gurgite lātō
> discernens pontī truculentum dīvidit aequor.
> An patris auxilium spērem? Quemne ipsa relīquī,   180
> respersum iuvenem frāternā caede secūta?

Coniugis an fīdō consōler mēmet amōre?
Quīne fugit lentōs incurvans gurgite remōs?
Praetereā nullō colitur sōla insula tectō,
nec patet ēgressus pelagī cingentibus undīs.   185
Nulla fugae ratiō, nullā spēs: omnia mūta,
omnia sunt dēserta, ostentant omnia lētum.

Notes: 171–176: **omnipotens (-entis)**: see Passage 2; **Gnōsius, -a, -um**: Cretan; **Cēcropius, -a, -um**: Athenian (Cecrops was the legendary founder of Athens); **puppis, -is (-ium)**, f: stern, ship; **indomitus, -a, -um**: untamed, fierce; **dīrus, -a, -um**: fearful, horrible; **stīpendium, -iī**, n: tax, contribution, pay; **taurus, -ī**, m: bull (referring to the Bull of Marathon who fathered the Minotaur); **perfidus, -a, -um**: faithless, treacherous; **Crēta, -ae**, f: Crete, the island kingdom where Ariadne's father, Minos, ruled and the center of Minoan culture; **religō, -āre, -āvī, -ātus**: bind fast, moor; **religā(vi)sset** (syncopated pluperfect subjunctive); **nāvita, -ae**, m: sailor; **fūnis, -is, (-ium)**, m: rope, line; **hic**: Theseus; **cēlō, -āre, -āvī, -ātus**: hide, conceal; **crūdēlis, -e**: cruel, bloodthirsty; **requiescō, -ere, -ēvī, -ētus**: rest; **requiē(vi)sset** (syncopated pluperfect subjunctive).

177–182: **quō**: where; **nītor, -ī, nixus sum**: lean on, depend on; **Īdaeus, -a, -um**: of Ida, a mountain in Crete sacred to Venus; **gurges, gurgitis**, m: whirlpool; **discernō, -ere, -crēvī, -crētus**: distinguish, separate; **truculentus, -a, -um**: ferocious; **dīvidō, -ere, -vīsī, -vīsus**: divide, distribute; **spērō, -āre, -āvī, -ātus**: praise, extol; **respergō, -ere, -spersī, -spersus**: sprinkle, spatter; **frāternus, -a, -um**: brotherly; **fīdus, -a, -um**: trusty, faithful, loyal; **consōlor, -ārī, consōlātus sum**: console, alleviate, allay; **-met**: intensive enclitic (*mēmet*: "me, myself").

183–188: **lentus, -a, -um**: slow; **incurvō, -āre, -āvī, -ātus**: cause to bend; **rēmus, -ī**, m: oar; **praeterea**: moreover; **ēgressus, -ūs**: departure, flight; **pelagus, -ī**, n: open sea; **fuga, -ae**, f: flight; **mūtus, -a, -um**: silent; **dēsertus, -a, -um**: lonely, deserted; **ostentō, -āre, -āvī, -ātus**: display, offer; **lētum, -ī**, n: death.

4. **Ovid,** *Metamorphoses* **6.349–65.** After giving birth to Apollo and Artemis (Diana), Latona finds herself wandering in Lycia (Turkey). The day is hot, and the goddess comes upon an inviting pool of water, but the mean-hearted Lycians refuse her a simple drink. After a vitriolic rant on "water rights" (recounted here), Latona turns the villains into frogs, a fitting punishment. Meter: dactylic hexameter.

"Quid prohibētis aquīs? Ūsus commūnis aquārum est.
Nec sōlem proprium nātūra nec āëra fēcit   350
nec tenuēs undās: ad pūblica mūnera vēnī;

quae tamen ut dētis, supplex petō. Nōn ego nostrōs
abluere hīc artūs lassātaque membra parābam,
sed relevāre sitim. Caret ōs ūmōre loquentis,
et faucēs ārent, vixque est via vōcis in illīs.   355
Haustus aquae mihi nectar erit, vītamque fatēbor
accēpisse simul: vītam dederītis in undā.

Hī quoque vōs moveant, quī nostrō bracchia tendunt
parva sinū," et cāsū tendēbant bracchia nātī.
Quem nōn blanda deae potuissent verba movēre?   360
Hī tamen ōrantem perstant prohibēre mināsque,
nī procul abscēdat, convīciaque insuper addunt.
Nec satis est, ipsōs etiam pedibusque manūque
turbāvēre lacūs īmōque ē gurgite mollem
hūc illūc līmum saltū movēre malignō.   365

Notes: 349–57: **quid**: why; **commūnis, -e**: universal, public; **proprius, -a, -um**: exclusively its own; **āera** (Greek accusative); **tenuis, -e**: thin, fine, delicate; **supplex (-icis)**: suppliant, begging; **petō**: the final -o in *peto* scans short in order for the meter to work out correctly; **abluō, -ere, -luī, -lūtus**: wash; **artus, -ūs**, m: joint, limb; **lassō, -āre, -āvī, -ātus**: tire, exhaust; **membrum, -ī**, n: limb; **relevō, -āre, -āvī, -ātus**: lift, lighten, be free from; **sitis, -is (-ium)**, f: thirst; **ōs, oris**, n: mouth, face; **ūmor, -ōris**, m: moisture; **faucēs, -ium**, f (plural): throat; **āreō, -ēre, -uī**: be parched; **haustus, -ūs**, m: drink; **nectar, -aris**, n: nectar, the drink of the gods.

358–65: **hī**: baby Apollo and Diana; **cāsū**: by chance; **brācchium, -iī**, n: arm, forearm; **blandus, -a, -um**: alluring, enticing; **hī**: the rustic rabble; **perstō, -āre, -stitī, -stātus**: stand firm; **minae, -ārum**, f (plural): threat; **abscēdō, -ere, -cessī, -cessus**: go away, depart; **convīcium, -iī**, n: clamor, reproach, insult; **insuper**: above, in addition; **gurges, gurgitis**, m: whirlpool, eddy, abyss; **illūc**: there; **līmus, -ī**, m: mud, slime; **saltus, -ūs**, m: leap, jump; **malignus, -a, -um**: wicked, mean-hearted.

5. Juvenal, *Saturae* 3.41–57. One of Juvenal's overarching themes was moral decline. Here he complains that there is no place in the city for honest men who live according to old-fashioned Roman *mōs māiōrum*. Rome, instead, fosters liars, quacks, and scam artists. Meter: dactylic hexameter.

Quid Rōmae faciam? Mentīrī nescio; librum,
sī malus est, nequeō laudāre et poscere; mōtūs
astrōrum ignōrō; fūnūs prōmittere patris

nec volo nec possum; rānārum viscera numquam
inspexī; ferre ad nuptam quae mittit adulter,   45
quae mandat, nōrunt aliī; mē nēmo ministrō
fūr erit, atque ideō nullī comes exeo tamquam
mancus et extinctae corpus nōn ūtile dextrae.

Quis nunc dīligitur nisi conscius et cui fervens
aestuat occultīs animus semperque tacendīs?   50
Nīl tibi sē dēbēre putat, nīl conferet umquam,
participem quī tē secrētī fēcit honestī.
Cārus erit Verrī quī Verrem tempore quō vult
accūsāre potest. Tantī tibi nōn sit opācī
omnis harēna Tagī quodque in mare volvitur aurum,   55
ut somnō careās pōnendaque praemia sūmās
tristis et ā magnō semper timeāris amīcō.

Notes: 41–48: **Rōmae**: "at Rome" (locative); **mentior, -īrī, mentītus sum**: assert falsely, lie; **nescio**: the final -o in *nescio* scans short in order for the meter to work out correctly **nequeō, -īre, -īvī** or **-iī, -itus**: be unable; **mōtus, -ūs**, m: motion; **astrum, -ī**, n: star, constellation (although astrology was a rigorous mathematical science and some practitioners were honest, many were not; astrologers were usually Greek or Egyptian and therefore mistrusted by conservative Romans); **ignōrō, -āre, -āvī, -ātus**: be ignorant of; **prōmittō, -ere, -mīsī, -missus**: send forth, promise; **volo**: the final -o in *volo* scans short in order for the meter to work out correctly; **rāna, -ae**, f: frog (surely a joke, as the entrails of a frog would be too tiny to examine with any authority. With some skepticism, Cicero, *de Divinatione* 1.15, mentions the Etruscan practice of divination by frog-croak. Roman priests, however, more commonly and less comically, examined the entrails of large sacrificial hoofstock); **viscus, visceris**, n: entrails, inner parts; **inspiciō, -ere, -spexī, -spectus**: examine; **nupta, -ae**, f: bride, wife; **adulter, adulterī**, m: adulterer; **mandō, -āre, -āvī, -ātus**: commit, entrust, order; **nō(vē)runt** (syncopated perfect); **minister, ministrī**, m: subordinate, attendant, servant; **fūr, fūris**, m: thief; **exeo**: the final o scans schort in order for the scansion to work out properly; **mancus, -a, -um**: lame, crippled; **extinguō, -ere, -tinxī, -tinctus**: extinguish, kill, destroy.

49–57: **conscius, -iī**, m/f: accomplice, accessory, partner; **cui** scans as two short syllables in order for the meter to work out correctly; **ferveō, -ēre, ferbuī**: boil, seethe; **aestuō, -āre, -āvī, -ātus**: burn; **occultus, -a, -um**: hidden, secret; **nīl** = *nihil*; **particeps (-ipis)** (+ genitive): sharing in; **secrētus, -a, -um**: private, remote, secret (*secrētīs*: substantive); **Verres, Verris**, m: governor of Sicily whom Cicero stunningly prosecuted for the flagrant extortion and plundering of his province in 70 BCE (*NLP* 15.9); **accūsō, -āre, -āvī, -ātus**: blame, find fault, impugn, reprimand; **opācus, -a, -um**: dark, shadowy, obscure; **harēna, -ae**, f: sand; **Tagus, -ī**, m: a river in Spain and Portugal renowned for gold panning; **aurum, -ī**, n: gold; **volvō, -ere, volvī, volūtus**: roll, revolve, consider.

6. **Propertius,** *Elegiae* **2.12.** Imagining an exquisite artistic depiction of Cupid (Amor), Propertius laments that he receives nothing but torment from this god whom he honors with his verse. Meter: elegiac couplets.

Quīcumque ille fuit, puerum quī pinxit Amōrem,
    nonne putās mīrās hunc habuisse manūs?
Is prīmum vīdit sine sensū vīvere amantīs,
    et levibus cūrīs magna perīre bona.
Īdem nōn frustrā ventōsās addidit ālās,   5
    fēcit et hūmānō corde volāre deum:
scīlicet alternā quoniam iactāmur in undā,
    nostraque nōn ullīs permanet aura locīs.
Et meritō hāmātīs manus est armāta sagittīs,
    et pharetra ex umerō Cnōsia utrōque iacet: 10
ante ferit quoniam, tūtī quam cernimus hostem,
    nec quisquam ex īllō vulnere sānus abit.

In mē tēla manent, manet et puerīlis imāgo:
    Sed certē pennās perdidit ille suās;
ēvolat heu nostrō quoniam dē pectore nusquam,   15
    assiduusque meō sanguine bella gerit.
Quid tibi iūcundum est siccīs habitāre medullīs?
    Sī pudor est, aliō trāĭce tēla una!
Intactōs istō satius temptāre venēnō:
    nōn ego, sed tenuis vāpulat umbra mea.   20
Quam sī perdideris, quis erit quī tālia cantet,
    (haec mea Mūsa levis glōria magna tua est),
quī caput et digitōs et lūmina nigra puellae,
    et canat ut soleant molliter īre pedēs?

Notes: 1–12: **pingō, -ere, pinxī, pictus:** paint, represent; **nonne:** surely; **mīrus, -a, -um:** wonderful, astonishing; **amantīs** (substantive); **ventōsus, -a, -um:** windy, swift; **āla, -ae,** f: wing; **volō, -āre, -āvī, -ātus:** fly, flutter, flit; **alternus, -a, -um:** alternating; **iactō, -āre, -āvī, -ātus:** throw, scatter, toss; **permaneō, -ēre, -mansī, -mansus:** remain, last; **aura, -ae,** f: air, breeze; **meritō:** deservedly, rightly; **hāmātus, -a, -um:** hooked; **armō, -āre, -āvī, -ātus:** arm, equip; **sagitta, -ae,** f: arrow; **pharetra, -ae,** f: quiver; **umerus, -ī,** m: shoulder; **Cnōsius, -a, -um:** related to Cnossus, the capital city of Crete, an island sacred to Cupid's mother Venus; **ante . . . quam:** before (tmesis); **feriō, -īre, -īvī, -ītus:** strike, smite, knock, wound.

13–24: **puerīlis, -e**: youthful; **penna, -ae**, f: wing; **ēvolō, -āre, -āvī, -ātus**: rush forth, fly away; **heu**: alas; **nusquam** = *numquam*; **assiduus, -a, -um**: constant, persistent; **quid**: why; **iūcundus, -a, -um**: pleasant, agreeable; **siccus, -a, -um**: dry; **medulla, -ae**, f: marrow, heart; **pudor, -ōris**, m: shame; **aliō** (*locō*); **trāiciō, -ere, -iēcī, -iectus**: throw/shoot across; **intactus, -a, -um**: untouched, virgin (i.e., fresh victims not yet vanquished by *Amor*); **satius** (*est*); **temptō, -āre, -āvī, -ātus**: try, test, prove; **tenuis, -e**: thin, fine, slight; **vāpulō, -āre, -āvī, -ātus**: be beaten, be flogged; **quam** (*umbram*); **digitus, -ī**, m: finger.

Précis of Latin Forms

SUMMARY OF THE LATIN NOUN

FIRST DECLENSION

Case	puella, -ae, f: girl	poēta, -ae, m: poet
Singular		
Nominative	puella	poēta
Genitive	puellae	poētae
Dative	puellae	poētae
Accusative	puellam	poētam
Ablative	puellā	poētā
Vocative	puella	poēta
Plural		
Nominative	puellae	poētae
Genitive	puellārum	poētārum
Dative	puellīs	poētīs
Accusative	puellās	poētās
Ablative	puellīs	poētīs
Vocative	puellae	poētae

SECOND DECLENSION

Case	annus, -ī, m: year	laurus, -ī, f: laurel tree	vir, virī, m: man	ager, agrī, m: field	vīnum, -ī, n: wine
Singular					
Nominative	ann**us**	laur**us**	vir	ager	vīn**um**
Genitive	ann**ī**	laur**ī**	vir**ī**	agr**ī**	vīn**ī**
Dative	ann**ō**	laur**ō**	vir**ō**	agr**ō**	vīn**ō**
Accusative	ann**um**	laur**um**	vir**um**	agr**um**	vīn**um**
Ablative	ann**ō**	laur**ō**	vir**ō**	agr**ō**	vīn**ō**
Vocative	ann**e**	laur**e**	vir	ager	vīn**um**
Plural					
Nominative	ann**ī**	laur**ī**	vir**ī**	agr**ī**	vīn**a**
Genitive	ann**ōrum**	laur**ōrum**	vir**ōrum**	agr**ōrum**	vīn**ōrum**
Dative	ann**īs**	laur**īs**	vir**īs**	agr**īs**	vīn**īs**
Accusative	ann**ōs**	laur**ōs**	vir**ōs**	agr**ōs**	vīn**a**
Ablative	ann**īs**	laur**īs**	vir**īs**	agr**īs**	vīn**īs**
Vocative	ann**ī**	laur**ī**	vir**ī**	agr**ī**	vīn**a**

THIRD DECLENSION

Case	māter, mātris, f: mother	rex, rēgis, m: king	corpus, corporis, n: body
Singular			
Nominative	māter	rex	corpus
Genitive	mātr**is**	rēg**is**	corpor**is**
Dative	mātr**ī**	rēg**ī**	corpor**ī**
Accusative	mātr**em**	rēg**em**	corpus
Ablative	mātr**e**	rēg**e**	corpor**e**
Vocative	māter	rex	corpus
Plural			
Nominative	mātr**ēs**	rēg**ēs**	corpor**a**
Genitive	mātr**um**	rēg**um**	corpor**um**
Dative	mātr**ibus**	rēg**ibus**	corpor**ibus**
Accusative	mātr**ēs**	rēg**ēs**	corpor**a**
Ablative	mātr**ibus**	rēg**ibus**	corpor**ibus**
Vocative	mātr**ēs**	rēg**ēs**	corpor**a**

THIRD DECLENSION i-STEM

Case	urbs, urbis (-ium), f: city	ignis, ignis (-ium), m: fire	mare, maris (-ium), n: sea
Singular			
Nominative	urbs	ignis	mare
Genitive	urbis	ignis	maris
Dative	urbī	ignī	marī
Accusative	urbem	ignem	mare
Ablative	urbe	igne (ignī)	marī
Vocative	urbs	ignis	mare
Plural			
Nominative	urbēs	ignēs	maria
Genitive	urbium	ignium	marium
Dative	urbibus	ignibus	maribus
Accusative	urbēs (urbīs)	ignēs (ignīs)	maria
Ablative	urbibus	ignibus	maribus
Vocative	urbēs	ignēs	maria

FOURTH DECLENSION

Case	lacus, lacūs, m: lake	manus, manūs, f: hand	cornū, cornūs, n: horn
Singular			
Nominative	lacus	manus	cornū
Genitive	lacūs	manūs	cornūs
Dative	lacuī	manuī	cornū
Accusative	lacum	manum	cornū
Ablative	lacū	manū	cornū
Vocative	lacus	manus	cornū
Plural			
Nominative	lacūs	manūs	cornua
Genitive	lacuum	manuum	cornuum
Dative	lacibus	manibus	cornibus
Accusative	lacūs	manūs	cornua
Ablative	lacibus	manibus	cornibus
Vocative	lacūs	manūs	cornua

FIFTH DECLENSION

Case	rēs, reī, f: thing	diēs, diēī, m: day
Singular		
Nominative	rēs	diēs
Genitive	reī	diēī
Dative	reī	diēī
Accusative	rem	diem
Ablative	rē	diē
Vocative	rēs	diēs
Plural		
Nominative	rēs	diēs
Genitive	rērum	diērum
Dative	rēbus	diēbus
Accusative	rēs	diēs
Ablative	rēbus	diēbus
Vocative	rēs	diēs

SUMMARY OF THE LATIN ADJECTIVE

FIRST AND SECOND DECLENSION ADJECTIVES

Case	Masculine	Feminine	Neuter
Singular			
Nominative	bonus	bona	bonum
Genitive	bonī	bonae	bonī
Dative	bonō	bonae	bonō
Accusative	bonum	bonam	bonum
Ablative	bonō	bonā	bonō
Vocative	bone	bona	bonum
Plural			
Nominative	bonī	bonae	bona
Genitive	bonōrum	bonārum	bonōrum
Dative	bonīs	bonīs	bonīs
Accusative	bonōs	bonās	bona
Ablative	bonīs	bonīs	bonīs
Vocative	bonī	bonae	bona

FIRST AND SECOND DECLENSION ADJECTIVES
(WITH A STEM CHANGE)

Case	Masculine	Feminine	Neuter
Singular			
Nominative	noster	nostra	nostrum
Genitive	nostrī	nostrae	nostrī
Dative	nostrō	nostrae	nostrō
Accusative	nostrum	nostram	nostrum
Ablative	nostrō	nostrā	nostrō
Vocative	noster	nostra	nostrum
Plural			
Nominative	nostrī	nostrae	nostra
Genitive	nostrōrum	nostrārum	nostrōrum
Dative	nostrīs	nostrīs	nostrīs
Accusative	nostrōs	nostrās	nostra
Ablative	nostrīs	nostrīs	nostrīs
Vocative	nostrī	nostrae	nostra

THIRD DECLENSION ADJECTIVES

Case	Masculine	Feminine	Neuter
Singular			
Nominative	brevis	brevis	breve
Genitive	brevis	brevis	brevis
Dative	brevī	brevī	brevī
Accusative	brevem	brevem	breve
Ablative	brevī	brevī	brevī
Vocative	brevis	brevis	breve
Plural			
Nominative	brevēs	brevēs	brevia
Genitive	brevium	brevium	brevium
Dative	brevibus	brevibus	brevibus
Accusative	brevēs/brevīs	brevēs/brevīs	brevia
Ablative	brevibus	brevibus	brevibus
Vocative	brevēs	brevēs	brevia

PRONOMINAL ADJECTIVES

Case	Masculine	Feminine	Neuter
Singular			
Nominative	sōlus	sōla	sōlum
Genitive	sōl**īus**	sōl**īus**	sōl**īus**
Dative	sōl**ī**	sōl**ī**	sōl**ī**
Accusative	sōl**um**	sōlam	sōl**um**
Ablative	sōlō	sōlā	sōlō
Vocative	sōl**e**	sōla	sōl**um**
Plural			
Nominative	sōlī	sōlae	sōla
Genitive	sōl**ōrum**	sōl**ārum**	sōl**ōrum**
Dative	sōlīs	sōlīs	sōlīs
Accusative	sōlōs	sōlās	sōla
Ablative	sōlīs	sōlīs	sōlīs
Vocative	sōlī	sōlae	sōla

COMPARATIVE FORMS OF REGULAR LATIN ADJECTIVES

Case	Masculine	Feminine	Neuter
Singular			
Nominative	brev**ior**	brev**ior**	brev**ius**
Genitive	brev**iōris**	brev**iōris**	brev**iōris**
Dative	brev**iōrī**	brev**iōrī**	brev**iōrī**
Accusative	brev**iōrem**	brev**iōrem**	brev**ius**
Ablative	brev**iōre** or brev**iōrī**	brev**iōre** or brev**iōrī**	brev**iōre** or brev**iōrī**
Vocative	brev**ior**	brev**ior**	brev**ius**
Plural			
Nominative	brev**iōrēs**	brev**iōrēs**	brev**iōra**
Genitive	brev**iōrum**	brev**iōrum**	brev**iōrum**
Dative	brev**iōribus**	brev**iōribus**	brev**iōribus**
Accusative	brev**iōrēs** or brev**iōrīs**	brev**iōrēs** or brev**iōrīs**	brev**iōra**
Ablative	brev**iōribus**	brev**iōribus**	brev**iōribus**
Vocative	brev**iōrēs**	brev**iōrēs**	brev**iōra**

SUPERLATIVE FORMS OF REGULAR LATIN ADJECTIVES

Case	Masculine	Feminine	Neuter
Singular			
Nominative	brevissimus	brevissima	brevissimum
Genitive	brevissimī	brevissimae	brevissimī
Dative	brevissimō	brevissimae	brevissimō
Accusative	brevissimum	brevissimam	brevissimum
Ablative	brevissimō	brevissimā	brevissimō
Vocative	brevissime	brevissima	brevissimum
Plural			
Nominative	brevissimī	brevissimae	brevissima
Genitive	brevissimōrum	brevissimārum	brevissimōrum
Dative	brevissimīs	brevissimīs	brevissimīs
Accusative	brevissimōs	brevissimās	brevissima
Ablative	brevissimīs	brevissimīs	brevissimīs
Vocative	brevissimī	brevissimae	brevissima

COMPARISON OF IRREGULAR ADJECTIVES

Positive	Comparative	Superlative
bonus, -a, -um (good)	melior, melius (better)	optimus, -a, -um (best)
magnus, -a, -um (big)	māior, māius (bigger)	maximus, -a, -um (biggest)
malus, -a, -um (bad)	pēior, pēius (worse)	pessimus, -a, -um (worst)
multus, -a, -um (much)	—, plūs (more)	plūrimus, -a, -um (most)
parvus, -a, -um (small)	minor, minus (smaller)	minimus, -a, -um (smallest)
superus, -a, -um (high)	superior, superius (higher)	summus, -a, -um suprēmus, -a, -um (highest)

COMPARISON OF SPECIAL ADJECTIVES IN -er

Positive	Comparative	Superlative
līber, -a, -um (free)	līberior, līberius	līber**rimus, -a, -um**
sacer, sacra, sacrum (sacred)	sacrior, sacrius	sacer**rimus, -a, -um**
pulcher, -chra, -chrum (beautiful)	pulchrior, pulchrius	pulcher**rimus, -a, -um**
ācer, ācris, ācre (sharp, fierce)	ācrior, ācrius	ācer**rimus, -a, -um**
celer, celeris, celere (swift)	celerior, celerius	celer**rimus, -a, -um**

COMPARISON OF SPECIAL ADJECTIVES IN -lis

Positive	Comparative	Superlative
facilis, -e (easy)	facilior, facilius	facil**limus, -a, -um**
difficilis, -e (difficult)	difficilior, difficilius	difficil**limus, -a, -um**
similis, -e (similar)	similior, similius	simil**limus, -a, -um**
dissimilis, -e (dissimilar)	dissimilior, dissimilius	dissimil**limus, -a, -um**
gracilis, -e (graceful)	gracilior, gracilius	gracil**limus, -a, -um**
humilis, -e (low, humble)	humilior, humilius	humil**limus, -a, -um**

COMPARISON OF REGULAR ADVERBS FROM ADJECTIVES

Adjective	Positive Adverb	Comparative Adverb	Superlative Adverb
doctus, -a, -um (learned)	doctē	doct**ius**	doct**issimē**
brevis, -e (brief)	breviter	brev**ius**	brev**issimē**
pulcher, -chra, -chrum (pretty)	pulchrē	pulchr**ius**	pulch**errimē**
ācer, -cre (sharp)	ācriter	acr**ius**	ac**errimē**
facilis, -e (easy)	faciliter	facil**ius**	facil**limē**

COMPARISON OF IRREGULAR ADVERBS FROM ADJECTIVES

Positive Adjective	Positive Adverb	Comparative Adverb	Superlative Adverb
bonus, -a, -um	bene (well)	melius (better)	optimē (best)
magnus, -a, -um	magnopere (greatly)	magis (more)	maximē (most)
malus, -a, -um	malē (badly)	pēius (worse)	pessimē (worst)
multus, -a, -um	multum (much)	plūs (more)	plūrimē (most)
parvus, -a, -um	parum (little)	minus (less)	minimē (least)

CARDINAL NUMBERS

ūnus, -a, -um: one

Case	Masculine	Feminine	Neuter
Nominative	ūnus	ūna	ūnum
Genitive	ūnīus	ūnīus	ūnīus
Dative	ūnī	ūnī	ūnī
Accusative	ūnum	ūnam	ūnum
Ablative	ūnō	ūnā	ūnō

duo, duae, duo: two

Case	Masculine	Feminine	Neuter
Nominative	duo	duae	duo
Genitive	duōrum	duārum	duōrum
Dative	duōbus	duābus	duōbus
Accusative	duōs / duo	duās	duo
Ablative	duōbus	duābus	duōbus

trēs, tria: three

Case	Masculine	Feminine	Neuter
Nominative	trēs	trēs	tria
Genitive	trium	trium	trium
Dative	tribus	tribus	tribus
Accusative	trēs / trīs	trēs / trīs	tria
Ablative	tribus	tribus	tribus

SUMMARY OF LATIN PRONOUNS

Personal Pronouns

FIRST PERSON PRONOUNS

Case	Singular	Plural
Nominative	ego	nōs
Genitive	meī	nostrum (nostrī)
Dative	mihi (mihī, mī)	nōbīs
Accusative	mē	nōs
Ablative	mē	nōbīs

SECOND PERSON PRONOUNS

Case	Singular	Plural
Nominative	tū	vōs
Genitive	tuī	vestrum (vestrī)
Dative	tibi (tibī)	vōbīs
Accusative	tē	vōs
Ablative	tē	vōbīs

THIRD PERSON PRONOUNS

Case	Masculine	Feminine	Neuter
Singular			
Nominative	is	ea	id
Genitive	eius	eius	eius
Dative	eī	eī	eī
Accusative	eum	eam	id
Ablative	eō	eā	eō
Plural			
Nominative	eī	eae	ea
Genitive	eōrum	eārum	eōrum
Dative	eīs	eīs	eīs
Accusative	eōs	eās	ea
Ablative	eīs	eīs	eīs

THIRD PERSON REFLEXIVE PRONOUNS

Case and Number	
Genitive singular and plural	suī
Dative singular and plural	sibi (sibī)
Accusative singular and plural	sē (sēsē)
Ablative singular and plural	sē (sēsē)

Intensive Pronoun

ipse, ipsa, ipsum: him-/her-/itself; themselves

Case	Masculine	Feminine	Neuter
Singular			
Nominative	ipse	ipsa	ipsum
Genitive	ipsīus	ipsīus	ipsīus
Dative	ipsī	ipsī	ipsī
Accusative	ipsum	ipsam	ipsum
Ablative	ipsō	ipsā	ipsō
Plural			
Nominative	ipsī	ipsae	ipsa
Genitive	ipsōrum	ipsārum	ipsōrum
Dative	ipsīs	ipsīs	ipsīs
Accusative	ipsōs	ipsās	ipsa
Ablative	ipsīs	ipsīs	ipsīs

Demonstrative Pronouns

hic, haec, hoc: this, these

Case	Masculine	Feminine	Neuter
Singular			
Nominative	hic	haec	hoc
Genitive	huius	huius	huius
Dative	huic	huic	huic
Accusative	hunc	hanc	hoc
Ablative	hōc	hāc	hōc
Plural			
Nominative	hī	hae	haec
Genitive	hōrum	hārum	hōrum
Dative	hīs	hīs	hīs
Accusative	hōs	hās	haec
Ablative	hīs	hīs	hīs

ille, illa, illud: that, those

Case	Masculine	Feminine	Neuter
Singular			
Nominative	ille	illa	illud
Genitive	illīus	illīus	illīus
Dative	illī	illī	illī
Accusative	illum	illam	illud
Ablative	illō	illā	illō
Plural			
Nominative	illī	illae	illa
Genitive	illōrum	illārum	illōrum
Dative	illīs	illīs	illīs
Accusative	illōs	illās	illa
Ablative	illīs	illīs	illīs

īdem, eadem, idem: the same

Case	Masculine	Feminine	Neuter
Singular			
Nominative	īdem	eadem	idem
Genitive	eiusdem	eiusdem	eiusdem
Dative	eīdem	eīdem	eīdem
Accusative	eundem	eandem	idem
Ablative	eōdem	eādem	eōdem
Plural			
Nominative	eīdem *or* iīdem	eaedem	eadem
Genitive	eōrundem	eārundem	eōrundem
Dative	eīsdem *or* īsdem	eīsdem *or* īsdem	eīsdem *or* īsdem
Accusative	eōsdem	eāsdem	eadem
Ablative	eīsdem *or* īsdem	eīsdem *or* īsdem	eīsdem *or* īsdem

aliquis, aliqua, aliquid: some

Case	Masculine	Feminine	Neuter
Singular			
Nominative	aliquis	aliqua	aliquid
Genitive	alicuius	alicuius	alicuius
Dative	alicui	alicui	alicui
Accusative	aliquem	aliquam	aliquid
Ablative	aliquō	aliquā	aliquō
Plural			
Nominative	aliquī	aliquae	aliqua
Genitive	aliquōrum	aliquārum	aliquōrum
Dative	aliquibus	aliquibus	aliquibus
Accusative	aliquōs	aliquās	aliqua
Ablative	aliquibus	aliquibus	aliquibus

quīdam, quaedam, quiddam: a certain

Case	Masculine	Feminine	Neuter
Singular			
Nominative	quīdam	quaedam	quiddam
Genitive	cuiusdam	cuiusdam	cuiusdam
Dative	cuidam	cuidam	cuidam
Accusative	quendam	quandam	quiddam
Ablative	quōdam	quādam	quōdam
Plural			
Nominative	quīdam	quaedam	quaedam
Genitive	quōrundam	quārundam	quōrundam
Dative	quibusdam	quibusdam	quibusdam
Accusative	quōsdam	quāsdam	quaedam
Ablative	quibusdam	quibusdam	quibusdam

RELATIVE PRONOUN

Case	Masculine	Feminine	Neuter
Singular			
Nominative	quī	quae	quod
Genitive	cuius	cuius	cuius
Dative	cui	cui	cui
Accusative	quem	quam	quod
Ablative	quō	quā	quō
Plural			
Nominative	quī	quae	quae
Genitive	quōrum	quārum	quōrum
Dative	quibus	quibus	quibus
Accusative	quōs	quās	quae
Ablative	quibus	quibus	quibus

INTERROGATIVE PRONOUN

Case	Masculine	Feminine	Neuter
Singular			
Nominative	quis	quis	quid
Genitive	cuius	cuius	cuius
Dative	cui	cui	cui
Accusative	quem	quem	quid
Ablative	quō	quā	quō
Plural			
Nominative	quī	quae	quae
Genitive	quōrum	quārum	quōrum
Dative	quibus	quibus	quibus
Accusative	quōs	quās	quae
Ablative	quibus	quibus	quibus

SUMMARY OF LATIN VERBS

Regular Verbs

PRESENT TENSE OF REGULAR VERBS

PRESENT ACTIVE INDICATIVE

	1st Conj.	2nd Conj.	3rd Conj.	3rd Conj. (-io)	4th Conj.
Singular					
1st	amō: I love	doceō: I teach	mittō: I send	capiō: I take	audiō: I hear
2nd	amās: you love	docēs: you teach	mittis: you send	capis: you take	audīs: you hear
3rd	amat: he/she/it loves	docet: he/she/it teaches	mittit: he/she/it sends	capit: he/she/it takes	audit: he/she/it hears
Plural					
1st	amāmus: we love	docēmus: we teach	mittimus: we send	capimus: we take	audīmus: we hear
2nd	amātis: you love	docētis: you teach	mittitis: you send	capitis: you take	audītis: you hear
3rd	amant: they love	docent: they teach	mittunt: they send	capiunt: they take	audiunt: they hear

PRESENT PASSIVE INDICATIVE

	1st Conj.	2nd Conj.	3rd Conj.	3rd Conj. (-io)	4th Conj.
Singular					
1st	amor: I am loved	doceor: I am taught	mittor: I am sent	capior: I am taken	audior: I am heard
2nd	amāris/ amāre: you are loved	docēris/ docēre: you are taught	mitteris/ mittere: you are sent	caperis/ capere: you are taken	audīris/ audīre: you are heard
3rd	amātur: he/she/it is loved	docētur: he/she/it is taught	mittitur: he/she/it is sent	capitur: he/she/it is taken	audītur: he/she/it is heard
Plural					
1st	amāmur: we are loved	docēmur: we are taught	mittimur: we are sent	capimur: we are taken	audīmur: we are heard
2nd	amāminī: you are loved	docēminī: you are taught	mittiminī: you are taught	capiminī: you are taken	audīminī: you are heard
3rd	amantur: they are loved	docentur: they are taught	mittuntur: they are sent	capiuntur: they are taken	audiuntur: they are heard

PRESENT ACTIVE SUBJUNCTIVE

	1st Conj.	2nd Conj.	3rd Conj.	3rd Conj. (-io)	4th Conj.
Singular					
1st	amem	doceam	mittam	capiam	audiam
2nd	amēs	doceās	mittās	capiās	audiās
3rd	amet	doceat	mittat	capiat	audiat
Plural					
1st	amēmus	doceāmus	mittāmus	capiāmus	audiāmus
2nd	amētis	doceātis	mittātis	capiātis	audiātis
3rd	ament	doceant	mittant	capiant	audiant

PRESENT PASSIVE SUBJUNCTIVE

	1st Conj.	2nd Conj.	3rd Conj.	3rd Conj. (-io)	4th Conj.
Singular					
1st	amer	docear	mittar	capiar	audiar
2nd	amēris/ amēre	doceāris/ doceāre	mittāris/ mittāre	capiāris/ capiāre	audiāris/ audiāre
3rd	amētur	doceātur	mittātur	capiātur	audiātur
Plural					
1st	amēmur	doceāmur	mittāmur	capiāmur	audiāmur
2nd	amēminī	doceāminī	mittāminī	capiāminī	audiāminī
3rd	amentur	doceantur	mittantur	capiantur	audiantur

IMPERFECT TENSE OF REGULAR VERBS

IMPERFECT ACTIVE INDICATIVE

	1st Conj.	2nd Conj.	3rd Conj.	3rd Conj. (-io)	4th Conj.
Singular					
1st	amābam: I was loving	docēbam: I was teaching	mittēbam: I was sending	capiēbam: I was taking	audiēbam: I was hearing
2nd	amābās: you were loving	docēbās: you were teaching	mittēbās: you were sending	capiēbās: you were taking	audiēbās: you were hearing
3rd	amābat: he/she/it was loving	docēbat: he/she/it was teaching	mittēbat: he/she/it was sending	capiēbat: he/she/it was taking	audiēbat: he/she/it was hearing
Plural					
1st	amābāmus: we were loving	docēbāmus: we were teaching	mittēbāmus: we were sending	capiēbāmus: we were taking	audiēbāmus: we were hearing
2nd	amābātis: you were loving	docēbātis: you were teaching	mittēbātis: you were sending	capiēbātis: you were taking	audiēbātis: you were hearing
3rd	amābant: they were loving	docēbant: they were teaching	mittēbant: they were sending	capiēbant: they were taking	audiēbant: they were hearing

IMPERFECT PASSIVE INDICATIVE

	1st Conj.	2nd Conj.	3rd Conj.	3rd Conj. (-io)	4th Conj.
Singular					
1st	amā**bar**: I was (being) loved	docē**bar**: I was (being) taught	mittē**bar**: I was (being) sent	capiē**bar**: I was (being) taken	audiē**bar**: I was (being) heard
2nd	amā**bāris**/ amā**bāre**: you were (being) loved	docē**bāris**/ docē**bāre**: you were (being) taught	mittē**bāris**/ mittē**bāre**: you were (being) sent	capiē**bāris**/ capiē**bāre**: you were (being) taken	audiē**bāris**/ audiē**bāre**: you were (being) heard
3rd	amā**bātur**: he/she/it was (being) loved	docē**bātur**: he/she/it was (being) taught	mittē**bātur**: he/she/it was (being) sent	capiē**bātur**: he/she/it was (being) taken	audiē**bātur**: he/she/it was (being) heard
Plural					
1st	amā**bāmur**: we were (being) loved	docē**bāmur**: we were (being) taught	mittē**bāmur**: we were (being) sent	capiē**bāmur**: we were (being) taken	audiē**bāmur**: we were (being) heard
2nd	amā**bāminī**: you were (being) loved	docē**bāminī**: you were (being) taught	mittē**bāminī**: you were (being) sent	capiē**bāminī**: you were (being) taken	audiē**bāminī**: you were (being) heard
3rd	amā**bantur**: they were (being) loved	docē**bantur**: they were (being) taught	mittē**bantur**: they were (being) sent	capiē**bantur**: they were (being) taken	audiē**bantur**: they were (being) heard

IMPERFECT ACTIVE SUBJUNCTIVE

	1st Conj.	2nd Conj.	3rd Conj.	3rd Conj. (-io)	4th Conj.
Singular					
1st	amā**rem**	docē**rem**	mitte**rem**	cape**rem**	audī**rem**
2nd	amā**rēs**	docē**rēs**	mitte**rēs**	cape**rēs**	audī**rēs**
3rd	amā**ret**	docē**ret**	mitte**ret**	cape**ret**	audī**ret**
Plural					
1st	amā**rēmus**	docē**rēmus**	mitte**rēmus**	cape**rēmus**	audī**rēmus**
2nd	amā**rētis**	docē**rētis**	mitte**rētis**	cape**rētis**	audī**rētis**
3rd	amā**rent**	docē**rent**	mitte**rent**	cape**rent**	audī**rent**

IMPERFECT PASSIVE SUBJUNCTIVE

	1st Conj.	2nd Conj.	3rd Conj.	3rd Conj. (-io)	4th Conj.
Singular					
1st	amārer	docērer	mitterer	caperer	audīrer
2nd	amārēris/ amārēre	docērēris/ docērēre	mitterēris/ mitterēre	caperēris/ caperēre	audīrēris/ audīrēre
3rd	amārētur	docērētur	mitterētur	caperētur	audīrētur
Plural					
1st	amārēmur	docērēmur	mitterēmur	caperēmur	audīrēmur
2nd	amārēminī	docērēminī	mitterēminī	caperēminī	audīrēminī
3rd	amārentur	docērentur	mitterentur	caperentur	audīrentur

FUTURE TENSE OF REGULAR VERBS

FUTURE ACTIVE INDICATIVE

	1st Conj.	2nd Conj.	3rd Conj.	3rd Conj. (-io)	4th Conj.
Singular					
1st	amābō: I shall love	docēbō: I shall teach	mittam: I shall send	capiam: I shall take	audiam: I shall hear
2nd	amābis: you will love	docēbis: you will teach	mittēs: you will send	capiēs: you will take	audiēs: you will hear
3rd	amābit: he/she/it will love	docēbit: he/she/it will teach	mittet: he/she/it will send	capiet: he/she/it will take	audiet: he/she/it will hear
Plural					
1st	amābimus: we shall love	docēbimus: we shall teach	mittēmus: we shall send	capiēmus: we shall take	audiēmus: we shall hear
2nd	amābitis: you will love	docēbitis: you will teach	mittētis: you will send	capiētis: you will take	audiētis: you will hear
3rd	amābunt: they will love	docēbunt: they will teach	mittent: they will send	capient: they will take	audient: they will hear

FUTURE PASSIVE INDICATIVE

	1st Conj.	2nd Conj.	3rd Conj.	3rd Conj. (-io)	4th Conj.
Singular					
1st	ama**bor**: I shall be loved	doce**bor**: I shall be taught	mitt**ar**: I shall be sent	capi**ar**: I shall be taken	audi**ar**: I shall be heard
2nd	ama**beris**/ ama**bere**: you will be loved	doce**beris**/ doce**bere**: you will be taught	mitt**ēris**/ mitt**ēre**: you will be sent	capi**ēris**/ capi**ēre**: you will be taken	audi**ēris**/ audi**ēre**: you will be heard
3rd	ama**bitur**: he/she/it will be loved	doce**bitur**: he/she/it will be taught	mitt**ētur**: he/she/it will be sent	capi**ētur**: he/she/it will be taken	audi**ētur**: he/she/it will be heard
Plural					
1st	ama**bimur**: we shall be loved	doce**bimur**: we shall be taught	mitt**ēmur**: we shall be sent	capi**ēmur**: we shall be taken	audi**ēmur**: we shall be heard
2nd	ama**biminī**: you will be loved	doce**biminī**: you will be taught	mitt**ēminī**: you will be sent	capi**ēminī**: you will be taken	audi**ēminī**: you will be heard
3rd	ama**buntur**: they will be loved	doce**buntur**: they will be taught	mitt**entur**: they will be sent	capi**entur**: they will be taken	audi**entur**: they will be heard

Perfect System of Regular Latin Verbs

PERFECT TENSE OF REGULAR VERBS

PERFECT ACTIVE INDICATIVE

	1st Conj.	2nd Conj.	3rd Conj.	3rd Conj. (-io)	4th Conj.
Singular					
1st	amāvī: I have loved	docuī: I have taught	mīsī: I have sent	cēpī: I have taken	audīvī: I have heard
2nd	amā**vistī**: you have loved	docu**istī**: you have taught	mīs**istī**: you have sent	cēp**istī**: you have taken	audī**vistī**: you have heard
3rd	amā**vit**: he/she/it has loved	docu**it**: he/she/it has taught	mīs**it**: he/she/it has sent	cēp**it**: he/she/it has taken	audī**vit**: he/she/it has heard

Plural					
1st	amāv**imus**: we have loved	docu**imus**: we have taught	mīs**imus**: we have sent	cēp**imus**: we have taken	audīv**imus**: we have heard
2nd	amāv**istis**: you have loved	docu**istis**: you have taught	mīs**istis**: you have sent	cēp**istis**: you have taken	audīv**istis**: you have heard
3rd	amāv**ērunt**/ amāv**ēre**: they have loved	docu**ērunt**/ docu**ēre**: they have taught	mīs**ērunt**/ mīs**ēre**: they have sent	cēp**ērunt**/ cēp**ēre**: they have taken	audīv**ērunt**/ audīv**ēre**: they have heard

PERFECT PASSIVE INDICATIVE

	1st Conj.	2nd Conj.	3rd Conj.	3rd Conj. (-io)	4th Conj.
Singular					
1st	amāt**us**, **-a**, **-um** **sum**: I have been loved	doct**us**, **-a**, **-um** **sum**: I have been taught	miss**us**, **-a**, **-um** **sum**: I have been sent	capt**us**, **-a**, **-um** **sum**: I have been taken	audīt**us**, **-a**, **-um** **sum**: I have been heard
2nd	amāt**us**, **-a**, **-um** **es**: you have been loved	doct**us**, **-a**, **-um** **es**: you have been taught	miss**us**, **-a**, **-um** **es**: you have been sent	capt**us**, **-a**, **-um** **es**: you have been taken	audīt**us**, **-a**, **-um** **es**: you have been heard
3rd	amāt**us**, **-a**, **-um** **est**: he/she/it has been loved	doct**us**, **-a**, **-um** **est**: he/she/it has been taught	miss**us**, **-a**, **-um** **est**: he/she/it has been sent	capt**us**, **-a**, **-um** **est**: he/she/it has been taken	audīt**us**, **-a**, **-um** **est**: he/she/it has been heard
Plural					
1st	amāt**ī**, **-ae**, **-a** **sumus**: we have been loved	doct**ī**, **-ae**, **-a** **sumus**: we have been taught	miss**ī**, **-ae**, **-a** **sumus**: we have been sent	capt**ī**, **-ae**, **-a** **sumus**: we have been taken	audīt**ī**, **-ae**, **-a** **sumus**: we have been heard
2nd	amāt**ī**, **-ae**, **-a** **estis**: you have been loved	doct**ī**, **-ae**, **-a** **estis**: you have been taught	miss**ī**, **-ae**, **-a** **estis**: you have been sent	capt**ī**, **-ae**, **-a** **estis**: you have been taken	audīt**ī**, **-ae**, **-a** **estis**: you have been heard
3rd	amāt**ī**, **-ae**, **-a** **sunt**: they have been loved	doct**ī**, **-ae**, **-a** **sunt**: they have been taught	miss**ī**, **-ae**, **-a** **sunt**: they have been sent	capt**ī**, **-ae**, **-a** **sunt**: they have been taken	audīt**ī**, **-ae**, **-a** **sunt**: they have been heard

PERFECT ACTIVE SUBJUNCTIVE

	1st Conj.	2nd Conj.	3rd Conj.	3rd Conj. (-io)	4th Conj.
Singular					
1st	amāv**erim**	docu**erim**	mīs**erim**	cēp**erim**	audīv**erim**
2nd	amāv**eris**	docu**eris**	mīs**eris**	cēp**eris**	audīv**eris**
3rd	amāv**erit**	docu**erit**	mīs**erit**	cēp**erit**	audīv**erit**
Plural					
1st	amāv**erimus**	docu**erimus**	mīs**erimus**	cēp**erimus**	audīv**erimus**
2nd	amāv**eritis**	docu**eritis**	mīs**eritis**	cēp**eritis**	audīv**eritis**
3rd	amāv**erint**	docu**erint**	mīs**erint**	cēp**erint**	audīv**erint**

PERFECT PASSIVE SUBJUNCTIVE

	1st Conj.	2nd Conj.	3rd Conj.	3rd Conj. (-io)	4th Conj.
Singular					
1st	amāt**us, -a, -um** sim	doct**us, -a, -um** sim	miss**us, -a, -um** sim	capt**us, -a, -um** sim	audīt**us, -a, -um** sim
2nd	amāt**us, -a, -um** sīs	doct**us, -a, -um** sīs	miss**us, -a, -um** sīs	capt**us, -a, -um** sīs	audīt**us, -a, -um** sīs
3rd	amāt**us, -a, -um** sit	doct**us, -a, -um** sit	miss**us, -a, -um** sit	capt**us, -a, -um** sit	audīt**us, -a, -um** sit
Plural					
1st	amāt**ī, -ae, -a** sīmus	doct**ī, -ae, -a** sīmus	miss**ī, -ae, -a** sīmus	capt**ī, -ae, -a** sīmus	audīt**ī, -ae, -a** sīmus
2nd	amāt**ī, -ae, -a** sītis	doct**ī, -ae, -a** sītis	miss**ī, -ae, -a** sītis	capt**ī, -ae, -a** sītis	audīt**ī, -ae, -a** sītis
3rd	amāt**ī, -ae, -a** sint	doct**ī, -ae, -a** sint	miss**ī, -ae, -a** sint	capt**ī, -ae, -a** sint	audīt**ī, -ae, -a** sint

PLUPERFECT TENSE OF REGULAR VERBS

PLUPERFECT ACTIVE INDICATIVE

	1st Conj.	2nd Conj.	3rd Conj.	3rd Conj. (-io)	4th Conj.
Singular					
1st	amāv**eram**: I had loved	docu**eram**: I had taught	mīs**eram**: I had sent	cēp**eram**: I had taken	audīv**eram**: I had heard
2nd	amāv**erās**: you had loved	docu**erās**: you had taught	mīs**erās**: you had sent	cēp**erās**: you had taken	audīv**erās**: you had heard
3rd	amāv**erat**: he/she/it had loved	docu**erat**: he/she/it had taught	mīs**erat**: he/she/it had sent	cēp**erat**: he/she/it had taken	audīv**erat**: he/she/it had heard

Plural					
1st	amāve**rāmus**: we had loved	docue**rāmus**: we had taught	mīse**rāmus**: we had sent	cēpe**rāmus**: we had taken	audīve**rāmus**: we had heard
2nd	amāve**rātis**: you had loved	docue**rātis**: you had taught	mīse**rātis**: you had sent	cēpe**rātis**: you had taken	audīve**rātis**: you had heard
3rd	amāve**rant**: they had loved	docue**rant**: they had taught	mīse**rant**: they had sent	cēpe**rant**: they had taken	audīve**rant**: they had heard

PLUPERFECT PASSIVE INDICATIVE

	1st Conj.	2nd Conj.	3rd Conj.	3rd Conj. (-io)	4th Conj.
Singular					
1st	amāt**us, -a, -um eram**: I had been loved	doct**us, -a, -um eram**: I had been taught	miss**us, -a, -um eram**: I had been sent	capt**us, -a, -um eram**: I had been taken	audīt**us, -a, -um eram**: I had been heard
2nd	amāt**us, -a, -um erās**: you had been loved	doct**us, -a, -um erās**: you had been taught	miss**us, -a, -um erās**: you had been sent	capt**us, -a, -um erās**: you had been taken	audīt**us, -a, -um erās**: you had been heard
3rd	amāt**us, -a, -um erat**: he/she/it had been loved	doct**us, -a, -um erat**: he/she/it had been taught	miss**us, -a, -um erat**: he/she/it had been sent	capt**us, -a, -um erat**: he/she/it had been taken	audīt**us, -a, -um erat**: he/she/it had been heard
Plural					
1st	amāt**ī, -ae, -a erāmus**: we had been loved	doct**ī, -ae, -a erāmus**: we had been taught	miss**ī, -ae, -a erāmus**: we had been sent	capt**ī, -ae, -a erāmus**: we had been taken	audīt**ī, -ae, -a erāmus**: we had been heard
2nd	amāt**ī, -ae, -a erātis**: you had been loved	doct**ī, -ae, -a erātis**: you had been taught	miss**ī, -ae, -a erātis**: you had been sent	capt**ī, -ae, -a erātis**: you had been taken	audīt**ī, -ae, -a erātis**: you had been heard
3rd	amāt**ī, -ae, -a erant**: they had been loved	doct**ī, -ae, -a erant**: they had been taught	miss**ī, -ae, -a erant**: they had been sent	capt**ī, -ae, -a erant**: they had been taken	audīt**ī, -ae, -a erant**: they had been heard

PLUPERFECT ACTIVE SUBJUNCTIVE

	1st Conj.	2nd Conj.	3rd Conj.	3rd Conj. (-io)	4th Conj.
Singular					
1st	amāv**issem**	docu**issem**	mīs**issem**	cēp**issem**	audīv**issem**
2nd	amāv**issēs**	docu**issēs**	mīs**issēs**	cēp**issēs**	audīv**issēs**
3rd	amāv**isset**	docu**isset**	mīs**isset**	cēp**isset**	audīv**isset**
Plural					
1st	amāv**issēmus**	docu**issēmus**	mīs**issēmus**	cēp**issēmus**	audīv**issēmus**
2nd	amāv**issētis**	docu**issētis**	mīs**issētis**	cēp**issētis**	audīv**issētis**
3rd	amāv**issent**	docu**issent**	mīs**issent**	cēp**issent**	audīv**issent**

PLUPERFECT PASSIVE SUBJUNCTIVE

	1st Conj.	2nd Conj.	3rd Conj.	3rd Conj. (-io)	4th Conj.
Singular					
1st	amāt**us, -a, -um** essem	doct**us, -a, -um** essem	miss**us, -a, -um** essem	capt**us, -a, -um** essem	audīt**us, -a, -um** essem
2nd	amāt**us, -a, -um** essēs	doct**us, -a, -um** essēs	miss**us, -a, -um** essēs	capt**us, -a, -um** essēs	audīt**us, -a, -um** essēs
3rd	amāt**us, -a, -um** esset	doct**us, -a, -um** esset	miss**us, -a, -um** esset	capt**us, -a, -um** esset	audīt**us, -a, -um** esset
Plural					
1st	amāt**ī, -ae, -a** essēmus	doct**ī, -ae, -a** essēmus	miss**ī, -ae, -a** essēmus	capt**ī, -ae, -a** essēmus	audīt**ī, -ae, -a** essēmus
2nd	amāt**ī, -ae, -a** essētis	doct**ī, -ae, -a** essētis	miss**ī, -ae, -a** essētis	capt**ī, -ae, -a** essētis	audīt**ī, -ae, -a** essētis
3rd	amāt**ī, -ae, -a** essent	doct**ī, -ae, -a** essent	miss**ī, -ae, -a** essent	capt**ī, -ae, -a** essent	audīt**ī, -ae, -a** essent

FUTURE PERFECT TENSE OF REGULAR VERBS

FUTURE PERFECT ACTIVE INDICATIVE

	1st Conj.	2nd Conj.	3rd Conj.	3rd Conj. (-io)	4th Conj.
Singular					
1st	amāv**erō:** I shall have loved	docu**erō:** I shall have taught	mīs**erō:** I shall have sent	cēp**erō:** I shall have taken	audīv**erō:** I shall have heard
2nd	amāv**eris:** you will have loved	docu**eris:** you will have taught	mīs**eris:** you will have sent	cēp**eris:** you will have taken	audīv**eris:** you will have heard
3rd	amāv**erit:** he/she/it will have loved	docu**erit:** he/she/it will have taught	mīs**erit:** he/she/it will have sent	cēp**erit:** he/she/it will have taken	audīv**erit:** he/she/it will have heard

Plural					
1st	amāverimus: we shall have loved	docuerimus: we shall have taught	mīserimus: we shall have sent	cēperimus: we shall have taken	audīverimus: we shall have heard
2nd	amāveritis: you will have loved	docueritis: you will have taught	mīseritis: you will have sent	cēperitis: you will have taken	audīveritis: you will have heard
3rd	amāverint: they will have loved	docuerint: they will have taught	mīserint: they will have sent	cēperint: they will have taken	audīverint: they will have heard

FUTURE PERFECT PASSIVE INDICATIVE

	1st Conj.	2nd Conj.	3rd Conj.	3rd Conj. (-io)	4th Conj.
Singular					
1st	amātus, -a, -um erō: I shall have been loved	doctus, -a, -um erō: I shall have been taught	missus, -a, -um erō: I shall have been sent	captus, -a, -um erō: I shall have been taken	audītus, -a, -um erō: I shall have been heard
2nd	amātus, -a, -um eris: you will have been loved	doctus, -a, -um eris: you will have been taught	missus, -a, -um eris: you will have been sent	captus, -a, -um eris: you will have been taken	audītus, -a, -um eris: you will have been heard
3rd	amātus, -a, -um erit: he/she/it will have been loved	doctus, -a, -um erit: he/she/it will have been taught	missus, -a, -um erit: he/she/it will have been sent	captus, -a, -um erit: he/she/it will have been taken	audītus, -a, -um erit: he/she/it will have been heard
Plural					
1st	amātī, -ae, -a erimus: we shall have been loved	doctī, -ae, -a erimus: we shall have been taught	missī, -ae, -a erimus: we shall have been sent	captī, -ae, -a erimus: we shall have been taken	audītī, -ae, -a erimus: we shall have been heard
2nd	amātī, -ae, -a eritis: you will have been loved	doctī, -ae, -a eritis: you will have been taught	missī, -ae, -a eritis: you will have been sent	captī, -ae, -a eritis: you will have been taken	audītī, -ae, -a eritis: you will have been heard
3rd	amātī, -ae, -a erunt: they will have been loved	doctī, -ae, -a erunt: they will have been taught	missī, -ae, -a erunt: they will have been sent	captī, -ae, -a erunt: they will have been taken	audītī, -ae, -a erunt: they will have been heard

Deponent Verbs

PRESENT TENSE OF DEPONENT VERBS

PRESENT INDICATIVE OF DEPONENT TENSE

	1st Conj.	2nd Conj.	3rd Conj.	3rd Conj. (-io)	4th Conj.
Singular					
1st	cōnor: I try	polliceor: I promise	loquor: I speak	ingredior: I enter	orior: I rise
2nd	cōnāris/ cōnāre: you try	pollicēris/ pollicēre: you promise	loqueris/ loquere: you speak	ingrederis/ ingredere: you enter	orīris/ orīre: you rise
3rd	cōnātur: he/she/it tries	pollicētur: he/she/it promises	loquitur: he/she/it speaks	ingreditur: he/she/it enters	orītur: he/she/it rises
Plural					
1st	cōnāmur: we try	pollicēmur: we promise	loquimur: we speak	ingredimur: we enter	orīmur: we rise
2nd	cōnāminī: you try	pollicēminī: you promise	loquiminī: you speak	ingrediminī: you enter	orīminī: you rise
3rd	cōnantur: they try	pollicentur: they promise	loquuntur: they speak	ingrediuntur: they enter	oriuntur: they rise

PRESENT SUBJUNCTIVE OF DEPONENT VERBS

	1st Conj.	2nd Conj.	3rd Conj.	3rd Conj. (-io)	4th Conj.
Singular					
1st	cōner	pollicear	loquar	ingrediar	oriar
2nd	cōnēris/ cōnēre	polliceāris/ polliceāre	loquāris/ loquāre	ingrediāris/ ingrediāre	oriāris/ oriāre
3rd	cōnētur	polliceātur	loquātur	ingrediātur	oriātur
Plural					
1st	cōnēmur	polliceāmur	loquāmur	ingrediāmur	oriāmur
2nd	cōnēminī	polliceāminī	loquāminī	ingrediāminī	oriāminī
3rd	cōnentur	polliceantur	loquantur	ingrediantur	oriantur

IMPERFECT TENSE OF DEPONENT VERBS

IMPERFECT INDICATIVE OF DEPONENT TENSE

	1st Conj.	2nd Conj.	3rd Conj.	3rd Conj. (-io)	4th Conj.
Singular					
1st	cōnā**bar**: I was trying	pollicē**bar**: I was promising	loquē**bar**: I was speaking	ingrediē**bar**: I was entering	oriē**bar**: I was rising
2nd	cōnā**bāris** / cōnābā**re**: you were trying	pollicē**bāris** / pollicēbā**re**: you were promising	loquē**bāris** / loquēbā**re**: you were speaking	ingrediē**bāris** / ingrediēbā**re**: you were entering	oriē**bāris** / oriēbā**re**: you were rising
3rd	cōnā**bātur**: he/she/it was trying	pollicē**bātur**: he/she/it was promising	loquē**bātur**: he/she/it was speaking	ingrediē**bātur**: he/she/it was entering	oriē**bātur**: he/she/it was rising
Plural					
1st	cōnā**bāmur**: we were trying	pollicē**bāmur**: we were promising	loquē**bāmur**: we were speaking	ingrediē**bāmur**: we were entering	oriē**bāmur**: we were rising
2nd	cōnā**bāminī**: you were trying	pollicē**bāminī**: you were promising	loquē**bāminī**: you were speaking	ingrediē**bāminī**: you were entering	oriē**bāminī**: you were rising
3rd	cōnā**bantur**: they were trying	pollicē**bantur**: they were promising	loquē**bantur**: they were speaking	ingrediē**bantur**: they were entering	oriē**bantur**: they were rising

IMPERFECT SUBJUNCTIVE OF DEPONENT VERBS

	1st Conj.	2nd Conj.	3rd Conj.	3rd Conj. (-io)	4th Conj.
Singular					
1st	cōnā**rer**	pollicē**rer**	loquē**rer**	ingredē**rer**	orī**rer**
2nd	cōnārē**ris** / cōnārē**re**	pollicērē**ris** / pollicērē**re**	loquērē**ris** / loquērē**re**	ingredērē**ris** / ingredērē**re**	orīrē**ris** / orīrē**re**
3rd	cōnārē**tur**	pollicērē**tur**	loquērē**tur**	ingredērē**tur**	orīrē**tur**
Plural					
1st	cōnārē**mur**	pollicērē**mur**	loquērē**mur**	ingredērē**mur**	orīrē**mur**
2nd	cōnārē**minī**	pollicērē**minī**	loquērē**minī**	ingredērē**minī**	orīrē**minī**
3rd	cōnāre**ntur**	pollicēre**ntur**	loquēre**ntur**	ingredēre**ntur**	orīre**ntur**

FUTURE TENSE OF DEPONENT VERBS

FUTURE INDICATIVE OF DEPONENT VERBS

	1st Conj.	2nd Conj.	3rd Conj.	3rd Conj. (-io)	4th Conj.
Singular					
1st	cōnābor: I shall try	pollicēbor: I shall promise	loquar: I shall speak	ingrediar: I shall enter	oriar: I shall rise
2nd	cōnāberis / cōnābere: you will try	pollicēberis / pollicēbere: you will promise	loquēris / loquēre: you will speak	ingrediēris / ingrediēre: you will enter	oriēris / oriēre: you will rise
3rd	cōnābitur: he/she/it will try	pollicēbitur: he/she/it will promise	loquētur: he/she/it will speak	ingrediētur: he/she/it will enter	oriētur: he/she/it will rise
Plural					
1st	cōnābimur: we shall try	pollicēbimur: we shall promise	loquēmur: we shall speak	ingrediēmur: we shall enter	oriēmur: we shall rise
2nd	cōnābiminī: you will try	pollicēbiminī: you will promise	loquēminī: you will speak	ingrediēminī: you will enter	oriēminī: you will rise
3rd	cōnābuntur: they will try	pollicēbuntur: they will promise	loquentur: they will speak	ingredientur: they will enter	orientur: they will rise

Perfect System of Deponent Latin Verbs

PERFECT TENSE OF DEPONENT VERBS

PERFECT INDICATIVE OF DEPONENT VERBS

	1st Conj.	2nd Conj.	3rd Conj.	3rd Conj. (-io)	4th Conj.
Singular					
1st	cōnātus, -a, -um **sum:** I have tried	pollicitus, -a, -um **sum:** I have promised	locūtus, -a, -um **sum:** I have spoken	ingressus, -a, -um **sum:** I have entered	ortus, -a, -um **sum:** I have risen
2nd	cōnātus, -a, -um **es:** you have tried	pollicitus, -a, -um **es:** you have promised	locūtus, -a, -um **es:** you have spoken	ingressus, -a, -um **es:** you have entered	ortus, -a, -um **es:** you have risen
3rd	cōnātus, -a, -um **est:** he/she/it has tried	pollicitus, -a, -um **est:** he/she/it has promised	locūtus, -a, -um **est:** he/she/it has spoken	ingressus, -a, -um **est:** he/she/it has entered	ortus, -a, -um **est:** he/she/it has risen

Plural					
1st	cōnātī, -ae, -a **sumus:** we have tried	pollicitī, -ae, -a **sumus:** we have promised	locūtī, -ae, -a **sumus:** we have spoken	ingressī, -ae, -a **sumus:** we have entered	ortī, -ae, -a **sumus:** we have risen
2nd	cōnātī, -ae, -a **estis:** you have tried	pollicitī, -ae, -a **estis:** you have promised	locūtī, -ae, -a **estis:** you have spoken	ingressī, -ae, -a **estis:** you have entered	ortī, -ae, -a **estis:** you have risen
3rd	cōnātī, -ae, -a **sunt:** they have tried	pollicitī, -ae, -a **sunt:** they have promised	locūtī, -ae, -a **sunt:** they have spoken	ingressī, -ae, -a **sunt:** they have entered	ortī, -ae, -a **sunt:** they have risen

PERFECT SUBJUNCTIVE OF DEPONENT VERBS

	1st Conj.	2nd Conj.	3rd Conj.	3rd Conj. (-io)	4th Conj.
Singular					
1st	cōnātus, -a, -um **sim**	pollicitus, -a, -um **sim**	locūtus, -a, -um **sim**	ingressus, -a, -um **sim**	ortus, -a, -um **sim**
2nd	cōnātus, -a, -um **sīs**	pollicitus, -a, -um **sīs**	locūtus, -a, -um **sīs**	ingressus, -a, -um **sīs**	ortus, -a, -um **sīs**
3rd	cōnātus, -a, -um **sit**	pollicitus, -a, -um **sit**	locūtus, -a, -um **sit**	ingressus, -a, -um **sit**	ortus, -a, -um **sit**
Plural					
1st	cōnātī, -ae, -a **sīmus**	pollicitī, -ae, -a **sīmus**	locūtī, -ae, -a **sīmus**	ingressī, -ae, -a **sīmus**	ortī, -ae, -a **sīmus**
2nd	cōnātī, -ae, -a **sītis**	pollicitī, -ae, -a **sītis**	locūtī, -ae, -a **sītis**	ingressī, -ae, -a **sītis**	ortī, -ae, -a **sītis**
3rd	cōnātī, -ae, -a **sint**	pollicitī, -ae, -a **sint**	locūtī, -ae, -a **sint**	ingressī, -ae, -a **sint**	ortī, -ae, -a **sint**

PLUPERFECT TENSE OF DEPONENT VERBS

PLUPERFECT INDICATIVE OF DEPONENT VERBS

	1st Conj.	2nd Conj.	3rd Conj.	3rd Conj. (-io)	4th Conj.
Singular					
1st	cōnātus, -a, -um eram: I had tried	pollicitus, -a, -um eram: I had promised	locūtus, -a, -um eram: I had spoken	ingressus, -a, -um eram: I had entered	ortus, -a, -um eram: I had risen
2nd	cōnātus, -a, -um erās: you had tried	pollicitus, -a, -um erās: you had promised	locūtus, -a, -um erās: you had spoken	ingressus, -a, -um erās: you had entered	ortus, -a, -um erās: you had risen
3rd	cōnātus, -a, -um erat: he/she/it had tried	pollicitus, -a, -um erat: he/she/it had promised	locūtus, -a, -um erat: he/she/it had spoken	ingressus, -a, -um erat: he/she/it had entered	ortus, -a, -um erat: he/she/it had risen
Plural					
1st	cōnātī, -ae, -a erāmus: we had tried	pollicitī, -ae, -a erāmus: we had promised	locūtī, -ae, -a erāmus: we had spoken	ingressī, -ae, -a erāmus: we had entered	ortī, -ae, -a erāmus: we had risen
2nd	cōnātī, -ae, -a erātis: you had tried	pollicitī, -ae, -a erātis: you had promised	locūtī, -ae, -a erātis: you had spoken	ingressī, -ae, -a erātis: you had entered	ortī, -ae, -a erātis: you had risen
3rd	cōnātī, -ae, -a erant: they had tried	pollicitī, -ae, -a erant: they had promised	locūtī, -ae, -a erant: they had spoken	ingressī, -ae, -a erant: they had entered	ortī, -ae, -a erant: they had risen

PLUPERFECT SUBJUNCTIVE OF DEPONENT VERBS

	1st Conj.	2nd Conj.	3rd Conj.	3rd Conj. (-io)	4th Conj.
Singular					
1st	cōnātus, -a, -um essem	pollicitus, -a, -um essem	locūtus, -a, -um essem	ingressus, -a, -um essem	ortus, -a, -um essem
2nd	cōnātus, -a, -um essēs	pollicitus, -a, -um essēs	locūtus, -a, -um essēs	ingressus, -a, -um essēs	ortus, -a, -um essēs
3rd	cōnātus, -a, -um esset	pollicitus, -a, -um esset	locūtus, -a, -um esset	ingressus, -a, -um esset	ortus, -a, -um esset
Plural					
1st	cōnātī, -ae, -a essēmus	pollicitī, -ae, -a essēmus	locūtī, -ae, -a essēmus	ingressī, -ae, -a essēmus	ortī, -ae, -a essēmus
2nd	cōnātī, -ae, -a essētis	pollicitī, -ae, -a essētis	locūtī, -ae, -a essētis	ingressī, -ae, -a essētis	ortī, -ae, -a essētis
3rd	cōnātī, -ae, -a essent	pollicitī, -ae, -a essent	locūtī, -ae, -a essent	ingressī, -ae, -a essent	ortī, -ae, -a essent

FUTURE PERFECT TENSE OF DEPONENT VERBS

FUTURE PERFECT INDICATIVE OF DEPONENT VERBS

	1st Conj.	2nd Conj.	3rd Conj.	3rd Conj. (-io)	4th Conj.
Singular					
1st	cōnātus, -a, -um **erō:** I shall have tried	pollicitus, -a, -um **erō:** I shall have promised	locūtus, -a, -um **erō:** I shall have spoken	ingressus, -a, -um **erō:** I shall have entered	ortus, -a, -um **erō:** I shall have risen
2nd	cōnātus, -a, -um **eris:** you will have tried	pollicitus, -a, -um **eris:** you will have promised	locūtus, -a, -um **eris:** you will have spoken	ingressus, -a, -um **eris:** you will have entered	ortus, -a, -um **eris:** you will have risen
3rd	cōnātus, -a, -um **erit:** he/she/it will have tried	pollicitus, -a, -um **erit:** he/she/it will have promised	locūtus, -a, -um **erit:** he/she/it will have spoken	ingressus, -a, -um **erit:** he/she/it will have entered	ortus, -a, -um **erit:** he/she/it will have risen
Plural					
1st	cōnātī, -ae, -a **erimus:** we shall have tried	pollicitī, -ae, -a **erimus:** we shall have promised	locūtī, -ae, -a **erimus:** we shall have spoken	ingressī, -ae, -a **erimus:** we shall have entered	ortī, -ae, -a **erimus:** we shall have risen
2nd	cōnātī, -ae, -a **eritis:** you will have tried	pollicitī, -ae, -a **eritis:** you will have promised	locūtī, -ae, -a **eritis:** you will have spoken	ingressī, -ae, -a **eritis:** you will have entered	ortī, -ae, -a **eritis:** you will have risen
3rd	cōnātī, -ae, -a **erunt:** they will have tried	pollicitī, -ae, -a **erunt:** they will have promised	locūtī, -ae, -a **erunt:** they will have spoken	ingressī, -ae, -a **erunt:** they will have entered	ortī, -ae, -a **erunt:** they will have risen

Irregular Latin Verbs

PRESENT TENSE OF IRREGULAR VERBS

PRESENT INDICATIVE OF IRREGULAR VERBS

	sum	possum	volō	mālō	nōlō	eō	fīō
Singular							
1st	sum: I am	possum: I am able	volō: I want	mālō: I prefer	nōlō: I do not want	eō: I go	fīō: I become/ am made
2nd	es: you are	potes: you are able	vīs: you want	māvīs: you prefer	nōn vīs: you do not want	īs: you go	fīs: you become/ are made
3rd	est: he/she/it is	potest: he/she/it is able	vult: he/she/it wants	māvult: he/she/it prefers	nōn vult: he/she/it does not want	it: he/she/it goes	fit: he/she/it becomes/ is made
Plural							
1st	sumus: we are	possumus: we are able	volumus: we want	mālumus: we prefer	nōlumus: we do not want	īmus: we go	fīmus: we become/ are made
2nd	estis: you are	potestis: you are able	vultis: you want	māvultis: you prefer	nōn vultis: you do not want	ītis: you go	fītis: you become/ are made
3rd	sunt: they are	possunt: they are able	volunt: they want	mālunt: they prefer	nōlunt: they do not want	eunt: they go	fiunt: they become/ are made

PRESENT SUBJUNCTIVE OF IRREGULAR VERBS

	sum	possum	volō	mālō	nōlō	eō	fiō
Singular							
1st	sim	possim	velim	mālim	nōlim	eam	fiam
2nd	sīs	possīs	velīs	mālīs	nōlīs	eās	fiās
3rd	sit	possit	velit	mālit	nōlit	eat	fiat
Plural							
1st	sīmus	possīmus	velīmus	mālīmus	nōlīmus	eāmus	fiāmus
2nd	sītis	possītis	velītis	mālītis	nōlītis	eātis	fiātis
3rd	sint	possint	velint	mālint	nōlint	eant	fiant

IMPERFECT TENSE OF IRREGULAR VERBS

IMPERFECT INDICATIVE OF IRREGULAR VERBS

	sum	possum	volō	mālō	nōlō	eō	fiō
Singular							
1st	eram: I was	poteram: I was able	volēbam: I was wanting	mālēbam: I was preferring	nōlēbam: I was not wanting	ībam: I was going	fiēbam: I became / was made
2nd	erās: you were	poterās: you were able	volēbās: you were wanting	mālēbās: you were preferring	nōlēbās: you were not wanting	ībās: you were going	fiēbās: you became / were made
3rd	erat: he/she/it was	poterat: he/she/it was able	volēbat: he/she/it was wanting	mālēbat: he/she/it was preferring	nōlēbat: he/she/it was not wanting	ībat: he/she/it was going	fiēbat: he/she/it became / was made
Plural							
1st	erāmus: we were	poterāmus: we were able	volēbāmus: we were wanting	mālēbāmus: we were preferring	nōlēbāmus: we were not wanting	ībāmus: we were going	fiēbāmus: we became / were made
2nd	erātis: you were	poterātis: you were able	volēbātis: you were wanting	mālēbātis: you were preferring	nōlēbātis: you were not wanting	ībātis: you were going	fiēbātis: you became / were made
3rd	erant: they were	poterant: they were able	volēbant: they were wanting	mālēbant: they were preferring	nōlēbant: they were not wanting	ībant: they were going	fiēbant: they became / were made

IMPERFECT SUBJUNCTIVE OF IRREGULAR VERBS

	sum	possum	volō	mālō	nōlō	eō	fīō
Singular							
1st	essem	possem	vellem	mällem	nōllem	īrem	fīerem
2nd	essēs	possēs	vellēs	mällēs	nōllēs	īrēs	fīerēs
3rd	esset	posset	vellet	mället	nōllet	īret	fīeret
Plural							
1st	essēmus	possēmus	vellēmus	mällēmus	nōllēmus	īrēmus	fīerēmus
2nd	essētis	possētis	vellētis	mällētis	nōllētis	īrētis	fīerētis
3rd	essent	possent	vellent	mällent	nōllent	īrent	fīerent

FUTURE TENSE OF IRREGULAR VERBS

FUTURE INDICATIVE OF IRREGULAR VERBS

	sum	possum	volō	mālō	nōlō	eō	ferō	fīō
Singular								
1st	erō: I shall be	poterō: I shall be able	volam: I shall want	mālam: I shall prefer	nōlam: I shall not want	ībō: I shall go	feram: I shall carry	fīam: I shall become/ be made
2nd	eris: you will be	poteris: you will be able	volēs: you will want	mālēs: you will prefer	nōlēs: you will not want	ībis: you will go	ferēs: you will carry	fīēs: you will become/ be made
3rd	erit: he/she/it will be	poterit: he/she/it will be able	volet: he/she/it will want	mālet: he/she/it will prefer	nōlet: he/she/it will not want	ībit: he/she/it will go	feret: he/she/it will carry	fīet: he/she/it will become/ be made

Plural								
1st	erimus: we will be	poterimus: we shall be able	volēmus: we shall want	mālēmus: we shall prefer	nōlēmus: we shall not want	ībimus: we shall go	ferēmus: we will carry	fīēmus: we shall become/ be made
2nd	eritis: you will be	poteritis: you will be able	volētis: you will want	mālētis: you will prefer	nōlētis: you will not want	ībitis: you will go	ferētis: you will carry	fīētis: you will become/ be made
3rd	erunt: they will be	poterunt: they will be able	volent: they will want	mālent: they will prefer	nōlent: they will not want	ībunt: they will go	ferent: they will carry	fīent: they will become/ be made

FERŌ

INDICATIVE

	Present Active	Present Passive	Imperfect Active	Imperfect Passive	Future Active	Future Passive
Singular						
1st	ferō: I carry	feror: I am carried	ferēbam: I was carrying	ferēbar: I was (being) carried	feram: I shall carry	ferar: I shall be carried
2nd	fers: you carry	ferris / ferre: you are carried	ferēbās: you were carrying	ferēbāris / ferēbāre: you were (being) carried	ferēs: you will carry	ferēris / ferēre: you will be carried
3rd	fert: he/she/it carries	fertur: he/she/it is carried	ferēbat: he/she/it was carrying	ferēbātur: he/she/it was (being) carried	feret: he/she/it will carry	ferētur: he/she/it will be carried
Plural						
1st	ferimus: we carry	ferimur: we are carried	ferēbāmus: we were carrying	ferēbāmur: we were (being) carried	ferēmus: we shall carry	ferēmur: we will be carried
2nd	fertis: you carry	feriminī: you are carried	ferēbātis: you were carrying	ferēbāminī: you were (being) carried	ferētis: you will carry	ferēminī: you will be carried
3rd	ferunt: they carry	feruntur: they are carried	ferēbant: they were carrying	ferēbantur: they were (being) carried	ferent: they will carry	ferentur: they will be carried

SUBJUNCTIVE

	Present Active	Present Passive	Imperfect Active	Imperfect Passive
Singular				
1st	feram	ferar	ferrem	ferrer
2nd	ferās	ferāris / ferāre	ferrēs	ferrēris / ferrēre
3rd	ferat	ferātur	ferret	ferrētur
Plural				
1st	ferāmus	ferāmur	ferrēmus	ferrēmur
2nd	ferātis	ferāminī	ferrētis	ferrēminī
3rd	ferant	ferantur	ferrent	ferrentur

SUMMARY OF LATIN INFINITIVES

INFINITIVE OF REGULAR VERBS

	1st Conj.	2nd Conj.	3rd Conj.	3rd Conj. (-io)	4th Conj.
Present Active	amāre: to love	docēre: to teach	mittere: to send	capere: to take	audīre: to hear
Present Passive	amārī: to be loved	docērī: to be taught	mittī: to be sent	capī: to be taken	audīrī: to be heard
Perfect Active	amāvisse: to have loved	docuisse: to have taught	mīsisse: to have sent	cēpisse: to have taken	audīvisse: to have heard
Perfect Passive	amātus, -a, -um esse: to have been loved	doctus, -a, -um esse: to have been taught	missus, -a, -um esse: to have been sent	captus, -a, -um esse: to have been taken	audītus, -a, -um esse: to have been heard
Future Active	amātūrus, -a, -um esse: to be about to love	doctūrus, -a, -um esse: to be about to teach	missūrus, -a, -um esse: to be about to send	captūrus, -a, -um esse: to be about to take	audītūrus, -a, -um esse: to be about to hear
Future Passive	amātum īrī: to be about to be loved	doctum īrī: to be about to be taught	missum īrī: to be about to be sent	captum īrī: to be about to be taken	audītum īrī: to be about to be heard

INFINITIVES OF DEPONENT VERBS

	1st Conj.	2nd Conj.	3rd Conj.	3rd Conj. (-io)	4th Conj.
Present Deponent	cōnārī: to try	pollicērī: to promise	loquī: to speak	ingredī: to enter	orīrī: to rise
Perfect Deponent	cōnātus, -a, -um esse: to have tried	pollicitus, -a, -um esse: to have promised	locūtus, -a, -um esse: to have spoken	ingressus, -a, -um esse: to have entered	ortus, -a, -um esse: to have risen
Future Deponent	cōnātūrus, -a, -um esse: to be about to try	pollicitūrus, -a, -um esse: to be about to promise	locūtūrus, -a, -um esse: to be about to speak	ingressūrus, -a, -um esse: to be about to enter	ortūrus, -a, -um esse: to be about to rise

INFINITIVES OF IRREGULAR VERBS

	sum	possum	volō	mālō	nōlō	eō	fiō
Present	esse: to be	posse: to be able	velle: to want	mālle: to prefer	nōlle: to be unwilling	īre: to go	fierī: to become
Perfect	fuisse: to have been	potuisse: to have been able	voluisse: to have wanted	māluisse: to have preferred	nōluisse: to have been unwilling	īvisse: to have gone	factus, -a, -um esse: to have become
Future	futūrus, -a, -um esse: to be about to be	——	——	——	——	itūrus, -a, -um esse: to be about to go	——

INFINITIVES OF FERRE

Present Active	Present Passive	Perfect Active	Perfect Passive	Future Active	Future Passive
ferre: to carry	ferrī: to be carried	tulisse: to have carried	lātus, -a, -um esse: to have been carried	lātūrus, -a, -um esse: to be about to carry	lātum īrī: to be about to be carried

SUMMARY OF LATIN IMPERATIVES

IMPERATIVE OF REGULAR VERBS

	Present Singular Active	Present Plural Active	Present Singular Passive	Present Plural Passive	Future Singular Active	Future Plural Active
1st Conj.	amā: love!	amāte: love!	amāre: be loved!	amāminī: be loved!	amātō: love! / you will love	amātōte: love! / you will love
2nd Conj.	docē: teach!	docēte: teach!	docēre: be taught!	docēminī: be taught!	docētō: teach! / you will teach	docētōte: teach! / you will teach
3rd Conj.	mitte: send!	mittite: send!	mittere: be sent!	mittiminī: be sent!	mittitō: send! / you will send	mittitōte: send! / you will send
3rd Conj. (-io)	cape: take!	capite: take!	capere: be taken!	capiminī: be taken!	capitō: take! / you will take	capitōte: take! / you will take
4th Conj.	audī: hear!	audīte: hear!	audīre: be heard!	audīminī: be heard!	audītō: listen! / you will listen	audītōte: listen! / you will listen

PRESENT IMPERATIVE OF DEPONENT VERBS

	1st Conj.	2nd Conj.	3rd Conj.	3rd Conj. (-io)	4th Conj.
2nd Singular	cōnāre: try!	pollicēre: promise!	loquere: speak!	ingredere: enter!	orīre: rise!
2nd Plural	cōnāminī: try!	pollicēminī: promise!	loquiminī: speak!	ingrediminī: enter!	orīminī: rise!

PRESENT IMPERATIVES OF IRREGULAR VERBS

	sum, esse	nōlō	eō	dīcō	dūcō	faciō	ferō
Singular	es: be!	nōlī: don't want (to)!	ī: go!	dīc: speak!	dūc: lead!	fac: make! do!	fer: carry!
Plural	este: be!	nōlīte: don't want to!	īte: go!	dīcite: speak!	dūcite: lead!	facite: make! do!	ferte: carry!

Summary of Latin Participles

PARTICIPLES OF REGULAR VERBS

	1st Conj.	2nd Conj.	3rd Conj.	3rd Conj. (-io)	4th Conj.
Present Active	amans, amantis: loving	docens, docentis: teaching	mittens, mittentis: sending	capiens, capientis: seizing	audiens, audientis: hearing
Perfect Passive	amātus, -a, -um: having been loved	doctus, -a, -um: having been taught	missus, -a, -um: having been sent	captus, -a, -um: having been seized	audītus, -a, -um: having been heard
Future Active	amātūrus, -a, -um: about to love	doctūrus, -a, -um: about to teach	missūrus, -a, -um: about to send	captūrus, -a, -um: about to seize	audītūrus, -a, -um: about to hear
Future Passive (Gerundive)	amandus, -a, -um: about to be loved	docendus, -a, -um: about to be taught	mittendus, -a, -um: about to be sent	capiendus, -a, -um: about to be seized	audiendus, -a, -um: about to be heard

PARTICIPLES OF DEPONENT VERBS

	1st Conj.	2nd Conj.	3rd Conj.	3rd Conj. (-io)	4th Conj.
Present Deponent	cōnans, cōnantis: trying	pollicens, pollicentis: promising	loquens, loquentis: speaking	ingrediens, ingredientis: entering	oriens, orientis: rising
Perfect Deponent	cōnātus, -a, -um: having tried	pollicitus, -a, -um: having promised	locūtus, -a, -um: having spoken	ingressus, -a, -um: having entered	ortus, -a, -um: having risen
Future Deponent	cōnātūrus, -a, -um: about to try	pollicitūrus, -a, -um: about to promise	locūtūrus, -a, -um: about to speak	ingressūrus, -a, -um: about to enter	ortūrus, -a, -um: about to rise
Future Passive (Gerundive)	cōnandus, -a, -um: about to be tried	pollicendus, -a, -um: about to be promised	loquendus, -a, -um: about to be spoken	ingrediendus, -a, -um: about to be entered	oriendus, -a, -um: about to be raised

PARTICIPLES OF IRREGULAR VERBS

	volō, velle	mālō, mālle	nōlō, nolle	eō, īre	fiō, fierī
Present Active	volens, volentis: wanting	mālens, mālentis: preferring	nōlens, nōlentis: not wanting	iens, ientis: going	fiens, fientis: becoming
Future Active	——	——	——	itūrus, -a, -um	——

GERUNDS OF REGULAR VERBS

Case	1st Conj.	2nd Conj.	3rd Conj.	3rd Conj. (-io)	4th Conj.
Nominative	——	——	——	——	——
Genitive	ama**ndī**	doce**ndī**	mitte**ndī**	capie**ndī**	audie**ndī**
Dative	ama**ndō**	doce**ndō**	mitte**ndō**	capie**ndō**	audie**ndō**
Accusative	ama**ndum**	doce**ndum**	mitte**ndum**	capie**ndum**	audie**ndum**
Ablative	ama**ndō**	doce**ndō**	mitte**ndō**	capie**ndō**	audie**ndō**

SUPINES OF REGULAR VERBS

Case	1st Conj.	2nd Conj.	3rd Conj.	3rd Conj. (-io)	4th Conj.
Accusative	amā**tum**	doc**tum**	mis**sum**	cap**tum**	audī**tum**
Ablative	amā**tū**	doc**tū**	mis**sū**	cap**tū**	audī**tū**

SUPINES OF DEPONENT VERBS

Case	1st Conj.	2nd Conj.	3rd Conj.	3rd Conj. (-io)	4th Conj.
Accusative	cōnā**tum**	pollici**tum**	locū**tum**	ingres**sum**	or**tum**
Ablative	cōnā**tū**	pollici**tū**	locū**tū**	ingres**sū**	or**tū**

Basic Guide to
Latin Meter and Scansion

LATIN POETRY FOLLOWS a strict rhythm based on the quantity of the vowel in each syllable. Each line of poetry divides into a number of feet (analogous to the measures in music). The syllables in each foot scan as "long" or "short" according to the parameters of the meter that the poet employs.

A vowel scans as "long" if

(1) it is long by nature (e.g., the ablative singular ending in the first declension: *puellā*);

(2) it is a diphthong: AE (*saepe*), AU (*laudat*), EI (*deinde*), EU (*neuter*), OE (*poena*), UI (*cui*);

(3) it is long by position—these vowels are followed by double consonants (*cantātae*) or a consonantal I (*Trōia*), X (*flexibus*), or Z.

All other vowels scan as "short."
A few other matters often confuse beginners:

(1) QU and GU count as single consonants (*sīc aquilam*; *linguā*);

(2) H does NOT affect the quantity of a vowel (*Bellus homō*: Martial 1.9.1, the -us in *bellus* scans as short);

(3) if a mute consonant (B, C, D, G, K, Q, P, T) is followed by L or R, the preceding vowel scans according to the demands of the meter, either long (*omnium patrōnus*: Catullus 49.7, the -a in *patrōnus* scans as long to accommodate the hendecasyllabic meter) OR short (*prō patriā*: Horace, *Carmina* 3.2.13, the first -a in *patriā* scans as short to accommodate the Alcaic strophe).

When two vowels elide, the first vowel drops out and does not affect the quantity of the elided syllable. Elision in Latin occurs if

(1) one word ends in a vowel or diphthong and the next one begins in a vowel (*Lesbia, atque amēmus*: Catullus 5.1);

(2) one word ends in a vowel or diphthong and the next one begins with H (*atque hīc*: Vergil, *Aeneid* 8.655); or

(3) one word ends in -UM, -AM, or -EM and the next word begins in a vowel (*quantum est*: Catullus 3.2).

An elided syllable scans according to the quantity of the **second** vowel. A hiatus (or very abrupt break in the scansion of a line) results from a failure to elide.

Most Latin meters utilize five different types of measures (the macron indicates a long vowel, the micron a short vowel):

- dactyl: — ∪ ∪   (example: *Lesbia*)
- spondee: — —   (example: *quārē*)
- iamb: ∪ —   (example: *regō*)
- trochee: — ∪   (example: *praeda*)
- choriamb: — ∪ ∪ — (example: *dēliciae*)

Note the following conventions:

- | marks the division between feet in dactylic lines
- ‖ marks the pause (hiatus) within a line
- x marks a syllable that can scan either long or short

There are thirteen meters represented in *NLP*:

Dactylic hexameter: six feet of dactyls. The first four feet can be either dactyls or spondees; the fifth foot is usually a dactyl; and the last foot scans as a spondee whether the last syllable is short or long.

$$- \overline{\cup\cup} \mid - \overline{\cup\cup} \mid - \overline{\cup\cup} \mid - \overline{\cup\cup} \mid - \cup\cup \mid - x$$

Elegiac couplets: alternating lines of dactylic hexameter and dactylic pentameter. In the pentameter line, the first two feet may be dactyls or spondees, but the rest of the line follows a set pattern.

$$- \overline{\cup\cup} \mid - \overline{\cup\cup} \mid - \overline{\cup\cup} \mid - \overline{\cup\cup} \mid - \cup\cup \mid - \text{x}$$
$$- \overline{\cup\cup} \mid - \overline{\cup\cup} \mid - \| - \cup\cup \mid - \cup\cup \mid \text{x}$$

Hendecasyllabics: lines of eleven syllables in five feet. The first foot may be a spondee, iamb, or trochee, followed by a dactyl, two trochees, and finally a spondee or trochee.

$$\underline{\cup} \, \overline{\cup} - \cup\cup - \cup - \cup - \text{x}$$

Limping iambics (known also as choliambics or scazons): five iambs capped off with a trochee or spondee. A spondee may be substituted in the first and third foot.

$$\overline{\cup} - \cup - \overline{\cup} - \cup - \cup - - \text{x}$$

Iambic Trimeter: three pairs of iambs with flexibility to substitute spondees in the first, third, and fifth foot.

$$\overline{\cup} - \cup - \overline{\cup} \| - \cup - \overline{\cup} - \cup \, \text{x}$$

Iambic strophe: alternating lines of iambic trimeter (three pairs of iambs) and iambic dimeter (two pairs of iambs) with flexibility to substitute spondees in the first, third, and fifth foot of the trimeter line, and in the first and third foot of the dimeter line.

$$\overline{\cup} - \cup - \overline{\cup} \| - \cup - \overline{\cup} - \cup \, \text{x}$$
$$\overline{\cup} - \cup - \overline{\cup} - \cup \, \text{x}$$

Galliambics: meter used in Catullus 63 (*NLP* 36.15) to celebrate the goddess Cybele. The name refers to the Galli, a retinue of castrated priests devoted to her worship.

$$\cup\cup - \cup - \cup - - \| \cup\cup - \cup\cup\cup\cup \, \text{x}$$

Sapphic strophe (in honor of Sappho of Lesbos, fl. seventh–sixth century BCE): a four-verse stanza, with the same metrical pattern in the first three lines.

$$- \cup - - - \parallel \cup \cup - \cup - \text{x}$$
$$- \cup - - - \parallel \cup \cup - \cup - \text{x}$$
$$- \cup - - - \parallel \cup \cup - \cup - \text{x}$$
$$- \cup \cup - \text{x}$$

Alcaic strophe (in honor of the Greek poet Alcaeus of Lesbos, born c. 630 BCE): a four-verse stanza, with the same metrical pattern in the first two lines.

$$\text{x} - \cup - - \parallel - \cup \cup - \cup \text{x}$$
$$\text{x} - \cup - - \parallel - \cup \cup - \cup \text{x}$$
$$\text{x} - \cup - - - \cup - \text{x}$$
$$- \cup \cup - \cup \cup - \cup - \text{x}$$

First Asclepiadean (in honor of the Greek poet Asclepiades of Samos, fl. 290 BCE): a spondee followed by two choriambs, capped off with an iamb.

$$- - - \cup \cup - \parallel - \cup \cup - \cup \text{x}$$

Second Asclepiadean (likewise inspired by the Greek poet Asclepiades): a Glyconic line (see this example) followed by a line of First Asclepiadean.

$$- - - \cup \cup - \cup \text{x}$$
$$- - - \cup \cup - \parallel - \cup \cup - \cup \text{x}$$

Fourth Asclepiadean (likewise inspired by the Greek poet Asclepiades): two lines of First Asclepiadean, followed by one Pherecratean line and one Glyconic line.

$$- - - \cup \cup - \parallel - \cup \cup - \cup \text{x}$$
$$- - - \cup \cup - \parallel - \cup \cup - \cup \text{x}$$
$$- - - \cup \cup - \text{x}$$
$$- - - \cup \cup - \cup \text{x}$$

Alcmanic Strophe (in honor of the Greek poet Alcman of Sparta, fl. 7th century BCE): one line of dactylic hexameter followed by one line of dactylic tetrameter.

$$- \overline{\cup \cup} \mid - \overline{\cup \cup} \mid - \overline{\cup \cup} \mid - \overline{\cup \cup} \mid - \cup \cup \mid - \text{x}$$
$$- \overline{\cup \cup} \mid - \overline{\cup \cup} \mid - \cup \cup \mid - \text{x}$$

APPENDIX C

Common Rhetorical Devices

THE FACT THAT LATIN is inflected allows for flexibility in word order, and Latin authors take full advantage of this pliability by using literary devices. Here follows a list of some of the more common rhetorical devices that are featured in *NLP*.

Alliteration: The repetition of the same sound.
> Horace, *Carmina* 4.1.2 (*NLP* 4.13): *Parce, precor, precor.*

Anaphora: The repetition of a word or phrase in successive phrases, clauses, or lines.
> *CIL* VI 29609 (*NLP* 1.14): *Cinis sum. Cinis terra est.*
>
> Pliny the Younger, *Epistulae* 2.1.12 (*NLP* 9.15): <u>*Vergīnium*</u> *cōgitō,* <u>*Vergīnium*</u> *videō,* <u>*Vergīnium*</u> *iam vānīs imāginibus.*

Anastrophe: An inversion of normal word order.
> Livy, *ab Urbe Condita* 9.13.2 (*NLP* 7.5): *Vādunt igitur in proelium urgentēs signiferōs.* (The verb usually comes at the end, not beginning, of a Latin sentence.)

Antithesis: An opposition or contrast of ideas or words.
> Ovid, *Amores* 1.9.1 (*NLP* 4.9): *Mīlitat omnis amans.* (Lovers are not usually soldiers.)

Apostrophe: An exclamatory address to a third party.
> Catullus 9.5 (*NLP* 13.6): *Ō mihi nuntiī beātī!*

Asyndeton: A lack of conjunctions.
> *CIL* VI 15258 (*NLP* 2.15): *Balnea, vīna, Venus corrumpunt corpora nostra.*

Chiasmus: The ABBA arrangement of corresponding pairs of words in opposite order (from the shape of the Greek letter *chi*, X).

Vergil, *Aeneid* 11.583 (*NLP* 5.13): <u>Aeternum</u> <u>tēlōrum</u> *et* <u>virginitātis</u> <u>amōrem</u>.

Hyperbaton: The separation of a noun from the adjective that agrees with it.

Ovid, *Ars Amatoria* 1.116 (*NLP* 3.5): <u>Cupidās</u> *iniciuntque* <u>manūs</u>.

Hyperbole: Rhetorical exaggeration.

Cicero, *Philippica* 13.45 (*NLP* 9.6): *Omnēs tē dī, hominēs, summī, mediī, infimī, cīvēs, peregrīnī, virī, mulierēs, līberī, servī odērunt. Sensimus hoc nūper falsō nuntiō, vērō propediem sentiēmus.*

Litotes: Rhetorical understatement, often the affirmation of an idea by denying its opposite.

Catullus 6.2 (*NLP* 26.1): *Nī sint illepidae atque inēlegantēs.*

Metonymy: The substitution of one word for another that it suggests.

Martial 1.61.1 (*NLP* 11.9): *Vērōna doctī syllabās amat vātis.* (i.e., the **people** of Verona love their bard, not the place which here stands in for its population).

Onomatopoeia: The use of words to imitate natural sounds.

Pliny the Elder, *Naturalis Historia* 8.95 (*NLP* 19.3): *Hinnītū* (a hippopotamus's whinnying)

Personification: The attribution of personality to an impersonal object.

Catullus 42.10 (*NLP* 4.4): *Circumsistite eam, et reflāgitāte.* (Here Catullus enjoins his lines of verse to retrieve the stolen notebooks.)

Polysyndeton: The use of unnecessary conjunctions.

Juvenal, *Saturae* 6.85 (*NLP* 5.8): *Inmemor illa domūs <u>et</u> coniugis <u>atque</u> sorōris.*

Prolepsis: The use of a word before it is logically appropriate.

Pliny the Elder, *Naturalis Historia* 29.15 (*NLP* 33.4): *Subicit enim <u>quā</u> <u>medicīnā</u> sē et coniugem usque ad longam senectam perduxerit.*

Simile: An explicit comparison (cf. **METAPHOR**: An implied comparison).

Vergil, *Aeneid* 2.795 (*NLP* 6.8): *Pār levibus ventīs volucrīque simillima somnō.*

Ovid, *Metamorphoses* 6.63–64 (*NLP* 16.6): <u>*Quālis*</u> *ab imbre solet percussīs sōlibus arcus / inficere ingentī longum curvāmine caelum.*

Synchysis: Interlocked word order (ABAB).

Statius, *Silvae* 5.3.28 (*NLP* 6.1): *Dā <u>vōcem</u> <u>magnō</u>, pater, <u>ingeniumque</u> <u>dolōrī</u>.*

Synechdoche: The use of a part of an object to represent the entire object.

Vergil, *Aeneid* 5.115 (*NLP* 14.13): *Quattuor ex omnī dēlectae classe carīnae* (i.e., the keels represent entire ships).

The Roman Calendar

THE PRE-JULIAN ROMAN calendar consisted of twelve lunar months of 29 or 30 days (the lunar month is 28.5 days), supplemented by an occasional "intercalary" month to harmonize the calendar with the solar year (approximately 365.25 days). These intercalary months were proclaimed by the consuls during the Republic, though not always consistently. In 46 BCE, Julius Caesar commissioned Alexandrian astronomers to reform the Roman calendar. This reform resulted in twelve months whose length varied from 28 days (February), to 30 (April, June, September, November) and 31 days (January, March, May, July, August, October, December). An intercalary day was added to February to make up for the extra quarter day. This calendar remained in use for over 1,600 years, until the Gregorian reform in 1582.

The Roman calendar was organized around three important days in the month:

Kalends: the first day of the Roman month, originally the day of the new moon. So called from the phrase *kalō Iuno Novella* ("I call/announce new Juno"), and proclaimed by the pontiffs on the Capitoline Hill (Varro, *de Lingua Latina* 6.27).

Nones: the day of the half moon (the 5th or 7th of the month; the 9th day before the Ides—counting inclusively).

Ides: the day of the full moon (the 13th or 15th of the month).

In **March**, **May**, **July**, and **October**, the Nones fell on the 7th, and the Ides fell on the 15th. In all other months, the Nones fell on the 5th and the Ides fell on the 13th.

Events that occur **on** the Kalends, Nones, or Ides are specified as follows:

Claudius was born on the Kalends of August (August 1).

Vergil was born on the Ides of October (October 15).

Julius Caesar was assassinated on the Ides of March (March 15).

Events that occur **the day before** the Kalends, Nones, or Ides are specified as follows:

Caligula was born the day before the Kalends of September (pridie Kal. Sept.: August 31).

The Romans calculated other calendar days by counting inclusively and backward from the Kalends, Nones, or Ides. Consider the following:

The city of Rome was founded 11 days before the Kalends of May (April 21).

The Battle of Actium occurred 4 days before the Nones of September (September 2).

Years were marked in two ways: from the foundation of the city (a.u.c. *ab urbe conditā* = 753 BCE) and by consular year. Consider the following:

The Republic was founded in 244 a.u.c. (509 BCE).

Julius Caesar was killed in 709 a.u.c. (44 BCE).

Pompey and Crassus vanquished Spartacus when Lentulus and Orestes were consuls (71 BCE).

The Catilinarian conspiracy occurred when Marcus Tullius Cicero and Gaius Antonius Hybrida were consuls (63 BCE).

Publius Clodius Pulcher was murdered when Quintus Caecilius Metellus Pius Scipio Nasica and Gnaeus Pompeius Magnus (Pompey the Great) were consuls (52 BCE).

SUGGESTIONS FOR FURTHER READING:

Feeney, Denis. *Caesar's Calendar: Ancient Time and the Beginnings of History*. University of California, 2008.

Hannah, Robert. *Greek and Roman Calendars: Constructions of Time in the Classical World*. Duckworth, 2005.

Hannah, Robert. *Time in Antiquity*. Routledge, 2009.

Salzman, Michele Renee. *On Roman Time: The Codex-Calendar of 354 and the Rhythms of Urban Life in Late Antiquity*. University of California, 1991.

Vocabulary Building
Compounds and Derivatives

Many Latin prepositions also serve as verb prefixes that add meaning or emphasis to the root verbs. Thus, new vocabulary can be quickly mastered by breaking down compound words into more familiar component parts. The following is merely a sample, drawn from required vocabulary, vocabulary featured in the passages, the Dickinson College Latin Core Vocabulary List (*http://dcc.dickinson .edu/latin-vocabulary-list*), and Richard E. Prior and Joseph Wohlberg, eds, *501 Latin Verbs* (2nd ed., Barron's, 2008).

LIST 1: COMMON PREFIXES AND THEIR BASIC MEANINGS

ā/ab (ap-/au-): away
ad (ac-/af-/ag-/ar-): toward
circum: around
co (col-/con-/com-/cor-): with
dē: down from
dis (di-/dif-): apart
ē/ex: away
in (im-): in, on, not
inter (intro-): between
ob (o-/oc-/of-/op-): over, before
per: through, thoroughly
prae: before, in front of
praeter: in front of, beside
prō: in front of
re: back
sub (suc-/suf-/sup-/sus-): under
super: above
trans (tra-): across

LIST 2: COMPOUND VERBS

agō, -ere, ēgī, actus: do, drive, accomplish, guide, spend, act
    cogō: force
    exigō: drive out
    peragō: complete

cadō, -ere, cecidī, cāsus: fall
    accidō: happen
    incidō: come upon
    occidō: fall

capiō, -ere, cēpī, captus: take, seize, capture
    accipiō: receive
    concipiō: begin
    excipiō: remove
    incipiō: begin
    praecipiō: anticipate
    rēcipiō: receive
    suscipiō: undertake

cēdō, -ere, cessī, cessus: proceed
    accēdō: approach
    concēdō: yield
    discēdō: depart
    prōcēdo: go forward

currō, -ere, cucurrī, cursus: run, rush
    occurrō: meet
    succurrō: run to help

dīcō, -ere, dixī, dictus: say
    benedīcō: praise (speak well of)
    ēdicō: declare
    indīcō: declare
    interdīcō: forbid
    maledīcō: curse (speak badly of)
    praedīcō: say beforehand

dō, dare, dedī, datus: give
    addō: add
    perdō: destroy
    prōdō: betray
    reddō: restore
    trādō: hand over

dūcō, -ere, duxī, ductus: lead
    addūcō: lead to
    dēdūcō: lead away
    dīdūcō: draw apart
    ēdūcō: lead out

eō, -īre, -īvī or -iī, -itus: go
    abeō: go away, depart
    adeō: approach
    exeō: leave
    pereō: die
    praetereō: pass by
    redeō: return
    subeō: come close to
    transeō: cross

faciō, -ere, fēcī, factus: make, do
    afficiō: influence
    conficiō: finish
    dēficiō: fall short
    efficiō: bring about
    interficiō: kill
    patefaciō: open up

ferō, ferre, tulī, lātus: bring
    afferō: carry to
    auferō: carry away
    conferō: carry together
    dēferō: bring down
    differō: disperse
    inferō: bring against
    offerō: offer
    perferō: endure
    praeferō: carry in front
    referō: bring back
    transferō: bring across

fugiō, fugere, fūgī: flee
    effugiō: flee, escape
    perfugiō: flee, desert
    refugiō: flee back

-gradior, -gredī, -gressus sum: enter
   dēgredior: step down
   ēgredior: leave
   ingredior: enter
   regredior: step back
   transgredior: cross over

habeō, -ēre, habuī, habitus: have
   adhibeō: apply to
   exhibeō: display
   prohibeō: hinder

iaciō, -ere, iēcī, iactus: throw
   disiiciō: scatter

legō, -ere, lēgī, lectus: pick, choose, read
   colligō: gather
   dīligō: cherish
   ēligō: select
   intellegō: understand

mittō, -ere, mīsī, missus: send, let go
   āmittō: send away, lose
   committō: join
   dīmittō: send away
   permittō: allow
   prōmittō: promise

pellō, -ere, pepulī, pulsus: strike, drive away
   appellō: call
   impellō: incite

pōnō, -ere, posuī, positus: put, place
   compōnō: put together
   impōnō: put on
   prōpōnō: display

rapiō, -ere, -uī, raptus: tear away, seize
   ēripiō: snatch away

spectō, -āre, -āvī, -ātus: observe
   exspectō: wait for

-spiciō, -ere, -spexī, -spectus: observe, see
   aspiciō: look at
   respiciō: look back

stō, stāre, stetī, stātus: stand
    constō: agree
    praestō: excel
sum, esse, fuī, futūrus: be
    absum: be away
    adsum: be present
    dēsum: fail
    insum: be in
    intersum: be among
    possum: be able
    praesum: be in charge
    prōsum: be useful
    supersum: survive
tendō, -ere, tetendī, tentus: stretch
    intendō: aim
    ostendō: display
veniō, -īre, vēnī, ventus: come
    adveniō: arrive
    circumveniō: surround
    conveniō: assemble
    inveniō: find
    perveniō: arrive
vertō, -ere, vertī, versus: turn
    advertō: turn towards
    animadvertō: notice (turn one's mind towards)
    convertō: turn around
    revertō: turn back

LIST 3: SOME NOUNS AND ADJECTIVES GENERATED FROM COMMON VERBS

agō, -ere, ēgī, actus: do, drive, accomplish, guide, spend, act
    actiō, -iōnis, f: deed, action
    actor, -ōris, m: actor, player
    agitātor, -ōris, m: driver, charioteer
    agmen, -inis, n: stream, band
cadō, -ere, cecidī, cāsus: fall
    cāsus, -ūs, m: accident

occāsiō, -iōnis, f: opportunity

occāsus, -ūs, m: setting, west (where the sun falls)

crēdō, -ere, crēdidī, crēditus (+ dative): believe

crēdibilis, -e: believable

crēdulus, -a, -um: trusting

incrēdibilis, -e: unbelievable

cupiō, -ere, -īvī, -ītus: wish

cupīditās, -ātis, f: desire, greed

cupīdō, -inis, f: desire

cupīdus, -a, -um: desirous, greedy

currō, -ere, cucurrī, cursus: run

curriculum, -ī, n: course

currus, -ūs, m: chariot

cursus, -ūs, m: course, running, race

faciō, -ere, fēcī, factus: make, do

artifex, -icis, m: craftsman

beneficium, -iī, n: favor, kindness

difficilis, -e: hard

facilis, -e: easy

facinus, -ōris, n: crime

factiō, -iōnis, f: band, group

factum, -ī, n: deed

pontifex, -icis, m: priest

sacrificium, -iī, n: sacrifice

fugiō, fugere, fūgī: flee

fuga, -ae, f: flight

fugax (-ācis): swift

fugitīvus, -a, -um: fugitive

fugō, -āre, -āvī, -ātus: rout, put to flight

iaciō, -ere, iēcī, iactus: throw

iaculum, -ī, n: javelin (something thrown)

legō, -ere, lēgī, lectus: pick, choose, read

legātus, -ī, m: envoy, delegate

legiō, -iōnis, f: legion

morior, -ī, mortuus sum: die

immortālis, -e: immortal, deathless

mortālis, -e: mortal, transitory, human

mors, mortis (-ium), f: death

mortifer, -fera, -ferum: deadly

mortuus, -a, -um: dead

noscō, -ere, nōvī, nōtus: learn, get to know

ignōtus, -a, -um: unknown

nōtitia, -iae, f: fame

nōtus, -a, -um: well known

petō, -ere, -īvī/iī, -ītus: seek

impetus, -ūs, m: attack

petitiō, -iōnis, f: claim

rapiō, -ere, -uī, raptus: tear away, seize

rapax (-ācis): grasping

rapidus, -a, -um: swift

rapīna, -ae, f: pillage

regō, -ere, rexī, rectus: rule, guide

rector, -ōris, m: guide

rectus, -a, -um: straight

rēgālis, -e: royal

rēgīna, -ae, f: queen

regiō, -iōnis, f: boundary, region

rēgius, -a, -um: royal

regnum, -ī, n: kingdom, realm, sovereignty

rex, rēgis, m: king

spectō, -āre, -āvī, -ātus: observe

aspectus, -ūs: look, appearance

auspicium, -iī, n: augury

conspectus, -ūs, m: view

perspicuus, -a, -um: transparent

speciēs, -iēī, f: appearance

spectāculum, -ī, n: spectacle

speculum, -ī, n: mirror

stō, stāre, stetī, stātus: stand

constantia, -iae, f: steadiness

stabilis, -e: steady

statiō, -iōnis, f: station

superstes (-itis): surviving

ūtor, -ī, ūsus sum (+ ablative): use

    inūtilis, -e: useless

    ūsus, -ūs, m: practice, skill, exercise, use, need

    ūtilis, -e: useful, advantageous, helpful

    ūtilitās, -ātis, f: usefulness

vehō, -ere, vexī, vectus: carry

    vectābilis, -e: portable

    vectigal, -ālis, n: tax

    vectūra, -ae, f: transportation

    vehiculum, -ī, n: vehicle

vertō, -ere, vertī, versus: turn

    adversus, -a, -um: opposing

    controversia, -iae, f: dispute

    ūniversus, -a, -um: general

    versus, -ūs, m: verse

Glossary of Required Vocabulary: Latin to English

ā/ab (+ ablative): from, away from, by (3)

abeō, -īre, -īvī or **-iī, -itus**: go away (15)

absolvō, -ere, -solvī, -solūtus: release (from), set free (from); complete, finish (3)

absum, -esse, āfuī, āfutūrus: be absent, be removed (25)

ac: and in addition, and also, and (5)

accēdō, -ere, -cessī, -cessus: approach (28)

accidit, -ere, accidit: it happens (20)

accipiō, -ere, -cēpī, -ceptus: receive, accept (7)

ācer, acris, acre: sharp, vigorous, brave, bitter (19)

aciēs, aciēī, f: edge, battleline, battle (18)

ad (+ accusative): to, toward, for (the purpose of) (3)

addō, -ere, -didī, -ditus: bring, add, join, place (27)

addūcō, -ere, -duxī, -ductus: bring, lead (35)

adeō, -īre, -iī, -itus: approach (30)

adeō: thus far, truly (23)

adflātus, -ūs, m: blowing, breathing, sea breeze (10)

adhūc: thus far, to this point, still (16)

adloquor, -loquī, adlocūtus sum: speak, address (21)

adsum, adesse, adfuī: be present, be at hand (9)

adversus (+ accusative): against (25)

aedēs, -is (-ium), f: temple, shrine; room, house, home (18)

aeger, aegra, aegrum: sick, weary (31)

aequor, -oris, n: level surface, sea (22)

aequus, -a, -um: equal, fair, evenly matched (*in aequō*: on level ground) (14)

āēr, āeris, m: air, atmosphere (16)

aetās, -ātis, f: lifetime, generation, age (26)

aeternus, -a, -um: eternal (26)

aevum, -ī, n: lifetime, age (34)

afficiō, -ere, -fēcī, -fectus: influence, affect (29)

ager, agrī, m: field (2)

agitātor, -ōris, m: driver, charioteer (14)

agmen, agminis, n: stream, band, column, army in marching order (29)

agō, -ere, ēgī, actus: do, drive, accomplish, guide, spend, act (3)

ait: he said (**aiunt**: they said) (25)

albus, -a, -um: white (14)

aliēnus, -a, -um: of another, strange, foreign (33)

aliquī, aliqua, aliquod: some, any (adjective) (15)

aliquis, aliqua, aliquid: someone, something; anyone, anything (pronoun) (15)

aliter: otherwise (34)

alius, alia, aliud: other, another (**aliī . . . aliī**: some . . . others) (6)

alō, -ere, -uī, alitus: nourish (31)

alter, altera, alterum: one of two, second, the other (**alter . . . alter**: the one . . . the other) (10)

altus, -a, -um: high, lofty (8)

ambō, ambae, ambō: both, two (14)

amīcus, -a, -um: friendly (**amīcus, -ī**, m and **amīca, -ae**, f: friend) (6)

āmittō, -ere, -mīsī, -missus: send away, let go, lose (17)

amnis, -is (-ium), m: river (10)

amō, -āre, -āvī, -ātus: like, love (1)

amoenus, -a, -um: beautiful, pleasant, charming (10)

amor, -ōris, m: love (4)

amphitheātrum, -ī, n: amphitheater (14)

amplus, -a, -um: large, spacious (13)

an: or (11)

anima, -ae, f: soul, spirit (26)

animal, -ālis (-ium), n: a living being, an animal (7)

animus, -ī, m: soul, mind (2)

annus, -ī, m: year (2)

ante (+ accusative): before, in front of; beforehand (as an adverb) (8)

antīquus, -a, -um: ancient, old (18)

aperiō, -īre, -uī, -pertus: uncover, lay open, reveal (26)

appellō, -āre, -āvī, -ātus: call, name (8)

aprīcus, -a, -um: sunny (10)

aptus, -a, -um (+ dative): fitting (for) (36)

apud (+ accusative): at, among, in the case of, at the house of (13)

aqua, -ae, f: water (and by extension "aqueduct") (7)

āra, -ae, f: altar (8)

arbitror, -ārī, arbitrātus sum: think, perceive, judge (36)

arbor, -oris, f: tree, "mast" (of a ship) (34)

arcessō, -ere, -īvī, -ītus: send for, summon (36)

arcus, -ūs, m: arch, vault, bow (17)

ardor, -ōris, m: passion, eagerness (21)

arma, -ōrum, n (plural): arms, weapons (3)

arō, -āre, -āvī, -ātus: plow (22)

ars, artis (-ium), f: skill (13)

arvum, -ī, n: region, country, field (22)

arx, arcis (-ium), f: citadel, fortress (35)

at: but (8)

atque: and also (4)

auctor, -ōris, m: originator, proposer, founder (18)

auctōritās, -ātis, f: responsibility, authority (18)

audax (audācis): bold, daring, courageous, foolhardy (20)

audeō, -ēre, ausus sum: dare (21)

audiō, -īre, -īvī, -ītus: hear (1)

auferō, -ferre, abstulī, ablātus: carry away, take away, remove (35)

aureus, -a, -um: golden (18)

auris, -is (-ium), f: ear (22)

aut: or (**aut . . . aut:** either . . . or) (4)

autem: however, moreover, but (9)

auxilium, -iī, n: aid, help (17)

avis, -is (-ium), f: bird (19)

beātus, -a, -um: happy, fortunate (23)

bellum, -ī, n: war (**bellum gerere:** to wage war) (3)

bellus, -a, -um: pretty, handsome (11)

bēlua, -ae, f: beast, large animal (19)

bene: well (5)

beneficium, -iī, n: favor, kindness, service (25)

bestia, -iae, f: wild beast (14)

bis: two times (14)

bonus, -a, -um: good; **bona, -ōrum,** n (plural): goods, possessions (substantive) (2)

bōs, bovis, m/f: ox, bull, cow (24)

brevis, -e: short (3)

Britannia, -iae, f: Britain (29)

cadō, -ere, cecidī, cāsus: fall, be killed, abate (13)

caedēs, -is (-ium), f: killing, slaughter (24)

caedō, -ere, cecīdī, caesus: cut down, strike, beat, kill (18)

caelum, -ī, n: sky (6)

campus, -ī, m: plain, field (23)

canis, -is, m/f: dog (13)

canō, -ere, cecinī, cantus: sing, prophesy (24)

cantō, -āre, -āvī, -ātus: sing, play (4)

capiō, -ere, cēpī, captus: take, seize, capture (1)

caput, capitis, n: head (3)

careō, -ēre, -uī (+ ablative): lack, be without (33)

carmen, carminis, n: song, poem (4)

cārus, -a, -um (+ dative): dear (9)

castitās, -ātis, f: chastity, virtue (5)

castra, -ōrum, n (plural): (military) camp (7)

castus, -a, -um: pure, chaste, innocent, virtuous (26)

cāsus, -ūs, m: misfortune, fall (31)

causā (+ genitive): for the sake of (5)

causa, -ae, f: cause, reason, legal case (9)

caveō, -ēre, cāvī, cautus: be on guard, beware (13)

cēdō, -ere, cessī, cessus: proceed, yield (22)

celebrō, -āre, -āvī, -ātus: practice, repeat, celebrate, make known (23)

celer, celeris, celere: quick, fast, rapid, swift (19)

cēnō, -āre, -āvī, -ātus: dine, eat (13)

censeō, -ēre, -uī, census: advise, resolve, think, express an opinion (36)

centēsimus, -a, -um: hundredth (14)

centum: one hundred (14)

cernō, -ere, crēvī, crētus: discern, distinguish, see (22)

certus, -a, -um: certain, resolved, decided (2)

cēterum: in addition, however (16)

cēterus, -a, -um: other, the rest (18)

cibus, -ī, m: food (33)

cingō, -ere, cinxī, cinctus: gird, wreathe, crown (22)

cinis, cineris, m/f: ash (33)

circā (+ accusative): around, about (*circā* can also be used alone as an adverb) (15)

circiter: about, approximately (10)

circum (+ accusative): around (31)

circumveniō, -īre, -vēnī, -ventus: surround, encircle (32)

cīvis, -is (-ium), m/f: citizen (9)

cīvitās, -ātis, f: citizenship, state (9)

clāmor, -ōris, m: cry, shout (27)

clārus, -a, -um: bright, clear, loud, distinct, distinguished (29)

classis, -is (-ium), f: fleet (14)

claudō, -ere, clausī, clausus: close, shut (13)

coepī, -isse, coeptus: begin (20)

cōgitō, -āre, -āvī, -ātus: think, reflect (9)

cognoscō, -ere, -nōvī, -nitus: learn, understand, perceive (9)

cōgō, -ere, coēgī, coactus: compel, force (30)

cohors, cohortis (-ium), f: troop, company, cohort (32)

cohortor, -ārī, cohortātus sum: encourage, incite (30)

collis, -is (-ium), m: hill, high ground (10)

collum, -ī, n: neck (36)

colō, -ere, coluī, cultus: inhabit, cultivate, worship (5)

color, -ōris, m: color, hue, complexion (6)

coma, -ae, f: hair, foliage (26)

comes, comitis, m/f: companion, associate (29)

commendō, -āre, -āvī, -ātus: commit, entrust (6)

committō, -ere, -mīsī, -missus: join, entrust to, bring together in a contest (35)

commūnis, -e: shared, universal, general (30)

comparō, -āre, -āvī, -ātus: provide, furnish, prepare (28)

compōnō, -ere, -posuī, -positus: bring together, collect, arrange, settle (27)

concēdō, -ere, -cessī, -cessus: yield, grant (35)

concipiō, -ere, -cēpī, -ceptus: absorb, receive, grasp (34)

condemnō, -āre, -āvī, -ātus: condemn, blame, disprove (5)

conditiō (condiciō), -iōnis, f: stipulation, provision, state, condition (29)

condō, -ere, -didī, -ditus: build, found; plunge, conceal, hide, store (22)

conferō, -ferre, -tulī, -lātus: bring together, collect, apply, devote (26)

conficiō, -ere, -fēcī, -fectus: complete, carry out (32)

confiteor, -ērī, confessus sum: confess, reveal, acknowledge (35)

coniunx, coniugis, m/f: spouse, husband, wife (5)

coniūrātiō, -iōnis, f: conspiracy (30)

conligō (colligō), -ere, -lēgī, -lectus: gather together, collect, infer (32)

cōnor, -ārī, cōnātus sum: try (21)

consequor, -sequī, consecūtus sum: follow, go after (21)

consilium, -iī, n: plan, counsel, good judgment, advice (5)

constat, -āre, constitit/constātum est: it is agreed, it is well known (20)

constituō, -ere, -stituī, -stitūtus: place, establish, decide (7)

constō, -stāre, -stitī, -status: agree, stand together, stand firm (32)

consul, consulis, m: a high political office in Rome (23)

consulō, -ere, -uī, -sultus: consult (35)

contemnō, -ere, -tempsī, -temptus: despise (18)

contingō, -ere, -tigī, -tactum: touch (13)

contrā (+ accusative): against, opposite (adverb and preposition) (34)

conveniō, -īre, -vēnī, -ventus: come together, meet with (28)

cōpia, -iae, f: abundance, troops (9)

cor, cordis, n: heart (29)

cornū, -ūs, n: horn, wing of an army (10)

corpus, corporis, n: body (3)

corrumpō, -ere, -rūpī, -ruptus: destroy, weaken, mar, spoil (26)

crās: tomorrow (24)

crēdō, -ere, crēdidī, crēditus (+ dative): believe, trust (6)

creō, -āre, -āvī, -ātus: create, make (25)

crēscō, -ere, crēvī, crētus: grow (12)

crīmen, crīminis, n: crime, guilt, charge (20)

cruor, -ōris, m: blood, gore (28)

culpa, -ae, f: blame, fault (17)

cum (+ ablative): with (3)

cum: when, since, although (11)

cum . . . tum: both . . . and; not only . . . but also (25)

cunctus, -a, -um: entire, the whole (singular); all (plural) (27)

cupīdō, cupīdinis, f: desire (34)

cupiō, -ere, -īvī, -ītus: wish, long for, desire (12)

cūr: why (28)

cūra, -ae, f: concern, care, trouble, distress (23)

cūrō, -āre, -āvī, -ātus: care for, attend to (24)

currō, -ere, cucurrī, cursus: run, rush (22)

currus, -ūs, m: chariot (18)

cursus, -ūs, m: course, running, race (22)

damnō, -āre, -āvī, -ātus: condemn, discredit (29)

dē (+ ablative): down from, about, concerning (7)

dēbeō, -ēre, -uī, -itus: owe, ought to (17)

decem: ten (14)

dēcernō, -ere, -crēvī, -crētus: decide, settle, propose (25)

decet, -ēre, -uit: it is proper, it is seemly, it is fitting (20)

decimus, -a, -um: tenth (14)

decus, decoris, n: honor, glory (4)

dēferō, -ferre, -tulī, -lātus: bring down, hand over (18)

dēficiō, -ere, -fēcī, -fectus: fail, run short (25)

dēgredior, -gredī, dēgressus sum: step down, depart for (21)

deinde or **dein**: then, next (3)

dēlātor, -ōris, m: informer (27)

dēnique: finally, at last, further (25)

dēscīscō, -ere, -scīvī, -scītus: desert, withdraw, revolt, break away (25)

dēserō, -ere, -seruī, -sertus: desert, abandon, leave, forsake (26)

deus, deī, m: god (4)

dexter, dext(e)ra, dext(e)rum: skillful, right (hand) (27)

Dī Mānēs, m (plural): the spirits of the dead (6)

dīcō, -ere, dixī, dictus: say, speak (of), mention, call, appoint (4)

dīdūcō, -ere, -duxī, -ductus: draw apart, separate (17)

diēs, diēī, m: day (10)

difficilis, -e: difficult, obstinate (26)

dignus, -a, -um (+ ablative): worthy (17)

dīligō, -ere, -lexī, -lectus: cherish, esteem (15)

dīmittō, -ere, -mīsī, -missus: send away, lose (30)

Dīs, Dītis, m: Pluto, god of the underworld (6)

discēdō, -ere, -cessī: depart, go away (30)

discō, -ere, didicī: learn, get to know (19)

disiiciō, -ere, -iēcī, -iectus: scatter, rout, destroy (22)

dissimilis, -e: dissimilar (19)

diū: for a long time (4)

dīves (dīvitis): rich (11)

dīvitiae, -iārum, f (plural): riches, wealth (20)

dīvus, -a, -um: divine, deified (18)

dō, dare, dedī, datus: give (1)

doceō, -ēre, docuī, doctus: teach, instruct (1)

doctus, -a, -um: learned, clever (4)

doleō, -ēre, -uī, -itus: suffer pain, grieve (27)

dolor, -ōris, m: pain, grief (5)

dolus, -ī, m: deceit, trick (28)

domina, -ae, f: mistress, lady friend (23)

dominus, -ī, m: household master, lord (15)

domus, -ī or **-ūs**, f: house, home (13)

dōnec: until (27)

dōnō, -āre, -āvī, -ātus: present, bestow, award, consecrate (27)

dōnum, -ī, n: gift (20)

dormiō, -īre, -īvī: sleep (12)

dubitō, -āre, -āvī, -ātus: waver, hesitate (28)

dubius, -a, -um: doubtful, uncertain, wavering (31)

dūcō, -ere, duxī, ductus: lead; think, consider (13)

dulcis, -e: sweet, pleasant (4)

dum: while, as long as, provided that (13)

dummodo: provided that (36)

duo, duae, duo: two (14)

duodecim: twelve (14)

duodecimus, -a, -um: twelfth (14)

duodēvīcēsimus, -a, -um: eighteenth (14)

duodēvīgintī: eighteen (14)

dūrus, -a, -um: hard, inflexible, harsh (22)

dux, ducis, m/f: leader, general (5)

ē/ex (+ ablative): out of, from, on account of, by reason of (5)

ecce: behold! (11)

ēdō, -ere, -didī, -ditus: bring forth, explain, emit (24)

ēdūcō, -ere, -duxī, -ductus: lead out, march out (36)

efficiō, -ere, -fēcī, -fectus: bring about, render, complete (9)

effundō, -ere, -fūdī, -fūsus: pour out, squander, waste (31)

ego: I (12)

ēgregius, -a, -um: distinguished, extraordinary (36)

ēligō, -ere, -lēgī, -lectus: choose, select (34)

em: here; often followed by the dative case (*em tibi* = "here you are!") (15)

enim: for, indeed (6)

eō, īre, īvī or **iī, itus**: go (11)

eō: there (29)

eō . . . quō: the more . . . the more; there . . . where (25)

epistula, -ae, f: letter (9)

eques, equitis, m: horseman, knight (7)

equitātus, -ūs, m: cavalry (32)

equus, -ī, m: horse (7)

ergō: therefore (6)

ēripiō, -ere, -uī, -reptus: snatch, tear away (28)

errō, -āre, -āvī, -ātus: wander, stray (22)

et: and (**et . . . et**: both . . . and) (1)

etiam: as yet, still, but also (6)

exemplum, -ī, n: example, sample (27)

ex(s)pectō, -āre, -āvī, -ātus: await, dread (32)

exeō, -īre, -īvī or **-iī, -itus**: go out (30)

exercitātiō, -iōnis, f: exercise, practice (33)

exercitus, -ūs, m: army (18)

exigō, -ere, -ēgī, -actus: demand, discover (17)

exiguus, -a, -um: small, scanty (25)

existimō, -āre, -āvi, -ātus: value, esteem, judge, think (25)

extrā (+ accusative): beyond, outside (17)

extrēmus, -a, -um: last, uttermost, lengthy, furthest (14)

faciēs, faciēī, f: shape, form, appearance (22)

facilis, -e: easy (19)

faciō, -ere, fēcī, factus: make, do (2)

factiō, -iōnis, f: band, group, team (14)

fallō, -ere, fefellī, falsus: deceive, cheat, be mistaken (16)

falsus, -a, -um: deceptive, false, fake (24)

fāma, -ae, f: rumor, fame, name (11)

famēs, -is (-ium), f: hunger (31)

familia, -iae, f: household, household slave, band of household slaves, family (15)

familiāris, -e: belonging to the household (9)

fās, n (indeclinable): in accord with divine law (20)

fateor, -ērī, fassus sum: confess, acknowledge (32)

fātum, -ī, n: fate (24)

fax, facis (-ium), f: torch (24)

febris, -is (-ium), m: fever (33)

fēlix (fēlicis): fertile, favorable, lucky (34)

fēmina, -ae, f: woman (2)

fenestra, -ae, f: window (23)

ferē: nearly, almost (18)

ferō, ferre, tulī, lātus: bring, carry, bear, endure, say (11)

ferrum, -ī, n: iron, sword (27)

fertilis, -e: abundant, fruitful (10)

ferus, -a, -um: savage, wild (36)

fessus, -a, -um: tired, weary, worn out, exhausted (21)

fidēs, fideī, f: faith, trust (20)

fīlia, -iae, f: daughter (5)

fīlius, -iī, m: son (13)

fingō, -ere, finxī, fictus: shape, invent (28)

fīnis, -is (-ium), m: boundary, end, territory (9)

fīō, fierī, factus sum: become (20)

flamma, -ae, f: flame, blaze, torch (20)

flōs, flōris, m: flower (26)

fluctus, -ūs, m: wave (19)

flūmen, flūminis, n: river, stream (10)

fluō, -ere, fluxī, fluxus: flow (29)

fons, fontis (-ium), m: spring, fountain (17)

fore = *futūrus, -a, -um esse* (24)

forma, -ae, f: shape, beauty (8)

forsitan: perhaps (31)

fortasse: perhaps (26)

fortis, -e: brave (19)

fortūna, -ae, f: fortune (6)

forum, -ī, n: forum, open square, marketplace (27)

frāter, frātris, m: brother (3)

frons, frontis (-ium), m: brow, forehead (5)

frūmentum, -ī, n: grain (32)

frustrā: in vain (22)

frux, frūgis, f: crops, fruit (10)

fugiō, fugere, fūgī: flee, escape, run away (1)

fūnus, fūneris, n: funeral, burial (25)

gaudeō, -ēre, gāvīsus sum: rejoice, delight in (21)

geminus, -ī, m: twin (15)

genitor, -ōris, m: father (36)

gens, gentis (-ium), f: family, clan, race (10)

genus, generis, n: origin, lineage, kind (6)

gerō, -ere, gessī, gestus: carry on, manage, wear, endure, suffer (3)

gignō, -ere, genuī, genitus: bear, bring forth (24)

gladiātor, -ōris, m: gladiator (14)

gladius, -iī, m: sword (27)

glōria, -iae, f: glory, fame, ambition, renown (9)

gracilis, -e: graceful (19)

grandis, -e: large (12)

grātiā (+ genitive): for the sake of (5)

grātia, -iae, f: favor, esteem, regard (**grātiās agere**: to give thanks) (20)

grātus, -a, -um (+ dative): pleasing, welcome, agreeable (19)

gravis, -e: heavy, serious, painful (4)

habeō, -ēre, habuī, habitus: have, consider, wear (3)

habitō, -āre, -āvī, -ātus: live, dwell (1)

haud: by no means, not at all (22)

hērēs, hērēdis, m: heir (35)

hīc: here (1)

hic, haec, hoc: this, these (15)

hinc: from here; **hinc . . . hinc**: here and there (16)

hodiē: today (11)

homo, hominis, m: human being (7)

honestus, -a, -um: respectable, honorable, proper, virtuous (23)

honor, -ōris, m: honor, glory, mark of respect or distinction (13)

hōra, -ae, f: hour (29)

hortor, -ārī, hortātus sum: encourage, urge, exhort (22)

hospes, hospitis, m: guest, host, stranger (34)

hostis, -is (-ium), m/f: enemy (7)

hūc: here, to this place (19)

hūmānus, -a, -um: human (7)

humilis, -e: low, humble (19)

iaceō, -ēre, iacuī: lie down (16)

iaciō, -ere, iēcī, iactus: throw, hurl (18)

iam: now, already (**nōn iam**: no longer) (5)

iānua, -ae, f: door (26)

ibi: there (10)

īdem, eadem, idem: the same (15)

ideō: therefore, for this reason (16)

igitur: therefore (21)

ignis, ignis (-ium), m: fire (3)

ille, illa, illud: that, those (15)

imāgō, imāginis, f: image, likeness, copy (18)

imber, imbris (-ium), m: shower, storm (16)

immineō, -ēre: overhang, threaten (23)

immolō, -āre, -āvī, -ātus: sacrifice (36)

impellō, -ere, -pulī, -pulsus: incite, impel (30)

imperātor, -ōris, m: commander-in-chief, emperor, victorious general (17)

imperium, -iī, n: command, dominion, power (3)

imperō, -āre, -āvī, -ātus (+ dative): command, control (6)

impetus, -ūs, m: attack, assault, charge (23)

impleō, -ēre, -ēvī, -ētus: fill in/up, complete (19)

impōnō, -ere, -posuī, -positus: place upon, impose (28)

īmus, -a, -um: lowest, deepest (22)

in (+ ablative): in, on (2)

in (+ accusative): into, onto, against (2)

incipiō, -ere, -cēpī, -ceptus: begin (8)

inde: from there, from then (9)

indīcō, -ere, -dixī, -dictus: declare, point out (18)

inferus, -a, -um: low, southern (29)

ingenium, -iī, n: talent, ability, nature, character (26)

ingens (-entis): huge, enormous (13)

ingrātus, -a, -um: unpleasant, thankless (36)

ingredior, -gredī, ingressus sum: enter (21)

inimīcus, -a, -um (+ dative): hostile (26)

initium, -iī, n: beginning (18)

iniūria, -iae, f: injury, wrong, injustice (19)

inpluō, -ere, -uī: rain (16)

inquit (defective verb): he/she said (9)

insignis, -e: notable, remarkable (31)

instituō, -ere, -stituī, -stitūtus: position, place, establish, decide (32)

insula, -ae, f: island, apartment block (10)

insum, -esse, -fuī: be in (34)

intellegō, -ere, -lexī, -lectus: understand (15)

intendō, -ere, -tendī, -tentus: aim, stretch, strain, exert (28)

inter (+ accusative): between, among, during (8)

interficiō, -ere, -fēcī, -fectus: destroy, kill (32)

interim: meanwhile (15)

interrogō, -āre, -āvī, -ātus: examine, question (35)

intrō, -āre, -āvī, -ātus: enter (12)

inveniō, -īre, -vēnī, -ventus: come upon, find, meet (17)

ipse, ipsa, ipsum: himself, herself, itself, themselves (12)

īra, -ae, f: wrath, anger (16)

īrascor, -ī, īrātus sum: be angry (33)

īrātus, -a, -um: angry (29)

is, ea, id: he, she, it; this, that (12)

iste, ista, istud: that (of yours), those (of yours) (15)

ita: thus, so

itaque: and so, therefore (12)

item: likewise (16)

iter, itineris, n: journey, route (7)

iterum: again (19)

iubeō, -ēre, iussī, iussus: order, command (13)

iūdicium, -iī, n: trial, legal investigation, decision (35)

iugum, -ī, n: yoke, team, crossbar, ridge (23)

iūs, iūris, n: right, law (35)

iustus, -a, -um: just (17)

iuvenis, -is, m: youth (5)

iuventus, iuventūtis, f: youth, the prime of life (31)

labor, -ōris, m: work, toil, effort (10)

labōrō, -āre, -āvī, -ātus: work (36)

lacrima, -ae, f: tear (9)

lacus, -ūs, m: lake (10)

laedō, -ere, laesī, laesus: hurt, wound, injure (31)

laetor, -ārī, laetus sum: rejoice, be glad (23)

laetus, -a, -um: glad, joyful, happy (13)

lapis, lapidis, m: stone (24)

lateō, -ēre, -uī: lie hidden (31)

lātus, -a, -um: broad, wide (23)

latus, lateris, n: side, flank (19)

laudo, -āre, -āvī, -ātus: praise, commend (11)

laus, laudis, f: praise (25)

lectus, -ī, m: bed, couch, sofa (13)

lēgātus, -ī, m: envoy, delegate (23)

legiō, -iōnis, f: legion (7)

legō, -ere, lēgī, lectus: pick, choose, read (6)

levis, -e: light, unambitious, fickle (6)

lēvis, -e: smooth, delicate (31)

lex, lēgis, f: law (9)

libellus, -ī, m: little book (4)

liber, librī, m: book (17)

līber, lībera, līberum: free (19)

līberī, līberōrum, m (plural): children (8)

līberta, -ae, f: freedwoman (12)

lībertīnus, -ī, m: freedman (35)

lībertus, -ī, m: freedman (12)

libet, -ēre, libuit/libitum est: it pleases (20)

lībidō, lībidinis, f: desire, lust, passion (33)

licet, -ere, -uit/licitum est: it is permitted (20)

licet: although, granted that (29)

līmen, līminis, n: threshold, entrance, home (28)

lingua, -ae, f: tongue, language (4)

littera, -ae, f: letter of the alphabet; in plural: dispatch, epistle (18)

lītus, lītoris, n: seashore, beach (19)

locus, -ī, m: place (7)

longē: by far (19)

longus, -a, -um: long, vast, spacious (2)

loquor, -ī, locūtus sum: speak, mention, say, address (21)

lūmen, lūminis, n: light, eye (36)

lūna, -ae, f: moon (16)

lupus, -ī, m: wolf (28)

lux, lūcis, f: light (12)

magis: more, to a greater extent (17)

magnitūdō, magnitūdinis, f: size, bulk, greatness (19)

magnopere: greatly (19)

magnus, -a, -um: great (2)

māior, māius: bigger (19)

māior, -ōris, m/f: ancestor (from comparative adjective of *magnus*: "the greater ones") (20)

malē: badly (19)

mālō, malle, māluī: prefer, choose (11)

malus, -a, -um: bad, evil (2)

maneō, -ēre, mansī, mansus: remain, stay (23)

mānēs, -ium, m (plural): spirits of the dead (6)

manus, -ūs, f: hand, band or force (of men) (10)

mare, maris (-ium), n: sea (3)

marītus, -ī, m: husband (28)

māter, mātris, f: mother (3)

māteria, -iae, f: subject matter (35)

maximē: most especially, certainly (9)

maximus, -a, -um: biggest (19)

medicāmentum, -ī, n: drug, remedy (33)

medicīna, -ae, f: treatment, remedy (33)

medicus, -ī, m: doctor, physician (24)

medius, -a, -um: middle, mid- (8)

melior, melius: better (19)

melius: better (19)

meminī, -isse (+ genitive): remember, recall (20)

memoria, -iae, f: recollection, memory (7)

memorō, -āre, -āvī, -ātus: remind, relate (31)

mens, mentis (-ium), f: mind, understanding, judgment, attention (8)

mensa, -ae, f: table, course, meal (31)

mereō, -ēre, -uī, -itus: deserve, earn,
obtain (26)

metuō, -ere, -uī, -ūtus: to fear, to dread (16)

metus, -ūs, m: fear, dread (18)

meus, -a, -um: mine (2)

mīles, mīlitis, m: soldier; soldiery (7)

mille: one thousand (14)

mille passūs: a thousand paces,
mile (10)

millēsimus, -a, -um: thousandth (14)

milliārium, -iī, n: milestone (17)

minimē: least (19)

minimus, -a, -um: smallest (19)

minor, minus: smaller (19)

minus: less (19)

mīrābilis, -e: extraordinary,
unusual (36)

mīror, -ārī, mīrātus sum: wonder (at),
marvel (at) (21)

misceō, -ēre, -uī, mixtus: mix,
mingle (22)

miser, misera, miserum: wretched, unhappy, miserable (2)

miseret, -ēre, miseruit/miseritum est: it
distresses, it induces pity (20)

mittō, -ere, mīsī, missus: send, let
go (1)

modo: just now (4)

modus, -ī, m: way, method, manner,
measure, rhythm (4)

moenia, -ium, n (plural): walls,
fortifications (20)

mollis, -e: soft, supple (22)

moneō, -ēre, -uī: advise, warn (32)

mons, montis (-ium), m: mountain (10)

monumentum, -ī, n: memorial,
monument (35)

mora, -ae, f: delay, hindrance (33)

morbus, -ī, m: sickness, disease, illness (33)

morior, -ī, mortuus sum: die (24)

mors, mortis (-ium), f: death (6)

mortālis, -e: mortal, transitory,
human (25)

mōs, mōris, m: custom, habit; (plural)
character (10)

moveō, -ēre, mōvī, mōtus: move (4)

mox: soon (18)

mulier, mulieris, f: woman (24)

multitūdo, multitūdinis, f: multitude,
number (5)

multō: by far, by much (12)

multum: much (19)

multus, -a, -um: great, many, many a (5)

mundus, -ī, m: universe, world (32)

mūnus, mūneris, n: duty, gift, show,
performance, spectacle, function (14)

murmur, murmuris, n: murmur, roar,
rumble (22)

mūrus, -ī, m: wall (32)

Mūsa, -ae, f: Muse, a goddess of artistic
inspiration (4)

mūtō, -āre, -āvī, -ātus: change, alter, shift
(18)

nam, namque: for, indeed, really (5)

nascor, -ī, nātus sum: be born, come into
existence (24)

nātūra, -ae, f: nature, character, temperament (8)

nātus, -ī, m: son (15)

nāvālis, -e: naval (14)

nāvis, -is (-ium), f: ship (15)

-ne: introduces a question that expects a positive answer (13)

nē: lest, so that . . . not (26)

nec: and . . . not (2)

necesse est: it is necessary (20)

necessitās, -ātis, f: necessity, need, poverty, difficult situation (29)

nefās (indeclinable): a violation of divine law, an impious act (32)

negō, -āre, -āvī, -ātus: deny, refuse (11)

nēmō, nēminis, m/f: no one (9)

nemus, nemoris, n: grove, forest (16)

nepōs, nepōtis, m: grandson, descendent (14)

neque: and not (**neque . . . neque**: neither . . . nor) (6)

nesciō, -īre, -īvī, -ītus: not to know, be unfamiliar, be ignorant of (33)

nī: if not, unless (26)

niger, nigra, nigrum: black, dark-colored (34)

nihil: nothing (1)

nisi: if not, unless, except (11)

nōbilis, -e: distinguished, noble, famous (10)

noceō, -ēre, -uī: hurt, harm, injure (17)

nocturnus, -a, -um: by night, nocturnal (32)

nōlō, nolle, nōluī: be unwilling, not want (11)

nōmen, nōminis, n: name (3)

nōn: not (1)

nōndum: not yet (33)

nōn sōlum . . . sed etiam: not only . . . but also (7)

nōn sōlum . . . vērum etiam: not only . . . but also (9)

nōnāgēsimus, -a, -um: ninetieth (14)

nōnāgintā: ninety (14)

nōnus, -a, -um: ninth (14)

nōs: we, us (12)

noscō, -ere, nōvī, nōtus: learn, get to know (16)

noster, nostra, nostrum: our (2)

novem: nine (14)

novus, -a, -um: new (4)

nox, noctis (-ium) f: night (8)

noxius, -a, -um: hurtful, injurious (10)

nūbila, -ōrum, n (plural): clouds (16)

nūdus, -a, -um: plain, mere (35)

nullus, -a, -um: not any, no (13)

nūmen, nūminis, n: divine spirit (25)

numerus, -ī, m: number (7)

numquam: never (15)

nunc: now (4)

nuntiō, -āre, -āvī, -ātus: announce (24)

ob (+ accusative): against, on account of (13)

oblīviscor, -ī, oblītus sum (+ genitive): forget (21)

occupō, -āre, -āvī, -ātus: take possession, seize (30)

ōceanus, -ī, m: ocean, the sea that surrounds the Earth (10)

octāvus, -a, -um: eighth (14)

octō: eight (14)

octōgēsimus, -a, -um: eightieth (14)

octōgintā: eighty (14)

oculus, -ī, m: eye (13)

ōdī, ōdisse (defective verb): hate, detest (27)

odium, -iī, n: hatred (27)

offerō, -ferre, obtulī, oblātus: present, offer (24)

officium, -iī, n: service, duty (7)

ōlim: once (21)

omnis, -e: whole, entire, every (singular), all (plural) (3)

oportet, -ere, -uit: it is fitting (20)

oppidum, -ī, n: town (7)

ops, opis, f: power, means (25)

optimē: best (19)

optimus, -a, -um: best (19)

optō, -āre, -āvī, -ātus: wish for, desire (8)

opus, operis, n: work, task, labor (4)

ōrātiō, -iōnis, f: speech (25)

orbis, -is (-ium) m: circle, disk; globe, earth, world (16)

ordō, ordinis, m: series, row, rank (30)

orior, -īrī, ortus sum: rise, begin, spring forth (from) (21)

ōrō, -āre, -āvī, -ātus: speak, beg (30)

ortus, -ūs, m: rising, origin (10)

ōs, ōris, n: mouth, face (23)

os, ossis, n: bone (32)

ostendō, -ere, -tendī, -tensus: show, display (32)

p(a)ene: nearly, almost (29)

paenitet, -ēre: it causes regret (20)

pār (paris): equal, pair (14)

parcō, -ere, pepercī (+ dative): spare, refrain from injuring (30)

parens, -entis, m/f: parent (20)

pariō, -ere, peperī, partus: bring forth, bear, give birth (to) (24)

parō, -āre, -āvī, -ātus: prepare (8)

pars, partis (-ium), f: part (5)

parum: (too) little (19)

parvus, -a, -um: small (10)

passus, -ūs, m: step, pace, "foot" (10)

pateō, -ēre, -uī: lie open (26)

pater, patris, m: father, senator (3)

patior, -ī, passus sum: suffer, endure, allow (22)

patria, -iae, f: fatherland, country (2)

paucī, -ae, -a (plural): few (16)

paulō, paulum: a little (24)

pauper (-eris): poor (26)

paveō, -ēre, pāvī: be scared (of), be terrified (at) (32)

pavor, -ōris, m: fear, dread (32)

pax, pācis, f: peace, harmony (18)

pectus, pectoris, n: breast, heart, soul (19)

pecūnia, -iae, f: money (9)

pecus, pecoris, n: flock (32)

pēior, pēius: worse (19)

pēius: worse (19)

pellō, -ere, pepulī, pulsus: strike, drive away, dislodge (32)

penātēs, -ium, m (plural): the gods of the home, hearth, or family line (13)

pendō, -ere, pependī, pensus: pay, weigh out (30)

per (+ accusative): through (3)

perdō, -ere, -didī, -ditus: destroy, ruin (34)

pereō, -īre, -iī, -ītus: waste, be lost, perish (23)

pergō, -ere, perrexī, perrectus: continue, proceed, go on with (20)

perīculum, -ī, n: danger (7)

perpetuus, -a, -um: continuous, uninterrupted (30)

persuādeō, -ēre, -suāsī, -suāsus (+ dative): convince, prevail upon (30)

perveniō, -īre, -vēnī, -ventus: come to, reach, arrive at (17)

pēs, pedis, m: foot, foot soldier (24)

pessimē: worst (19)

pessimus, -a, -um: worst (19)

petō, -ere, -īvī/iī, -ītus: seek, demand, ask, beg (17)

pietās, -ātis, f: responsibility, sense of duty, piety (9)

piget, -ēre, -uī: it displeases (20)

piscīna, -ae, f: fishpond (17)

pius, pia, pium: dutiful, devoted, affectionate (19)

placeō, -ēre, -uī (+ dative): please (11)

placet, -ēre, -uit/placitum est: it pleases, it is agreeable (20)

plānē: clearly (12)

plēnus, -a, -um (+ ablative): full (27)

plērumque: for the most part, commonly, generally (20)

plūrimē: most (19)

plūrimus, -a, -um: most (19)

plūs (plūris): more (18)

plūs: more (19)

poena, -ae, f: punishment, penalty (*poenam dare*: to pay the penalty) (30)

poēta, -ae, m: poet (2)

polliceor, -ērī, pollicitus sum: offer, promise (21)

pondus, ponderis, n: weight (33)

pōnō, -ere, posuī, positus: put, place, put aside, consider (**castra pōnere**: to pitch camp) (15)

pontus, -ī, m: sea (22)

populus, -ī, m: people (3)

porta, -ae, f: gate, strait (8)

poscō, -ere, poposcī: demand, inquire (20)

possum, posse, potuī: be able, can (11)

post (+ accusative): after, behind (8)

posteā: afterwards (18)

posterī, -ōrum, m (plural): posterity, descendants (12)

posterus, -a, -um: following, next (27)

postquam: after, when (20)

postulō, -āre, -āvī, -ātus: demand (30)

potens (-entis): powerful (22)

potestās, -ātis, f: power, control, authority (18)

praecipuus, -a, -um: particular, special (33)

praeclārus, -a, -um: bright, distinguished, excellent (28)

praemium, -iī, n: prize, reward (14)

praesidium, -iī, n: defense, protection, guard (4)

praestō, -āre, -stitī, -stitus: offer, excel (32)

praesum, -esse, -fuī (+ dative): be in charge (34)

praeter (+ accusative): beyond, except, in addition to, in front of (20)

praetor, -ōris, m: leader, military leader, magistrate at Rome with the constitutional authority to lead an army (20)

prasinus, -a, -um: green (14)

premō, -ere, pressī, pressus: press, oppress, control, pursue (4)

pretium, -iī, n: price, reward (23)

prex, precis, f: request, entreaty (23)

prīmum or **prīmō**: at first, for the first time (13)

prīmus, -a, -um: first (14)

princeps, principis, m: leader, chief, emperor (14)

priusquam: before (30)

prō (+ ablative): for, on behalf of, in place of, in front of (5)

probō, -āre, -āvī, -ātus: prove, approve (34)

prōcēdō, -ere, -cessī, -cessus: proceed, advance (25)

procul: from a distance (23)

prodest, -esse, -fuit: it is useful, it is advantageous, it benefits (20)

prōdigium, -iī, n: prodigy, portent (24)

prōdō, -ere, -didī, -ditus: put forth, proclaim, abandon, betray (27)

proelium, -iī, n: battle (7)

proficiscor, proficiscī, profectus sum: set out, depart (21)

prohibeō, -ēre, -uī, -itus: restrain, hinder (23)

prōnuntiō, -āre, -āvī, -ātus: declare (30)

prope (+ accusative): near (also can function as an adverb) (30)

properō, -āre, -āvī, -ātus: hurry (25)

prōpōnō, -ere, -posuī, -positus: expose, display (35)

propter (+ accusative): because of (12)

prōsequor, -sequī, prōsecūtus sum: follow, accompany, attend (21)

prōtinus: immediately (28)

prōvincia, -iae, f: command, province, the backwoods (21)

proximus, -a, -um: closest (13)

pūblicus, -a, -um: public, at public expense (8)

pudet: it shames, it disgraces (20)

puella, -ae, f: girl (2)

puer, puerī, m: boy (4)

pugnō, -āre, -āvī, -ātus: fight (14)

pulcher, pulchra, pulchrum: pretty (19)

pūrus, -a, -um: upright, faultless (36)

putō, -āre, -āvī, -ātus: think, suppose, consider (5)

quā: where, how (23)

quadrāgēsimus, -a, -um: fortieth (14)

quadrāgintā: forty (14)

quaerō, -ere, quaesīvī, quaesītus: look for, seek (29)

quālis, -e (+ dative): of what sort/kind as, just like (19)

quam: than (19)

quamquam: although, however (26)

quamvīs: although, however much (19)

quandō: when (20)

quantus, -a, -um: how much (25)

quārē: why (31)

quartus, -a, -um: fourth (14)

quartus decimus, -a, -um: fourteenth (14)

quasi: as if (18)

quattuor: four (14)

quattuordecim: fourteen (14)

-que: and (2)

-que . . . -que: both . . . and (2)

queror, -querī, questus sum: complain (26)

quī, quae, quod: who, what (16)

quia: because (11)

quīcumque, quaecumque, quodcumque: whoever, whatever (33)

quīdam, quaedam, quiddam: a certain one; a certain thing (pronoun) (15)

quīdam, quaedam, quoddam: a certain (adjective) (15)

quidem: certainly, at least, indeed (7)

quindecim: fifteen (14)

quingentēsimus, -a, -um: five hundredth (14)

quingentī, -ae, -a: five hundred (14)

quinquāgēsimus, -a, -um: fiftieth (14)

quinquāgintā: fifty (14)

quinque: five (14)

quintus, -a, -um: fifth (14)

quintus decimus, -a, -um: fifteenth (14)

quippe: certainly, to be sure (29)

quis, quid: who? what? (16)

quisquam, quicquam/quidquam: any (single) person, anyone at all (18)

quisque, quaeque, quidque: each (20)

quisquis, quaeque, quicquid or **quidquid**: whoever, whatever (27)

quō modō or **quōmodō**: how (31)

quō: where, to what place (31)

quod: because, the fact that (6)

quondam: once, formerly (18)

quoniam: since, because (19)

quoque: also (6)

rāmus, -ī, m: branch, bough (36)

rapiō, -ere, -uī, raptus: tear away, seize, snatch (19)

rārus, -a, -um: scattered (31)

ratiō, -iōnis, f: account, reckoning, reasoning, method (22)

recipiō, -ere, -cēpi, -ceptus: take back, receive (16)

reddō, -ere, -didī, -ditus: return, give back (15)

redeō, -īre, -iī or **īvī, -itus**: go back, return (16)

referō, -ferre, -tulī, -lātus: bring back, return, report (35)

refert, -ferre, -tulit: it matters (20)

rēgīna, -ae, f: queen (31)

regiō, -iōnis, f: boundary, region (10)

rēgius, -a, -um: royal (31)

regnum, -ī, n: kingdom, realm, sovereignty (3)

regō, -ere, rexī, rectus: rule, guide (19)

regredior, -gredī, regressus sum: step back, retreat (21)

religiō, -iōnis, f: obligation, scruples, observance of a religious ceremony (36)

relinquō, -ere, relīquī, relictus: leave behind, desert, abandon (2)

reliquus, -a, -um: remaining, left (19)

removeō, -ēre, -mōvī, -mōtus: move back, withdraw, be distant (36)

reor, rērī, ratus sum: think, suppose, judge, consider (21)

repetō, -ere, -īvī/iī, -ītus: seek again, recall (27)

requīrō, -ere, -quīsīvī, -quisītus: seek again, search for (31)

rēs, reī, f: thing, object, matter, affair, circumstance (10)

rescrībō, -ere, -scripsī, -scriptus: write back, answer a petition (35)

respiciō, -ere, -spexī, -spectus: look back (31)

respondeō, -ēre, -spondī, -sponsus: answer, reply (9)

rex, rēgis, m: king (3)

rīdeō, -ēre, rīsī, rīsus: laugh, laugh at (15)

rīvus, -ī, m: stream (17)

rogō, -āre, -āvī, -ātus: ask, ask for, endorse (3)

Rōma, -ae, f: the city of Rome (4)

Rōmānus, -a, -um: Roman (3)

rursus or **rursum**: back, again (9)

rūs, rūris, n: country, countryside (7)

russātus, -a, -um: red (14)

sacer, sacra, sacrum: holy, consecrated, accursed (4)

sacerdōs, -ōtis, m/f: priest(ess), bishop (29)

sacerdōtium, -iī, n: priesthood (20)

saepe: often (7)

saevus, -a, -um: fierce, raging, violent (23)

sanctus, -a, -um: holy, sacred, blameless (4)

sanguis, sanguinis, m: blood (16)

sānus, -a, -um: sound, healthy, sane (28)

sapientia, -iae, f: wisdom, discernment, prudence (25)

satis or **sat**: enough, sufficiently (25)

saxum, -ī, n: rock, cliff (16)

scelus, sceleris, n: crime (3)

scīlicet: evidently, certainly, of course (28)

sciō, -īre, -īvī, -ītus: know (1)

scrībō, -ere, scripsī, scriptus: write (5)

secundus, -a, -um: second, favorable (26)

sed: but (2)

sēdecim: sixteen (14)

sēdēs, -is (-ium), f: seat, base, home (21)

semel: once (24)

semper: always, every time (19)

senātus, -ūs, m: Senate (18)

senex, senis, m: old man (34)

sensus, -ūs, m: feeling, sense, understanding (31)

sententia, -iae, f: opinion, judgment (9)

sentiō, -īre, sensī, sensus: perceive, feel (9)

septem: seven (14)

septendecim: seventeen (14)

septimus, -a, -um: seventh (14)

septimus decimus, -a, -um: seventeenth (14)

septuāgēsimus, -a, -um: seventieth (14)

septuāgintā: seventy (14)

sequor, sequī, secūtus sum: follow, accompany, attend, yield, aim at (21)

sermō, -ōnis, m: conversation, discourse (7)

servō, -āre, -āvī, -ātus: observe, watch over, keep, protect (20)

servus, -ī, m: slave (9)

seu: whether, or if (31)

sex: six (14)

sexāgēsimus, -a, -um: sixtieth (14)

sexāgintā: sixty (14)

sextus, -a, -um: sixth (14)

sextus decimus, -a, -um: sixteenth (14)

sī: if (6)

sīc: thus, in this manner (6)

sīcut: as, just as (17)

sīdus, sīderis, n: star, constellation, planet (16)

signum, -ī, n: sign, standard, mark (7)

silva, -ae, f: woods, forest (10)

similis, -e (+ dative): like, similar (6)

simul: at once, at the same time (24)

sine (+ ablative): without (6)

singulī, -ae, -a (plural): each, one by one, one each (33)

singulus, -a, -um: single, separate, one at a time (19)

sinō, -ere, sīvī, situs: allow, leave; place, lay down, bury (18)

sinus, -ūs, m: bend, curve, fold, bay; lap, bosom, embrace (10)

sīve . . . sīve: whether . . . or (23)

socius, -iī, m: ally, follower (30)

sōl, sōlis, m: the sun (7)

soleō, -ēre, solitus sum: be accustomed (21)

solum, -ī, n: land, soil (10)

sōlus, -a, -um: alone, only (12)

solvō, -ere, solvī, solūtus: break, weaken, loosen, relax (17)

somnus, -ī, m: sleep (23)

sonō, -āre, -āvī, -ātus: resound, make a sound (26)

soror, sorōris, f: sister (3)

sors, sortis (-ium), f: lot, chance, oracular response (36)

spatium, -iī, n: space (10)

speciēs, speciēī, f: appearance, kind, type (17)

spectāculum, -ī, n: spectacle, performance, show (14)

spectō, -āre, -āvī, -ātus: observe, watch (12)

spēs, spēī, f: hope (31)

spīritus, -ūs, m: breath, spirit, soul (20)

statim: immediately (21)

statuō, -ere, -uī, -ūtus: establish, settle, decide (32)

stella, -ae, f: star (16)

stō, stāre, stetī, stātus: stand (29)

studeō, -ēre, -uī (+ dative): strive for, be devoted to, study (35)

studium, -iī, n: pursuit, enthusiasm, zeal (8)

suādeō, -ēre, suāsī, suāsus (+ dative): advise, persuade, urge (30)

suāvis, -e: sweet, agreeable, pleasant (28)

sub (+ ablative): under (8)

subeō, -īre, -īvī or -iī, -itus: approach, undergo, endure (35)

subitō: suddenly (24)

suī, sibi, sē, sē: him-, her-, it-, themselves (12)

sum, esse, fuī, futūrus: be (1)

summus, -a, -um: highest, most distinguished (19)

sūmō, -ere, sumpsī, sumptus: take up, put on (8)

super (+ accusative): above (13)

superī, -ōrum, m (plural): gods (16)

superior, superius: higher (19)

superō, -āre, -āvī, -ātus: overcome, conquer (36)

supersum, -esse, -fuī, -futūrus: remain, abound (26)

superus, -a, -um: high (19)

suprā (+ accusative): above (as adverb: "previously", "above") (6)

suprēmus, -a, -um: highest (19)

surgō, -ere, surrexī, surrectus: rise (28)

suscipiō, -ere, -cēpī, -ceptus: accept, receive, maintain, undertake (19)

sustineō, -ēre, -uī, -tentus: hold back, support, sustain (20)

suus, sua, suum: his/her/its/their own (12)

taceō, -ēre, -uī, -itus: be silent (24)

taedet, -ēre, taeduit/taesum est: it bores, it disgusts (20)

tālis, -e: of such a kind (20)

tālis . . . quālis: such . . . as (25)

tam: so (13)

tam . . . quam: as . . . as (25)

tamen: nevertheless, nonetheless, however, but (2)

tamquam: just as, so as, as it were, so to speak, as if (10)

tandem: finally (11)

tangō, -ere, tetigī, tactus: touch, reach, border on, affect (20)

tantō . . . quantō: the more . . . the more (25)

tantum: only (5)

tantus, -a, -um: so great, so much (5)

tantus . . . quantus: so great . . . as (25)

tardus, -a, -um: slow, sluggish, dull (34)

tectum, -ī, n: roof, building, house (13)

tegō, -ere, texī, tectus: cover, hide (22)

tellus, tellūris, f: earth (32)

tēlum, -ī, n: missile, dart, javelin, spear (19)

temperiēs, temperiēī, f: proper mixture, mildness (10)

tempestās, -ātis, f: period of time, season; bad weather, storm (16)

templum, -ī, n: temple (8)

tempus, temporis, n: time (**brevī tempore**: soon); (plural) temples (of head) (7)

tendō, -ere, tetendī, tentus: stretch, hasten, direct (31)

tenebrae, -ārum, f (plural): darkness, gloom (33)

teneō, -ēre, tenuī, tentus: hold, maintain, detain (2)

tener, tenera, tenerum: delicate, tender, soft (4)

ter: three times (14)

tergum, -ī, n: back (33)

terra, -ae, f: land (6)

terreō, -ēre, -uī: frighten, terrify (24)

terror, -ōris, m: dread, terror (32)

tertius, -a, -um: third (14)

tertius decimus, -a, -um: thirteenth (14)

testis, -is (-ium), m/f: witness (29)

timeō, -ēre, -uī: fear, dread (17)

timor, -ōris, m: fear, dread (32)

tollō, -ere, sustulī, sublātus: lift up (25)

tot: so many (10)

tot ... quot: so much/as many ... as (25)

totiens ... quotiens: so often ... as (25)

tōtus, -a, -um: all, entire, complete (7)

trādō, -ere, trādidī, trāditus: hand over, yield (9)

trahō, -ere, traxī, tractus: draw, drag, derive, prolong (29)

trans (+ accusative): across (11)

transeō, -īre, -īvī or -iī, -itus: cross (30)

transferō, -ferre, -tulī, -lātus: transfer, carry over (34)

transgredior, -gredī, transgressus sum: cross over, pass over to (21)

tredecim: thirteen (14)

trēs, tria: three (14)

tribūnus, -ī, m: tribune, representative (30)

trīcēsimus, -a, -um: thirtieth (14)

trīgintā: thirty (14)

tristis, -e: sad, gloomy (24)

tū: you (singular) (12)

tum: then (15)

tunc: then, at that time (8)

turba, -ae, f: crowd (23)

turbō, -āre, -āvī, -ātus: disturb, throw into confusion (24)

turpis, -e: disgraceful, shameful, ugly (15)

tūs, tūris, n: incense, frankincense (36)

tūtus, -a, -um: safe, protected, secure (19)

tuus, -a, -um: your (singular) (2)

ubi: where, when (13)

ubique: everywhere (28)

ulciscor, -ī, ultus sum: avenge, take vengeance, punish (21)

ullus, -a, -um: any (18)

ultimus, -a, -um: farthest, most distant, highest, greatest (36)

ultrā (+ accusative): on the other side; beyond, farther (as an adverb) (22)

umbra, -ae, f: shade, shadow (13)

umquam: ever (26)

ūnā: together (with) (30)

unda, -ae, f: water, stream, wave (2)

unde: from where, whence (19)

undecim: eleven (14)

undecimus, -a, -um: eleventh (14)

undēvīcēsimus, -a, -um: nineteenth (14)

undēvīgintī: nineteen (14)

undique: from all sides, on all sides (7)

ūnus, -a, -um: one, only, alone (ūnā: at the same time) (8)

urbs, urbis (-ium), f: city (3)

usque: continuously, all the way (23)

ūsus, -ūs, m: practice, skill, exercise, use, need (19)

ut/utī: as, like (with indicative verbs); so that (with subjunctive verbs); how (28)

uterque, utraque, utrumque: each (of two), both (16)

ūtilis, -e: useful, advantageous, helpful (33)

utinam: would that (26)

ūtor, -ī, ūsus sum (+ ablative): use (21)

utrum . . . an: whether . . . or (15)

uxor, uxōris, f: wife (3)

vacuus, -a, -um: empty, idle (28)

vagus, -a, -um: wandering, roving (32)

valeō, -ēre, -uī: be strong, be able, fare well, prevail (20)

valētūdō, valētūdinis, f: health, soundness (33)

vallum, -ī, n: wall, entrenchment (32)

varius, -a, -um: varied, different (31)

-ve: or (28)

vehō, -ere, vexī, vectus: convey, carry (35)

vel: or, for instance (7)

vel . . . vel: either . . . or (7)

velut: just as, just like (26)

vēnātiō, -iōnis, f: staged hunt (14)

venēnum, -ī, n: poison (33)

venetus, -a, -um: blue (14)

veniō, -īre, vēnī, ventus: come (5)

ventus, -ī, m: wind (16)

verbum, -ī, n: word (4)

vereor, -ērī, veritus sum: revere, respect, fear, dread (32)

vērō: in fact, certainly, without doubt (7)

vertō, -ere, vertī, versus: turn, destroy (23)

vērus, -a, -um: true (11)

vester, vestra, vestrum: your (plural) (2)

vestīgium, -iī, n: track, trace, mark (20)

vestis, -is (-ium), f: garment, covering (36)

vetō, -āre, vetuī, vetitus: forbid (32)

vetus (veteris): old, ancient (17)

via, viae, f: path, road, street (8)

vīcēsimus, -a, -um: twentieth (14)

viciens: twenty times (14)

vīcīnus, -a, -um: neighboring, near (16)

victor, -ōris, m: conqueror, winner (12)

victōria, -iae, f: victory (29)

videō, -ēre, vīdī, vīsus: see, look at, watch (1)

vīgintī: twenty (14)

villa, -ae, f: country house, estate (13)

vincō, -ere, vīcī, victus: conquer (12)

vīnum, -ī, n: wine (2)

vir, virī, m: man, husband (2)

virgō, virginis, f: maiden, virgin (4)

virtūs, -ūtis, f: valor, manliness, virtue (6)

vīs, vīris (-ium), f: force, strength, power (9)

vīta, -ae, f: life (2)

vitium, -iī, n: fault, vice (17)

vīvō, -ere, vixī, victus: live, be alive (6)

vix: scarcely, hardly (12)

vocō, -āre, -āvī, -ātus: call, summon (3)

volō, velle, voluī: wish (11)

voluptās, -ātis, f: pleasure, enjoyment (22)

vōs: you (plural) (12)

vōtum, -ī, n: vow, solemn promise (25)

vox, vōcis, f: voice (6)

vulgus, -ī, n: the people, the public, the crowd (21)

vulnus, vulneris, n: wound (14)

vultus, -ūs, m: face, appearance (22)

xystus, -ī, m: open colonnade, walk planted with trees, promenade (13)

Glossary of Required Vocabulary: English to Latin

abandon: **relinquō** (2), **dēserō** (26)

above: **super** (13), **suprā** (6)

absent (be): **absum** (25)

accept: **accipiō** (7)

accompany: **sequor** (21), **prōsequor** (21)

accursed: **sacer** (4)

accustomed (be): **soleō** (21)

across: **trans** (11)

act: **agō** (3)

add: **addō** (27)

advise: **suādeō** (30), **censeō** (36)

affect: **afficiō** (29)

after: **post** (8), **postquam** (20)

afterward: **posteā** (18)

again: **iterum** (19)

against, opposite: **contrā** (+ accusative) (adv. and prep.) (34)

against: **in** (2), **ob** (13), **adversus** (25)

age: **aetās** (26), **aevum** (34)

agree: **constō** (32)

aim: **intendō** (28)

air: **āēr** (16)

all: **omnis** (3), **tōtus** (7), **cunctus** (27)

allow: **sinō** (18)

ally: **socius** (30)

almost: **ferē** (18), **p(a)ene** (29)

alone: **sōlus** (12)

already: **iam** (5)

also: **quoque** (6)

altar: **āra** (8)

although: **cum** (11), **licet** (29), **quamquam** (26), **quamvīs** (19)

always: **semper** (19)

among: **apud** (13)

amphitheater: **amphitheātrum** (14)

ancestor: **maiōr** (20)

and: **et** (1), **-que** (2)

and also: **atque** (4)

and in addition: **ac** (5)

and not: **neque** (6)

and . . . not: **nec** (2)

anger: **īra** (16)

angry: **īrātus** (29); become angry: **īrascor** (33)

animal: **animal** (7)

announce: **nuntiō** (24)

another: **alius** (6)

answer: **respondeō** (9), **rescrībō** (35)

any (single) person, anyone at all: **quisquam, quicquam/quidquam** (18) any: **ullus** (18)

apartment (block): **insula** (10)

appearance: **faciēs** (22)

approach: **accēdō** (28), **adeō** (30),
   subeō (35)

approve: **probō** (34)

approximately: **circiter** (10)

arch: **arcus** (17)

army: **exercitus** (18)

army in marching order: **agmen** (29)

around: **circā** (15), **circum** (31)

arrange: **compōnō** (27)

arrive at: **perveniō** (17)

as if: **quasi** (18)

as, like (with indicative verbs): **ut/uti** (28)

as . . . as: **tam . . . quam** (25)

as yet, still, but also: **etiam** (6)

ash: **cinis** (33)

ask: **rogō** (3)

at the same time: **ūnā** (8), **simul** (24)

attack: **impetus** (23)

authority: **auctōritās** (18)

avenge: **ulciscor** (21)

await, dread: **ex(s)pectō** (32)

back: **rursus, rursum** (9)

back: **tergum** (33)

bad, evil: **malus** (2)

bad weather: **tempestās** (16)

badly: **malē** (19)

band or force (of men): **manus** (10)

band: **agmen** (29)

base: **sēdēs** (21)

battle: **proelium** (7)

battle line: **aciēs** (18)

bay: **sinus** (10)

be: **sum, esse, fuī, futūrus** (1)

be in: **insum** (34)

be in charge: **praesum** (34)

bear: **pariō** (24), **gignō** (24)

beast: **bestia** (14), **bēlua** (19)

beautiful: **amoenus** (10)

beauty: **forma** (8)

because: **quia** (11)

because of: **propter** (12)

become: **fiō** (20)

bed: **lectus** (13)

before: **ante** (8), **priusquam** (30)

beg: **orō** (30)

begin: **incipiō** (8), **coepī** (20)

beginning: **initium** (18)

behind: **post** (8)

behold!: **ecce** (11)

believe: **crēdō** (6)

belonging to the household: **familiāris** (9)

best: **optimus** (19)

bestow: **dōnō** (27)

betray: **prōdō** (27)

better: **melius** (19)

between: **inter** (8)

beware: **caveō** (13)

beyond: **extrā** (17), **praeter** (20), **ultrā** (22)

big: **magnus** (2), **grandis** (12)

bigger: **māior** (19)

biggest: **maximus** (19)

bird: **avis** (19)

bitter: **ācer** (19)

black: **niger** (34)

blame: **culpa** (17)

blood: **sanguis** (16), **cruor** (28)

blue: **venetus** (14)

body: **corpus** (3)

bold: **audax** (20)

bone: **os** (32)

book: **liber** (17)

born (be): **nascor** (24)

both: **ambō** (14), **uterque** (16)

both . . . and: **et . . . et** (1), **-que . . . -que** (2)

boundary: **fīnis** (9)

bow: **arcus** (17)

boy: **puer** (4)

branch: **rāmus** (36)

brave: **fortis** (19)

break: **solvō** (17)

breast: **pectus, -oris**, n (19)

breath: **spīritus** (20)

breathing: **adflātus** (10)

bright: **praeclārus** (28), **clārus** (29)

Britain: **Britannia** (29)

brother: **frāter** (3)

but: **sed** (2), **at** (8)

by far: **multō** (12), **longē** (19)

by no means: **haud** (22)

call: **vocō** (3), **appellō** (8)

camp: **castra** (7)

can: **possum** (11)

capture: **capiō** (1)

care: **cūra** (23)

care for: **cūrō** (24)

carry: **ferō** (11)

cause: **causa** (9)

cavalry: **equitātus** (32)

celebrate: **celebrō** (23)

certain, sure: **certus** (2)

certain: **quīdam** (15)

certainly: **quidem** (7), **vērō** (7), **maximē** (9), **quippe** (29)

chance: **sors** (36)

change: **mūtō** (18)

character: **nātūra** (8), **ingenium** (26)

charge: **crīmen** (20)

chariot: **currus** (18)

charioteer: **agitātor** (14)

chaste: **castus** (26)

chastity: **castitās** (5)

cheat: **fallō** (16)

cherish: **dīligō** (15)

children: **līberī** (8)

choose: **legō** (6), **ēligō** (34)

circle: **orbis** (16)

circumstance: **rēs, reī**, f (10)

citadel: **arx** (35)

citizen: **cīvis** (9)

city: **urbs** (3)

clearly: **plānē** (12)

clever: **doctus** (4)

close: **claudō** (13)

closest: **proximus** (13)

clouds: **nūbila** (16)

cohort: **cohors** (32)

collect: **conferō** (26), **compōnō** (27), **conligō** (32)

color: **color** (6)

column: **agmen** (29)

come: **veniō** (5)

command: **imperō** (6)

companion: **comes, -itis**, m/f (29)

complain: **queror** (26)

complete: **efficiō** (9), **conficiō** (32)

conceal: **condō** (22)

concerning: **dē** (7)

condemn: **condemnō** (5), **damnō** (29)

confess: **fateor** (32), **confiteor** (35)

conquer: **vincō** (12), **superō** (36)

consider: **habeō** (3), **pōnō** (15)

conspiracy: **coniūrātiō** (30)

consul: **consul** (23)

consult: **consulō** (35)

continuous: **perpetuus** (30)

continuously: **usque** (23)

conversation: **sermō** (7)

convey: **vehō** (35)

convince: **persuādeō** (30)

countryside: **rūs** (7)

course: **cursus** (22)

cover: **tegō** (22)

create: **creō** (25)

crime: **scelus** (3), **crīmen** (20)

crops: **frux** (10)

cross: **transeō** (30)

cross over: **transgredior** (21)

crowd: **vulgus** (21), **turba** (23)

cultivate: **colō** (5)

custom: **mōs, mōris,** m (10)

danger: **perīculum** (7)

dare: **audeō** (21)

darkness: **tenebrae** (33)

daughter: **fīlia** (5)

day: **diēs** (10)

dear: **cārus** (9)

death: **mors** (6)

deceit: **dolus** (28)

deceive: **fallō** (16)

deceptive: **falsus** (24)

decide: **constituō** (7), **dēcernō** (25), **instituō** (32), **statuō** (32)

decision: **iūdicium** (35)

declare: **indīcō** (18), **prōnuntiō** (30)

defense: **praesidium** (4)

delay: **mora** (33)

delicate: **tener** (4), **lēvis** (31)

demand: **exigō** (17), **petō** (17), **poscō** (20), **postulō** (30)

deny: **negō** (11)

depart: **proficiscor** (21), **discēdō** (30)

descendants: **posterī** (12)

deserve: **mereō** (26)

desire: **cupiō** (12)

desire: **lībidō** (33), **cupīdō** (34)

despise: **contemnō** (18)

destroy: **corrumpō** (26)

die: **morior** (24)

difficult: **difficilis** (26)

discern: **cernō** (22)

discover: **exigō** (17)

disgraceful: **turpis** (15)

display: **ostendō** (32), **prōpōnō** (35)

dissimilar: **dissimilis** (19)

disturb: **turbō** (24)

divine: **dīvus** (18)

divine spirit: **nūmen** (25)

do: **faciō** (2), **agō** (3)

dog: **canis** (13)

door: **iānua, -ae,** f (26)

doubtful: **dubius** (31)

drag: **trahō** (29)

dread: **terror** (32)

drive: **agō** (3)

dutiful: **pius** (19)

duty: **officium** (7), **mūnus** (14)

dwell: **habitō** (1)

each (of two): **uterque** (16)

each: **quisque, quaeque, quidque** (20)

each: **singulī** (33)

ear: **auris** (22)

earth: **tellus** (32)

easy: **facilis** (19)

eat: **cēnō** (13)

edge: **aciēs** (18)

either . . . or: **aut . . . aut** (4), **vel . . . vel** (7)

embrace: **sinus** (10)

emperor: **princeps** (14), **imperātor** (17)

empty: **vacuus** (28)

encourage: **hortor** (22), **cohortor** (30)

endure: **gerō** (3), **ferō** (11), **patior** (22)

enemy: **hostis** (7)

enough: **satis** or **sat** (25)

enter: **intrō** (12), **ingredior** (21)

enthusiasm: **studium** (8)

entire: **omnis** (3)

entrance: **līmen** (28)

entrenchment: **vallum** (32)

entrust: **commendō** (6), **committō** (35)

envoy: **legātus** (23)

epistle: **litterae** (18)

equal: **aequus** (14), **pār** (14)

establish: **constituō** (7), **statuō** (32)

estate: **villa** (13)

eternal: **aeternus** (26)

ever: **umquam** (26)

everywhere: **ubique** (28)

evidently: **scīlicet** (28)

example: **exemplum** (27)

excel: **praestō** (32)

exercise: **usus** (19), **exercitātiō** (33)

explain: **ēdō** (24)

expose: **prōpōnō** (35)

extraordinary: **ēgregius** (36), **mīrābilis** (36)

eye: **oculus** (13), **lūmen** (36)

face: **ōs** (23), **vultus** (22)

fail: **dēficiō** (25)

faith: **fidēs** (20)

fall: **cadō** (13)

fall: **cāsus** (31)

family: **gens** (10)

farthest: **ultimus** (36)

fate: **fātum** (24)

father: **pater** (3), **genitor** (36)

fatherland: **patria** (2)

faultless: **pūrus** (36)

favor: **grātia** (20)

favorable: **secundus** (26)

fear: **metuō** (16), **timeō** (17), **vereor** (32), **metus** (18), **timor** (32)

feel: **sentiō** (9)

feeling: **sensus** (31)

fever: **febris** (33)

few: **paucī** (16)

field: **ager** (2), **arvum** (22), **campus** (23)

fierce: **saevus** (23)

fight: **pugnō** (14)

fill in: **impleō** (19)

finally: **tandem** (11), **dēnique** (25)

find: **inveniō** (17)

fire: **ignis** (3)

first: **prīmum, prīmō** (13), **prīmus** (14)

fishpond: **piscīna** (17)

fitting (for): **aptus** (36)

flame: **flamma** (20)

flee: **fugiō** (1)

fleet: **classis** (14)

flock: **pecus** (32)

flow: **fluō** (29)

flower: **flōs** (26)

fold: **sinus** (10)

follow: **sequor** (21), follow: **prōsequor** (21), **consequor** (21)

food: **cibus** (33)

foot: **pēs** (24)

foot soldier: **pēs** (24)

for a long time: **diū** (4)

for the sake of: **causā** (5), **grātiā** (5)

forbid: **vetō** (32)

force: **cōgō** (30)

force: **vīs** (9)

forehead: **frons** (5)

foreign: **aliēnus** (33)

forest: **silva** (10)

forget: **oblīviscor** (21)

form: **faciēs** (22)

formerly: **quondam** (18)

fortress: **castrum** (15)

fortunate: **beātus** (23)

fortune: **fortūna** (6)

found: **condō** (22)

founder: **auctor** (18)

fountain: **fons** (17)

free: **līber** (19)

freedman: **lībertus** (12), **lībertinus** (35)

freedwoman: **līberta** (12)

friend: **amīcus, amīca** (6)

friendly: **amīcus** (6)

frighten: **terreō** (24)

from: **ā/ab** (3), **ē/ex** (5)

from a distance: **procul** (23)

from all sides: **undique** (7)

from here: **hinc** (16)

from then: **inde** (9)

from there: **inde** (9)

from where: **unde** (19)

fruitful: **fertilis** (10)

full: **plēnus** (27)

funeral: **fūnus** (25)

garment: **vestis** (36)

gate: **porta** (8)

general: **dux** (5), **imperātor** (17)

generally: **plērumque** (20)

generation: **aetās** (26)

gift: **mūnus** (14), **dōnum** (20)

gird: **cingō** (22)

girl: **puella** (2)

give: **dō** (1)

give thanks: **grātiās agere** (20)

glad: **laetus** (13)

gladiator: **gladiātor** (14)

glory: **glōria** (9)

go: **eō** (11)

go away: **abeō** (15)

go out: **exeō** (30)

god: **deus** (4)

gods: **superī** (16)

gods of the home: **penātēs** (13)

golden: **aureus** (18)

good: **bonus** (2)

goods: **bona** (2)

graceful: **gracilis** (19)

grain: **frūmentum** (32)

grandson: **nepōs** (14)

great: **magnus** (2)

greatly: **magnopere** (19)

green: **prasinus** (14)

grief: **dolor** (5)

grieve: **doleō** (27)

grove: **nemus** (16)

grow: **crēscō** (12)

guest: **hospes** (34)

guide: **regō** (19)

hair: **coma** (26)

hand: **manus** (10)

hand over: **trādō** (9), **dēferō** (18)

happy: **laetus** (13)

hard: **dūrus** (22)

hardly: **vix** (12)

hasten: **tendō** (31)

hate: **ōdī** (27)

hatred: **odium** (27)

have: **habeō** (3)

he, she, it; this, that: **is, ea, id** (12)

he/she said: **inquit** (9), **ait** (25)

head: **caput** (3)

health: **valētūdō** (33)

healthy: **sānus** (28)

hear: **audiō** (1)

heart: **cor** (29)

heavy: **gravis** (4)

heir: **hēres** (35)

help: **auxilium** (17)

here: **em** (15), **hīc** (1), **hūc** (19)

hesitate: **dubitō** (28)

hide: **tegō** (22)

high: **altus** (8), **superus** (19)

higher: **superior** (19)

highest: **summus** (19), **suprēmus** (19)

hill: **collis** (10)

himself, herself, itself, themselves: **ipse, ipsa, ipsum** (12)

hinder: **prohibeō** (23)

his/her/its/their own: **suus** (12)

hold: **teneō** (2)

hold up: **sustineō** (20)

holy: **sacer** (4), **sanctus** (4)

home: **sēdēs** (21)

honor: **decus** (4), **honor** (13)

hope: **spēs** (31)

horn: **cornū** (10)

horse: **equus** (7)

horseman: **eques** (7)

host: **hospes** (34)

hostile: **inimīcus** (26)

hour: **hōra** (29)

house: **aedēs** (18), **domus** (13)

household: **familia** (15)

household master: **dominus** (15)

how: **quā** (23)

how: **quō modō, quōmodō** (31), **utī** (31)

how much: **quantus** (25)

however: **cēterum** (16)

huge: **ingens** (13)

human: **homo** (7), **hūmānus** (7), **mortālis** (25)

humble: **humilis** (19)

hunger: **famēs** (31)

hurry: **properō** (25)

hurt: **noceō** (17), **laedō** (31)

hurtful: **noxius** (10)

husband: **vir** (2), **marītus** (28)

I: **ego** (12)

if: **sī** (6)

(be) ignorant: **nesciō** (33)

illness: **morbus** (33)

image: **imāgō, -inis**, f (18)

immediately: **statim** (21), **prōtinus** (28)

in: **in** (2)

in accord with divine law: **fās** (20)

in place of: **prō** (5)

in vain: **frustrā** (22)

incense: **tūs** (36)

incite: **impellō** (30)

indeed: **nam, namque** (5), **enim** (6)

informer: **dēlātor** (27)

injury: **iniūria** (19)

inquire: **poscō** (20)

into: **in** (2)

iron: **ferrum** (27)

island: **insula** (10)

it causes regret: **paenitet** (20)

it disgusts: **taedet** (20)

it displeases: **piget** (20)

it distresses: **miseret** (20)

it happens: **accidit** (20)

it is agreed: **constat** (20)

it is fitting: **oportet** (20)

it is necessary: **necesse est** (20)

it is permitted: **licet** (20)

it is proper: **decet** (20)

it is useful: **prōdest** (20)

it matters: **refert** (20)

it pleases: **placet** (20), **libet** (20)

it shames: **pudet** (20)

journey: **iter** (7)

just: **iustus** (17)

just as: **tamquam** (10), **sīcut** (17), **velut** (26)

just now: **modo** (4)

keep: **servō** (20)

kill: **caedō** (18), **interficiō** (32)

kind: **genus** (6), **speciēs, -ēī**, f (17)

kindness: **beneficium** (25)

king: **rex** (3)

kingdom: **regnum** (3)

know: **sciō** (1), **nōscō** (16)

lack: **careō** (33)

lake: **lacus** (10)

land: **terra** (6)

language: **lingua** (4)

large: **grandis** (12)

last: **extrēmus** (14)

laugh: **rīdeō** (15)

law: **lex** (9), **iūs** (35)

lead: **dūcō** (13), **addūcō** (35)

lead out: **ēdūcō** (36)

leader: **dux** (5), **princeps** (14)

learn: **discō** (19)

least: **minimē** (19)

leave: **relinquō** (2)

legal case: **causa** (9)

legion: **legiō** (7)

less: **minus** (19)

lest: **nē** (26)

letter: **epistula** (9), **littera** (18)

lie, rest on: **iaceō** (16)

lie hidden: **lateō** (31)

lie open: **pateō** (26)

life: **vīta** (2)

lifetime: **aetās** (26), **aevum** (34)

lift up: **tollō** (25)

light: **levis** (6)

light: **lux** (12), **lūmen** (36)

little: **parum** (19), **paulō**, **paulum** (24)

little book: **libellus** (4)

live: **vīvō** (6)

long: **longus** (2)

look back: **respiciō** (31)

loosen: **solvō** (17)

lord: **dominus** (15)

lose: **āmittō** (17), **dīmittō** (30)

love: **amō** (1)

love: **amor** (4)

low: **inferus** (29)

lowest: **īmus** (22)

lucky: **fēlix** (34)

maintain: **teneō** (2)

make: **faciō** (2)

man: **vir** (2)

manage: **gerō** (3)

many: **multus** (5)

marketplace: **forum** (27)

marvel (at): **mīror** (21)

matter: **rēs**, **reī**, f (10)

meal: **mensa** (31)

meanwhile: **interim** (15)

meet with: **conveniō** (28)

memorial: **monumentum** (35)

memory: **memoria** (7)

method: **modus** (4)

middle: **medius** (8)

mildness: **temperiēs** (10)

mile: **mille passūs** (10)

milestone: **milliārium** (17)

mind: **animus** (2), **mens** (8)

mine: **meus** (2)

miserable: **miser** (2)

misfortune: **cāsus** (31)

missile: **tēlum** (19)

mistress: **domina** (23)

mix: **misceō** (22)

money: **pecūnia** (9)

moon: **lūna** (16)

more: **magis** (17), **plūs** (18, 19)

moreover: **autem** (9)

most: **plūrimē** (19), **plūrimus** (19)

mother: **māter** (3)

mountain: **mons** (10)

mouth: **ōs** (23)

move: **moveō** (4)

much: **multum** (19)

multitude: **multitūdo** (5)

murmur: **murmur** (22)

Muse: **Mūsa** (4)

name: **nōmen** (3)

nature: **nātūra** (8)

naval: **nāvālis** (14)

near: **prope** (30)

nearly: **ferē** (18), **p(a)ene** (29)

neck: **collum** (36)

need: **necessitās** (29)

neighboring: **vīcīnus** (16)

neither . . . nor: **neque . . . neque** (6)

never: **numquam** (15)

nevertheless: **tamen** (2)

new: **novus** (4)

next: **deinde** or **dein** (3)

next: **posterus** (27)

night: **nox** (8)

no: **nullus** (13)

no longer: **nōn iam** (5)

no one: **nēmō** (9)

noble: **nōbilis** (10)

nocturnal: **nocturnus** (32)

not: **nōn** (1)

not only . . . but also: **cum . . . tum** (25),
   nōn sōlum . . . sed etiam (7), **nōn
   sōlum . . . vērum etiam** (9)

not yet: **nōndum** (33)

notable: **īnsignis** (31)

nothing: **nihil** (1)

nourish: **alō** (31)

now: **nunc** (4), **iam** (5)

number: **numerus** (7)

obligation: **religiō** (36)

observe: **spectō** (12), **servō** (20)

ocean: **ōceanus** (10)

offer: **offerō** (24), **praestō** (32)

often: **saepe** (7)

old: **vetus** (17), **antīquus** (18)

old man: **senex** (34)

on: **in** (2)

on all sides: **undique** (7)

on behalf of: **prō** (5)

once: **ōlim** (21), **quondam** (18),
   semel (24)

one: **ūnus** (8)

one of two: **alter** (10)

one . . . the other: **alter . . . alter** (10)

only, alone: **sōlus** (12), **ūnus** (8)

only, so (much): **tantum** (5)

onto: **in** (2)

opinion: **sententia** (9)

or: **an** (11), **aut** (4), **-ve** (28), **vel** (7)

order: **iubeō** (13)

origin: **genus** (6), **ortus** (10)

other: **alius** (6), **alter** (10), **cēterus** (18)

otherwise: **aliter** (34)

ought to: **dēbeō** (17)

our: **noster** (2)

out of: **ē/ex** (5)

owe: **dēbeō** (17)

ox: **bōs** (24)

pain: **dolor** (5)

painful: **gravis** (4)

parent: **parens** (20)

part: **pars** (5)

passion: **ardor** (21)

pay: **pendō** (30)

peace: **pax** (18)

perhaps: **fortasse** (26), **forsitan** (31)

perceive: **cognoscō** (24)

penalty: **poena** (30)

people: **populus** (3)

perish: **pereō** (23)

physician: **medicus** (24)

pitch camp: **castra pōnere** (15)

place: **locus** (7)

place: **constituō** (7), **pōnō** (15), **instituō** (32)

place upon: **impōnō** (28)

plain: **nūdus** (35)

plan: **consilium** (5)

pleasant: **dulcis** (4)

please: **placeō** (11)

pleasing: **grātus** (19)

pleasure: **voluptās** (22)

plow: **arō** (22)

Pluto: **Dīs** (6)

poem: **carmen** (4)

poet: **poēta** (2)

poison: **venēnum** (33)

poor: **pauper** (26)

possessions: **bona** (2)

power: **imperium** (3), **potestās** (18),
    ops (25)

powerful: **potens** (22)

practice: **exercitātiō** (33), **usus** (19)

praetor: **praetor** (20)

praise: **laudo** (11)

praise: **laus** (25)

prefer: **mālō** (11)

prepare: **parō** (8)

present (be): **adsum** (9)

press: **premō** (4)

pretty: **bellus** (11), **pulcher** (19)

prevail: **valeō, -ēre, -uī** (20)

price: **pretium** (23)

priest(ess): **sacerdōs** (29)

priesthood: **sacerdōtium** (20)

prize: **praemium** (14)

proceed: **pergō** (20), **cēdō** (22),
    prōcēdō (25)

proclaim: **prōdō** (27)

prodigy: **prōdigium** (24)

promenade: **xystus** (13)

promise: **polliceor** (21)

prophesy: **canō** (24)

propose: **dēcernō** (25)

protect: **servō** (20)

provide: **comparō** (28)

provided that: **dummodo** (36)

province: **prōvincia** (21)

provision: **conditiō** (29)

public: **pūblicus** (8)

queen: **rēgīna** (31)

question: **interrogō** (35)

quick: **celer** (19)

race (contest): **cursus** (22)

race (ethnicity): **gens** (10)

rain: **inpluō** (16)

read: **legō** (6)

reasoning: **ratiō** (22)

receive: **recipiō** (16), **concipiō** (34)

red: **russātus** (14)

region: **regiō** (10)

rejoice: **gaudeō** (21), **laetor** (23)

remain: **maneō** (23), **supersum** (26)

remaining: **reliquus** (19)

remedy: **medicāmentum** (33),
    medicīna (33)

remember: **meminī** (20)

remind: **memorō** (31)

remove: **auferō** (35)

report: **referō** (35)

request: **prex** (23)

resound: **sonō** (26)

respectable: **honestus** (23)

rest (the): **cēterus** (18)

retreat: **regredior** (21)

return, come back: **redeō** (16), **referō** (35)

return, give back: **reddō** (15)

reveal: **aperiō** (26)

reward: **praemium** (14), **pretium** (23)

rich: **dīves** (11)

riches, wealth: **dīvitiae** (20)

right: **iūs** (35)

right (hand): **dexter** (27)

rise: **orior** (21), **surgō** (28)

river: **amnis** (10)

road: **via** (8)

rock: **saxum** (16)

Roman: **Rōmānus** (3)

Rome: **Rōma** (4)

roof: **tectum** (13)

row: **ordo** (30)

royal: **rēgius** (31)

ruin: **perdō** (34)

rule: **regō** (19)

rumble: **murmur** (22)

rumor: **fāma** (11)

run: **currō** (22)

sacred: **sanctus** (4)

sacrifice: **immolō** (36)

sad: **tristis** (24)

safe: **tūtus** (19)

same (the): **īdem** (15)

say: **dīcō** (4)

say: **ferō** (11)

scanty: **exiguus** (25)

scatter: **disiiciō** (22)

scattered: **rārus** (31)

sea: **aequor** (22)

sea: **mare** (3), **pontus** (22)

search for: **requīrō** (31)

seashore: **lītus** (19)

season: **tempestās** (16)

seat: **sēdēs** (21)

second, following: **secundus** (14)

second, other: **alter** (10)

see: **videō** (1), **cernō** (22)

seek: **quaerō** (29)

seek again: **repetō** (27)

seize: **occupō** (30)

Senate: **senātus** (18)

senator: **pater** (3)

send: **mittō** (1)

sense of duty: **pietās** (9)

separate: **dīdūcō** (17)

serious: **gravis** (4)

set free (from): **absolvō** (3)

shadow: **umbra** (13)

shape: **fingō** (28)

shape: **forma** (8), **faciēs** (22)

ship: **nāvis** (15)

short: **brevis** (3)

shout: **clāmor** (27)

show: **mūnus** (14), **spectāculum** (14)

shower: **imber** (16)

shrine: **aedēs** (18)

side: **latus** (19)

sign: **signum** (7)

silent (be): **taceō** (24)

similar: **similis** (6)

since: **cum** (11), **quoniam** (19)

sing: **cantō** (4), **canō** (24)

single: **singulus** (19)

sister: **soror** (3)

size: **magnitūdō** (19)

skill: **ars** (13), **usus** (19)

skillful: **dexter** (27)

sky: **caelum** (6)

slaughter: **caedēs** (24)

slave: **servus** (9)

sleep: **dormiō** (12), **somnus** (23)

slow: **tardus** (34)

small: **parvus** (10)

smaller: **minor** (19)

smallest: **minimus** (19)

snatch: **rapiō** (19)

so, then: **tam** (13)

so great: **tantus** (5)

so great . . . as: **tantus . . . quantus** (25)

so many: **tot** (10)

so much . . . as: **tot . . . quot** (25)

so often . . . as: **totiens . . . quotiens** (25)

so that: **ut/utī** (28)

soft: **mollis** (22)

soil: **solum** (10)

soldier: **mīles** (7)

some: **aliqui** (15)

some . . . others: **aliī . . . aliī** (6)

someone: **aliquis** (15)

son: **fīlius** (13), **nātus** (15)

soon: **brevī tempore** (7), **mox** (18)

soul: **animus** (2), **anima** (26)

space: **spatium** (10)

spacious: **amplus** (13)

spare: **parcō** (30)

speak: **adloquor** (21), **loquor** (21)

special: **praecipuus** (33)

speech: **ōrātiō** (25)

spirit: **anima** (26)

spirits of the dead: **mānēs** (6)

spouse: **coniunx** (5)

squander: **effundō** (31)

staged hunt: **vēnātiō** (14)

stand: **stō** (29)

star: **sīdus** (16), **stella** (16)

state: **cīvitās** (9)

step: **passus** (10)

step down, depart for: **dēgredior** (21)

still: **adhūc** (16)

stone: **lapis** (24)

storm: **tempestās** (16)

strange: **aliēnus** (33)

stream: **flūmen** (10), **rīvus** (17)

stretch: **tendō** (31)

strike: **pellō** (32)

study: **studeō** (35)

subject matter: **māteria** (35)

such a kind: **tālis** (20)

such . . . as: **talis . . . qualis** (25)

suddenly: **subitō** (24)

suffer: **gerō** (3), **patior** (22)

summon: **arcessō** (36)

sun: **sōl** (7)

sunny: **aprīcus** (10)

surround: **circumveniō** (32)

sweet: **dulcis** (4), **suāvis** (28)

sword: **gladius** (27)

table: **mensa** (31)

take up: **sūmō** (8)

talent: **ingenium** (26)

teach: **doceō** (1)

team: **factiō** (14)

tear (weeping): **lacrima** (9)

tear away: **ēripiō** (28)

temple: **templum** (8), **aedēs** (18)

temples (of head): **tempora** (7)

than: **quam** (19)

that (of yours), those (of yours): **iste** (15)

that, those: **ille, illa, illud** (15)

the more . . . the more: **tantō . . . quantō** (25), **eō . . . quō** (25)

then: **deinde** or **dein** (3), **tunc** (8), **tum** (15)

there: **ibi** (10), **eō** (29)

there . . . where: **eō . . . quō** (25)

therefore: **ergō** (6), **ideō** (16), **igitur** (21), **itaque** (12)

they said: **aiunt** (25)

thing: **rēs, reī**, f (10)

think: **arbitror** (36), **cōgitō** (9), **dūcō** (13), **existimō** (25), **putō** (5), **reor** (21)

third: **tertius** (14)

this, these: **hīc** (15)

threaten: **immineō** (23)

three times: **ter** (14)

through: **per** (3)

throw: **iaciō** (18)

thus: **sīc** (6), **ita** (7)

thus far: **adeō** (23)

time: **tempus** (7)

tired: **fessus** (21)

today: **hodiē** (11)

together (with): **ūnā** (30)

tomorrow: **crās** (24)

torch: **fax** (24)

touch: **contingō** (13), **tangō** (20)

toward: **ad** (3)

town: **oppidum** (7)

trace: **vestīgium** (20)

transfer: **transferō** (34)

tree: **arbor** (34)

trial: **iūdicium** (35)

tribune: **tribūnus** (30)

troops: **cōpia** (9)

true: **vērus** (11)

truly, thus far: **adeō** (23)

trust: **crēdō** (6)

try: **cōnor** (21)

turn: **vertō** (23)

twin: **geminus** (15)

two: **duo** (14)

two times: **bis** (14)

under: **sub** (8)

understand: **cognoscō** (9), **intellegō** (15)

understanding: **mens** (8)

undertake: **suscipiō** (19)

universal: **commūnis** (30)

unless: **nisi** (11)

unpleasant: **ingrātus** (36)

until: **dōnec** (27)

unwilling (be): **nōlō** (11)

use, need: **usus** (19)

use: **ūtor** (21)

useful: **ūtilis** (33)

varied: **varius** (31)

vice: **vitium** (17)

victory: **victōria** (29)

violation of divine law: **nefās** (32)

virgin: **virgō** (4)

virtue: **virtūs** (6)

virtuous: **sanctus** (25)

voice: **vōx** (6)

vow: **vōtum** (25)

wage war: **bellum gerere** (3)

wall(s): **moenia** (20), **mūrus** (32)

wander: **errō** (22)

wandering: **vagus** (32)

war: **bellum** (3)

warn: **moneō** (32)

water: **aqua** (7)

wave: **unda** (2), **fluctus** (19)

we/us: **nōs** (12)

weaken: **solvō** (17)

weapons: **arma, -ōrum**, n (plural) (3)

wear: **gerō** (3), **habeō** (3)

weary: **aeger, aegra, aegrum** (31)

weight: **pondus** (33)

well: **bene** (5)

what sort/kind as: **quālis** (19)

when: **cum** (11), **ubi** (13), **quandō** (20)

when: **postquam** (20)

where: **ubi** (13), **quā** (23), **quō** (31)

whether: **seu** (31)

whether . . . or: **utrum . . . an** (15),
   sīve . . . sīve (23)

while: **dum** (13)

white: **albus** (14)

who, what: **quī, quae, quod** (16)

who? what?: **quis, quid** (16)

whoever, whatever: **quisquis** (27),
   quīcumque (33)

why: **cūr** (28), **quārē** (31)

wide: **lātus** (23)

wife: **uxor** (3)

wild: **ferus** (36)

wind: **ventus** (16)

window: **fenestra** (23)

wine: **vīnum** (2)

wing: **cornū** (10)

winner: **victor** (12)

wisdom: **sapientia** (25)

wish: **volō** (11)

wish for: **optō** (8)

with: **cum** (3)

withdraw: **dēsciscō** (25), **removeō** (36)

without: **sine** (6)

witness: **testis** (29)

wolf: **lupus** (28)

woman: **fēmina** (2), **mulier** (24)

word: **verbum** (4)

work: **labōrō** (36)

work: **opus** (4), **labor** (10)

world: **mundus** (32), **orbis** (16)

worse: **pēior** (19)

worst: **pessimus** (19)

worthy: **dignus** (17)

wound: **vulnus** (14)

write: **scrībō** (5)

year: **annus** (2)

yield: **concēdō** (35)

yoke: **iugum** (23)

you: **tū** (singular), **vōs** (plural) (12)

your: **tuus** (singular), **vester** (plural) (2)

youth: **iuvenis** (5)

Extra Glossary of
High Frequency Vocabulary

MASTERY OF THE most common vocabulary is a tremendous asset in reading unfamiliar authors and unfamiliar works of literature. In generating the required vocabulary lists for each lesson, we worked very closely with the Dickinson College Latin Core Vocabulary List (*http://dcc.dickinson.edu/latin-vocabulary-list*), which distills Latin vocabulary into a manageable "core vocabulary" of the one thousand words that appear most frequently in standard Latin texts. Our aim was to develop Required Vocabulary lists of a reasonable length (about 25 to 30 words per lesson) that privileged the "high-frequency" words appearing in the reading selections.

Below we offer a list of the 155 "high frequency" words that did not make it into the Required Vocabulary lists. You should find many of these words familiar, since quite a few of them have appeared in passages throughout the *Primer*.

LIST 1 (HIGH-FREQUENCY WORDS: 201–500)

adversus, -a, -um: facing, opposed, unfavorable

afferō, -ferre, attulī, allātus: bring to

amīcitia, -iae, f: friendship

aurum, -ī, n: gold

dēsum, -esse, -fuī: be lacking

excipiō, -ere, -cēpī, -ceptus: take out

exerceō, -ēre, -cuī, -itus: train, exercise, carry on

frangō, -ere, frēgī, frāctus: break, shatter

fuga, -ae, f: flight, route

iūdicō, -āre, -āvī, -ātus: judge, decide

iuvō, -āre, iūvī, iūtus: help, assist, please, delight

lībertās, -ātis, f: freedom

plēbs, -is, f: the common people

prior, -ius: earlier, preceding

prōsum, prōdesse, prōfuī (+ dative): be of use, do good, help

salūs, -ūtis, f: health, safety

sapiens (-entis): wise

tentō, -āre, -āvī, -ātus: try, test

LIST 2 (COMMON WORDS: 501–1000)

adhibeō, -ēre, -uī, -itus: apply

adveniō, -īre, -vēnī, -ventus: come to, arrive at

advertō, -ere, -ī, -versus: turn towards

aes, aeris, n: copper, bronze

aethēr, aetheris, n: pure, upper air, ether, heaven, sky

agitō, -āre, -āvī, -ātus: drive

aliquandō: at some time, at length

antequam: before

aperiō, -īre, -uī, apertus: open

ardeō, -ēre, arsī, arsus: blaze, glow, be eager

argentum, -ī, n: silver, money

ascendō, -ere, -scendī, -scēnsus: climb up, ascend

aspiciō, -ere, -spēxī, -spectus: look to/at, behold

astrum, -ī, n: star, constellation

augeō, -ēre, auxī, auctus: increase

aura, -ae, f: breeze

barbarus, -ī, m: foreigner, barbarian

caecus, -a, -um: blind, unseeing, dark, obscure

caelestis, -e: from or of heaven; **caelestēs**: the gods

candidus, -a, -um: white, fair

certō, -āre, -āvī, -ātus: decide by contest, fight, compete

citō: swiftly

cītus, -a, -um: swift

colligō, -ere, -lēgī, -lēctus: gather together, collect

consistō, -sistere, -stitī (+ ablative): take position, consist

consuētūdō, -inis, f: custom, habit

consūmō, -ere, -sūmpsī, -sūmptus: use up, consume

contineō, -tinēre, -tinuī, -tentus: contain, restrain

convertō, -ere, -vertī, -versus: turn about, turn, change

convīvium, -iī, n: banquet, feast

cūstōs, cūstōdis, m: guardian

damnum, -ī, n: damage, injury

dēdūcō, -ere, -dūxī, -ductus: launch, lead away

dēfendō, -ere, -fendī, -fēnsus: defend, ward off

dēscendō, -ere, -scendi -scēnsus: climb down, descend

dēsīderō, -āre, -āvī, -ātus: long for, desire, greatly

dēsinō, -ere, -sīvī, -situs: leave off, cease

differō, -ferre, distulī, dīlātus: scatter, publish, divulge, differ, defer, postpone

dīgnitās, -ātis, f: worth, reputation, honor

dīsciplīna, -ae, f: training, instruction, learning, discipline

dīversus, -a, -um: different, diverse

dīvidō, -ere, dīvīsī, dīvīsus: divide, separate

ēdīcō, -ere, -dīxī, -dictus: declare

ēgredior, -ī, ēgressus sum (+ ablative): stride out, depart, disembark

experior, -īrī, expertus sum: try thoroughly, test, experience

exsilium, -iī, n: exile, banishment

fabula, -ae, f: account, tale, story

facinus, facinoris, n: deed, crime

factum, -ī, n: deed, accomplishment

fidēlis, -e: faithful

fleō, flēre, flēvī, flētus: weep

foedus, -a, -um: foul

for, fārī, fātus sum: report, say

fors, fortis, f: chance

forte: by chance

frequens (-entis): in large numbers, often

fructus, -ūs, m: fruit, crops, enjoyment, delight

fruor, fruī, frūctus sum (+ ablative): enjoy

fugō, -āre, -āvī, -ātus: put to flight

fundō, -ere, fūdī, fūsus: pour, scatter

furor, -ōris, m: rage, fury

gaudium, -iī, n: delight, joy, pleasure

gladius, -iī, m: sword

gradus, -ūs, m: step, pace, grade, rank

hiems, hiemis, f: winter

humus, -ī, f: ground; **humī**: on the ground

ictus, -ūs, m: blow, stroke

illīc: at that place, there

illinc: from that place

illūc: to that place

incidō, -ere, incidī: fall upon, fall into, happen

inferō, -ferre, intulī, illātus: bring upon, against; **bellum inferre**: to attack in war

integer, -gra, -grum: untouched, fresh, complete, whole

intersum, -esse, -fuī (+ genitive): be between, it is in the interest of

intrā (+ accusative): within

invidia, -iae, f: envy, jealousy, hatred

item: likewise

iūdex, iūdicis, m: judge, juror

iungō, -ere, iūnxī, iūnctus: join

iūrō, -āre, -āvī, -ātus: take an oath, swear; **iūs iūrandum**: oath

maestus, -a, -um: sad, sorrowful, depressing

magister, magistrī, m: master, chief

membrum, -ī, m: limb, member of the body

moror, -ārī, morātus sum: delay

narrō, -āre, -āvī, -ātus: relate, recount

negōtium, -iī, n: business

nimius, -a, -um: too much, excessive

nimis or **nimium**: excessively

nōtus, -a, -um: well-known

num: interrogative particle implying negative answer

nuntius, -iī, m: messenger, news

occīdō, -ere, -cīdī, -cīsus: kill, cut down

occurrō, -ere, -cucurrī, -cursus: run to meet, come into one's mind

onus, oneris, n: load, burden

opera, -ae, f: labor, activity, work

otium, -iī, n: leisure

pāreō, parēre, pāruī (+ dative): obey

peccō, -āre, -āvī, -ātus: commit a wrong, injure

permittō, -ere, -mīsī, -missus: yield, allow, permit

pertineō, -ēre, -tinuī: tend to, refer to, pertain to, be the business of

portō, -āre, -āvī, -ātus: carry (a load)

potis, -e: powerful, able

praebeō, -ēre, -uī, -itus: furnish, supply, render

praeceptum, -i, n: rule, command

praecipiō, -ere, -cēpī, -ceptus: anticipate, advise, warn

praeda, -ae, f: booty, prey

praesens, -entis: present, in person, ready

praetereā: besides, moreover

precor, -ārī, precātus sum: pray, invoke

principium, -iī, n: beginning

prīvātus, -a, -um: personal, private

prodō, -ere, prodidī, proditus: publish, hand down, betray

prōmittō, -ere, -mīsī, -missus: send forth, offer

proprius, -a, -um: one's own, peculiar

pudor, pudōris, m: sense of shame, modesty, propriety

pugna, -ae, f: fist-fight, battle

quantum: how much? how greatly? how much! how greatly!

quemadmodum: in what manner, how

quiēscō, -ere, quiēvī, quiētus: keep quiet, sleep

quīn: indeed, in fact (as adverb); so that . . . not (+ subjunctive)

quotiēns: how many times?

recēdō, -ere, -cessī, -cessus: step back, recoil, recede, withdraw

recens (-entis): fresh, new

rectus, -a, -um: straight, direct

reperiō, -īre, reperī, repertus: find, find out

repetō, -ere, -petīvī, -petītus: demand, recollect, repeat

retineō, -ēre, -tinuī, -tentus: hold back, keep

reus, -ī, m: defendant

revertō, -ere, -vertī: turn back

revocō, -āre, -āvī, -ātus: call back, recall

ripa, -ae, f: bank of a river

rumpō, -ere, rūpī, ruptus: break, rupture

saeculum, -ī, n: generation, age, century

scientia, -iae, f: knowledge

sēcūrus, -ā -um: free from care, tranquil, careless

sedeō, -ēre, sēdī, sessus: sit

sepulcrum, -ī, n: place of burial, tomb, grave

serviō, -īre (+ dative): be a slave, serve

spargō, -ere, sparsī, sparsus: scatter

spērō, -āre, -āvī, -ātus: hope

superbus, -a, -um: overbearing, proud, haughty

supplicium, -iī, n: punishment, penalty

tribūnus, -ī, m: tribune, title of various Roman officials

vacō, -āre, -āvī, -ātus: be empty, open, unoccupied

validus, -a, -um: strong

vanus, -a, -um: empty, false, deceitful

vates, -is, m: poet, bard

vinculum, -ī, n: bond, fetter, tie

vītō, -āre, -āvī, -ātus: avoid, shun

volucer, -cris, -cre: flying

volucris, -is, m/f: bird

voluntās, -ātis, f: wish, desire

Index of Latin Grammar
and Syntax

INDEX OF LATIN AUTHORS CITED IN *NLP*

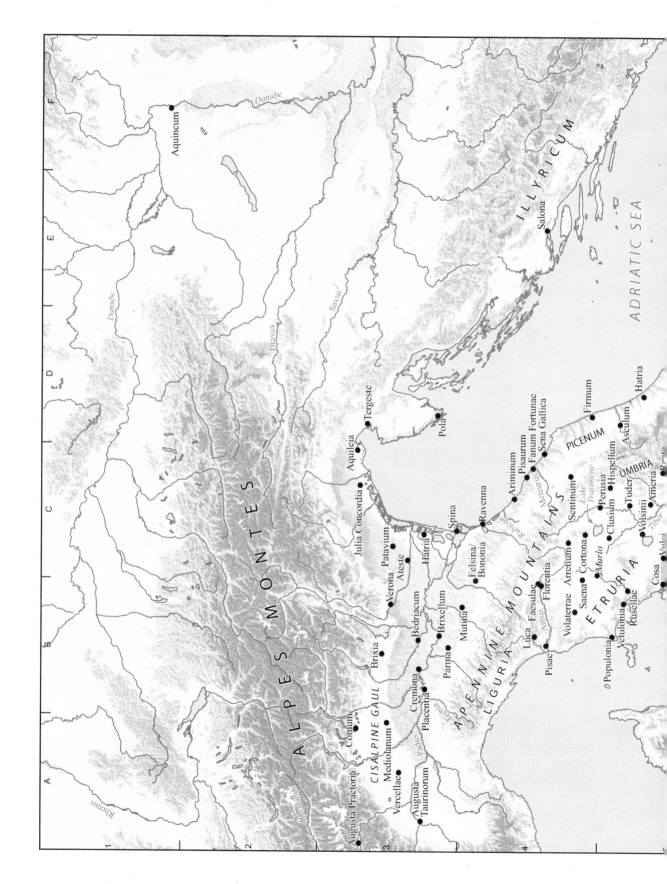